Teacher's Guide

GRADE 1 • VOLUME 1

Authors and Advisors

Alma Flor Ada • Kylene Beers • F. Isabel Campoy
Joyce Armstrong Carroll • Nathan Clemens
Anne Cunningham • Martha Hougen
Elena Izquierdo • Carol Jago • Erik Palmer
Robert Probst • Shane Templeton • Julie Washington

Contributing Consultants

David Dockterman • Mindset Works
Jill Eggleton

Welcome to
HMH Into Reading™

Houghton Mifflin Harcourt is delighted to welcome you to our brand-new literacy program. *HMH Into Reading*™ combines the best practices of balanced literacy with comprehensive coverage of **English Language Arts curriculum standards**.

The authors and consultants who contributed to *Into Reading* share a deep commitment to education and a passion for learning. We look forward to sharing the story of our program with you—and to helping all of your students get *Into Reading* and become lifelong learners.

CONTENTS
PROGRAM OVERVIEW

Authors and Advisors . . . . iv–v

Develop Collaborative,
Self-Directed Learners . . . . vi–vii

Build Content Knowledge
Through Multi-Genre Text Sets . . . . viii–ix

Support Vocabulary and Language
Development x

Build Foundational Reading Skills xi

Foster Critical Thinking and
Deep Analysis of Text . . . . xii–xiii

Notice & Note: Strategies for
Close Reading xiii

Make Meaningful Connections Between
Reading and Writing . . . . xiv–xv

Maximize Growth Through Data-Driven
Differentiation and Assessment . . . . xvi–xvii

Respond to the Needs of
All Learners . . . . xviii–xix

Foster a Mindset for Learning xx

Connect with Families and Community xx

Build a Culture of Professional Growth xxi

Student and Teacher Materials . . . . xxii–xxiii

Volume Contents . . . . xxiv–xxxv

Small-Group Reading xxxvi

HMH Into Reading™ Authors and Advisors

Kylene Beers, Ed.D.
Nationally known lecturer and author on reading and literacy; national and international consultant dedicated to improving literacy, particularly for striving readers; coauthor of *Disruptive Thinking, Notice & Note: Strategies for Close Reading,* and *Reading Nonfiction: Notice & Note Stances, Signposts, and Strategies*

Joyce Armstrong Carroll, Ed.D., H.L.D.
Nationally known consultant on the teaching of writing, with classroom experience in every grade from primary through graduate school, codirector of Abydos Literacy Learning, which trains teachers in writing instruction; coauthor of *Acts of Teaching: How to Teach Writing*

Nathan Clemens, Ph.D.
Associate Professor, University of Texas, Austin; researcher and educator with a focus on improving instruction, assessment, and intervention for students with reading difficulties in kindergarten through adolescence

Anne Cunningham, Ph.D.
Professor, University of California, Berkeley; nationally recognized researcher on literacy and development across the life span; coauthor of *Book Smart: How to Develop and Support Successful, Motivated Readers*

Martha C. Hougen, Ph.D.
Teacher educator focused on reforming educator preparation to better address the diverse needs of students; coeditor and contributing author of *Fundamentals of Literacy Instruction & Assessment Pre-K–6*

Carol Jago, M.A.
Nationally known author and lecturer on reading and writing with 32 years of classroom experience; author of *With Rigor for All* and the forthcoming *The Book in Question: How and Why Reading Is in Crisis*; national consultant who focuses on text complexity, genre instruction, and the use of appropriate literature in the K–12 classroom

Erik Palmer, M.A.
Veteran teacher and consultant whose work focuses on how to teach oral communication and good thinking (argument, persuasion, and reasoning), and how to use technology in the classroom to improve instruction; author of *Well Spoken* and *Good Thinking*

Robert E. Probst, Ph.D.
Professor Emeritus, Georgia State University; nationally known literacy consultant to national and international schools; author of *Response and Analysis* and coauthor of *Disruptive Thinking, Notice & Note: Strategies for Close Reading,* and *Reading Nonfiction: Notice & Note Stances, Signposts, and Strategies*

Shane Templeton, Ph.D.
Foundation Professor Emeritus of Literacy Studies at the University of Nevada, Reno; researcher and practitioner with a focus on developmental word knowledge; author of *Words Their Way*

Julie Washington, Ph.D.
Professor, Georgia State University; researcher with an emphasis on the intersection of cultural dialect use, literacy attainment, and academic performance; author of numerous articles on language and reading development, and on language disorders in urban children growing up in poverty; consultant for *iRead, System 44,* and *READ 180* Universal

Into Reading and *¡Arriba la lectura!*

Alma Flor Ada, Ph.D.
Professor Emerita, University of San Francisco; internationally renowned expert in bilingual literature and literacy; author of over 200 award-winning books, both academic and for young readers; a leading mentor in transformative education

F. Isabel Campoy
Award-winning bilingual author of over 150 children's books of poetry, theater, stories, biographies, art, and culture; internationally recognized scholar, educator, and translator; a member of the North American Academy of Spanish Language

Elena Izquierdo, Ph.D.
Associate Professor of teacher education at the University of Texas, El Paso; researcher and practitioner with a focus on dual-language education, biliteracy, and educational equity for English learners

Contributing Consultants

David Dockterman, Ed.D.
Lecturer at Harvard University Graduate School of Education whose work focuses on turning research into effective, innovative practice to meet the variable needs of all learners; advisor on *MATH 180* and *READ 180* Universal

Jill Eggleton, QSO (Queen's Service Order in Literacy and Education), Ed.D.
Leading balanced-literacy expert, international consultant, and teacher with over 35 years of teaching and administration experience; trains and inspires educators in how to incorporate balanced-literacy methods in the classroom; Adjunct Professor, Sioux Falls University; Margaret Mahy Literacy Medal award winner; author of over 1000 children's books, poetry, and teacher resources

Develop Collaborative, Self-Directed Learners

Into Reading's **Workshop Model** utilizes a gradual release of responsibility that sets students on a path to mastery and success.

Reading Workshop

A quick whole-group minilesson is followed by small-group and independent application time, during which students practice collaboratively and on their own.

WHOLE-GROUP MINILESSON

Learn Together 15–20 minutes

Whole-Group Minilesson

Students are introduced to skills via **Anchor Charts** and the shared reading of a common text.

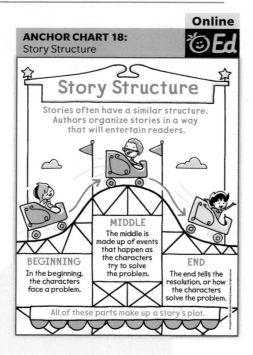

ANCHOR CHART 18:
Story Structure

Online **Ed**

Story Structure

Stories often have a similar structure. Authors organize stories in a way that will entertain readers.

BEGINNING
In the beginning, the characters face a problem.

MIDDLE
The middle is made up of events that happen as the characters try to solve the problem.

END
The end tells the resolution, or how the characters solve the problem.

All of these parts make up a story's plot.

Small-Group Instruction

Multiple options for small-group instruction allow teachers to meet the needs of diverse learners.

GUIDED READING WITH LEVELED LIBRARY
Advance student ability with texts that engage and challenge readers at their instructional level.

FOUNDATIONAL SKILLS DEVELOPMENT
Build students' foundational reading skills through reading decodable texts and other support activities based on need.

SKILL AND STRATEGY LESSONS
Provide targeted support in specific skills and strategies based on individual student needs.

SUPPORT FOR ENGLISH LEARNERS
Provide instruction and practice in a safe, risk-free setting, allowing English learners to experiment with language.

COLLABORATIVE WORK

INDEPENDENT PRACTICE

WHOLE-GROUP WRAP-UP

TEACHER-LED SMALL GROUPS

Small-Group and Independent Work 45–60 minutes

Wrap-Up 5 minutes

Independent and Collaborative Work

Opportunities for independent work allow students to practice and apply targeted knowledge and skills.

LITERACY CENTERS

Engaging activities across a variety of instructional contexts allow students to synthesize information and solidify their understanding.

 WORD WORK

 CREATIVITY CORNER

 DIGITAL STATION

 READING CORNER

 TEAMWORK TIME

*my*BOOK

Write-in student text offers opportunities to read, write, and respond to complex texts.

GENRE STUDY BOOK CLUBS

Conversation about books fosters excitement about reading and writing.

STUDENT CHOICE LIBRARY BOOKS

Self-selected reading creates an authentic opportunity for students to practice new skills and heighten reading engagement.

INQUIRY AND RESEARCH PROJECT

Research- and inquiry-based activities are consistent with project-based learning.

Build Content Knowledge Through Multi-Genre Text Sets

Authentic and **award-winning texts** build topic knowledge expertise and support reading growth for all students.

The selections in each module purposefully contribute to students' overall content and genre knowledge.

Introduce and spark interest in the **module topic**.

Build and **activate background knowledge** about the module topic.

Model **fluent reading** and promote listening comprehension.

Interact with complex texts by annotating, taking notes, and marking text evidence in the Student *my*Book.

Grade 1 *Teacher's Guide*, Volume 2, Module 3

MODULE 3

Welcome to the Module

Teaching with Text Sets

Carefully selected, content-rich text sets help children build topic knowledge and reading skills.

WEEK 1

GET CURIOUS VIDEO — Online Ed

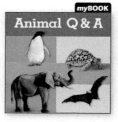
Animal Q & A — *my*BOOK

Best Foot Forward — BIG BOOK

The Nest — *my*BOOK

Hidden Animals
Children view and respond to the video *Hidden Animals* to learn more about animals and camouflage.

Genre: Informational Text
Lexile Measure: 310L
Guided Reading Level: E

Genre: Informational Text
Lexile Measure: NC920L

Genre: Realistic Fiction
Lexile Measure: 260L
Guided Reading Level: F

WEEK 2

Whose Eye Am I? — READ ALOUD BOOK

Blue Bird and Coyote — *my*BOOK

Have You Heard the Nesting Bird? — *my*BOOK

Genre: Informational Text
Lexile Measure: AD770L

Genre: Folktale
Lexile Measure: 310L
Guided Reading Level: F

Genre: Narrative Nonfiction
Lexile Measure: AD430L
Guided Reading Level: G

Amazing Animals

? **Essential Question**
All texts in this set address the question:
How do animals' bodies help them?

Inspire inquiry and set a purpose for reading.

WEEK 3

Genre: Fantasy
Lexile Measure: AD570L

Genre: Procedural Text
Lexile Measure: 480L
Guided Reading Level: H

Genre: Video

WRITING FOCAL TEXT

Genre: Informational Text
Lexile Measure: 330L
Guided Reading Level: C

Launch **Writer's Workshop** with high-interest trade books.

Support Vocabulary and Language Development

Learning flows through language. As students engage in **academic discussion**, **construct meaning from texts**, and **put their own ideas into writing**, they embrace the power of using language to communicate effectively.

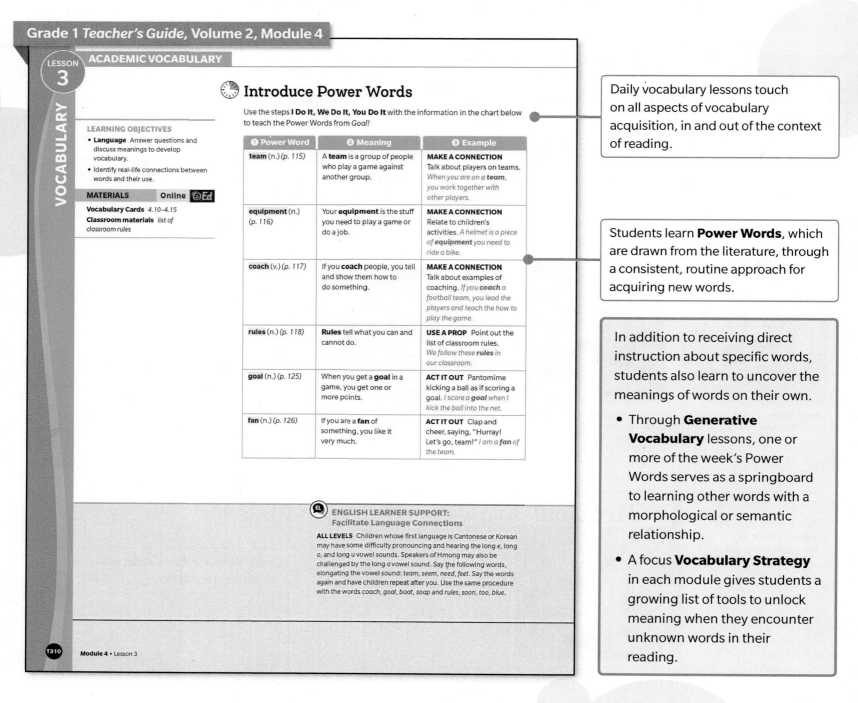

Grade 1 *Teacher's Guide*, Volume 2, Module 4

LESSON 3

VOCABULARY

ACADEMIC VOCABULARY

🕐 **Introduce Power Words**

Use the steps **I Do It, We Do It, You Do It** with the information in the chart below to teach the Power Words from *Goal!*

LEARNING OBJECTIVES
- **Language** Answer questions and discuss meanings to develop vocabulary.
- Identify real-life connections between words and their use.

MATERIALS Online 🔵*Ed*

Vocabulary Cards 4.10–4.15
Classroom materials *list of classroom rules*

❶ Power Word	❷ Meaning	❸ Example
team (n.) *(p. 115)*	A **team** is a group of people who play a game against another group.	**MAKE A CONNECTION** Talk about players on teams. *When you are on a **team**, you work together with other players.*
equipment (n.) *(p. 116)*	Your **equipment** is the stuff you need to play a game or do a job.	**MAKE A CONNECTION** Relate to children's activities. *A helmet is a piece of **equipment** you need to ride a bike.*
coach (v.) *(p. 117)*	If you **coach** people, you tell and show them how to do something.	**MAKE A CONNECTION** Talk about examples of coaching. *If you **coach** a football team, you lead the players and teach the how to play the game.*
rules (n.) *(p. 118)*	**Rules** tell what you can and cannot do.	**USE A PROP** Point out the list of classroom rules. *We follow these **rules** in our classroom.*
goal (n.) *(p. 125)*	When you get a **goal** in a game, you get one or more points.	**ACT IT OUT** Pantomime kicking a ball as if scoring a goal. *I score a **goal** when I kick the ball into the net.*
fan (n.) *(p. 126)*	If you are a **fan** of something, you like it very much.	**ACT IT OUT** Clap and cheer, saying, "Hurray! Let's go, team!" *I am a **fan** of the team.*

🔵 **ENGLISH LEARNER SUPPORT:**
Facilitate Language Connections

ALL LEVELS Children whose first language is Cantonese or Korean may have some difficulty pronouncing and hearing the long e, long o, and long u vowel sounds. Speakers of Hmong may also be challenged by the long o vowel sound. Say the following words, elongating the vowel sound: *team, seem, need, feet.* Say the words again and have children repeat after you. Use the same procedure with the words *coach, goal, boat, soap* and *rules, soon, too, blue.*

T310 Module 4 • Lesson 3

Daily vocabulary lessons touch on all aspects of vocabulary acquisition, in and out of the context of reading.

Students learn **Power Words**, which are drawn from the literature, through a consistent, routine approach for acquiring new words.

In addition to receiving direct instruction about specific words, students also learn to uncover the meanings of words on their own.

- Through **Generative Vocabulary** lessons, one or more of the week's Power Words serves as a springboard to learning other words with a morphological or semantic relationship.

- A focus **Vocabulary Strategy** in each module gives students a growing list of tools to unlock meaning when they encounter unknown words in their reading.

Build Foundational Reading Skills

Explicit and systematic instruction in phonological awareness, phonics, fluency, and spelling provides students with the **critical building blocks** to become confident, independent readers and writers.

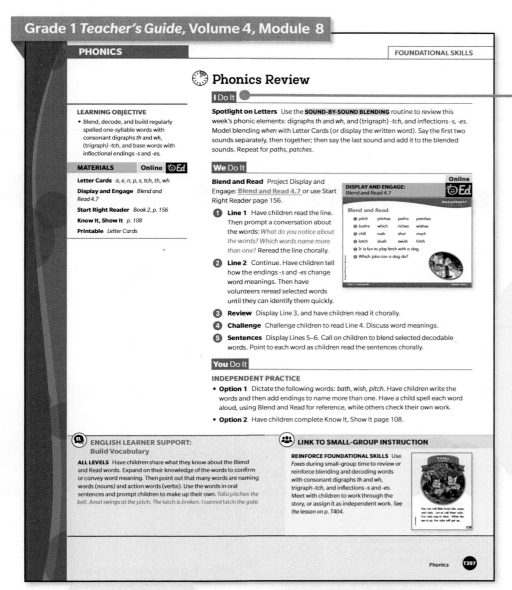

Grade 1 *Teacher's Guide*, Volume 4, Module 8

I Do It, We Do It, You Do It lesson format ensures consistent delivery of instruction to students, followed by immediate guided and independent practice.

START RIGHT READER

In the **Start Right Reader**, students apply what they have learned about phonics and fluency to reading decodable texts. These texts contain only previously taught phonic elements and high-frequency words, and they feature a connected storyline or topic across the week's texts to build students' interest and anticipation.

Foster Critical Thinking and Deep Analysis of Text

The **myBook** is a student component that provides opportunities for write-in text interactions, such as note-taking, annotating, and responding.

The companion **Teaching Pal** offers point-of-use teacher-directed instructional questions and prompts that encourage critical thinking and deep analysis of the *my*Book student texts.

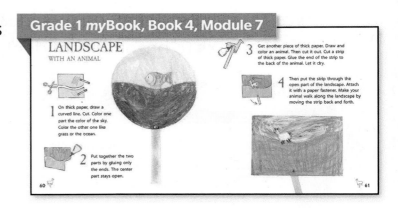

Grade 1 *my*Book, Book 4, Module 7

📖 READ FOR UNDERSTANDING

During a first reading of the text, guide students to respond to questions, prompts, and annotation tips designed to help them **arrive at the gist of the text**.

🔍 TARGETED CLOSE READ

During subsequent readings, students **closely analyze the text** to apply skills and demonstrate knowledge.

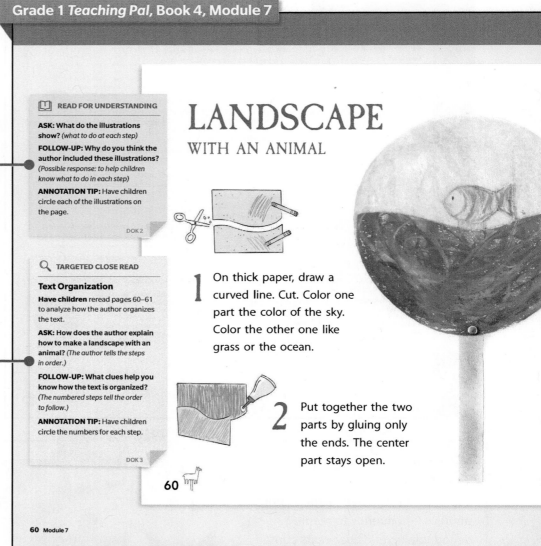

Grade 1 *Teaching Pal*, Book 4, Module 7

📖 **READ FOR UNDERSTANDING**

ASK: What do the illustrations show? *(what to do at each step)*

FOLLOW-UP: Why do you think the author included these illustrations? *(Possible response: to help children know what to do in each step)*

ANNOTATION TIP: Have children circle each of the illustrations on the page.

DOK 2

🔍 **TARGETED CLOSE READ**

Text Organization

Have children reread pages 60–61 to analyze how the author organizes the text.

ASK: How does the author explain how to make a landscape with an animal? *(The author tells the steps in order.)*

FOLLOW-UP: What clues help you know how the text is organized? *(The numbered steps tell the order to follow.)*

ANNOTATION TIP: Have children circle the numbers for each step.

DOK 3

LANDSCAPE
WITH AN ANIMAL

1 On thick paper, draw a curved line. Cut. Color one part the color of the sky. Color the other one like grass or the ocean.

2 Put together the two parts by gluing only the ends. The center part stays open.

60 Module 7

Notice & Note

Use these notes to help students **deepen their understanding** as they learn to look for signposts in the text in order to create meaning.

3 Get another piece of thick paper. Draw and color an animal. Then cut it out. Cut a strip of thick paper. Glue the end of the strip to the back of the animal. Let it dry.

4 Then put the strip through the open part of the landscape. Attach it with a paper fastener. Make your animal walk along the landscape by moving the strip back and forth.

Notice & Note

Numbers and Stats

• **Remind children** that when an author uses numbers in a text, they should stop to notice and note. Explain that understanding why the author included these numbers can help them summarize.

• **Have children** explain why they might use this strategy on pages 60–61. *(The author uses numbers to show the order in which to do something.)*

• **Remind them** of the Anchor Question: **What does this make me wonder about?** *(Possible response: How else could the author have written the steps if she didn't use numbers?)*

DOK 2

📖 **READ FOR UNDERSTANDING**

Summarize

MODEL SUMMARIZING

🗨 **THINK ALOUD** *When I read, I ask myself, what have I learned so far? I can summarize the important details from the words and pictures. I have learned you can use paper and other materials to make an animal that moves through a landscape.*

DOK 2

🦙 **61**

Handmade **61**

Notice & Note

Strategies for Close Reading

Develop attentive, critical readers using the powerful work of Kylene Beers and Robert E. Probst. Notice & Note introduces Signposts and Anchor Questions that help readers understand and respond to critical aspects of both fiction and nonfiction texts.

SIGNPOSTS

Signposts alert readers to significant moments in a text and encourage students to read closely.

Fiction

• Contrast & Contradictions
• Words of the Wiser
• Aha Moment
• Again & Again
• Memory Moment
• Tough Questions

Nonfiction

• Contrast & Contradictions
• Extreme or Absolute Language
• Numbers and Stats
• Quoted Words
• Word Gaps

Kylene Beers and Robert E. Probst

Make Meaningful Connections Between Reading and Writing

During **close reading of the *myBook***, students identify and annotate literary elements, genre characteristics, and evidence of author's purpose and craft. This analysis **supports their own development as writers** across multiple forms and genres.

Writing in Response to Reading

Students engage in deep analysis of literary and informational texts as well as media selections.

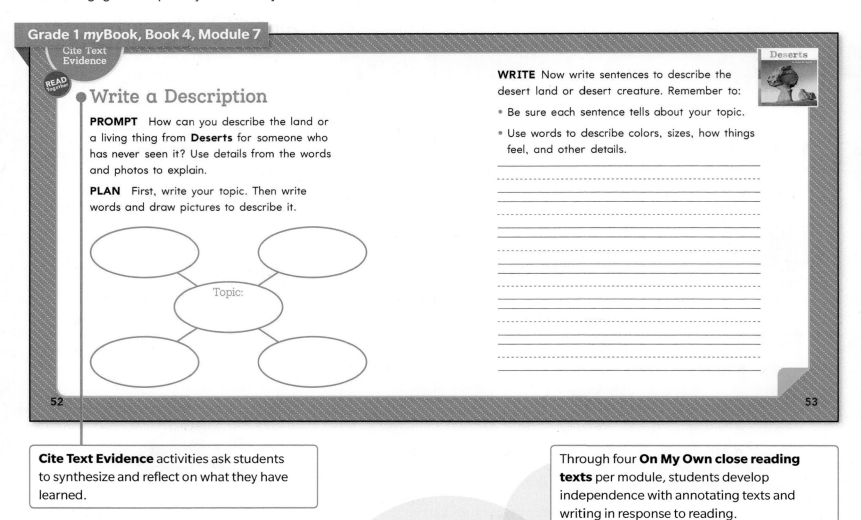

Grade 1 *myBook*, Book 4, Module 7

Cite Text Evidence

READ Together

Write a Description

PROMPT How can you describe the land or a living thing from **Deserts** for someone who has never seen it? Use details from the words and photos to explain.

PLAN First, write your topic. Then write words and draw pictures to describe it.

Topic:

WRITE Now write sentences to describe the desert land or desert creature. Remember to:

• Be sure each sentence tells about your topic.

• Use words to describe colors, sizes, how things feel, and other details.

Deserts

52

53

Cite Text Evidence activities ask students to synthesize and reflect on what they have learned.

Through four **On My Own close reading texts** per module, students develop independence with annotating texts and writing in response to reading.

"Writing as a process means giving students time to prewrite, write, postwrite, proofread, and edit their papers. It means teaching writing, not just assigning it. It means teaching the various forms of writing so students think through their meaning, their purpose, the needs of their audience to determine the most appropriate genre."

—*Dr. Joyce Armstrong Carroll*

Writing Workshop

Into Reading employs a Writing Workshop method of instruction that is student centered, process driven, and collaborative.

Writing Workshop made explicit:

- Instruction, activities, and routines for every stage of the writing process
- Extensive teacher modeling and tips
- Digitally projectable instruction at point of use

The **Writer's Notebook** directly supports the act of writing by allowing students to set and evaluate personal goals, interact with writing models, use a variety of prewriting strategies, and confer with peers.

Focal Texts connect to module topics and serve as a springboard for discussion around the module topic and writing prompt.

Maximize Growth Through Data-Driven Differentiation and Assessment

Meaningful data insights help teachers determine a daily skills focus for minilessons and small-group needs.

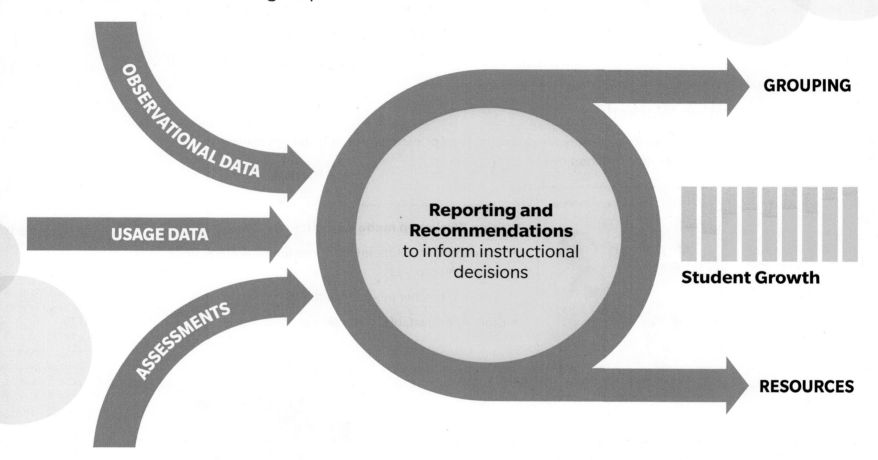

OBSERVATIONAL DATA

USAGE DATA

ASSESSMENTS

Reporting and Recommendations
to inform instructional decisions

GROUPING

Student Growth

RESOURCES

Actionable reports drive grouping, reading, and instructional recommendations appropriate for each learner.

REPORTS

Multiple report views allow teachers to **see the gaps and gains** of the class at any moment throughout the school year.

GROUPING

Data-driven recommendations dynamically assign students to groups, allowing teachers to target learning needs and differentiate instruction.

RESOURCE RECOMMENDATIONS

Based on data, resources are recommended to **target students' individual learning needs**.

ASSESSMENTS AND PROGRESS MONITORING

Adaptive Growth Measure and Guided Reading Benchmark

3 times
per year

Adaptive Growth Measure and Guided Reading Benchmark allows teachers to gain an understanding of where students are on the learning continuum and identify students in need of intervention or enrichment.

Module Assessment

12 times
per year

Module Assessments, given every three weeks, assess mastery of skills covered during the course of the module across all literacy strands.

Ongoing Feedback from Daily Classroom Activities

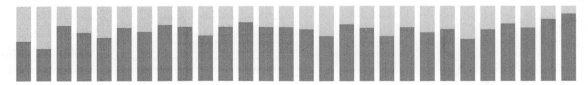

Formative Assessment data, collected across a variety of student activities, help teachers to make informed instructional decisions. Data sources include:

- Weekly Assessments
- Selection and Leveled Reader Quizzes
- Independent Reading
- Skills Practice

- Usage Data
- Teacher Observations
- Running Records
- Inquiry and Research Projects

Respond to the Needs of All Learners

Into Reading's **Tabletop Toolkit** makes it easier for teachers to differentiate instruction and meet the individual needs of all students.

Intervention

TABLETOP MINILESSONS: INTERVENTION

Provide Tier 2 intervention support with daily minilessons targeting prerequisite foundational skills, academic language, and critical thinking.

Scaffolding and Enrichment

TABLETOP MINILESSONS: READING

Target grade-level skills and strategies to address students' needs and optimize small-group learning.

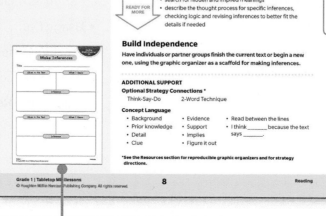

Minilessons can be used with **ANY text**.

Suggestions for differentiation include scaffolded support for students who are **"Almost There"** as well as more challenging prompts for those who are **"Ready for More."**

Teach key reading skills and strategies through **Anchor Charts** in a small-group setting.

Graphic organizers support student interactions with texts.

Supporting English Learners

Throughout *Into Reading,* embedded supports **facilitate students' effective expression at each level of English language proficiency** and across instructional contexts.

TABLETOP MINILESSONS: ENGLISH LANGUAGE DEVELOPMENT

English learners engage in small groups to practice and **apply language functions** across the four domains—listening, speaking, reading, writing— and collaborative problem solving.

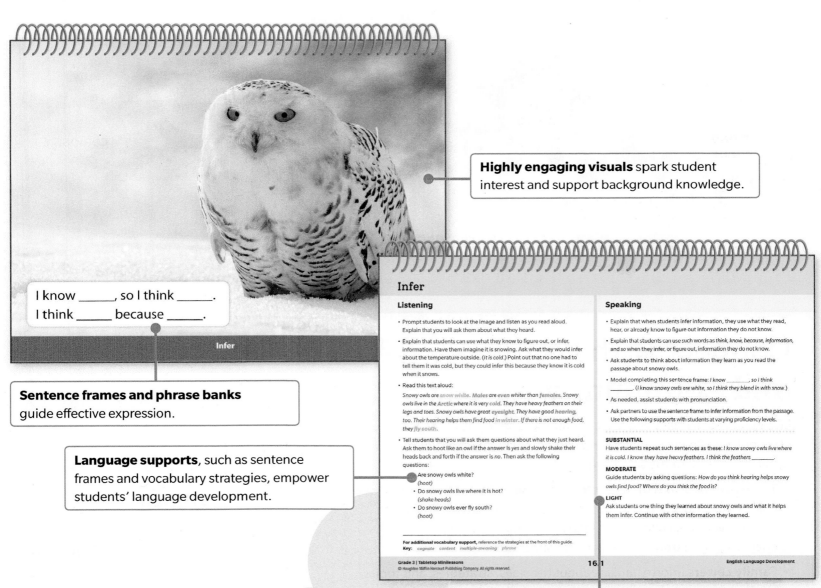

Highly engaging visuals spark student interest and support background knowledge.

I know _____, so I think _____.
I think _____ because _____.

Sentence frames and phrase banks guide effective expression.

Language supports, such as sentence frames and vocabulary strategies, empower students' language development.

Infer

Listening

- Prompt students to look at the image and listen as you read aloud. Explain that you will ask them about what they heard.

- Explain that students can use what they know to figure out, or infer, information. Have them imagine it is snowing. Ask what they would infer about the temperature outside. (*It is cold.*) Point out that no one had to tell them it was cold, but they could infer this because they know it is cold when it snows.

- Read this text aloud:
  Snowy owls are snow white. Males are even whiter than females. Snowy owls live in the Arctic where it is very cold. They have heavy feathers on their legs and toes. Snowy owls have great eyesight. They have good hearing, too. Their hearing helps them find food in winter. If there is not enough food, they fly south.

- Tell students that you will ask them questions about what they just heard. Ask them to hoot like an owl if the answer is yes and slowly shake their heads back and forth if the answer is *no.* Then ask the following questions:
  - Are snowy owls white?
    (hoot)
  - Do snowy owls live where it is hot?
    (shake heads)
  - Do snowy owls ever fly south?
    (hoot)

For additional vocabulary support, reference the strategies at the front of this guide.
Key: *cognate content multiple-meaning phrase*

Grade 3 | Tabletop Minilessons
© Houghton Mifflin Harcourt Publishing Company. All rights reserved.
16.1
English Language Development

Speaking

- Explain that when students infer information, they use what they read, hear, or already know to figure out information they do not know.

- Explain that students can use such words as *think, know, because, information,* and so when they infer, or figure out, information they do not know.

- Ask students to think about information they learn as you read the passage about snowy owls.

- Model completing this sentence frame: *I know _____, so I think _____.* (*I know snowy owls are white, so I think they blend in with snow.*)

- As needed, assist students with pronunciation.

- Ask partners to use the sentence frame to infer information from the passage. Use the following supports with students at varying proficiency levels.

SUBSTANTIAL
Have students repeat such sentences as these: *I know snowy owls live where it is cold. I know they have heavy feathers. I think the feathers _____.*

MODERATE
Guide students by asking questions: *How do you think hearing helps snowy owls find food? Where do you think the food is?*

LIGHT
Ask students one thing they learned about snowy owls and what it helps them infer. Continue with other information they learned.

Scaffolded instruction supports students at their language proficiency level and provides opportunities for growth.

Foster a Mindset for Learning

Through a partnership with **Mindset Works**®, *Into Reading* incorporates the latest research, strategies, and practices to build a community of resilient, curious learners.

- Introduce the learning mindsets: **growth mindset**, **relevance**, **belonging**, and **purpose** to help students better understand their self-perception and attitudes toward learning.

- Establish the **tenets of growth mindset**, so that each student understands that he or she has the capacity to learn and grow.

- Target the research-based stances and skills that are key to **student agency**, **engagement**, and **academic success**.

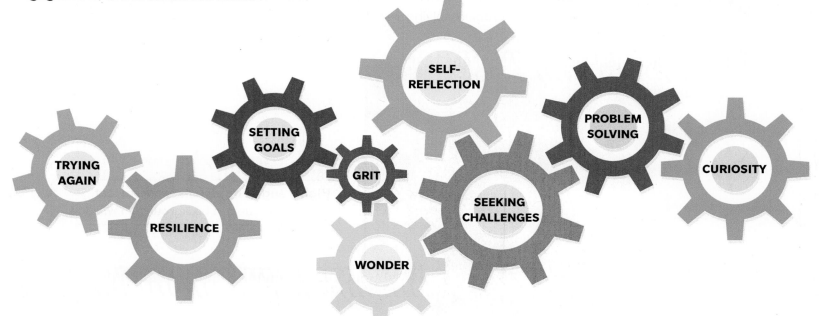

Connect with Families and Community

Engaging with families and the community is critical to student success in school. *Into Reading* provides resources to help teachers interact with families throughout the school year.

- **The write-in format of *myBook*** gives families a front-row seat to their child's thinking and progress over time. Upon completion of each *myBook* volume, children can take home and share literature, encouraging a strong home-school connection.

- **Family Letters** inform families about the skills, strategies, and topics students are encountering at school, extending rich dialogue beyond the classroom.

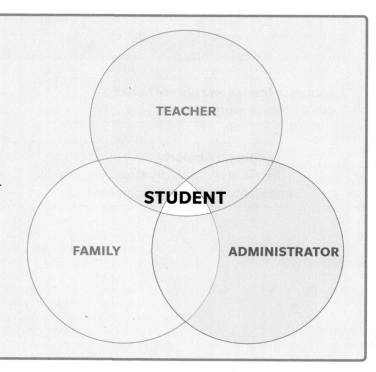

Build a Culture of Professional Growth

Embedded and ongoing **Professional Learning** empowers and supports teachers to be developers of high-impact learning experiences that provide all students with opportunities for reading and writing success.

Build Agency with Purposeful, Embedded Support

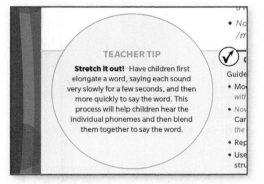

TEACHER TIPS

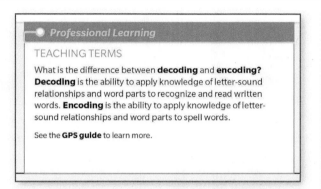

PROFESSIONAL LEARNING REFERENCES

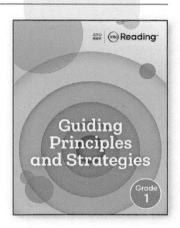

CLASSROOM VIDEOS

ON-DEMAND PROFESSIONAL LEARNING MODULES

Grow Your Practice with Personalized Blended Professional Learning

- **Getting Started and Professional Learning Guide:** Learn the program components, pedagogy, and digital resources to successfully teach with *Into Reading*.

- **Follow-Up:** Choose from a variety of instructional topics to design a personalized in-person or live online Follow-Up experience to deepen program mastery and enhance teaching practices.

- **Coaching and Modeling:** Experience just-in-time support to ensure continuous professional learning that is student centered and grounded in data.

- **askHMH:** Get on-demand access to program experts who will answer questions and provide personalized conferencing and digital demonstrations to support implementation.

- **Technical Services:** Plan, prepare, implement, and operate technology with ease.

- **International Center for Leadership in Education (ICLE):** Partner with ICLE to strengthen rigor and relevance in the literacy classroom.

Student and Teacher Materials

Student Materials

ONLINE STUDENT MANAGEMENT CENTER
Online
Ed

- Access all program materials
- Complete and submit assignments and assessments
- Track progress

*my*Book: 5 Books

Read Aloud Books: 20 Books

Big Books: 10 Books

Teacher Materials

ONLINE STUDENT MANAGEMENT CENTER
Online
Ed

- Access all program materials
- Plan lessons
- Assign materials
- View reports
- Group children

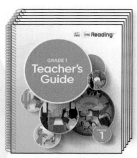

Teacher's Guide: 6 Volumes

Writing Workshop Teacher's Guide: 1 Volume

Vocabulary Cards

Anchor Charts

Teaching Pal: 5 Books

BookStix

Teacher Resource Book

Display and Engage

FOUNDATIONAL SKILLS

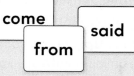

s i t

Letter Cards

come from said

Word Cards

Start Right Reader: 6 Books

Sound/Spelling Cards

Picture Cards

iRead

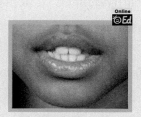

Articulation Videos

SMALL-GROUP AND INDEPENDENT APPLICATION

Student Choice Library:
6 copies of each title

Rigby®
LEVELED LIBRARY

Know It, Show It

Writer's Notebook

Printables include:

- Readers' Theater
- Reading Remake
- Graphic Organizers
- Reading Log
- Listening Log
- Spelling & Handwriting
- Word Lists
- Anchor Charts

Take and Teach Lessons:
Leveled Readers

Take and Teach Lessons:
Genre Study

Tabletop Minilessons:
Reading

Tabletop Minilessons:
English Language Development

Tabletop Minilessons:
Intervention

ASSESSMENTS

Data & Reporting:

- Adaptive Growth Measure
- Guided Reading Benchmark Assessment Kit

Program Assessments:

- Leveled Reader Quizzes
- Weekly Assessments
- Module Assessments

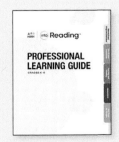

PROFESSIONAL LEARNING & IMPLEMENTATION SUPPORT

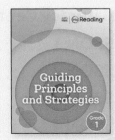

Professional Learning Guide

Guiding Principles and Strategies

Welcome to *HMH Into Reading*™

MODULE 1

Nice to Meet You!

Module Overview T1

myBook, Book 1

MODULE 1

Nice to Meet You!

SOCIAL STUDIES CONNECTION:
New Friends and Experiences 8

My First Day 12
REALISTIC FICTION

Try This! 14
by Pam Muñoz Ryan
NARRATIVE NONFICTION

› On My Own
We Try, We Paint 28

My School Trip 32
by Aly G. Mays • illustrated by Elisa Chavarri
REALISTIC FICTION

› On My Own
A Trip to a Garden 46

4

A Kids' Guide to Friends 50
by Trey Amico
INFORMATIONAL TEXT

› On My Own
Good Friends 64

Big Dilly's Tale 68
by Gail Carson Levine • illustrated by Jui Ishida
FAIRY TALE

› On My Own
The Map 82

I'm Me 86
by The FuZees
MEDIA: SONG

Let's Wrap Up! 90

5

WEEK 1

Weekly Planning T21
  • Essential Skills
  • Week at a Glance
  • Preview Lesson Texts
  • Literacy Centers

LESSON 1 .... T28

LESSON 2 .... T44

LESSON 3 .... T58

LESSON 4 .... T70

LESSON 5 .... T82

WEEK 2

Weekly Planning T95
  • Essential Skills
  • Week at a Glance
  • Preview Lesson Texts
  • Literacy Centers

LESSON 6 .... T102

LESSON 7 .... T118

LESSON 8 .... T132

LESSON 9 .... T144

LESSON 10 .... T156

WEEK 3

Weekly Planning T169
  • Essential Skills
  • Week at a Glance
  • Preview Lesson Texts
  • Literacy Centers

LESSON 11 .... T176

LESSON 12 .... T192

LESSON 13 .... T206

LESSON 14 .... T220

LESSON 15 .... T232

Resources R1

MODULE 2

My Family, My Community

Module Overview

Module Overview T245

myBook, Book 1

MODULE 2
My Family, My Community

🔊 SOCIAL STUDIES CONNECTION: Communities 92

Kids Speak Up! 96
OPINION WRITING

Dan Had a Plan 98
by Wong Herbert Yee
REALISTIC FICTION

› On My Own
Together 116

On the Map! 120
by Lisa Fleming
INFORMATIONAL TEXT

› On My Own
Neighborhoods 130

Places in My Neighborhood 134
by Shelly Lyons
INFORMATIONAL TEXT

› On My Own
What Is This Place? 148

Who Put the Cookies in
the Cookie Jar? 152
by George Shannon • illustrated by Julie Paschkis
INFORMATIONAL TEXT

› On My Own
Kids Can Help 174

Curious About Jobs 178
MEDIA: VIDEO

Let's Wrap Up! 182
Glossary 184
Index of Titles and Authors 195

6   7

WEEK 1	WEEK 2	WEEK 3
Weekly Planning T265	**Weekly Planning** T341	**Weekly Planning** T417
• Essential Skills	• Essential Skills	• Essential Skills
• Week at a Glance	• Week at a Glance	• Week at a Glance
• Preview Lesson Texts	• Preview Lesson Texts	• Preview Lesson Texts
• Literacy Centers	• Literacy Centers	• Literacy Centers

WEEK 1	WEEK 2	WEEK 3
LESSON 1 .... T272	**LESSON 6** T348	**LESSON 11** T424
LESSON 2 .... T288	**LESSON 7** T364	**LESSON 12** T440
LESSON 3 .... T302	**LESSON 8** T378	**LESSON 13** T454
LESSON 4 .... T316	**LESSON 9** T392	**LESSON 14** T468
LESSON 5 .... T328	**LESSON 10** T404	**LESSON 15** T480

Resources R1

MODULE 3

Amazing Animals

Module Overview T1

myBook, Book 2

MODULE 3

Amazing Animals

✂ **SCIENCE CONNECTION:** How Animals Live 8

Animal Q & A 12
INFORMATIONAL TEXT

The Nest 14
by Carole Roberts • illustrated by Nina de Polonia
REALISTIC FICTION

> On My Own
> The Pet Plan 34

Blue Bird and Coyote 38
by James Bruchac • illustrated by Chris Lensch
FOLKTALE

> On My Own
> The Nut 52

**Have You Heard
the Nesting Bird?** 56
by Rita Gray • illustrated by Kenard Pak
NARRATIVE NONFICTION

> On My Own
> Bird News 78

**Step-by-Step Advice from
the Animal Kingdom** 82
by Steve Jenkins and Robin Page
PROCEDURAL TEXT

> On My Own
> Pop-Up Armadillo 96

Beaver Family 100
from National Geographic Kids
MEDIA: VIDEO

Let's Wrap Up! 104

4

5

WEEK 1

Weekly Planning T21
- Essential Skills
- Week at a Glance
- Preview Lesson Texts
- Literacy Centers

LESSON 1 .... T28
LESSON 2 .... T44
LESSON 3 .... T58
LESSON 4 .... T72
LESSON 5 .... T84

WEEK 2

Weekly Planning T97
- Essential Skills
- Week at a Glance
- Preview Lesson Texts
- Literacy Centers

LESSON 6 .... T104
LESSON 7 .... T120
LESSON 8 .... T134
LESSON 9 .... T148
LESSON 10 .... T160

WEEK 3

Weekly Planning T173
- Essential Skills
- Week at a Glance
- Preview Lesson Texts
- Literacy Centers

LESSON 11 .... T180
LESSON 12 .... T196
LESSON 13 .... T210
LESSON 14 .... T224
LESSON 15 .... T236

Resources R1

MODULE 4

Better Together

Module Overview

Module Overview T249

myBook, Book 2

MODULE 4

Better Together

🔵 **SOCIAL STUDIES CONNECTION:**
Being Good Citizens 106

Good Sports 110
OPINION WRITING

Goal! 112
by Jane Medina • illustrated by Maine Diaz
INFORMATIONAL TEXT

› On My Own
Chess Fan 130

Get Up and Go! 134
by Rozanne Lanczak Williams
INFORMATIONAL TEXT

› On My Own
Play Tag! 148

A Big Guy Took My Ball! 152
by Mo Willems
FANTASY

› On My Own
Biggy-Big-Big! 186

If You Plant a Seed 190
by Kadir Nelson
FANTASY

› On My Own
Fox and Crow 212

Color Your World with Kindness 216
from BetterWorldians Foundation
MEDIA: VIDEO

Let's Wrap Up! 220

Glossary 222

Index of Titles and Authors 233

6   7

WEEK 1

Weekly Planning T269
- Essential Skills
- Week at a Glance
- Preview Lesson Texts
- Literacy Centers

LESSON 1 .... T276
LESSON 2 .... T292
LESSON 3 .... T306
LESSON 4 .... T320
LESSON 5 .... T332

WEEK 2

Weekly Planning T345
- Essential Skills
- Week at a Glance
- Preview Lesson Texts
- Literacy Centers

LESSON 6 .... T352
LESSON 7 .... T368
LESSON 8 .... T382
LESSON 9 .... T396
LESSON 10 .... T408

WEEK 3

Weekly Planning T421
- Essential Skills
- Week at a Glance
- Preview Lesson Texts
- Literacy Centers

LESSON 11 .... T428
LESSON 12 .... T444
LESSON 13 .... T458
LESSON 14 .... T472
LESSON 15 .... T484

Resources R1

MODULE 5

Now You See It, Now You Don't

Module Overview...T1

*my*Book, Book 3

MODULE 5

Now You See It, Now You Don't

🌱 **SCIENCE CONNECTION:** Light and Dark.............................8

Super Shadows!............................12
INFORMATIONAL TEXT

Blackout...................................14
by John Rocco
REALISTIC FICTION

› On My Own
Lin and the Stars........................40

Day and Night.............................44
by Margaret Hall
INFORMATIONAL TEXT

› On My Own
Rainbows.................................58

The Best Season...........................62
by Nina Crews
OPINION WRITING

› On My Own
My Great Town...........................80

Waiting Is Not Easy!......................84
by Mo Willems
FANTASY

› On My Own
Liz's Shadow............................114

I'm So Hot................................118
from StoryBots
MEDIA: SONG

Let's Wrap Up!...........................122

4

5

WEEK 1

Weekly Planning........T21
- Essential Skills
- Week at a Glance
- Preview Lesson Texts
- Literacy Centers

LESSON 1...............T28
LESSON 2...............T44
LESSON 3...............T58
LESSON 4...............T72
LESSON 5...............T84

WEEK 2

Weekly Planning........T97
- Essential Skills
- Week at a Glance
- Preview Lesson Texts
- Literacy Centers

LESSON 6...............T104
LESSON 7...............T120
LESSON 8...............T134
LESSON 9...............T148
LESSON 10..............T160

WEEK 3

Weekly Planning........T173
- Essential Skills
- Week at a Glance
- Preview Lesson Texts
- Literacy Centers

LESSON 11..............T180
LESSON 12..............T196
LESSON 13..............T210
LESSON 14..............T224
LESSON 15..............T236

Resources...R1

MODULE 6

Celebrate America

Module Overview

Module Overview T249

myBook, Book 3

MODULE 6
Celebrate America

🌐 **SOCIAL STUDIES CONNECTION:**
Holidays and Symbols 124

State the Facts! 128
INFORMATIONAL TEXT

Monument City 130
by Jerdine Nolen • illustrated by Joe Cepeda
DRAMA
› On My Own
Mount Rushmore 156

The Contest 160
by Libby Martinez • illustrated by Nina de Polonia
OPINION WRITING
› On My Own
A Great Day 178

The Statue of Liberty 182
by Tyler Monroe
INFORMATIONAL TEXT
› On My Own
The Plant Doctor 196

Hooray for Holidays! 200
by Pat Cummings • illustrated by John Herzog
REALISTIC FICTION
› On My Own
Arbor Day 214

Patriotic Poems 218
illustrated by Amanda Lima
POETRY

Let's Wrap Up! 226
Glossary 228
Index of Titles and Authors 239

6   7

WEEK 1	WEEK 2	WEEK 3
Weekly Planning T269	**Weekly Planning** T345	**Weekly Planning** T421
• Essential Skills	• Essential Skills	• Essential Skills
• Week at a Glance	• Week at a Glance	• Week at a Glance
• Preview Lesson Texts	• Preview Lesson Texts	• Preview Lesson Texts
• Literacy Centers	• Literacy Centers	• Literacy Centers

WEEK 1	WEEK 2	WEEK 3
LESSON 1 .... T276	**LESSON 6** T352	**LESSON 11** T428
LESSON 2 .... T292	**LESSON 7** T368	**LESSON 12** T444
LESSON 3 .... T306	**LESSON 8** T382	**LESSON 13** T458
LESSON 4 .... T320	**LESSON 9** T396	**LESSON 14** T472
LESSON 5 .... T332	**LESSON 10** T408	**LESSON 15** T484

Resources R1

MODULE 7

The Big Outdoors

Module Overview T1

myBook, Book 4

MODULE 7
The Big Outdoors
🔬 **SCIENCE CONNECTION:** The Natural World 8

Storm Report 12
OPINION WRITING

Sam & Dave Dig a Hole 14
by Mac Barnett • illustrated by Jon Klassen
FANTASY
› On My Own
   Ron and Tron 32

Deserts 36
by Quinn M. Arnold
INFORMATIONAL TEXT
› On My Own
   How an Island Is Made 54

Handmade 58
by Guadalupe Rodríguez
PROCEDURAL TEXT
› On My Own
   Be a Bird Helper 68

Grand Canyon 72
by Sara Gilbert
INFORMATIONAL TEXT
› On My Own
   Grand Canyon Fossils 88

Water Cycle 92
by The Bazillions
MEDIA: SONG

Let's Wrap Up! 96

4

WEEK 1

Weekly Planning T21
• Essential Skills
• Week at a Glance
• Preview Lesson Texts
• Literacy Centers

LESSON 1 .... T28
LESSON 2 .... T44
LESSON 3 .... T58
LESSON 4 .... T72
LESSON 5 .... T84

WEEK 2

Weekly Planning T97
• Essential Skills
• Week at a Glance
• Preview Lesson Texts
• Literacy Centers

LESSON 6 .... T104
LESSON 7 .... T120
LESSON 8 .... T134
LESSON 9 .... T148
LESSON 10 .... T160

WEEK 3

Weekly Planning T173
• Essential Skills
• Week at a Glance
• Preview Lesson Texts
• Literacy Centers

LESSON 11 .... T180
LESSON 12 .... T196
LESSON 13 .... T210
LESSON 14 .... T224
LESSON 15 .... T236

Resources R1

MODULE 8

Tell Me a Story

Module Overview

Module Overview T249

myBook, Book 4

MODULE 8

Tell Me a Story

 SOCIAL STUDIES CONNECTION:
What Stories Teach Us 98

Follow the Story Path 102
INFORMATIONAL TEXT

Interrupting Chicken 104
by David Ezra Stein
FANTASY

> On My Own
   Hansel and Gretel Two 134

Little Red Riding Hood 138
by Lisa Campbell Ernst • illustrated by Jesús Aguado
DRAMA

> On My Own
   Keep Trying 158

The Grasshopper & the Ants 162
by Jerry Pinkney
FABLE

> On My Own
   A Tale of Two Mice 188

Thank You, Mr. Aesop 192
by Helen Lester • illustrated by Roberto Weigand
INFORMATIONAL TEXT

> On My Own
   Make Stories Come Alive 202

The Tortoise and the Hare 206
from Speakaboos, adapted by Amy Kraft
MEDIA: VIDEO

Let's Wrap Up! 210

Glossary 212

Index of Titles and Authors 223

6   7

WEEK 1

Weekly Planning T269
- Essential Skills
- Week at a Glance
- Preview Lesson Texts
- Literacy Centers

LESSON 1 . . . . T276
LESSON 2 . . . . T292
LESSON 3 . . . . T306
LESSON 4 . . . . T320
LESSON 5 . . . . T332

WEEK 2

Weekly Planning T345
- Essential Skills
- Week at a Glance
- Preview Lesson Texts
- Literacy Centers

LESSON 6 . . . . T352
LESSON 7 . . . . T368
LESSON 8 . . . . T382
LESSON 9 . . . . T396
LESSON 10 . . . . T408

WEEK 3

Weekly Planning T421
- Essential Skills
- Week at a Glance
- Preview Lesson Texts
- Literacy Centers

LESSON 11 . . . . T428
LESSON 12 . . . . T444
LESSON 13 . . . . T458
LESSON 14 . . . . T472
LESSON 15 . . . . T484

Resources R1

MODULE 9

Grow, Plants, Grow!

Module Overview T1

myBook, Book 5

MODULE 9

Grow, Plants, Grow!

🌱 SCIENCE CONNECTION: Plants and Gardens 8

Plant Pairs 12
POETRY

So You Want to Grow a Taco? 14
by Bridget Heos • illustrated by Daniele Fabbri
PROCEDURAL TEXT

› On My Own
1, 2, 3, Salsa! 36

Which Part Do We Eat? 40
by Katherine Ayres • illustrated by Hazel Quintanilla
POETRY

› On My Own
Pie Poems 50

The Talking Vegetables 54
by Won-Ldy Paye and Margaret H. Lippert •
illustrated by Julie Paschkis
FOLKTALE

› On My Own
The Little Red Hen 80

Yum! ¡MmMm! ¡Qué rico!:
Americas' Sproutings 84
by Pat Mora • illustrated by Rafael López
POETRY

› On My Own
Garden Poems 94

A Year in the Garden 98
by Brad Hiebert
MEDIA: VIDEO

Let's Wrap Up! 102

4

5

WEEK 1

Weekly Planning T21
- Essential Skills
- Week at a Glance
- Preview Lesson Texts
- Literacy Centers

LESSON 1 .... T28
LESSON 2 .... T44
LESSON 3 .... T58
LESSON 4 .... T72
LESSON 5 .... T84

WEEK 2

Weekly Planning T97
- Essential Skills
- Week at a Glance
- Preview Lesson Texts
- Literacy Centers

LESSON 6 .... T104
LESSON 7 .... T120
LESSON 8 .... T134
LESSON 9 .... T148
LESSON 10 .... T160

WEEK 3

Weekly Planning T173
- Essential Skills
- Week at a Glance
- Preview Lesson Texts
- Literacy Centers

LESSON 11 .... T180
LESSON 12 .... T196
LESSON 13 .... T210
LESSON 14 .... T224
LESSON 15 .... T236

Resources R1

Dare to Dream

Module Overview T249

myBook, Book 5

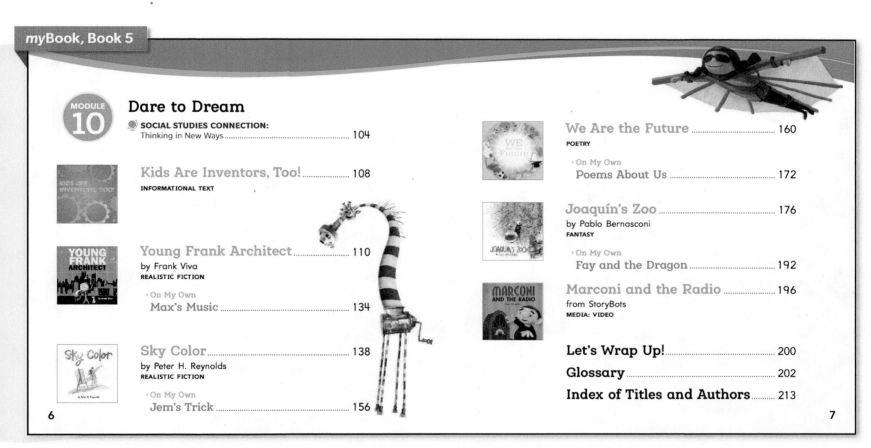

MODULE 10

Dare to Dream

🌐 **SOCIAL STUDIES CONNECTION:**
Thinking in New Ways 104

Kids Are Inventors, Too! 108
INFORMATIONAL TEXT

Young Frank Architect 110
by Frank Viva
REALISTIC FICTION

› On My Own
Max's Music 134

Sky Color 138
by Peter H. Reynolds
REALISTIC FICTION

› On My Own
Jem's Trick 156

We Are the Future 160
POETRY

› On My Own
Poems About Us 172

Joaquín's Zoo 176
by Pablo Bernasconi
FANTASY

› On My Own
Fay and the Dragon 192

Marconi and the Radio 196
from StoryBots
MEDIA: VIDEO

Let's Wrap Up! 200

Glossary 202

Index of Titles and Authors 213

6

7

WEEK 1

Weekly Planning T269
- Essential Skills
- Week at a Glance
- Preview Lesson Texts
- Literacy Centers

LESSON 1 .... T276
LESSON 2 .... T292
LESSON 3 .... T306
LESSON 4 .... T320
LESSON 5 .... T332

WEEK 2

Weekly Planning T345
- Essential Skills
- Week at a Glance
- Preview Lesson Texts
- Literacy Centers

LESSON 6 .... T352
LESSON 7 .... T368
LESSON 8 .... T382
LESSON 9 .... T396
LESSON 10 .... T408

WEEK 3

Weekly Planning T421
- Essential Skills
- Week at a Glance
- Preview Lesson Texts
- Literacy Centers

LESSON 11 .... T428
LESSON 12 .... T444
LESSON 13 .... T458
LESSON 14 .... T472
LESSON 15 .... T484

Resources R1

MODULE 11

Genre Study: Nonfiction

Module Overview T1

WEEK 1

Weekly Planning T5
- Essential Skills
- Week at a Glance

LESSON 1 .... T8
LESSON 2 .... T18
LESSON 3 .... T26
LESSON 4 .... T34
LESSON 5 .... T40

WEEK 2

Weekly Planning T47
- Essential Skills
- Week at a Glance

LESSON 6 .... T50
LESSON 7 .... T60
LESSON 8 .... T68
LESSON 9 .... T76
LESSON 10 .... T82

WEEK 3

Weekly Planning T89
- Essential Skills
- Week at a Glance

LESSON 11 .... T92
LESSON 12 .... T102
LESSON 13 .... T110
LESSON 14 .... T118
LESSON 15 .... T124

Resources R1

Genre Study: Literary Texts

Module Overview T131

WEEK 1

Weekly Planning T135
  • Essential Skills
  • Week at a Glance

LESSON 1 .... T138
LESSON 2 .... T148
LESSON 3 .... T156
LESSON 4 .... T164
LESSON 5 .... T170

WEEK 2

Weekly Planning T177
  • Essential Skills
  • Week at a Glance

LESSON 6 .... T180
LESSON 7 .... T190
LESSON 8 .... T198
LESSON 9 .... T206
LESSON 10 .... T212

WEEK 3

Weekly Planning T219
  • Essential Skills
  • Week at a Glance

LESSON 11 .... T222
LESSON 12 .... T232
LESSON 13 .... T240
LESSON 14 .... T248
LESSON 15 .... T254

Resources R1

Small-Group Reading

The Rigby Leveled Library offers a carefully controlled continuum of texts, spanning a range of levels, topics, and genres.

Rigby®
LEVELED LIBRARY

GUIDED READING LEVEL	⟵ C D E F G H I J K ⟶
	10 TITLES PER LEVEL

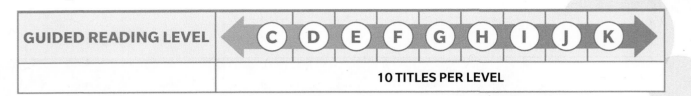

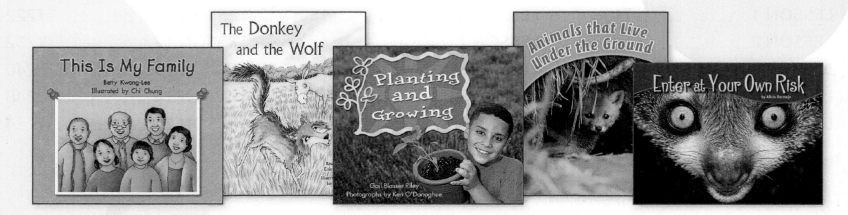

Nice to Meet You!

? **Essential Question**

How can making new friends and learning new things help us?

 SOCIAL STUDIES CONNECTION:

New Friends and Experiences

The start of a new school year is an exciting time for children. They will meet new people. They will try and learn new things. For some children, though, this time of year can also be challenging.

In this module, children will read about how the people they meet and the experiences they have can help them. Children will read about the different activities they can do at school. They also will read about what makes a good friend, the many different types of friends they can have, and what makes each person special.

Building Knowledge Networks

As children read, view, and interact with the texts and media in this module, they build deep topic knowledge about building friendships and the lessons we can learn from friends.

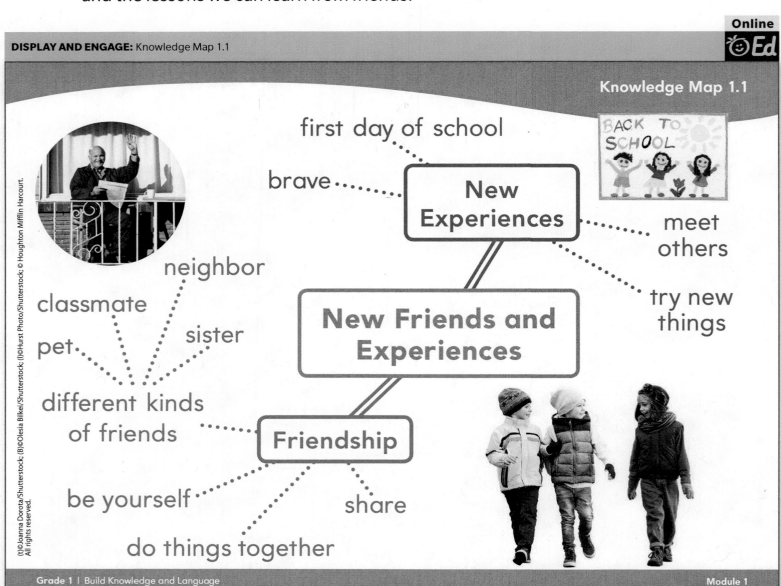

Knowledge Map 1.1

first day of school

brave

New Experiences

BACK TO SCHOOL

meet others

try new things

neighbor

classmate

pet

sister

New Friends and Experiences

different kinds of friends

Friendship

be yourself

share

do things together

(t)©Joanna Dorota/Shutterstock; (B)©Olesia Bilkei/Shutterstock; (l)©Hurst Photo/Shutterstock; © Houghton Mifflin Harcourt. All rights reserved.

Grade 1 | Build Knowledge and Language

Module 1

Synthesize Knowledge

1 At the beginning of the module, introduce the module topic. Use Display and Engage: **Knowledge Map 1.1** to preview what children can expect to learn about making new friends and experiencing new things.

2 After reading each text, share the Knowledge Map again to help children visualize the ways that they can make new friends and the things that new friends can teach us.

3 At the end of the module, have children synthesize what they have learned about the topic during **Let's Wrap Up!**

Fostering a Learning Mindset

Throughout this module, look for the Learning Mindset feature to introduce the Learning Mindset focus—**seeking challenges**—and use the suggestions to weave it throughout children's literacy instruction as they encounter new texts and practice new skills.

Key Messages

- It is important to learn how to do new things. However, sometimes learning new things can be challenging.
- Everyone has challenges, but overcoming these challenges helps people grow.
- School is a place where you can seek new challenges and find opportunities to grow!
- Display <u>Anchor Chart 53: My Learning Mindset</u> throughout the year. Refer to it to introduce seeking challenges.
- Recognize when children consistently exhibit a Learning Mindset focus, using Printable: <u>Learning Mindset Certificate</u>.

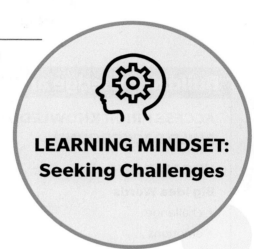

**LEARNING MINDSET:
Seeking Challenges**

Online
Ed

ANCHOR CHART 53: My Learning Mindset

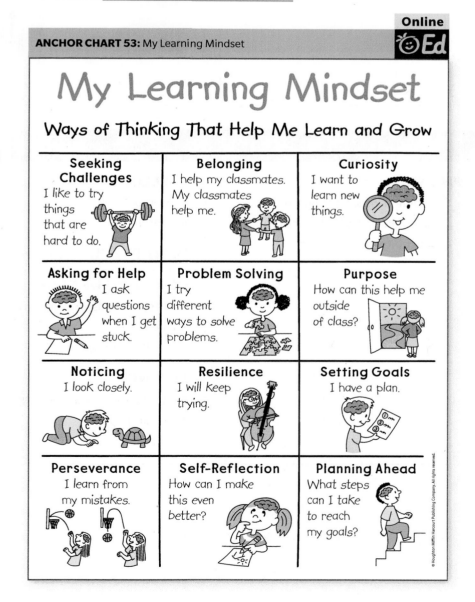

Developing Knowledge and Skills

Children build topic knowledge and develop foundational reading, writing, and oral language skills through daily whole- and small-group instruction.

? Essential Question
How can making new friends and learning new things help us?

LEARNING MINDSET:
Seeking Challenges

Build Knowledge and Language

ACCESS PRIOR KNOWLEDGE/ BUILD BACKGROUND

VOCABULARY

Big Idea Words
- challenge
- emotions
- friendship

MULTIMEDIA

Active Listening and Viewing
- Get Curious Video: *First Day Friends*

Online
Ed
GET CURIOUS VIDEO

Foundational Skills

PHONOLOGICAL AWARENESS
- Blend Onset and Rime
- Segment Syllables, Onset/Rime
- Alliteration; Isolate Phonemes
- Blend Phonemes
- Segment Onset and Rime
- Alliteration; Segment Phonemes
- Segment Phonemes
- Isolate Phonemes: Identify Vowel

PHONICS
- Consonants *m, s, t, b*; Short *a*
- Consonants *n, d, p, c* /**k**/; Short *a*
- Consonants *r, f, s* /**z**/; Short *i*

SPELLING
- Short *a*
- Short *i*

HIGH-FREQUENCY WORDS

CONCEPTS OF PRINT
- Letters, Words, and Sentences
- Directionality
- End Punctuation

FLUENCY
- Accuracy and Self-Correction
- Reading Rate
- Phrasing

Reading Workshop & Vocabulary

VOCABULARY

Power Words

Reader's Vocabulary

Generative Vocabulary

- Words About Feelings
- Inflection -ed

Vocabulary Strategy

- Classify and Categorize

MULTIPLE GENRES

Discuss Genre Characteristics

- Realistic Fiction
- Fantasy
- Narrative Nonfiction
- Informational Text
- Fairy Tale
- Song

SPEAKING AND LISTENING

- Collaborative Conversations

COMPREHENSION

Use Metacognitive Skills

- Ask and Answer Questions
- Monitor and Clarify
- Make Inferences

Literary Elements/Author's Purpose and Craft

- Story Structure
- Elements of Poetry
- Author's Purpose
- Central Idea
- Characters

RESPONSE TO TEXT

- Interact with Sources
- Written Response

FLUENCY

- Accuracy and Self-Correction
- Reading Rate
- Phrasing

Writing Workshop

WRITING FORM

Oral Story

FOCAL TEXT

Ralph Tells a Story by Abby Hanlon

GRAMMAR MINILESSONS

- Common Nouns: People and Animals
- Common Nouns: Places and Things
- Action Verbs

Demonstrate Knowledge

INQUIRY & RESEARCH PROJECT

- "Celebrate Us!" Profiles

ASSESS LEARNING

Formative Assessments

- Selection Quizzes
- Weekly Assessments

Performance-Based Assessments

- Narrative Writing
- Inquiry and Research Project

Summative Assessment

- Module Assessments
- Summative Assessments

Teaching with Text Sets

Carefully selected, content-rich text sets help children build topic knowledge and reading skills.

WEEK 1

First Day Friends

Children view and respond to the video *First Day Friends* to learn more about making new friends.

Genre: Realistic Fiction
Lexile Measure: 150L
Guided Reading Level: E

Genre: Fantasy
Lexile Measure:
AD430L

Genre: Narrative Nonfiction
Lexile Measure: 60L
Guided Reading Level: D

WEEK 2

Genre: Fantasy
Lexile Measure: AD510L

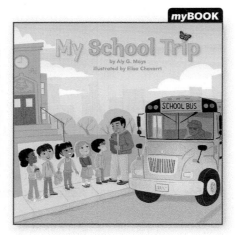

Genre: Realistic Fiction
Lexile Measure: 140L
Guided Reading Level: E

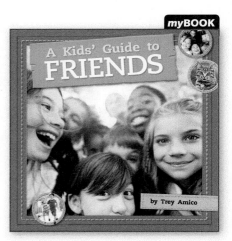

Genre: Informational Text
Lexile Measure: 230L
Guided Reading Level: F

Essential Question
All texts in this set address the question:
How can making new friends and learning new things help us?

WEEK 3

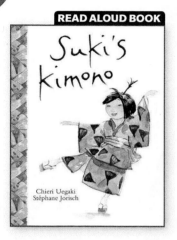

READ ALOUD BOOK

Genre: Realistic Fiction
Lexile Measure: 690L

*my*BOOK

Genre: Fairy Tale
Lexile Measure: 360L
Guided Reading Level: F

*my*BOOK   Online Ed

Genre: Song

WRITING FOCAL TEXT

Genre: Realistic Fiction
Lexile Measure: 460L
Guided Reading Level: G

Reading Workshop

During Reading Workshop, children will engage daily in a variety of whole-group, small-group, and independent literacy activities. Multiple options for differentiated instruction allow teachers to tailor instruction based on student need.

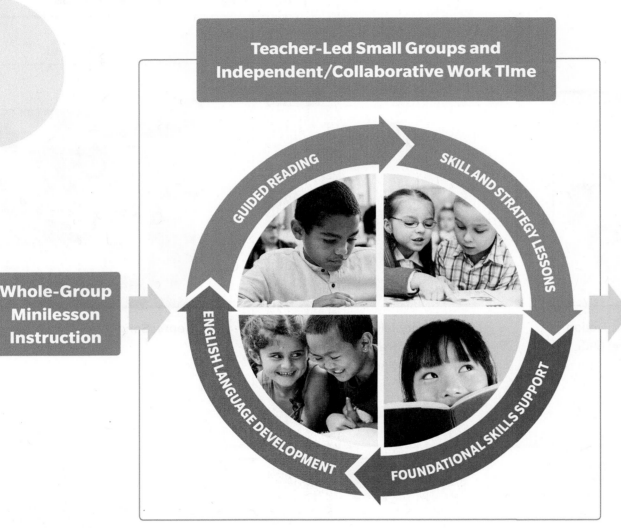

Teacher-Led Small Groups and Independent/Collaborative Work Time

Whole-Group Minilesson Instruction

GUIDED READING · SKILL AND STRATEGY LESSONS · FOUNDATIONAL SKILLS SUPPORT · ENGLISH LANGUAGE DEVELOPMENT

Wrap Up and Share

GUIDED READING

Teacher works with children at their instructional guided reading level.

Using the Rigby Leveled Library, pull just-right books to facilitate guided reading lessons.

SKILL AND STRATEGY LESSONS

Teacher works with small groups to reinforce reading skills and strategies.

Group children for targeted support. Lessons may be connected to the daily whole-group minilesson or based on student need.

FOUNDATIONAL SKILLS SUPPORT

Teacher works with needs-based groups.

Group children according to need to reinforce foundational skills through additional lessons and activities.

ENGLISH LANGUAGE DEVELOPMENT

Teacher works with small groups to support English language acquisition.

Lessons provide children with opportunities to engage in language skills across all the literacy domains in a safe small-group environment.

Forming Small Groups

Guided Reading Groups

- Assess children periodically, using running records or other diagnostic assessments to determine each child's guided reading level.

- Choose books from the Rigby Leveled Library based on reading level, or choose strategies that you plan to teach or practice with each group.

- Use assessment data and information from conferences to frequently regroup children based on reading level.

- Refer to Take & Teach lessons to guide reading instruction, check comprehension, and extend learning.

- Access online Printables, comprehension quizzes, and additional resources that promote revisiting the Leveled Readers for multiple purposes.

English Language Development

- Use Tabletop Minilessons: English Language Development to teach and practice language skills. Guide children to apply them to each lesson's text at their identified language proficiency level

- Access online Printables for children to apply the skill to an independent reading book.

Skill and Strategy Groups

- Observe children during whole-group minilessons to determine who may benefit from targeted support or extension of the day's reading skill. Use assessment data and information to pull groups according to need.

- Use Tabletop Minilessons: Reading to scaffold children's understanding of the skill through an Anchor Chart and supporting lesson.

- Access online Printables for children to apply their understanding of the skill to an independent reading book.

Foundational Skills Support

- Guide children to apply phonics and fluency skills in the Start Right Reader decodable texts and connect the related texts from across the week.

- Use the suggestions in Make Minutes Count to reinforce other foundational skills from the lesson, as needed.

SETTING READING GOALS AND CONFERRING

- Talk to children about their strengths and areas for growth during conferences.

- Work with children to set realistic reading goals that will support them with reaching the next guided reading level.

- Teach strategies that will help children achieve their goals, and remind them to use the strategies when they read. Review strategies frequently with different books.

。

Writing Workshop

Children will engage in the full writing process to produce an oral story during this three-week module. The Writing Workshop Teacher's Guide provides explicit instruction and ample opportunity for children to write daily.

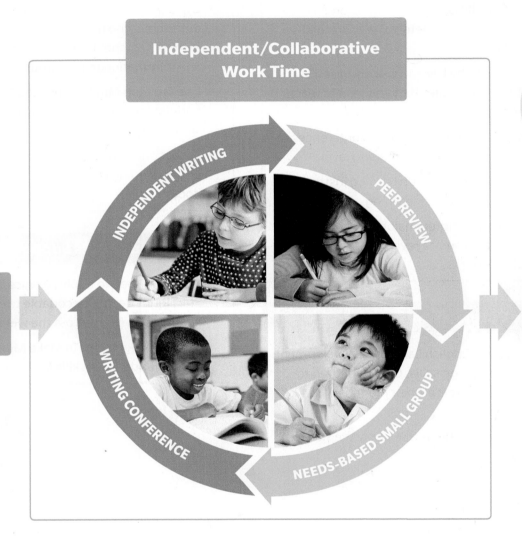

Independent/Collaborative Work Time

Launch Writing Workshop

Share

INDEPENDENT WRITING · PEER REVIEW · WRITING CONFERENCE · NEEDS-BASED SMALL GROUP

INDEPENDENT WRITING

Children work independently to:
- generate ideas/research
- prewrite
- draft
- write
- revise and edit
- publish

PEER REVIEW

Children work in small groups to peer edit. Children engage in analytic talk and clocking activities to provide comments and suggestions that peers may consider incorporating into their writing.

NEEDS-BASED SMALL GROUP

Teacher works with small needs-based groups on grammar and writing skills. Targeted minilessons support development of writing and grammar skills in areas of need.

WRITING CONFERENCE

One-on-One Conferring Teachers meet with children one-on-one to set writing goals and to provide feedback throughout the writing process.

Oral Story Writing Module Overview

Writing Workshop Teacher's Guide, pp. W1–W16

WEEK 1
- Introducing the Focal Text
- The Read
- Vocabulary
- Finding a Topic
- Beginning Oral Storytelling

WEEK 2
- Telling and Listening to Stories I
- Telling and Listening to Stories II
- Prewriting: A Written Class Story
- Drafting I: Developing the Class Story
- Drafting II: Assessing the Story

WEEK 3
- Revising I: Adding Detail
- Revising II: Finding the Right Words
- Editing: Capitalizing Proper Nouns
- Publishing
- Sharing

Ralph Tells a Story by Abby Hanlon

WRITING MODE Narrative Writing

WRITING FORM Oral Story

FOCAL STATEMENT Everyone has a story to tell.

FOCAL TEXT

Writing Prompt

- **TELL** a story about a moment in your life.

Assessment and Progress Monitoring

Ongoing formative assessment guides daily instruction while performance-based assessments demonstrate student progress toward mastery of module skills and standards.

Selection Quizzes

Assess comprehension of the *my*Book text selections.

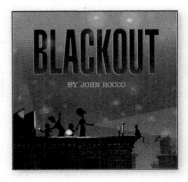   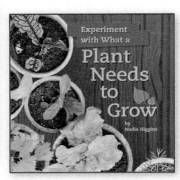

Weekly Assessments

Assess children's understanding of the key Reading, Writing, and Foundational Skills covered during each week of instruction.

Ongoing Formative Assessment Tools

- Leveled Readers
- Comprehension Quizzes
- Running Records
- 1:1 Observation Records
- Daily Lesson Checks and Correct & Redirect opportunities in the Teacher's Guide

Module Assessment

Measure children's proficiency in the critical skills covered in this module:

- Foundational Skills
- Generative Vocabulary
- Vocabulary Strategies
- Comprehension/Literary Analysis
- Grammar
- Writing

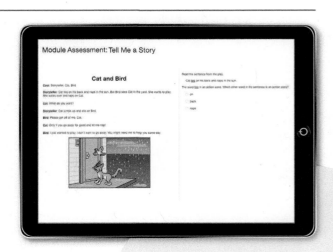

Performance-Based Assessments

Children synthesize what they have learned from the module's text set and demonstrate their topic knowledge by completing one of the module's culminating activities. An optional written Performance Task is also provided at the end of each module in the Teacher's Guide.

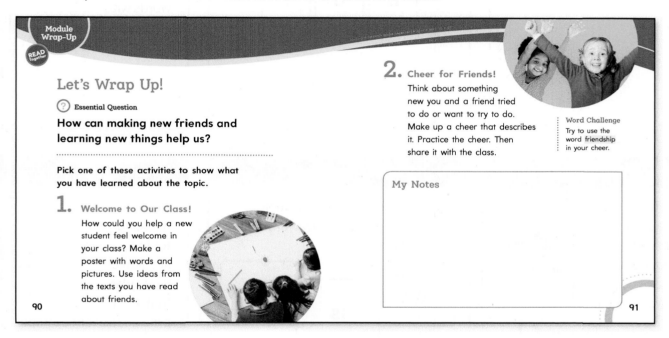

Writing Assessment

Throughout the course of the module, children work through the stages of the writing process in Writing Workshop. Children's writing can be evaluated according to the rubric provided for the module's writing form in the Teacher Resource Book.

Teaching with Instructional Routines

Use recursive, research-informed instructional routines to support lesson planning and maximize children's learning.

Active Viewing

Build and extend children's knowledge about the module topic by actively viewing and responding to the Get Curious Videos at the beginning of each module.

FOCUS ROUTINE

Blending: Sound-by-Sound

Lead children to decode unfamiliar one-syllable words, using consistent language.

Blending: Continuous Blending

Provide this intermediate strategy as a transition between sound-by-sound blending and reading words with automaticity.

Blending: Vowel-First Blending

Provide additional support to children who have difficulty with the other types of blending and need to focus on vowel sounds.

High-Frequency Words

Teach children to read and spell common high-frequency words with automaticity.

Vocabulary

Explicitly teach the meaning of topic-related and academic vocabulary words from the texts, provide relevant examples, and practice using the words in familiar contexts.

Additional Routines

ENGAGEMENT ROUTINES
- Choral Reading
- Partner Reading
- Echo Reading
- Turn and Talk
- Write and Reveal
- Think-Pair-Share
- Share Chair

CLASSROOM MANAGEMENT ROUTINES
- Quiet Cue
- Silent Signals
- Give Me Five!
- Ask Three, Then Me
- Partner Up

Refer to the **GPS guide** for support with using the **ENGAGEMENT** routines and **CLASSROOM MANAGEMENT** routines embedded throughout the lessons.

FOCUS ROUTINE

Blending: Sound-by-Sound

Use the **BLENDING: SOUND-BY-SOUND** routine to

- explicitly teach whole class or small groups to blend words with a target short vowel, consonant digraph, or long vowel spellings.

- model precise and consistent hand motions to blend words.

- provide opportunities to practice blending words with target sound-spellings.

- support children in building word knowledge and rich vocabularies that contribute to future reading success.

ROUTINE MATERIALS

Use the **Letter Cards** when teaching children to blend words.

- Gather the Letter Cards before the lesson and put them in order of the words to blend.

- Display each Letter Card in a pocket chart or on the chalkboard ledge as you ask children to say the sound and blend the letter sounds.

ROUTINE IN ACTION

ROUTINE STEP	MODEL LANGUAGE
1 **Display the cards in order.** Say the first letter and sound.	*What is the letter?* (s) *What sound?* (/s/) s i t
2 **Slide the second letter over.** Say its sound. Then blend the two sounds.	*Sound?* (ĭ) *What sound?* (/sssĭĭĭ/) s i t ⟶
3 **Slide the last letter over.** Say its sound. Say the first two blended sounds, the last sound, and the blended word.	*Sound?* (t) *What sound?* (/sssĭĭĭt/) *What's the word?* (sit) s i t ⟶

BEST PRACTICES

When children are first learning to read or if they are struggling with reading, it is recommended that teachers use the **SOUND-BY-SOUND BLENDING** routine to model blending. The **CONTINUOUS BLENDING** routine provides children with an intermediate strategy as a transition between sound-by-sound blending and reading words with automaticity.

See the **GPS guide** to learn more.

IMPLEMENTATION SUPPORT

Consider these tips when you teach and practice blending:

- Use precise language for blending. For example, say "/f/ sound" and not "*f* sound," since *f* is a letter and not a sound.

- Be careful not to add sounds that make blending difficult. For example, be careful not to add a vowel sound after consonant sounds ("buh" for /b/ and "puh" for /p/).

- If children blend incorrectly, stop and model blending the word. Then guide children to blend the word again.

- Connect to word meaning using context sentences, Picture Cards, or actions to ensure that children are building oral language and understanding during instruction.

Inquiry and Research Project

"CELEBRATE US!" PROFILES Over the next three weeks, children will collaborate to generate ideas, research, complete, and present an inquiry-based project.

WEEK 1

Launch the Project

LEARNING OBJECTIVES

- Participate in shared research projects.
- Generate questions for inquiry and develop a research plan.
- Gather information and evidence from sources.

MATERIALS

- Chart paper
- Informational books
- Approved websites

WEEKLY FOCUS Set a Goal and Gather Information

Build Background Remind children that they will be learning about themselves and others in this module.

- Tell children that the beginning of the school year is a great time to make new friends and find out what makes everyone in the class special.

- Help children start thinking about themselves by brainstorming ideas about what it means to be a good friend and what they want to do and learn this year.

Clarify Project Goals Tell children that over the next few weeks they will create and write illustrated profiles about themselves. The profiles will include a self-portrait and sentences that tell about themselves. They will compile their profiles into a class book and share their self-portraits and sentences with the class.

Generate Research Questions Use the **THINK-PAIR-SHARE** routine to have children brainstorm research questions about friends and themselves that they hope their research will help answer. Make a note of children's questions to revisit after they have completed their projects.

Develop a Research Plan Guide children to come up with a research plan that will help them answer their research questions. Prompt children to ask themselves questions about what they like to do, what they want to learn, and what it means to be a good friend. They can look in magazines for images that illustrate what it means to be a good friend or what they want to be when they grow up.

Create Curiosity Boards Have children start researching.

- Create a classroom Curiosity Board on which groups can post images or write other ideas about themselves and being a good friend. Discuss the display with children, and explain how you would like them to use it.

- As children post to the board, have them think about things that make them special and words that describe what they like and do or what they want to be.

(EL) ENGLISH LEARNER SUPPORT: Share Ideas

Help children think about the things they like to do. Allow children to act out activities or provide sentence frames: *I like _____. I want to _____.*

WEEK 2 Take Action

LEARNING OBJECTIVE
- Record information in simple visual formats.

MATERIALS
- Chart paper
- Pencils and crayons

WEEKLY FOCUS Develop Ideas

Plan to Write Help children plan their profiles.

- Provide sentence frames to help students begin writing: *My name is _____. I like _____. A friend is someone who _____. I am a good friend when I _____. Something new I want to try is _____. I wish _____.*

- Have children begin writing their ideas and planning what they will draw.

Create a Self-Portrait Have children draw their pictures and write complete sentences. Clarify that they do not have to include every sentence.

- When children have completed their self-portraits, work with the class to compile them into a print or eBook. Tell children that they will present their portraits to the class.

- As an extension, children can add to their self-portraits throughout the year, telling about new things they have tried or learned.

 ENGLISH LEARNER SUPPORT: Generate Ideas

Work with children to complete the sentence frames. If necessary, they can provide words in their home language or act out activities. You can help record them in English.

WEEK 3 Present and Reflect

LEARNING OBJECTIVE
- Participate in a presentation.

MATERIALS
- List of research questions from Week 1
- Self-portraits from Week 2

WEEKLY FOCUS Practice and Present

Practice Presenting Have children practice presenting with a small group.

- Tell children in each group to take turns "introducing" themselves using their self-portraits and the sentences they wrote about themselves.

Present and Reflect Establish a time for children to compile their class book and then present their profiles to the whole class, using the **SHARE CHAIR** routine.

- Tell presenters to speak loudly and clearly. Children can respond to and ask questions after each presentation.

- Revisit the research questions children generated in Week 1 and discuss which ones they were able to answer.

✓ ASSESS LEARNING   Online **Ed**

See the **Inquiry and Research Project Rubric**.

 ENGLISH LEARNER SUPPORT: Present Ideas

Help children practice their presentations. Work with children to self-correct or help pronounce words.

Introduce this module's Signposts, using these lessons. Revisit the Anchor Charts, as needed, as you encounter the Signposts during Shared Reading.

FICTION Contrasts and Contradictions

INTRODUCE THE SIGNPOST

- Tell children that sometimes the way a character acts contrasts, or is different from, the way the reader would expect someone to act. The character may also act in the opposite way he or she has been acting up to that point. These contrasts tell something important about the character, plot, setting, or theme.

- **Look for Clues!** Explain that there are usually clues in the story that help readers identify the Contrasts and Contradictions Signpost. For example, a character might suddenly act or think in a different or new way, or there is something about the setting that seems strange.

NOTICE & NOTE IN ACTION!

- Tell children that you will pause as you read certain *my*Book stories in this module to prompt them to notice the Contrasts and Contradictions Signpost and explain how they would apply it to that page or pages. You will also ask children to note in their books things in the text or pictures that will help them remember the Signpost and why it is important to the story.

ANCHOR QUESTION

- Display **Anchor Chart 59: Contrasts and Contradictions**, and discuss the Anchor Question. Tell children that they will ask themselves this question after noticing the Contrasts and Contradictions Signpost. Answering this question will help children better understand a character or setting. The question will also encourage children to think about why the characters do what they do.

ANCHOR CHART 59: Contrasts and Contradictions

Online Ⓔⓓ

Contrasts and Contradictions

Why would the character feel or act this way?

This module's Signposts are featured with the texts below, which contain strong examples of the Signposts as well as complementary comprehension skills. Encourage children to use their growing bank of known Signposts as they read different texts.

LESSON	TEXT	GENRE	COMPREHENSION SKILL	SIGNPOST
3	Try This!	Narrative Nonfiction	Ask and Answer Questions	3 Big Questions
7	My School Trip	Realistic Fiction	Monitor and Clarify	Contrasts and Contradictions
9	A Kids' Guide to Friends	Informational Text	Make Inferences	3 Big Questions
12	Big Dilly's Tale	Fairy Tale	Ask and Answer Questions	Contrasts and Contradictions

● *Professional Learning*

RESEARCH FOUNDATIONS

"When you introduce a child to a good story, you do more than introduce him to a plot and characters. You introduce him to a world that begins on a page, moves into his head, and potentially ends in his heart."

—Beers & Probst (2017)

See the **GPS guide** to learn more.

NONFICTION 3 Big Questions

INTRODUCE

- Explain to children that when they read nonfiction texts, it is important to remember that the author is saying something about the world or a certain topic. Readers cannot assume that everything the author says is true or correct. The author might include his or her opinions. Readers should question what the author says and how it relates to what they already know.

NOTICE & NOTE IN ACTION!

- Tell children that you will pause as you read certain *my*Book selections in this module to prompt them to ask themselves the 3 Big Questions about a page or pages. You will also ask children to note in their books things in the text or pictures that will help them remember the questions, help them answer the questions, or tell why the questions are important to the text.

ANCHOR QUESTIONS

- Display <u>Anchor Chart 65: 3 Big Questions</u>, and discuss the Anchor Questions. Share that children will ask themselves these questions when they see new, confusing, or challenging information in a nonfiction text.

Online

ANCHOR CHART 65: 3 Big Questions

Kicking Off the Module!

Get started with Module 1 by setting goals with children and connecting with families.

Set Goals with Children

Tell children that over the next few weeks they will build and strengthen their reading, writing, listening, and speaking skills as they explore new friends and experiences:

- Encourage children to reflect on their prior learning and set personal goals for the upcoming module.

- Share the sentence frames to the right to support children with setting goals. Model examples and record goals for each child.

- Revisit children's goals throughout the module to help them track progress and reflect on their learning.

> I want to read stories about _____.
>
> I want to learn about _____.
>
> I will _____ so I can _____.

Connect with Families

Share Printable: **Family Letter 1** to support children's learning at home:

- Offer support to help families discuss the module topic and the module's Big Idea Words.

- Encourage children to read at home with their families, and provide ideas for families to talk about books together.

- Suggest word play activities to support literacy development.

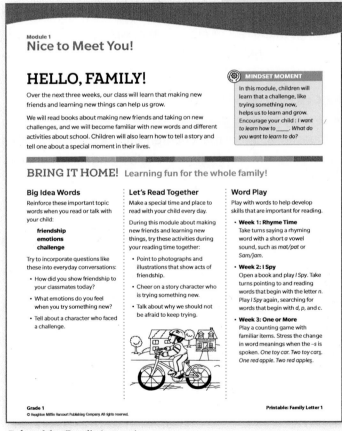

Printable: Family Letter 1

 SOCIAL STUDIES CONNECTION:
New Friends and Experiences

Nice to Meet You!

 Essential Question How can making new friends and learning new things help us?

Essential Skills

FOUNDATIONAL SKILLS

- Phonics: Consonants *m, s, t, b*; Short *a*
- High-Frequency Words: *go, is, like, see, the, this, to, we*
- Fluency: Accuracy and Self-Correction
- Spelling: Short *a*

VOCABULARY

- Power Words: *enjoy, excited, noisy, favorite, furry, goodness, great, hall, library, nervous, new, try*
- Generative Vocabulary: Words About Feelings
- Vocabulary Strategy: Classify and Categorize

READING WORKSHOP

- Story Structure
- Elements of Poetry
- Ask and Answer Questions
- Author's Purpose
- Speaking and Listening: Collaborative Conversations

WRITING WORKSHOP

- Writing Form: Oral Story
- Grammar Minilessons: Common Nouns: People and Animals

LEARNING MINDSET:
Seeking Challenges

THIS WEEK'S TEXTS

My First Day

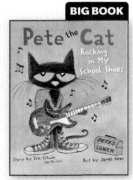

Pete the Cat: Rocking in My School Shoes

Try This!

Decodable Texts
The Mat
Sam at Bat
Tab at Bat
Tam at Bat

Rigby®
LEVELED LIBRARY

Suggested Daily Times

- **BUILD KNOWLEDGE & LANGUAGE/ VOCABULARY** — 10–15 minutes
- **FOUNDATIONAL SKILLS** — 15–30 minutes
- **READING WORKSHOP** — 60–75 minutes
- **WRITING WORKSHOP** — 20–30 minutes

This Week's Words

BIG IDEA WORDS

challenge	emotions	friendship

POWER WORDS

enjoy	excited	favorite
furry	goodness	great
hall	library	nervous
new	noisy	try

HIGH-FREQUENCY WORDS

go	is	like	see
the	this	to	we

READER'S VOCABULARY

adjective	alliteration	author's purpose
categorize	classify	detail
entertain	event	evidence
formal language	genre	inform
informal language	pattern	persuade
repetition	rhyme	sequence

Assessment Options

 Online **Ed**

- ✓ **Selection Quiz: Try This!**
- ✓ **Weekly Assessment**
  - High-Frequency Words
  - Phonics: Consonants *m, s, t, b*; Short *a*
  - Comprehension: Story Structure; Author's Purpose
  - Generative Vocabulary: Words About Feelings
  - Vocabulary Strategy: Categorize and Classify
  - Grammar: Common Nouns: People and Animals

Intervention

For children needing strategic intervention, use *Tabletop Minilessons: Intervention.*

- Module 1, Week 1 Daily Lessons

LESSON 1

BUILD KNOWLEDGE & LANGUAGE

Module Launch, pp. T28–T29   *Teaching Pal*

- Introduce the Topic: New Friends and Experiences
- Big Idea Words: *challenge, emotions, friendships*

FOUNDATIONAL SKILLS

Word Work Warm-Up, pp. T30–T31

- High-Frequency Words: *go, is, like, see, the, this, to, we*
- Phonological Awareness

Phonics, pp. T32–T33

- Consonants *m, s, t, b*; Short *a*

Spelling, pp. T34–T35

- Short *a*

READING WORKSHOP

My First Day   *Teaching Pal*
GENRE Realistic Fiction
Shared Reading: MINILESSON, pp. T36–T37

- Connect and Teach: Story Structure
- Apply to Text: *My First Day*
- Engage and Respond: Speaking & Listening

SMALL-GROUP INSTRUCTION

Options for Differentiation

- Guided Reading Groups, p. T38
- English Learner Support: Seek Information, p. T38
- Reinforce Story Structure, p. T39
- Reinforce Foundational Skills: Read *The Mat*, pp. T40–T41

Options for Independent and Collaborative Work, pp. T42–T43

WRITING WORKSHOP

Oral Story, p. W2

- Introducing the Focal Text

Grammar, p. W241

- Nouns

LESSON 2

FOUNDATIONAL SKILLS

Word Work Warm-Up, pp. T44–T45

- High-Frequency Words: *go, is, like, see, the, this, to, we*
- Phonological Awareness

Phonics, pp. T46–T47

- Consonants *m, s, t, b*; Short *a*

VOCABULARY

Academic Vocabulary, pp. T48–T49

- Introduce Oral Language: *noisy, furry, hall, library, goodness, favorite*

READING WORKSHOP

Pete the Cat: Rocking in My School Shoes   *Book Stix*
GENRE Fantasy
Shared Reading: MINILESSON, pp. T50–T51

- Connect and Teach: Elements of Poetry
- Apply to Text: *Pete the Cat: Rocking in My School Shoes*
- Engage and Respond: Writing

SMALL-GROUP INSTRUCTION

Options for Differentiation

- Guided Reading Groups, p. T52
- English Learner Support: Seek Information, p. T52
- Reinforce Elements of Poetry, p. T53
- Reinforce Foundational Skills: Read *Sam at Bat*, pp. T54–T55

Options for Independent and Collaborative Work, pp. T56–T57

WRITING WORKSHOP

Oral Story, p. W3

- The Read

Grammar, p. W242

- Words That Name People

LESSON 3

FOUNDATIONAL SKILLS

Word Work Warm-Up, p. T58
- High-Frequency Words: *go, is, like, see, the, this, to, we*
- Phonological Awareness

Fluency, p. T59
- Accuracy and Self-Correction

VOCABULARY

Academic Vocabulary, pp. T60–T61
- Introduce Power Words: *try, new, great, enjoy, excited, nervous*

READING WORKSHOP

Try This!
GENRE Narrative Nonfiction
Shared Reading: MINILESSON,
pp. T62–T63
- Connect and Teach: Ask and Answer Questions
- Apply to Text: *Try This!*
- Engage and Respond: Speaking & Listening

SMALL-GROUP INSTRUCTION

Options for Differentiation
- Guided Reading Groups, p. T64
- English Learner Support: Seek Information, p. T64
- Reinforce Ask and Answer Questions, p. T65
- Reinforce Foundational Skills: Read *Tab at Bat*, pp. T66–T67

Options for Independent and Collaborative Work, pp. T68–T69

WRITING WORKSHOP

Oral Story, p. W4
- Vocabulary

Grammar, p. W243
- Words That Name Animals

LESSON 4

FOUNDATIONAL SKILLS

Word Work Warm-Up, p. T70
- High-Frequency Words: *go, is, like, see, the, this, to, we*
- Phonological Awareness

Phonics, p. T71
- Phonics Review

VOCABULARY

Academic Vocabulary, p. T72
- Review Power Words: *try, new, great, enjoy, excited, nervous*

Generative Vocabulary, p. T73
- Words About Feelings

READING WORKSHOP

Try This!
GENRE Narrative Nonfiction
Shared Reading: MINILESSON,
pp. T74–T75
- Connect and Teach: Author's Purpose
- Apply to Text: *Try This!*
- Engage and Respond: Writing

SMALL-GROUP INSTRUCTION

Options for Differentiation
- Guided Reading Groups, p. T76
- English Learner Support: Seek Information, p. T76
- Reinforce Author's Purpose, p. T77
- Reinforce Foundational Skills: Read *Tam at Bat*, pp. T78–T79

Options for Independent and Collaborative Work, pp. T80–T81

WRITING WORKSHOP

Oral Story, p. W5
- Finding a Topic

Grammar, p. W259
- Spiral Review: Proper Nouns and Capitalization

LESSON 5

FOUNDATIONAL SKILLS

Word Work Warm-Up, p. T82
- High-Frequency Words: *go, is, like, see, the, this, to, we*
- Phonological Awareness

Spelling, p. T83
- Spelling Assessment

VOCABULARY

Vocabulary Strategy, pp. T84–T85
- Classify and Categorize

READING WORKSHOP

Speaking & Listening: MINILESSON,
pp. T86–T87
- Connect and Teach: Collaborative Conversations
- Apply to Text
- Engage and Respond: Writing

SMALL-GROUP INSTRUCTION

Options for Differentiation
- Guided Reading Groups, p. T88
- English Learner Support: Seek Information, p. T88
- Reinforce Collaborative Conversations, p. T89
- Reinforce Foundational Skills: Make Connections, pp. T90–T91

Options for Independent and Collaborative Work, pp. T92–T93

WRITING WORKSHOP

Oral Story, p. W6
- Beginning Oral Storytelling

Grammar, p. W245
- Connect to Writing: Using Nouns

Preview Lesson Texts

Build understanding of this week's texts so that you can best support children in making connections, understanding key ideas, and becoming lifelong readers.

myBOOK

My First Day

GENRE Realistic Fiction

WHY THIS TEXT?

Children should readily identify with the content of this story in which a young girl writes about her first day of first grade. Children can consider their own first day of school in relation to that of this fictional student.

KEY LEARNING OBJECTIVES

- Identify features of realistic fiction.
- Use details in the text and illustrations to describe key events in the beginning, middle, and end of a story.

TEXT COMPLEXITY

LEXILE MEASURE 150L • **GUIDED READING LEVEL** E

OVERALL RATING Simple

The story describes a common experience in chronological order.

MAKE CONNECTIONS

🔗 **BUILD KNOWLEDGE AND LANGUAGE**

- **Social Studies Connection:** New Friends and Experiences

🔗 **FOUNDATIONAL SKILLS**

- **High-Frequency Words:** *see, to, we*
- **Consonants *m, s, t, b*; Short *a*:** *first, goodbye, it, last, much, my, said, sang, school, see, so, story, to, tomorrow*

📖 TEXT X-RAY

KEY IDEAS	🔵 LANGUAGE
Key Idea *p. 12* The first day of school was busy. **Key Idea** *p. 13* The children sang, listened to a story, did work, and played. They said goodbye and looked forward to seeing each other the next day.	**Order Words** ***first, next, then, last*** (p. 13): The author uses these words to indicate the order in which events happen during the first day of school.

CULTURAL REFERENCES

goodbye (p. 13): Explain that "goodbye" is the word people use when they are leaving one another or ending a phone conversation. Have children share words that have the same meaning in their primary language, such as *adiós*.

Try This! by Pam Muñoz Ryan

GENRE Narrative Nonfiction

WHY THIS TEXT?

Sam and his classmates try out and enjoy many new activities as they begin a new school year. They think school is great, and hopefully readers will too as they see and reflect on the positive experiences of other children their age!

KEY LEARNING OBJECTIVES

- Identify characteristics of narrative nonfiction.

- Ask and answer questions about a text before, during, and after reading, using text evidence to support responses.

- Determine and discuss the author's purpose for writing a text.

TEXT COMPLEXITY

LEXILE MEASURE 60L • **GUIDED READING LEVEL** D

OVERALL RATING Simple

Photos of familiar childhood experiences support the simple, patterned text.

MAKE CONNECTIONS

🔗 **BUILD KNOWLEDGE AND LANGUAGE**

- **Social Studies Connection:** New Friends and Experiences

🔗 **VOCABULARY**

- **Words About Feelings:** *great*

🔗 **FOUNDATIONAL SKILLS**

- **High-Frequency Words:** *go, is, like, this, to, we*
- **Consonants *m, s, t, b*; Short *a*:** *at, bat, bus, great, outside, paint, Sam, school, this, to, try*

TEXT X-RAY

KEY IDEAS	🗨 LANGUAGE
Key Idea *pp. 16–19* Sam is about to have new experiences at school. First, he tries taking a bus to school.	**Multiple Meanings** ***great:*** Children may be familiar with this word in conjunction with things that are large, as in "a great big bug." Here, however, *great* has the meaning of "very good" or "excellent."
Key Idea *pp. 20–23* Next, Sam tries painting and playing games outside with classmates.	**CULTURAL REFERENCES**
Key Idea *p. 24* Sam and his friends like school and the new things they are trying and learning.	***Try to bat*** (p. 23): If children are unfamiliar with the game of baseball, describe the general rules and the equipment that players use, including a bat. Explain that in the photo, the children are playing tee ball. This game is similar to baseball but is easier because the batter hits the ball off of a stationary tee, or stand, instead of trying to hit a ball thrown by a pitcher.

Literacy Centers

While you meet with small groups, have children work independently in Literacy Centers. At the beginning of the week, explain what is expected of children in each center. Post a daily rotation schedule.

WORD WORK

Word Hunt

- Provide clipboards (or another writing surface) in the center. Also display the Word Cards for this week's High-Frequency Words.

- Have children copy two words and then try to find them in another place in the room, either on a word wall, on bulletin boards, or in books. When they find a word, they should copy it again and tell where they found it.

- For an extra challenge, have children find another mystery word in the classroom.

go	is	like	see

the	this	to	we

Short *a*

- Display the week's Spelling Words and copies of Printable: **Spelling & Handwriting**. Have children choose one of the activities to practice writing this week's Spelling Words in their best handwriting.

- Have children complete the activity on a separate sheet of paper.

Printable: Spelling & Handwriting

CREATIVITY CORNER

Readers' Theater

- Preview Printable: **Readers' Theater 1**, "The New School," and assign parts to mixed-ability groups of five children. The part of Pam Cat is ideal for a struggling reader; the part of Nat Cat can be read by a proficient reader.

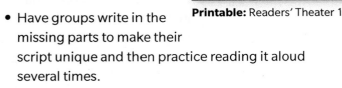

Printable: Readers' Theater 1

- Have groups write in the missing parts to make their script unique and then practice reading it aloud several times.

- Remind children to read their lines loudly and clearly.

Reading Remake

- Display in the center and have children complete the activity for *Try This!* on Printable: **Make an Ad**.

- Tell partners to explain to one another how their ad shows their understanding of the selection.

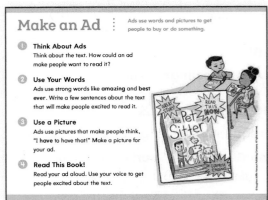

Printable: Make an Ad

DIGITAL STATION

Listener's Choice

- Have children listen to the Big Book *Pete the Cat: Rocking in My School Shoes* or a Leveled Reader of their choice.

- Tell them to add the book to their Printable: **Listening Log**, as well as the active listening skills they used, a summary, and a question they have about the book.

Phonics Practice

- Have children continue their personalized, adaptive learning for foundational skills in *iRead*.

TEAMWORK TIME

Inquiry and Research Project: "Celebrate Us!" Profiles

- Have groups begin work on the module project.

- Remind children that their focus this week is to think about what makes them special and post their ideas to the Curiosity Board. *See pp. T16–T17.*

READING CORNER

Independent Reading

- Have children self-select or continue reading an independent reading book.

- Remind children to set a purpose for reading and to record their progress on their Printable: **Reading Log**.

- You may want to choose from these additional options to have children interact with their books:

  » **Read for Fluency** Children use the **PARTNER READING** routine to practice the week's fluency skill, accuracy and self-correction, or another area of need.

  » **Annotate the Text** Children practice a strategy and use sticky notes to record questions or what they are thinking as they read. Review the sticky notes while you confer with children.

  » **Response Journal** Children draw or write about what they read.

Student Choice Library

Introduce the Topic: New Friends and Experiences

LEARNING OBJECTIVES

- **Language** Answer questions using multi-word responses.
- Share information and ideas about a topic under discussion.
- Identify real-life connections between words and their use.

MATERIALS   Online

Display and Engage *Knowledge Map 1.1*

Teaching Pal *Book 1, pp. 8–11*

myBook *Book 1, pp. 8–11*

Get Curious Video *First Day Friends*

Vocabulary Cards *1.1–1.3*

Access Prior Knowledge

- Reveal the module topic by projecting Display and Engage: **Knowledge Map 1.1**. Point to the center of the Knowledge Map. Tell children that the texts they will read about all relate to new friends and experiences. Use the Knowledge Map to point out some things that children can expect to read about in this module.

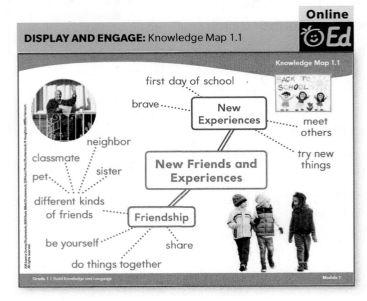

DISPLAY AND ENGAGE: Knowledge Map 1.1

- Have children brainstorm word associations for *new friends and experiences* and add them to a web.

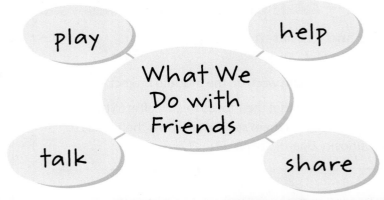

 LEARNING MINDSET

Seeking Challenges

Introduce Tell children that a challenge is a task that takes extra effort. When we seek a challenge, we try something that might be hard to do. Relate the concept to facing challenges at the beginning of the year. *There are lots of new things to figure out when we begin a school year. These are challenges! Did you know that your brain grows when you try new things? That's good news!*

Point out examples of challenges as children encounter them throughout the module.

Professional Learning

RESEARCH FOUNDATIONS

Learning mindsets are a set of beliefs—including growth mindset, belonging, purpose, and relevance—that have been shown to increase academic performance. Research has shown that children who have positive learning mindsets are more likely to take on challenges, persist after an initial failure, and achieve academic success.

See the **GPS guide** to learn more.

Teaching Pal, pp. 8–9

Build Background

In your Teaching Pal, pages 8–11, use the prompts to begin developing the module topic as children follow along in their *my*Book.

- **Discuss the Quotation** Lead a discussion about the familiar quotation (*p. 8*).

- **Essential Question** Introduce the Essential Question: *How can making new friends and learning new things help us?* Then use the **ACTIVE VIEWING** routine with the Get Curious Video: <u>First Day Friends</u> (*p. 9*).

- **Big Idea Words** Use the **VOCABULARY** routine and Vocabulary Cards 1.1–1.3 to introduce the Big Idea Words: *friendship, emotions, challenge.* Then have children begin the Vocabulary Network (*pp. 10–11*). Encourage them to add to it throughout the module.

Online
ⓔEd
GET CURIOUS VIDEO

Vocabulary Cards

EL **ENGLISH LEARNER SUPPORT:**
Facilitate Discussion

SUBSTANTIAL
To facilitate discussion about the topic, ask *yes/no* questions: *Do you have a friend at school? Point to your friend. Do you know your friend's name?*

MODERATE
Provide these frames: *My friend is _____. We like to _____.*

LIGHT
To elicit discussion about the topic, ask open-ended questions: *How do friends have fun? How do friends help each other?*

Professional Learning

BEST PRACTICES

Parents, caretakers, and friends are critical to the learning process. Communication with those at home is essential to building a successful classroom environment. Caretakers should be aware of the topics and skills children are learning about at school. Children should be encouraged to use vocabulary, practice reading skills, and discover new reasons to read at home.

See the **GPS guide** to learn more.

WORD WORK WARM-UP

FOUNDATIONAL SKILLS

LEARNING OBJECTIVES

- Identify and read high-frequency words.
- **Language** Recognize, recite, and write basic sight vocabulary.
- Orally blend onsets and rimes in one-syllable words.
- Segment syllables in multisyllabic words.
- Orally segment onsets and rimes in one-syllable words.

MATERIALS   Online

Word Cards *go, is, like, see, the, this, to, we*

Know It, Show It *p. 4*

Picture Cards *cat, dots, elephant, flowers, hammer, hat, map, mitt, nightlight, pen, rainbow, slippers, tub*

Classroom materials *index cards with holes punched in one corner, ring clips (one per child)*

 # High-Frequency Words

Teach the Words

Use Word Cards *go, is, like, see, the, this, to,* and *we* and the **HIGH-FREQUENCY WORDS** routine below to introduce the week's High-Frequency sight words.

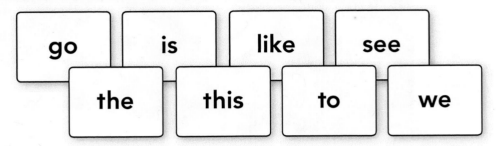

① **See the word.** Display a Word Card. Say the word, and have children repeat it twice.

② **Say the word.** Have children repeat it chorally. Use the word in a sentence or two. *I will go to my desk. Where will you go?* (Use pantomime.)

③ **Spell the word.** Point to the letters, and have children spell the word aloud. Point out any familiar spelling patterns. *Go begins with g. Who has a name that begins with G? Do you know any other words that begin with g?*

④ **Write and check the word.** Hide the word, and have children use the **WRITE AND REVEAL** routine to write the word. Then have them check it against the Word Card.

Tell children that they will be making Word Rings for words they will be learning to read and write this year. Distribute index cards and ring clips. Tell children that writing the words for their Word Rings will help them learn the words. They can use the Word Rings to practice reading the words and as reference for using the words in their writing.

Have children write a word on the front of each card and on the back of the card to write or draw a picture that will help them remember the word. When children finish, have them clip the cards together with the ring clip. Tell children that they will be adding new words to the Word Rings throughout the year.

Alternatively, you may have children complete Know It, Show It page 4.

● Getting Started

ENGAGEMENT ROUTINE

Teach and practice the steps for **WRITE AND REVEAL**.

1. Follow directions to partner.
2. Listen to the question.
3. Think about the answer.
4. Take turns answering the question.
5. Share with the group.

See the **GPS guide** to learn more.

 CORRECT & REDIRECT

Guide children who have trouble identifying any of the words. Say the correct word, and have children repeat it. Example:

- *This. What is the word?* (this)
- Have children spell the word. (t-h-i-s) *How do we say the word?* (this)
- Have children reread all the cards in random order.

Phonological Awareness

Blend Onset and Rime

- Tell children that listening for and working with the sounds in words they hear can help them learn to read and write words. Explain that saying words in chunks can help them notice the sounds in words.

- Display Picture Cards *cat, dots, hat, map, mitt, pen,* and *tub.*

- Tell children that you will say words in chunks and that they will put together, or blend, the chunks to say the words. Display Picture Card *map* and model: *I will say this picture name in two chunks. First, I will say the beginning, and then I will say the rest of the word. You blend the beginning chunk with the rest of the word to say the word. I will do the first one and give you a hint by showing a picture of the word. Listen to the two chunks of this word: /m/ /ăp/. I can blend the two chunks to say the word: /m/ /ăp/, /m-ăp/,* map. *The word is* map. Point to Picture Card *map.*

- *Now you try it. I will say the name of one of these pictures in two chunks, the beginning and the rest of the word. You blend the word chunks and say the word. I will call on someone to point to the matching Picture Card. Listen: /k/ /ăt/. What is the word? (cat) Who can give me the card that matches?*

- Continue having children blend onset and rime to say a Picture Card name. Call a volunteer to bring you the card for each word children say: /p/ /ĕn/ (pen), /d/ /ŏts/ (dots), /h/ /ăt/ (hat), /m/ /ĭt/ (mitt), /t/ /ŭb/ (tub).

Segment Syllables, Onset/Rime

- Tell children that we can break longer words into parts, called syllables. They will clap for each syllable they hear in the words that you say. Say: *For each syllable in a word, clap one time.* Display Picture Card *rainbow. Listen as I say this word:* rainbow, rain-bow. Clap for each syllable. *The first part is* rain-. *The second part is* -bow. *The syllables in* rainbow *are* rain- *and* -bow.

- Display Picture Cards *elephant, flowers, hammer, nightlight,* and *slippers. Now let's do one together. Listen to the picture name. Then clap for each part:* flowers, flow-ers. *How many times did we clap? (two times) What are the two parts of* flowers? *(flow-ers)*

- *Your turn! I'll say a picture name. You repeat the word and clap for each part:* nightlight, night-light. *How many claps? (two) What are the two parts of* nightlight? *(night-light)*

- *Let's keep going. Remember to clap for each word part you hear:* slippers *(slip-pers),* elephant *(el-e-phant),* hammer *(ham-mer).*

- Point out to children that just as they can blend the beginning chunk and the rest of a word, they can break a word into its beginning and the rest of the word. Model: girl. *The beginning sound is /g/. The rest of the word is /ûrl/.* Girl, /g/ /ûrl/.

- Have children segment these words into onset and rime: chip (/ch/ /ĭp/), fox (/f/ /ŏks/), sun (/s/ /ŭn/), cast (/k/ /ăst/), help (/h/ /ĕlp/).

ENGLISH LEARNER SUPPORT:
Build Vocabulary

ALL LEVELS Use gestures to help reinforce word meanings. For example, point to your eyes and look toward a map hanging on the wall as you say this: *I see the map.* Then have children take turns pointing to and naming Picture Cards used in the activity.

CORRECT & REDIRECT

If children have trouble segmenting onset and rime, guide them to first say the beginning sound and then say the rest of the word. Have children repeat after you. Example:

Sun. I hear /s/ at the beginning of sun. *Say it with me:* sun, /s/. *The rest of the word is /ŭn/. Say it with me: /ŭn/.* Sun, /s/ *at the beginning, and the rest /ŭn/. Let's say* sun *in two parts. (/s/ /ŭn/)*

Consonants *m, s, t, b*; Short *a*

Spotlight on Sounds

- Tell children that they will be reading words with the short *a* sound and the sounds for the letters *m, s, t,* and *b*. Then have them practice identifying the beginning sounds in words you say. *I am going to say a word, and you will say the beginning sound. I will do the first one. Listen: the word is* mat. *The beginning sound in* mat *is /m/. Listen again, and repeat after me:* mat, /m/. *Now listen to each word and then say the beginning sound:* sat (/s/); bat (/b/); tap (/t/); man /m/).

- Next, have children suggest words with specific beginning sounds. Say: *Think of words you know that begin with /m/.* Repeat for the sounds /s/, /t/, /b/.

- Conclude by modeling how to identify the final sound in *am, /m/.* Have children say the final sounds in these words: *mat (/t/); tab (/b/); gas (/s/); ram (/m/).*

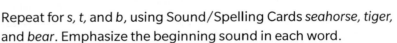
I Do It

Spotlight on Letters Explain that the alphabet includes vowels (*a, e, i, o, u*) and consonants (the other letters). *Let's talk about some of the consonants.*

Display the Sound/Spelling Card for *m: moth.* Name the picture, say the sound, and give the spelling. *Moth begins with the sound /m/, and the letter* m *stands for that sound. Listen: /m/, mmmoth, m. Say that with me: /m/, moth, m.*

Repeat for *s, t,* and *b,* using Sound/Spelling Cards *seahorse, tiger,* and *bear.* Emphasize the beginning sound in each word.

Next, display the Sound/Spelling Card for short *a: alligator. The letter* a *is a vowel. Vowels stand for many sounds. One of this letter's sounds is the short* a *sound, /ă/. Alligator begins with /ă/. The letter* a *can stand for /ă/ at the beginning or in the middle of a word.*

Have children use Printable: <u>Letter Cards</u>. Say: *Listen as I say the sounds of the letters again. Hold up the letter card that stands for the sound I say: /m/ (m); /s/ (s); /ă/ (a); /b/ (b); /t/ (t).*

LEARNING OBJECTIVES

- Learn the sound-spellings for short *a* and the consonants *m, s, t, b.*
- **Language** Recognize sound-letter relationships and use them to decode words.
- Blend sounds and decode regularly spelled one-syllable words with /ă/, /m/, /s/, /t/, and /b/.

MATERIALS   Online ⊙*Ed*

Sound/Spelling Cards *alligator, bear, moth, seahorse, tiger*
Printable *Letter Cards*
Letter Cards *a, m, S, s, t, b*
Articulation Videos /ă/, /b/, /m/, /s/, /t/

TEACHER TIP

Now decodable! After this lesson, children will be able to decode the High-Frequency Words *am* and *at*! Children will practice these words along with the other High-Frequency Words for this week to build fluent word recognition.

EL **ENGLISH LEARNER SUPPORT: Facilitate Language Connections**

ALL LEVELS Because short *a* is not a sound in Spanish, Vietnamese, Cantonese, or Korean, some children may not know how to hold their mouths when saying the sound. Say /ă/ several times while children focus on your mouth. Then play the <u>Articulation Video</u> for /ă/. Have children use mirrors to see how their mouths look as they say /ă/.

If children need practice with the consonant sounds, see the other <u>Articulation Videos</u> in the Materials list.

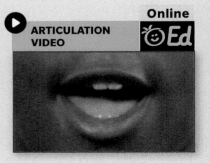
ARTICULATION VIDEO   Online ⊙*Ed*

We Do It

Write *mat,* and use Letter Cards *m, a, t* with the **SOUND-BY-SOUND BLENDING** routine below to model blending the word.

1 **Display** cards as shown. Point to the vowel. *When there is only one vowel and it is followed by a consonant, the vowel usually stands for its short sound.* Say the first letter and sound.

2 **Slide** the second letter over. Say its sound. Then blend the two sounds.

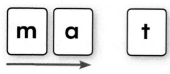

3 **Slide** the last letter over. Say its sound. Say the first two blended sounds, the last sound, and the blended word: /mǎ//t/, mat.

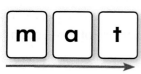

Sound-by-Sound Blending Repeat the **SOUND-BY-SOUND BLENDING** routine with cards for the words *bat* and *Sam,* having children say the sounds and blend.

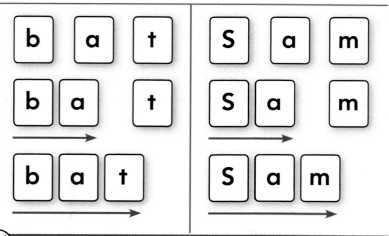

You Do It

INDEPENDENT PRACTICE

Blending Practice Write the words below. Then choose a volunteer to model the activity. Say: *Find a word that begins with the letter* m *and read it.* Repeat the blending routine as needed. Continue asking children to find and read words that begin or end with the letters *a, m, s, t, b* until each child has had a turn and all the words have been read.

mat	bat	tab	Tam
Sam	sat	at	am

✓ CORRECT & REDIRECT

- If a child mispronounces a word during Blending Practice, make note of the error type and address it.
- If a child reads *am* when directed to read a word that begins with the letter *m,* explain that *am* ends with *m.* Point to and identify the beginning letter in *mat, bat,* and *tab.* Have the child name the beginning letter in the remaining words. Then have the child go back and read a word that begins with *m.*
- If a child reads *mat* as *tam,* cover the word and blend it together as you uncover one letter at a time, left to right. Then have the child blend and read the word.

👥 LINK TO SMALL-GROUP INSTRUCTION

REINFORCE FOUNDATIONAL SKILLS
Use *The Mat* during small-group time to review or reinforce blending and decoding words with short *a* and consonants *m, s, t, b.* Meet with children to work through the story, or assign it as independent work. *See the lesson on p. T40.*

FOUNDATIONAL SKILLS

LEARNING OBJECTIVES

- Spell words with short *a* (closed syllables).
- **Language** Identify relationships between sounds and letters.
- Develop handwriting by printing *a, d*.

MATERIALS Online Ed

Sound/Spelling Card *alligator*
Printables *Manuscript Aa, Dd; Word List 1*
Know It, Show It *p. 5*

DICTATION SENTENCES

BASIC

1. **mat** Wipe your feet on the *mat*.
2. **sat** We *sat* on the couch.
3. **bat** The ball player has a *bat*.
4. **Sam** That boy is named *Sam*.
5. **am** I *am* in first grade.
6. **at** We are *at* school now.

🕐 Short *a*

Administer the Pretest

- Read the first Spelling Word and the Dictation Sentence. Repeat the word as children write it.
- Write the word, and have children correct their spelling if needed. Repeat for words 2–6.

Teach the Principle

- Write *mat* on the board, underlining *a*, and read it aloud. Explain that the /ă/ sound can be spelled with the letter *a*.
- Tell children that this week all the Spelling Words have the short *a* sound, /ă/, spelled *a*. Explain that short *a* sound can be at the beginning or in the middle of a word.
- If children have difficulty, review Sound/Spelling Card *alligator*. Remind them that *a* is a vowel that can stand for many sounds and that one of those sounds is /ă/ as in *alligator*.

Model Handwriting

- Model how to write lowercase *a* and *d*. *a: Start just below the middle line. Pull back, around, up to the middle line, and then down. d: Start just below the middle line. Pull back, around, up to the top line, and then down.*
- Have children describe what they notice about the letters *a* and *d*. (*They are both formed in a similar way, and they look similar to each other.*) Model writing one or more of the Spelling Words that include *a*.
- Have children use the **WRITE AND REVEAL** routine to practice writing words that include lowercase *a* and *d*. As needed, distribute the handwriting models on Printable: **Manuscript Aa, Dd**. Printables for Continuous Stroke letter forms are also available online.

TEACHER TIP

Take it from the middle! Some children may start writing *d* at the top of the middle line. Remind them that *d* is similar to *a*, and like *a*, the starting point for *d* is just below the middle line. Point out that to write a letter correctly from memory, children have to remember where to begin forming it.

○ *Getting Started*

ENGAGEMENT ROUTINE

Model and practice engagement routines until they are automatic. For example, role-play with a few children **WRITE AND REVEAL** to show the whole class the benefits of all of you displaying the information at the same time instead of taking turns to do so.

See the **GPS guide** to learn more.

Word Sort

1 **Introduce** Display the Spelling Word cards from Printable: Word List 1. Explain that today's word sort will focus on words that have the short *a* sound.

2 **Column 1** Display and read *am*. On chart paper, model identifying the short *a*. Point out that the short *a* sound is at the beginning of the word *am*. Post the card as the heading for words that have the same vowel sound at the beginning.

3 **Column 2** Repeat for *mat*, and start a column for words that have the short *a* sound in the middle of the word.

4 **Continue** Sort the other words. Model if necessary. Example: *At. I'll listen for the place where I hear the /ă/ sound. Is it at the beginning of the word or in the middle of the word? Aaaam. The short a sound, /ă/, is at the beginning of the word. It is in the same place as in the word am. So I'll put at under am.* Repeat the procedure for *sat*, placing it under *mat*.

5 **Discuss** Read each column together. Discuss what children notice about the words in each column. If no one mentions it, point out that the short *a* sound can appear in the beginning of words or in the middle. Tell children they can think about this pattern when they spell words with short *a*.

6 **Repeat** Have children work together to repeat the sort, using the Spelling Word cards from Printable: Word List 1. Remind children to save the rest of the page and the Spelling Word Cards for use all week.

am	mat
at	sat
	bat
	Sam

INDEPENDENT PRACTICE

For additional practice, have children complete Know It, Show It page 5. Encourage them to use their best handwriting and pay particular attention to writing the letter *a* correctly.

 ENGLISH LEARNER SUPPORT:
Facilitate Language Connections

ALL LEVELS The short *a* sound does not exist in Cantonese. Have speakers of this language listen and watch your mouth position as you say the short *a* sound. Ask children to repeat the vowel sound after you a few times. Correct their pronunciation as necessary.

 LEARNING MINDSET

Seeking Challenges

Model Help children understand that when we look for challenges and try new things, our brains grow! Use the following example. *When I come across a word I don't know, I think of it as a challenge. I don't know how to spell some of this week's Spelling Words, but I want to learn how. I think that there are always words and other things I don't know, so it's important to challenge myself into learning as much I can!*

READING WORKSHOP

Story Structure

Step 1 Connect and Teach

LEARNING OBJECTIVES

- Recognize characteristics of realistic fiction.
- Identify and describe story events in order.
- **Language** Describe events in order using sequence words.
- Share ideas in cooperative learning interactions.

MATERIALS   Online **Ed**

Anchor Chart 18 *Story Structure*

Printable *Anchor Chart 18: Story Structure*

Teaching Pal *Book 1, pp. 12–13*

myBook *My First Day, Book 1, pp. 12–13*

READER'S VOCABULARY

- **event** something that happens in a story
- **sequence** an order of events (beginning, middle, and end) in a story

- Explain that we usually do things in a certain order. Give an example, such as waking up at the beginning of the day, going to school in the middle of the day, and going to bed at the end of the day.

- Then project or display **Anchor Chart 18: Story Structure**.

- Point out that things in stories also happen in a certain order. Tell children that a thing that happens in a story is called an **event**. Events in a story are told in order, or in a **sequence**.

- Explain that identifying and describing the most important events in the beginning, middle, and end of a story helps readers understand it better.

- Finally, tell children that readers can use details in both the text and pictures, and the words *first, next,* and *last* to identify and describe the most important events in a story.

- Tell children they will practice identifying and describing important events when they read a story called *My First Day.*

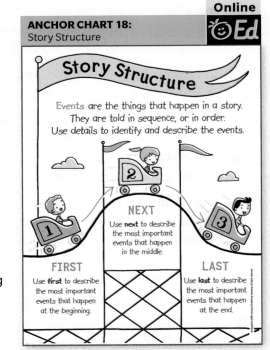

ANCHOR CHART 18:
Story Structure

Online **Ed**

TEACHER TIP

Order matters! Recite a familiar nursery rhyme out of order, for example: *Gently down the stream; Life is but a dream; Merrily, merrily, merrily, merrily; Row, row, row your boat.* Discuss why the rhyme doesn't make sense in this order. Have children tell the correct order of the lines.

 ENGLISH LEARNER SUPPORT: Support Comprehension

ALL LEVELS Help children understand how to use the words *first, next,* and *last.* Have children form a line. Then tap children as you tell their order: *(Juan) is first. (Lin) is next. (Tanu) is next. (Maria) is last.* Then have the group break into lines of three to five and have children tell who is *first, next,* and *last.*

Online

ANNOTATE IT!

Children may use the annotation
tools in their eBook.

Step 2 Apply to Text

 In your Teaching Pal, pages 12–13 use the blue **READ FOR
UNDERSTANDING** prompts to guide discussion of *My First
Day* as children follow along in their *my*Book.

- **Genre Study** Tell children that realistic fiction stories are
made up but could happen in real life. Have them preview
the title and illustrations, and tell whether the events could
happen in real life.

- **Set a Purpose** Prompt children to set their own purpose for
reading, based on their preview. As needed, use this model:
*I'll read to find out what the girl does on her first day. I'll pay
attention to what happens in the beginning, middle, and end of
her school day.*

- **Read and Comprehend** Guide children to read the selection
all the way through. Pause occasionally, using the prompts in
your Teaching Pal to gauge children's understanding, and to
have them identify story events at the beginning, middle, and
end of the day. Refer back to the Anchor Chart, and discuss
what happens first, next, and last.

Step 3 Engage and Respond

INDEPENDENT PRACTICE: Speaking & Listening

- Remind children of the Essential Question: *How can making
new friends and learning new things help us?* Then have children
look at *My First Day* again to see if they can find any
information that helps them answer the question.

- Have partners use the **THINK-PAIR-SHARE** routine to discuss
their ideas and then share with the group. Remind children to
listen carefully and look at the person speaking to show they
are listening.

- You may want to have children conduct their discussions
during daily small-group time.

Getting Started

ENGAGEMENT ROUTINE

Teach and practice the steps for **THINK-PAIR-SHARE.**

1. Think: Listen to a question and think about your answer.

2. Pair: Take turns answering the question.

3. Share: Share with the group.

See the **GPS guide** to learn more.

 LINK TO SMALL-GROUP INSTRUCTION

REINFORCE STORY STRUCTURE Review or extend the skill as
needed during small-group time to support children's need for
differentiation. *See the lesson on p. T39.*

Options for Differentiation

As the class engages in independent and collaborative work, meet with Guided Reading Groups or differentiate instruction based on student need.

GUIDED READING GROUPS

Match Children to Books + Instruction

- Choose just-right books based on level, skill, topic, or genre.

C — D — E — F — G — H — I — J — K →

Leveled Readers

- Deliver instruction with each book's Take and Teach Lesson, choosing appropriate sessions based on need.

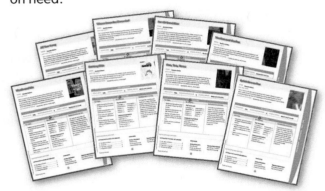

- Check comprehension, reinforce instruction, and extend learning with suggested supporting activities.

Rigby
LEVELED LIBRARY

EL ENGLISH LEARNER SUPPORT

Seek Information

- Use **Tabletop Minilessons: English Language Development 1.1 (Listening)** to introduce and practice the language skill.

Tabletop Minilessons: English Language Development

- Then use the following text-based prompts with *My First Day* to guide application of the language skill. Begin with the prompt at the child's identified language proficiency level. As children are able, use lighter supports to encourage increased language proficiency.

SUBSTANTIAL
Review question words with children by asking them to identify information in the story. Ask: *Where are the children? What are they doing in this picture?* Allow students to point to words or pictures to answer.

MODERATE
Model asking a question about the story such as: *What is this girl doing?* Then have children ask and answer questions about the story using these frames: *Where _____? What _____?*

LIGHT
Ask children to formulate a question about each scene. Encourage children to use a variety of structures such as: *What is _____? What does _____? How does _____? How many _____?* and so on.

REINFORCE STORY STRUCTURE

Demonstrate

- Use **Tabletop Minilessons: Reading 18** to remind children that the **events** are what happens in a story. The **sequence** of events is the order: what happens at the beginning, in the middle, and at the end of a story. Remind children to use details in the pictures and in the text to help them understand the events. They can use the words *first, next, then,* and *last* to identify important events and the order of the events.

- Model filling out Printable: **Reading Graphic Organizer 23** to identify and describe the sequence of events in *My First Day*.

Tabletop Minilessons: Reading

Apply to Independent Reading

- Now have children identify and describe the sequence of events in an appropriate just-right book that they are reading independently. Customize these prompts to the books children choose.

  » *What are the events in this story?*

  » *What happens first?*

  » *What happens next?*

  » *What happens last?*

- Have children complete Printable: **Reading Graphic Organizer 23** for their independent reading book.

Printable:
Reading Graphic Organizer 23

ALMOST THERE
↓
READY FOR MORE

SCAFFOLD AND EXTEND

- Help children use the pictures to identify the sequence of events of the story.

- Describe the beginning of the story. Then ask children whether this event happened *first* or *last*.

- Have children discuss the words that help them know the order in which the events happen in the story.

 ENGLISH LEARNER SUPPORT

SUBSTANTIAL

Ask children to identify what happens first in the story by pointing to pictures or text or answer orally. Then ask what happens next and last. Model answering in short sentences.

MODERATE

Briefly relate an event from the story. Then ask: *Does this event happen in the beginning, in the middle, or at the end?*

LIGHT

Have children work with a partner to retell the events of the story. Prompt them to use the terms *first, next, then,* and *last*.

👥 SMALL-GROUP INSTRUCTION

Options for Differentiation

The Mat, Start Right Reader, *Book 1*, pp. 4–11

REINFORCE FOUNDATIONAL SKILLS

Read Decodable Text

Get Started Have children turn to Start Right Reader page 4. Explain that this week's stories about two friends named Sam and Tab. Have children share things they like to do with their friends. Then read page 4 together and discuss the questions.

Preview the Story Draw attention to page 5, the title page. Read aloud the title and have children look at the pictures on the first few pages. Have them predict what will happen to the mat.

Concepts of Print: Letters, Words, and Sentences
Use page 5 to model identifying letters, words, and sentences. Point to individual letters, and use your fingers to frame words and then sentences. Point out the narrow space between each letter in a word and the larger space between each word in a sentence. Have children place a finger on the space between *Sam* and *sat*.

Fluency Focus: Accuracy and Self-Correction
Read aloud page 7 as children follow along. Misread *to* as *on* and then model self-correcting. Ask children what they noticed about your reading. *(You corrected yourself.)*

Point out that it is important to read each word accurately, or correctly, for the text to make sense. Then lead children in reading page 7.

Reflect on Reading Have children use a finger to track the words from left to right as they read each page silently. Then have them read the page chorally. Pause for these prompts:

- **Page 5:** *What are Sam and Tab doing? (They are sitting and having a picnic.)*

- **Pages 6–7:** *What happens to the mat? (It blows into a tree.)*

- **Page 9:** *What does "Bam! Bam! Bam!" mean? (It is the sound of Tab nailing down the mat.)*

- **Page 10:** *What do you think Sam and Tab will do next? (play baseball) Why do you think so? (Sam says, "Go to bat, Tab" and Tab is holding a bat in the picture.)*

Rhyming Word Hunt Read aloud the directions on page 11. Have children read the clues, look through the story for the answers, and write the answers on a sheet of paper. *(Sam; mat; sat)*

Tab! Tab!

Bam! Bam! Bam!
Bam! Bam! Bam!

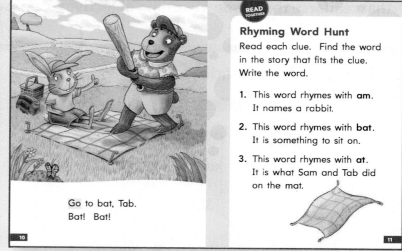

Go to bat, Tab.
Bat! Bat!

READ TOGETHER

Rhyming Word Hunt
Read each clue. Find the word in the story that fits the clue. Write the word.

1. This word rhymes with **am**. It names a rabbit.

2. This word rhymes with **bat**. It is something to sit on.

3. This word rhymes with **at**. It is what Sam and Tab did on the mat.

⏱ Make Minutes Count

As you meet with small groups to read *The Mat*, use one or more of these related activities, as needed, at the beginning or the end of the small-group session.

- **Connect to Phonics** Use Letter Cards *a, b, m, s,* and *t* to review letter sounds. Then use the Letter Cards to build these words: *bat, mat, sat, Tab.* Have each child choose a word, model blending, and then say the word smoothly.

- **Connect to Spelling** Play Raise the Roof. Write a Spelling Word on the board or on chart paper. As you point to each letter in the word, have children name it with you and push up toward the ceiling, one push for each letter. Repeat the procedure for the remaining Spelling Words.

- **Connect to Handwriting** Draw a triple-track line on the board, and write the letters *a* and *d* on the track. Discuss how the letters are formed in a similar way. Reinforce that when forming *d*, they should begin just below the middle line, not at the top. Then have children "air write" the letters *a* and *d*.

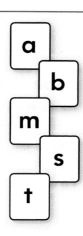

Options for Independent and Collaborative Work

While you meet with small groups, have other children engage in literacy activities that reinforce the lesson's learning objectives. Choose from these options.

Independent Reading

Student Choice Library

Rigby LEVELED LIBRARY

APPLY READING SKILL

Story Structure Children complete Printable: **Reading Graphic Organizer 23** for an independent reading book.

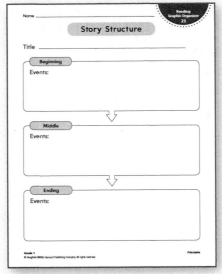

Printable: Reading Graphic Organizer 23

APPLY LANGUAGE SKILL

Seek Information Children complete Printable: **Language Graphic Organizer 12** for an independent reading book.

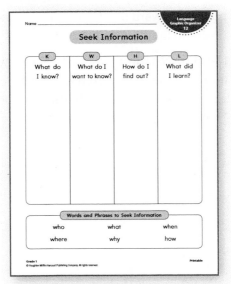

Printable: Language Graphic Organizer 12

Literacy Centers

See pp. T26–T27.

 WORD WORK

 CREATIVITY CORNER

 DIGITAL STATION

 READING CORNER

 TEAMWORK TIME

Start Right Reader

The Mat
by Edward Ruiz
illustrated by David Bucs

Sam sat.
Tab sat.

5

Read Decodable Text *The Mat*, Book 1: pp. 4–11

Speaking & Listening

Partners use Think-Pair-Share to discuss the Essential Question. *See Engage & Respond, p. T37.*

Additional Skills Practice

HIGH-FREQUENCY WORDS

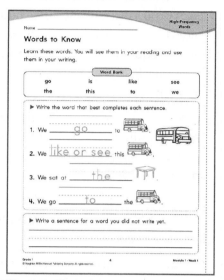

Name _____

High-Frequency Words

Words to Know

Learn these words. You will see them in your reading and use them in your writing.

Word Bank

go	is	like	see
the	this	to	we

▶ Write the word that best completes each sentence.

1. We __go__ to 🚌
2. We __like or see__ this 🚌
3. We sat at __the__ 🪑
4. We go __to__ the 🚌

▶ Write a sentence for a word you did not write yet.
_____

Grade 1
© Houghton Mifflin Harcourt Publishing Company. All rights reserved.   4   Module 1 • Week 1

Know It, Show It, p. 4

SPELLING

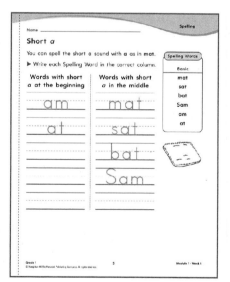

Name _____

Spelling

Short a

You can spell the short a sound with a as in mat.

▶ Write each Spelling Word in the correct column.

Words with short a at the beginning	Words with short a in the middle
am	mat
at	sat
	bat
	Sam

Spelling Words

Basic
mat
sat
bat
Sam
am
at

Grade 1
© Houghton Mifflin Harcourt Publishing Company. All rights reserved.   5   Module 1 • Week 1

Know It, Show It, p. 5

Wrap-Up
Share Time

At the end of Reading Workshop, have children reflect on their learning by sharing how they applied **Story Structure** or another area of focus during independent work time. Choose from these options:

- **SHARE CHAIR** Select a reader each day to come to the front of the class and tell what he or she learned from the reading by using a skill or strategy.

- **THINK-PAIR-SHARE** Children share their thinking with a partner. Select a few children each day to share with the whole class.

- **RETURN TO ANCHOR CHART** Have children add sticky notes about their independent reading book to the Story Structure Anchor Chart. Call on a few children to explain what they added.

ANCHOR CHART 18: Story Structure

Online Ed

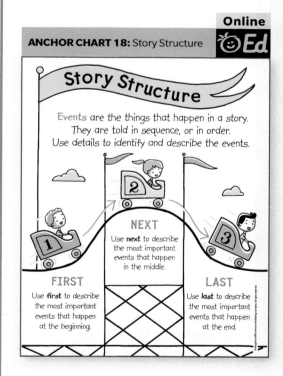

Story Structure

Events are the things that happen in a story. They are told in sequence, or in order. Use details to identify and describe the events.

FIRST Use **first** to describe the most important events that happen at the beginning.

NEXT Use **next** to describe the most important events that happen in the middle.

LAST Use **last** to describe the most important events that happen at the end.

LEARNING OBJECTIVES

- Identify and read high-frequency words.
- **Language** Recognize, recite, and spell basic sight vocabulary.
- **Language** Compose oral sentences using basic sight vocabulary.
- Orally blend onsets and rimes in one-syllable words.
- Segment syllables in multisyllabic words.
- Orally segment onsets and rimes in one-syllable words.

MATERIALS   Online

Word Cards *am, at, go, is, like, see, the, this, to, we*

Printable *Word List 1*

Picture Cards *bat (animal), butterfly, cherries, kangaroo, log, web*

 # High-Frequency Words

Review the Words

Repeat the **HIGH-FREQUENCY WORDS** routine to review this week's High-Frequency Words: *go, is, like, see, the, this, to,* and *we,* and the decodable High-Frequency Words *am* and *at.*

Card Flip

- Have children work in small groups. Each group will use one set of cutout High-Frequency and decodable High-Frequency Word cards from Printable: **Word List 1**. Have children place the cards face up in a row.

- One child chooses a word, without picking up or pointing to the word card, and says a sentence using that word. (Example: *I like playing baseball.*)

- The other group members find the word card for the word used in the sentence, and flip it over so it is face down.

- Children take turns saying sentences using the High-Frequency Words until all cards have been flipped over.

Printable: Word List 1

TEACHER TIP

Two-card flip! Challenge children to suggest sentences that use two High-Frequency Words. If sentences correctly use two words, other group members flip over both word cards.

Professional Learning

BEST PRACTICES

Using the routines embedded in the lessons will help build a classroom that is both student-friendly and academically successful. Choose a few key routines and begin using them early on. Add to those routines each month. Effective teachers know that routines make all the difference!

See the **GPS guide** to learn more.

Phonological Awareness

Blend Onset and Rime

- Remind children that they can listen for and pay attention to the sounds in words. Remind them that they know how to blend the beginning chunk of a word with the rest of it to say the word.

- Display Picture Cards *bat (animal), log,* and *web.*

- Tell children they are going to blend the word chunks you say and say the words. Model: *I am trying to say a word. Listen: /b//ăt/. I can blend the chunks to say the word: /b//ăt/,* bat. *The word is* bat. Point to Picture Card *bat.*

- *Your turn! Blend these word chunks to say a word. Then point to the picture that matches the word you said. Listen to these word chunks: /l//ŏg/. What is the word? (log) Blend these chunks: /w//ĕb/. What is the word? (web)*

- *Now let's practice blending word chunks to say words: /sh//ĕl/ (shell), /j//ēnz/ (jeans), /sh//ōōz/ (shoes), /ch//ärt/ (chart), /m//outh/ (mouth), /ch//īld/ (child).*

Segment Syllables, Onset/Rime

- Remind children that longer words have parts called syllables, and that they have practiced breaking words into their syllables. Say: *I will say a word. You will say the word and clap once for each syllable you say. Listen as I do the first one:* backpack, back-pack. Clap for each syllable. *I clapped two times.* Backpack *has two syllables. The first part is* back-. *The second part is* -pack. Backpack, back-pack.

- *Now you try it. I'll hold up a Picture Card and say the picture name. Then you say the word and clap for each part you say:* butterfly. *(but-ter-fly) I heard three claps. What are the three parts of* butterfly? *(but-ter-fly)*

- *Let's try more. Clap for each word part you hear:* cherries *(cher-ries),* kangaroo *(kan-ga-roo).*

- Remind children that they can also break words into chunks: the beginning and the rest of the word. Model: tap. *The beginning chunk is /t/, and the rest of the word is /ăp/.* Tap, */t//ăp/.*

- *Now you try:* big. *(/b//ĭg/)*

- Have children continue segmenting onset/rime with the names of classroom objects. Use the following object words, and then ask children to suggest others: desk *(/d//ĕsk/)*, pad *(/p//ăd/)*, book *(/b//ōōk/)*.

 ENGLISH LEARNER SUPPORT:
Build Vocabulary

SUBSTANTIAL
Ask *yes/no* questions about the words in the Phonological Awareness activities. For example: *Can you write with a pen? Can you read a desk?*

MODERATE
Have children answer *either/or* questions about the words. *Does a spider make a bat or a web? Is a butterfly or a kangaroo a kind of bug?*

LIGHT
Supply children with sentence frames to complete that name a classmate and a classroom object: _____ *has a* _____ *on her desk.*

 CORRECT & REDIRECT

If children blend onset and rime incorrectly, model the task by stepping out the process and reminding the child of the word part they are to blend to say the word, as in the example below.

- Say the onset and rime: */j//ēnz/*. Have the child repeat. *(/j//ēnz/)*

- Ask: *What is the beginning part? (/j/) Here are the sounds again: /j//ēnz/. What is the rest of the word? (/ēnz/)*

- Ask the child to blend the beginning part and the rest of the word. *(jeans) Yes! /j/ and /ēnz/ make* jeans!

- Continue as needed using other words from the blending activity.

LEARNING OBJECTIVES

- Blend, build, and decode regularly spelled one-syllable words with short *a* and consonants *m, s, t, b.*
- **Language** Recognize sound-letter relationships and use them to decode words.

MATERIALS   Online

Sound/Spelling Cards *alligator, bear, moth, seahorse, tiger*

Letter Cards *a, b, m, s, t*

Display and Engage *Blend and Read 1.2*

Start Right Reader Book 1, p. 12

Printable *Letter Cards*

Know It, Show It p. 6

Consonants *m, s, t, b;* Short *a*

Spotlight on Sounds

- Remind children that they have been learning about the short a vowel sound, /ă/. Guide them to listen for short *a* in the middle of words. *I will say two words. You will tell me which word has the short a sound, /ă/.*

- *I will do the first one. Listen:* man, mane. **Repeat, emphasizing the vowel sounds:** *Man, mane. Man has the short a sound, /ă/, in the middle.*

- *Now you try it. Tell me which word has the short a sound in the middle, and say the sound:* mad/made (mad, /ă/), pan/pane (pan, /ă/); bake/back (back, /ă/); came/Cam (Cam, /ă/); mat/mate (mat, /ă/); paid/pad (pad, /ă/).

I Do It

Spotlight on Letters Review Sound/Spelling Cards *alligator, bear, moth, seahorse,* and *tiger. Remember, a is one of the vowel letters. These other letters are consonants.*

Write *tab* for children to see, and use the **SOUND-BY-SOUND BLENDING** routine below to model blending the word using Letter Cards *t, a, b.*

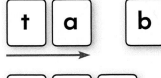

1. **Display** Letter Cards as shown. Say the first letter and sound.

2. **Slide** the second letter over. Say its sound. Then blend the two sounds.

3. **Slide** the last letter over. Say its sound. Say the first two blended sounds, the last sound, and the blended word: /tă//b/, tab. *Who knows what a tab is? (a flap at the edge of a page or a folder; the part you pull to open a can)*

Repeat the routine with the cards for *mat* and *sat.*

Professional Learning

RESEARCH FOUNDATIONS

"Depending on the interactional context, learners are likely to notice the corrective quality of recasts (Oliver & Mackey 2003), especially in cases where the recasts have been shortened and/ or provided with added stress to highlight the error."
   —Dr. Roy Lyster, Dr. Kazuya Siato, & Dr. Masatoshi Sato (2013)

See the **GPS guide** to learn more.

 ENGLISH LEARNER SUPPORT: Build Vocabulary

SUBSTANTIAL
   Discuss the meaning of each Blend and Read word. Point out that *Tam, Sam,* and *Tab* are names and that *bam* names a sound.

MODERATE
   Explain that some words, such as *bat* and *mat,* have multiple meanings. Guide children to understand each meaning.

LIGHT
   Have children identify the Blend and Read words with multiple meanings.

We Do It

Blend and Read

Project Display and Engage: **Blend and Read 1.2** or use Start Right Reader page 12.

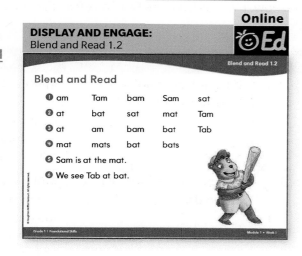

DISPLAY AND ENGAGE:
Blend and Read 1.2

Online
Ed

Blend and Read 1.2

Blend and Read

❶ am   Tam   bam   Sam   sat
❷ at   bat   sat   mat   Tam
❸ at   am   bam   bat   Tab
❹ mat   mats   bat   bats
❺ Sam is at the mat.
❻ We see Tab at bat.

Grade 1 | Foundational Skills   Module 1 • Week I

❶ **Line 1** Have children read the line. Then prompt a conversation about the words: *How are some of the words the same or different? What do you notice?* If necessary, lead children to compare the words: beginning sound (*Sam, sat*); ending sounds/rhyming words (*am, Tam, bam, Sam*). Point to each word, and have children read the line chorally. Provide corrective feedback as needed.

❷ **Line 2** Continue with these words. Then call on volunteers to reread selected words until children can identify the words quickly.

❸ **Review** For Line 3, have children read the words chorally.

❹ **Challenge** If children are ready for a challenge, have them read the words in Line 4 and share how they figured out the ones ending with -*s*.

❺ **Sentences** For Lines 5–6, call on children to blend selected decodable words. Then have the group read the sentences chorally.

You Do It

INDEPENDENT PRACTICE

- **Option 1** Model how to write and spell the word *Sam* sound by sound. Then have children identify sounds and use Printable: **Letter Cards** to form these words: *am, mat, bam*. Have a child spell each word aloud while others check their own work.

- **Option 2** Children complete Know It, Show It page 6.

 CORRECT & REDIRECT

- If a child mispronounces a word during the Blend and Read, make note of the error type and address it.
- If a child has trouble blending a word, have the child use letter cards to display the word. Help the child name each letter and sound, and then guide the child through the sound-by-sound blending routine to blend the word.

 LINK TO SMALL-GROUP INSTRUCTION

REINFORCE FOUNDATIONAL SKILLS
Use *Sam at Bat* during small-group time to review or reinforce blending and decoding words with short a and consonants *m, s, t, b*. Meet with children to work through the story, or assign it as independent work. *See the lesson on p. T54.*

Sam at Bat
by Edward Ruiz
illustrated by David Baca

Sam is at bat.
Bat, Sam. Bat!

LEARNING OBJECTIVES

- **Language** Answer questions and discuss meanings to develop vocabulary.
- Identify real-life connections between words and their use.

MATERIALS   Online

Vocabulary Cards *1.4–1.9*
Big Book *Pete the Cat: Rocking in My School Shoes*
Classroom materials *crayon*

 # Introduce Oral Language

Use the steps **I Do It, We Do It, You Do It** with the information in the chart below to teach the oral Power Words from the Big Book *Pete the Cat: Rocking in My School Shoes.*

① Power Word	② Meaning	③ Example
noisy (adj.) *(p. 13)*	If something is **noisy**, it is loud and full of sounds.	**MAKE A CONNECTION** Name school activities that can be noisy. *Sometimes it gets **noisy** when everyone talks in the lunchroom.*
furry (adj.) *(p. 3)*	If something is **furry**, it is covered in soft, thick hair.	**MAKE A CONNECTION** Connect the concept of furry to common animals. *Cats and dogs are **furry** animals.*
hall (n.) *(p. 6)*	A **hall** is a long walkway that is not wide and is inside a building.	**ACT IT OUT** Walk out the door and stand in the hall. *When I go out the door, I am in the **hall**.*
library (n.) *(p. 8)*	A **library** is a place where books are kept for people to use or borrow.	**MAKE A CONNECTION** Point out the books in the classroom library. *We have a lot of books in our **library**.*
goodness (n.) *(p. 9)*	People say **"goodness!"** when they are surprised about something.	**ACT IT OUT** Make a surprised expression. ***Goodness**, I didn't know it would rain today!*
favorite (adj.) *(p. 9)*	Your **favorite** thing is the one you like best.	**USE A PROP** Hold up a favorite color of crayon. *This is my **favorite** color. I like it the most because ___.*

TEACHER TIP

More surprises! After discussing *goodness,* ask children to share other expressions they might use when they are surprised, such as *wow, gosh, I don't believe it, really,* and *oh my.* Have volunteers use the expressions in sentences and act out feeling surprised. Encourage them to include other Power Words in their sentences.

 ## LEARNING MINDSET

Seeking Challenges

Model When we read, we may come to words we don't know. We can think of these words as challenges. Here's an example: *I've never seen this word before. I'm going to take time and figure it out. I'll look for word parts and read each part. Then I'll try to read the whole word. If it's the meaning I don't know, I can look for clues to figure it out.*

I Do It

Use the **VOCABULARY** routine and Vocabulary Cards 1.4–1.9 to introduce the oral Power Words from *Pete the Cat: Rocking in My School Shoes*. You may wish to display the corresponding Vocabulary Card for each word as you discuss it.

noisy

Vocabulary Cards

1 **Say the Power Word.** Ask children to repeat it.

2 **Explain the meaning.** Read aloud the student-friendly meaning.

3 **Talk about examples.** Use the image or a strategy to give examples of the word.

We Do It

Guide children to make connections between each word's meaning and how they can use it in their own lives. Use these prompts. Encourage children to explain or justify their answers.

- *Name some things that are **furry**.*

- *What do you do when you go to a **library**?*

- *When you walk down a **hall** at school, what do you see?*

- *Tell about a time when you could say, **"Goodness!"***

- *What are some **noisy** sounds that you can hear outside?*

- *Name your **favorite** food. Tell why it is your favorite.*

You Do It

INDEPENDENT PRACTICE

Have partners work together to complete each of the activities below. Circulate and observe partners as they work, providing corrective feedback as necessary.

- **Draw** *Draw a picture that shows your **favorite furry** animal.*

- **Compare** *Tell what it is like to walk down a **hall** alone. Then tell what it is like to walk down a hall with lots of other people.*

- **Role-Play** *Imagine you won a big prize. Show how you would look. Say the word **"Goodness!"** to show how you feel.*

- **Discuss** *Is a **library** quiet or **noisy**? Tell why.*

Professional Learning

RESEARCH FOUNDATIONS

"Important research-based practices include encouraging students to play with and explore words, actively teaching students new vocabulary, helping students build strategies to learn new words independently, reading to students, and encouraging students to read widely."

—Dr. Camille L. Z. Blachowicz and Dr. Peter Fisher (2004)

See the **GPS guide** to learn more.

Elements of Poetry

LEARNING OBJECTIVES

- Recognize characteristics of fantasy.
- Identify and discuss repetition, rhyme, and alliteration in poems.
- **Language** Discuss the poet's use of rhyme, repetition, and alliteration, using those terms.
- Use text evidence to draw and write about a character's actions.

MATERIALS   Online

Anchor Chart 36
Elements of Poetry

Printable *Anchor Chart 36: Elements of Poetry*

Big Book *Pete the Cat: Rocking in My School Shoes*

BookStix *1.1*

READER'S VOCABULARY

- **alliteration** repetition of the same sound(s) or letter(s) at the beginning of words
- **pattern** a repeated set of words, sounds, or beats in a piece of writing
- **repetition** the same word or sound appears over and over to show something is important or to add rhythm
- **rhyme** the repetition of the same sound(s) at the end of words

- Tell children that poets use words in special ways to make poems sound good and fun to read.

- Project or display <u>Anchor Chart 36: Elements of Poetry</u>. Read and explain each part of the chart.

- Explain that **alliteration** is the repetition of the same sounds at the beginning of words. Explain that the repeating sounds make a **pattern**.

- Point out that poets sometimes use **repetition**, or the inclusion of the same word over and over, to help readers understand what is most important in a poem.

- Finally, explain that **rhyme** is the repetition of the same sound or sounds at the end of words. Point out that rhymes also create a pattern of sounds.

- Tell children they will talk about rhyme, repetition, and alliteration as they listen to a Big Book called *Pete the Cat: Rocking in My School Shoes.*

Online

ANCHOR CHART 36: Elements of Poetry

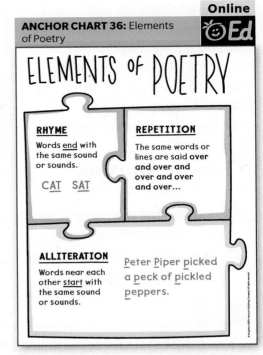

 Professional Learning

RESEARCH FOUNDATIONS

"In kindergarten and early first grade, the use of big books supports the primary literacy goals. The instructional support provided by the teacher in the whole-class setting [during shared reading] provides the bridge that enables a student to gain new insights that later allows him or her to successfully engage in the reading process independently."

—Dr. Katherine Dougherty Stahl (2012)

See the **GPS guide** to learn more.

LEARNING MINDSET

Seeking Challenges

Reflect Review pages 13–15 of the Big Book. Discuss how Pete embraces a new challenge: *Pete is about to eat in a big, noisy room. How do you think he feels? What does he do?* Guide children to conclude that Pete is willing to try new things.

Then review pages 29–32. Discuss how Pete shows that he is ready and willing to learn. *When Pete says he'll do it again tomorrow and it's all good, what does that tell you about how he feels?*

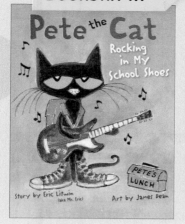

**Go to
BookStix 1.1**

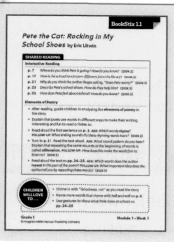

Step 2 Apply to Text

- **Genre Study** Read aloud the title *Pete the Cat: Rocking in My School Shoes,* and introduce the book. *We are going to read a book that is a fantasy written as a poem.* Have children look at the cover and first two pages. Ask: *Who do you think the story is about? What will the cat do?*

- **Set a Purpose** Tell children that one purpose for reading fantasy is to be entertained. *As we read, listen for funny or interesting things that happen to the characters.*

- **Model Fluency** Tell children that as you read, you are going to demonstrate how to read words correctly and correct yourself if you make a mistake. Demonstrate by rereading the title, misreading *shoes,* and self-correcting.

- **Concepts of Print** As you read, point out the differences between letters, words, and sentences. Have children find examples of each.

- **Read and Comprehend** Do a shared reading of the Big Book with children using BookStix 1.1. Pause occasionally to ask the questions and to have children analyze how alliteration, repetition, and rhyme add meaning to the poem and make it more interesting and fun to read and listen to. Refer back to the Anchor Chart, as needed.

Step 3 Engage and Respond

INDEPENDENT PRACTICE: Writing

- Remind children that in the Big Book *Pete the Cat: Rocking in My School Shoes,* the poet repeats the words, "I'm (doing something) in my school shoes."

- Have children draw a picture of one of the things Pete does in his school shoes. Have them label their picture by completing the sentence frame: *I'm _____ in my school shoes.* Encourage children to include details from the book in their pictures.

- Ask partners to share and compare their responses. Encourage them to recognize how their responses are similar or different.

- You may want to have children complete their writing during daily small-group time.

ENGLISH LEARNER SUPPORT:
Build Background

SUBSTANTIAL
Take a picture walk. Name key objects and locations, for example, the *books* in the *library,* and have children repeat the words.

MODERATE
Page through the book and have children name each place and what Pete is doing there: *Pete is in the _____. He is _____.*

LIGHT
Display the frame: *I am _____ing in my school shoes.* Page through the book and have children use the frame to tell what Pete is doing.

LINK TO SMALL-GROUP INSTRUCTION

REINFORCE ELEMENTS OF POETRY Review or extend the skill as needed during small-group time to support children's need for differentiation. *See the lesson on p. T53.*

👥 SMALL-GROUP INSTRUCTION

Options for Differentiation

As the class engages in independent and collaborative work, meet with Guided Reading Groups or differentiate instruction based on student need.

GUIDED READING GROUPS

Match Children to Books + Instruction

- Choose just-right books based on level, skill, topic, or genre.

C D E F G H I J K →

Leveled Readers

- Deliver instruction with each book's Take and Teach Lesson, choosing appropriate sessions based on need.

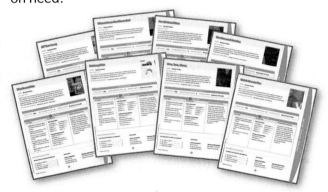

- Check comprehension, reinforce instruction, and extend learning with suggested supporting activities.

Rigby®
LEVELED LIBRARY

🔵 EL ENGLISH LEARNER SUPPORT

Seek Information

- Use **Tabletop Minilessons: English Language Development 1.1 (Speaking)** to reinforce and practice the language skill.

Tabletop Minilessons: English Language Development

- Then use the following text-based prompts with *Pete the Cat: Rocking in My School Shoes* to guide application of the language skill. Begin with the prompt at the child's identified language proficiency level. As children are able, use lighter supports to encourage increased language proficiency.

SUBSTANTIAL
Show children the front cover. Point to Pete's shoes, backpack, guitar, and lunchbox. Say each word and have children repeat. Then ask what color each item is.

MODERATE
Look at page 6 and model asking a question using *where.* Then supply the frame: *Where is _____?* and have children ask their own question about that page. Repeat with other pages and question words.

LIGHT
Have children take turns asking questions about the story using *who, where, how many,* and *why.* Allow children to answer their peers' questions. Correct and model accurate questions and answers as necessary.

REINFORCE ELEMENTS OF POETRY

Demonstrate

- Use **Tabletop Minilessons: Reading 36** to remind children that authors use different techniques to make poems interesting. **Repetition** helps readers understand what the most important ideas are. **Rhyme** is the repetition of certain sounds at the end of words. **Alliteration** is the repetition of certain sounds at the beginning of words. Rhyming words and alliteration make patterns of sounds.

- Model filling out Printable: <u>**Reading Graphic Organizer 15**</u> to identify elements of poetry in *Pete the Cat: Rocking in My School Shoes.*

Tabletop Minilessons: Reading

Apply to Independent Reading

- Now have children identify elements of poetry in an appropriate just-right book that they are reading independently. Customize these prompts to the books children choose.

  » *Does your book have rhyming words? What are they?*

  » *Does your book have alliteration? What sound do you hear at the beginning of the words?*

  » *Are any of the sounds, words, or phrases repeated? Which ones?*

- Have children complete Printable: <u>**Reading Graphic Organizer 15**</u> for their independent reading book.

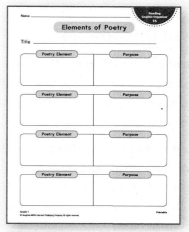

Printable:
Reading Graphic Organizer 15

ALMOST THERE

READY FOR MORE

SCAFFOLD AND EXTEND

- Identify the rhyme, alliteration, and repetition for children. Prompt them to discuss how each technique adds meaning to the poems.

- Guide children to identify the elements of poetry in their books. Prompt them to discuss how they add meaning to the poems.

- Have children discuss the elements of poetry in their poems. Have them tell how each adds meaning to the poems.

(EL) ENGLISH LEARNER SUPPORT

SUBSTANTIAL

Point to and read aloud a rhyming pair in a poem, emphasizing the rhyme. Have children repeat the words and sounds after you. Repeat for alliteration and repetition.

MODERATE

Give children a word from the poem and guide them to identify the word it rhymes with. Have them repeat the rhyming pair. Repeat for alliteration and repetition.

LIGHT

Prompt children to isolate the rhyme in rhyming words. Repeat for alliteration and repetition.

Options for Differentiation

Sam at Bat, Start Right Reader, *Book 1,* pp. 12–19

REINFORCE FOUNDATIONAL SKILLS

Read Decodable Text

Blend and Read Have children turn to Start Right Reader page 12. Use the **CHORAL READING** routine to read aloud the Blend and Read lines. Use challenge line 4 with children who are ready.

Preview the Story Read aloud the title on page 13 and have children look at the picture and identify the characters as Sam and Tab from *The Mat.* Call attention to the baseball diamond in the picture and ask children to share what they know about baseball. Then have children look at the pictures on the first few pages and predict what might happen when Sam and Tab play baseball.

Fluency Focus: Accuracy and Self-Correction
Read aloud page 14 as children follow along. Misread *Bam!* as *Bat!* and discuss what you should do to self-correct. Ask: *Did I read this word correctly? (no) The word is* Bam! *I said* Bat! *What should I do? (reread to say the correct word)* Lead children in reading the page chorally, with accuracy.

Reflect on Reading Have children use a finger to track the words from left to right as they read each page silently. Then have them read the page chorally. Pause for these prompts:

- **Page 14:** *Who hits the ball? (Sam) Who tries to catch the ball? (Tab)*

- **Pages 15–16:** *What happens to the ball? (It falls into a big hole.) Is this what you predicted would happen? Explain. (Responses will vary.)*

- **Pages 17–18:** *What does Sam do? (He dives into the hole and gets the ball out.)*

What Is the Word? Read aloud the directions and clues on page 19. Have children find and read the matching words in the story. *(bat; Bam!)* Then have them page through the story for ideas for their own clue writing. Have partners find and read the words that match each other's clues.

Sam! Sam!
See this, Sam?

Sam! Sam! Sam!

16 | 17

See, Tab?

READ TOGETHER

What Is the Word?
Use the clues to find words in the story.

Clue 1: tells what Sam does
Clue 2: rhymes with **mat**
What is the word?

Clue 1: names a loud sound
Clue 2: rhymes with **Sam**
What is the word?

Now you do it! Give two clues about a story word. Can a partner find it?

18 | 19

⏱ Make Minutes Count

As you meet with small groups to read *Sam at Bat*, use one or more of these related activities, as needed, at the beginning or the end of the small-group session.

- **Connect to Phonics** Play Letter Swap. Have partners take turns building words using Letter Cards *a, b, m, s, t.* One partner builds a word. Then the other partner adds, removes, or replaces one consonant to form a new word. Have partners write each word they build. At the end of the activity, have partners read aloud their lists.

- **Connect to Spelling** Play Word Jar. Place the Spelling Word cards from Printable: Word List 1 in a jar or box. Have children take turns choosing a word and spelling it aloud. Continue until all the words have been selected.

- **Connect to Handwriting** Write the words *am* and *at* on the board. As you model, reinforce the correct starting point for the letter *a*. Then have children write each word two times in their best handwriting. As they write, check their pencil grip and paper position, correcting as needed. Have children put a star next to the words that best match the models.

a	m
b	a	m
b	a	t
s	a	t

LESSON 2

READING WORKSHOP

Options for Independent and Collaborative Work

While you meet with small groups, have other children engage in literacy activities that reinforce the lesson's learning objectives. Choose from these options.

Independent Reading

Student Choice Library

Rigby
LEVELED LIBRARY

APPLY READING SKILL

Elements of Poetry Children complete Printable: **Reading Graphic Organizer 15** for an independent reading book.

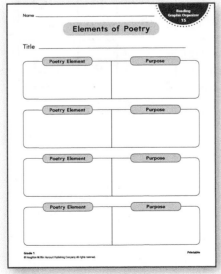

Printable: Reading Graphic Organizer 15

APPLY LANGUAGE SKILL

Seek Information Children complete Printable: **Language Graphic Organizer 12** for an independent reading book.

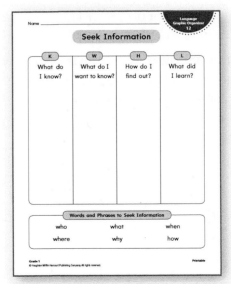

Printable: Language Graphic Organizer 12

Literacy Centers

See pp. T26–T27.

 WORD WORK

 CREATIVITY CORNER

 DIGITAL STATION

 READING CORNER

 TEAMWORK TIME

Start Right Reader

Sam is at bat.
Bat, Sam. Bat!

Read Decodable Text *Sam at Bat,* Book 1: pp. 12–19

Additional Skills Practice

PHONICS

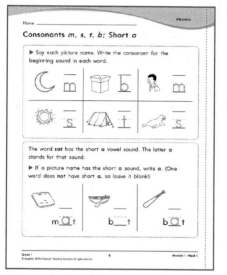

Know It, Show It, p. 6

Writing

Children use details from the Big Book to draw a picture and complete a sentence frame that partners then share and compare. *See Engage & Respond, p. T51.*

Wrap-Up
Share Time

At the end of Reading Workshop, have children reflect on their learning by sharing how they applied **Elements of Poetry** or another area of focus during independent work time. Choose from these options:

- **SHARE CHAIR** Select a reader each day to come to the front of the class and tell what he or she learned from the reading by using a skill or strategy.

- **THINK-PAIR-SHARE** Children share their thinking with a partner. Select a few children each day to share with the whole class.

- **RETURN TO ANCHOR CHART** Have children add sticky notes about their independent reading book to the Elements of Poetry Anchor Chart. Call on a few children to share what information they added.

ANCHOR CHART 36: Elements of Poetry

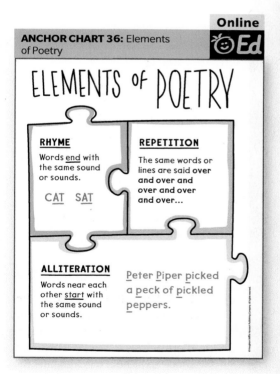

LESSON 3

FOUNDATIONAL SKILLS

LEARNING OBJECTIVES

- Identify and read high-frequency words.
- **Language** Recite and spell basic sight vocabulary.
- Recognize spoken alliteration.
- Isolate initial and final phoneme in spoken one-syllable words.
- Blend phonemes to say one-syllable words.

MATERIALS   Online

Word Cards *am, at, go, is, like, see, the, this, to, we*

Picture Cards *boat, cup, log, pin, tub*

 # High-Frequency Words

Review the Words

Repeat the **HIGH-FREQUENCY WORDS** routine to review the week's High-Frequency Words: *go, is, like, see, the, this, to,* and *we,* and the decodable High-Frequency Words *am* and *at.*

> **am**

Blast Off!

- Have children crouch down on the floor. Say a High-Frequency Word. Ask children to repeat the word and spell it. Then have them jump up and "blast off" as they say the word again.
- Repeat for the remaining words.

Phonological Awareness

Alliteration; Isolate Phonemes

- Tell children that you will say sets of words, and they will give a thumbs-up if all the words in a set begin with the same sound and a thumbs-down if they do not. Say: *I will do the first set:* water, willow, wash. *Thumbs up! I hear /w/ at the beginning of all three words.* Continue with these word sets: call, kitchen, couch (*up*); red, round, bean (*down*); half, hot, hungry (*up*); van, zebra, very (*down*).
- Display the Picture Cards. Model how to isolate initial sounds: *The word is* tap. *The beginning sound in tap is /t/. Tub has the same beginning sound as tap, /t/.*
- *Now you try! Listen: What is the beginning sound in bed? (/b/) Which Picture Card word begins with the same sound? (boat) Let's keep going:* cow (/k/, *cup*); late (/l/, *log*); part (/p/, *pin*).
- Adapt and repeat the activity to have children isolate final sounds in these words: sit (/t/, *boat*); nap (/p/ *cup*); cab (/b/, *tub*); rag (/g/, *log*); fine (/n/, *pin*).

Blend Phonemes

- Tell children that they can blend sounds to say words. Say: *I will say the sounds in a word, and you will blend the sounds to say the word, like this: /w/ /ĭ/ /g/,* wig.
- *Now it's your turn:* /ā/ /t/ (*ate*), /p/ /ĕ/ /t/ (*pet*), /ĭ/ /n/ (*in*), /h/ /ō/ /p/ (*hope*), /m/ /ŭ/ /d/ (*mud*).

TEACHER TIP

Stretch it out! Have children first elongate a word, saying each sound very slowly for a few seconds, and then more quickly to say the word. This process will help children hear the individual phonemes and then blend them together to say the word.

 CORRECT & REDIRECT

Guide children who have trouble isolating initial and final phonemes.

- Model the task. *Listen as I say the word* part. *The sound at the beginning of part is /p/. Say it with me:* part, /p/.
- *Now let's find the Picture Card whose name begins with the same sound, /p/.* Display Picture Card *pin*. *This is a pin. The sound at the beginning of pin is /p/. Do pin and part begin with the same sound, /p/? Yes!*
- Repeat for cow (/k/, *cup*) and late (/l/, *log*).
- Use a similar modeling and support for identifying final phonemes for children who struggle isolating sounds at the end of words.

Accuracy and Self-Correction

I Do It

LEARNING OBJECTIVE

• Read on-level text accurately by using context to self-correct.

MATERIALS Online Ed

Start Right Reader Book 1, pp. 13–18

• Explain to children that good readers think about what they are reading and whether the words make sense. They ask themselves questions, such as these: *Does that sound right? Does that make sense? What would make sense here?*

• Ask children to follow along and to pay attention to whether the words make sense as you read Start Right Reader page 13 (*Sam at Bat*). Model misreading the first sentence, pointing to each word. Sam is ate bat. *Does that sound right? No, the word* ate *doesn't make sense in that sentence. I'll try again.* Reread the sentence correctly: Sam is at bat. *The word is* at, *not* ate. *That makes much more sense!*

We Do It

• Have children return to Start Right Reader page 13 (*Sam at Bat*). Model misreading *bat* in the last line as *bait* and then self-correcting. Bait, Sam. Bait *doesn't make sense. I'll take another look. Oh, it's* bat. Bat, Sam. Bat *makes sense.* Ask a volunteer to restate the process you used when you read a word that didn't make sense.

• Have children use the **PARTNER READING** routine to take turns reading pages 14 and 15 to each other. As you circulate and listen, coach children to use context to confirm or self-correct their word recognition. Encourage partners to help each other go back and find the words that caused difficulty and reread them correctly.

You Do It

INDEPENDENT PRACTICE

• Have children use the **PARTNER READING** routine to reread one of this week's Start Right Reader stories about Sam and Tab or *Try This!* from their *my*Book. Point out that rereading and self-correcting when things do not make sense will help them become better readers.

Getting Started

ENGAGEMENT ROUTINE

Teach and practice **PARTNER READING**:

• Pair students strategically and assign numbers (1/2) to decide who goes first.

• Tell partners who will read first and how much of the text to read.

• Model taking turns reading and listening.

• Have partners take turns reading the text.

See the **GPS guide** to learn more.

LINK TO SMALL-GROUP INSTRUCTION

REINFORCE FOUNDATIONAL SKILLS

Use *Tab at Bat* during small-group time to review or reinforce blending and decoding words with short *a*, and consonants *m, s, t,* and *b*. Meet with children to work through the story, or assign it as independent work. *See the lesson on p. T66.*

LEARNING OBJECTIVES

- **Language** Answer questions and discuss meanings to develop vocabulary.
- Identify real-life connections between words and their use.

MATERIALS   Online Ed

Vocabulary Cards *1.10–1.15*

Classroom materials *a new book*

 Introduce Power Words

Use the steps **I Do It, We Do It, You Do It** with the information in the chart below to teach the Power Words from *Try This!*

❶ Power Word	❷ Meaning	❸ Example
try (v.) *(p. 17)*	When you **try** to do something, you work at doing it.	**ACT IT OUT** Reach down to touch your toes. *I will* **try** *to touch my toes.*
new (adj.) *(p. 17)*	When something is **new**, you have never seen, had, or done it before.	**USE A PROP** Hold up a new book. *We got a* **new** *book for our classroom library.*
great (adj.) *(p. 19)*	Something that is **great** is better than good.	**MAKE A CONNECTION** Make a comparison to everyday experiences. *That music was not just good, it was* **great***!*
enjoy (v.)	If you **enjoy** doing something, you really like it.	**MAKE A CONNECTION** Name an activity you *enjoy* doing at home. *I* **enjoy** *walking my dog.*
excited (adj.)	When you feel **excited**, you are very happy.	**MAKE A CONNECTION** Relate feeling excited to children's experiences. *I am* **excited** *to make new friends today.*
nervous (adj.)	When you feel **nervous**, you are worried about what might happen.	**ACT IT OUT** Show a worried look on your face. *I felt* **nervous** *about coming to the first day of school.*

 Professional Learning

TEACHING TERMS

A **student-friendly explanation** for a word gives the meaning in everyday, accessible language and a familiar sentence structure.

See the **GPS guide** to learn more.

EL **ENGLISH LEARNER SUPPORT:**
Build Vocabulary

SUBSTANTIAL
Model showing facial expressions for *excited* and *nervous*. Have children do the same and repeat the words after you.

MODERATE
Supply frames such as these: *I feel* **excited** *when* _____. *I feel* **nervous** *when* _____.

LIGHT
Ask children to use a Power Word in a phrase or short sentence to explain how they are feeling. Encourage them to elaborate.

I Do It

Use the **VOCABULARY** routine and Vocabulary Cards 1.10–1.15 to introduce the Power Words from *Try This!* You may wish to display the corresponding Vocabulary Card for each word as you discuss it.

Vocabulary Cards

1. **Say the Power Word.** Ask children to repeat it.

2. **Explain the meaning.** Read aloud the student-friendly meaning.

3. **Talk about examples.** Use the image or a strategy to give examples of the word.

We Do It

Guide children to make connections between each word's meaning and how they can use it in their own lives. Use these prompts. Encourage children to explain or justify their answers.

- *When did you **try** something **new** at school?*

- *Can you feel **excited** and **nervous** at the same time? Why?*

- *What types of food do you **enjoy** the most?*

- *If you think something is **great**, do you like it or not like it? Explain.*

You Do It

INDEPENDENT PRACTICE

Have partners work together to complete each of the activities below. Circulate and observe partners as they work, providing corrective feedback as necessary.

- **Draw** *Draw a picture of something that you **enjoy** doing at recess.*

- **Describe** *Tell what it is like when you **try** something **new**. Describe what you do and how you feel.*

- **Role-Play** *Show how you look when you feel **excited**. Then show how you look when you feel **nervous**.*

- **Discuss** *Tell about a TV show or movie that you think is **great**.*

TEACHER TIP

Illustrate emotions! Use illustrations in classroom books or magazines to focus on words that show emotions, such as *nervous* and *excited*. Have children use details in the illustrations to describe why the person might be feeling this way.

READING WORKSHOP

Ask and Answer Questions

Step 1 Connect and Teach

Step 1 Connect and Teach

LEARNING OBJECTIVES

- Identify the features of narrative nonfiction.
- Generate questions about a text before, during, and after reading.
- **Language** Ask and answer questions about key ideas in a text.
- Listen carefully to others.

MATERIALS · Online

Anchor Chart 1 *Ask and Answer Questions*

Printable *Anchor Chart 1: Ask and Answer Questions*

Teaching Pal *Book 1, pp. 14–25*

myBook *Try This!, Book 1, pp. 14–25*

 READER'S VOCABULARY

- **evidence** clues or details in the text that support an answer or idea
- **detail** small bit of information that supports a central idea or describes something in a text

- Tell children that good readers "stay awake" and think about what they are reading. Explain that one way of showing that you are "awake" and thinking is by asking questions about what you are reading.

- Project or display <u>Anchor Chart 1: Ask and Answer Questions</u>.

- As you point to the different parts of the Anchor Chart, explain that readers ask questions before, during, and after reading to get information and to help them understand a text. Explain that they ask questions by putting into words the things they wonder about or are curious about.

- Point to the chart and explain that starting questions with the words *who, what, where, why, when,* or *how* can help readers ask different kinds of questions and get different kinds of information.

- Finally, tell children that readers use **evidence** and **details** in the text, to help them answer questions.

- Tell children they will practice asking and answering questions when they read narrative nonfiction called *Try This!*

ANCHOR CHART 1: Ask and Answer Questions · Online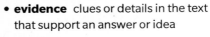

Notice & Note

Big Questions

- The Teaching Pal prompts in this lesson feature the **Notice & Note Big Questions** for nonfiction.
- As needed, refer to p. T19 to review the Big Questions with children.

✓ ASSESSMENT OPTION

Assign the <u>Selection Quiz</u> to check comprehension of *Try This!*

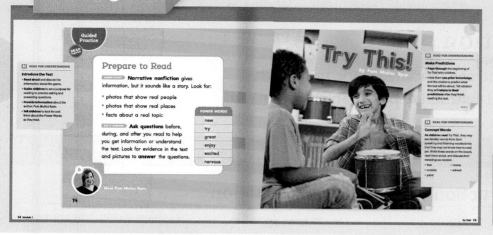

ANNOTATE IT!

Online
Ed

Children may use the annotation tools in their eBook.

Step 2 Apply to Text

 In your Teaching Pal, pages 14–25, use the blue **READ FOR UNDERSTANDING** prompts to read *Try This!* with children as they follow along and annotate in their *my*Book.

- **Genre Study** Read the genre information on page 14. Discuss the differences between narrative nonfiction and a fiction story with children.

- **Set a Purpose** Read the Set a Purpose section on page 14. Prompt children to set their own purpose for reading *Try This!*

- **Meet the Author** Play the audio about Pam Muñoz Ryan. Help children describe what they learned about her and explain some questions they would like to ask her.

- **Read and Comprehend** Guide children to read the text all the way through. Pause occasionally, using the prompts in your Teaching Pal to gauge children's understanding and to have them ask and answer questions. As children ask questions, have them refer back to the Anchor Chart to note when, why, and how to ask questions.

Step 3 Engage and Respond

INDEPENDENT PRACTICE: Speaking & Listening

- Use the **TURN AND TALK** routine with the questions on Teaching Pal and *my*Book page 25. Remind children to use details from the words and pictures as evidence to explain their responses.

- Read the Listening Tip. Remind children to follow agreed-upon rules of discussion, such as looking at their partners when they are speaking and listening carefully to what they say.

- You may want to have children conduct their discussions during daily small-group time.

 ENGLISH LEARNER SUPPORT: Facilitate Discussion

SUBSTANTIAL
Rephrase the second Turn and Talk question: *Look at page 24. Does Sam feel happy? excited? proud? scared? nervous? Point to show how you know.*

MODERATE
Provide sentence frames: *Sam feels _____ at the end of the story. I know because he _____.*

LIGHT
Have children describe the picture of Sam on page 24 before they answer the question.

LINK TO SMALL-GROUP INSTRUCTION

REINFORCE ASK AND ANSWER QUESTIONS Review or extend the skill as needed during small-group time to support children's need for differentiation. *See the lesson on p. T65.*

👥 SMALL-GROUP INSTRUCTION

Options for Differentiation

As the class engages in independent and collaborative work, meet with Guided Reading Groups or differentiate instruction based on student need.

GUIDED READING GROUPS

Match Children to Books + Instruction

- Choose just-right books based on level, skill, topic, or genre.

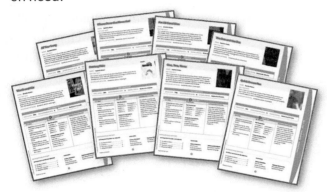

C D E F G H I J K

Leveled Readers

- Deliver instruction with each book's Take and Teach Lesson, choosing appropriate sessions based on need.

- Check comprehension, reinforce instruction, and extend learning with suggested supporting activities.

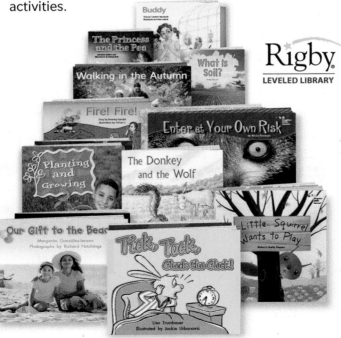

Rigby® LEVELED LIBRARY

🔵 ENGLISH LEARNER SUPPORT

Seek Information

- Use **Tabletop Minilessons: English Language Development 1.2 (Reading)** to reinforce and practice the language skill.

It is the first day of school. Jordan is worried. She walks into her class. She sees Tom, Sam, and Nate!

Seek Information

Tabletop Minilessons: English Language Development

- Then use the following text-based prompts with *Try This!* to guide application of the language skill. Begin with the prompt at the child's identified language proficiency level. As children are able, use lighter supports to encourage increased language proficiency.

SUBSTANTIAL

Reread page 17. Ask: *What is his name? What is Sam holding? Where is Sam going?* Allow children to respond using single words or short phrases. Model complete answers, such as: *His name is Sam.*

MODERATE

Have children ask questions about the ways the children in the text get to school. Supply sentence frames: *How does _____? How do _____?*

LIGHT

Have children ask questions about Sam and the other children in the text. Guide them to use *how, how many, what,* and *why* as they ask questions.

REINFORCE ASK AND ANSWER QUESTIONS

Demonstrate

- Use **Tabletop Minilessons: Reading 1** to remind children that they can ask questions before, during, and after reading. Asking questions will help them understand a text. When they ask questions, they are staying "awake" and thinking about the text. They can use *who, what, where, when, why,* and *how* to ask questions about a text. Tell children that they can answer their questions about the text by looking for evidence, or details in the text and pictures.

- Model filling out Printable: **Reading Graphic Organizer 1** to ask and answer questions about *Try This!*

Apply to Independent Reading

- Now have children ask and answer questions about an appropriate just-right book that they are reading independently. Customize these prompts to the books children choose.

  » *Look at the cover. What question do you have about what you see there? How can you find out the answers to your questions?*

  » *Now that you've read the beginning of this book, what questions do you have? Read that section again and find the answers to your questions.*

  » *Now that you've finished the book, what questions do you have? How can you answer them?*

- Have children complete Printable: **Reading Graphic Organizer 1** for their independent reading book.

Tabletop Minilessons: Reading

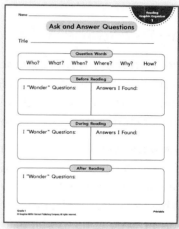

Printable:
Reading Graphic Organizer 1

ALMOST THERE

READY FOR MORE

SCAFFOLD AND EXTEND

- Have children ask *who, where,* and *what* questions. Then guide them to find answers in the text.

- Help children formulate additional *who, where,* or *what* questions about the book and answer them based on information in it.

- Encourage children to formulate questions using *how, why,* and *I wonder whether.* Have children answer the questions using text evidence.

EL ENGLISH LEARNER SUPPORT

SUBSTANTIAL
Point to details and ask: *Who is _____ ?* or *What is _____ ?* Provide the frame *This is _____* to help children respond.

MODERATE
Have children ask and answer questions. Supply frames such as: *Who is/are _____ ? Where is/are _____ ? Why is/are _____ ? Why does/do___?*

LIGHT
As children answer prompts, encourage them to explain where they found answers to their questions. Have them ask an open-ended question, such as: *What do you think _____ ?*

Options for Differentiation

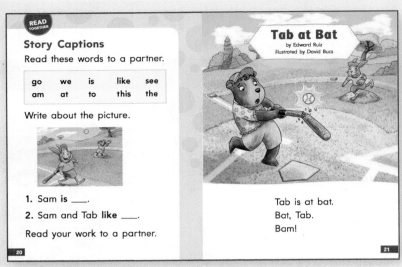

Tab at Bat, Start Right Reader, *Book 1,* pp. 20–27

REINFORCE FOUNDATIONAL SKILLS

Read Decodable Text

Story Captions: High-Frequency Word Review
Have children turn to Start Right Reader page 20. Have partners read the boxed words and then use the words and the sentence starters to write about the picture.

Preview the Story Call attention to page 21. Have children read the title and identify Tab and Sam in the picture. Remind them that Sam was previously at bat. Then have children look at the pictures on the first few pages and predict the problem in the story.

Concepts of Print: Letters, Words, and Sentences
Have children use a finger to point to individual letters and words on pages 22–23. Have them also finger trace along entire sentences. Periodically prompt: *What is the first word in this sentence? What is the first letter in that word? What is the last word in this sentence? Put your finger on the end punctuation.*

Fluency Focus: Accuracy and Self-Correction Read aloud page 21 as children follow along. Remind them that they should read each word accurately and self-correct when something they read does not make sense. Help children read the page chorally with accuracy.

Reflect on Reading Have children use a finger to track the words from left to right as they read each page silently. Then have them read the page chorally. Pause for these prompts:

- **Page 21:** *What happens to Tab's bat? (It breaks.)*

- **Page 23:** *What does Sam say to Tab? ("See this, Tab?") What does he want Tab to see? (a roll of tape) What do you think Sam plan to do? (Possible response: use the tape to fix Tab's bat)*

- **Pages 24–25:** *Do Sam and Tab fix the bat? (No; it breaks again.)*

Story Events Read aloud the directions on page 27. Then have partners use the pictures to tell about *The Mat, Sam at Bat,* and *Tab at Bat.* Have them discuss what they think will happen next.

Go, Sam!

Bat, Tab. Bat!
Bam!

24   25

Sam sat.
Tab sat.

Story Events
Use the pictures to tell a friend
about the stories so far.

What do you think
will happen next? Share
ideas with your friend.

26   27

Make Minutes Count

As you meet with small groups to read *Tab at Bat,* use one or more of these related
activities, as needed, at the beginning or the end of the small-group session.

- **Connect to Phonics** Play Hot Potato. Write the following on the board or chart
  paper: *m-a-t, b-a-t, s-a-t, T-a-b, S-a-m.* Have children gather in a circle. Then take a
  soft item, such as a beanbag, and hand it to a child. Have children pass the
  beanbag around the circle until you say, "Hot potato!" Then whoever has the
  beanbag must blend and read the sounds you point to. Repeat until each child has
  had a turn.

- **Connect to Spelling** Play Eruption. Write the Spelling Words on the board or
  chart paper. Point to a word and have children spell it in a whisper. Then have
  children pretend they are a volcano erupting as they raise their arms and spell the
  word in a normal speaking voice. Continue with the remaining words.

- **Connect to High-Frequency Words** Play Point It Out. Place the High-Frequency
  Word cards from Printable: **Word List 1** face up on the tabletop. Call out a word
  and have children point to the correct card as quickly as possible. Continue until all
  the words have been called.

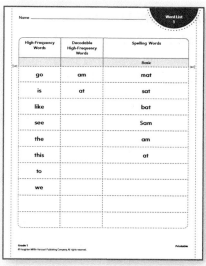

Printable: Word List 1

👥 INDEPENDENT APPLICATION

Options for Independent and Collaborative Work

While you meet with small groups, have other children engage in literacy activities that reinforce the lesson's learning objectives. Choose from these options.

Independent Reading

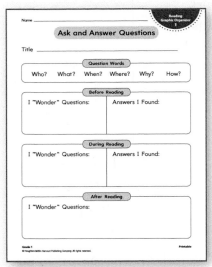

Student Choice Library

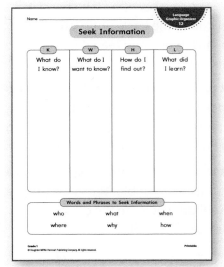

Rigby
LEVELED LIBRARY

APPLY READING SKILL

Ask and Answer Questions Children complete Printable: **Reading Graphic Organizer 1** for an independent reading book.

Printable: Reading Graphic Organizer 1

APPLY LANGUAGE SKILL

Seek Information Children complete Printable: **Language Graphic Organizer 12** for an independent reading book.

Printable: Language Graphic Organizer 12

Notice & Note

Big Questions

Encourage children to ask the Big Questions for nonfiction while reading: *What surprised me? What did the author think I already knew? What challenged, changed, or confirmed what I already knew?*

Literacy Centers

See pp. T26–T27.

 WORD WORK

 CREATIVITY CORNER

 DIGITAL STATION

 READING CORNER

 TEAMWORK TIME

Start Right Reader

Read Decodable Text *Tab at Bat,* Book 1: pp. 20–27

Speaking & Listening

Partners discuss the Turn and Talk questions while using words and pictures as evidence to explain their responses. *See Engage & Respond, p. T63.*

Additional Skills Practice

SPELLING

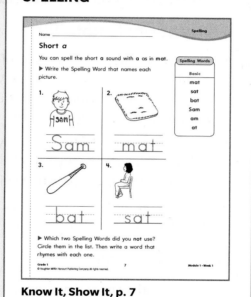

Know It, Show It, p. 7

Wrap-Up
Share Time

At the end of Reading Workshop, have children reflect on their learning by sharing how they applied **Ask and Answer Questions** or another area of focus during independent work time. Choose from these options:

- **SHARE CHAIR** Select a reader each day to come to the front of the class and tell what he or she learned from the reading by using a skill or strategy.

- **THINK-PAIR-SHARE** Children share their thinking with a partner. Select a few children each day to share with the whole class.

- **RETURN TO ANCHOR CHART** Have children add sticky notes about their independent reading book to the Ask and Answer Questions Anchor Chart. Call on a few children to explain what they added.

ANCHOR CHART 1: Ask and Answer Questions

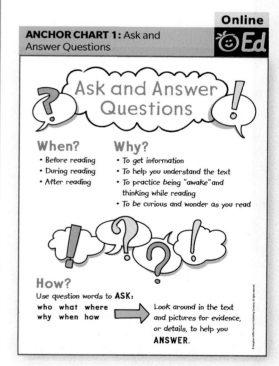

LESSON 4

FOUNDATIONAL SKILLS

LEARNING OBJECTIVES

- Identify and read high-frequency words.
- **Language** Recognize and recite basic sight vocabulary.
- Recognize spoken alliteration.
- Isolate initial and final phoneme in spoken one-syllable words.
- Blend phonemes to say one-syllable words.

MATERIALS

Online

Word Cards *am, at, go, is, like, see, the, this, to, we*

Printable *Word List 1*

Picture Cards *can, cat, cup, kite, map, mitt, moon, pan, pot*

Classroom materials *bean bag or other soft object*

 # High-Frequency Words

Review the Words

Repeat the **HIGH-FREQUENCY WORDS** routine to review this week's High-Frequency Words: *go, is, like, see, the, this, to,* and *we,* and the decodable High-Frequency Words *am* and *at.*

Hot Potato

- Display the Word Cards for this week's High-Frequency Words and decodable High-Frequency Words. Have children sit in a circle.

- Take a soft object, such as a beanbag, and hand it to a child. Tell children to pass the "hot potato" around the circle until you say, "Hot potato!" Then point to a Word Card, and say "Hot Potato!" Whoever has the "hot potato" must read the High-Frequency Word you point to. Continue the game until each child has had the chance to read at least two High-Frequency Words.

 # Phonological Awareness

Alliteration; Isolate Phonemes

- Tell children that you will say sets of words, and they will say "yes" if the first sound in all the words is the same. Model: *Listen:* lonely little lion. *Yes, I hear /l/ at the beginning of all three words.* Have children continue: dirty dishes, big bad wolf, perfect pink pony, purple bird beaks, ten tall tigers, five fearless fish.

- Ask children to sort Picture Cards by beginning sound. Model with *can: What is the beginning sound in can? (/k/)* Call on children to choose a card, say the beginning sound, and tell whether it goes with *can* or needs to be in a new pile.

- Repeat the activity for final sounds. Model: *Now, listen for the sound at the end of each word. Here's the first one:* map. *I hear /p/ at the end of* map.

Blend Phonemes

- Model blending phonemes to say a word. Say: *I will say each sound in a word and then blend the sounds to say the word. Listen: /ĭ/ /t/, /ĭ-t/,* it. *The word is* it.

- Then children blend the sounds you say. *Listen to each sound and then blend the sounds together:* /ŭ/ /p/ (up), /r/ /ă/ /t/ (rat), /f/ /ī/ /t/ (fight), /j/ /ō/ /k/ (joke).

TEACHER TIP

Spell it! For additional practice with the High-Frequency Words, provide letter cards and have children use them to spell and read this week's High-Frequency Words.

 CORRECT & REDIRECT

Guide children who have trouble isolating initial or final phonemes.

- Model the task. Display Picture Card *kite. Listen for the beginning sound as I say the word* kite. *The sound at the beginning of* kite *is /k/. Say it with me:* kite, /k/.

- *Does* kite *have the same beginning sound as* can? *Listen as I say the words:* kite, can. *Yes,* kite *and* can *begin with the same sound, /k/.* Repeat with *cat* and *pot.*

- Repeat the above process to isolate the final sounds in *cup* and *moon* and compare them to *map.*

Phonics Review

LEARNING OBJECTIVES
- Blend, build, and decode regularly spelled one-syllable words with short *a* and consonants *m, s, t, b*.

MATERIALS Online

Letter Cards *a, b, m, s, t*

Display and Engage *Blend and Read 1.3*

Start Right Reader *Book 1, p. 28*

Know It, Show It *p. 8*

I Do It

Spotlight on Letters Use the **SOUND-BY-SOUND BLENDING** routine to review this week's phonic elements: short *a, m, s, t, b*. Model blending *sat* with Letter Cards (or display the written word). Say the first two sounds separately, then together; then say the last sound and add it to the blended sounds. Repeat for *bam*.

We Do It

Blend and Read Project Display and Engage: **Blend and Read 1.3** or use Start Right Reader page 28.

DISPLAY AND ENGAGE:
Blend and Read 1.3

Online

Blend and Read 1.3

Blend and Read

❶ at	sat	am	Sam	Tam
❷ bam	bat	tab	Tam	am
❸ sat	mat	bat	at	am
❹ at	mat	bat	mats	bats
❺ We like Tam.				
❻ Tab / is at bat.				

Grade 1 | Foundational Skills   Module 1 • Week 1

1. **Line 1** Have children read the line. Then prompt a conversation about the words. Ask: *How are all the words alike? Which words have short a in the middle? Which words have short a at the beginning?* Have children read the line chorally.

2. **Line 2** Continue. Then have volunteers reread selected words until they can identify them quickly.

3. **Review** Display Line 3, and have children read it chorally.

4. **Challenge** Challenge children to read Line 4 and tell which words refer to more than one item.

5. **Sentences** Display Lines 5–6. Call on children to blend selected words. Point to each word as children read the sentences chorally.

You Do It

INDEPENDENT PRACTICE

- **Option 1** Have partners write *Tam* and then find and write three words from the Blend and Read lines that rhyme with *Tam*. (*am, Sam, bam*) Repeat for the word *bat*. (*at, mat, sat*)

- **Option 2** Have children complete Know It, Show It page 8.

 ENGLISH LEARNER SUPPORT:
Support Language Transfer

ALL LEVELS Vietnamese and Hmong speakers may have trouble writing words that end in -*at* because of difficulty perceiving and/or pronouncing the sound /t/. Review the /t/ sound with these children, asking them to repeat the sound after you. Then have them practice saying *at, bat, mat,* and *sat*.

 LINK TO SMALL-GROUP INSTRUCTION

REINFORCE FOUNDATIONAL SKILLS
Use *Tam at Bat* during small-group time to review or reinforce blending and decoding words with short *a* and consonants *m, s, t, b*. Meet with children to work through the story, or assign it as independent work. *See the lesson on p. T78.*

Tam at Bat
by Edward Ruiz
Illustrated by David Buco

Sam sat.
Tab sat.
Tam sat.

LEARNING OBJECTIVES

- **Language** Ask and answer questions using multi-word responses.
- Use newly acquired vocabulary to identify real-life connections between words and their use.
- Identify and use words that name actions.

MATERIALS   Online Ed

Vocabulary Cards *1.10–1.15*
Know It, Show It *p. 9*

Review Power Words

Revisit the Power Words

- Use Vocabulary Cards 1.10–1.15 to review the Power Words from *Try This!*
- Guide children to discuss how the image helps them understand each word's meaning.

Vocabulary Cards

Vocabulary Chat

- Read aloud the following questions:

  1. *Would you be **excited** or **nervous** if you saw a snake in the woods? Explain.*

  2. *What **new** food would you like to **try**?*

  3. *Do you **enjoy** watching or playing a sport? Which sport do you enjoy?*

  4. *What **great** joke or riddle do you know?*

- After you read aloud each question, have children use the **THINK-PAIR-SHARE** routine to discuss. Call on pairs to share their answers. Use positive feedback to reinforce correct usages of words.

- **Get Up and Move!** *Think of a musical instrument that you would like to **try** to play. Act it out.* Have a volunteer act out playing the instrument, and ask others to guess what the instrument is.

- For additional practice with the Power Words from *Try This!*, have children complete Know It, Show It page 9.

Getting Started

ENGAGEMENT ROUTINE

Use **THINK-PAIR-SHARE** to encourage strong responses. When children share, listen intently to a child who displays low confidence about speaking aloud to the class. Validate a strong response, provide support as needed, and ask that child to share a rehearsed response with the class.

See the **GPS guide** to learn more.

ENGLISH LEARNER SUPPORT: Facilitate Discussion

SUBSTANTIAL
Say: *Show how your face would look if you saw a snake. Are you **excited** or **nervous**?*

MODERATE
Supply these frames: *I would like to **try** _____. I **enjoy** (watching/playing) _____.*

LIGHT
Ask: *What do you feel **excited** about? What do you **enjoy** doing?* Have children respond using complete sentences.

Words About Feelings

I Do It

- Project Display and Engage: **Generative Vocabulary 1.4**. Read aloud the introduction.

- Discuss the example *excited*. Point out the boy's expression in the photo. Explain that the word *excited* is an **adjective** that describes how the boy feels.

- Then model determining the meaning of a word about feelings. *The word is excited. I can see that the boy has a big smile on his face. He looks very happy. The way he looks helps me understand that* excited *must mean "very happy."*

- Continue by reading the remaining examples, and discussing each word's meaning. If children don't know the meaning of a word, tell them they can look it up in a print or online dictionary. Model looking up one of the examples in the dictionary.

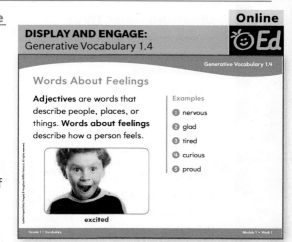

Online

DISPLAY AND ENGAGE:
Generative Vocabulary 1.4

Generative Vocabulary 1.4

Words About Feelings

Adjectives are words that describe people, places, or things. **Words about feelings** describe how a person feels.

Examples
1. nervous
2. glad
3. tired
4. curious
5. proud

excited

We Do It

- Guide children to name other words about feelings they know. Prompt them with questions, such as these: *How do you feel when you play with a friend? How do you feel when you work hard?* Write a list of children's responses.

- Ask volunteers to demonstrate the meaning of each word. Coach children to look up the meaning of unknown words in a dictionary.

You Do It

INDEPENDENT PRACTICE

- **Option 1** Have children choose a feeling word and draw a picture to show its meaning. Have partners exchange pictures and guess the feeling that the pictures show. Have children look up unknown words in the dictionary. Then have children label their picture with the feeling word.

- **Option 2** Have children complete Know It, Show It page 10.

LEARNING OBJECTIVES

- Understand and use words about feelings.
- **Language** Describe feelings using adjectives.
- Use a dictionary to find the meaning of unknown words.

MATERIALS   Online

Display and Engage *Generative Vocabulary 1.4*

Know It, Show It *p. 10*

 READER'S VOCABULARY

- **adjective** a word that describes people, places, or things

---

 ENGLISH LEARNER SUPPORT:
Build Vocabulary

SUBSTANTIAL
Say feeling words such as *excited, nervous,* and *sad*. Ask children to repeat and demonstrate how they look when they feel that way.

MODERATE
Supply these frames: *I feel excited when _____. I feel nervous when _____.*

LIGHT
Ask children to use feeling words to describe experiences, for example: *I was sad when I lost my favorite toy.*

Professional Learning

TEACHING TERMS

Generative vocabulary instruction helps children recognize word parts and how words work in order to unlock meanings of new, unfamiliar words when they encounter them in reading. This type of instruction exposes children to networks of words that have morphological or semantic connections.

See the **GPS guide** to learn more.

Author's Purpose

LEARNING OBJECTIVES

- Determine the author's purpose for writing a text, using the genre and text evidence.
- **Language** Discuss the author's purpose for writing a text.
- Write a caption to retell part of a text, using evidence to support ideas.

MATERIALS   Online

Anchor Chart 12
Author's Purpose

Printable *Anchor Chart 12: Author's Purpose*

Teaching Pal *Book 1, pp. 14–27*

myBook Try This!, Book 1, pp. 14–27

Know It, Show It *p. 11*

READER'S VOCABULARY

- **author's purpose** the author's reason for writing
- **persuade** to try to convince someone of an idea or to try to get someone to do something
- **inform** to give facts about a topic
- **entertain** to bring joy and fun to the reader through a story
- **genre** a type or category of writing, such as fiction, informational text, or opinion writing

- Tell children that, like them, authors have reasons for writing. Explain that an author's reason for writing is called the **author's purpose**.

- Project or display <u>Anchor Chart 12: Author's Purpose</u>. Give examples of each purpose on the Anchor Chart.

- Explain that an author who writes to **persuade** might write an opinion on why spaghetti is the best lunch.

- Explain that an author who writes to **inform** might write about how an animal lives or how a machine works.

- Explain that an author who writes to **entertain** might write an exciting story, or a story that teaches a lesson in a fun way.

- Finally, point out that thinking about the **genre**, or type of writing, of a text can help children figure out the author's purpose: informative texts inform, opinions persuade, and fiction entertains. Knowing the author's purpose will help children understand more about what they're reading and what the author wants them to know or learn.

- Tell children they will reread parts of *Try This!* to practice determining the author's purpose.

ANCHOR CHART 12:
Author's Purpose

TEACHING TERMS

Anchor charts are engaging, visual representations of skills, strategies, concepts, or processes that can be prepared by the teacher or co-created during a lesson by the teacher and class. Anchor Charts are displayed in the classroom to make thinking visible, to keep learning relevant, and to help to build a collaborative culture of literacy.

See the **GPS guide** to learn more.

 ENGLISH LEARNER SUPPORT:
Facilitate Language Connections

ALL LEVELS For Spanish-speaking children, point out that the English words *author, purpose, inform, entertain,* and *persuade* have the following Spanish cognates: *autor, propósito, informar, entretener,* and *persuadir.*

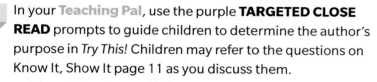

We go to new rooms.

20

This is new.
Try to paint, Sam!

21

Go to Your Teaching Pal

ANNOTATE IT!
Online **Ed**

Children may use the annotation tools in their eBook.

Step 2 Apply to Text

In your Teaching Pal, use the purple **TARGETED CLOSE READ** prompts to guide children to determine the author's purpose in *Try This!* Children may refer to the questions on Know It, Show It page 11 as you discuss them.

- Read aloud the first question on Teaching Pal page 20 and have children answer it based on evidence from the text and pictures. *(new things kids can do at school)*

- Then read the follow-up question. Tell children to use clues from the text to make an inference, or a smart guess, to answer the question. *(She wants to tell readers what new things might happen on their first few days of school.)*

- Read aloud the questions on Teaching Pal page 24. Have children use what they know about the genre and text evidence to answer. *(Possible response: to give facts about new things kids can do at school; that it is good to try new things)*

- Refer back to the Anchor Chart to support the discussion. Children may add sticky notes to the chart, adding genre and answer clues that helped them decide on the author's purpose in *Try This!*

Step 3 Engage and Respond

INDEPENDENT PRACTICE: Writing

- Read aloud the prompt on Teaching Pal page 26. Have children use the planning space to draw something Sam does.

- Then have children write their responses to the prompt. Remind children to refer back to *Try This!* and use the words and pictures from the text for ideas. Then have children complete the sentence frame to write a caption for the picture.

- You may want to have children complete their writing during daily small-group time.

Getting Started

CLASSROOM MANAGEMENT

The instructional notes in your Teaching Pal are color-coded for different purposes. Refer to them in the moment of teaching as you read the text with children. Add your own sticky notes to tailor the shared reading for your students' particular needs.

See the **GPS guide** to learn more.

 LINK TO SMALL-GROUP INSTRUCTION

REINFORCE AUTHOR'S PURPOSE Review or extend the skill as needed during small-group time to support children's need for differentiation. *See the lesson on p. T77.*

👥 SMALL-GROUP INSTRUCTION

Options for Differentiation

As the class engages in independent and collaborative work, meet with Guided Reading Groups or differentiate instruction based on student need.

GUIDED READING GROUPS

Match Children to Books + Instruction

- Choose just-right books based on level, skill, topic, or genre.

C   D   E   F   G   H   I   J   K ⟶

Leveled Readers

- Deliver instruction with each book's Take and Teach Lesson, choosing appropriate sessions based on need.

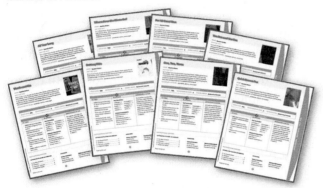

- Check comprehension, reinforce instruction, and extend learning with suggested supporting activities.

Rigby®
LEVELED LIBRARY

🔵EL ENGLISH LEARNER SUPPORT

Seek Information

- Use **Tabletop Minilessons: English Language Development 1.2 (Writing)** to reinforce and practice the language skill.

Tabletop Minilessons: English Language Development

- Then use the following text-based prompts with *Try This!* to guide application of the language skill. Begin with the prompt at the child's identified language proficiency level. As children are able, use lighter supports to encourage increased language proficiency.

SUBSTANTIAL
Lead children to ask questions about Sam. Supply these frames: *Is Sam _____? Does Sam _____?* Echo and/or model correctly formed answers. For example, *Yes, Sam is outside.*

MODERATE
Have children ask and answer questions about Sam. Select one or two questions to write down. Then have children write or copy the question word.

LIGHT
Have children ask questions about Sam using *who, what,* and *where.* Then help them write their questions.

REINFORCE AUTHOR'S PURPOSE

Demonstrate

- Use **Tabletop Minilessons: Reading 12** to remind children that an **author's purpose** is the reason why he or she wrote the text. Authors choose to write texts of different **genres** for different reasons. They write stories to **entertain**, informational texts to teach or **inform** readers about a topic or idea, and opinion writing to give an opinion or **persuade** the reader to change his or her mind about something. Knowing the author's purpose helps readers understand the texts better and know what the author wants readers to learn from them.

- Model filling out Printable: **Reading Graphic Organizer 11** to identify and explain the author's purpose in *Try This!*

Apply to Independent Reading

- Now have children identify the author's purpose in an appropriate just-right book that they are reading independently. Before children read their books, guide them to set a purpose for reading. Remind them to think about why the author wrote it. Customize these prompts to the books children choose.

  » *Does the book tell a story, give information, or give an opinion?*

  » *Why do you think the author wrote this book?*

  » *What does the author want you to learn from reading this book?*

- Have children complete Printable: **Reading Graphic Organizer 11** for their independent reading book.

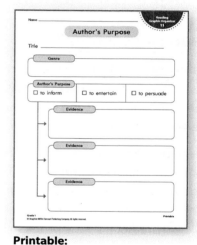

Tabletop Minilessons: Reading

Printable:
Reading Graphic Organizer 11

ALMOST THERE → READY FOR MORE

SCAFFOLD AND EXTEND

- Guide children to decide whether the author's purpose is to entertain, to persuade, or to inform.

- Have children identify whether their book contains facts, opinions, or is make-believe.

- Ask children to discuss why the author includes certain people, events, or ideas in the text. Ask children to use their own words to explain.

EL ENGLISH LEARNER SUPPORT

SUBSTANTIAL

Hold up several books and guide children to identify the author's name on the cover. Model: *The author of this book is _____.*

MODERATE

After reading a book, have students make a statement using this frame: *The author's purpose for writing this book is _____.*

LIGHT

As children discuss the author's purpose, ask them to identify text or pictures that help show the author's purpose.

Options for Differentiation

Tam at Bat, Start Right Reader, *Book 1,* pp. 28–35

REINFORCE FOUNDATIONAL SKILLS

Read Decodable Text

Blend and Read Have children turn to Start Right Reader page 28. Use the **CHORAL READING** routine to read aloud the Blend and Read lines. Use challenge line 4 with children who are ready.

Preview the Story Help children recall the problem from *Tab at Bat.* (Tab's bat broke.) Then call attention to page 29 and have them read the title and tell who they think is the new character in the picture. *(Tam)* Have children predict how the problem of the broken bat will be solved.

Fluency Focus: Accuracy and Self-Correction
Read aloud page 29 as children follow along. Model misreading a character's name and self-correcting. Point out that you self-corrected to make sure that you read each character's name correctly. Then have children read the selection, paying attention to accuracy and self-correcting as needed.

Reflect on Reading Have children read to find out how Tam will help Tab. Have them read each page silently and then chorally. Pause for these prompts:

- **Page 30:** *What do Tab and Sam show Tam? (the broken bat)*

- **Page 32:** *Tam is a beaver, and beavers chew wood. Look at the picture. Why is Tam chewing the log? (He is making a new bat.)*

- **Page 33:** *Why do you think Sam and Tab say "We like Tam!"? (They are happy that Tam made them a new bat.)*

- **Page 34:** *How was the story's problem solved? (Tam made a new bat.) Is this what you predicted? Explain. (Responses will vary.)*

What If? Allow time for partners to reread the week's four Start Right Reader stories. Then have them answer the questions on page 35. Encourage children to share story details that helped them answer the "what if" questions.

Tam, Tam!
Tam, Tam!

We like this bat!
We like Tam!
Tam! Tam! Tam! Tam!

Tam is at bat.
Bat, Tam. Bat!
Bam!

READ TOGETHER

What If?
Reread the week's stories.

1. What if Tam were a deer, not a beaver? How would **Tam at Bat** be different?

2. What if Sam, Tab, and Tam were real children? What would change in the stories? What would stay the same?

Talk about your answers with a partner.

(?) Make Minutes Count

As you meet with small groups to read *Tam at Bat*, use one or more of these related activities, as needed, at the beginning or the end of the small-group session.

- **Connect to Phonics** Have children go on a word hunt in *Tam at Bat*. Choose a few pages for children to reread. Have them hunt for words with the short *a* sound and write the words they find.

- **Connect to Spelling** Play Wordhead. Write the Spelling Words on self-stick notes and place them sticky-side up in the center of the table. One child selects a note, and without looking at the word, sticks the note on his or her forehead. The other group members provide clues about the word without saying the word, for example: *It begins with the letter* m; *it names something you can sit on.* The child must guess the word on his or her forehead and then spell it. Continue until all of the self-stick notes have been selected.

- **Connect to High-Frequency Words** Play Card Flip. Spread out the High-Frequency Word cards from Printable: **Word List 1** face up on the tabletop. Say a sentence that contains one of the High-Frequency Words. Call on a child to find the correct High-Frequency Word and flip over the card. Continue until all of the cards are flipped over.

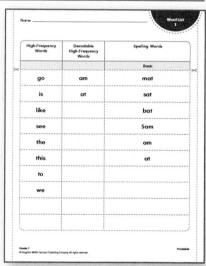

Printable: Word List 1

High-Frequency Words	Decodable High-Frequency Words	Spelling Words
		Basic
go	am	mat
is	at	sat
like		bat
see		Sam
the		am
this		at
to		
we		

Options for Independent and Collaborative Work

While you meet with small groups, have other children engage in literacy activities that reinforce the lesson's learning objectives. Choose from these options.

Independent Reading

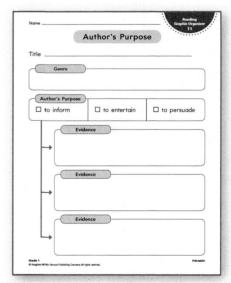

Student Choice Library

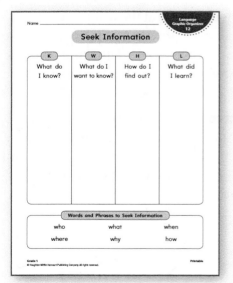

Rigby LEVELED LIBRARY

APPLY READING SKILL

Author's Purpose Children complete Printable: **Reading Graphic Organizer 11** for an independent reading book.

Printable: Reading Graphic Organizer 11

APPLY LANGUAGE SKILL

Seek Information Children complete Printable: **Language Graphic Organizer 12** for an independent reading book.

Printable: Language Graphic Organizer 12

Literacy Centers

See pp. T26–T27.

 WORD WORK

 CREATIVITY CORNER

 DIGITAL STATION

 READING CORNER

 TEAMWORK TIME

Start Right Reader

Read Decodable Text *Tam at Bat,* Book 1: pp. 28–35

Writing

Children write a caption for a picture about something Sam does. *See Engage & Respond, p. T75.*

Close Reading

***my*Book, Book 1, pp. 28–31**

Additional Skills Practice

PHONICS AND VOCABULARY

Know It, Show It, p. 8

Know It, Show It, pp. 9–10

Wrap-Up
Share Time

At the end of Reading Workshop, have children reflect on their learning by sharing how they applied **Author's Purpose** or another area of focus during independent work time. Choose from these options:

- **SHARE CHAIR** Select a reader each day to come to the front of the class and tell what he or she learned from the reading by using a skill or strategy.

- **THINK-PAIR-SHARE** Children share their thinking with a partner. Select a few each day to share with the whole class.

- **RETURN TO ANCHOR CHART** Have children add sticky notes about their independent reading book to the Author's Purpose Anchor Chart. Call on a few children to explain what they added.

ANCHOR CHART 12: Author's Purpose

WORD WORK WARM-UP

LEARNING OBJECTIVES

- Identify and read high-frequency words.
- **Language** Recognize, recite, and spell basic sight vocabulary.
- **Language** Compose oral sentences using basic sight vocabulary.
- Orally blend and segment onsets and rimes in one-syllable words.
- Segment syllables in multisyllabic words.
- Recognize spoken alliteration.
- Isolate initial and final phoneme in spoken one-syllable words.
- Blend phonemes to say one-syllable words.

MATERIALS   Online

Word Cards *am, at, go, is, like, see, the, this, to, we*

Printables *Phonological Awareness 1; Word List 1*

Classroom materials *bean bag or other soft object*

 # High-Frequency Words

Children's Choice

- Remind children of the High-Frequency Words they have been practicing this week: *go, is, like, see, the, this, to,* and *we,* and the decodable High-Frequency Words *am* and *at*.

- Review any words that posed difficulty for children this week, using Word Cards and the **HIGH-FREQUENCY WORDS** routine.

- In Lessons 2–4, children used these practice activities: Card Flip (p. T44), Blast Off! (p. T58), and Hot Potato (p. T70). Have children vote on their favorite, and use it to review the week's words for word recognition fluency.

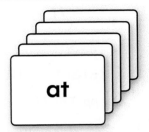

Phonological Awareness

Teacher's Choice

- In Lessons 1–4, children practiced blending onset and rime, segmenting syllables, and segmenting onset and rime (pp. T31, T45). They also practiced alliteration, isolating phonemes, and blending phonemes (pp. T58, T70).

- Use the following examples to gauge which tasks need reinforcement.

  » **Blend Onset and Rime** Ask children to blend the following word chunks to say words: /b/ /ŭg/ (bug), /t/ /ĕn/ (ten).

  » **Segment Onset and Rime** Have children say the beginning sound and then the rest of the word for these words: bat (/b/ /ăt/), fit (/f/ /ĭt/).

  » **Blend Phonemes** Have children blend phonemes to say these words: /p/ /ĕ/ /t/ (pet), /f/ /ī/ /n/ (fine).

- Use Printable: **Phonological Awareness 1** for reinforcement.

  » **Segment Syllables** Have children repeat each word you say, clapping for each syllable: sidewalk (*side-walk*), beautiful (*beau-ti-ful*).

  » **Alliteration** Use these word sets to check children's recognition of alliteration: mop, mask, mouse; ring, rabbit, rug.

  » **Isolate Phonemes** Initial: sing (/s/), call (/k/); Final: ran (/n/), mad (/d/)

 ENGLISH LEARNER SUPPORT:
Build Vocabulary

SUBSTANTIAL
Have children use sentence frames with the decodable High-Frequency Word *am* to identify themselves. *I am [name].*

MODERATE
Have children complete this sentence frame to tell about themselves. Example: *I am _____. (in first grade)*

LIGHT
Ask children to complete the sentence frame *I am _____* and then say another sentence that tells about something they like to do.

 CORRECT & REDIRECT

If children have difficulty, have them practice these skills.

- Blend onset and rime. Model: *Listen: /b/ /ŭg/. The word is bug. Blend with me: /b/ /ŭg/. What is the word? (bug)*

- Isolate initial sounds. Model: *We listen and say the sound at the beginning of a word. The word is sing. The first sound is /s/. Say it with me: /s/. What is the first sound in sing? (/s/)*

- Isolate final sounds. Model: *We can say the sound at the end of a word. Listen: pet. The last sound is /t/. What is the last sound in pet? (/t/)*

Short *a*

Spelling Assessment

LEARNING OBJECTIVE

- Spell words with short *a* (closed syllables).

DICTATION SENTENCES

BASIC

1. **mat** Wipe your feet on the *mat*.
2. **sat** We *sat* on the couch.
3. **bat** The ball player has a *bat*.
4. **Sam** That boy is named *Sam*.
5. **am** I *am* in first grade.
6. **at** We are *at* school now.

1 Say each Spelling Word, and read the Dictation Sentence. Repeat the word, and then have children write it. Remind them to use their best handwriting.

2 Review any words that children misspell. If they miss two or more words, then revisit the Lesson 1 Word Sort activity on page T35.

1. mat
2. sat
3. bat
4. am
5. ___
6. ___
7. ___
8. ___
9. ___
10. ___

VOCABULARY STRATEGY

 # Classify and Categorize

 READER'S VOCABULARY

- **classify** to sort words into groups
- **categorize** to name a group of words in a way that describes how they are alike

I Do It

- Project Display and Engage: **Vocabulary Strategy 1.5**. Read aloud the first section.

- Explain to children that they can **classify** and **categorize** words to help them better understand their meanings.

- Say: *You can use the categories and other information you know about the words to explain them to yourself or to someone else.*

- Read aloud Example 1. Model identifying how the words are alike. *The words* run, kick, *and* jump *belong together because they all name actions, or things that someone or something does. I can add other words like* play, skip, *and* swim *to the list.*

- Use the category and what you know about the word to model how to define it. *The word* run *is an action word that means walking fast.*

- Continue with Examples 2 and 3 in the same way, reading the words in each group, identifying the category they belong to, and using that information to define one or two words from each category.

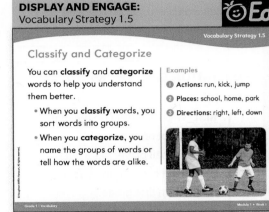

Online

DISPLAY AND ENGAGE:
Vocabulary Strategy 1.5

Vocabulary Strategy 1.5

Classify and Categorize

You can **classify** and **categorize** words to help you understand them better.

- When you **classify** words, you sort words into groups.
- When you **categorize**, you name the groups of words or tell how the words are alike.

Examples
1. **Actions:** run, kick, jump
2. **Places:** school, home, park
3. **Directions:** right, left, down

 LEARNING MINDSET

Seeking Challenges

Model Tell children that sometimes we need to think about words in different ways, like thinking about how they are alike. That can be a challenge when learning something new. *When I think about learning something new, I know it might be hard at first, but I'll take my time and do my best work.*

We Do It

Write the following words on the board, and read them aloud to children.

around	theater	out
up	hospital	library

- Help children think about how some words are alike. Prompt them to explain their reasoning.

- Work with children to classify the words into two groups. Guide them in identifying each category: *Words That Name Places* and *Words That Name Directions*. Write the correct words in a list under each category.

- Prompt children to use the categories and information they know about the words to define one or two of them: *The word* library *is a word that names a place where you can get books.*

You Do It

INDEPENDENT PRACTICE

- **Option 1** Have partners choose one of the following categories: actions, places, or directions. Have them name words that belong in that category. Then ask them to think of another category and write several words that belong in that category on a sheet of paper. Have children define one word from each group by using the category and other information they know about the word.

- **Option 2** Have children complete Know It, Show It page 12.

ENGLISH LEARNER SUPPORT:
Build Vocabulary

ALL LEVELS Use pictures or realia to explain the meanings of the words in the We Do It activity. Have children name the places or directions as you point to each one using single words, short phrases, or complete sentences depending on their English proficiency.

─● *Professional Learning*

RESEARCH FOUNDATIONS

"Children learn best when words are presented in integrated contexts that make sense to them. A set of words connected to a category such as 'energy' can help children remember not only the words themselves but the linkages in meaning between them."
—Dr. Susan B. Neuman and Dr. Tanya S. Wright (2014)

See the **GPS guide** to learn more.

Collaborative Conversations

LEARNING OBJECTIVES

- Share information in a discussion, following agreed-upon rules and conventions of language.
- Listen actively, speak clearly, and elaborate on answers.
- **Language** Discuss ideas and opinions in cooperative learning interactions.

MATERIALS   Online

Anchor Chart 43
Collaborative Conversations

Printable
Anchor Chart 43:
Collaborative
Conversations

myBook *Try This!*, Book 1, pp. 14–27

Know It, Show It pp. 13–14

Classroom materials *digital tool, such as a computer or tablet*

READER'S VOCABULARY

- **formal language** a style for speaking or writing, following the rules of English
- **informal language** a style for speaking or writing that you use with people you know, like friends and family

- Remind children that they read the selection *Try This!* about some children's first day at school. Explain that one thing that happens at the beginning of the year is that everyone learns the rules of school.

- Project or display <u>Anchor Chart 43: Collaborative Conversations</u>. Explain that the chart shows important rules to remember when having a conversation with teachers or classmates at school.

- Discuss the rules on the Anchor Chart. Point out the difference between **formal language** and **informal language**. Give examples of each, for example, *Please pass me a marker* or *Hey, toss me that marker.*

- Explain that the reason for these rules is to help the group share thoughts in a way that is fair and polite and that keeps the conversation going.

- Tell children they will have a chance to practice following the rules in a discussion about *Try This!*

Online
ANCHOR CHART 43:
Collaborative Conversations

Step 2 Apply to Text

- Write the following questions about *Try This!* on the board:

> Which of the new things in <u>Try This!</u> did you try this year? How did it feel to try them?

- Tell children they will discuss the new things the children do in *Try This!* Form small groups and have children look through and discuss the text.

- Then read aloud the questions on the board. Have a volunteer work with you to demonstrate having an exchange about each question. Refer back to the Anchor Chart as you demonstrate each rule.

- Then have small groups discuss the questions. Circulate and prompt children to follow the rules of discussion, referring back to the Anchor Chart as needed.

Step 3 Engage and Respond

INDEPENDENT PRACTICE: Writing

- **Option 1** Have partners discuss which rules for conversations they think are the most important. Encourage them to follow the rules they learned in their discussions. Have them work together to illustrate it and write something about it.

- **Option 2** Have children complete Know It, Show It pages 13–14.

 ENGLISH LEARNER SUPPORT:
Facilitate Discussion

As children discuss new things they did, use the following prompts.

SUBSTANTIAL
Encourage children to pantomime or use single words to tell about things they tried, and how it felt. Help them name actions and feelings.

MODERATE
Supply these frames: *I tried _____. (Before/After) I tried, I felt _____.*

LIGHT
Ask: *What did you learn from trying something new?*

 LINK TO SMALL-GROUP INSTRUCTION

REINFORCE COLLABORATIVE CONVERSATIONS Review or extend the skill as needed during small-group time to support children's need for differentiation. *See the lesson on p. T89.*

👥 SMALL-GROUP INSTRUCTION

Options for Differentiation

As the class engages in independent and collaborative work, meet with Guided Reading Groups or differentiate instruction based on student need.

GUIDED READING GROUPS

Match Children to Books + Instruction

- Choose just-right books based on level, skill, topic, or genre.

C D E F G H I J K

Leveled Readers

- Deliver instruction with each book's Take and Teach Lesson, choosing appropriate sessions based on need.

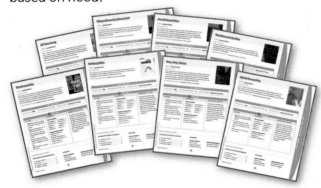

- Check comprehension, reinforce instruction, and extend learning with suggested supporting activities.

Rigby®
LEVELED LIBRARY

🔵 EL ENGLISH LEARNER SUPPORT

Seek Information

- Use **Tabletop Minilessons: English Language Development 1.3 (Collaborative Problem Solving)** to reinforce and practice the language skill.

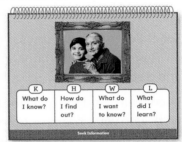

Tabletop Minilessons: English Language Development

- Then use the following text-based prompts with *Try This!* to guide application of the language skill. Begin with the prompt at the child's identified language proficiency level. As children are able, use lighter supports to encourage increased language proficiency.

SUBSTANTIAL
Have children practice collaborating to find information. Supply frames: _____ *does this mean?* _____ *do you say this?* Model pointing to pictures and text, and asking and answering questions. Allow children to answer briefly or use their home language.

MODERATE
Have children collaborate to identify and discuss details in the text. Supply these frames: *Why is he _____? What does he _____? Who is this _____?*

LIGHT
Have children work with a partner to ask and answer questions about the text. Supply these frames: *Why do you think _____? What is happening _____? Why are _____?*

REINFORCE COLLABORATIVE CONVERSATIONS

Demonstrate

- Use **Tabletop Minilessons: Reading 43** as you remind children that *Try This!* is about the first day of school. Explain that rules and routines are taught at the beginning of the school year. One important routine to learn is how to have conversations with classmates and teachers. Some rules for having conversations include: **listen** to others; **ask questions** when you don't understand something; **answer questions** giving enough information; **speak up** in a loud, clear voice so that others can hear; **take turns** speaking; **add your ideas** to a conversation; talk about the **topic**, not other things. Talk to children about the difference between **formal** and **informal** language.

- Lead a collaborative conversation about *Try This!*, guiding children and modeling as needed.

Tabletop Minilessons: Reading

Apply to Independent Reading

- Now have children practice following the rules for collaborative conversations while they have a discussion about an appropriate just-right book that they are reading independently. Customize these prompts as needed.

  » *What can you add to the conversation?*

  » *How can you let a classmate know that you agree or disagree with what he or she just said?*

  » *Do you understand what _____ just said? How can you ask for more information?*

ALMOST THERE

↓

READY FOR MORE

SCAFFOLD AND EXTEND

- Model how to show attentive listening. Serve as moderator, if necessary, to help children take turns.

- Prompt children to ask questions to get more information. Help children identify when they can add an idea to extend the conversation.

- Have children discuss what they can do to make sure everyone participates in a conversation. Ask them to think about and describe a good conversation.

(EL) ENGLISH LEARNER SUPPORT

SUBSTANTIAL
Model speaking loudly enough to be heard by others. Have children practice answering a simple question in a loud-enough voice.

MODERATE
Model stating that you don't understand something using this frame: *I don't understand _____. Could you say that again?*

LIGHT
Prompt children to contribute their ideas to others' ideas to keep the conversation going by agreeing, disagreeing, or offering an opinion.

Options for Differentiation

Start Right Reader, *Book 1*, pp. 4–35

REINFORCE FOUNDATIONAL SKILLS

Read Decodable Text

Review Remind children of the Start Right Reader stories they read this week about the characters Sam, Tab, and Tam.

- *The Mat*
- *Sam at Bat*
- *Tab at Bat*
- *Tam at Bat*

Allow a few minutes for children to page through the stories to recall what they are about.

Make Text Connections Prompt children to explain how the four stories are connected.

- *Which characters appear in all four stories? (Sam and Tab)*

- *What is the main thing that each story is about? (Possible responses: In* The Mat, *Sam and Tab are at a picnic when their mat is blown away; in* Sam at Bat, *Sam and Tab play baseball; in* Tab at Bat, *Tab breaks the bat; in* Tam at Bat, *Tam makes a new bat and the three friends play baseball.)*

- *What problem in* Tab at Bat *has a solution in* Tam at Bat? *What is the solution? (Tab breaks the bat; Tam makes a new bat.)*

- *How do the characters help one another? (Possible responses: Tab gets the mat down from the tree; Sam gets the ball from in the hole; Tam makes a new bat.)*

- *What might happen to Sam, Tab, and Tam in a new story about them? (Accept reasonable responses.)*

Reread for Fluency Have partners select one of the stories to reread. Have them use the **PARTNER READING** routine and focus on reading with accuracy, self-correcting as needed.

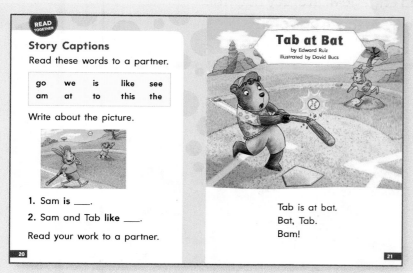

Story Captions

Read these words to a partner.

go	we	is	like	see
am	at	to	this	the

Write about the picture.

1. Sam is ___.
2. Sam and Tab like ___.

Read your work to a partner.

20

Tab at Bat
by Edward Ruiz
illustrated by David Bucs

Tab is at bat.
Bat, Tab.
Bam!

21

Blend and Read

1. at   sat   am   Sam   Tam
2. bam   bat   tab   Tam   am
3. sat   mat   bat   at   am
4. at   mat   bat   mats   bats
5. We like Tam.
6. Tab is at bat.

28

Tam at Bat
by Edward Ruiz
illustrated by David Bucs

Sam sat.
Tab sat.
Tam sat.

29

Make Minutes Count

As you meet with small groups to review the week's decodable stories, use one or both of these related activities, as needed, at the beginning or the end of the small-group session.

- **Connect to Phonics** Play Word Match. Use two sets of the Spelling Word cards from Printable: Word List 1. Shuffle the cards and place them face down in a grid on the tabletop. Children take turns selecting two cards, turning them over, and reading the words. If the words match, the child leaves the cards facing up. If the words do not match, the child turns the cards face down again and the next player takes a turn. Play continues until all of the words are matched.

- **Connect to Handwriting** Draw a triple-track line on the board, and write this sentence on the track: *Tab is sad.* Read the sentence aloud. Then remind children that the starting point for *a* and *d* is just below the middle line. Have children write the sentence two times in their best handwriting. Have them self-assess their letter formation and word spacing and draw a star next to the sentence that most closely matches the model.

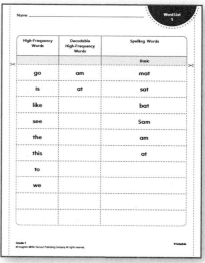

High-Frequency Words	Decodable High-Frequency Words	Spelling Words
		Basic
go	am	mat
is	at	sat
like		bat
see		Sam
the		am
this		at
to		
we		

Printable: Word List 1

👥 INDEPENDENT APPLICATION

Options for Independent and Collaborative Work

While you meet with small groups, have other children engage in literacy activities that reinforce the lesson's learning objectives. Choose from these options.

Independent Reading

Student Choice Library

Rigby
LEVELED LIBRARY

APPLY READING SKILL

Ask and Answer Questions Children complete Printable: **Reading Graphic Organizer 1** for an independent reading book.

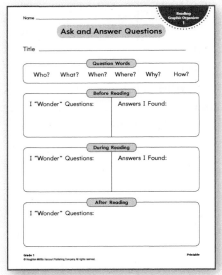

Printable: Reading Graphic Organizer 1

APPLY LANGUAGE SKILL

Seek Information Children complete Printable: **Language Graphic Organizer 12** for an independent reading book.

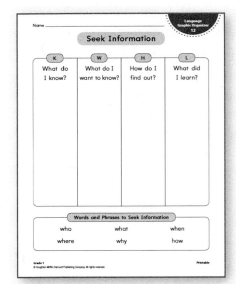

Printable: Language Graphic Organizer 12

Literacy Centers

See pp. T26–T27.

 WORD WORK

 CREATIVITY CORNER

 DIGITAL STATION

 READING CORNER

 TEAMWORK TIME

Start Right Reader

Read Decodable Text Book 1: pp. 4–35

Speaking & Listening

Children act out conversations or complete the Know It, Show It pp. *See Engage & Respond, p. T87.*

Additional Skills Practice

VOCABULARY STRATEGY

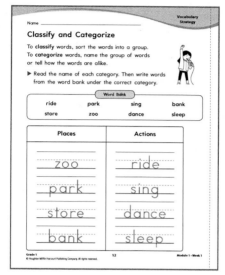

Know It, Show It, p. 12

SPEAKING AND LISTENING

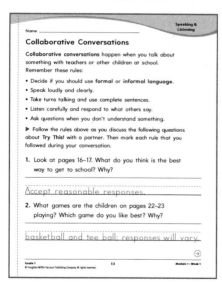

Know It, Show It, pp. 13–14

Wrap-Up
Share Time

At the end of Reading Workshop, have children reflect on their learning by sharing how they applied **Collaborative Conversations** or another area of focus during independent work time. Choose from these options:

- **SHARE CHAIR** Select a reader each day to come to the front of the class and tell what he or she learned about the skill.

- **THINK-PAIR-SHARE** Children share their thinking with a partner. Select a few children each day to share with the whole class.

- **RETURN TO ANCHOR CHART** Revisit the Collaborative Conversations Anchor Chart. Call on a few children to explain what they learned.

ANCHOR CHART 43:
Collaborative Conversations

Notes

 SOCIAL STUDIES CONNECTION:
New Friends and Experiences

Nice to Meet You!

 Essential Question How can making new friends and learning new things help us?

Essential Skills

FOUNDATIONAL SKILLS

- Phonics: Consonants *n, d, p, c /k/*; Short *a*
- High-Frequency Words: *a, first, good, had, he, I, my, was*
- Fluency: Reading Rate
- Spelling: Short *a*

VOCABULARY

- Power Words: *accept, calm, happened, introduce, kinds, last, partner, ridiculous, search, together, trip, wished*
- Generative Vocabulary: Inflection *-ed*

READING WORKSHOP

- Story Structure
- Monitor and Clarify
- Author's Purpose
- Make Inferences
- Central Idea

WRITING WORKSHOP

- Writing Form: Oral Story
- Grammar Minilessons: Common Nouns: Places and Things

LEARNING MINDSET:
Seeking Challenges

THIS WEEK'S TEXTS

READ ALOUD BOOK

You Will Be My Friend!

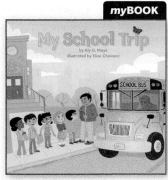

My School Trip

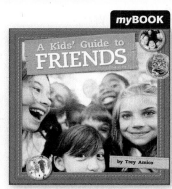

A Kids' Guide to Friends

START RIGHT READER

Decodable Texts
Dan Can Tap, Tap, Tap
Tab Can Tap, Tap, Tap
Map Nap
Can Tab Nap?

LEVELED LIBRARY

Suggested Daily Times

- VOCABULARY — 10–15 minutes
- FOUNDATIONAL SKILLS — 15–30 minutes
- READING WORKSHOP — 60–75 minutes
- WRITING WORKSHOP — 20–30 minutes

This Week's Words

BIG IDEA WORDS

challenge	emotions	friendship

POWER WORDS

accept	calm	happened
introduce	kinds	last
partner	ridiculous	search
together	trip	wished

HIGH-FREQUENCY WORDS

a	first	good	had
he	I	my	was

READER'S VOCABULARY

author's purpose	background	knowledge
central idea	clarify	detail
entertain	event	evidence
genre	inference	inform
monitor	persuade	reread
sequence	supporting evidence	topic
verb	visual	

Assessment Options

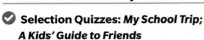 Online **Ed**

✓ Selection Quizzes: *My School Trip; A Kids' Guide to Friends*

✓ Weekly Assessment
- High-Frequency Words
- Phonics: Consonants *n, d, p, c* /k/; Short *a*
- Comprehension: Author's Purpose; Central Idea
- Generative Vocabulary: Inflection *-ed*
- Grammar: Common Nouns: Places and Things

Intervention

For children needing strategic intervention, use Tabletop Minilessons: Intervention.

- Module 1, Week 2 Daily Lessons

LESSON 6

FOUNDATIONAL SKILLS

Word Work Warm-Up, pp. T102–T103
- High-Frequency Words: *a, first, good, had, he, I, my, was*
- Phonological Awareness

Phonics, pp. T104–T105
- Consonants *n, d, p, c* /k/; Short *a*

Spelling, pp. T106–T107
- Short *a*

VOCABULARY

Academic Vocabulary, pp. T108–T109
- Introduce Oral Language: *search, introduce, ridiculous, clam, happened, accept*

READING WORKSHOP

You Will Be My Friend! Book Stix
GENRE Fantasy
Read Aloud: MINILESSON, pp. T110–T111
- Connect and Teach: Story Structure
- Apply to Text: *You Will Be My Friend!*
- Engage and Respond: Writing

SMALL-GROUP INSTRUCTION

Options for Differentiation
- Guided Reading Groups, p. T112
- English Learner Support: Infer, p. T112
- Reinforce Story Structure, p. T113
- Reinforce Foundational Skills: Read *Dan Can Tap, Tap, Tap,* pp. T114–T115

Options for Independent and Collaborative Work, pp. T116–T117

WRITING WORKSHOP

Oral Story, p. W7
- Telling and Listening to Stories I

Grammar, p. W246
- Nouns

LESSON 7

FOUNDATIONAL SKILLS

Word Work Warm-Up, pp. T118–T119
- High-Frequency Words: *a, first, good, had, he, I, my, was*
- Phonological Awareness

Phonics, pp. T120–T121
- Consonants *n, d, p, c* /k/; Short *a*

VOCABULARY

Academic Vocabulary, pp. T122–T123
- Introduce Power Words: *trip, partner, wished, last, kinds, together*

READING WORKSHOP

My School Trip Teaching Pal
GENRE Realistic Fiction
Shared Reading: MINILESSON, pp. T124–T125
- Connect and Teach: Monitor and Clarify
- Apply to Text: *My School Trip*
- Engage and Respond: Speaking & Listening

SMALL-GROUP INSTRUCTION

Options for Differentiation
- Guided Reading Groups, p. T126
- English Learner Support: Infer, p. T126
- Reinforce Monitor and Clarify, p. T127
- Reinforce Foundational Skills: Read *Tab Can Tap, Tap, Tap,* pp. T128–T129

Options for Independent and Collaborative Work, pp. T130–T131

WRITING WORKSHOP

Oral Story, p. W8
- Telling and Listening to Stories II

Grammar, p. W247
- Words That Name Places

LESSON 8

FOUNDATIONAL SKILLS

Word Work Warm-Up, p. T132
- High-Frequency Words: *a, first, good, had, he, I, my, was*
- Phonological Awareness

Fluency, p. T133
- Reading Rate

VOCABULARY

Academic Vocabulary, pp. T134–T135
- Review Power Words: *trip, partner, wished, last*

READING WORKSHOP

My School Trip
GENRE Realistic Fiction
Shared Reading: MINILESSON, pp. T136–T137

Teaching Pal

- Connect and Teach: Author's Purpose
- Apply to Text: *My School Trip*
- Engage and Respond: Writing

SMALL-GROUP INSTRUCTION

Options for Differentiation
- Guided Reading Groups, p. T138
- English Learner Support: Infer, p. T138
- Reinforce Author's Purpose, p. T139
- Reinforce Foundational Skills: Read *Map Nap*, pp. T140–T141

Options for Independent and Collaborative Work, pp. T142–T143

WRITING WORKSHOP

Oral Story, p. W9
- Prewriting: Developing a Written Class Story

Grammar, p. W248
- Words That Name Things

LESSON 9

FOUNDATIONAL SKILLS

Word Work Warm-Up, p. T144
- High-Frequency Words: *a, first, good, had, he, I, my, was*
- Phonological Awareness

Phonics, p. T145
- Phonics Review

VOCABULARY

Generative Vocabulary, pp. T146–T147
- Inflection *-ed*

READING WORKSHOP

A Kids' Guide to Friends
GENRE Informational Text
Shared Reading: MINILESSON, pp. T148–T149

Teaching Pal

- Connect and Teach: Make Inferences
- Apply to Text: *A Kids' Guide to Friends*
- Engage and Respond: Speaking & Listening

SMALL-GROUP INSTRUCTION

Options for Differentiation
- Guided Reading Groups, p. T150
- English Learner Support: Infer, p. T150
- Reinforce Make Inferences, p. T151
- Reinforce Foundational Skills: Read *Can Tab Nap?*, pp. T152–T153

Options for Independent and Collaborative Work, pp. T154–T155

WRITING WORKSHOP

Oral Story, p. W10
- Drafting I: Developing the Story

Grammar, p. W244
- Spiral Review: Nouns

LESSON 10

FOUNDATIONAL SKILLS

Word Work Warm-Up, p. T156
- High-Frequency Words: *a, first, good, had, he, I, my, was*
- Phonological Awareness

Spelling, p. T157
- Spelling Assessment

VOCABULARY

Academic Vocabulary, pp. T158–T159
- Review Power Words: *kinds, together*

READING WORKSHOP

A Kids' Guide to Friends
GENRE Informational Text
Shared Reading: MINILESSON, pp. T160–T161

Teaching Pal

- Connect and Teach: Central Idea
- Apply to Text: *A Kids' Guide to Friends*
- Engage and Respond: Writing

SMALL-GROUP INSTRUCTION

Options for Differentiation
- Guided Reading Groups, p. T162
- English Learner Support: Infer, p. T162
- Reinforce Central Idea, p. T163
- Reinforce Foundational Skills: Make Connections, pp. T164–T165

Options for Independent and Collaborative Work, pp. T166–T167

WRITING WORKSHOP

Oral Story, p. W11
- Drafting II: Assessing the Story

Grammar, p. W250
- Connect to Writing: Using Nouns

Preview Lesson Texts

Build understanding of this week's texts so that you can best support children in making connections, understanding key ideas, and becoming lifelong readers.

My School Trip by Aly G. Mays

GENRE Realistic Fiction

WHY THIS TEXT?

A first-grade class takes a field trip to a butterfly garden. Children will easily relate to the story's content: riding on a bus, being a new student, making new friends, and enjoying nature.

KEY LEARNING OBJECTIVES

- Identify features of realistic fiction.

- Monitor comprehension and use different strategies, such as rereading, when something in the text doesn't make sense.

- Determine and discuss the author's purpose for writing a text.

TEXT COMPLEXITY

LEXILE MEASURE 140L • **GUIDED READING LEVEL** E

OVERALL RATING Simple

The story is told in chronological order through simple, patterned sentences.

MAKE CONNECTIONS

🔗 **BUILD KNOWLEDGE AND LANGUAGE**

- **Social Studies Connection:** New Friends and Experiences

🔗 **VOCABULARY**

- **Inflection -ed:** wished

🔗 **FOUNDATIONAL SKILLS**

- **High-Frequency Words:** *a, first, had, I, my, was*

- **Consonants n, d, p, c /k/; Short a:** *at, Dan, friend, garden, had, happy, last, mad, Nan, new, Pam, partner, sad, trip*

📖 TEXT X-RAY

KEY IDEAS	LANGUAGE
Key Idea *pp. 34–37* A group of first-graders takes a class trip to a butterfly garden. A new student, Nan, is shy and quiet.	**Idiom** **at last** (p. 41): Explain that this phrase means "after a long time" or "finally."
Key Idea *pp. 38–40* Butterflies land on several of the children. Nan is sad because she thinks that no butterfly has landed on her.	**CULTURAL REFERENCES**
Key Idea *pp. 41–42* The narrator spots a butterfly on Nan's back and moves it to her arm, where she can see it. Now Nan is happy, and the two girls become friends.	**Butterfly Garden** (p. 37): Be sure children understand that this is a different type of garden than the kind they have probably seen, where people grow flowers or vegetables. The garden the children visit in this story is an enclosed space where many kinds of butterflies fly about freely and are protected and studied.

A Kids' Guide to Friends by Trey Amico

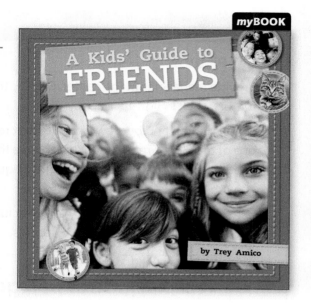

GENRE Informational Text

WHY THIS TEXT?

In this informational text with strong photographic support, the author explains who can be a friend, some fun activities friends can do together, and how to be a good friend. Building lasting friendships is an important life skill for everyone!

KEY LEARNING OBJECTIVES

- Identify characteristics of informational texts.

- Make inferences, using prior knowledge along with evidence from the text and illustrations.

- Identify the central, or main, idea of a text, using text evidence and supporting details.

TEXT COMPLEXITY

LEXILE MEASURE 230L • **GUIDED READING LEVEL** F

OVERALL RATING Slightly Complex

Simple text features help the reader navigate the content and identify the text's concrete purpose.

MAKE CONNECTIONS

🔗 BUILD KNOWLEDGE AND LANGUAGE

- **Social Studies Connection:** New Friends and Experiences

🔗 FOUNDATIONAL SKILLS

- **High-Frequency Words:** *a, good*

- **Consonants *n, d, p, c* /k/; Short *a*:** *around, ask, can, cat, classmate, Dad, dig, do, find, friends, fun, good, Grandma, happy, help, jump, Kids', kinds, neighbor, new, nice, one, place, play, read, ride, run, up*

TEXT X-RAY

KEY IDEAS	**LANGUAGE**
Key Idea *pp. 52–53* There are many kinds of friends. Friends are nice and enjoy being with you.	**Phrasal Verb** **_look around_** (p. 56): Explain that if you "look around," you move through or around a place to see what is there.
Key Idea *pp. 54–55* Friends have fun. They do things together, such as run, read, and laugh.	**Idioms** **_take turns_** (p. 58): Demonstrate the meaning of this phrase, perhaps by taking turns bouncing a ball.
Key Idea *pp. 56–57* There are different ways to find and make new friends.	**_cheer [someone] up_** (p. 58): Tell children that when you cheer someone up, you do something to make that person happy.
Key Idea *pp. 58–60* You can be a good friend by doing certain things, such as sharing and helping. Good friends try to make their friends happy!	

While you meet with small groups, have children work independently in Literacy Centers. At the beginning of the week, explain what is expected of children in each center. Post a daily rotation schedule.

WORD WORK

Word Pictures

- Provide magazines in the center. Display the Word Cards for this week's High-Frequency Words.

- Have children find or draw a picture that reminds them of one of the High-Frequency Words. Have them write a caption or label containing the High-Frequency Word to go with their picture.

- For an extra challenge, have children include two High-Frequency Words in their captions.

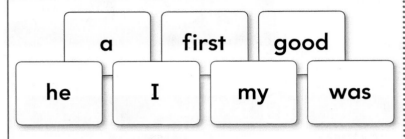

Short *a*

- Display the week's Spelling Words and copies of Printable: **Spelling & Handwriting**. Have children choose one of the activities to practice writing this week's Spelling Words in their best handwriting.

- Have children complete the activity on a separate sheet of paper.

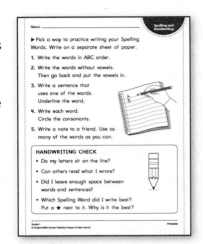

Printable: Spelling & Handwriting

CREATIVITY CORNER

Readers' Theater

- Have children read Printable: **Readers' Theater 1**, "The New School." Ask them to think of props to use in the production, such as cat ears and whiskers.

- Point out the importance of reading with accuracy. Then read aloud the Performance Tip and the Read with Fluency tip, and have groups rehearse.

- Encourage children to identify unfamiliar words in the script and ask them to make a note about their pronunciations in their scripts.

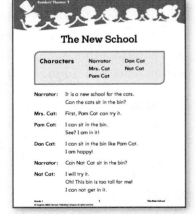

Printable: Readers' Theater 1

Reading Remake

- Display in the center and have children complete the activity for *My School Trip* on Printable: **Make a Map**.

- Tell partners to explain to one another how their map shows their understanding of the selection.

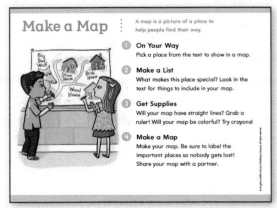

Printable: Make a Map

DIGITAL STATION

Listener's Choice

Online Ed

- Have children listen to the Read Aloud *You Will Be My Friend!* or a Leveled Reader of their choice.

- Tell them to add the book to their Printable: **Listening Log**, as well as the active listening skills they used, a summary, and a question they have about the book.

Phonics Practice

- Have children continue their personalized, adaptive learning for foundational skills in *iRead*.

TEAMWORK TIME

Inquiry and Research Project: "Celebrate Us!" Profiles

- Have groups continue work on the module project.

- Remind children that their focus this week is to write a sentence about and draw a picture of themselves to add to a class book. *See pp. T16–T17.*

 READING CORNER

Independent Reading

- Have children self-select or continue reading an independent reading book.

- Remind children to set a purpose for reading and to record their progress on their Printable: **Reading Log**.

- You may want to choose from these additional options to have children interact with their books:

  » **Read for Fluency** Children use the **PARTNER READING** routine to practice the week's fluency skill, reading rate, or another area of need.

  » **Annotate the Text** Children practice a strategy and use sticky notes to record questions or what they are thinking as they read. Review the sticky notes while you confer with children.

  » **Response Journal** Children draw or write about what they read.

Student Choice Library

Rigby
LEVELED LIBRARY

FOUNDATIONAL SKILLS

LEARNING OBJECTIVES

- Identify and read high-frequency words.
- **Language** Recognize, recite, and write basic sight vocabulary.
- Blend onsets and rimes to say one-syllable words.
- Blend phonemes to say one-syllable words.

MATERIALS — Online

Word Cards *a, first, good, had, he, I, my, was*

Know It, Show It p. 15

Picture Cards *bat (baseball), bell, eel, gate, kite, pen*

 # High-Frequency Words

Teach the Words

Use Word Cards *a, first, good, had, he, I, my,* and *was* and the **HIGH-FREQUENCY WORDS** routine below to introduce the week's High-Frequency sight words.

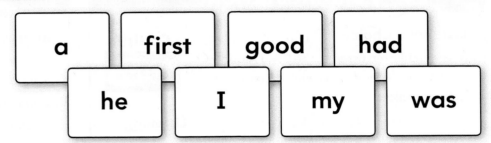

1. **See the word.** Display a Word Card. Say the word, and have children repeat it twice.

2. **Say the word.** Have children repeat it chorally. Use the word in a sentence or two. *I am the first person in line. I like to be first.* (Use pantomime.)

3. **Spell the word.** Point to the letters, and have children spell the word aloud. Point out any familiar spelling patterns. *My begins with* m. *Can you think of an animal name that begins with* m? *(monkey, moose) Do you know any other words that begin with* m?

4. **Write and check the word.** Hide the word, and have children use the **WRITE AND REVEAL** routine to write the word. Then have them check it against the Word Card.

Have children add this week's words to their individual Word Rings. Tell them to write a word on the front of each card and write a sentence or draw a picture about the word on the back. Alternatively, you may have children complete Know It, Show It page 15.

 ENGLISH LEARNER SUPPORT: Build Vocabulary

ALL LEVELS Use gestures to help reinforce word meanings. For example, point to yourself as you say, *My name is [name]. I am [name].* Then have children take turns introducing themselves in the same way.

 CORRECT & REDIRECT

Guide children who have trouble identifying any of the words. Say the correct word, and have children repeat it. Example:

- *Had. What is the word?* (had)
- Have children spell the word. *(h-a-d) How do we say this word?* (had)
- Have children reread all the cards in random order.

Phonological Awareness

Blend Onset and Rime

- Remind children that words are made of sounds and that working with the sounds in words can help them read and write better.

- Remind children that words can be broken into chunks and that they know how to blend word chunks to say words.

- Display Picture Cards *bat (baseball), kite,* and *pen.*

- Tell children they are going to help you say some words. Model: *I will say a word in two chunks: the beginning and the rest of the word. I want you to help me say the word. Listen while I do the first one: /k/ /ärd/. I can blend the two chunks together to say the word. /k/ /ärd/, card. The word is card.*

- *Now you try it: /m/ /ān/. What is the word? (main)*

- *Great! Let's keep going. As you blend word chunks to say words, see if the words you say match any of the Picture Cards. Not all the words you say will have a Picture Card match. Blend these word chunks to say the word: /p/ /ĕn/ (pen), /m/ /ŏp/ (mop), /t/ /āp/ (tape), /k/ /īt/ (kite), /s/ /ăd/ (sad), /n/ /ōz/ (nose), /b/ /ăt/ (bat).*

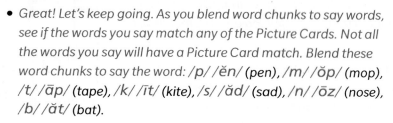

Blend Phonemes

- Remind children that they also know how to blend all the sounds in a word to say the word.

- Say: *I will say all the sounds in a word, and you will blend the sounds to say the word. I will do the first one. Listen, the sounds are: /ĭ/ /n/. When I blend /ĭ/ and /n/, I say the word in. /ĭ/ /n/, in.*

- *Are you ready to try? Listen: /ă/ /t/. What's the word? (at) Very good!*

- Display Picture Cards *bell, eel,* and *gate.*

- *Let's see if you can blend the sounds to say these words. As you blend and say a word, see if the word you say matches any of the Picture Cards. Not every word you say has a Picture Card match, so pay attention. Ready? Blend these sounds: /ē/ /l/ (eel), /ŏ/ /n/ (on), /b/ /ĕ/ /l/ (bell), /f/ /ŭ/ /n/ (fun), /ĕ/ /g/ (egg), /f/ /ĭ/ /l/ (fill), /g/ /ā/ /t/ (gate).*

 ENGLISH LEARNER SUPPORT: Build Vocabulary

ALL LEVELS Ensure that children are familiar with the meaning of each word in the Phonological Awareness activities (*pen, mop, tape, kite,* and so on). Use the Picture Cards to reinforce the meanings of words shown on the cards and gestures and examples for some of the other words.

 CORRECT & REDIRECT

For children who blend incorrectly, differentiate instruction by modeling. Enunciate the sounds separately, and then say them more closely together before finally blending them. Example for onset and rime:

The first chunk in my word is /p/. The next chunk is /ĕn/. Say the chunks with me: /p/, /ĕn/. Listen as I blend them together: /p/ /ĕn/, /p-ĕn/, pen. What is the word for the word chunks /p/ and /ĕn/? (pen)

FOUNDATIONAL SKILLS

 ## Consonants *n, d, p, c* /k/; Short *a*

Spotlight on Sounds

LEARNING OBJECTIVES

- Learn the sound-spellings for short *a* and consonants *n, d, p, c* /k/.

- **Language** Recognize sound-letter relationships and use them to decode words.

- Blend and decode regularly spelled one-syllable words with /ă/, /n/, /d/, /p/, and *c* /k/.

MATERIALS Online

Sound/Spelling Cards *alligator, cat, duck, nest, porcupine*

Letter Cards *a, b, c, d, D, n*

Articulation Videos /ă/, /k/, /n/, /d/, /p/

- Tell children that they will be reading words with the short *a* sound and the sounds for the letters *n, d, p,* and *c*. As a warm-up, have them practice identifying the beginning sounds in words you say. *I am going to say a word, and you will say the beginning sound. I will do the first one. Listen: the word is pan. The beginning sound in pan is /p/. Listen again, and repeat after me: pan, /p/. Now listen to each word and say the beginning sound: sad (/s/); cat (/k/); nap (/n/).*

- Next, have children suggest words with beginning sounds you specify. Say: *Think of words you know that begin with /n/.* Repeat for the sounds /d/, /p/, /k/. For /k/, accept words that begin with *c* /k/ or *k* /k/.

- Conclude the activity by modeling how to identify the ending sound in *mad*. Have children repeat the word and ending sound. Then have children listen for the ending sound in the words *tap* (/p/), *Dan* (/n/), and *pad* (/d/).

I Do It

Spotlight on Letters Display the Sound/Spelling Card for short *a: alligator*. Name the picture, say the sound, and give the spelling. *Alligator begins with the short a sound, /ă/. The letter a can stand for the sound /ă/ at the beginning or in the middle of a word.*

Write *at*. Say the letter sounds and blend the word: /ă/ /t/, at. Point out the vowel and consonant. Say: *Remember, a is a vowel, so it can stand for many sounds, and t is a consonant. When there is only one vowel in a word, and it is followed by a consonant, the vowel usually stands for the short vowel sound.*

Repeat for *c* /k/ (hard *c*), *d, n,* and *p,* using Sound/Spelling Cards *cat, duck, nest,* and *porcupine* and the words *cat, dad, Nan,* and *pan.*

 Professional Learning

BEST PRACTICES

When children are first learning to read or if they are struggling with reading, it is recommended that teachers use the **SOUND-BY-SOUND BLENDING** routine to model blending. The **CONTINUOUS BLENDING** routine provides children with an intermediate strategy as a transition between sound-by-sound blending and reading words with automaticity.

See the **GPS guide** to learn more.

EL **ENGLISH LEARNER SUPPORT:**
Facilitate Language Connections

Online

ALL LEVELS English learners may have trouble with the /n/ sound. Play the <u>Articulation Video</u> for /n/. Have children practice the sound in isolation and with these words: *nap, no, not nut, net.* For practice with the other sounds, see the <u>Articulation Videos</u> in the Materials list.

ARTICULATION VIDEO

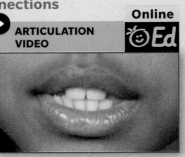

We Do It

Write *nap* and use Letter Cards *n, a, p* with the <mark>SOUND-BY-SOUND BLENDING</mark> routine below to model blending the word.

1 **Display** ccards as shown. Say the first letter and sound.

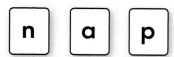

2 **Slide** the second letter over. Say its sound. Then blend the two sounds.

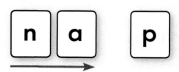

3 **Slide** the last letter over. Say its sound. Say the first two blended sounds, the last sound, and the blended word: /nă//p/, nap.

Sound-by-Sound Blending Repeat the <mark>SOUND-BY-SOUND BLENDING</mark> routine with cards for the words *can* and *Dan*, having children say the sounds and blend.

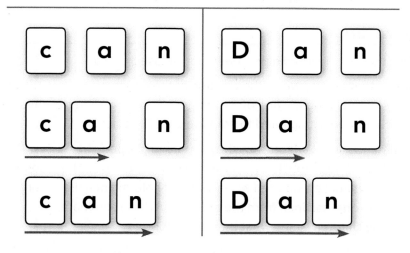

You Do It

INDEPENDENT PRACTICE

Blending Practice Write the words below. Then choose a volunteer to model the activity. Explain that you will point to two words in random order and the child will read them aloud. Repeat the blending routine as needed. Continue until each child has had a turn.

sad	pan	map	cat
tan	mat	pat	bad

✔ CORRECT & REDIRECT

- If a child mispronounces a word during Blending Practice, make note of the error type and address it.
- If a child reads *mat* as *mate,* explain that the vowel letter's name is *a* but that the sound it stands for in this word is the short *a* sound, /ă/. Use Sound/Spelling Card *alligator* to reinforce the /ă/ sound. Use sound-by-sound blending to read the word *mat,* and then have the child repeat the steps after you.
- If a child reads *pat* as *tap,* cover the word and blend it together as you uncover one letter at a time, left to right. Then have the child blend and read the word.

👥 LINK TO SMALL-GROUP INSTRUCTION

REINFORCE FOUNDATIONAL SKILLS Use *Dan Can Tap, Tap, Tap* during small-group time to review or reinforce blending and decoding words with short *a* and consonants *n, d, p, c* /k/. Meet with children to work through the story, or assign it as independent work. *See the lesson on p. T114.*

Dan Can Tap, Tap, Tap
by Margaret Fetty
Illustrated by Rob McClurkan

I am Dan.

FOUNDATIONAL SKILLS

 Short a

Administer the Pretest

- Read the first Spelling Word and the Dictation Sentence. Repeat the word as children write it.

- Write the word, and have children correct their spelling if needed. Repeat for words 2–6 and for the Review Words.

- Assign the Basic and Review Words as needed for practice this week. If children do well on the pretest, assign the Challenge Words.

LEARNING OBJECTIVES

- Spell words with short *a* (closed syllables).
- **Language** Identify relationships between sounds and letters.
- Develop handwriting by using correct paper position and pencil grip.

MATERIALS   Online ⏺ Ed

Sound/Spelling Card *alligator*
Picture Cards *can, cat, pan*
Printable *Word List 2*
Know It, Show It *p. 16*

DICTATION SENTENCES

BASIC

1. **an**   I ate *an* orange.
2. **bad**   The milk had gone *bad*.
3. **can**   Mom opened a *can* of peas.
4. **nap**   The tired baby took a *nap*.
5. **cat**   My *cat* is named Fluffy.
6. **pan**   He cooked eggs in a *pan*.

REVIEW

7. **am**   I *am* in first grade.
8. **at**   We are *at* school now.
9. **sat**   We *sat* on the couch.
10. **bat**   The ball player has a *bat*.

CHALLENGE

11. **trap**   The fish got caught in a *trap*.
12. **lamp**   The *lamp* is very bright.

Teach the Principle

- Remind children that they have learned to read and spell some words with short a. Write *bad* on the board, underlining *a*, and read it aloud. Remind children that the /ă/ sound can be spelled with the letter *a*.

- Tell children that this week all the Spelling Words have the short *a* sound, /ă/, spelled *a*. Remind them that short *a* sound can be at the beginning or in the middle of a word.

- If children have difficulty, review Sound/Spelling Card *alligator*. Remind them that *a* is a vowel that can stand for many sounds and that one of those sounds is /ă/ as in *alligator*.

Model Handwriting

- Remind children that they learned how to write lowercase *a* and *d*.

- Explain to children that as they write, the position of the paper is important. The paper should be slanted along the line of the child's writing arm, and the child should use his or her non-writing hand to hold the paper in place.

- Tell children that handedness affects how they should grip a pencil. Right-handed writers should hold the pencil at the edge of the paint line, about one inch from the lead tip. Left-handed writers should hold the pencil farther back, about one-and-one-half inch from the tip. This will help eliminate smudging and allow children to see what they are writing.

- Ask both right- and left-handed volunteers to model the correct paper position and pencil grip. Have children follow these models as they write the Spelling Words.

---● *Professional Learning*

RESEARCH FOUNDATIONS

"Handwriting and spelling made statistically significant contributions to written expression, demonstrating the importance of these lower-order transcription skills to higher order text-generation skills from a very early age."

—Dr. Cynthia Puranik and Dr. Stephanie Al Otaiba (2012)

See the **GPS guide** to learn more.

 ENGLISH LEARNER SUPPORT:
Build Vocabulary

ALL LEVELS Make sure children understand the meaning of the Spelling Words and Dictation Sentences. Display Picture Cards *can*, *cat*, and *pan*. Have children say the Spelling Words as they match the words to the pictures. Then discuss the meanings of the remaining words.

Word Sort

1 **Introduce** Display the Spelling Word cards from Printable: Word List 2. Explain that today's word sort will focus on words that have the short *a* sound.

2 **Column 1** Display and read *pan*. Model identifying the short *a*. Point out that *pan* ends with the letters *an* and the sounds /ăn/. Post the card as the heading for words that end with the same letters and sounds.

3 **Column 2** Repeat for *cat*, and start a column for words that end with the letters *at* and the sounds /ăt/.

4 **Column 3** Write *other* as a third column heading for words that do not belong in columns 1 or 2.

5 **Continue** Sort the remaining words, including the Review Words. Model if necessary. Example: *Can. Can ends with the letters an and the sounds /ăn/. So I'll put can under pan.* Repeat the procedure for *at*, placing it under *cat*, and for *bad*, placing it under *other*.

6 **Discuss** Read each column together. Discuss what children notice about the words in each column. If no one mentions it, point out that the words in column 1 rhyme and the words in column 2 rhyme. Tell children they can think about these patterns when they spell words with short *a*.

7 **Repeat** Have children work together to repeat the sort, using the Spelling Word cards from Printable: Word List 2. Remind children to save the rest of the page and the Spelling Word cards for use all week.

pan	cat	other
an	at	bad
can	sat	nap
	bat	am

INDEPENDENT PRACTICE

For additional practice, have children complete Know It, Show It page 16. Encourage them to use their best handwriting and pay particular attention to the position of their papers and their pencil grip.

(EL) ENGLISH LEARNER SUPPORT:
Facilitate Language Connections

ALL LEVELS If English learners pronounce the short vowel sound /ă/ as /ŏ/, help them practice correct pronunciation. Read the list of Spelling Words, elongating the short *a* sound in each word (baaaad). Then read the words normally. Have children repeat the words after you.

Professional Learning

BEST PRACTICES

Have children explore words and their patterns through the process of comparing, contrasting, and analyzing in interactive word sort activities. Word sorts engage and motivate children, and the discussions allow children to share insights and discover generalizations about words. Word sorting combines student-exploratory and teacher-directed learning.

See the **GPS guide** to learn more.

LEARNING OBJECTIVES

- **Language** Answer questions and discuss meanings to develop vocabulary.
- Identify real-life connections between words and their use.

MATERIALS Online Ed

Vocabulary Cards *1.16–1.21*
Read Aloud Book *You Will Be My Friend!*
Classroom materials *book*

Introduce Oral Language

Use the steps **I Do It, We Do It, You Do It** with the information in the chart below to teach the oral Power Words from the Read Aloud Book *You Will Be My Friend!*

❶ Power Word	❷ Meaning	❸ Example
search (n.) (*p. 6*)	When you go on a **search**, you are looking for someone or something.	**ACT IT OUT** Look around the classroom for an object. *My **search** for a pencil ended when I found one in my desk.*
introduce (v.) (*p. 11*)	When you **introduce** yourself, you tell someone your name.	**ACT IT OUT** Introduce yourself to a student and shake hands. *Let me **introduce** myself. I am _____.*
ridiculous (adj.) (*p. 15*)	If you feel **ridiculous**, you feel very silly.	**MAKE A CONNECTION** Give an example of feeling ridiculous. *I felt **ridiculous** when I had to wear a silly hat.*
calm (v.) (*p. 22*)	If you **calm** yourself down, you become quiet and peaceful.	**ACT IT OUT** Take a deep breath. *I take a deep breath when I want to **calm** myself.*
happened (v.) (*p. 28*)	If something **happened**, it took place.	**MAKE A CONNECTION** Connect *happened* to a recent school event. *Do you remember what **happened** at school yesterday? We read a new book.*
accept (v.) (*p. 31*)	When you **accept** something, you say "yes" or agree to it.	**USE A PROP** Hold up a book and gesture to a child. *Will you **accept** my invitation to read together?*

● *Getting Started*

CLASSROOM MANAGEMENT

While planning your lesson, note which materials you will need for the lesson to make the preparation easier. Include which cards, books, digital materials, and basic classroom supplies will be needed.

See the **GPS guide** to learn more.

 LEARNING MINDSET

Seeking Challenges

Model Remind children that part of the challenge of reading is learning and understanding new words. Every reader faces this challenge, but learning new words makes reading fun and exciting. *I've heard the word* ridiculous, *but I haven't really thought about its meaning. I'll listen to the meaning and think about how it applies to my own life. I'll challenge myself and ask, "Can I think of a time when I felt* ridiculous?"

I Do It

Use the **VOCABULARY** routine and Vocabulary Cards 1.16–1.21 to introduce the oral Power Words from *You Will Be My Friend!* You may wish to display the corresponding Vocabulary Card for each word as you discuss it.

Vocabulary Cards

1. **Say the Power Word.** Ask children to repeat it.

2. **Explain the meaning.** Read aloud the student-friendly meaning.

3. **Talk about examples.** Use the image or a strategy to give examples of the word.

We Do It

Guide children to make connections between each word's meaning and how they can use it in their own lives. Use these prompts. Encourage children to explain or justify their answers.

- *What steps would you take on a **search** for something you lost?*

- *When might you need to **introduce** yourself?*

- *Would you feel **ridiculous** if you went to school in your pajamas? Why or why not?*

- *What special place makes you feel **calm**?*

- *Tell about something that **happened** at school yesterday.*

- *When would you or your friends **accept** a gift?*

You Do It

INDEPENDENT PRACTICE

Have partners work together to complete each of the activities below. Circulate and observe partners as they work, providing corrective feedback as necessary.

- **Discuss** *Talk about a time you felt **ridiculous**. Tell what **happened**.*

- **Role-Play** *Act out how you would **accept** an invitation to a birthday party.*

- **Role-Play** *Show how you would **introduce** yourself to a new classmate. Take turns so you each get to practice a few times.*

- **Discuss** *Talk about what it is like to go on a **search** for something. Do you feel **calm** or nervous? Why?*

 **ENGLISH LEARNER SUPPORT: Facilitate Discussion**

SUBSTANTIAL
Ask *yes/no* questions: *Would you **introduce** yourself to an old friend? If you **accept** something, are you giving it away?*

MODERATE
Supply these frames: *I feel **calm** when _____. I feel **ridiculous** when _____.*

LIGHT
Point out that the words *calm* and *ridiculous* express feelings. Ask children to explain when they might experience these feelings.

TEACHER TIP

Glad to meet you! Discuss different situations when people introduce themselves to each other, such as at school or sports events, parties, or family gatherings. Emphasize that it is important to learn and remember a person's name. Model an introduction, such as this: *Hello, my name is (Mr. Allen). What's your name? It's nice to meet you!* Ask volunteers to role-play similar situations.

READ ALOUD   **MINILESSON**

LEARNING OBJECTIVES

- Recognize characteristics of fantasy.
- Identify and describe story events in order.
- **Language** Describe events in order, using sequence words.
- Write the events in a story in order.

MATERIALS   Online

Anchor Chart 18
Story Structure

Anchor Chart 69
Parts of a Book

Printables *Anchor Chart 18: Story Structure; Anchor Chart 69: Parts of a Book; Reading Graphic Organizer 23: Story Structure*

Read Aloud Book *You Will Be My Friend!*

BookStix *1.2*

READER'S VOCABULARY

- **event** something that happens in a story
- **sequence** an order of events (beginning, middle, and end) in a story

---

Story Structure

Step **1** Connect and Teach

- Remind children that in stories, things happen in a certain order. Project or display **Anchor Chart 18: Story Structure**.

- Review that things that happen in a story are called **events** and that the order in which they happen is the **sequence**. Explain that identifying and describing important events in order helps readers understand a story better.

- Remind children that they can use details in the text and pictures to figure out each important event at the beginning, in the middle, and at the end of a story.

- Finally, point out the sequence words on the chart and explain that children can use the words *first, next,* and *last* to tell the order of events.

- Tell children they will practice identifying and describing important events in order when they listen to a story called *You Will Be My Friend!*

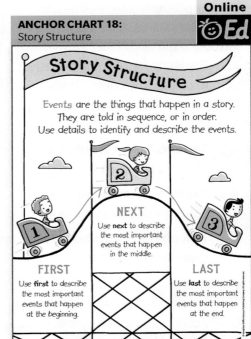

ANCHOR CHART 18:
Story Structure   Online

LEARNING MINDSET

Seeking Challenges

Reflect Discuss with children how Lucy had a goal to find a friend. Talk about the difficulties that Lucy had in meeting her goal. Point out how she keeps trying even when she fails, and how she eventually ends up reaching her goal—and makes a new friend. Remind children that it is important to set goals for yourself, even if it might be difficult to achieve them.

EL ENGLISH LEARNER SUPPORT:
Facilitate Language Connections

ALL LEVELS For Spanish-speaking children, point out that the English words *event* and *sequence* have the following Spanish cognates: *evento* and *sequencia.*

Go to Your
BookStix 1.2

Step 2 Apply to Text

- **Genre Study** Read aloud the title *You Will Be My Friend!* and introduce the book. *Today we will read a fantasy, or a made-up story.* Have children examine the cover. Prompt them to think about what the book will be about. Ask: *Who is the story about? What do you think the bear wants to do?*

- **Set a Purpose** Preview a few pages in the book and ask: *Do you think the bear will find a friend?* Have children use their predictions to set a purpose for reading.

- **Model Fluency** Tell children that as you read, you will show them how to read at a rate, or speed, that fits the kind of text you are reading. Demonstrate reading at a smooth, steady pace—not too fast or too slow—so you sound natural, as if you were talking.

- **Concepts of Print** Project or display **Anchor Chart 69: Parts of a Book**. Review the information each part of a book provides, print directionality, and the difference between letters, words, and sentences.

- **Read and Comprehend** Read aloud the book for children, pausing occasionally to ask the questions on BookStix 1.2 and to have them identify important events at the beginning, middle, and end of the story. Refer back to the Anchor Chart to discuss story structure in *You Will Be My Friend!*

Step 3 Engage and Respond

INDEPENDENT PRACTICE: Writing

- Remind children that in the Read Aloud Book *You Will Be My Friend!*, Lucy wants to find a friend.

- Have children use Reading Graphic Organizer 23 to write or draw the important events at the beginning, middle, and end of the story.

- Ask children to use their completed graphic organizers to write about the important events of the story in order. Remind them to use the words *first, next,* and *last* to tell about the events.

- You may want to have children complete their writing during daily small-group time.

 LINK TO SMALL-GROUP INSTRUCTION

REINFORCE STORY STRUCTURE Review or extend the skill as needed during small-group time to support children's need for differentiation. *See the lesson on p. T113.*

👥 SMALL-GROUP INSTRUCTION

Options for Differentiation

As the class engages in independent and collaborative work, meet with Guided Reading Groups or differentiate instruction based on student need.

GUIDED READING GROUPS

Match Children to Books + Instruction

- Choose just-right books based on level, skill, topic, or genre.

C **D** **E** **F** **G** **H** **I** **J** **K** ➡

Leveled Readers

- Deliver instruction with each book's Take and Teach Lesson, choosing appropriate sessions based on need.

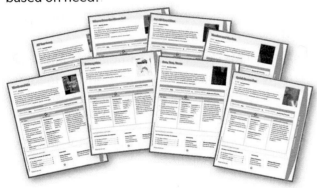

- Check comprehension, reinforce instruction, and extend learning with suggested supporting activities.

Rigby LEVELED LIBRARY

🔵 ENGLISH LEARNER SUPPORT

Infer

- Use **Tabletop Minilessons: English Language Development 2.1 (Listening)** to introduce and practice the language skill.

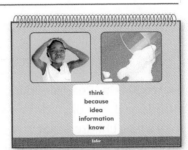

Tabletop Minilessons: English Language Development

- Then use the following text-based prompts with *You Will Be My Friend!* to guide application of the language skill. Begin with the prompt at the child's identified language proficiency level. As children are able, use lighter supports to encourage increased language proficiency.

SUBSTANTIAL

Display the cover. Ask: *How does Lucy feel? How do the other animals feel?* Repeat on page 11, with Lucy and the giraffe. Allow children to respond with a thumbs up or down, or with single words or simple phrases.

MODERATE

Ask children to make inferences about the characters on pages 7–9, using these frames: *Lucy probably thinks ___. The frogs might feel ___. Lucy looks ___.*

LIGHT

Ask children to make inferences about how the characters feel or what they think by looking at the pictures. Have them respond in complete sentences.

REINFORCE STORY STRUCTURE

Demonstrate

- Use **Tabletop Minilessons: Reading 18** to remind children that the **events**, or what happens in a story, are told in **sequence**, or in the order in which they happen. Identifying and describing what happens at the beginning, in the middle, and at the end of a story helps readers understand it better. Readers can use evidence or details in the text and pictures, and the words *first, next,* and *last,* to identify and describe the most important events in a story.

- Model filling out Printable: **Reading Graphic Organizer 23** to identify and describe the story structure in *You Will Be My Friend!*

Tabletop Minilessons: Reading

Apply to Independent Reading

- Now have children describe the story structure by identifying the events at the beginning, middle, and end in an appropriate just-right book that they are reading independently. Before children read their books, guide them to set a purpose for reading. Remind them to think about story events. Customize these prompts to the books children choose.

  » *What happens at the beginning of the story?*

  » *What happens in the middle of the story?*

  » *What happens at the end of the story?*

- Have children complete Printable: **Reading Graphic Organizer 23** for their independent reading book.

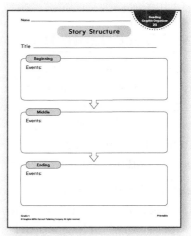

Printable:
Reading Graphic Organizer 23

ALMOST THERE

READY FOR MORE

SCAFFOLD AND EXTEND

- Read the first important event in the book and ask: *Does this event happen in the beginning, middle, or end of the book?* Repeat with other events.

- Have children retell an event that happens at the beginning, middle, and end of the story.

- Ask children which part of the story is usually the most exciting: beginning, middle, or end? Have them tell why.

 ENGLISH LEARNER SUPPORT

SUBSTANTIAL

Display pages 2–5. Ask: *Which event happened first?* Have children use *first* as they point to the appropriate picture.

MODERATE

Ask: *What happens at the beginning? in the middle? at the end?* Have children give simple responses.

LIGHT

Have children describe an event or illustration they like. Have them tell whether it is from the beginning, middle, or end.

Small-Group Instruction **T113**

Options for Differentiation

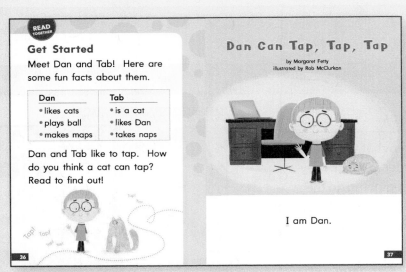 

Dan Can Tap, Tap, Tap, Start Right Reader, *Book 1*, pp. 36–43

REINFORCE FOUNDATIONAL SKILLS

Read Decodable Text

Get Started Have children turn to Start Right Reader page 36. Explain that this week's stories are about a boy named Dan and his cat, Tab. Talk with children about how a cat might get the name Tab. Explain that there is a kind of cat called a tabby cat. Then read page 36 together and discuss the question.

Preview the Story Draw attention to page 37, the title page. Read aloud the title and have children look at the pictures on the first few pages. Have them predict what Dan will tap.

Concepts of Print: Directionality Use pages 38–39 to model how to track print from left to right and from top to bottom. As children track the print, periodically call out words for them to locate on the page.

Fluency Focus: Reading Rate Read aloud page 40 as children follow along. Point out that you read the words at the same speed, or rate, as you would say them. Lead children in reading page 40 chorally with fluency and at an appropriate rate.

Reflect on Reading Have children use a finger to track the words from left to right as they read each page silently. Then have them read the page chorally. Pause for these prompts:

- **Pages 37–38:** *Who are the characters? (Dan, Tab)*

- **Page 39:** *Now do you know what Dan is tapping? What does he tap? (yes; a computer) Is this what you predicted? Explain. (Responses will vary.)*

- **Page 41:** *What is Dan making? (a map)*

Short *a* Word Hunt Read aloud the first numbered item on page 43. Have children look through the story for words with short *a* and write the words they find on a sheet of paper. Then read the second numbered item. Allow time for children to read their lists and circle words that rhyme with *Dan*. Call on children to tell which words they circled.

Dan can tap.
Tap, Dan! Tap, tap, tap!

40

Dan had a map.
Can Dan tap at the map?
He can. Tap, tap, tap!

41

A good map, Dan!

42

READ TOGETHER

Short a Word Hunt

1. Look in the story for words with short **a**. Write each word you find.

2. Look at your list of short **a** words. Circle the words that rhyme with the boy's name.

43

(?) Make Minutes Count

As you meet with small groups to read *Dan Can Tap, Tap, Tap,* use one or more of these related activities, as needed, at the beginning or the end of the small-group session.

- **Connect to Phonics** Use Letter Cards *a, c, d, n, p* to review letter sounds. Then use the Letter Cards to build these words: *can, cap, nap, pad, pan.* Have each child choose a word, model blending, and then say the word smoothly.

- **Connect to Spelling** Have children sort the Spelling Word cards from Printable: <u>Word List 2</u> into two categories: words that rhyme with *man* and words that do not. Have them explain how the words that rhyme with *man* are the same. *(They all end with the letters -an and the sounds /ăn/.)*

- **Connect to Handwriting** Have children write their first and last names three times each. Monitor their pencil grip and paper position. If necessary, help children adjust their grip for left- and right-handedness.

High-Frequency Words	Decodable High-Frequency Words	Spelling Words	
		Basic	Review
a	an	an	am
first	can	bad	at
good	man	can	sat
had		nap	bat
he		cat	
I		pan	
my			
was			
			Challenge
			trap
			lamp

Printable: Word List 2

Options for Independent and Collaborative Work

While you meet with small groups, have other children engage in literacy activities that reinforce the lesson's learning objectives. Choose from these options.

Independent Reading

Student Choice Library

APPLY READING SKILL

Story Structure Children complete Printable: **Reading Graphic Organizer 23** for an independent reading book.

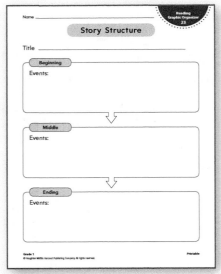

Printable: Reading Graphic Organizer 23

APPLY LANGUAGE SKILL

Infer Children complete Printable: **Language Graphic Organizer 7** for an independent reading book.

Printable: Language Graphic Organizer 7

Literacy Centers

See pp. T100–T101.

 WORD WORK

 CREATIVITY CORNER

 DIGITAL STATION

 READING CORNER

 TEAMWORK TIME

Start Right Reader

Read Decodable Text *Dan Can Tap, Tap, Tap*, Book 1: pp. 36–43

Writing

Children write numbered steps to share and discuss with partners.
See Engage & Respond, p. T111.

Additional Skills Practice

HIGH-FREQUENCY WORDS

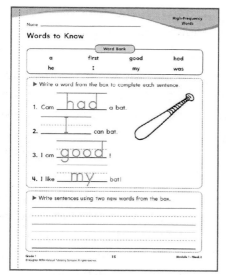

Know It, Show It, p. 15

SPELLING

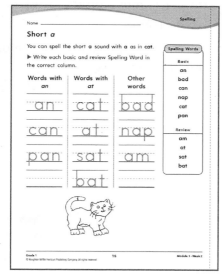

Know It, Show It, p. 16

Wrap-Up
Share Time

At the end of Reading Workshop, have children reflect on their learning by sharing how they applied **Story Structure** or another area of focus during independent work time. Choose from these options:

- **SHARE CHAIR** Select a reader each day to come to the front of the class and tell what he or she learned from the reading by using a skill or strategy.

- **THINK-PAIR-SHARE** Children share their thinking with a partner. Select a few children each day to share with the whole class.

- **RETURN TO ANCHOR CHART** Have children add sticky notes about their independent reading book to the Story Structure Anchor Chart. Call on a few children to explain what they added.

ANCHOR CHART 18: Story Structure   **Online** Ed

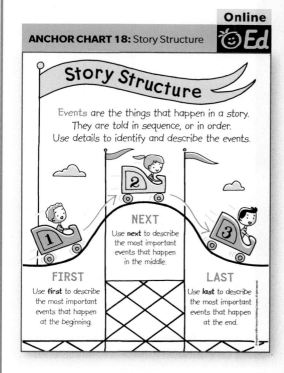

FOUNDATIONAL SKILLS

LEARNING OBJECTIVES

- Identify and read high-frequency words.
- **Language** Recognize, recite, and write basic sight vocabulary.
- Blend onsets and rimes to say one-syllable words.
- Blend phonemes to say one-syllable words.

MATERIALS   Online

Word Cards *a, an, can, first, good, had, he, I, man, my, was*

Printable *Word List 2*

Picture Cards *ax, cup, fox, goat, map, mitt, pen, tub, yak*

 # High-Frequency Words

Review the Words

Repeat the **HIGH-FREQUENCY WORDS** routine to review this week's High-Frequency Words: *a, first, good, had, he, I, my,* and *was,* and the decodable High-Frequency Words *an, can,* and *man.*

Word-O Game

- Have children cut out cards for the High-Frequency Words and decodable High-Frequency Words from Printable: Word List 2.

- On a separate sheet of paper, have each child create a grid by drawing two lines down and two lines across to make nine squares. Tell children to write one High-Frequency Word in each square in any order, using any nine words.

- Help children form small groups to play Word-O. Players take turns reading a word card aloud. Other players look to see if the word is on their grids. If it is, they place their word card on the grid.

- Play continues until one player makes three matches in a row and calls "Word-O!" To win, the player must correctly read the three words aloud.

- Tell children to save the word cards to use throughout the week.

Printable: Word List 2

Word-O

man	was	my
good	first	an
can	I	had

TEACHER TIP

Game night! Consider sending Printable: Word List 2 and the Word-O grids home with children. Game night could be word practice night!

 LEARNING MINDSET

Seeking Challenges

Normalize Explain to children that learning how to read and spell words can seem hard and can sometimes be frustrating, but that when they try to learn new things, their brains grow. Say: *If you have trouble remembering one or more of the words, think of it as a challenge. There will always be words or things we don't know, so it's important to challenge ourselves into learning as much as we can! Think of how proud you will be once you have learned the words that were hard for you!*

Phonological Awareness

Blend Onset and Rime

- Remind children that they know how to blend word chunks to say words.

- Display Picture Cards *ax, goat, map,* and *tub.*

- Tell children they are going to help you say some words: *I will say a word in two chunks: the beginning, and the rest of the word. Then you can blend the chunks to say the word. Listen as I do the first one. I am trying to say a word. Listen to the chunks: /t/ /ŭb/. I can blend the chunks to say the word: /t/ /ŭb/, tub. The word is tub. Does tub have a Picture Card match? Yes.* Point to Picture Card *tub.*

- *Your turn. Listen and blend the word chunks. Then tell whether there is a Picture Card match. Here are the chunks for the first word: /n/ /ăp/. What is the word?* (nap) *Great! Does the word nap have a Picture Card match?* (no) *That's right. Not all the words you say will have a Picture Card match.*

- *Let's keep going: /ă/ /ks/ (ax), /j/ /ŭg/ (jug), /m/ /ăp/ (map), /h/ /ŏt/ (hot), /m/ /āl/ (mail), /g/ /ōt/ (goat).*

Blend Phonemes

- Then remind children that they not only know how to blend word chunks, they also know how to blend individual sounds to say words. Say: *I will say all the sounds in a word, and you will blend the sounds to say the word. Listen as I do the first one: /m/ /ĕ/ /t/, met. When I blend /m/, /ĕ/, and /t/, I say the word met; /m/ /ĕ/ /t/, met.*

- *Are you ready? Listen: /p/ /ă/ /d/ (pad), /b/ /ŏ/ /ks/ (box), /l/ /ĭ/ /p/ (lip), /r/ /ă/ /n/ (ran), /f/ /ŭ/ /n/ (fun), /d/ /ŏ/ /g/ (dog), /p/ /ă/ /k/ (pack).*

- Then distribute Picture Cards *cup, fox, mitt, pen,* and *yak* to five children. Have them stand in front of the group. Explain that all children will blend more sounds to say words and when they say a word with a Picture Card match, they should tell the child with the card to hold it up high.

- Use the following phoneme sets, and explain that not all words have a matching Picture Card image: /k/ /ŭ/ /p/ (cup), /f/ /ŏ/ /ks/ (fox), /n/ /ī/ /f/ (knife), /p/ /ĭ/ /t/ (pit), /p/ /ĕ/ /n/ (pen), /l/ /ĕ/ /g/ (leg), /y/ /ă/ /k/ (yak), /ch/ /ĭ/ /k/ (chick), /m/ /ĭ/ /t/ (mitt).

- When there is a Picture Card match, have the group tell the child with the matching Picture Card to hold up the card and say the word one more time.

ENGLISH LEARNER SUPPORT:
Build Vocabulary

SUBSTANTIAL
Use the Picture Cards to help children learn word meanings. For words without Picture Card matches, use gestures or quick sketches to help.

MODERATE
Provide sentence frames for children to complete using words pictured on Picture Cards. Example: *I use an _____ to chop wood.*

LIGHT
Have children say a sentence that uses one of the words from today's Phonological Awareness activities.

CORRECT & REDIRECT

To support children who blend phonemes incorrectly, model the task by saying the sounds more and more closely together, as in the example below.

- Say each sound in the word: /k/ /ŭ/ /p/. Have the child repeat. (/k/ /ŭ/ /p/)

- Repeat, each time blending the sounds a little more closely together, and then say the word: /k/ /ŭ/ /p/, /k-ŭ-p/, cup.

- Ask the child to blend and say the word.

- Have children blend individual sounds to say other words.

FOUNDATIONAL SKILLS

Consonants n, d, p, c /k/; Short a

Spotlight on Sounds

- Guide children to listen for and distinguish vowel sounds. *Today I will say pairs of words. The words will have different vowel sounds. You repeat the words and say which word has the short a sound, /ă/.*

- *I will do the first one. Listen:* cap, cape. Repeat, emphasizing the vowel sounds. *Cap, cape. Cap is the word with /ă/, the short a sound.*

- Extend the activity by having children say the following word pairs, tell which word has the /ă/ sound, and say the sound: Sam/same (Sam, /ă/); ate/at (at, /ă/); hate/hat (hat, /ă/); am/aim (am, /ă/); mat/mate (mat, /ă/); aid/add (add, /ă/).

LEARNING OBJECTIVES

- Blend, build, and decode regularly spelled one-syllable words with short *a* and consonants *n, d, p, c /k/*.

- **Language** Recognize sound-letter relationships and use them to decode words.

MATERIALS   Online

Sound/Spelling Cards
alligator, cat, duck, nest, porcupine

Letter Cards *a, c, d, n, p*

Display and Engage *Blend and Read 1.6*

Start Right Reader *Book 1, p. 44*

Printable *Letter Cards*

Know It, Show It *p. 17*

I Do It

Spotlight on Letters Review Sound/Spelling Cards *alligator, cat, duck, nest,* and *porcupine.*

Write *pan* for children to see, and use the **SOUND-BY-SOUND BLENDING** routine below to model blending the word using Letter Cards *p, a, n.*

1 **Display** Letter Cards as shown. Say the first letter and sound.

2 **Slide** the second letter over. Say its sound. Then blend the two sounds.

3 **Slide** the last letter over. Say its sound. Say the first two blended sounds, the last sound, and the blended word: /pă//n/, pan.

Repeat the routine with the cards for *pad* and *can.*

● *Professional Learning*

RESEARCH FOUNDATIONS

"Without well-developed phonological awareness, receiving the common suggestion to 'sound it out,' will make little sense to a child who is attempting to read or spell."

—Dr. Anne E. Cunningham and Dr. Jamie Zibulsky (2014)

See the **GPS guide** to learn more.

EL ENGLISH LEARNER SUPPORT:
Build Vocabulary

SUBSTANTIAL
Help children understand Blend and Read words with sketches (*pan, cap*), gestures (*pat, nap*), or sentences (*I am a teacher*).

MODERATE
Some Blend and Read words, such as *bat* and *can*, have multiple meanings. Help children demonstrate or explain each meaning.

LIGHT
Challenge children to identify the Blend and Read words with multiple meanings.

We Do It

Blend and Read

Project Display and Engage: **Blend and Read 1.6** or use Start Right Reader page 44.

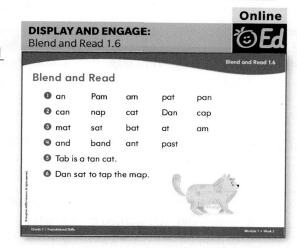

DISPLAY AND ENGAGE:
Blend and Read 1.6

Online **Ed**

Blend and Read 1.6

Blend and Read

1. an   Pam   am   pat   pan
2. can   nap   cat   Dan   cap
3. mat   sat   bat   at   am
4. and   band   ant   past
5. Tab is a tan cat.
6. Dan sat to tap the map.

1. **Line 1** Have children read the line. Then prompt a conversation about the words: *How are some of the words the same or different? What do you notice?* If necessary, lead children to compare the words: beginning sound *(an, am; Pam, pat, pan)*; rhyming *(an, pan; Pam, am)*. Point to each word, and have children read the line chorally. Provide corrective feedback as needed.

2. **Line 2** Continue with these words. Then call on volunteers to reread selected words until children can identify the words quickly.

3. **Review** For Line 3, have children read the words chorally.

4. **Challenge** If children are ready for a challenge, have them read the words with final consonant blends in Line 4 and share how they figured them out.

5. **Sentences** For Lines 5–6, call on children to blend selected decodable words. Then have the group read the sentences chorally.

You Do It

INDEPENDENT PRACTICE

- **Option 1** Model how to write and spell the word *nap* sound by sound. Then have children identify sounds and use Printable: **Letter Cards** to form these words: *can, pad, Dan*. Have a child spell each word aloud while others check their own work.

- **Option 2** Children complete Know It, Show It page 17.

 CORRECT & REDIRECT

- If a child mispronounces a word in the Blend and Read lines, say the word, call attention to the mispronounced phonic element, and help the child blend the word. Have the child practice rereading the whole line, and be sure to celebrate improvements in decoding fluency!

- If a child reads *pan* as *nap*, cover the word and blend it together as you uncover one letter at a time, left to right. Then have the child blend and read the word.

LINK TO SMALL-GROUP INSTRUCTION

REINFORCE FOUNDATIONAL SKILLS Use *Tab Can Tap, Tap, Tap* during small-group time to review or reinforce blending and decoding words with short *a* and consonants *n, d, p, c/k/*. Meet with children to work through the story, or assign it as independent work. *See the lesson on p. T128.*

Tab Can Tap, Tap, Tap
by Margaret Fetty
Illustrated by Rob McClurkan

Tab sat.

LEARNING OBJECTIVES

- **Language** Answer questions and discuss meanings to develop vocabulary.
- Identify real-life connections between words and their use.

MATERIALS   Online

Vocabulary Cards 1.22–1.27
Classroom materials *a thick book*

 # Introduce Power Words

Use the steps **I Do It, We Do It, You Do It** with the information in the chart below to teach the Power Words from *My School Trip* and *A Kids' Guide to Friends*.

❶ Power Word	❷ Meaning	❸ Example
trip (n.) *(p. 34)*	When you go on a **trip**, you go from one place to another.	**MAKE A CONNECTION** Relate a trip to a specific location. *I went on a **trip** to _____.*
partner (n.) *(p. 35)*	A **partner** is someone you work with or play with.	**ACT IT OUT** Pantomime dancing a waltz. *I need a **partner** to dance with me.*
wished (v.) *(p. 39)*	If you **wished** for something, you wanted it to happen.	**MAKE A CONNECTION** Talk about things you have wished for. *I **wished** that the sun would shine today.*
last (n.) *(p. 41)*	When something happens at **last**, it happens after a long time.	**USE A PROP** Hold up a thick book. *It took a long time, but I finished reading this book at **last**!*
kinds (n.) *(p. 53)*	If there are many **kinds** of something, there are many different groups of it.	**MAKE A CONNECTION** Give examples of different kinds of things. *Celery, carrots, and broccoli are different **kinds** of vegetables.*
together (adv.) *(p. 54)*	When friends do things **together**, they do them with each other.	**ACT IT OUT** Ask several children to form a circle with you. *We are standing **together** in a circle.*

● *Professional Learning*

TEACHING TERMS

Most of the Power Words in this program are **Tier-Two words**, which are the best candidates for explicit instruction. Tier-Two words occur frequently in texts, are used across several content areas, and are recognized by mature readers. They are not unique to specific contexts or subjects.

See the **GPS guide** to learn more.

ENGLISH LEARNER SUPPORT: Build Vocabulary

SUBSTANTIAL
   Have children act out meanings. For example, ask two partners to stand next to each other. Ask three children to stand together.

MODERATE
   Ask questions such as these: *What different **kinds** of fruit are there? What **kinds** of fruit do you like?*

LIGHT
   Ask children to use four of the Power Words in their own sentences.

I Do It

Use the **VOCABULARY** routine and Vocabulary Cards 1.22–1.27 to introduce the Power Words from *My School Trip* and *A Kids' Guide to Friends*. You may wish to display the corresponding Vocabulary Card for each word as you discuss it.

trip

Vocabulary Cards

1. **Say the Power Word.** Ask children to repeat it.

2. **Explain the meaning.** Read aloud the student-friendly meaning.

3. **Talk about examples.** Use the image or a strategy to give examples of the word.

We Do It

Guide children to make connections between each word's meaning and how they can use it in their own lives. Use these prompts. Encourage children to explain or justify their answers.

- *Would you rather go on a **trip** to the mountains or to the ocean? Why?*

- *What can you do better with a **partner** instead of by yourself? Why?*

- *If you **wished** for something to happen today, what would it be?*

- *When people say "at **last**," did something happen after a short time or a long time?*

- *What **kinds** of music do you like?*

- *When we read **together**, do we read alone or with others?*

You Do It

INDEPENDENT PRACTICE

Have partners work together to complete each of the activities below. Circulate and observe partners as they work, providing corrective feedback as necessary.

- **Draw** *Draw a picture of a place where you would like to go on a **trip**.*

- **Discuss** *What do you like to do with a **partner** at recess? How do you play **together**?*

- **Role-Play** *Imagine you **wished** you could finish a big job, and you finally did. Show how your face would look as you say "at **last**!"*

- **Draw** *Draw a picture of different **kinds** of pets.*

TEACHER TIP

More than one meaning! Children are probably more familiar with the meaning of *last* as "at the end." Tell children that one word can have several meanings. Ask volunteers to explain how the meanings for this word are different.

READING WORKSHOP

Monitor and Clarify

LEARNING OBJECTIVES

- Identify the features of realistic fiction.
- Monitor comprehension and use strategies to clarify understanding.
- **Language** Explain the use of strategies to clarify understanding.
- Ask questions to clarify understanding.

MATERIALS   Online

Anchor Chart 2
Monitor and Clarify

Printable *Anchor Chart 2: Monitor and Clarify*

Teaching Pal *Book 1, pp. 32–43*

myBook *My School Trip, Book 1, pp. 32–43*

📖 READER'S VOCABULARY

- **monitor** to check for understanding while reading
- **clarify** to try to fix up what you don't understand in your reading
- **reread** to read something again
- **background knowledge** what you already know about a topic
- **visual** a picture, drawing, or illustration

Step 1   Connect and Teach

- Project or display <u>Anchor Chart 2: Monitor and Clarify</u>.

- Read aloud the introduction. Tell children that they should **monitor**, or make sure they understand, what they read. Point out that if something doesn't make sense, they should stop and **clarify**, or "fix up," what they do not understand.

- Point to each part of the chart as you read and explain the different things children can do if they do not understand something they read.

- Tell children that they can **reread** the part of the text they do not understand.

- Explain that children can also use their **background knowledge**, or what they already know, to help them understand what confuses them.

- Point out that children should also look at the **visuals** on a page, such as a picture or illustration, to see if it gives information about the part of the text they do not understand.

- Finally, tell children they can use the words *who, what, where, when, how,* and *why* to ask themselves questions about anything they do not understand. Point out that asking questions can sometimes help readers figure out what confuses them.

- Tell children they will practice how to monitor and clarify as they read realistic fiction called *My School Trip.*

ANCHOR CHART 2:
Monitor and Clarify

Online 🍊Ed

Monitor & Clarify

Pay attention as you read.
If something doesn't make sense,
try these things to help you understand.

REREAD the part of the text that you don't understand.

Use what you already know to **CONNECT** to the text. This part reminds me of . . .

ASK QUESTIONS about the part you don't understand.
What was that paragraph mostly about?
Why did the main character say that?

Look for **VISUAL CLUES.**
How can the headings, captions, pictures, or special type help me?

Notice Note

Contrasts and Contradictions

- The Teaching Pal prompts in this lesson feature the **Notice & Note signpost: Contrasts and Contradictions**.

- As needed, refer to p. T19 to review the signpost with children.

✓ ASSESSMENT OPTION

Assign the <u>Selection Quiz</u> to check comprehension of *My School Trip.*

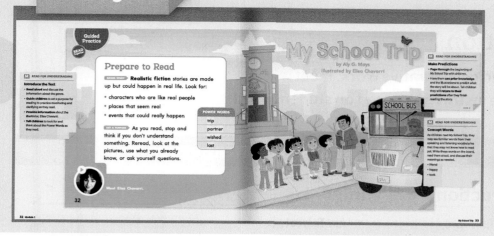

ANNOTATE IT!

Children may use the annotation tools in their eBook.

Step 2 Apply to Text

 In your Teaching Pal, pages 32–43, use the blue **READ FOR UNDERSTANDING** prompts to read *My School Trip* with children as they follow along and annotate in their *my*Book.

- **Genre Study** Read the genre information on page 32. Discuss the kinds of things children would expect to find in a realistic fiction story and compare them with what they might find in a fantasy story like *You Will Be My Friend!*

- **Set a Purpose** Read the Set a Purpose section on page 32. Prompt children to set their own purpose for reading *My School Trip.*

- **Meet the Illustrator** Play the audio about **Elisa Chavarri**. Help children make connections between the information about Elisa Chavarri and experiences in their own lives.

- **Read and Comprehend** Guide children to read the story all the way through. Pause occasionally, using the prompts in your Teaching Pal to gauge children's understanding and to have them monitor what they read and clarify what they do not understand. Have children refer back to the Anchor Chart to choose and use a fix-up strategy.

Step 3 Engage and Respond

INDEPENDENT PRACTICE: Speaking & Listening

- Use the **TURN AND TALK** routine with the questions on Teaching Pal and *my*Book page 43. Remind children that they can refer to the Anchor Chart as they explain how they figured out parts of the story they did not understand.

- Read the Talking Tip. Remind children that they can ask questions if they do not understand something their partner says. Tell them to use the sentence frame to help them ask their questions.

- You may want to have children conduct their discussions during daily small-group time.

 ENGLISH LEARNER SUPPORT:
Build Background

SUBSTANTIAL
Act out the meanings of *sad, mad,* and *happy.* Children can repeat the actions and name the feeling words.

MODERATE
Preview the illustrations and discuss important details. Ask: *What is a school trip? Where do the children go? What do you think Nan is feeling?*

LIGHT
Before reading, have partners preview the illustrations and describe what is happening in them.

LINK TO SMALL-GROUP INSTRUCTION

REINFORCE MONITOR AND CLARIFY Review or extend the skill as needed during small-group time to support children's need for differentiation. *See the lesson on p. T127.*

LESSON 7

READING WORKSHOP

Options for Differentiation

As the class engages in independent and collaborative work, meet with Guided Reading Groups or differentiate instruction based on student need.

GUIDED READING GROUPS

Match Children to Books + Instruction

- Choose just-right books based on level, skill, topic, or genre.

C D E F G H J K →

Leveled Readers

- Deliver instruction with each book's Take and Teach Lesson, choosing appropriate sessions based on need.

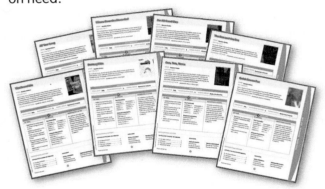

- Check comprehension, reinforce instruction, and extend learning with suggested supporting activities.

Buddy

The Princess and the Pea

Walking in the Autumn

What Is Soil?

Rigby LEVELED LIBRARY

Fire! Fire!

Enter at Your Own Risk

Planting and Growing

The Donkey and the Wolf

Our Gift to the Bear

Tick, Tock, Check the Clock!

Little Squirrel Wants to Play

EL ENGLISH LEARNER SUPPORT

Infer

- Use **Tabletop Minilessons: English Language Development 2.1 (Speaking)** to reinforce and practice the language skill.

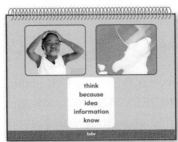

Tabletop Minilessons: English Language Development

- Then use the following text-based prompts with *My School Trip* to guide application of the language skill. Begin with the prompt at the child's identified language proficiency level. As children are able, use lighter supports to encourage increased language proficiency.

SUBSTANTIAL
Have children look at page 36 and point to Nan. Ask children whether they think Nan is sad or mad. Provide this frame: *I think Nan is _____.*

MODERATE
Have children turn to page 37. Point to several characters in the picture and ask how children think each child feels. Provide this frame: *I think he/she feels _____.* Provide feeling words, as needed.

LIGHT
Have children turn to pages 40–41. Ask: *How does Nan feel in each picture?* Have children tell what they learn about both girls from looking at the two pictures on page 41.

REINFORCE MONITOR AND CLARIFY

Demonstrate

- Use **Tabletop Minilessons: Reading 2** to remind children to pay attention as they read and **monitor** their understanding. If they don't understand something, they should stop and think. To try to **clarify**, or "fix up" what doesn't make sense, they can **reread**, think about what they already know, look at **visuals** (pictures) for clues, and ask themselves questions.

- Model filling out Printable: **Reading Graphic Organizer 2** to monitor and clarify understanding of *My School Trip*.

Apply to Independent Reading

- Now have children monitor and clarify their understanding of an appropriate just-right book that they are reading independently. Before children read their books, guide them to set a purpose for reading. Remind them to think about what they do not understand and which "fix up" strategies they can use. Customize these prompts to the books children choose.

  » *What parts can you reread to help you understand what you are reading better?*

  » *What did you already know?*

  » *What clues or information can you find in the pictures?*

  » *What questions can you ask yourself?*

- Have children complete Printable: **Reading Graphic Organizer 2** for their independent reading book.

Tabletop Minilessons: Reading

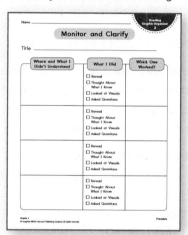

Printable:
Reading Graphic Organizer 2

ALMOST THERE	**SCAFFOLD AND EXTEND**

↓

SCAFFOLD AND EXTEND

- Prompt children to use this frame to ask themselves questions: *What do I know about _____?*

- Prompt children to ask questions about their books. Then direct them to check visuals for the answers.

- Have children list what they already know about their book's topic before reading. Have them write questions they want their books to answer.

READY FOR MORE

 ENGLISH LEARNER SUPPORT

SUBSTANTIAL
Ask children to point to words they do not know. Lead them to use the visuals to help them find out their meanings.

MODERATE
Have children complete these frames: *This book is about _____. I already knew _____. Now I know _____.*

LIGHT
Ask children what their book is about. Then ask: *What part of the book did you understand? What part did you not understand?*

SMALL-GROUP INSTRUCTION

Options for Differentiation

Tab Can Tap, Tap, Tap, *Start Right Reader, Book 1,* pp. 44–51

REINFORCE FOUNDATIONAL SKILLS

Read Decodable Text

Blend and Read   Have children turn to Start Right Reader page 44. Use the **CHORAL READING** routine to read aloud the Blend and Read lines. Use challenge line 4 with children who are ready.

Preview the Story   Call attention to page 45. Have children read the title, look at the picture, and identify the cat as Tab from *Dan Can Tap, Tap, Tap.* Have children look at the pictures on the first two pages and predict what Tab will tap.

Fluency Focus: Reading Rate   Read aloud page 47 as children follow along. Point out that you read at a speed, or rate, that sounds smooth and natural—you read the words at the same rate you would use to say them. Then lead children in reading the page chorally.

Reflect on Reading   Have children use a finger to track the words from left to right as they read each page silently. Then have them read the page chorally. Pause for these prompts:

- **Page 45:** *What do you think Tab is sitting on? (Dan's map)*

- **Page 48:** *How can Tab "tap like Dan"? (Dan is using his fingers to tap on the computer keyboard. Tab is using his paw to tap the map.) Is this what you predicted Tab would tap? Explain. (Responses will vary.)*

- **Page 49:** *Look at the picture. What is happening to Dan's map? (Tab is playing with it and wrinkling it.)*

- **Page 50:** *Do you think Dan knows what Tab is doing? Explain. (Possible response: No; Dan is tapping on the computer and does not see that Tab is playing with the map.) How might Dan feel when he sees what Tab did to the map? Why? (Possible response: upset, because Tab messed up the map)*

Short a Picture Hunt   Read aloud the directions and boxed words on page 51. Explain that not all of the words name things shown in the pictures. On a sheet of paper, have children write the words they find pictured in the story. (*bat, cat, Dan, man, map, Tab*) Have partners compare lists.

Tap! Tap! Tap!
Tab can tap like Dan!

Tap, Tab! Tap!
Tab can tap the map!

48

49

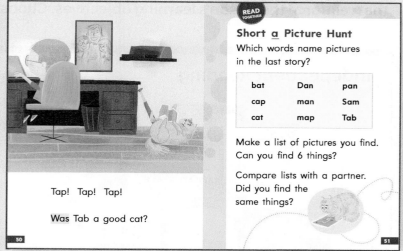

Tap! Tap! Tap!

Was Tab a good cat?

50

READ TOGETHER

Short a Picture Hunt

Which words name pictures in the last story?

bat	Dan	pan
cap	man	Sam
cat	map	Tab

Make a list of pictures you find. Can you find 6 things?

Compare lists with a partner. Did you find the same things?

51

⏱ Make Minutes Count

As you meet with small groups to read *Tab Can Tap, Tap, Tap,* use one or more of these related activities, as needed, at the beginning or the end of the small-group session.

- **Connect to Phonics** Play Letter Swap. Use Letter Cards to build *cap*. Have children blend and read the word. Ask what letter must be swapped in order to change *cap* to *can*. Make the change, and have children blend and read *can*. Continue with the words *pan, pad, dad,* and *bad*.

- **Connect to Spelling** Give each child a Spelling Word card from Printable: Word List 2. Have children draw a picture on a sheet of paper that illustrates the assigned Spelling Word. Then have partners trade pictures, identify the illustrated Spelling Word, and spell it. Have partners use the word cards to check each other's spelling.

- **Connect to Handwriting** Say the letters *a* and *d*, and have children write the letters from memory. Then have them write each letter three times in their best handwriting. Reinforce proper pencil grip and paper position.

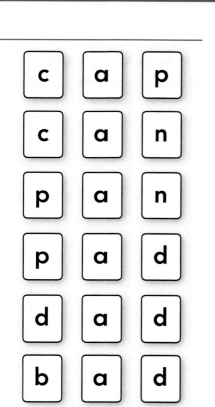

c	a	p
c	a	n
p	a	n
p	a	d
d	a	d
b	a	d

👥 **INDEPENDENT APPLICATION**

Options for Independent and Collaborative Work

While you meet with small groups, have other children engage in literacy activities that reinforce the lesson's learning objectives. Choose from these options.

Independent Reading

Student Choice Library

Rigby®
LEVELED LIBRARY

APPLY READING SKILL

Monitor and Clarify Children complete Printable: **Reading Graphic Organizer 2** for an independent reading book.

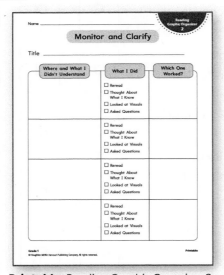

Printable: Reading Graphic Organizer 2

APPLY LANGUAGE SKILL

Infer Children complete Printable: **Language Graphic Organizer 7** for an independent reading book.

Printable: Language Graphic Organizer 7

Notice 8 Note

Contrasts and Contradictions

When children encounter this signpost in their independent reading, encourage them to ask the Anchor Question: *Why would the character act (feel) this way?*

Literacy Centers

See pp. T100–T101.

 WORD WORK

 CREATIVITY CORNER

 DIGITAL STATION

 READING CORNER

 TEAMWORK TIME

Start Right Reader

Read Decodable Text *Tab Can Tap, Tap, Tap,* Book 1: pp. 44–51

Speaking & Listening

Partners discuss the Turn and Talk Questions to monitor and clarify their understanding. *See Engage & Respond, p. T125.*

Additional Skills Practice

PHONICS

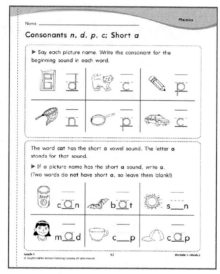

Know It, Show It, p. 17

Wrap-Up
Share Time

At the end of Reading Workshop, have children reflect on their learning by sharing how they applied **Monitor and Clarify** or another area of focus during independent work time. Choose from these options:

- **SHARE CHAIR** Select a reader each day to come to the front of the class and tell what he or she learned from the reading by using a skill or strategy.

- **THINK-PAIR-SHARE** Children share their thinking with a partner. Select a few children each day to share with the whole class.

- **RETURN TO ANCHOR CHART** Have children add sticky notes about their independent reading book to the Monitor and Clarify Anchor Chart. Call on a few children to explain what they added.

ANCHOR CHART 2:
Monitor and Clarify

Online Ed

FOUNDATIONAL SKILLS

LEARNING OBJECTIVES

- Identify and read high-frequency words.
- **Language** Recognize and recite basic sight vocabulary.
- Orally segment onsets and rimes in one-syllable words.

MATERIALS   Online

Word Cards *a, an, can, first, good, had, he, I, man, my, was*

Printable *Word List 2*

Classroom materials *large jar or other container*

 # High-Frequency Words

Review the Words

Repeat the **HIGH-FREQUENCY WORDS** routine to review this week's High-Frequency Words: *a, first, good, had, he, I, my,* and *was* and the decodable High-Frequency Words *an, can,* and *man.*

had

Word Jar

- Use a set of the week's High-Frequency Words and decodable High-Frequency Words from Printable: . Place the Word Cards in a large jar.
- Display Word Cards *a, an, can, first, good, he, I, man, my,* and *was* where all children can see them.
- Have children take turns pulling out a word and reading it to the class. Then call on another child to find and hold up the matching large Word Card for the class to read.

Phonological Awareness

Segment Onset and Rime

- Remind children that they know how to work with sounds in words, including separating words into chunks or individual sounds.
- Explain: *I will say a word, and you will separate the word into two chunks: the beginning sound and the rest of the word.*
- Model: *Listen as I do the first one:* man. *I hear* /m/ *at the beginning of* man, *and the rest of the word is* /ăn/. Man, /m/ /ăn/.
- *Let's do it together. I will say a word and separate the beginning sound from the rest of the word. Listen:* tape. *The beginning sound in* tape *is* /t/. *What is the rest of the word?* (/āp/) *That's right!* Tape, /t/ /āp/.
- *Now you separate these words into two chunks: the beginning sound and the rest of the word.* Use the following words: moon (/m/ /ōōn/), nice (/n/ /īs/), home (/h/ /ōm/), lap (/l/ /ăp/), pet (/p/ /ĕt/), not (/n/ /ŏt/).

TEACHER TIP

Extra practice! Play segmenting games like this at transition times, too. Practicing segmenting will help children become good spellers.

 CORRECT & REDIRECT

Guide children who have trouble identifying any of the High-Frequency Words.

- *The word is* good. *What is the word?* (*good*)
- *Have children spell the word.* (*g-o-o-d*) *How do we say this word?* (*good*)
- Have children reread all the Word Cards as you display them one at a time.

Reading Rate

I Do It

- Explain that with practice, good readers learn to read at a smooth, regular rate, reading the words at about the same speed as when they are talking naturally. Explain that this pace helps both the reader and listeners understand what is happening in a story or other text.

- Ask children to follow along and to pay attention to your pace as you read Start Right Reader pages 45–47 (*Tab Can Tap, Tap, Tap*) at an appropriate rate. Point out that you used the end punctuation as a signal to pause at the end of each sentence. Then use the **CHORAL READING** routine to reread the pages with children.

We Do It

- Ask children to follow along as you read aloud page 48 as a guide to appropriate rate and attention to punctuation.

- Have children use the **PARTNER READING** routine to read pages 49 and 50 to each other. As you circulate and listen, coach children to use a smooth, regular rate to make the reading sound natural.

You Do It

INDEPENDENT PRACTICE

- Have children use the **ECHO READING** routine to reread one of the week's Start Right Reader stories about Dan and Tab or *My School Trip* from their *my*Book. Remind children to track the print from left to right and to read at a rate that a listener can easily understand.

LEARNING OBJECTIVE

- Read fluently and at an appropriate rate.

MATERIALS   Online Ed

Start Right Reader *Book 1, pp. 45–50*

Getting Started

ENGAGEMENT ROUTINE

Remind children about the **PARTNER READING** routine and practice it.

- Model taking turns reading and listening.
- Have partners take turns reading the text.

See the **GPS guide** to learn more.

LINK TO SMALL-GROUP INSTRUCTION

REINFORCE FOUNDATIONAL SKILLS Use *Map Nap* during small-group time to review or reinforce blending and decoding words with short *a*, and the consonants *n*, *d*, *p*, and *c* /k/. Meet with children to work through the story, or assign it as independent work. *See the lesson on p. T140.*

Map Nap
by Margaret Fetty
illustrated by Rob McClurkan

Tab can nap.

Review Power Words

Revisit the Power Words

- Revisit the Power Words from *My School Trip*. Display the questions and sentence frames below word by word.

- Model the task for the first word, using a child as your partner. Read aloud the question, and have the child repeat it. Respond using the sentence frame.

- Have partners use the **TURN AND TALK** routine to respond to each question using the sentence frame.

- For each word, ask one or two children to share their responses with the class. Then have them discuss the next question.

Power Word	Question	Sentence Frame
trip	If you took a **trip** through space, what would you like to see?	*If I took a **trip** through space, I would like to see _____.*
partner	What would you like to do with a **partner** today?	*I would like to _____ with a **partner**.*
wished	If you **wished** for a gift, what would it be?	*If I **wished** for a gift, it would be a _____.*
last	When might you say "at **last**"?	*I might say "at **last**" when I _____.*

 ENGLISH LEARNER SUPPORT:
Elicit Participation

SUBSTANTIAL
Say: *Show me what you would do to get ready for a **trip**. Now show me how you would work with a **partner**.*

MODERATE
Ask: *Where would you go on a **trip**? What would you do with a **partner**?*

LIGHT
Have children work in pairs: *Tell about something you **wished** for. Tell about a **trip** you took.*

Vocabulary Guess

- Display the Power Words. Have children break into small groups.

- One child in each group gives clues about a Power Word without saying the word itself. These children are encouraged to say words that have similar or opposite meanings, provide examples, or describe times they used or might use the Power Word.

- For example, for the Power Word *partner*, children can say, "This word means someone who works with another person," or "I would use this word to talk about a friend that I want to read with."

- The rest of the group guesses the word. If necessary, children may ask the speaker questions to get clarification about the word or what he/she is saying.

- Have children continue the activity until all the words have been guessed.

- For additional practice with the Power Words from *My School Trip*, have children complete Know It, Show It page 19.

LEARNING MINDSET

Seeking Challenges

Normalize Remind children that it is normal to feel frustrated when they face challenges as they read and come across words they don't understand. *When we learn and use a new word, we might not get it right the first time, or even the second time. But when we keep trying, we get better and better!*

TEACHER TIP

It's exciting! Explain to children that people use different words and expressions to show excitement or surprise. Work together to make a list of examples, such as *awesome, that's great, amazing,* and *at last*. Ask volunteers to use the words during the day, and ring a bell to celebrate when they do!

READING WORKSHOP

LEARNING OBJECTIVES

- Determine the author's purpose for writing a text, using the genre and text evidence.
- **Language** Share text evidence that shows the author's purpose for writing.
- Write a list of details, using evidence from a story.

MATERIALS   Online

Anchor Chart 12
Author's Purpose

Printable *Anchor Chart 12: Author's Purpose*

Teaching Pal *Book 1, pp. 32–45*

myBook *My School Trip, Book 1, pp. 32–45*

Know It, Show It *p. 20*

READER'S VOCABULARY

- **author's purpose** the author's reason for writing
- **persuade** to try to convince someone of an idea or to try to get someone to do something
- **inform** to give facts about a topic
- **entertain** to bring joy and fun to the reader through a story
- **genre** a type or category of writing, such as fiction, informational text, or opinion writing

Author's Purpose

Step 1   Connect and Teach

- Remind children that an author writes for a reason, or the **author's purpose**.

- Then project or display <u>Anchor Chart 12: Author's Purpose</u>. Explain the different purposes for writing on the Anchor Chart.

- Remind children that an author who writes to **persuade** gives an opinion and tries to change a reader's mind; an author who writes to **inform** gives facts about a topic; and an author who writes to **entertain** writes to give readers something fun to read.

- Finally, remind children that thinking about the **genre** of a text can help children figure out the author's purpose. Informative text gives information, persuasive text tells someone's opinion, and fiction can entertain and teach a lesson. Explain that knowing the author's purpose can help children understand more about what they're reading and what the author wants them to know or learn.

- Tell children they will reread parts of *My School Trip* to practice determining the author's purpose.

Online

ANCHOR CHART 12:
Author's Purpose

TEACHER TIP

Get to know genres! As you read new books with children or discuss ones you've already read, talk about the genre of each. Discuss with children what they think the author's purpose was for each story.

● *Professional Learning*

BEST PRACTICES

Distribute the printable version of each Anchor Chart when you introduce it for the first time. Have children collect the Anchor Charts in a notebook. Children may "make them their own" by coloring them or adding notes to them. Encourage children to refer to their Anchor Chart notebook during small-group lessons or independent reading, as needed.

See the **GPS guide** to learn more.

ANNOTATE IT!

Online
Ed

Children may use the annotation tools in their eBook.

Step 2 Apply to Text

 In your Teaching Pal, use the purple **TARGETED CLOSE READ** prompts to guide children to apply the author's purpose skill to *My School Trip*. Children may refer to the questions on Know It, Show It page 20 as you discuss them.

- Tell children you will start looking for clues about the author's purpose for writing. Read aloud the first question on Teaching Pal page 38. Have children use what they already know about genres to answer it. (*Sample responses: realistic fiction; a make-believe story*)

- Then read the follow-up question. Tell children to look for evidence of the text's genre. (*Sample response: The kids act like real kids but they aren't real.*)

- Read aloud the questions on Teaching Pal page 42. Tell children to look for evidence to help them answer the questions. (*Possible responses: to tell a nice story about how two girls become friends; that being kind to someone who is new at school can make everyone happy*)

- Refer back to the Anchor Chart to support the discussion. Children may add sticky notes to the chart to show which genre or story details helped them figure out the author's purpose for writing *My School Trip*.

Step 3 Engage and Respond

INDEPENDENT PRACTICE: Writing

- Read aloud the prompt on Teaching Pal page 44. Have children use the planning space to draw or write things the girl likes about her trip.

- Then have children write their responses to the prompt. Remind children to refer back to *My School Trip* and use the words and pictures from the story for ideas. Then have children use their ideas to make a list of the things the girl likes about her trip. Remind them to give the list a title.

- You may want to have children complete their writing during daily small-group time.

 ENGLISH LEARNER SUPPORT:
Scaffold Writing

SUBSTANTIAL
Have children point to parts of the text that show what the girl likes. Prompt them to say a word or phrase about what they are pointing to.

MODERATE
Have children complete the sentence frame: *The girl likes _____.*

LIGHT
Have children write their lists or label their drawings. Circulate and coach them on using English sound/spelling correspondences as they write.

LINK TO SMALL-GROUP INSTRUCTION

REINFORCE AUTHOR'S PURPOSE Review or extend the skill as needed during small-group time to support children's need for differentiation. *See the lesson on p. T139.*

Options for Differentiation

As the class engages in independent and collaborative work, meet with Guided Reading Groups or differentiate instruction based on student need.

GUIDED READING GROUPS

Match Children to Books + Instruction

- Choose just-right books based on level, skill, topic, or genre.

C D E F G H I J K

Leveled Readers

- Deliver instruction with each book's Take and Teach Lesson, choosing appropriate sessions based on need.

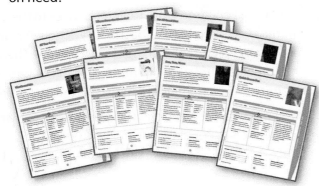

- Check comprehension, reinforce instruction, and extend learning with suggested supporting activities.

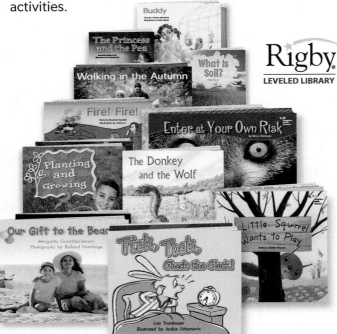

Rigby® LEVELED LIBRARY

🔵 ENGLISH LEARNER SUPPORT

Infer

- Use **Tabletop Minilessons: English Language Development 2.2 (Reading)** to reinforce and practice the language skill.

The children have a new game to play.
This new game is fun.
"What is 5 + 3?" asks Mia.

Infer

Tabletop Minilessons: English Language Development

- Then use the following text-based prompts with *My School Trip* to guide application of the language skill. Begin with the prompt at the child's identified language proficiency level. As children are able, use lighter supports to encourage increased language proficiency.

SUBSTANTIAL
Have children look at page 34 and make inferences about the children. Supply these frames: *I think he/she is _____. I think this boy/girl thinks _____.*

MODERATE
Have children make inferences about Nan's thoughts on various pages of the story. Supply these frames: *I think she thinks _____ because _____. The text says _____, so I think _____.*

LIGHT
Have children look at page 35. Ask children to make inferences about what the two girls think about being partners during the school trip.

REINFORCE AUTHOR'S PURPOSE

Demonstrate

- Use **Tabletop Minilessons: Reading 12** to remind children that the **author's purpose** is the reason the author wrote the book. The author's purpose might be to **entertain** readers with a fun story, to **inform** readers about a topic or idea, or to **persuade** readers to agree with an opinion or idea. To better understand a text, readers can think about what the author wants them to know or learn.

- Model filling out Printable: <u>**Reading Graphic Organizer 11**</u> to identify the author's purpose in *My School Trip*.

Apply to Independent Reading

- Now have children identify the author's purpose in an appropriate just-right book that they are reading independently. Customize these prompts to the books children choose.

  » *What do you think the author wants you to know?*

  » *What clues can you find to help you find the author's purpose?*

  » *Does this book give information, give an opinion, or tell a story?*

  » *What does this book teach you? Why might the author have wanted to teach readers about that topic?*

- Have children complete Printable: <u>**Reading Graphic Organizer 11**</u> for their independent reading book.

Tabletop Minilessons: Reading

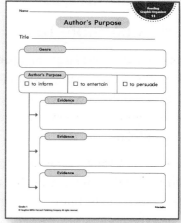

Printable:
Reading Graphic Organizer 11

ALMOST THERE	**SCAFFOLD AND EXTEND**

SCAFFOLD AND EXTEND

- Help children determine whether the author's purpose is mostly to entertain, inform, or persuade. Lead children to identify a detail that reveals the author's purpose.

- Guide children to identify two or three details that show the author's purpose.

- Ask children what they would add to the book to further enhance the author's purpose.

READY FOR MORE

ENGLISH LEARNER SUPPORT

SUBSTANTIAL

Ask: *What does the author want readers to know about?* Have children tell you or point to the most important details. Have children answer briefly or use their home language.

MODERATE

Review the words *entertain, inform,* and *persuade.* Supply this frame: *The author wrote this book to _____.*

LIGHT

Have children use the words *entertain, inform,* and *persuade* in sentences to tell about different books they have read.

Options for Differentiation

Map Nap, *Start Right Reader, Book 1,* pp. 52–59

REINFORCE FOUNDATIONAL SKILLS

Read Decodable Text

Sentence Starters: High-Frequency Word Review
Have children turn to Start Right Reader page 52. Have partners read the boxed words and then use the words and the sentence starters to talk about *Dan Can Tap, Tap, Tap* and *Tab Can Tap, Tap, Tap.*

Preview the Story Focus on pages 53–54. Have children read the title, look at the pictures, and identify Dan and Tab. Have children predict what will happen between the characters.

Concepts of Print: Directionality Have children use a finger to show the direction they will follow to read the story. Have them track the print from left to right, showing where they go next as they come to the end of each line and each page.

Fluency Focus: Reading Rate Read aloud page 55 as children follow along. Remind them that reading should be at the same speed, or rate, as talking. Then help children read the page chorally at an appropriate rate.

Reflect on Reading Have children read to find out what happens between Dan and Tab, reading each page silently and then chorally. Pause for these prompts:

- **Page 54:** *Uh-oh! What is under Tab? (Dan's map) What is Tab doing? (napping on the map)*

- **Pages 56–57:** *What happens when Tab sits up? (Dan sees the map.) How does Dan feel when he sees the map? How can you tell? (Possible response: He is upset; he looks like he is yelling in the pictures.)*

- **Page 58:** *What question does the author ask? ("Was Tab a bad cat?") What is your answer to the question? Why do you feel that way? (Responses will vary.)*

Story Clues Have children read the clue on page 59 and answer it. *(Tab)* Then have them page through the story for ideas for their clue writing. Have partners listen to and answer each other's clues.

Pat Tab, Dan.
Pat, pat. Pat, pat, pat.
Tab can nap.

56

Tab sat.
Dan can see the map!

57

Tab! My first map!
I am mad, Tab!

Was Tab a bad cat?

58

READ TOGETHER

Story Clues

1. Read the clue.

   I am tan. I can nap.

   Who or what is the clue about?

2. Pick something in the story. Write a clue and read it to a friend. Can your friend find it?

59

Make Minutes Count

As you meet with small groups to read *Map Nap*, use one or more of these related activities, as needed, at the beginning or the end of the small-group session.

- **Connect to Phonics** Play Picture Match. Arrange the basic and review Spelling Word cards from Printable: Word List 2 face up on the tabletop. Then display the *bat* Picture Card. Call on a child to match the correct Spelling Word to the Picture Card. Repeat the process for these Picture Cards: *can, cat, pan*. After all of the Picture Cards are matched, have children read the words chorally.

- **Connect to Spelling** Use Letter Cards to build the word *bat*. Then have children use their knowledge of letter-sounds to write these words as you say them: *at, cat, sat*.

- **Connect to High-Frequency Words** Have children turn to page 58 of the Start Right Reader. Call out the word *my* and have children point to the word on the page and then read it aloud. Repeat the process for the words *first* and *was*.

Options for Independent and Collaborative Work

While you meet with small groups, have other children engage in literacy activities that reinforce the lesson's learning objectives. Choose from these options.

Independent Reading

Student Choice Library

Rigby
LEVELED LIBRARY

APPLY READING SKILL

Author's Purpose Children complete Printable: **Reading Graphic Organizer 11** for an independent reading book.

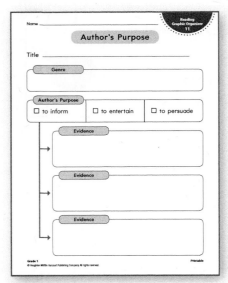

Printable: Reading Graphic Organizer 11

APPLY LANGUAGE SKILL

Infer Children complete Printable: **Language Graphic Organizer 7** for an independent reading book.

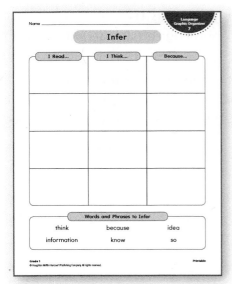

Printable: Language Graphic Organizer 7

Literacy Centers

See pp. T100–T101.

 WORD WORK

 CREATIVITY CORNER

 DIGITAL STATION

 READING CORNER

 TEAMWORK TIME

Start Right Reader

Read Decodable Text *Map Nap,* Book 1: pp. 52–59

Writing

Children write a list based on words and pictures from the story. *See Engage & Respond, p. T137.*

Close Reading

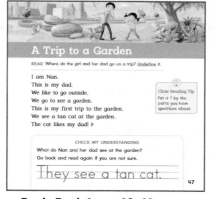

myBook, Book 1, pp. 46–49

Additional Skills Practice

SPELLING AND VOCABULARY

Know It, Show It, p. 18

Know It, Show It, p. 19

Wrap-Up
Share Time

At the end of Reading Workshop, have children reflect on their learning by sharing how they applied **Author's Purpose** or another area of focus during independent work time. Choose from these options:

- **SHARE CHAIR** Select a reader each day to come to the front of the class and tell what he or she learned from the reading by using a skill or strategy.

- **THINK-PAIR-SHARE** Children share their thinking with a partner. Select a few children each day to share with the whole class.

- **RETURN TO ANCHOR CHART** Have children add sticky notes about their independent reading book to the Author's Purpose Anchor Chart. Call on a few children to explain what they added.

Online **Ed**

ANCHOR CHART 12: Author's Purpose

WORD WORK WARM-UP

LEARNING OBJECTIVES

- Identify and read high-frequency words.
- **Language** Recite and spell basic sight vocabulary.
- Orally segment onsets and rimes in one-syllable words.

MATERIALS   Online

Word Cards *a, an, can, first, good, had, he, I, man, my, was*

Printable *Word List 2*

High-Frequency Words

Review the Words

Repeat the **HIGH-FREQUENCY WORDS** routine to review this week's High-Frequency Words: *a, first, good, had, he, I, my,* and *was,* and the decodable High-Frequency Words *an, can,* and *man.*

Chant and Cheer

- Have children set out the word cards they saved from Printable: <u>Word List 2</u> so that they can see all the words.

- Choose one child at a time to be the Caller, who will choose a word card to "call." The Caller will spell the word with the class in a call-and-response pattern. As the Caller calls out each letter of the word, the class echoes: *Give me a* **C!** *(C!) Give me an* **A!** *(A!) Give me an* **N!** *(N!) What does that spell? (CAN!)*

- Have children hold up the correct word card as they say the word at the end of the cheer.

Phonological Awareness

Segment Onset and Rime

- Tell children that they will be breaking words into two chunks: the beginning sound and the rest of the word.

- Explain: *I will say a word, and you will separate it into two chunks: the beginning sound and the rest of the word.*

- Model: *Listen as I do the first one. The word is pat. I hear /p/ at the beginning of pat. Pat. The rest of the word is /ăt/. Listen again: pat, /p/ /ăt/.*

- *Let's do it together. I will say a word and separate it into two chunks: the beginning sound and the rest of the word. Listen: coat. The beginning sound in coat is /k/. What is the rest of the word? (/ōt/) Good job. Coat, /k/ /ōt/.*

- *Now you do it! Say each word in two chunks: the beginning sound and the rest of the word.* Use the following words: cape (/k/ /āp/), sick (/s/ /ĭk/), bus (/b/ /ŭs/), bed (/b/ /ĕd/), top (/t/ /ŏp/), same (/s/ /ām/).

TEACHER TIP

Get moving! Have the Caller perform simple motions as they call out each letter in their chosen High-Frequency Word. Guide the other children to copy the Caller's movements as they spell the word.

 CORRECT & REDIRECT

If children segment incorrectly, say the word repeatedly, emphasizing the onset or rime each time. Example:

- *The word is cape.*
- */k-āp/: The beginning sound is /k/.*
- */k-āp/: The rest of the word is /āp/.*

Phonics Review

I Do It

Spotlight on Letters Use the **SOUND-BY-SOUND BLENDING** routine to review this week's phonic elements: short *a*; *n, d, p, c /k/* (hard *c*). Model blending *can* with Letter Cards (or display the written word). Say the first two sounds separately, then together; then say the last sound and add it to the blended sounds. Repeat for *pad*.

We Do It

Blend and Read Project Display and Engage: <u>Blend and Read 1.7</u> or use Start Right Reader page 60.

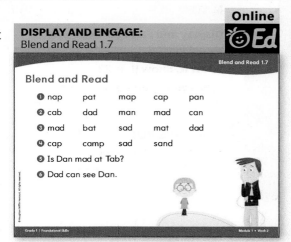

DISPLAY AND ENGAGE:
Blend and Read 1.7

Online

Blend and Read 1.7

Blend and Read

❶ nap	pat	map	cap	pan
❷ cab	dad	man	mad	can
❸ mad	bat	sad	mat	dad
❹ cap	camp	sad	sand	

❺ Is Dan mad at Tab?
❻ Dad can see Dan.

Grade 1 | Foundational Skills   Module 1 • Week 2

1 **Line 1** Have children read the line. Then prompt a conversation about the words. Ask: *Do any words have the same consonant? Where is it in each word?* Reread the line chorally.

2 **Line 2** Continue. Then have volunteers reread selected words until they can identify them quickly.

3 **Review** Display Line 3, and have children read it chorally.

4 **Challenge** Children who are ready for a challenge can read Line 4, tell how the words in columns 2 and 4 differ from the ones in columns 1 and 3, and demonstrate how they blended the words with four letters.

5 **Sentences** Display Lines 5–6. Call on children to blend selected words. Point to each word as children read the sentences chorally.

You Do It

INDEPENDENT PRACTICE

- **Option 1** Have partners write *nap, dad, cap, can*. Have them check their spelling using the Blend and Read lines, draw a picture for each word, and share.

- **Option 2** Have children complete Know It, Show It page 21.

 ENGLISH LEARNER SUPPORT:
Build Vocabulary

ALL LEVELS Have children share what they know about each Blend and Read word. Confirm or clarify word meanings as needed. Then provide oral clues, and have children find and read the word that matches the clue: *I may do this when I am tired. (nap) I can wear this on my head. (cap) This is another word for* father *or* papa. *(dad)*

LINK TO SMALL-GROUP INSTRUCTION

REINFORCE FOUNDATIONAL SKILLS Use *Can Tab Nap?* during small-group time to review or reinforce blending and decoding words with short *a* and consonants *n, d, p, c /k/*. Meet with children to work through the story, or assign it as independent work. *See the lesson on p. T152.*

Can Tab Nap?
by Margaret Petty
illustrated by Rob McClurkan

Tab sat.
Tab was sad.

LEARNING OBJECTIVES
- Blend, build, and decode regularly spelled one-syllable words with short *a* and consonants *n, d, p, c /k/.*

MATERIALS   Online

Letter Cards *a, c, d, n, p*
Display and Engage *Blend and Read 1.7*
Start Right Reader *Book 1, p. 60*
Know It, Show It *p. 21*

Inflection -ed

I Do It

LEARNING OBJECTIVES

- **Language** Define verbs with the inflection -*ed*.
- Use verbs with the ending -*ed* in phrases and sentences to tell about things that happened in the past.

MATERIALS   Online

Display and Engage *Generative Vocabulary 1.8*

Know It, Show It *p. 22*

Classroom materials *note cards*

READER'S VOCABULARY

- **verb** an action word

- Project Display and Engage: **Generative Vocabulary 1.8**. Read aloud the introductory text.

- Explain that when -*ed* is added to the end of a **verb**, or action word, it means that the action happened in the past.

- Discuss the example, *wished*. Tell children that *wish* is a verb that tells about something that is happening now, like in the sentence *I wish you would listen carefully.* Explain that when the ending -*ed* is added to the verb *wish*, it changes *wish* to *wished*. *Wished* is a verb that tells about something that happened in the past, like in this sentence: *Last year, I wished for a kitten.*

- Read Example 1 aloud. Model determining the meaning of *jumped* by thinking about its base word and ending. *Jumped is made from the verb* jump *and the ending -ed.* Jump *tells about something that is happening now.* Jumped *tells about something that happened in the past.*

- Continue in the same way with the remaining examples.

DISPLAY AND ENGAGE:
Generative Vocabulary 1.8

Online
Ed

Generative Vocabulary 1.8

Inflection -*ed*

A **verb** is an action word. The ending -*ed* can be added to a verb to tell that something happened in the past.

wished

Examples
1 jump + ed   = jumped
2 play + ed   = played
3 look + ed   = looked
4 park + ed   = parked
5 camp + ed   = camped

| Verb | Ending | | |
| wish | + | ed | = | wished |

TEACHER TIP

Practice past tense! Look for opportunities during the day to point out and emphasize past-tense verbs. For example, after you read a story, ask questions that use past-tense verbs. Point out when children use past-tense verbs to answer the questions. Then ask: *Did that action happen now or in the past?*

Professional Learning

BEST PRACTICES

When presenting new concepts and skills for the first time, use the lesson structure of I Do It, We Do It, and You Do It to promote a gradual release of responsibility from teacher to children. This lesson structure incorporates explicit instruction and guided practice before children are expected to apply a skill independently.

See the **GPS guide** to learn more.

We Do It

- Write the following words on the board and read them aloud with children: *walk, cook, learn,* and *talk.*

- Use the word *walk* in a sentence: *I walk around the classroom. Does this tell about something happening now or in the past?*

- Ask a volunteer to add *-ed* to the end of the word. Guide another volunteer to use the new word *walked* in a sentence. Prompt children to tell whether the word tells about something that is happening now or in the past.

- Continue in the same way with the remaining words. Prompt children to explain the meanings of the words as you talk about them.

You Do It

INDEPENDENT PRACTICE

- **Option 1** Write the following words on note cards: *fill, plant, turn,* and *clean.* Have one partner choose a card, read the word, and add *-ed* to the end. Have the other partner use the word in a sentence. Then have partners switch roles. Finally, have each pair draw a picture to illustrate two of the words. Ask them to share their drawings with the class and explain the meaning of the words.

- **Option 2** Have children complete Know It, Show It page 22.

 ENGLISH LEARNER SUPPORT: Facilitate Language Connections

ALL LEVELS Children whose first language is Cantonese, Haitian Creole, Hmong, Khmer, Korean, Tagalog, or Vietnamese, might omit the *-ed* ending in past-tense verbs because verbs in their primary language do not change form to express tense. Model using the verbs *walk* and *walked* in sentences that include time clues, such as *today* and *yesterday*. Have children repeat the sentences after you.

Getting Started

CLASSROOM MANAGEMENT

Project a stopwatch or timer as a visual cue of time remaining for group and partner work. You can also either play music or give children a verbal reminder of time remaining when the allotted time for a task is nearly finished.

See the **GPS guide** to learn more.

READING WORKSHOP

LEARNING OBJECTIVES

- Identify the features of informational text.
- Make inferences based on text evidence and personal knowledge.
- **Language** Explain evidence and background knowledge that support inferences.
- Explain ideas and feelings clearly and take turns speaking.

MATERIALS Online

Anchor Chart 6
Make Inferences
Printable *Anchor Chart 6: Make Inferences*
Teaching Pal *Book 1, pp. 50–61*
myBook *A Kids' Guide to Friends, Book 1, pp. 50–61*

READER'S VOCABULARY

- **inference** a smart guess that readers make, based on clues in the text and what they already know
- **evidence** clues or details in the text that support an answer or idea

 Make Inferences

Step 1 Connect and Teach

- Tell children that an author doesn't always tell readers everything they need to know to understand a text.

- Writers expect good readers to use clues to figure out some things on their own. This is called making an **inference**.

- Project or display **Anchor Chart 6: Make Inferences**.

- Explain that to make an inference, readers use **evidence**, or clues, in the text.

- Point out that the clues may be from the text or the pictures. Readers may also use clues from things that they already know from their own lives.

- Tell children they will practice making inferences when they read an informational text called *A Kids' Guide to Friends*.

Online

ANCHOR CHART 6:
Make Inferences

Make Inferences

When you make inferences, you use clues to make a smart guess about something the author doesn't tell you.

CLUES FROM THE TEXT AND PICTURES

CLUES FROM WHAT I ALREADY KNOW

INFERENCE

Notice & Note

Big Questions

- The Teaching Pal prompts in this lesson feature the **Notice & Note Big Questions** for nonfiction.
- As needed, refer to p. T19 to review the Big Questions with children.

 ASSESSMENT OPTION

Assign the **Selection Quiz** to check comprehension of *A Kids' Guide to Friends*.

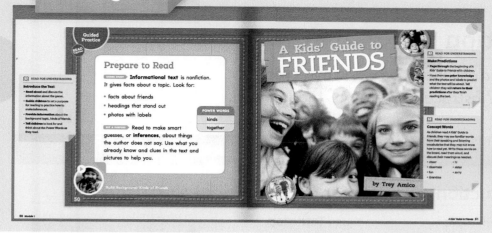

ANNOTATE IT!

Online
Ed

Children may use the annotation tools in their eBook.

Step 2 Apply to Text

 In your Teaching Pal, pages 50–61, use the blue **READ FOR UNDERSTANDING** prompts to read *A Kids' Guide to Friends* with children as they follow along and annotate in their *my*Book.

- **Genre Study** Read the genre information on page 50. Discuss the kinds of things children would expect to find in informational text and compare these things to a fiction story such as *My School Trip*.

- **Set a Purpose** Read the Set a Purpose section on page 50. Prompt children to set their own purpose for reading *A Kids' Guide to Friends*.

- **Build Background** Play the audio **Kinds of Friends**. Have children predict what kinds of friends they might read about in *A Kids' Guide to Friends*.

- **Read and Comprehend** Guide children to read the text all the way through. Pause occasionally, using the prompts in your Teaching Pal to gauge children's understanding and to have them make inferences. Have children refer back to the Anchor Chart to tell about the text evidence and what they already knew that helped them make each inference.

Step 3 Engage and Respond

INDEPENDENT PRACTICE: Speaking & Listening

- Use the **TURN AND TALK** routine with the questions on Teaching Pal and *my*Book page 61. Have children point out evidence or background knowledge that helped them make an inference.

- Read the Talking Tip. Remind children to speak one at a time, and to explain their ideas and feelings clearly to their partners. Tell children to use the sentence frame as they tell about their feelings.

- You may want to have children conduct their discussions during daily small-group time.

 ENGLISH LEARNER SUPPORT: Build Background

ALL LEVELS As you play the audio *Kinds of Friends* to build background for the text, have children signal when they don't understand something. Pause to clarify, repeating or writing phrases and sentences as needed. Develop meaning for unknown words or concepts by pantomiming or sketching ideas. Play the audio several times.

 LINK TO SMALL-GROUP INSTRUCTION

REINFORCE MAKE INFERENCES Review or extend the skill as needed during small-group time to support children's need for differentiation. *See the lesson on p. T151.*

👥 **SMALL-GROUP INSTRUCTION**

Options for Differentiation

As the class engages in independent and collaborative work, meet with Guided Reading Groups or differentiate instruction based on student need.

GUIDED READING GROUPS

Match Children to Books + Instruction

- Choose just-right books based on level, skill, topic, or genre.

C D E F G H I J K

Leveled Readers

- Deliver instruction with each book's Take and Teach Lesson, choosing appropriate sessions based on need.

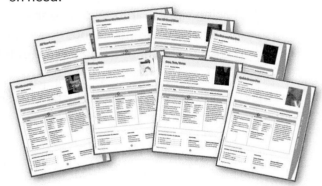

- Check comprehension, reinforce instruction, and extend learning with suggested supporting activities.

Rigby
LEVELED LIBRARY

EL ENGLISH LEARNER SUPPORT

Infer

- Use **Tabletop Minilessons: English Language Development 2.2 (Writing)** to reinforce and practice the language skill.

The children have a new game to play. This new game is fun. "What is 5 + 3?" asks Mia.

Tabletop Minilessons: English Language Development

- Then use the following text-based prompts with *A Kids' Guide to Friends* to guide application of the language skill. Begin with the prompt at the child's identified language proficiency level. As children are able, use lighter supports to encourage increased language proficiency.

SUBSTANTIAL
Point to the photo of children on the cover and ask: *How do these children feel about each other?* Provide this frame: *These children are/feel _____.*

MODERATE
Point to the cover and ask: *How do you think these children feel about each other? Why do you think so?* Provide this frame: *I think these children feel _____ because they _____.*

LIGHT
Have children infer how the children on the cover feel about each other and why they think they feel that way.

REINFORCE MAKE INFERENCES

Demonstrate

Tabletop Minilessons: Reading

- Use **Tabletop Minilessons: Reading 6** to remind children that an **inference** is a smart guess about something the author doesn't tell you. Readers use clues, or **evidence**, from the text and pictures to make inferences. Readers can also think about what they already know and use that information to make inferences about what they read.

- Model filling out Printable: **Reading Graphic Organizer 10** to make inferences about *A Kids' Guide to Friends*.

Apply to Independent Reading

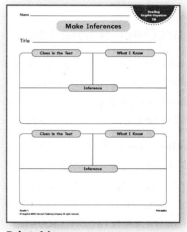

Printable:
Reading Graphic Organizer 10

- Now have children make inferences about an appropriate just-right book that they are reading independently. Before children read their books, guide them to set a purpose for reading. Remind them to use clues from the text and pictures to make smart guesses about it. Customize these prompts to the books children choose.

  » *What clues in the pictures can you use to make an inference?*

  » *What clues in the text can you use to make an inference?*

  » *What information that you already know can help you make a smart guess about the text?*

- Have children complete Printable: **Reading Graphic Organizer 10** for their independent reading book.

ALMOST THERE

READY FOR MORE

SCAFFOLD AND EXTEND

- Prompt children to look at the cover and infer what the book is about.

- Tell children that sometimes the text tells what it is about and sometimes the pictures do. Ask: *What do you learn from the pictures in this book?*

- Ask children to think of a picture they could add to the book. Have them tell what the picture would show and what readers could infer from the picture.

 ENGLISH LEARNER SUPPORT

SUBSTANTIAL

Ask children to choose a picture from the book. Ask what they see and what they infer. Supply these frames: *This picture shows _____. I infer that _____.*

MODERATE

Point to a picture that is not explained by the text on the page. Ask: *What does this picture tell you about the story/topic?*

LIGHT

Ask: *What information do you get from the words in the text? What information do you get from the pictures?*

Options for Differentiation

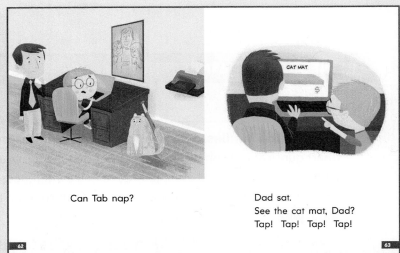

Can Tab Nap?, Start Right Reader, *Book 1*, pp. 60–67

REINFORCE FOUNDATIONAL SKILLS

Read Decodable Text

Blend and Read Have children turn to Start Right Reader page 60. Use the **CHORAL READING** routine to read aloud the Blend and Read lines. Use challenge line 4 with children who are ready.

Preview the Story Ask: *What did Tab do to Dan's map? How did Dan respond? (Tab played with and napped on Dan's map, wrinkling it; Dan picked up the map and was mad.)* Then have children read the title on page 61 and look at the pictures on pages 65-66. Ask: *What do you think Tab wants to do? (find a place to nap)*

Fluency Focus: Reading Rate Read aloud page 63 as children follow along. Point out that you read smoothly, with no long pauses between words in a sentence. Then have children read the page chorally.

Reflect on Reading Have children read to find the answer to the question in the story's title. Have them read each page silently and then chorally. Pause for these prompts:

- **Pages 62–63:** *What new character is introduced? (Dad) What do Dad and Dan do to help Tab? (order a cat mat)*

- **Pages 64–65:** *How do you think Tab feels about the new mat? How can you tell? (Possible response: I think Tab is curious about it; Tab looks at the mat and taps it.)*

- **Page 66:** *Can Tab nap? (Yes; Tab naps on the mat.)*

Show What You Know Allow time for children to reread the week's four Start Right Reader stories. Then have them answer the questions on page 67.

Tab, I like this tan cat mat.

Tab had a tan cat mat.
Tap. Tap. Tap. Tap.
Can Tab nap?

64 65

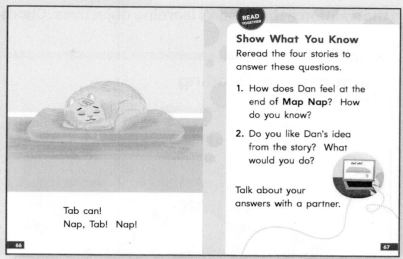

Tab can!
Nap, Tab! Nap!

Show What You Know
Reread the four stories to answer these questions.

1. How does Dan feel at the end of **Map Nap**? How do you know?

2. Do you like Dan's idea from the story? What would you do?

Talk about your answers with a partner.

66 67

Make Minutes Count

As you meet with small groups to read *Can Tab Nap?*, use one or more of these related activities, as needed, at the beginning or the end of the small-group session.

- **Connect to Phonics** Have children go on a word hunt in *Can Tab Nap?* Choose a few pages for them to reread. Have them hunt for words with short *a* and write the words they find.

- **Connect to Spelling** Have children draw a two-column chart on a sheet of paper and label one column *an* and the other *bad*. Explain that you will call out the Spelling Words. They should write Spelling Words that have the /ă/ sound at the beginning of the word in the first column and write Spelling Words that have the /ă/ sound in the middle of the word in the second column. Then call out the basic and review Spelling Words, allowing time between words for children to write them in the appropriate columns.

- **Connect to High-Frequency Words** Play What Am I Thinking? Display these High-Frequency Word cards from Printable: **Word List 2** face up on the tabletop: *first, good, he, my*. On a sheet of paper, have children write the numbers 1–4. Then give a clue about one of the words. For example: *Number 1: I am thinking of a word that is the opposite of* bad. *(good)* Children choose the High-Frequency Word that correctly answers the clue and write it next to the number 1. Continue for the other words. After all the clues have been given, review the answers and have children check their spelling.

first

good

he

my

👥 **INDEPENDENT APPLICATION**

Options for Independent and Collaborative Work

While you meet with small groups, have other children engage in literacy activities that reinforce the lesson's learning objectives. Choose from these options.

Independent Reading

Student Choice Library

Rigby LEVELED LIBRARY

APPLY READING SKILL

Make Inferences Children complete Printable: **Reading Graphic Organizer 10** for an independent reading book.

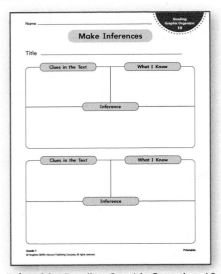

Printable: Reading Graphic Organizer 10

APPLY LANGUAGE SKILL

Infer Children complete Printable: **Language Graphic Organizer 7** for an independent reading book.

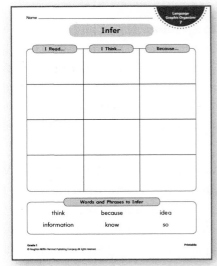

Printable: Language Graphic Organizer 7

Notice & Note

Big Questions

Encourage children to ask the Big Questions for nonfiction: *What surprised me? What did the author think I already knew? What challenged, changed, or confirmed what I already knew?*

Literacy Centers

See pp. T100–T101.

 WORD WORK

 CREATIVITY CORNER

 DIGITAL STATION

 READING CORNER

 TEAMWORK TIME

Start Right Reader

Read Decodable Text *Can Tab Nap?*, Book 1: pp. 60–67

Speaking & Listening

Partners discuss the Turn and Talk questions using evidence. *See Engage & Respond, p. T149.*

Additional Skills Practice

PHONICS

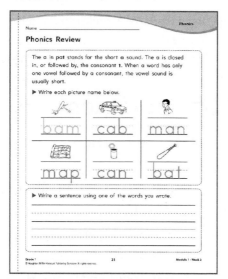

Know It, Show It, p. 21

GENERATIVE VOCABULARY

Know It, Show It, p. 22

Wrap-Up
Share Time

At the end of Reading Workshop, have children reflect on their learning by sharing how they applied **Make Inferences** or another area of focus during independent work time. Choose from these options:

- **SHARE CHAIR** Select a reader each day to come to the front of the class and tell what he or she learned from the reading by using a skill or strategy.

- **THINK-PAIR-SHARE** Children share their thinking with a partner. Select a few each day to share with the whole class.

- **RETURN TO ANCHOR CHART** Have children add sticky notes about their independent reading book to the Make Inferences Anchor Chart. Call on a few children to explain what they added.

Online **Ed**

ANCHOR CHART 6: Make Inferences

FOUNDATIONAL SKILLS

LEARNING OBJECTIVES

- Identify and read high-frequency words.
- **Language** Recognize, recite, write, and spell basic sight vocabulary.
- Blend onsets and rimes to say one-syllable words.
- Blend phonemes to say one-syllable words.
- Segment spoken one-syllable words into individual phonemes.

MATERIALS Online

Word Cards *a, an, can, first, good, had, he, I, man, my, was*

Printables *Phonological Awareness 2; Word List 2*

Classroom materials *large jar or other container*

 # High-Frequency Words

Children's Choice

- Remind children of the High-Frequency Words they have been practicing this week: *a, first, good, had, he, I, my,* and *was,* and the decodable High-Frequency Words *an, can,* and *man.*

- Review any words that posed difficulty for children this week, using Word Cards and the **HIGH-FREQUENCY WORDS** routine.

- In Lessons 7–9, children used these practice activities: Word-O Game (p. T118), Word Jar (p. T132), and Chant and Cheer (p. T144). Have children vote on their favorite, and use it to review the week's words for word recognition fluency.

> **was**

 # Phonological Awareness

Teacher's Choice

- In Lessons 6–9, children practiced blending onset and rime and blending phonemes (pp. T103, T119). They also practiced segmenting onset and rime (pp. T132, T144).

- Use Printable: **Phonological Awareness 2** to gauge which blending tasks need reinforcement.

  » **Blend Onset and Rime** Have children blend the chunks to say each word: /k/ /ŭp/ (cup), /m/ /ăn/ (man).

  » **Blend Phonemes** Have children blend phonemes to say each word: /m/ /ĭ/ /t/ (mitt), /n/ /ŭ/ /t/ (nut), /b/ /ŏŏ/ /k/ (book), /d/ /ŏ/ /g/ (dog).

- Have children segment the following words into onset and rime to determine whether reinforcement is needed for segmenting: safe (/s/ /āf/), net (/n/ /ĕt/), heat (/h/ /ēt/), page (/p/ /āj/), bat (/b/ /ăt/), lot (/l/ /ŏt/).

(EL) ENGLISH LEARNER SUPPORT:
Build Vocabulary

SUBSTANTIAL
Have children use the word *I* to begin a sentence about an action they perform, using gestures. Examples: *I write. I smile.*

MODERATE
Have children use a sentence frame to identify an object they once owned. For example: *I had a _____. (doll)*

LIGHT
Tell children to describe an object they once owned using this sentence frame: *I had a _____. (red toy truck)*

✓ CORRECT & REDIRECT

If children have difficulty, model the tasks by emphasizing the sounds. Examples:

- Model blending onset and rime. *Listen: /m/ /ăn/, /mmm/ /ăăănnn/. Say the chunks with me: /m/ /ăn/, /mmm/ /ăn/, /m/ /ăăănnn/, man. What is the word when we blend /m/ and /ăn/? (man)*

- Model segmenting onset and rime: *We can break a word into its beginning sound and the rest of the word. Listen: net, /nnn/ /ĕĕĕt/. I hear /nnn/ at the beginning. The rest of the word is /ĕĕĕt/. What are the chunks for net? (/n/ /ĕt/)*

Short a

Spelling Assessment

LEARNING OBJECTIVE

• Spell words with short *a* (closed syllables).

DICTATION SENTENCES

BASIC

1. **an** I ate *an* orange.
2. **bad** The milk had gone *bad*.
3. **can** Mom opened a *can* of peas.
4. **nap** The tired baby took a *nap*.
5. **cat** My *cat* is named Fluffy.
6. **pan** He cooked eggs in a *pan*.

REVIEW

7. **am** I *am* in first grade.
8. **at** We are *at* school now.
9. **sat** We *sat* on the couch.
10. **bat** The ball player has a *bat*.

CHALLENGE

11. **trap** The fish got caught in a *trap*.
12. **lamp** The *lamp* is very bright.

1 Say each Spelling Word, and read the Dictation Sentence. Repeat the word and then have children write it. Remind them to use their best handwriting.

2 Add the Surprise Words *mad, man,* and *tap*. If you prefer a shorter test, replace three of the Basic Words with the Surprise Words.

• **mad** She was *mad* when her team lost.

• **man** That *man* is his dad.

• **tap** She can *tap* lightly on the drum.

3 Include the Challenge Words for children who practiced them this week.

4 Review any words that children misspell. If they miss two or more words, then revisit the Lesson 6 Word Sort activity on page T107.

1. an
2. bad
3. can
4. nap
5.
6.
7.
8.
9.
10.

TEACHER TIP

Surprise! The Surprise Words are application words. Their purpose is to show whether children can apply the spelling principle, going beyond the memorization of specific words. After a while, kids will start trying to guess the surprise words early in the week.

LEARNING OBJECTIVES

- **Language** Respond and use grade-level vocabulary accurately.
- Use newly acquired vocabulary to identify real-life connections between words and their use.

MATERIALS   Online

Know It, Show It *p. 23*

 # Review Power Words

Revisit the Power Words

- Revisit the Power Words from *A Kids' Guide to Friends*. Display the questions and sentence frames below word by word.

- Model the task for the first word, using a child as your partner. Read aloud the question, and have the child repeat it. Respond using the sentence frame.

- Have partners use the **TURN AND TALK** routine to respond to each question using the sentence frame.

- For each word, ask one or two children to share their responses with the class. Then have them discuss the next question.

Power Word	Question	Sentence Frame
kinds	What **kinds** of books do you like to read?	*The **kinds** of books I like to read are _____.*
together	When is it helpful to work **together**?	*It's helpful to work **together** when _____.*

TEACHER TIP

It takes all kinds! Have children practice classifying *kinds* of objects in between activities or during small group time for early finishers. Have children practice different ways of grouping objects and ideas. Begin with classroom objects, using prompts such as these: *What **kinds** of art materials do we use? What **kinds** of games do we play at recess?*

● *Getting Started*

ENGAGEMENT ROUTINE

Model and practice engagement routines until they are automatic. For example, role-play **TURN AND TALK** in front of the class and show examples (and non-examples) of how to be a good partner.

See the **GPS guide** to learn more.

Vocabulary Chat

- Read aloud the following questions to have children use the Power Words in a different context:

  1 *What **kinds** of food do you like to eat for breakfast? What **kinds** of food do you like to eat for a special treat? How are these **kinds** of food different?*

  2 *What activities do we do **together** at school? What activities do you do **together** at home? When do you most like working **together** with someone?*

- After you read aloud each question, have children use the **THINK-PAIR-SHARE** routine to discuss. Call on pairs to share their answers. Use positive feedback to reinforce correct usages of words.

- For additional practice with the Power Words from *A Kids' Guide to Friends,* have children complete Know It, Show It page 23.

 ENGLISH LEARNER SUPPORT:
Build Vocabulary

SUBSTANTIAL
Restate children's responses to the Vocabulary Chat questions in complete sentences. Have them repeat the sentences after you.

MODERATE
Supply frames such as these: *The **kinds** of food I like are _____. We work **together** when _____.*

LIGHT
Have children think of other questions that use the Power Word *kinds*. Have them ask a partner their questions..

READING WORKSHOP

LEARNING OBJECTIVES

- Identify the central idea by using supporting evidence and details.
- **Language** State a central idea and explain supporting evidence.
- Write an opinion and a supporting reason in response to a text.

MATERIALS Online

Anchor Chart 13
Central Idea

Printable *Anchor Chart 13: Central Idea*

Teaching Pal *Book 1, pp. 50–63*

*my***Book** *A Kids' Guide to Friends, Book 1, pp. 50–63*

Know It, Show It *p. 24*

📖 READER'S VOCABULARY

- **topic** the person or thing a text is about
- **central idea** the big idea, or main idea, that readers should take away from reading a text
- **supporting evidence** detail in a text that helps to explain the central idea
- **detail** small bit of information that supports a central idea or describes something in a text

🕐 Central Idea

- Explain to children that it's important to figure out what the author wants them to gain from reading a text.

- Project or display <u>Anchor Chart 13: Central Idea</u>.

- Tell children that the **topic** of an informational text is the person or thing that the text is about.

- Explain that all informational texts have a **central idea**, or main idea, that the author wants readers to take away from reading the text. Point out that the central idea is a statement or a sentence about the topic.

- Point out that readers can use **supporting evidence** and **details** in the text to figure out the central idea.

- Tell children they will reread parts of *A Kids' Guide to Friends* to practice identifying the central idea.

ANCHOR CHART 13:
Central Idea

Online 🍊 **Ed**

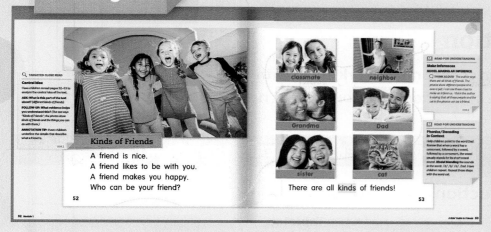

ANNOTATE IT!

Online
Ed

Children may use the annotation tools in their eBook.

Step 2 Apply to Text

 In your Teaching Pal, use the purple **TARGETED CLOSE READ** prompts to guide children to apply the central idea skill to *A Kids' Guide to Friends.* Children may refer to the questions on Know It, Show It page 24 as you discuss them.

- Read aloud the first question on Teaching Pal page 52 and have children use evidence to tell what this part of the text is about. *(different kinds of friends)*

- Then read the follow-up question. Tell children to look for evidence in the text and graphic features to answer the question. *(The text says "Kinds of Friends"; the photos show kinds of friends and things you can do with them.)*

- Read aloud the questions on Teaching Pal page 58. Tell children use details from the text and picture to figure out the central idea about friends. *(It's great to have friends and to be a good friend; the words say it feels good to be a friend; the photos show friends having fun together.)*

- Refer back to the Anchor Chart to support the discussion. Children may add sticky notes to the chart to add the topic, supporting evidence, and central idea of the selection *A Kids' Guide to Friends.*

Step 3 Engage and Respond

INDEPENDENT PRACTICE: Writing

- Read aloud the prompt on Teaching Pal page 62. Have children use the planning space to think about the ways the text shows how to make a friend, and which one they think is the best way.

- Then have children write their responses to the prompt. Remind children to refer back to *A Kids' Guide to Friends* and use the words and pictures to remind them of all the ideas for making friends.

- You may want to have children complete their writing during daily small-group time.

Professional Learning

RESEARCH FOUNDATIONS

"Close reading provides students with some needed structure to reread text with purpose, often using symbols and annotations to demonstrate their interaction with the text."

—Dr. Heather Dean (2017)

See the **GPS guide** to learn more.

 LINK TO SMALL-GROUP INSTRUCTION

REINFORCE CENTRAL IDEA Review or extend the skill as needed during small-group time to support children's need for differentiation. *See the lesson on p. T163.*

READING WORKSHOP

👥 SMALL-GROUP INSTRUCTION

Options for Differentiation

As the class engages in independent and collaborative work, meet with Guided Reading Groups or differentiate instruction based on student need.

GUIDED READING GROUPS

Match Children to Books + Instruction

- Choose just-right books based on level, skill, topic, or genre.

C D E F G H I J K

Leveled Readers

- Deliver instruction with each book's Take and Teach Lesson, choosing appropriate sessions based on need.

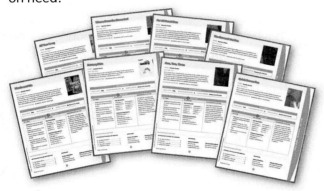

- Check comprehension, reinforce instruction, and extend learning with suggested supporting activities.

Rigby® LEVELED LIBRARY

Buddy
The Princess and the Pea
Walking in the Autumn
What is Soil?
Fire! Fire!
Enter at Your Own Risk
Planting and Growing
The Donkey and the Wolf
Our Gift to the Beach
Tick, Tock, Check the Clock!
Little Squirrel Wants to Play

🔵 EL ENGLISH LEARNER SUPPORT

Infer

- Use **Tabletop Minilessons: English Language Development 2.3 (Collaborative Problem Solving)** to reinforce and practice the language skill.

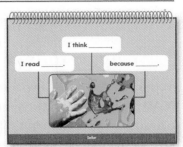

Tabletop Minilessons: English Language Development

- Then use the following text-based prompts with *A Kids' Guide to Friends* to guide application of the language skill. Begin with the prompt at the child's identified language proficiency level. As children are able, use lighter supports to encourage increased language proficiency.

SUBSTANTIAL
Direct children's attention to page 56. Then ask: *Is there only one place where you can make friends? Where else can you make friends?*

MODERATE
Direct children's attention to page 56. Then ask: *Are there other places to find a friend?* Then ask students to name places to find friends.

LIGHT
Direct children's attention to page 56. Ask: *Are there other places where you can make a friend? Which words in the text tell you there are?*

REINFORCE CENTRAL IDEA

Demonstrate

- Use **Tabletop Minilessons: Reading 13** to remind children that the **topic** is the person or thing the text is about. The **central idea** is what the author wants readers to take away from reading the text. To figure out the central idea, readers should look for **details** and **supporting evidence** in the text.

- Model filling out Printable: **Reading Graphic Organizer 12** to identify the central idea in *A Kids' Guide to Friends*.

Apply to Independent Reading

- Now have children determine the central idea in an appropriate just-right book that they are reading independently. Customize these prompts to the books children choose.

  » *What is the topic of this book?*

  » *What details about the topic can you find?*

  » *What does the author want you to know about the topic?*

- Have children complete Printable: **Reading Graphic Organizer 12** for their independent reading book.

Tabletop Minilessons: Reading

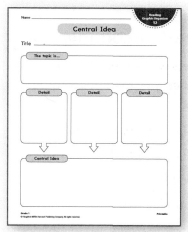

Printable:
Reading Graphic Organizer 12

ALMOST THERE ↓ READY FOR MORE	**SCAFFOLD AND EXTEND**

SCAFFOLD AND EXTEND

- Have children identify the central idea in smaller sections of the book before they move on to identifying its overall central idea.

- Prompt children to list important parts or sections of their books. Ask: *How are these parts connected? What big, or central, idea is the author sharing?*

- Ask: *What idea connects all the parts of your book?* Have children discuss why this is the central idea in the book.

ENGLISH LEARNER SUPPORT

SUBSTANTIAL

Ask children simple questions about the book's topic and central idea, such as *Is the book about (topic)? Is the central idea (say something specific about it)?*

MODERATE

Ask children questions about the book's topic and central idea. Provide these sentence frames: *This book is about _____. The details tell me that _____. The central idea is _____.*

LIGHT

Have children connect the book's topic and central idea. Prompt them to discuss using the academic vocabulary.

LESSON 10

READING WORKSHOP

Options for Differentiation

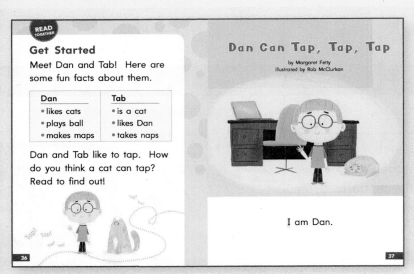

Start Right Reader, *Book 1*, pp. 36–67

REINFORCE FOUNDATIONAL SKILLS

Read Decodable Text

Review Remind children of the Start Right Reader stories they read this week about the characters Dan and Tab.

- *Dan Can Tap, Tap, Tap*
- *Tab Can Tap, Tap, Tap*
- *Map Nap*
- *Can Tab Nap?*

Allow a few minutes for children to page through the stories to recall what they are about.

Make Text Connections Prompt children to explain how the four stories are connected.

- *Who are the main characters in these stories? (Dan and Tab)*

- *What is the main thing that each story is about? (Possible responses: In* Dan Can Tap, Tap, Tap, *Dan makes a map on his computer; in* Tab Can Tap, Tap, Tap, *Tab plays with the map; in* Map Nap, *Tab naps on the map; in* Can Tab Nap?, *Tab naps on the new mat.)*

- *What problem in* Map Nap *has a solution in* Can Tab Nap? What is the solution? (Tab wrinkled Dan's map and then took a nap on it; Dan and Dad order a cat mat for Tab, and Tab naps on the mat.)*

- *How does Tab change from the first story to the last story? (Tab is happy because Tab has a place to nap.)*

- *What might happen to Dan and Tab in a new story about them? (Accept reasonable responses.)*

Reread for Fluency Select one of the stories to reread. Use the **CHORAL READING** routine and have children focus on reading at an appropriate rate.

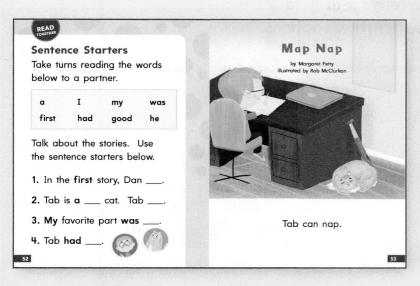

READ TOGETHER

Sentence Starters

Take turns reading the words below to a partner.

a	I	my	was
first	had	good	he

Talk about the stories. Use the sentence starters below.

1. In the **first** story, Dan ___.

2. Tab is **a** ___ cat. Tab ___.

3. **My** favorite part **was** ___.

4. Tab **had** ___.

Map Nap
by Margaret Fetty
illustrated by Rob McClurkan

Tab can nap.

52   53

Blend and Read

1. nap   pat   map   cap   pan
2. cab   dad   man   mad   can
3. mad   bat   sad   mat   dad
4. cap   camp   sad   sand
5. Is Dan mad at Tab?
6. Dad can see Dan.

Can Tab Nap?
by Margaret Fetty
illustrated by Rob McClurkan

Tab sat.
Tab was sad.

60   61

Make Minutes Count

As you meet with small groups to review the week's decodable stories, use one or both of these related activities, as needed, at the beginning or the end of the small-group session.

- **Connect to Phonics** Play Sentence Scramble. Write these words on separate index cards: *can, nap, Pam, Sam, sat.* Randomly place the cards face up on the tabletop. Say: *Sam can nap.* Have children work together to arrange the cards in the correct order to form the sentence. Repeat the process with *Pam sat.*

- **Connect to Handwriting** Write this sentence from *Can Tab Nap?* on the board: *See the cat mat, Dad?* Have children write the sentence. As they write, reinforce proper pencil grip and paper position. Then have children compare their sentence to the model and self-assess letter formation and word spacing.

Options for Independent and Collaborative Work

While you meet with small groups, have other children engage in literacy activities that reinforce the lesson's learning objectives. Choose from these options.

Independent Reading

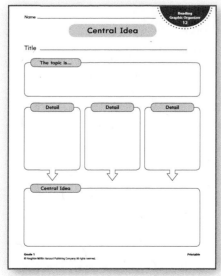

Student Choice Library

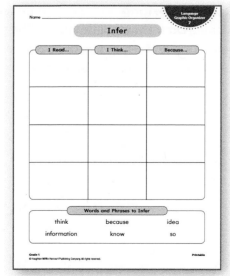

LEVELED LIBRARY

APPLY READING SKILL

Central Idea Children complete Printable: **Reading Graphic Organizer 12** for an independent reading book.

Printable: Reading Graphic Organizer 12

APPLY LANGUAGE SKILL

Infer Children complete Printable; **Language Graphic Organizer 7** for an independent reading book.

Printable: Language Graphic Organizer 7

Literacy Centers

See pp. T100–T101.

 WORD WORK

 CREATIVITY CORNER

 DIGITAL STATION

 READING CORNER

 TEAMWORK TIME

Start Right Reader

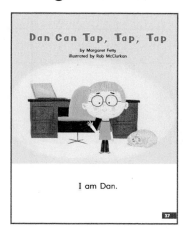

Read Decodable Text
Book 1: pp. 36–67

Writing

Children refer to pictures and words from the text to write about ways to make friends. *See Engage & Respond, p. T161.*

Close Reading

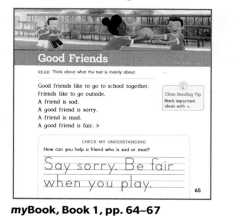

myBook, Book 1, pp. 64–67

Additional Skills Practice

VOCABULARY

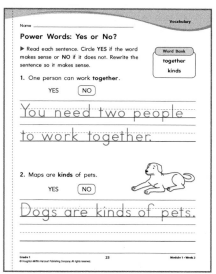

Know It, Show It, p. 23

Wrap-Up
Share Time

At the end of Reading Workshop, have children reflect on their learning by sharing how they applied **Central Idea** or another area of focus during independent work time. Choose from these options:

- **SHARE CHAIR** Select a reader each day to come to the front of the class and tell what he or she learned from the reading by using a skill or strategy.

- **THINK-PAIR-SHARE** Children share their thinking with a partner. Select a few children each day to share with the whole class.

- **RETURN TO ANCHOR CHART** Have children add sticky notes about their independent reading book to the Central Idea Anchor Chart. Call on a few children to explain what they added.

ANCHOR CHART 13: Central Idea

Notes

 SOCIAL STUDIES CONNECTION:
New Friends and Experiences

Nice to Meet You!

 Essential Question How can making new friends and learning new things help us?

Essential Skills

FOUNDATIONAL SKILLS

- Phonics: Consonants *r, f, s /z/*; Short *i*; Inflection *-s*
- High-Frequency Words: *and, find, for, just, many, one, she, then*
- Fluency: Phrasing
- Spelling: Short *i*

VOCABULARY

- Power Words: *approve, beautiful, changed, chilly, copied, flutter, folds, grumbled, paddled, quivered, swayed, ugly, weird*
- Generative Vocabulary: Inflection *-ed*

READING WORKSHOP

- Characters
- Ask and Answer Questions

WRITING WORKSHOP

- Writing Form: Oral Story
- Grammar Minilessons: Action Verbs

LEARNING MINDSET:
Seeking Challenges

THIS WEEK'S TEXTS

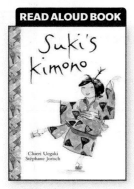
READ ALOUD BOOK

Suki's Kimono

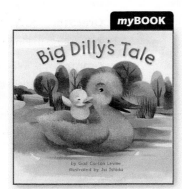
myBOOK

Big Dilly's Tale

myBOOK

I'm Me

START RIGHT READER

Decodable Texts
Tim and Pam
Dab, Dab, Dab!
Tin Cans Tip!
Fin

Rigby
LEVELED LIBRARY

Suggested Daily Times

- VOCABULARY — 10–15 minutes
- FOUNDATIONAL SKILLS — 15–30 minutes
- READING WORKSHOP — 60–75 minutes
- WRITING WORKSHOP — 20–30 minutes

This Week's Words

BIG IDEA WORDS

challenge	emotions	friendship

POWER WORDS

approve	beautiful	changed
chilly	copied	flutter
folds	grumbled	paddled
quivered	swayed	ugly
weird		

HIGH-FREQUENCY WORDS

and	find	for	just
many	one	she	then

READER'S VOCABULARY

action	character	detail
evidence	reason	verb

Assessment Options

Online **Ed**

✓ **Selection Quiz:** *Big Dilly's Tale*

✓ **Weekly Assessment**
- High-Frequency Words
- Phonics: Consonants *r, f, s* /z/; Short *i*; Inflection *-s*
- Comprehension: Characters
- Generative Vocabulary: Inflection *-ed*
- Grammar: Action Verbs

Intervention

For children needing strategic intervention, use *Tabletop Minilessons: Intervention.*

- Module 1, Week 3 Daily Lessons

LESSON 11

FOUNDATIONAL SKILLS

Word Work Warm-Up, pp. T176–T177
- High-Frequency Words: *and, find, for, just, many, one, she, then*
- Phonological Awareness

Phonics, pp. T178–T179
- Consonants *r, f, s* /z/; Short *i*

Spelling, pp. T180–T181
- Short *i*

VOCABULARY

Academic Vocabulary, pp. T182–T183
- Introduce Oral Language: *approve, weird, copied, quivered, flutter, folds, swayed, grumbled*

READING WORKSHOP

Suki's Kimono   Book Stix
GENRE Realistic Fiction
Read Aloud: MINILESSON,
pp. T184–T185
- Connect and Teach: Characters
- Apply to Text: *Suki's Kimono*
- Engage and Respond: Writing

SMALL-GROUP INSTRUCTION

Options for Differentiation
- Guided Reading Groups, p. T186
- English Learner Support: Describe, p. T186
- Reinforce Characters, p. T187
- Reinforce Foundational Skills: Read *Tim and Pam*, pp. T188–T189

Options for Independent and Collaborative Work, pp. T190–T191

WRITING WORKSHOP

Oral Story, p. W12
- Revising I: Adding Detail

Grammar, p. W286
- Action Verbs

LESSON 12

FOUNDATIONAL SKILLS

Word Work Warm-Up, pp. T192–T193
- High-Frequency Words: *and, find, for, just, many, one, she, then*
- Phonological Awareness

Phonics, pp. T194–T195
- Consonants *r, f, s* /z/; Short *i*

VOCABULARY

Academic Vocabulary, pp. T196–T197
- Introduce Power Words: *ugly, paddled, chilly, beautiful, changed*

READING WORKSHOP

Big Dilly's Tale   Teaching Pal
GENRE Fairy Tale
Shared Reading: MINILESSON,
pp. T198–T199
- Connect and Teach: Ask and Answer Questions
- Apply to Text: *Big Dilly's Tale*
- Engage and Respond: Speaking & Listening

SMALL-GROUP INSTRUCTION

Options for Differentiation
- Guided Reading Groups, p. T200
- English Learner Support: Describe, p. T200
- Reinforce Ask and Answer Questions, p. T201
- Reinforce Foundational Skills: Read *Dab, Dab, Dab!*, pp. T202–T203

Options for Independent and Collaborative Work, pp. T204–T205

WRITING WORKSHOP

Oral Story, p. W13
- Revising II: Finding the Right Words

Grammar, p. W287
- Action Words in the Present

LESSON 13

FOUNDATIONAL SKILLS

Word Work Warm-Up, p. T206
- High-Frequency Words: *and, find, for, just, many, one, she, then*
- Phonological Awareness

Fluency, p. T207
- Phrasing

Phonics, pp. T208–T209
- Inflection *-s*

VOCABULARY

Academic Vocabulary, pp. T210–T211
- Review Power Words: *ugly, paddled, chilly, beautiful, changed*

READING WORKSHOP

Big Dilly's Tale
GENRE Fairy Tale
Shared Reading: MINILESSON,
pp. T212–T213
- Connect and Teach: Characters
- Apply to Text: *Big Dilly's Tale*
- Engage and Respond: Writing

SMALL-GROUP INSTRUCTION

Options for Differentiation
- Guided Reading Groups, p. T214
- English Learner Support: Describe, p. T214
- Reinforce Characters, p. T215
- Reinforce Foundational Skills: Read *Tin Cans Tip!*, pp. T216–T217

Options for Independent and Collaborative Work, pp. T218–T219

WRITING WORKSHOP

Oral Story, p. W14
- Editing: Capitalizing Proper Nouns

Grammar, p. W288
- Using Action Words

LESSON 14

FOUNDATIONAL SKILLS

Word Work Warm-Up, p. T220
- High-Frequency Words: *and, find, for, just, many, one, she, then*
- Phonological Awareness

Phonics, p. T221
- Phonics Review

VOCABULARY

Generative Vocabulary, pp. T222–T223
- Inflection *-ed*

READING WORKSHOP

I'm Me
GENRE Song
Shared Reading: MINILESSON,
pp. T223–T225
- Connect and Teach: Characters
- Apply to Text: *I'm Me*
- Engage and Respond: Speaking & Listening

SMALL-GROUP INSTRUCTION

Options for Differentiation
- Guided Reading Groups, p. T226
- English Learner Support: Describe, p. T226
- Reinforce Characters, p. T227
- Reinforce Foundational Skills: Read *Fin*, pp. T228–T229

Options for Independent and Collaborative Work, pp. T230–T231

WRITING WORKSHOP

Oral Story, p. W15
- Publishing

Grammar, p. W279
- Sprial Review: Possessive Pronouns

LESSON 15

FOUNDATIONAL SKILLS

Word Work Warm-Up, p. T232
- High-Frequency Words: *and, find, for, just, many, one, she, then*
- Phonological Awareness

Spelling, p. T233
- Spelling Assessment

VOCABULARY

Academic Vocabulary, pp. T234–T235
- Cumulative Vocabulary Review

READING WORKSHOP

Module Wrap-Up,
pp. T236–T237
- Wrap Up the Topic
- Synthesize

SMALL-GROUP INSTRUCTION

Options for Differentiation
- Guided Reading Groups, p. T238
- English Learner Support: Describe, p. T238
- Reinforce Synthesize, p. T239
- Reinforce Foundational Skills: Make Connections, pp. T240–T241

Options for Independent and Collaborative Work, pp. T242–T243

WRITING WORKSHOP

Oral Story, p. W16
- Sharing

Grammar, p. W290
- Connect to Writing: Using Action Verbs

Build understanding of this week's texts so that you can best support children in making connections, understanding key ideas, and becoming lifelong readers.

myBOOK

Big Dilly's Tale by Gail Carson Levine

GENRE Fairy Tale

WHY THIS TEXT?

In this version of the classic fairy tale *The Ugly Duckling,* Dilly is called ugly but eventually learns that he is not a duck but is, instead, a graceful swan. Children understand how it feels to be made fun of and will learn important life lessons.

KEY LEARNING OBJECTIVES

- Identify features of fairy tales.

- Ask and answer questions about a text before, during, and after reading, using text evidence to support responses.

- Use details in the text and illustrations to identify and describe story characters and the reasons for their actions.

TEXT COMPLEXITY

LEXILE MEASURE 360L • **GUIDED READING LEVEL** F

OVERALL RATING Moderately Complex

The story contains a subtle theme but is accompanied by illustrations that directly support the text.

MAKE CONNECTIONS

BUILD KNOWLEDGE AND LANGUAGE

- **Social Studies Connection:** New Friends and Experiences

VOCABULARY

- **Inflection -ed:** *called, lived, looked, paddled, played, splashed, turned, wished*

FOUNDATIONAL SKILLS

- **High-Frequency Words:** *and, find, for, just, many, one, she, then*
- **Consonants r, f, s /z /; Short i:** *afraid, after, barn, big, chilly, Dilly, duckling, ever, farm, fast, find, for, found, friend, fun, girl, her, him, himself, his, lived, Minna, morning, other, spring, still, swans, was, wind, wished, with*
- **Inflection -s:** *ducks, swans, weeks*

TEXT X-RAY

KEY IDEAS

Key Idea *pp. 70–71*
Dilly doesn't look like the other ducklings. One duck calls him ugly. His friend Minna thinks he's cute.

Key Idea *pp. 72–73*
Dilly gets separated from the ducks; he is alone, lost, and afraid.

Key Idea *pp. 74–75*
Dilly follows a girl to her farm where he is warm and well cared for.

Key Idea *pp. 76–78*
In the spring, Dilly finds Minna and the other ducks. When he sees his reflection in the water, Dilly realizes that he is a lovely swan, not a duck after all!

LANGUAGE

Onomatopoeia
honk, quack, splashed, splat (p. 71): Help children understand that these words imitate the sounds of things happening in the story.

Common Expression
after all (p. 77): People use this phrase when something is the opposite of what they originally thought.

CULTURAL REFERENCES

Once upon a time (p. 70); ***lived happily ever after*** (p. 78): Expressions used to begin and end stories can vary from culture to culture. Explain the meanings of these common phrases, often used in fairy tales and other children's stories.

I'm Me by The FuZees

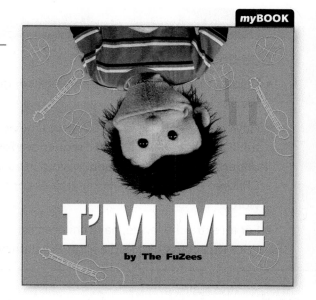

myBOOK

I'M ME
by The FuZees

GENRE Song

WHY THIS TEXT?

Children will enjoy this lively song, performed by two puppets. The song lyrics encourages them to think about and appreciate their own unique qualities as well as those of others.

KEY LEARNING OBJECTIVES

- Identify characteristics of songs.
- Use details in the text and illustrations to identify and describe story characters, including how they think and feel.

TEXT COMPLEXITY

LEXILE MEASURE N/A • **GUIDED READING LEVEL** N/A

OVERALL RATING Simple

The video uses easy-to-understand language and repeated sentences to explain its theme.

MAKE CONNECTIONS

🔗 **BUILD KNOWLEDGE AND LANGUAGE**

- **Social Studies Connection:** New Friends and Experiences

🔗 **FOUNDATIONAL SKILLS**

- **High-Frequency Words:** *and, for, one*
- **Consonants r, f, s /z/; Short i:** *as, characters, details, for, FuZees, him, in, pictures, think, understand, use, words*
- **Inflection -s:** *characters, likes, makes, pictures, words*

📖 TEXT X-RAY

KEY IDEAS	**EL LANGUAGE**
Key Idea Two brothers, Jacob and Josh, sing about how every person has a unique identity.	**Informal Language** ***woohoo:*** This word is an informal way to express joy, excitement, or approval. It's similar in meaning to *hooray*.
Key Idea Josh wonders what *unique* means, and Jacob explains its meaning.	***[things that we're] into:*** If you're "into" something, you like it a lot or enjoy doing it.
Key Idea Josh learns that his particular preferences make him unique.	***have no clue:*** Explain that when people "have no clue" about something, they don't know or understand anything about it.
Key Idea People are also unique because of the different things they enjoy doing.	***getting the hang of:*** If you're "getting the hang of" something, you're starting to understand it or know how to do it.

While you meet with small groups, have children work independently in Literacy Centers. At the beginning of the week, explain what is expected of children in each center. Post a daily rotation schedule.

WW WORD WORK

Title Challenge!

- Display the Word Cards for this week's High-Frequency Words.

- Have children list as many book and movie titles they can think of that contain a High-Frequency Word. Have them underline the High-Frequency Word in each title. Children may also write original titles containing the words.

- For an extra challenge, have children list book and movie titles that contain multiple High-Frequency Words.

and	find	for	just

many	one	she	then

Short *i*

- Display the week's Spelling Words and copies of Printable: **Spelling & Handwriting**. Have children choose one of the activities to practice writing this week's Spelling Words in their best handwriting.

- Have children complete the activity on a separate sheet of paper.

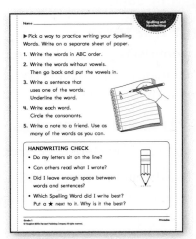

Printable: Spelling & Handwriting

😊 CREATIVITY CORNER

Readers' Theater

- As children practice reading Printable: **Readers' Theater 1**, "The New School," request that they pay attention to reading the script with accuracy. Encourage them to self-correct any errors they make while reading.

- Have groups of children perform the script. Then ask them to answer the questions on the last page of the script to assess their performance.

- Encourage group members to share what they liked best about the story.

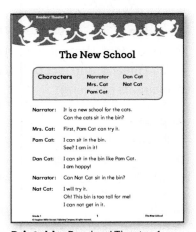

Printable: Readers' Theater 1

Reading Remake

- Display in the center and have children complete the activity for *Big Dilly's Tale* on Printable: **Make a Movie**.

- Tell partners to explain to one another how their movie shows their understanding of the selection.

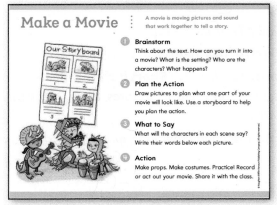

Printable: Make a Movie

DIGITAL STATION

Listener's Choice

Online Ed

- Have children listen to the Read Aloud Book *Suki's Kimono* or a Leveled Reader of their choice.

- Tell them to add the book to their Printable: <u>Listening Log</u>, as well as the active listening skills they used, a summary, and a question they have about the book.

Phonics Practice

- Have children continue their personalized, adaptive learning for foundational skills in *iRead*.

TEAMWORK TIME

Inquiry and Research Project: "Celebrate Us!" Profiles

- Have groups work on the module project.

- Remind children that their focus this week is to compile and present their class book. *See pp. T16–T17.*

READING CORNER

Independent Reading

- Have children self-select or continue reading an independent reading book.

- Remind children to set a purpose for reading and to record their progress on their Printable: <u>Reading Log</u>.

- You may want to choose from these additional options to have children interact with their books:

  » **Read for Fluency** Children use the **PARTNER READING** routine to practice the week's fluency skill, phrasing, or another area of need.

  » **Annotate the Text** Children practice a strategy and use sticky notes to record questions or what they are thinking as they read. Review the sticky notes while you confer with children.

  » **Response Journal** Children draw or write about what they read.

Student Choice Library

FOUNDATIONAL SKILLS

LEARNING OBJECTIVES

- Identify and read high-frequency words.
- **Language** Recognize, recite, and write basic sight vocabulary.
- Recognize spoken alliteration.
- Segment spoken one-syllable words into individual phonemes.
- Blend phonemes to say one-syllable words.

MATERIALS   Online :Ed

Word Cards *and, find, for, just, many, one, she, then*

Know It, Show It *p. 25*

Picture Cards *ball, bat (animal), boat, cape, keys, kite, map, maze, mule, peas, pool*

 # High-Frequency Words

Teach the Words

Use Word Cards *and, find, for, just, many, one, she,* and *then* and the **HIGH-FREQUENCY WORDS** routine below to introduce the week's High-Frequency sight words.

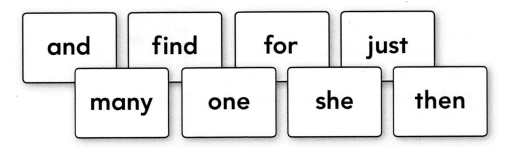

1   **See the word.** Display a Word Card. Say the word, and have children repeat it twice.

2   **Say the word.** Have children repeat it chorally. Use the word in a sentence or two. *This is for you. We are ready for action!* (Use gestures.)

3   **Spell the word.** Point to the letters, and have children spell the word aloud. Point out any familiar spelling patterns. *For begins with f. Does anyone in this class have a name that begins with F? Do you know any other words that begin with f?*

4   **Write and check the word.** Hide the word, and have children use the **WRITE AND REVEAL** routine to write the word. Then have them check it against the Word Card.

Have children add this week's words to their individual Word Rings. Tell them to write a word on the front of each card and write a sentence or draw a picture about the word on the back. Alternatively, you may have children complete Know It, Show It page 25.

● Getting Started

ENGAGEMENT ROUTINE

Use the **WRITE AND REVEAL** routine after practicing High-Frequency Words or after practicing words with a particular phonics skill. This is a good way to get a quick check of student progress.

See the **GPS guide** to learn more.

 CORRECT & REDIRECT

Guide children who have trouble identifying any of the words. Say the correct word, and have children repeat it. Example:

- *Find. What is the word?* (*find*)
- Have children spell the word. (*f-i-n-d*) *How do we say this word?* (*find*)
- Have children reread all the cards in random order.

Phonological Awareness

Alliteration; Segment Phonemes

- First, remind children that they can listen for and pay attention to the sounds in words. Tell children that you will say sets of words, and they will say "yes" if the first sound in all the words matches.

- Model: *Listen: four funny faces. Yes. I hear /f/ at the beginning of all three words, four funny faces.* Use these phrases for children to try: running rabbit, old brown boots, silly silver snake, deep dark cave, fine flat fork.

- Now remind children that they know how to segment, or break, words into their sounds.

- Display Picture Cards *ball, bat (animal), boat, cape, keys, kite, map, maze, mule, peas,* and *pool.* Choose a card and model how to segment the picture name into phonemes.

- Say: *Now we are going to say all of the sounds in a word. Listen carefully to the sounds as I say each word. Then say all the sounds you hear. I will do the first one: boat, /b/ /ō/ /t/. I hear /b/ at the beginning, /ō/ in the middle, and /t/ at the end. Boat, /b/ /ō/ /t/.* Repeat for the other Picture Cards, having volunteers choose the next card each time.

- *Are you ready to segment more words?* be (/b/ /ē/), few (/f/ /yoo/), ten (/t/ /ĕ/ /n/), hug (/h/ /ŭ/ /g/), low (/l/ /ō/), pin (/p/ /ĭ/ /n/).

Blend Phonemes

- Remind children that not only can they break words apart into sounds, but they also know how to blend sounds to say words. Tell them that now they will blend the sounds you say to say words.

- Say: *I will say each sound in a word, and you blend the sounds to say the word. I will do the first one: /g/ /ē/ /s/. Now listen as I blend the sounds: /g/ /ē/ /s/, /g-ē-s/, geese. What word did I say? (geese) That's right!*

- *Now you blend the sounds to say these words: /ĭ/ /t/ (it), /g/ /ŭ/ /m/ (gum), /ă/ /t/ (at), /z/ /ĭ/ /p/ (zip), /r/ /ē/ /l/ (real), /m/ /ŏ/ /m/ (mom).*

 ENGLISH LEARNER SUPPORT: Build Vocabulary

ALL LEVELS Ensure children are familiar with the meanings of the words in the Phonological Awareness activities (*boat, cape, few, hug, low,* and so on). The Picture Cards can help children make the connection to the meanings of some words. For other words, use gestures or examples as needed.

✓ **CORRECT & REDIRECT**

For children who blend incorrectly, differentiate instruction by modeling. Enunciate the sounds separately, then say them more closely together, and finally blend them to say the word. Example:

The sounds are /ĭ/ and /t/. The first sound is /ĭ/. Listen: /ĭĭĭ/. The next sound is /t/. Listen: /t/, /t/, /t/. Say each sound with me: /ĭ/ /t/. Now listen as I blend the two sounds together: /ĭ/ /t/, /ĭ-t/, it. What is the word? (it)

FOUNDATIONAL SKILLS

⏱ Consonants *r*, *f*, *s* /z/; Short *i*

Spotlight on Sounds

- Tell children that they will be reading words with a new vowel, short *i*, and the sounds for the consonants *r*, *f*, and *s* /z/. As a warm-up, have them practice identifying the beginning sounds in words you say. *I am going to say a word, and you will say the beginning sound. I will do the first one. Listen:* fit. *The beginning sound in* fit *is* /f/. *Listen again:* fit, /f/. *Now you try it. Listen to the words I say and say the beginning sound:* rip (/r/); sun (/s/); fill (/f/); sip (/s/); ride (/r/); fig (/f/).

- Next, have children suggest words with beginning sounds you specify. Say: *Think of words you know that begin with* /r/. *Repeat for the initial sound* /f/.

- Conclude by modeling how to identify the ending sound in his, /z/. Have children say the ending sound in these words: *fir* (/r/); *stiff* (/f/); *fans* (/z/); *has* (/z/).

▌I Do It

Spotlight on Letters Display the Sound/Spelling Card for short *i*: igloo. Name the picture, say the sound, and give the spelling. *Igloo begins with the short* i *sound,* /ĭ/. *The letter* i *can stand for the sound* /ĭ/ *at the beginning or in the middle of a word.*

Write *in*. Say the letter sounds and blend the word. Point out the vowel and consonant. *The letter* i *is a vowel and can stand for many sounds, and* n *is a consonant. When there is only one vowel and it is followed by a consonant, the vowel usually stands for the short vowel sound.*

Repeat for *r* and *f*, using Sound/Spelling Cards *raccoon* and *fish* and the words *rib* and *fit*.

Next, write *sip* and blend the word. Point to the *s*, and remind children that *s* can stand for the /s/ sound. Then point to *s* on the Sound/Spelling Card *zebra*. *The letter* s *can also stand for the* /z/ *sound at the end of words.*

Write and read *is*. *This is the word* is. *The letter* i *stands for the short* i *sound,* /ĭ/. *What sound does the* s *in* is *stand for?* (/z/) *Read the word with me:* /ĭ/ /z/, is.

EL **ENGLISH LEARNER SUPPORT: Facilitate Language Connections**

ALL LEVELS Since the sound /ĭ/ is not used in Spanish, Tagalog, Korean, Vietnamese, and Haitian Creole, some children may substitute long *e* for /ĭ/. Play the **Articulation Video** for /ĭ/. Then model the medial sound in *pit, pin, fin, tip, rip, lip*, and have children repeat.

▶ ARTICULATION VIDEO   Online ⓔ**Ed**

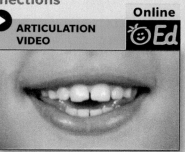

We Do It

Write *fin* and use Letter Cards *f, i, n* with the **SOUND-BY-SOUND BLENDING** routine below to model blending the word.

1 Display cards as shown. Say the first letter and sound.

2 Slide the second letter over. Say its sound. Then blend the two sounds.

3 Slide the last letter over. Say its sound. Say the first two blended sounds, the last sound, and the blended word: /fĭ/ /n/, fin.

Sound-by-Sound Blending Repeat the **SOUND-BY-SOUND BLENDING** routine with cards for the words *rip* and *is*, having children say the sounds and blend.

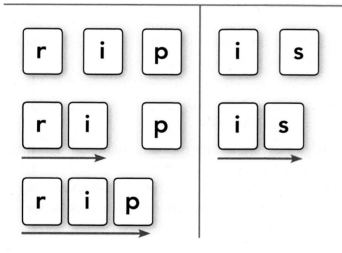

You Do It

INDEPENDENT PRACTICE

Blending Practice Write the words below. Then choose two volunteers to model the activity. Explain that you will point to a word in random order and the first child will say the separate beginning, middle, and ending sounds. The second child will read the word. Repeat the blending routine as needed. Continue until each child has had a turn.

fit	rip	is	pin
ran	fat	as	nap

✓ CORRECT & REDIRECT

- If a child mispronounces a word during Blending Practice, make note of the error type and address it.

- If a child reads *is* as *ice*, explain that the vowel letter's name is *i* but that the sound it stands for in this word is the short *i* sound, /ĭ/. Use Sound/Spelling Card *igloo* to reinforce the /ĭ/ sound. Use sound-by-sound blending to read the word *is*, and then have the child repeat the steps after you.

- If a child reads *pin* as *nip*, cover the word and blend it together as you uncover one letter at a time, left to right. Then have the child blend and read the word.

👥 LINK TO SMALL-GROUP INSTRUCTION

REINFORCE FOUNDATIONAL SKILLS Use *Tim and Pam* during small-group time to review or reinforce blending and decoding words with short *i* and consonants *r, f, s* /z/. Meet with children to work through the story, or assign it as independent work. *See the lesson on p. T188.*

Short *i*

Administer the Pretest

- Read the first Spelling Word and the Dictation Sentence. Repeat the word as children write it.

- Write the word, and have children correct their spelling if needed. Repeat for words 2–6 and for the Review Words.

- Assign the Basic and Review Words as needed for practice this week. If children do well on the pretest, assign the Challenge Words.

Teach the Principle

- Write *pin* on the board, underlining *i*, and read it aloud. Explain that the /ĭ/ sound can be spelled with the letter *i*.

- Tell children that this week all the Spelling Words have the short *i* sound, /ĭ/, spelled *i*. Explain that short *i* sound can be at the beginning or in the middle of a word.

- If children have difficulty, review Sound/Spelling Card *igloo*. Remind them that *i* is a vowel that can stand for many sounds and that one of those sounds is /ĭ/ as in *igloo*.

Model Handwriting

- Remind children that they have learned how to write lowercase *a* and *d*. Model how to write lowercase *i*, *l*, and *t*. *i: Start at the middle line. Pull down. Add a dot. l: Start at the top line. Pull down. t: Start just below the top line. Pull down and cross.*

- Have children describe what they notice about the letters *i*, *l*, and *t*. (*They are all formed by pulling down, and they are made up of straight lines.*) Model writing one or more of the Spelling Words that include *i* or *t*.

- Have children use the **WRITE AND REVEAL** routine to practice writing words that include lowercase *i* and *t*. Remind them to also use what they learned about the correct paper position and pencil grip. As needed, distribute the handwriting models on Printable: **Manuscript Ii, Ll, Tt**. Printables for Continuous Stroke letter forms are also available online.

LEARNING OBJECTIVES

- Spell words with short *i* (closed syllables).
- **Language** Identify relationships between sounds and letters.
- Develop handwriting by printing *i, t, l.*

MATERIALS   Online

Sound/Spelling Card *igloo*
Printables Manuscript *Ii, Ll, Tt;* Word List 3
Know It, Show It p. 26

DICTATION SENTENCES

BASIC
1. **it** Put *it* away.
2. **him** I gave *him* a gift.
3. **is** She *is* my best friend.
4. **sip** Take a *sip* of the drink.
5. **fit** All my markers *fit* in the box.
6. **pin** She uses a *pin* to hold her hair.

REVIEW
7. **pan** He cooked eggs in a *pan.*
8. **an** I ate *an* orange.
9. **nap** The tired baby took a *nap.*
10. **cat** My *cat* is named Fluffy.

CHALLENGE
11. **rich** The treat is *rich* and creamy.
12. **spin** *Spin* the top.

TEACHER TIP

Tall and short! Point out to children that when they write a "tall" lowercase letter, or a letter with an ascender such as *l*, the letter should touch all three lines. When they write a lowercase letter without an ascender, such as *i*, the letter should touch the middle line and the bottom line.

Getting Started

ENGAGEMENT ROUTINE

Use strategies that engage all children in listening and responding. For example, instead of having one child come to the board to practice writing, use **WRITE AND REVEAL** to have all children practice writing and reveal it to the teacher at the same time.

See the **GPS guide** to learn more.

Word Sort

1 **Introduce** Display both the basic and the review Spelling Word cards from Printable: **Word List 3** and read each one aloud.

2 **Columns 1 and 2** Display the word cards *is* and *an* as column headings. Explain: *I will put* is *at the top of one column and* an *at the top of another. I will read a word, and you will tell me if the vowel sound is the same as in* is *or in* an. *I'll sort the first word to show you.*

3 **Model** Display the word card *him* and read it aloud. Explain: Him. *Listen for the vowel sound.* Hiiiim. *That sounds the same as the vowel sound iiiis, so I'll put* him *under* is. Repeat for *nap*, placing it under *an*.

4 **Continue** Sort the other words. Model if necessary.

5 **Discuss** Read each column together. Discuss what children notice about the words in each column. If no one mentions it, guide children to identify the words in column 1 as having the short *i* sound and the words in column 2 as having the short *a* sound. Tell children they can think about this pattern when they spell words with short *i* and short *a*.

6 **Repeat** Have children work together to repeat the sort, using the Spelling Word cards from Printable: **Word List 3**. Remind children to save the rest of the page and the Spelling Word cards for use all week.

is	an
him	nap
sip	pan
pin	cat
it	
fit	

INDEPENDENT PRACTICE

For additional practice, have children complete Know It, Show It page 26. Encourage them to use their best handwriting and pay particular attention to writing the letters *i* and *t* correctly.

EL **ENGLISH LEARNER SUPPORT:**
Facilitate Language Connections

ALL LEVELS Some English learners may need support distinguishing the short vowel sound /ĭ/ from /ĕ/. Say the following pairs of words as children listen: *will/well, bill/bell, fill/fell*. Repeat the word pairs, one at a time. Ask children to raise a hand when they hear a word with /ĭ/. Have them say the word.

Professional Learning

RESEARCH FOUNDATIONS

"Handwriting is not merely a mechanical, motor skill, but rather a brain-based skill that facilitates meaning-making as writers externalize their cognitions through letter forms, the building blocks of written words and text."

—Dr. Todd L. Richards et al (2011)

See the **GPS guide** to learn more.

VOCABULARY

 ## Introduce Oral Language

Use the steps **I Do It, We Do It, You Do It** with the information in the chart below to teach the oral Power Words from the Read Aloud Book *Suki's Kimono*.

LEARNING OBJECTIVES

- **Language** Answer questions and discuss meanings to develop vocabulary.
- Identify real-life connections between words and their use.

MATERIALS   Online

Vocabulary Cards *1.28–1.35*
Read Aloud Book *Suki's Kimono*
Classroom materials *napkin, unusual object*

❶ Power Word	❷ Meaning	❸ Example
approve (v.) *(p. 3)*	If you **approve** of something, you think it is right or good.	**MAKE A CONNECTION** Tell about something you *approve* of. *I* **approve** *of your good work habits.*
weird (adj.) *(p. 3)*	Something or someone that is **weird** is odd or strange.	**USE A PROP** Display an unusual object. *This looks very* **weird**.
copied (v.) *(p. 7)*	If you **copied** someone, you did something the same way that person did.	**ACT IT OUT** Make simple movements and ask children to repeat. *You* **copied** *my movements.*
quivered (v.) *(p. 9)*	If you **quivered**, your body shook because you felt cold, scared, or excited.	**ACT IT OUT** Stand and shake your arms and legs. *I* **quivered** *before I jumped in the lake.*
flutter (v.) *(p. 12)*	If things **flutter**, they move back and forth quickly like wings.	**MAKE A CONNECTION** Connect *flutter* to animals that fly. *Bats' wings* **flutter** *quickly.*
folds (n.) *(p. 20)*	The **folds** in cloth are the curved shapes you see on parts that are not flat.	**USE A PROP** Fold a napkin twice. *This has two* **folds**.
swayed (v.) *(p. 22)*	If you **swayed** your arms, you moved them slowly back and forth.	**ACT IT OUT** Sway back and forth. *I* **swayed** *when I heard the music.*
grumbled (v.) *(p. 30)*	If you **grumbled**, you spoke in a low voice in an unhappy way.	**ACT IT OUT** Talk in a low voice. *I* **grumbled** *that the game was cancelled.*

TEACHER TIP

Words are powerful! Lead a discussion about the power of words and how they can affect others. Talk about why the word *weird* shouldn't be used for labeling other people. Reinforce the message that *weird* may be odd or strange, but odd and strange can be wonderful!

● *Professional Learning*

RESEARCH FOUNDATIONS

"The heart of language development is vocabulary learning."
—Dr. Linnea C. Ehri and Dr. Julie Rosenthal (2007)

See the **GPS guide** to learn more.

I Do It

Use the **VOCABULARY** routine and Vocabulary Cards 1.28–1.35 to introduce the oral Power Words from *Suki's Kimono.* You may wish to display the corresponding Vocabulary Card for each word as you discuss it.

Vocabulary Cards

1 **Say the Power Word.** Ask children to repeat it.

2 **Explain the meaning.** Read aloud the student-friendly meaning.

3 **Talk about examples.** Use the image or a strategy to give examples of the word.

We Do It

Guide children to make connections between each word's meaning and how they can use it in their own lives. Use these prompts. Encourage children to explain or justify their answers.

- *Would you* ***approve*** *if you saw a friend help someone? Explain.*

- *If you* ***grumbled****, would your voice be loud or soft?*

- *If you* ***swayed****, how would you move?*

- *Tell about a time when you* ***quivered****.*

- *Show how your arms can* ***flutter****.*

- *Tell about a time when you* ***copied*** *someone.*

- *Describe something* ***weird*** *you have seen.*

- *What do you have that has* ***folds****?*

You Do It

INDEPENDENT PRACTICE

Have partners work together to complete each of the activities below. Circulate and observe partners as they work, providing corrective feedback as necessary.

- **Draw** *Draw a picture of a* ***weird*** *outfit.*

- **Discuss** *Would you* ***approve*** *if someone* ***copied*** *your homework? Why or why not?*

- **Role-Play** *If a bird* ***quivered*** *in a nest, how would it move? How would a bird* ***flutter*** *its wings? Show how trees have* ***swayed*** *in the wind.*

- **Role-Play** *Demonstrate how to make* ***folds****.*

- **Discuss** *Tell how you felt when you* ***grumbled*** *about something.*

 ENGLISH LEARNER SUPPORT:
Build Vocabulary

SUBSTANTIAL
Have children act out the meanings of the words. Say each word and have children repeat it after you.

MODERATE
Supply these frames: *I* ***approve*** *means I* _____*. I* ***quivered*** *means I* _____*. I* ***copied*** *means I* _____*.*

LIGHT
Rephrase all the prompts as questions. If children respond with a phrase or short sentence, encourage them to elaborate.

READING WORKSHOP

Characters

Step 1 Connect and Teach

- Tell children that the **characters** in a story are the people, animals, or things that the story is about.

- Project or display <u>Anchor Chart 16: Characters</u>.

- As you point to the corresponding parts of the Anchor Chart, tell children that readers can "get to know" characters by paying attention to details in the words and pictures.

- Explain that these details can tell what the characters are like on the outside, or what they look like. They can also tell what the characters are like on the inside, or what they think or feel.

- Tell children that when they read a story, they should also think about the **reasons** for the characters' **actions**. Details in the story can help readers understand why characters do what they do.

- Tell children that they will practice describing characters and the reasons for their actions when they listen to a Read Aloud Book called *Suki's Kimono*.

Online

ANCHOR CHART 16: Characters

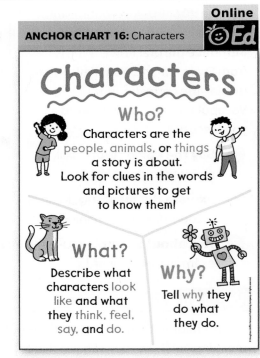

LEARNING OBJECTIVES

- Recognize characteristics of realistic fiction.
- Describe characters and the reasons for their actions.
- **Language** Explain the reasons for a character's feelings and actions.
- Write the reason for a character's action, citing text evidence.

MATERIALS   Online

Anchor Chart 16
Characters

Anchor Chart 69
Parts of a Book

Printable *Anchor Chart 16: Characters; Anchor Chart 69: Parts of a Book*

Read Aloud Book
Suki's Kimono

BookStix *1.3*

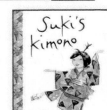

READER'S VOCABULARY

- **character** a person or animal in a story
- **reason** why or how something happened
- **action** what someone or something does

EL **ENGLISH LEARNER SUPPORT:**
Facilitate Language Connections

ALL LEVELS For Spanish-speaking children, point out that the English words *action* and *reason* have the following Spanish cognates: *acción* and *razón*.

Go to
BookStix 1.3

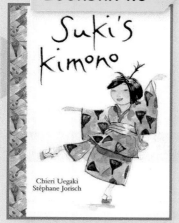

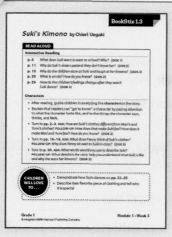

Step 2 Apply to Text

- **Genre Study** Read aloud the title *Suki's Kimono* and introduce the book. *Today we will read realistic fiction. A realistic fiction story is made up, but seems like it could happen in real life.* Have children examine the cover. Prompt them to think about what the book will be about.

- **Set a Purpose** Remind children that one of the purposes for reading realistic fiction is to find out what the characters will do. Ask: *What do you think Suki will do in the story? Use your answer to set a purpose for reading.*

- **Model Fluency** Tell children that you are going to show them how to read with good phrasing. Demonstrate by reading some of the story. As you read, chunk words and phrases naturally and pause in places where it makes sense, for example, at punctuation marks.

- **Concepts of Print** Project or display <u>Anchor Chart 69: Parts of a Book</u>. Review the information each part of a book provides, directionality of print, and the difference between letters, words, and sentences.

- **Read and Comprehend** Read aloud the book for children, pausing to ask the questions on BookStix 1.3. Have children describe characters and reasons for their actions. Refer back to the Anchor Chart. Have children ask and answer who, what, and why questions about characters in *Suki's Kimono*.

Step 3 Engage and Respond

INDEPENDENT PRACTICE: Writing

- Remind children that characters do many different actions in the Read Aloud Book *Suki's Kimono*.

- Have children draw a picture of Suki doing something from the story. Then have them compete this sentence frame to tell why she did it: *Suki _____ because _____.*

- Ask partners to share and compare their responses. Encourage them to discuss how what they wrote about is similar or different.

- You may want to have children complete their writing during daily small-group time.

 LEARNING MINDSET

Seeking Challenges

Reflect Remind children that having a learning mindset means seeking challenges and trying new things. Together, page through *Suki's Kimono* and talk about which of Suki's actions show that she is not afraid to do things that are new or different.

LINK TO SMALL-GROUP INSTRUCTION

REINFORCE CHARACTERS Review or extend the skill as needed during small-group time to support children's need for differentiation. *See the lesson on p. T187.*

👥 **SMALL-GROUP INSTRUCTION**

Options for Differentiation

As the class engages in independent and collaborative work, meet with Guided Reading Groups or differentiate instruction based on student need.

GUIDED READING GROUPS

Match Children to Books + Instruction

- Choose just-right books based on level, skill, topic, or genre.

C D E F G H I J K ➡
Leveled Readers

- Deliver instruction with each book's Take and Teach Lesson, choosing appropriate sessions based on need.

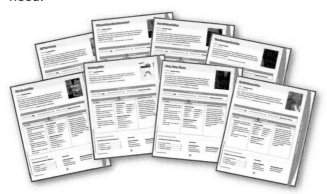

- Check comprehension, reinforce instruction, and extend learning with suggested supporting activities.

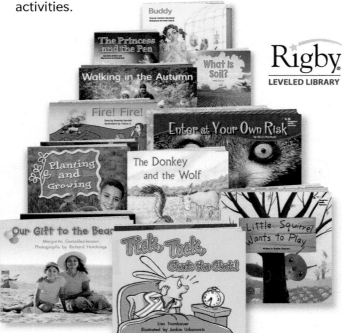

Rigby LEVELED LIBRARY

EL ENGLISH LEARNER SUPPORT

Describe

- Use **Tabletop Minilessons: English Language Development 3.1 (Listening)** to introduce and practice the language skill.

looks   feels   tastes   smells   sounds

Tabletop Minilessons: English Language Development

- Then use the following text-based prompts with *Suki's Kimono* to guide application of the language skill. Begin with the prompt at the child's identified language proficiency level. As children are able, use lighter supports to encourage increased language proficiency.

SUBSTANTIAL

Ask children simple questions to prompt them to describe what is happening on pages 6–7, such as: *Are the characters dancing? Do the characters hear music? Is it quiet or loud?*

MODERATE

Prompt children to describe what is happening on pages 6–7. Provide frames such as: *I see _____ and _____. The characters are _____. The characters hear _____.*

LIGHT

List describing words about pages 6–7 and have children use them in complete sentences to describe what is happening.

REINFORCE CHARACTERS

Demonstrate

- Use **Tabletop Minilessons: Reading 16** to remind children that they can get to know **characters** by looking for details in the pictures and text. Readers can look for information about the "outside" of characters to learn what characters look like and what they do. They can also look for details about the "inside" of characters to learn what characters think, feel, or want. Knowing how characters think or feel helps readers understand the **reasons** for their **actions**.

- Model filling out Printable: **Reading Graphic Organizer 25** to identify and describe the characters in *Suki's Kimono*.

Apply to Independent Reading

- Now have children identify and describe characters and the reasons for their actions in an appropriate just-right book that they are reading independently. Customize these prompts to the books children choose.

  » *What details tell or show what the characters are like on the outside?*

  » *What clues tell you how the characters think and feel?*

  » *Why does this character do this?*

- Have children complete Printable: **Reading Graphic Organizer 25** for their independent reading book.

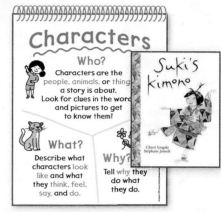

Tabletop Minilessons: Reading

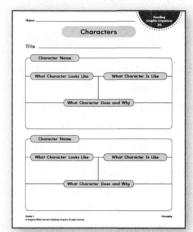

Printable:
Reading Graphic Organizer 25

ALMOST THERE

⬇

READY FOR MORE

SCAFFOLD AND EXTEND

- Have children choose a picture and describe the character(s) shown and what is happening.

- Guide children to use details from pictures and text to describe how a character's feelings are connected to the character's actions during a chosen part of the story.

- Have children describe a character based on the character's actions and the things he or she says.

🇪🇱 ENGLISH LEARNER SUPPORT

SUBSTANTIAL

Model describing a character's actions. Point to pictures and use simple descriptive words. Have children repeat after you.

MODERATE

Ask children to describe what a character is doing in a particular part of the story. Point to a picture. Ask: *What is this character doing?* Provide this frame: *This character is _____.*

LIGHT

Have children use details about the characters' thoughts or feelings to explain the characters' actions.

Options for Differentiation

Tim and Pam, Start Right Reader, *Book 1*, pp. 68–75

REINFORCE FOUNDATIONAL SKILLS

Read Decodable Text

Get Started Have children turn to Start Right Reader page 68. Explain that this week's stories are about a brother and sister, Tim and Pam, and their cat, Fin. Have children point to each character in the illustration. Then read page 68 together and discuss the question.

Preview the Story Draw attention to page 69, the title page. Read aloud the title and have children look at the pictures on the first few pages. Discuss that Tim is looking for something and have children predict what it is he wants to find.

Concepts of Print: End Punctuation Use page 69 to model identifying end punctuation. Explain that every sentence ends with a punctuation mark. Point out the end punctuation on page 69 and review what kind of sentence each mark signals. Remind children to pay attention to end punctuation as they read.

Fluency Focus: Phrasing Read aloud page 71 as children follow along. Point out that instead of reading word-by-word, like a robot, you grouped words into meaningful "chunks" and paused at end punctuation. Lead children in reading page 71 chorally with fluency and natural phrasing.

Reflect on Reading Have children read to find out what Tim is looking for, reading each page silently and then chorally. Pause for these prompts:

- **Page 69:** *What does the picture show about Tim? (Possible responses: He is a young boy; he is holding a baseball; he looks sad.) What do the words say about how Tim feels? ("Tim is sad.") What is Tim looking for? (a bat)*

- **Pages 70–71:** *Where do Tim and Pam look for the bat? (in a bin in the closet)*

- **Page 72:** *What question does the author ask? ("Is Tim sad?") What is the answer? How do you know? (No; he is smiling in the picture because he found the bat.)*

- **Pages 73–74:** *What is the "tan tip" Tim points to? (the tip of Fin's tail)*

Rhyming Word Hunt Read aloud the first numbered item on page 75. Have children look through the story and list words they find that rhyme with *cat* on a sheet of paper. Then read aloud item 2 and have children find and list words that rhyme with *pin*. Tell children to read their lists and circle the word that names a character. *(Fin)*

Tim, the bat is in it!

Is Tim sad?

72

Pam, Pam, Pam!
See the tan tip, Pam?
Is Fin in the bin?

73

Fin! It **is** Fin!
Pat Fin, Tim.
Pat Fin, Pam.

74

READ TOGETHER

Rhyming Word Hunt

1. Look in the story for words that rhyme with **cat**. Write each word you find.

2. Look in the story for words that rhyme with **pin**. Write each word you find.

3. Look at your list of words. Circle the word that names a character.

75

⏱ Make Minutes Count

As you meet with small groups to read *Tim and Pam*, use one or more of these related activities, as needed, at the beginning or the end of the small-group session.

- **Connect to Phonics** Gather Letter Cards *f, i, n, p, r, s, t*. Then divide the group into teams. Use the Letter Cards to build words such as *fit, is, pin, pit, rip, tip*. Call on children from alternating teams to blend and read a word. For each word blended correctly, the team gets one star or point.

- **Connect to Spelling** Play Tap and Clap. Display the basic and review Spelling Word cards from Printable: **Word List 3**. Point to each word and have children spell the word chorally with you, tapping the table for each consonant and softly clapping for each vowel.

- **Connect to Handwriting** Have children "air write" the letters *i, l, t*. Ask them to explain what they did to form each letter. Discuss how the formation of one letter is similar to and different from the formation of the other letters.

High-Frequency Words	Decodable High-Frequency Words	Spelling Words	
		Basic	Review
and	as	it	pan
find	if	him	an
for	in	is	nap
just	is	sip	cat
many	it	fit	
one		pin	
she			
then			
			Challenge
			rich
			spin

Printable: Word List 3

Options for Independent and Collaborative Work

While you meet with small groups, have other children engage in literacy activities that reinforce the lesson's learning objectives. Choose from these options.

Independent Reading

Student Choice Library

LEVELED LIBRARY

APPLY READING SKILL

Characters Children complete Printable: **Reading Graphic Organizer 25** for an independent reading book.

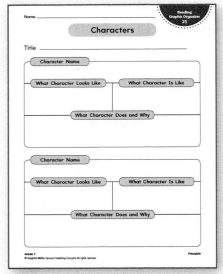

Printable: Reading Graphic Organizer 25

APPLY LANGUAGE SKILL

Describe Children complete Printable: **Language Graphic Organizer 6** for an independent reading book.

Printable: Language Graphic Organizer 6

Literacy Centers

See pp. T174–T175.

 WORD WORK

 CREATIVITY CORNER

 DIGITAL STATION

 READING CORNER

 TEAMWORK TIME

Start Right Reader

Read Decodable Text *Tim and Pam*, Book 1: pp. 68–75

Writing

Children write about what a character does and why. *See Engage & Respond, p. T185.*

Additional Skills Practice

HIGH-FREQUENCY WORDS

Know It, Show It, p. 25

SPELLING

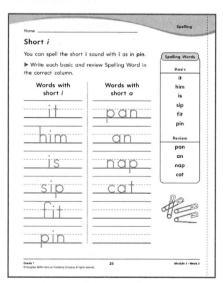

Know It, Show It, p. 26

Wrap-Up

Share Time

At the end of Reading Workshop, have children reflect on their learning by sharing how they applied **Characters** or another area of focus during independent work time. Choose from these options:

- **SHARE CHAIR** Select a reader each day to come to the front of the class and tell what he or she learned from the reading by using a skill or strategy.

- **THINK-PAIR-SHARE** Children share their thinking with a partner. Select a few children each day to share with the whole class.

- **RETURN TO ANCHOR CHART** Have children add sticky notes about their independent reading book to the Characters Anchor Chart. Call on a few children to explain what they added.

ANCHOR CHART 16: Characters

Online Ed

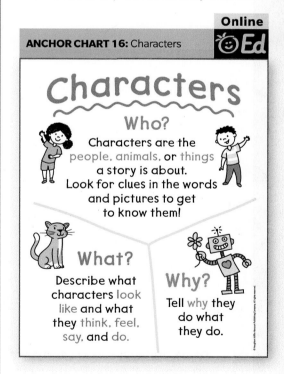

FOUNDATIONAL SKILLS

LEARNING OBJECTIVES

- Identify and read high-frequency words.
- **Language** Recognize, recite, and spell basic sight vocabulary.
- Recognize spoken alliteration.
- Segment spoken one-syllable words into individual phonemes.
- Blend phonemes to say one-syllable words.

MATERIALS   Online

Word Cards *and, as, find, for, if, in, is, it, just, many, one, she, then*

Printable *Word List 3*

Picture Cards *cup, dawn, duck, fish, gym, lamb, leash, lock, sheep*

 # High-Frequency Words

Review the Words

Repeat the **HIGH-FREQUENCY WORDS** routine to review this week's High-Frequency Words: *and, find, for, just, many, one, she,* and *then,* and the decodable High-Frequency Words *as, if, in, is,* and *it.*

Guess the Word

- Have children cut out cards for the High-Frequency Words and decodable High-Frequency Words from Printable: <u>Word List 3</u>.

- Write a dash on the board to represent each letter of one of the High-Frequency Words.

- Tell children that each dash stands for one letter of the "mystery word." Explain that they will take turns naming letters until they name all the letters and say the word.

- Have children refer to their word cards to play. Call on children to say a letter that appears in one of the words on their cards. If the letter is in the mystery word, write it on the appropriate dash.

- Continue until a child guesses the word. Have the class spell and read the word aloud as they hold up the correct word card.

- Repeat for the remaining words.

Printable: Word List 3

TEACHER TIP

Game strategy! Have children count the number of dashes for each word. Then have them find the word cards for all the words that have the same number of letters.

● Professional Learning

RESEARCH FOUNDATIONS

"If readers know words by sight and can recognize them automatically as they read text, then word reading operates unconsciously. In contrast, each of the other ways of reading words requires conscious attention. If readers attempt to decode words, to analogize, or to predict words, their attention is shifted from the text to the word itself to identify it, and this disrupts comprehension, at least momentarily."

—Dr. Linnea C. Ehri (2005)

Phonological Awareness

Alliteration; Segment Phonemes

- Tell children that you will say sets of words, and they should raise their hands if the first sound in all of the words is the same.

- Model: *Listen:* warm winter coat. Warm *and* winter *begin with* /w/. Coat *begins with* /k/. *I will not raise my hand.* Use these phrases for children to try: my marker, pink party hat, super stinky sock, tiny turtle town, eat each pear.

- Then display Picture Cards *cup, dawn, duck, fish, gym, lamb, leash, lock,* and *sheep.* Choose a card and model how to segment the picture name into phonemes. Hold onto the card and face the class.

- Have a child select a card and show it to the class. Have children say all the sounds in the word. If the card has the same initial sound as yours, have the child stand near you or go to a different part of the room if the sound is different. Continue in a similar manner for the remaining cards.

- After children segment the picture names and sort the cards, ask: *How many groups did you make? (six)* Point to each group and have the class say the beginning sound. Repeat the activity, sorting for ending sound this time.

- Say: *Now let's segment more words into their sounds. Ready?* deep (/d/ /ē/ /p/), aim (/ā/ /m/), by (/b/ /ī/), pit (/p/ /ĭ/ /t/), boss (/b/ /ŏ/ /s/), so (/s/ /ō/), type (/t/ /ī/ /p/)

Blend Phonemes

- Remind children that they know how to blend individual sounds to say words and that they will be blending phonemes to say words.

- Say: *Listen as I say each sound in a word and then blend the sounds to say the word. I will do the first one:* /v/ /ă/ /n/. *Now listen as I blend the sounds:* /v/ /ă/ /n/, van. *What word did I say? (van) That's right!*

- *Now you will blend the sounds to say each word:* /ĭ/ /f/ (if), /m/ /ŭ/ /g/ (mug), /ă/ /d/ (add), /f/ /ĭ/ /t/ (fit), /h/ /ĕ/ /n/ (hen), /j/ /ŏ/ /b/ (job), /n/ /ou/ (now), /k/ /ĭ/ /d/ (kid), /ā/ /k/ (ache), /r/ /ĕ/ /d/ (red), /g/ /ŏ/ /t/ (got). *Very good!*

 ENGLISH LEARNER SUPPORT:
Build Vocabulary

SUBSTANTIAL
Have children choose a Picture Card, say the name, and act out the word (pretend to drink from a cup, quack like a duck, and so on).

MODERATE
Provide sentence frames for children to complete with one of the Picture Card names. *A _____ can quack. I exercise in a _____.*

LIGHT
Have children silently choose a Picture Card and give clues about the word. *(It is an animal. It swims.)* Invite the group to guess the word.

✓ CORRECT & REDIRECT

To support children who blend incorrectly, model the task by saying the sounds more and more closely together, as in the example below.

- Say each sound in the word: /m/ /ŭ/ /g/. Have the child repeat. (/m/ /ŭ/ /g/)

- Repeat, each time blending the sounds a little more closely together, and then say the word: /m/, /ŭ/, /g/; /m/ /ŭ/ /g/; /m-ŭ-g/; mug.

- Ask the child to blend and say the word.

- Continue, having children blend individual sounds to say other words.

Consonants r, f, s /z/; Short i

Spotlight on Sounds

Remind children that they have been learning about the sounds for vowels and consonants. Guide children to listen for and distinguish vowel sounds in words. *Today I will say a word, and you will say the vowel sound and name the vowel.*

I will do the first one. Listen: the word is sit. Repeat, emphasizing the vowel sound: sit, /ĭ/, short i.

Now you try it. Repeat the word, say the vowel sound, and name the vowel: rap *(rap, /ă/, short a);* sat *(sat, /ă/, short a);* tip, *(tip, /ĭ/, short i);* sip, *(sip, /ĭ/, short i).*

LEARNING OBJECTIVES

- Blend, build, and decode regularly spelled one-syllable words with short *i* and consonants r, f, final s /z/.
- **Language** Recognize sound-letter relationships and use them to decode words.

MATERIALS   Online Ed

Sound/Spelling Cards *igloo, raccoon, fish, zebra*

Letter Cards *i ,d, f, r, s, t*

Display and Engage *Blend and Read 1.9*

Start Right Reader *Book 1, p. 76*

Printable *Letter Cards*

Know It, Show It *p. 27*

I Do It

Spotlight on Letters Review Sound/Spelling Cards *igloo, raccoon, fish, zebra.*

Write *rid* for children to see, and use the **SOUND-BY-SOUND BLENDING** routine below to model blending the word using Letter Cards *r, i, d.*

1 **Display** Letter Cards as shown. Say the first letter and sound.

2 **Slide** the second letter over. Say its sound. Then blend the two sounds.

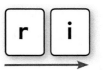

3 **Slide** the last letter over. Say its sound. Say the first two blended sounds, the last sound, and the blended word: /rĭ/ /d/, rid.

Repeat the routine with the cards for *is* and *fit.*

Professional Learning

RESEARCH FOUNDATIONS

"In addition to the role that phonological awareness plays in supporting children's ability to break the code, phonological awareness also plays an ongoing role in children's attempts to read and spell every word they encounter."

—Dr. Anne E. Cunningham and Dr. Jamie Zibulsky (2014)

See the **GPS guide** to learn more.

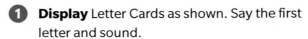 ENGLISH LEARNER SUPPORT: Build Vocabulary

SUBSTANTIAL
Act out sentence frames for children to complete with Blend and Read words: *I put the pencil _____ my desk. (in)*

MODERATE
Have partners take turns pointing to a Blend and Read word, reading it, and using it in an oral sentence.

LIGHT
Challenge children to use two Blend and Read words in a sentence.

We Do It

Blend and Read

Project Display and Engage: **Blend and Read 1.9** or use Start Right Reader page 76.

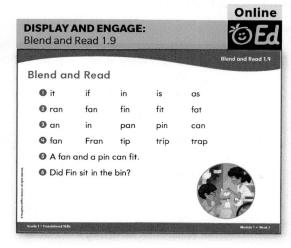

❶ **Line 1** Have children read the line. Then prompt a conversation about the words: *How are all the words alike? What is different about the words?* If necessary, lead children to compare the words (same: *have two letters; begin with a short vowel; end in one consonant;* different: *no short* i *in* as). Point to each word, and have children read the line chorally. Provide corrective feedback as needed.

❷ **Line 2** Continue with these words. Then call on volunteers to reread selected words until children can identify the words quickly.

❸ **Review** For Line 3, have children read the words chorally.

❹ **Challenge** Have children who are ready for a challenge read Line 4. Ask them to compare any two words that differ by one letter, and to demonstrate how they read words with consonant blends. Discuss word meanings with the group.

❺ **Sentences** For Lines 5–6, call on children to blend selected decodable words. Then have the group read the sentences chorally.

You Do It

INDEPENDENT PRACTICE

- **Option 1** 1 Model how to write and spell the word *fan* sound by sound. Then have children identify sounds and use Printable: **Letter Cards** to form these words: *fin, ran, pin.* Have a child spell each word aloud while others check their own work.

- **Option 2** Children complete Know It, Show It page 27.

✓ CORRECT & REDIRECT

- If a child mispronounces a word in the Blend and Read lines, say the word, call attention to the mispronounced phonic element, and help the child blend the word. Then have the child reread the whole line.

- If a child reads *is* as /ĭss/, use Sound/Spelling Card *zebra* to reinforce the /z/ sound for *s* at the end of some words. Then have the child blend and read the word again.

👥 LINK TO SMALL-GROUP INSTRUCTION

REINFORCE FOUNDATIONAL SKILLS Use *Dab, Dab, Dab!* during small-group time to review or reinforce blending and decoding words with short *i* and consonants *f, r,* and final *s* /z/. Meet with children to work through the story, or assign it as independent work. *See the lesson on p. T202.*

Dab, Dab, Dab!
by Rosa Chim
Illustrated by Nina de Polonia

See this tin can, Tim.
The rim is tan.

LEARNING OBJECTIVES

- **Language** Answer questions and discuss meanings to develop vocabulary.
- Identify real-life connections between words and their use.

MATERIALS Online

Vocabulary Cards *1.36–1.40*
Classroom materials *student artwork*

 Introduce Power Words

Use the steps **I Do It, We Do It, You Do It** with the information in the chart below to teach the Power Words from *Big Dilly's Tale*.

❶ Power Word	❷ Meaning	❸ Example
ugly (adj.) (p. 70)	If something is **ugly**, it is not nice to look at.	**ACT IT OUT** Scrunch up your face. *If I hear bad news, I might make an **ugly** face like this.*
paddled (v.) (p. 72)	If you **paddled** through water, you swam by moving your hands and feet.	**ACT IT OUT** Move your hands as if you were paddling in water. *Before I learned to swim, I kicked and **paddled** in the water.*
chilly (adj.) (p. 73)	When something is **chilly**, it is cold.	**MAKE A CONNECTION** Make a connection to the weather. *I enjoy **chilly** weather in the winter.*
beautiful (adj.)	Something that is **beautiful** is nice to look at.	**USE A PROP** Point to children's artwork displayed in your classroom. *These are a **beautiful** pieces of art.*
changed (v.)	If something **changed**, it became different from what it was.	**ACT IT OUT** Smile and then change your expression. *At first I looked happy, but I **changed** my expression. How do I feel now?*

 ENGLISH LEARNER SUPPORT:
Facilitate Language Connections

ALL LEVELS Children whose first language is Haitian Creole, Hmong, Khmer, Spanish, or Vietnamese may place adjectives in sentences after the nouns (e.g. *I saw a vase beautiful*). Adjectives commonly come after nouns in these languages. Model using the Power Words *beautiful, chilly,* and *ugly* in several sentences and have children repeat after you.

I Do It

Use the **VOCABULARY** routine and Vocabulary Cards 1.36–1.40 to introduce the Power Words from *Big Dilly's Tale*. You may wish to display the corresponding Vocabulary Card for each word as you discuss it.

Vocabulary Cards

1. **Say the Power Word.** Ask children to repeat it.

2. **Explain the meaning.** Read aloud the student-friendly meaning.

3. **Talk about examples.** Use the image or a strategy to give examples of the word.

We Do It

Guide children to make connections between each word's meaning and how they can use it in their own lives. Use these prompts. Encourage children to explain or justify their answers.

- *Tell about something **beautiful** you have seen.*
- *What do you wear in **chilly** weather?*
- *How has the weather **changed** this week?*
- *If you **paddled** in a lake, did you move or stay still? Explain.*
- *What might an **ugly** place look like?*

You Do It

INDEPENDENT PRACTICE

Have partners work together to complete each of the activities below. Circulate and observe partners as they work, providing corrective feedback as necessary.

- **Role-Play** *Show what you look like when you are **chilly**.*
- **Describe** *When have you **changed** your mind about an idea?*
- **Draw** *Draw something in nature that is **beautiful** and something in nature that is **ugly**.*
- **Discuss** *Name animals that have **paddled** in the water. What do they do?*

TEACHER TIP

Use specific words! Talk about how the word *beautiful* conveys a slightly different image than words such as *pretty* or *nice*. Give examples of when to use each word. Encourage children to use specific words as they write and speak.

READING WORKSHOP

 Ask and Answer Questions

Step **1** Connect and Teach

LEARNING OBJECTIVES

- Identify the features of fairy tales.
- Ask questions about a text before, during, and after reading.
- **Language** Ask and answer questions about key ideas in a text.
- Listen carefully and add to what others say.

MATERIALS   Online

Anchor Chart 1 *Ask and Answer Questions*
Printable *Anchor Chart 1: Ask and Answer Questions*
Teaching Pal *Book 1, pp. 68–79*
myBook *Big Dilly's Tale, Book 1, pp. 68–79*

📖 READER'S VOCABULARY

- **evidence** clues or details in the text that support an answer or idea
- **detail** small bit of information that supports a central idea or describes something in a text

- Remind children that good readers "stay awake" and think about what they are reading. Explain that one way of showing that you are "awake" and thinking is by asking questions about what you are reading.

- Project or display **Anchor Chart 1: Ask and Answer Questions**.

- As you point to the *when* and *why* parts of the Anchor Chart, explain that readers ask questions before, during, and after reading to get information and to help them understand a text. Explain that they ask questions by putting into words the things they wonder about or are curious about.

- As you point to the *how* part of the chart, explain that starting questions with the words *who, what, where, why, when,* or *how* can help readers ask different kinds of questions and get different kinds of information.

- Finally, tell children that readers use **evidence** and **details** in the text to help them answer questions about what they read.

- Tell children they will practice asking and answering questions when they read a fairy tale called *Big Dilly's Tale.*

Online

ANCHOR CHART 1: Ask and Answer Questions

Ask and Answer Questions

When?
- Before reading
- During reading
- After reading

Why?
- To get information
- To help you understand the text
- To practice being "awake" and thinking while reading
- To be curious and wonder as you read

How?
Use question words to **ASK:**
who   what   where
why   when   how
→ Look around in the text and pictures for evidence, or details, to help you **ANSWER**.

Notice & **Note**

Contrasts and Contradictions

- The Teaching Pal prompts in this lesson feature the **Notice & Note signpost: Contrasts and Contradictions**.
- As needed, refer to p. T19 to review the signpost with children.

 ASSESSMENT OPTION

Assign the **Selection Quiz** to check comprehension of *Big Dilly's Tale.*

Step 2 Apply to Text

 In your Teaching Pal, pages 68–79, use the blue **READ FOR UNDERSTANDING** prompts to read *Big Dilly's Tale* with children as they follow along and annotate in their *my*Book.

- **Genre Study** Read the genre information on page 68. Discuss the things children would expect to find in a fairy tale and compare them with a realistic fiction story like *Suki's Kimono*.

- **Set a Purpose** Read the Set a Purpose section on page 68. Prompt children to set their own purpose for reading *Big Dilly's Tale*.

- **Meet the Author** Play the audio about Gail Carson Levine. Help children describe what they learned about her and how she is similar to or different from other authors they have learned about.

- **Read and Comprehend** Guide children to read the selection all the way through. Pause occasionally, using the prompts in your Teaching Pal to gauge children's understanding and to have them ask and answer questions about the story. Have them refer back to the Anchor Chart for question words they can use.

Step 3 Engage and Respond

INDEPENDENT PRACTICE: Speaking & Listening

- Use the **TURN AND TALK** routine with the questions on Teaching Pal and *my*Book page 79. Remind children to use the questions words *who, what, where, when, why,* or *how*.

- Read the Talking Tip. Remind children to follow rules for discussion and listen carefully to their partners. Have children use the sentence frame to help them add to their partners' ideas.

- You may want to have children conduct their discussions during daily small-group time.

 ENGLISH LEARNER SUPPORT: Facilitate Discussion

SUBSTANTIAL
Have children point to the parts of the story they have questions about. Encourage them to use a question word—*who, what, when, where, why,* or *how*—about the page.

MODERATE
Model how to begin a question with *who, what, when, where, why,* or *how*. Then have children ask a question.

LIGHT
Have children ask questions using complete sentences.

LINK TO SMALL-GROUP INSTRUCTION

REINFORCE ASK AND ANSWER QUESTIONS Review or extend the skill as needed during small-group time to support children's need for differentiation. *See the lesson on p. T201.*

LESSON 12

READING WORKSHOP

Options for Differentiation

As the class engages in independent and collaborative work, meet with Guided Reading Groups or differentiate instruction based on student need.

GUIDED READING GROUPS

Match Children to Books + Instruction

- Choose just-right books based on level, skill, topic, or genre.

C D E F G H J K

Leveled Readers

- Deliver instruction with each book's Take and Teach Lesson, choosing appropriate sessions based on need.

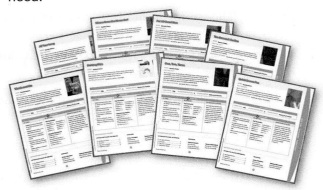

- Check comprehension, reinforce instruction, and extend learning with suggested supporting activities.

Rigby® LEVELED LIBRARY

Buddy
The Princess and the Pen
What Is Soil?
Walking in the Autumn
Fire! Fire!
Enter at Your Own Risk
Planting and Growing
The Donkey and the Wolf
Our Gift to the Bear
Tick, Tock, Check the Clock!
Little Squirrel Wants to Play

EL ENGLISH LEARNER SUPPORT

Describe

- Use **Tabletop Minilessons: English Language Development 3.1 (Speaking)** to reinforce and practice the language skill.

Tabletop Minilessons: English Language Development

- Then use the following text-based prompts *with Big Dilly's Tale* to guide application of the language skill. Begin with the prompt at the child's identified language proficiency level. As children are able, use lighter supports to encourage increased language proficiency.

SUBSTANTIAL
Display page 70. Prompt children to describe where the characters are. Repeat with page 72.

MODERATE
Show children pages 70 and 72. Ask them simple questions to prompt them to describe the setting. Allow them to use phrases or simple sentences.

LIGHT
Ask children to say a sentence to describe the place shown on page 70. Repeat with page 72.

REINFORCE ASK AND ANSWER QUESTIONS

Demonstrate

- Use **Tabletop Minilessons: Reading 1** to remind children to ask and answer questions before, during, and after reading, and to look for clues that can help answer those questions. Readers can "have a conversation" with a book by asking *who, what, where, when, why,* and *how* questions. They can look for details in the text and pictures to help answer those questions.

- Model filling out Printable: <u>**Reading Graphic Organizer 1**</u> to ask and answer questions about *Big Dilly's Tale.*

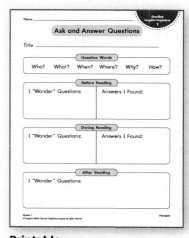

Tabletop Minilessons: Reading

Apply to Independent Reading

- Now have children ask and answer questions about an appropriate just-right book that they are reading independently. Customize these prompts to the books children choose.

  » *Look at the cover and the pictures inside. What questions can you ask about the book before you start reading it?*

  » *Read a few pages. What questions can you ask? Reread the pages to find answers to your questions.*

  » *Finish reading your book. What questions can you ask now? How can you answer your questions?*

- Have children complete Printable: <u>**Reading Graphic Organizer 1**</u> for their independent reading book.

Printable:
Reading Graphic Organizer 1

ALMOST THERE ↓ **READY FOR MORE**

SCAFFOLD AND EXTEND

- Have children stop after reading each page and ask themselves *What just happened?* Have children answer the question before they keep reading.

- Have children ask and answer one question before reading, one during reading, and one after reading.

- Have children work with a partner to ask and answer questions about how things in the story change or how they are connected.

 ENGLISH LEARNER SUPPORT

SUBSTANTIAL

Ask questions such as *What do you think this book is about?* Provide the sentence frame: *I think this book is about _____.*

MODERATE

Have children ask a *why* question about the picture on each page. For example: *Why does the character look [happy, sad, confused] in the picture?* Have children answer the questions.

LIGHT

Ask children to formulate *what* and *why* questions as they read using details from pictures and text.

Options for Differentiation

Dab, Dab, Dab!, *Start Right Reader, Book 1*, pp. 76–83

REINFORCE FOUNDATIONAL SKILLS

Read Decodable Text

Blend and Read Have children turn to Start Right Reader page 76. Use the **CHORAL READING** routine to read aloud the Blend and Read lines. Use challenge line 4 with children who are ready.

Preview the Story Call attention to page 77. Read aloud the title and have children identify the characters in the picture as Tim, Pam, and Fin from *Tim and Pam*. Then have children look at the pictures on the first few pages and predict what Tim and Pam will do in this story.

Fluency Focus: Phrasing Read aloud page 77 as children follow along. Point out that you read "See this tin can" as a group before pausing briefly at the comma. Lead children in reading the page chorally. Remind them to match your phrasing and pause at commas and end punctuation.

Reflect on Reading Have children use a finger to track the words from left to right as they read each page silently. Then have them read the page chorally. Pause for these prompts:

• **Page 78:** *What is in the tin cans? (paint)*

• **Page 79:** *What does Pam want Tim to do? (dip the tip of his paintbrush into the paint and then dab it onto the paper to paint) Is this what you predicted they would do? Explain. (Responses will vary.)*

• **Page 81:** *Who is the picture for? (Dad)*

• **Page 82:** *What happens to the picture? (It rips.) How do Pam and Tim feel about what happens? (Pam is sad and Tim is mad.)*

Story Word Clues Read aloud the directions on page 83. Then have children read the clues and find the word in the story that fits each clue. *(can; rip)*

Dab it, Tim!
Dab it, Pam!

This is for Dad.

Rip! Rip!
Pam is sad.
Tim is mad.

READ TOGETHER

Story Word Clues

Find the word in the story that answers each clue below.

1. This holds paint. It is made of tin. What is the word?

2. This word tells what happens to Pam and Tim's painting. What is it?

80   81   82   83

(?) Make Minutes Count

As you meet with small groups to read *Dab, Dab, Dab!*, use one or more of these related activities, as needed, at the beginning or the end of the small-group session.

- **Connect to Phonics** Play Letter Swap. Gather multiple Letter Cards for *f, i, m, n, p, r, s, t*. Have partners take turns building words that have short *i*. One partner builds a word. Then the other partner replaces one consonant with a different consonant to build a new word. Have partners write the words they build and read the list to the group.

- **Connect to Spelling** Play Robot. Write the Spelling Words on the board or on chart paper. Then call on volunteers to demonstrate a "robot" voice and body movements. Point to a Spelling Word and have children quietly spell the word with you, chanting each letter in a robotic voice and moving like a robot. Repeat for all of the week's words.

- **Connect to Handwriting** Draw a triple-track line on the board, and write these words on the track: *dip, lip, tip*. Read each word and have children repeat after you. Then have children point out which letters touch all three lines and which touch only the middle and bottom lines. Have children write each word two times. Check children's pencil grip and paper position, correcting as needed. Have them self-assess their letter formation and place a star next to the words that best match the models.

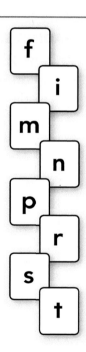

Options for Independent and Collaborative Work

While you meet with small groups, have other children engage in literacy activities that reinforce the lesson's learning objectives. Choose from these options.

Independent Reading

Student Choice Library

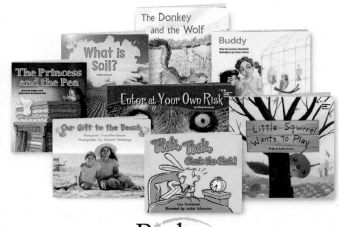

Rigby® LEVELED LIBRARY

APPLY READING SKILL

Ask and Answer Questions Children complete Printable: **Reading Graphic Organizer 1** for an independent reading book.

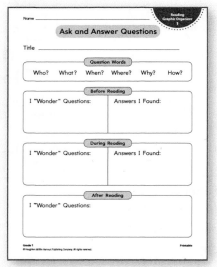

Printable: Reading Graphic Organizer 1

APPLY LANGUAGE SKILL

Describe Children complete Printable: **Language Graphic Organizer 6** for an independent reading book.

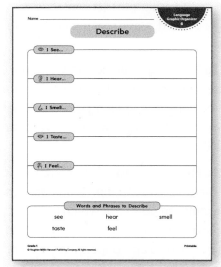

Printable: Language Graphic Organizer 6

Notice ⓼ Note

Contrasts and Contradictions

When children encounter this signpost in their independent reading, encourage them to ask the Anchor Question: *Why would the character act (feel) this way?*

Literacy Centers

See pp. T174–T175.

 WORD WORK

 CREATIVITY CORNER

 DIGITAL STATION

 READING CORNER

 TEAMWORK TIME

Start Right Reader

Read Decodable Text *Dab, Dab, Dab!*, Book 1: pp. 76–83

Speaking & Listening

Partners discuss the Turn and Talk questions using a sentence frame and question words to help them add to their ideas. *See Engage & Respond, p. T199.*

Additional Skills Practice

PHONICS

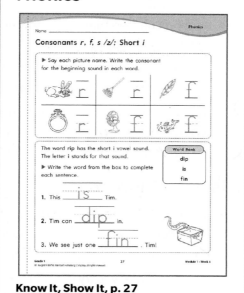

Know It, Show It, p. 27

Wrap-Up
Share Time

At the end of Reading Workshop, have children reflect on their learning by sharing how they applied **Ask and Answer Questions** or another area of focus during independent work time. Choose from these options:

- **SHARE CHAIR** Select a reader each day to come to the front of the class and tell what he or she learned from the reading by using a skill or strategy.

- **THINK-PAIR-SHARE** Children share their thinking with a partner. Select a few children each day to share with the whole class.

- **RETURN TO ANCHOR CHART** Have children add sticky notes about their independent reading book to the Ask and Answer Questions Anchor Chart. Call on a few children to explain what they added.

ANCHOR CHART 1: Ask and Answer Questions

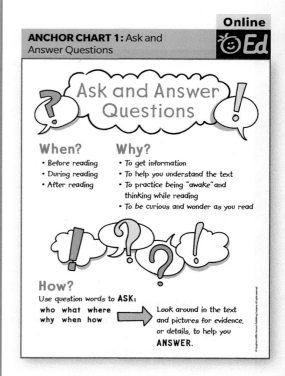

LEARNING OBJECTIVES

- Identify and read high-frequency words.
- **Language** Recognize and recite basic sight vocabulary.
- Segment spoken one-syllable words into individual phonemes.
- Isolate medial vowel sounds in spoken one-syllable words.

MATERIALS   Online

Word Cards *and, as, find, for, if, in, is, it, just, many, one, she, then*

 # High-Frequency Words

Review the Words

Repeat the **HIGH-FREQUENCY WORDS** routine to review this week's High-Frequency Words: *and, find, for, just, many, one, she,* and *then* and the decodable High-Frequency Words *as, if, in, is,* and *it*.

> if

I Spy

- Have children close their eyes as you place a Word Card somewhere in the room.
- Tell children to open their eyes and raise a hand when they see the Word Card.
- When most children have raised their hands, call on a child to read the word.

 # Phonological Awareness

Segment Phonemes

- Remind children that they know how to break words into individual sounds. Say: *First, I will say a word, and you will say the sounds in the word.*
- Model: *Listen as I do the first one:* my. *I hear /m/ at the beginning of* my. My, */m/ /ī/. The sounds in* my *are /m/ and /ī/.*
- *Now you try it! Listen to the word. Then say each sound:* it (/ĭ/ /t/), at (/ă/ /t/), on (/ŏ/ /n/), pan (/p/ /ă/ /n/), fit (/f/ /ĭ/ /t/), gem (/j/ /ĕ/ /m/), jug (/j/ /ŭ/ /g/), tape (/t/ /ā/ /p/), home (/h/ /ō/ /m/).

Isolate Phonemes: Identify Vowel

- Say: *Now I will say more words. This time, I want you tell me the sound you hear in the middle of each word. Let me do the first one.* Cap. *I hear /ă/ in the middle of* cap. *The middle sound in* cap *is /ă/.* Cap, /ăăă/.
- *Is everyone ready to try it? Listen to the word. What is the middle sound?* ran (/ă/), bad (/ă/), hip (/ĭ/), did (/ĭ/), tab (/ă/), rip (/ĭ/), sack (/ă/)

TEACHER TIP

Extra practice! Have children segment phonemes as part of your daily classroom routines. For example, call on children individually to say all the sounds in their names before lining up to leave the classroom.

 CORRECT & REDIRECT

If children have trouble identifying the middle sound in words, first segment the phonemes. Then emphasize and elongate the middle sound in the word. Example:

- *First, let's break the word into all of its sounds. Listen for the sounds:* ran, /r/ /ă/ /n/. *Say the sounds with me:* /r/ /ă/ /n/.
- *Now let's listen for just the middle sound:* /r/ /ăăă/ /n/. *What is the middle sound in* ran? (/ă/)

🕐 Phrasing

I Do It

- Explain that good readers pay attention to punctuation when they read. Tell children that punctuation can help them read more naturally and that pausing at periods and commas can help readers and listeners better understand what the author wrote.

Dab, Dab, Dab!
by Rosa Dunn
illustrated by Nina de Polonia

See this tin can, Tim.
The rim is tan.

77

- Have children look at the text on page 77 of the Start Right Reader (*Dab, Dab, Dab!*). Read the sentences, modeling how to pause as you read. Point to the comma and the period in the first sentence, tell children the name of each mark, and have them repeat. Explain that periods show where a sentence ends, so it helps to stop for a moment at every period. Commas show sentence parts, so it helps to pause at commas, too.

- Read the two sentences, running all the words together and not pausing between words. Point out that the sentences sounded better when you paused at the punctuation marks because it sounded more like speaking.

We Do It

- Ask children to follow along as you read aloud page 78 as a guide to appropriate phrasing. Read the two sentences as you point to and pause at the periods. Use the **ECHO READING** routine to have children follow your model to reread the sentences.

- Repeat with page 79, as children point to the period in each sentence.

You Do It

INDEPENDENT PRACTICE

- Have children use the **PARTNER READING** routine with one of the stories from this week's Start Right Reader selections or *Big Dilly's Tale* from their *my*Book. Circulate to coach children to read smoothly and accurately, paying attention to punctuation.

LEARNING OBJECTIVE

- Read aloud fluently and with appropriate phrasing (prosody).

MATERIALS   Online 🖲 **Ed**

Start Right Reader *Book 1, pp. 77–82*

 LEARNING MINDSET

Seeking Challenges

Reflect As children participate in partner reading, ask them to think about any challenges they may have had reading fluently. *Learning to read fluently can be a challenge. It may seem tricky to pay attention to the words and the punctuation, but if you keep trying, you will get better.*

Getting Started

ENGAGEMENT ROUTINE

Use the **PARTNER READING** routine when the text is familiar, such as decodable texts that have been read before. This allows the teacher to walk around and listen to readers and provide guidance when necessary.

See the **GPS guide** to learn more.

Inflection -s

Spotlight on Sounds

- Tell children that they will be reading words that name one item and words that mean more than one item. Explain that first, they will listen for the ending sound in words you say. *I am going to say two words. You will say the words and the sound you hear at the end of each one.*

- *I will do the first one. Listen:* cat, cats. Repeat the words, emphasizing the ending sounds. *I hear these ending sounds:* cat, */t/;* cats, */s/.*

- *Now you try it. Repeat these words and say the ending sound:* hat, hats (hat, */t/;* hats */s/);* web, webs (web, */b/;* webs, */z/);* car, cars (car, */r/;* cars, */z/);* rock, rocks (rock, */k/;* rocks, */s/);* dog, dogs (dog, */g/;* dogs, */z/).*

▌Do It

Spotlight on Letters Display the Sound/Spelling Card for /s/: *seahorse.* Name the picture and identify the sound. *Seahorse begins with the /s/ sound. The letter s is also an ending. Let's see what happens when we add the ending -s to words.*

Write *cat.* Read the word, and tell its meaning. *The word* cat *names one cat.*

Then write *cats.* Read the word, and circle the *-s* ending. *When I add the ending -s to* cat, *I change its meaning. The word* cats *means more than one cat.*

Repeat for Sound/Spelling Card *zebra* and the words *pan, pans.* Explain that the *-s* ending can also stand for the /z/ sound at the end of a word.

LEARNING OBJECTIVES

- **Language** Recognize inflection *-s* and use it to decode words.
- Blend and decode regularly spelled one-syllable words with inflection *-s.*

MATERIALS Online

Sound/Spelling Cards *seahorse, zebra*
Letter Cards *a, b, f, i, r, s, n, t,*

TEACHER TIP

The why of it! The consonant before *-s* dictates the inflection's pronunciation. Voiced consonants, which cause the vocal cords to vibrate, produce the voiced /z/ sound for the ending *-s.* They include *b, d, g, l, r, m, n, v, w, y.* Unvoiced consonants produce an unvoiced /s/ sound for the ending.

 ENGLISH LEARNER SUPPORT:
Facilitate Language Connections

ALL LEVELS In languages such as Cantonese, Haitian Creole, Hmong, Khmer, Korean, Tagalog, and Vietnamese, nouns do not change form to show the plural. English learners may need additional practice adding the inflection *-s* to mean more than one. Use classroom objects to reinforce meaning and to reinforce the sounds for *-s: one book, two books /s/; one pen, two pens /z/.*

We Do It

Write *fins* and use Letter Cards *f, i, n, s* with the **SOUND-BY-SOUND BLENDING** routine below to model blending the word.

1 **Display** cards as shown. Say the first letter and sound.

2 **Slide** the second letter over. Say its sound. Then blend the two sounds: /fĭ/. Continue with the third letter: /fĭ/ /n/, fin.

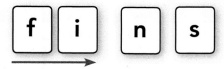

3 **Slide** the last letter over. The last letter over. Say its sound. Say the first three blended sounds, the last sound, and the blended word: /fĭn/ /z/, fins.

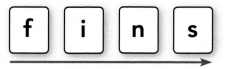

Sound-by-Sound Blending Repeat the **SOUND-BY-SOUND BLENDING** routine with cards for the words *bats* and *fans,* having children say the sounds and blend.

You Do It

INDEPENDENT PRACTICE

Blending Practice Write the words below. Then choose a volunteer to model the activity. Explain that you will point to a word pair, and the child will read it aloud and tell which word names more than one. Repeat the blending routine as needed. Continue, pointing to word pairs in random order, until each child has had a turn.

rib ribs	pin pins	cans can
pits pit	tins tin	pad pads

✓ CORRECT & REDIRECT

- If a child mispronounces a word during Blending Practice, make note of the error type and address it.
- If a child reads *ribs* as *rib*, say the word correctly. Point to the *-s* ending: *This word has the -s ending. Blend the word again and add the -s ending.* Have the child blend and read the word. Ask how the *-s* ending changes the word *rib*. *(It means more than one rib.)*

👥 LINK TO SMALL-GROUP INSTRUCTION

REINFORCE FOUNDATIONAL SKILLS Use *Tin Cans Tip!* during small-group time to review or reinforce blending and decoding words with short *i*, consonants *r, f, s* /z/, and inflection *-s*. Meet with children to work through the story, or assign it as independent work. *See the lesson on p. T216.*

Tin Cans Tip!
Pam finds a mat.
Can it fit?

Review Power Words

Revisit the Power Words

- Revisit the Power Words from *Big Dilly's Tale*. Display the questions and sentence frames below word by word.

- Model the task for the first word, using a child as your partner. Read aloud the question, and have the child repeat it. Respond using the sentence frame.

- Have partners use the **TURN AND TALK** routine to respond to each question using the sentence frame.

- For each word, ask one or two children to share their responses with the class. Then have them discuss the next question.

LEARNING OBJECTIVES

- **Language** Respond to questions using multi-word responses.
- Use newly acquired vocabulary to identify real-life connections between words and their use.

MATERIALS   Online

Know It, Show It *p. 29*

Power Word	Question	Sentence Frame
ugly	What **ugly** thing might you see in the trash?	*I might see an **ugly** _____ in the trash.*
paddled	Where have you **paddled** in water?	*I have **paddled** _____.*
chilly	What months usually have **chilly** weather?	*The weather is usually **chilly** during the months of _____.*
beautiful	What do you see in our classroom that is **beautiful**?	*I see a **beautiful** _____.*
changed	How have you **changed** since school started?	*I have **changed** _____.*

 ENGLISH LEARNER SUPPORT:
Build Vocabulary

SUBSTANTIAL
Ask: *When you are **chilly**, are you cold or hot? If you **paddled**, are you in water or on land?*

MODERATE
Supply frames such these: *We _____ in water. The _____ is **beautiful**.*

LIGHT
Point out that *beautiful* and *ugly* are opposites. Ask children to say the opposite of *chilly*.

Vocabulary Guess

- Display the Power Words. Have children break into small groups.

- One child in each group gives clues about a Power Word without saying the word itself. These children are encouraged to say words that have similar or opposite meanings, provide examples, or describe times they used or might use the Power Word.

- For example, for the Power Word *chilly*, children can say, "It means when the weather is cold," or "This word is the opposite of *warm*."

- The rest of the group guesses the word. If necessary, children may ask the speaker questions to get clarification about the word or what he/she is saying.

- Have children continue the activity until all the words have been guessed.

- For additional practice with the Power Words from *Big Dilly's Tale*, have children complete Know It, Show It page 29.

LEARNING MINDSET

Seeking Challenges

Reflect Encourage children to reflect on connections between learning and seeking challenges. *When you think of learning new words as a challenge, does it help you try to do your best? When you face a challenge, you want to try hard because you are learning something new. Every time you challenge yourself to try something new, your brain grows!*

LESSON 13

READING WORKSHOP

🕐 # Characters

Step 1 Connect and Teach

LEARNING OBJECTIVES

- Describe characters and the reasons for their actions.
- **Language** Explain the reasons for a character's actions.
- Write a description of a character, using evidence to support ideas.

MATERIALS Online 💿Ed

Anchor Chart 16
Characters

Printable *Anchor Chart 16: Characters*

Teaching Pal *Book 1, pp. 68–81*

myBook *Big Dilly's Tale, Book 1, pp. 68–81*

Know It, Show It *p. 30*

📖 READER'S VOCABULARY

- **character** a person or animal in a story
- **reason** why or how something happened
- **action** what someone or something does

- Remind children that the **characters** in a story are whom the story is about.

- Project or display <u>Anchor Chart 16: Characters</u>.

- As you point to the corresponding parts of the Anchor Chart, tell children that readers can "get to know" characters by looking for clues and paying attention to details in the words and pictures.

- Remind children that details can tell what the characters are like on the outside, or what they look like. They can also tell what they are like on the inside, or what they think or feel.

- Explain that understanding what a character is like can help readers describe the **reasons** for the characters' **actions**, or why they do what they do.

- Tell children they will reread parts of *Big Dilly's Tale* to practice describing characters and the reasons for their actions.

Online
💿Ed
ANCHOR CHART 16: Characters

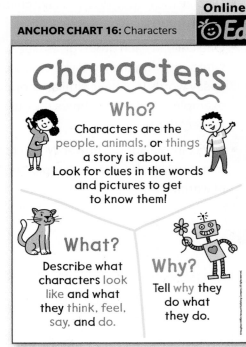

TEACHER TIP

Don't wear words out! Explain that words like *nice* are often overused when describing characters. Challenge children to describe characters using words that are more informative, such as *friendly, caring, polite, kind, fair,* or *helpful.*

⚙️ LEARNING MINDSET

Seeking Challenges

Normalize Writing can be frustrating! During work on Step 3, explain how children can get unstuck by talking through ideas and by viewing it as a challenge they can solve. *Sometimes writers get stuck, but they can look for ways to get unstuck. One way you can get unstuck is to explain to a friend or a favorite toy what it is that you want to say. What are other ways you could get unstuck on writing?*

Go to Your Teaching Pal

Once upon a time, Dilly was a
BIG duckling with a BIG beak.
A duck called him ugly.

His friend Minna called him cute.
Dilly splashed. Splat!

Honk! Ha!

Quack! Ha!

70 · 71

ANNOTATE IT!

Online Ed

Children may use the annotation tools in their eBook.

Step 2 | Apply to Text

 In your Teaching Pal, use the purple **TARGETED CLOSE READ** prompts to guide children to apply the describing characters skill to *Big Dilly's Tale*. Children may refer to the questions on Know It, Show It page 30 as you discuss them.

- Read aloud the first question on Teaching Pal page 70 and have children use details in the text and pictures to tell who the characters are. *(two friends, Dilly and Minna)*

- Then read the follow-up question. Tell children to look for evidence in the text and pictures that tells about the characters. *(Dilly looks different from Minna and the other ducks; Dilly and Minna like to have fun together.)*

- Read aloud the questions on Teaching Pal page 76. Tell children to use clues from the words and pictures to make an inference. *(because she is his friend; the words say that Minna thinks Dilly is cute; the pictures show that Dilly and Minna like spending time together)*

- Refer back to the Anchor Chart to support the discussion. Children may add sticky notes to the chart to describe the characters and the reasons for their actions.

Step 3 | Engage and Respond

INDEPENDENT PRACTICE: Writing

- Read aloud the prompt on Teaching Pal page 80. Have children use the planning space to record how Dilly looks, sounds, and acts. Then have them write their descriptions.

- Then have children write their responses to the prompt. Remind children to refer back to *Big Dilly's Tale* and use the words and pictures from the story for ideas.

- You may want to have children complete their writing during daily small-group time.

EL ENGLISH LEARNER SUPPORT: Scaffold Writing

SUBSTANTIAL
List and explain words that could describe Dilly, for example, *gray, different, playful, brave, loyal*. Have children choose and write a word, then find the part of the text that it goes with.

MODERATE
Provide sentence frames: *I know Dilly is _____ because he _____. He also _____.*

LIGHT
Have partners discuss and list describing words before beginning writing.

👥 LINK TO SMALL-GROUP INSTRUCTION

REINFORCE CHARACTERS Review or extend the skill as needed during small-group time to support children's need for differentiation. *See the lesson on p. T215.*

SMALL-GROUP INSTRUCTION

Options for Differentiation

As the class engages in independent and collaborative work, meet with Guided Reading Groups or differentiate instruction based on student need.

GUIDED READING GROUPS

Match Children to Books + Instruction

- Choose just-right books based on level, skill, topic, or genre.

C D E F G H I J K

Leveled Readers

- Deliver instruction with each book's Take and Teach Lesson, choosing appropriate sessions based on need.

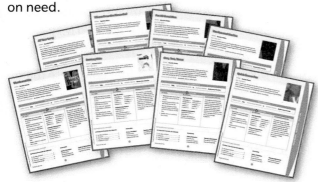

- Check comprehension, reinforce instruction, and extend learning with suggested supporting activities.

Rigby®
LEVELED LIBRARY

(EL) ENGLISH LEARNER SUPPORT

Describe

- Use **Tabletop Minilessons: English Language Development 3.2 (Reading)** to reinforce and practice the language skill.

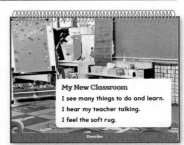

Tabletop Minilessons: English Language Development

- Then use the following text-based prompts with *Big Dilly's Tale* to guide application of the language skill. Begin with the prompt at the child's identified language proficiency level. As children are able, use lighter supports to encourage increased language proficiency.

SUBSTANTIAL
Prompt children to look at p. 70 of *Big Dilly's Tale*. Ask: *What word is used to describe Dilly?* Allow children to point to the word or answer aloud. Then ask: *What color is Dilly?* Provide children with the word *gray* if needed.

MODERATE
Ask children to describe the size of Dilly compared to the other ducks. Ask: *Is Dilly the smallest or the biggest animal?* Allow children to respond and have them point to the words in the text that help them decide.

LIGHT
Ask children to describe Dilly and the other characters in the story by using words such as *smaller/smallest*, *darker/darkest*, and so on. If needed, correct and model the correct form of words used to describe characters.

REINFORCE CHARACTERS

Demonstrate

- Use **Tabletop Minilessons: Reading 16** to remind children that details in the text and pictures help readers understand what the **characters** are like on the outside and on the inside. Thinking about these details helps readers understand what characters do and why.

- Model filling out Printable: **Reading Graphic Organizer 25** to identify and describe the characters and the reasons for their actions in *Big Dilly's Tale*.

Apply to Independent Reading

- Now have children identify and describe characters and the reasons for their actions in an appropriate just-right book that they are reading independently. Customize these prompts to the books children choose.

  » *Who are the characters?*

  » *How can you describe the outside of this character—how the character looks?*

  » *How can you describe the inside of this character—how the character thinks and feels?*

  » *Can you explain the reason for this character's actions?*

- Have children complete Printable: **Reading Graphic Organizer 25** for their independent reading book.

Tabletop Minilessons: Reading 16

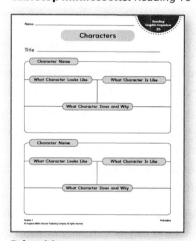

Printable:
Reading Graphic Organizer 25

ALMOST THERE

READY FOR MORE

SCAFFOLD AND EXTEND

- Have children describe what the characters are like on the outside and why they do what they do.

- Have children describe what one of the characters does at the beginning, middle, and end. Then have them tell why the character does what it does.

- Have children use details from the text and pictures to describe how the characters change, and give reasons for their actions.

ENGLISH LEARNER SUPPORT

SUBSTANTIAL

Point to a picture and tell what a character is doing with a simple sentence: *This character is _____.* Have students repeat your description as they point to the picture.

MODERATE

Have children describe characters' actions based on the pictures and identify words that connect to the actions.

LIGHT

Ask children to describe what characters do and why they do what they do.

LESSON 13

READING WORKSHOP

Options for Differentiation

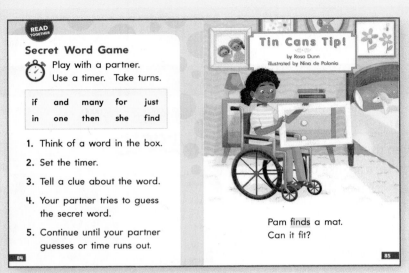

Tin Cans Tip!, *Start Right Reader, Book 1,* pp. 84–91

REINFORCE FOUNDATIONAL SKILLS

Read Decodable Text

Secret Word Game: High-Frequency Word Review Have children turn to Start Right Reader page 84. Have partners read the boxed words. Then have one partner think of a word in the box, set the timer, and give clues about the word until the other partner guesses the word or time runs out. Then have partners switch roles.

Preview the Story Call attention to page 85. Read aloud the title and have children look at the pictures on the first few pages. Remind them that in *Dab, Dab, Dab!*, Tim and Pam's picture ripped. Have children predict what might happen in this story.

Concepts of Print: End Punctuation As they read, periodically prompt: *Point to the end punctuation. What is this punctuation mark? What kind of sentence does it signal?*

Fluency Focus: Phrasing Read aloud page 87 as children follow along. Remind them that they should "chunk" words and phrases naturally and pause at punctuation marks. Help children read the page chorally with natural phrasing.

Reflect on Reading Have children read each page silently and then chorally. Pause for these prompts:

- **Page 85:** *What is Pam holding? (a mat) What do you think she will use the mat for? (Possible response: as a frame for a picture)*

- **Page 86:** *How does Pam fix the picture? (She tapes over the rip and pins the picture into the mat.)*

- **Pages 88–89:** *What happens when Pam tips one tin can? (Many cans tip and paint spills out. Some paint drips down onto Fin.)*

- **Page 90:** *Why does Pam say "Nab Fin, Tim!"? (She wants Tim to chase after Fin and catch him.) What do you think Pam and Tim will do next? (Possible response: clean Fin to get the paint off his fur)*

Cause and Effect Have children explain what happens in the pictures on page 91 and why it happens. Then have them draw a picture of what happens next and write why it happens. Have partners share their work and discuss how one thing leads to another.

Pam did it.
Then she tips one tin can.

88

Many tin cans tip.
Bam! Bam! Bam! Bam!

89

Fin ran!
Tim ran!
Nab Fin, Tim!

90

READ TOGETHER

Cause and Effect

1. Look at the pictures. Tell what happens and why. How does one thing lead to another?

2. Draw a picture of what happens next. Write why it happens.

3. Share your picture and writing. Talk about how one thing leads to another.

91

⏱ Make Minutes Count

As you meet with small groups to read *Tin Cans Tip!*, use one or more of these related activities, as needed, at the beginning or the end of the small-group session.

- **Connect to Phonics** Write these word pairs on separate index cards: *can, cans; cat, cats; fan, fans; pin, pins; tip, tips.* Hand each child one of the word pair cards. Have the child with the word pair *cat, cats* read aloud the words. Ask: *What is the difference between the two words? How does that difference change the meaning of the words?* (cats *ends with* -s; *it means more than one cat*) Repeat the process for each word pair.

- **Connect to Spelling** Play What Am I Thinking? Write the basic Spelling Words on the board. On a sheet of paper, have children write the numbers 1–6, with each number on a separate line. Then give a clue about a Spelling Word. For example: *Number 1: I am thinking of a word that names what you do when you tear paper.* (rip) Children choose the Spelling Word that correctly answers the clue and write it next to the number 1. Continue for the other Spelling Words. After all the clues have been given, review the answers and have children check their spelling.

- **Connect to High-Frequency Words** Play Fill in the Blank. Display these High-Frequency Word cards from Printable: **Word List 3**: *and, find, for, many, one, then.* Dictate a sentence for each word, replacing the High-Frequency Word with the word *blank*. Have children name the High-Frequency Word that completes the sentence and point to the corresponding card.

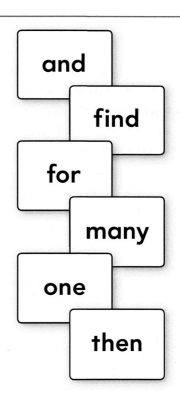

and

find

for

many

one

then

LESSON 13

READING WORKSHOP

Options for Independent and Collaborative Work

While you meet with small groups, have other children engage in literacy activities that reinforce the lesson's learning objectives. Choose from these options.

Independent Reading

Student Choice Library

LEVELED LIBRARY

APPLY READING SKILL

Characters Children complete Printable: <u>Reading Graphic Organizer 25</u> for an independent reading book.

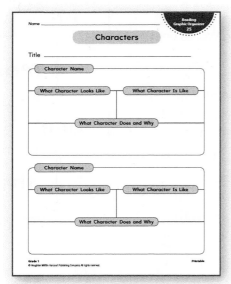

Printable: Reading Graphic Organizer 25

APPLY LANGUAGE SKILL

Describe Children complete Printable: <u>Language Graphic Organizer 6</u> for an independent reading book.

Printable: Language Graphic Organizer 6

Literacy Centers

See pp. T174–T175.

 WORD WORK

 CREATIVITY CORNER

 DIGITAL STATION

 READING CORNER

 TEAMWORK TIME

Start Right Reader

Tin Cans Tip!
by Rosa Dunn
illustrated by Nina de Polonia

Pam finds a mat.
Can it fit?

85

Read Decodable Text *Tin Cans Tip!*, Book 1: pp. 84–91

Writing

Children use evidence to write ideas about what Dilly is like. *See Engage & Respond, p. T213.*

Close Reading

The Map

READ How does Duck get to the farm? Underline words that tell.

Brave Duck took a trip to find new friends.
She had a map.
Tap, tap, tap, on the map!
The map took Duck to a farm.
Sad Cat was at the farm.
Sad Cat was happy to see Duck.
Duck had a new friend!

Close Reading Tip
Put a ? by the parts you have questions about.

CHECK MY UNDERSTANDING
Write a question you have about the story.

What will Duck and Cat do together?

83

myBook, Book 1, pp. 82–85

Additional Skills Practice

SPELLING AND VOCABULARY

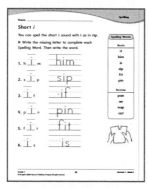

Name ____

Short i

You can spell the short i sound with i as in rip.

▶ Write the missing letter to complete each Spelling Word. Then write the word.

Spelling Words
Basic
it
him
is
sip
fit
pin
Review
pan
an
nap
cat

1. h i m   him
2. s i p   sip
3. i f   if
4. p i n   pin
5. f i t   fit
6. i s   is

Know It, Show It, p. 28

Name ____

Power Words: Match

Word Bank
ugly   beautiful   paddled   chilly   changed

▶ Write the Power Word from Big Dilly's Tale that best fits each item.

1. Which word would you use to tell about a very pretty picture?   beautiful
2. This word means to become different.   changed
3. Which word means not good-looking?   ugly
4. This word tells how something moved through water.   paddled
5. Which word means almost the same as cold?   chilly

Know It, Show It, p. 29

Wrap-Up

Share Time

At the end of Reading Workshop, have children reflect on their learning by sharing how they applied **Characters** or another area of focus during independent work time. Choose from these options:

- **SHARE CHAIR** Select a reader each day to come to the front of the class and tell what he or she learned from the reading by using a skill or strategy.

- **THINK-PAIR-SHARE** Children share their thinking with a partner. Select a few children each day to share with the whole class.

- **RETURN TO ANCHOR CHART** Have children add sticky notes about their independent reading book to the Characters Anchor Chart. Call on a few children to explain what they added.

ANCHOR CHART 16: Characters

Online
Ed

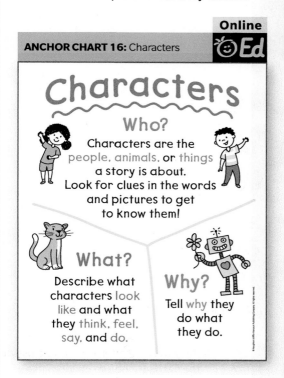

Characters

Who?
Characters are the people, animals, or things a story is about. Look for clues in the words and pictures to get to know them!

What?
Describe what characters look like and what they think, feel, say, and do.

Why?
Tell why they do what they do.

FOUNDATIONAL SKILLS

LEARNING OBJECTIVES

- Identify and read high-frequency words.
- **Language** Recognize and recite basic sight vocabulary.
- Segment spoken one-syllable words into individual phonemes.
- Isolate medial vowel sounds in spoken one-syllable words.

MATERIALS   Online

Word Cards *and, as, find, for, if, in, is, it, just, many, one, she, then*

Printable *Word List 3*

Classroom materials *flashlight*

 # High-Frequency Words

Review the Words

Repeat the **HIGH-FREQUENCY WORDS** routine to review this week's High-Frequency Words: *and, find, for, just, many, one, she,* and *then,* and the decodable High-Frequency Words *as, if, in, is,* and *it.*

Flashlight Game

- Display the High-Frequency Word Cards for the week's words, and have children take out their word cards from Printable: Word List 3. Turn off the classroom lights.

- Have one child at a time use a flashlight to shine a light on one of the Word Cards. Ask the rest of the class to read the word aloud and hold up the corresponding word card. Repeat until all children have had a turn.

 # Phonological Awareness

Segment Phonemes

- Tell children that they will be segmenting, or breaking, words you say into their individual sounds. Model: *Listen as I say all the sounds I hear in the word* bet. *I hear /b/ at the beginning, /ĕ/ in the middle, and /t/ at the end. The sounds in* bet *are /b/, /ĕ/, and /t/. Bet, /b/ /ĕ/ /t/.*

- Then have children segment the words you say: *Now it's your turn. Listen to the word. Then say each sound:* up (/ŭ/ /p/), an (/ă/ /n/), zip (/z/ /ĭ/ /p/), nod (/n/ /ŏ/ /d/), fin (/f/ /ĭ/ /n/), yes (/y/ /ĕ/ /s/), duck (/d/ /ŭ/ /k/), pole (/p/ /ō/ /l/), wave (/w/ /ā/ /v/).

Isolate Phonemes: Identify Vowel

- Remind children that they can also listen to the sounds in a word and say what sounds they hear in different parts of words. Tell them to listen for and say the sound they hear in the middle of each word you say. Model: *Listen: The word is* sick. *Let me say it again:* sick. *I hear /ĭ/ in the middle of* sick.

- *Now you try it! Listen to the word. What is the middle sound?* sip (/ĭ/), lap (/ă/), pad (/ă/), bin (/ĭ/), him (/ĭ/), tag (/ă/)

TEACHER TIP

Safety first! Model appropriate use of the flashlight before children use it. Tell them to only shine the light on the word cards and to be sure to keep the light from shining in classmates' eyes.

 CORRECT & REDIRECT

If children segment incorrectly, elongate the medial sound as you say the word and then identify each phoneme individually. Example:

- *Let's break the word* zip *into all of its sounds. Listen:* zip, /zĭĭĭp/, /z/ /ĭĭĭ/ /p/.

- Have children repeat the sounds as needed.

- *The sounds in* zip *are /z/, /ĭ/, and /p/. What is the middle sound in* zip? (/ĭ/)

Phonics Review

I Do It

Spotlight on Letters Use the **SOUND-BY-SOUND BLENDING** routine to review this week's phonic elements: short *i*; *r*, *f*, final *s* /*z*/; and inflection -*s*. Model blending *fibs* with Letter Cards (or display the written word). Say the first two sounds separately, then together; then say the next sound and add it to the blended sounds, and repeat with the final sound. Repeat for *rims*.

We Do It

Blend and Read Project Display and Engage: **Blend and Read 1.10** or use Start Right Reader page 92.

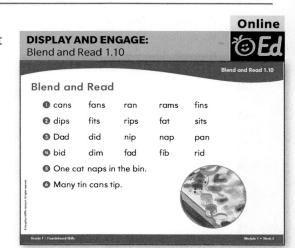

DISPLAY AND ENGAGE:
Blend and Read 1.10

Online
⊙ Ed

Blend and Read 1.10

Blend and Read

❶ cans	fans	ran	rams	fins
❷ dips	fits	rips	fat	sits
❸ Dad	did	nip	nap	pan
❹ bid	dim	fad	fib	rid

❺ One cat naps in the bin.

❻ Many tin cans tip.

1 **Line 1** Have children read the line. Ask: *What do you notice? Which words mean more than one?* Reread the line chorally.

2 **Line 2** Continue. Then have volunteers reread selected words until they can identify them quickly.

3 **Review** Display Line 3, and have children read it chorally.

4 **Challenge** Children who are ready for a challenge can read Line 4 and use the words in sentences or tell what they mean.

5 **Sentences** Display Lines 5–6. Call on children to blend selected words. Point to each word as children read the sentences chorally.

You Do It

INDEPENDENT PRACTICE

- **Option 1** Have each child choose a Blend and Read word, illustrate it, and draw blank lines to show the number of letters in the word. Partners can exchange drawings and write the word that names the picture. Have children check each other's spelling and discuss labels. Repeat for several more words.

- **Option 2** Have children complete Know It, Show It page 31.

 ENGLISH LEARNER SUPPORT:
Build Vocabulary

ALL LEVELS Ensure that children understand the meaning of the Blend and Read words by asking questions that have them choose between two words. Examples: *Which word names animals, rams or cans?* (*rams*) *Which word names things that keep you cool, fins or fans?* (*fans*)

 LINK TO SMALL-GROUP INSTRUCTION

REINFORCE FOUNDATIONAL SKILLS
Use *Fin* during small-group time to review or reinforce blending and decoding words with short *i*, consonants *r*, *f*, *s* /*z*/, and inflection -*s*. Meet with children to work through the story, or assign it as independent work. *See the lesson on p. T228.*

LEARNING OBJECTIVES

- **Language** Identify and determine the meaning of verbs with the inflection -ed.

- Read and write verbs that tell about actions in the past.

MATERIALS   Online

Display and Engage *Generative Vocabulary 1.11*

Know It, Show It *p. 32*

 READER'S VOCABULARY

- **verb** an action word

 Inflection -ed

I Do It

- Project Display and Engage: <u>Generative Vocabulary 1.11</u>. Read aloud the introductory text.

- Review that when -ed is added to the end of a **verb**, it means that the action happened in the past.

- Discuss the example *paddled*. Point out that the word *paddle* ends in *e*. Explain that when a word ends in *e*, you drop the *e* before adding -ed.

- Tell children that *paddle* is a verb that tells about something that is happening now: *I paddle in the pool.* Explain that when the ending -ed is added to the verb *paddle*, it changes *paddle* to *paddled*. *Paddled* is a verb that tells about something that happened in the past: *Yesterday, I paddled in the pool.*

- Read Example 1 aloud. Model determining the meaning of *picked* by thinking about its base word and ending: *Picked is made up of the verb* pick *and the ending* -ed. Pick *tells about something that is happening now.* Picked *tells about something that happened in the past.*

- Continue in the same way with the remaining examples.

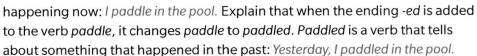

DISPLAY AND ENGAGE:
Generative Vocabulary 1.11

Online

Generative Vocabulary 1.11

Inflection -ed

A **verb** is an action word. The ending **-ed** can be added to a verb to tell when something happened.

Examples
1. pick + ed = picked
2. open + ed = opened
3. want + ed = wanted
4. need + ed = needed

paddled

Verb		Ending		
paddle	+	ed	=	paddled

TEACHER TIP

The past is the past! Use different time periods to reinforce past-tense verbs, such as *yesterday, last week, last month,* and *last spring.*

We Do It

Write the following words on the board and read them aloud with children: *wait, ask, kick,* and *thank*.

- Use the word *wait* in a sentence: *I wait for the school bus. Does this tell what I am doing now or in the past?*

- Ask a volunteer to add *-ed* to the end of the word. Help another volunteer use the new word, *waited,* in a sentence. Guide children to tell whether the word tells about something that is happening now or in the past.

- Continue in the same way with the remaining words.

You Do It

INDEPENDENT PRACTICE

- **Option 1** Have partners make a list of verbs with the ending *-ed.* Have one partner use a word in a sentence as the other partner acts it out and then explains the meaning. Then have them switch roles.

- **Option 2** Have children complete Know It, Show It page 32.

ENGLISH LEARNER SUPPORT:
Facilitate Language Connections

ALL LEVELS Children whose first language is Spanish, French, or Italian will be familiar with adding endings to conjugate verbs. They will likely have difficulty knowing which verbs in English are regular and which ones are not, so model conjugating and using irregular verbs if children incorrectly add the ending *-ed* to them.

Characters

LEARNING OBJECTIVES

• Identify the features of songs.
• Identify, describe, and compare characters.
• **Language** Share information about characters.
• Listen carefully and politely.

MATERIALS   Online Ed

Anchor Chart 17
Characters

Printable *Anchor Chart 17: Characters*

Teaching Pal *Book 1, pp. 86–89*

myBook *I'm Me, Book 1, pp. 86–89*

 READER'S VOCABULARY

• **character** a person or animal in a story

• **detail** small bit of information that supports a central idea or describes something in a text

• Remind children that when they read a story or listen to a song, they should think about the **characters** in them, what they are like, and the reasons for their actions.

• Project or display <u>Anchor Chart 17: Characters</u>. Remind children that the characters in a story or song are the people, animals, or things it is about.

• Remind children that readers can "get to know" characters by paying attention to **details**, or small pieces of information, in the words and pictures.

• Explain that looking for details that answer the questions on the Anchor Chart will help children know what the characters are like on the outside, or what they look like, and on the inside, or what they think or feel. They can also help tell why the characters do what they do.

• Tell children they will practice describing and comparing characters when they view *I'm Me*.

Online Ed

ANCHOR CHART 17: Characters

 ENGLISH LEARNER SUPPORT: Build Background

SUBSTANTIAL
Point to yourself and say *me*. Then point to a child and say *you*. Have children repeat after you.

MODERATE
Have children add gestures to the following sentences: *I'm me. You're you. I am unique.* Then have them sing the song with the gestures.

LIGHT
Have partners discuss the meaning of the word *unique*.

Go to Your
Teaching Pal

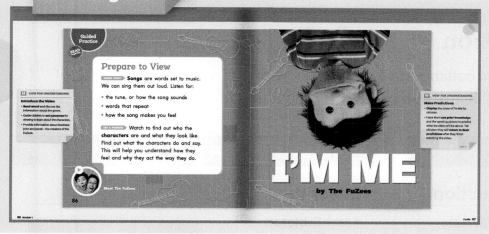

 I'M ME
by The FuZees

Step 2 Apply to Media

 In your Teaching Pal, pages 86–89, use the blue **VIEW FOR UNDERSTANDING** prompts to introduce and project *I'm Me* as children follow along in their *my*Book.

- **Genre Study** Read the genre information on page 86. Discuss the kinds of things children expect to find in a song. Remind children that the tune and the words work together to give listeners ideas and feelings.

- **Set a Purpose** Read the Set a Purpose section on page 86. Prompt children to set their own purpose for viewing *I'm Me*.

- **Meet the Creators** Play the audio about **The FuZees** to set up the topic of the song.

- **As You View** Read page 88. Guide children to watch the video all the way through. Pause occasionally to gauge children's understanding and to have them use details in the images and audio to identify, describe, and compare the characters. Children can refer back to the Anchor Chart as necessary.

Step 3 Engage and Respond

INDEPENDENT PRACTICE: Speaking & Listening

- Use the **TURN AND TALK** routine with the questions on Teaching Pal and *my*Book page 89. Remind children to use the details and other supporting evidence in the video to explain their responses.

- Read the Talking Tip. Remind children that it is important to follow agreed upon rules for discussion. Ask why it's important to listen carefully and look at your partner when talking.

- You may want to have children conduct their discussions during daily small-group time.

● *Getting Started*

ENGAGEMENT ROUTINE

Teach and practice **TURN AND TALK**:

- Read the question/topic to the class and make sure everyone understands it.

- Have partners share the answer or their ideas about the topic.

- Remind children that both people should have a chance to share.

- Ask partners to share their responses.

See the **GPS guide** to learn more.

👥 LINK TO SMALL-GROUP INSTRUCTION

REINFORCE CHARACTERS Review or extend the skill as needed during small-group time to support children's need for differentiation. *See the lesson on p. T227.*

LESSON 14

READING WORKSHOP

Options for Differentiation

As the class engages in independent and collaborative work, meet with Guided Reading Groups or differentiate instruction based on student need.

GUIDED READING GROUPS

Match Children to Books + Instruction

- Choose just-right books based on level, skill, topic, or genre.

C — D — E — F — G — H — I — J — K

Leveled Readers

- Deliver instruction with each book's Take and Teach Lesson, choosing appropriate sessions based on need.

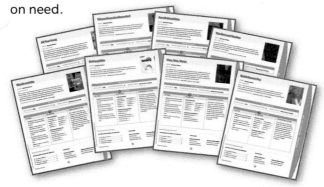

- Check comprehension, reinforce instruction, and extend learning with suggested supporting activities.

Rigby LEVELED LIBRARY

(EL) ENGLISH LEARNER SUPPORT

Describe

- Use **Tabletop Minilessons: English Language Development 3.2 (Writing)** to reinforce and practice the language skill.

Tabletop Minilessons: English Language Development

- Then use the following text-based prompts with *I'm Me* to guide application of the language skill. Begin with the prompt at the child's identified language proficiency level. As children are able, use lighter supports to encourage increased language proficiency.

SUBSTANTIAL

Have children draw the brothers in *I'm Me*. Using their drawings, have children describe the brothers. Ask: *Do they look the same? What is the same about them? What is different about them?* Allow children to point or to respond in single words or simple phrases.

MODERATE

Ask children to describe the brothers in *I'm Me* by focusing on what they look like, things they like, and what their favorite colors or items are. Supply these frames: *This brother has _____. That brother has _____. This brother likes _____. That brother likes _____. Their favorite colors are _____.*

LIGHT

Ask children to describe what things the brothers like to do with a partner. Encourage students to ask each other questions to enhance descriptions of the characters.

REINFORCE CHARACTERS

Demonstrate

- Use **Tabletop Minilessons: Reading 17** to remind children to "get to know" **characters** by paying attention to **details** in the words and pictures. By looking at and thinking about clues in the book, readers gain understanding of characters' thoughts and feelings.

- Model filling out Printable: <u>**Reading Graphic Organizer 25**</u> to identify and describe the characters in *I'm Me*.

Apply to Independent Reading

- Now have children identify and describe characters in an appropriate just-right book that they are reading independently. Customize these prompts to the books children choose.

  » *What details do you notice about the characters?*

  » *What does this character think and feel? Why?*

  » *What does the character do?*

- Have children complete Printable: <u>**Reading Graphic Organizer 25**</u> for their independent reading book.

Tabletop Minilessons: Reading

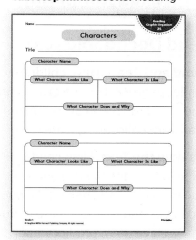

Printable:
Reading Graphic Organizer 25

ALMOST THERE ↓ READY FOR MORE

SCAFFOLD AND EXTEND

- Help children identify details in the pictures and text that tell about the characters' actions.

- Prompt children to use the pictures in the story to explain what the characters do in different parts of the story.

- Have children "introduce" a character to a classmate, as if the character were a friend.

EL **ENGLISH LEARNER SUPPORT**

SUBSTANTIAL

Point to a picture in the book. Use simple words and phrases to describe characters' actions. Have children repeat.

MODERATE

Have partners discuss the thoughts and/or feelings of characters in different parts of the book. Provide this frame: *This character thinks _____. This character feels _____.*

LIGHT

Ask: *What do you know about the main character at the beginning? At the end? How does the character change?*

Options for Differentiation

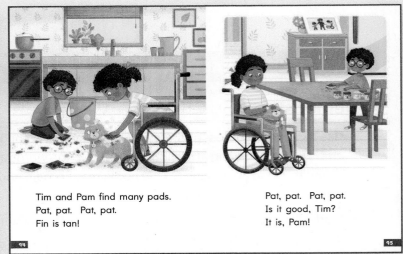

Fin, Start Right Reader, *Book 1,* pp. 92–99

REINFORCE FOUNDATIONAL SKILLS

Read Decodable Text

Blend and Read Have children turn to Start Right Reader page 92. Use the **CHORAL READING** routine to read aloud the Blend and Read lines. Use challenge line 4 with children who are ready.

Preview the Text Help children recall what happened to Fin in *Tin Cans Tip!* (Fin got paint on him and ran off. Tim tried to catch him.) Then read aloud the title on page 93 and have children look at the pictures on the first few pages. Have them predict what will happen to Fin.

Fluency Focus: Phrasing Read aloud page 94 as children follow along. Model grouping the words into natural phrases and pausing at punctuation. Then have children read the selection chorally, paying attention to their phrasing.

Reflect on Reading Have children read to find out what Tim, Pam, and Fin do in this story, reading each page silently and then chorally. Pause for these prompts:

- **Page 94:** *What do Tim and Pam do? (They use sponge pads to clean up the floor and Fin.)*

- **Page 97:** *What does Pam do to the bin? (She pins a "No Fin" sign on it.)*

- **Page 98:** *How is what happens on this page similar to something that happened before? (In* Tim and Pam, *Tim was also sad and looking for his bat.) Where should Tim and Pam look for the bat? Why? (In the bin in the closet; that is where they found it before, and it is pictured in the bin on page 97.)*

Think-Pair-Share Allow time for children to reread the week's four Start Right Reader stories. Then use the **THINK-PAIR-SHARE** routine to guide partners in answering the questions on page 99. Have partners share their ideas with the group.

Tim sits.
The tin cans fit in the bin.

96

Is this for Fin, Pam?
She pins it.

97

Pam sat. Tim ran in.
Tim is sad.
Did Pam see a bat for Tim?

98

READ TOGETHER

Think-Pair-Share
Reread the four stories. Think and then talk with your partner.

1. How does one thing lead to another in all the stories? Use details from each story in your answer.

2. How does *Fin* end? What do you think will happen next? Why?

Share your ideas with a group.

99

Make Minutes Count

As you meet with small groups to read *Fin*, use one or more of these related activities, as needed, at the beginning or the end of the small-group session.

- **Connect to Phonics** Write these words on separate index cards: *cats, pans, Sam, sip, sit, tips*. Have children read the words and sort them into two categories: words that start with *s* and words that end with *-s*. After children are finished sorting, have them read the words in each pile and explain the sound *s* makes in the words. (*In the words that start with s, s makes the /s/ sound. In the words that end with -s, s makes either the /s/ or the /z/ sound.*)

- **Connect to Spelling** Play Hot Potato. Have children gather in a circle. Take a soft item, such as a beanbag, and hand it to a child. Have children pass the beanbag around the circle until you say, "Hot potato!" Then whoever has the beanbag must spell the Spelling Word that you say. Repeat until each child has had a turn.

- **Connect to High-Frequency Words** Play Tic-Tac-Toe. Have partners draw a three-by-three grid and assign who will be *X* and who will be *O*. One partner points to a High-Frequency Word from Printable: **Word List 3** for the other partner to read. If the other partner reads the word correctly, he or she writes his or her assigned letter anywhere on the grid. Play continues until one partner has three *X*s or *O*s in a row.

Name _____

Word List 3

High-Frequency Words	Decodable High-Frequency Words	Spelling Words	
		Basic	Review
and	as	it	pan
find	if	him	an
for	in	is	nap
just	is	sip	cat
many	it	fit	
one		pin	
she			
then			
			Challenge
			rich
			spin

Grade 1
© Houghton Mifflin Harcourt Publishing Company. All rights reserved.   Printable

Printable: Word List 3

Options for Independent and Collaborative Work

While you meet with small groups, have other children engage in literacy activities that reinforce the lesson's learning objectives. Choose from these options.

Independent Reading

Student Choice Library

LEVELED LIBRARY

APPLY READING SKILL

Characters Children complete Printable: <u>Reading Graphic Organizer 25</u> for an independent reading book.

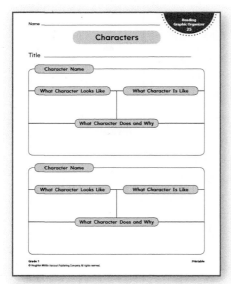

Printable: Reading Graphic Organizer 25

APPLY LANGUAGE SKILL

Describe Children complete Printable: <u>Language Graphic Organizer 6</u> for an independent reading book.

Printable: Language Graphic Organizer 6

Literacy Centers

See pp. T174–T175.

 WORD WORK

 CREATIVITY CORNER

 DIGITAL STATION

 READING CORNER

 TEAMWORK TIME

Start Right Reader

Fin? Fin?
Fin!
Fin is sad.

93

Read Decodable Text *Fin*,
Book 1: pp. 92–99

Speaking & Listening

Partners discuss the Turn and
Talk questions using evidence.
See Engage & Respond, p. T225.

Additional Skills Practice

PHONICS

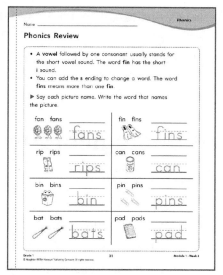

Know It, Show It, p. 31

GENERATIVE VOCABULARY

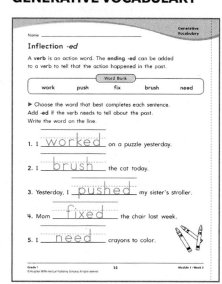

Know It, Show It, p. 32

Wrap-Up
Share Time

At the end of Reading Workshop, have
children reflect on their learning by
sharing how they applied **Characters** or
another area of focus during independent
work time. Choose from these options:

- **SHARE CHAIR** Select a reader each day
  to come to the front of the class and tell
  what he or she learned from the reading
  by using a skill or strategy.

- **THINK-PAIR-SHARE** Children share
  their thinking with a partner. Select a
  few children each day to share with the
  whole class.

- **RETURN TO ANCHOR CHART** Have
  children add sticky notes about their
  independent reading book to the
  Characters Anchor Chart. Call on a few
  children to explain what they added.

Online
Ed

ANCHOR CHART 17: Characters

FOUNDATIONAL SKILLS

WORD WORK WARM-UP

LEARNING OBJECTIVES

- Identify and read high-frequency words.
- **Language** Recognize, recite, and spell basic sight vocabulary.
- Recognize spoken alliteration.
- Segment spoken one-syllable words into individual phonemes.
- Blend phonemes to say one-syllable words.
- Isolate medial vowel sounds in spoken one-syllable words.

MATERIALS   Online

Word Cards *and, as, find, for, if, in, is, it, just, many, one, she, then*

Printables *Phonological Awareness 3; Word List 3*

Classroom materials *flashlight*

 # High-Frequency Words

Children's Choice

- Remind children of the High-Frequency Words they have been practicing this week: *and, find, for, just, many, one, she,* and *then,* and the decodable High-Frequency Words *as, if, in, is,* and *it.*

- Review any words that posed difficulty for children this week, using Word Cards and the **HIGH-FREQUENCY WORDS** routine.

- In Lessons 12–14, children used these practice activities: Guess the Word (p. T192), I Spy (p. T206), and Flashlight Game (p. T220). Have children vote on their favorite, and use it to review the week's words for word recognition fluency.

 # Phonological Awareness

Teacher's Choice

- In Lessons 11–14, children practiced alliteration, segmenting phonemes, and blending phonemes (pp. T177, T193, T206, T220). They also practiced isolating phonemes and identifying medial vowel sounds (pp. T206, T220).

- Use the following examples to gauge which isolation tasks need reinforcement.

  » **Isolate Phoneme: Identify Vowel** Have children practice isolating medial phonemes by identifying the vowel sounds in the middle of these words: pick (/ĭ/), bag (/ă/), jam (/ă/), will (/ĭ/).

- Use Printable: **Phonological Awareness 3** to gauge which tasks from the week need reinforcement.

  » **Alliteration; Segment Phonemes** Have children tell whether all the words in each word set have the same beginning sound: hand, house, heart *(yes)*; fan, snake, five *(no)*. Then have children segment the following words into phonemes and say how many sounds they hear: ax (/ă/ /ks/, *2*); pin (/p/ /ĭ/ /n/, *3*); toe (/t/ /ō/, *2*).

  » **Blend Phonemes** Have children blend the sounds to say these words: /l/ /ŏ/ /k/ (lock), /k/ /ē/ (key).

 ENGLISH LEARNER SUPPORT: Build Vocabulary

SUBSTANTIAL
Provide a set of small objects, such as paper clips. Have children use the objects to show the meaning of *one* and *many.*

MODERATE
Have children use sentence frames to reinforce the meanings of *one* and *many. I have one _____. I have many _____.*

LIGHT
Ask children to share sentences about something they have only done *one* time and something they have done *many* times.

✓ **CORRECT & REDIRECT**

If children have difficulty identifying alliteration, walk them through the process providing additional supports. Examples:

- *These are the words: hand, house, heart. Let's say each word and then say the beginning sound: hand (/h/); house (/h/); heart (/h/).*

- *Are the beginning sounds the same or different? (the same)*

- *Let's try the second set of words. What sound do you hear at the beginning of fan, snake, and five? fan (/f/); snake (/s/); five (/f/)*

- *Are the beginning sounds the same or different? (different; snake has a different beginning sound)*

Short *i*

Spelling Assessment

LEARNING OBJECTIVE

- Spell words with short *i* (closed syllables).

DICTATION SENTENCES

BASIC

1. **it** Put *it* away.
2. **him** I gave *him* a gift.
3. **is** She *is* my best friend.
4. **sip** Take a *sip* of the drink.
5. **fit** All my markers *fit* in the box.
6. **pin** She uses a *pin* to hold her hair.

REVIEW

7. **pan** He cooked eggs in a *pan*.
8. **an** I ate *an* orange.
9. **nap** The tired baby took a *nap*.
10. **cat** My *cat* is named Fluffy.

CHALLENGE

11. **rich** The treat is *rich* and creamy.
12. **spin** *Spin* the top.

1 Say each Spelling Word, and read the Dictation Sentence. Repeat the word and then have children write it. Remind them to use their best handwriting.

2 Add the Surprise Words *sit, dip,* and *tin.* If you prefer a shorter test, replace three of the Basic Words with the Surprise Words.

- **sit** He will *sit* on the couch.
- **dip** I like to *dip* chips in salsa.
- **tin** She put the muffins in a *tin*.

3 Include the Challenge Words for children who practiced them this week.

4 Review any words that children misspell. If they miss two or more words, then revisit the Lesson 11 Word Sort activity on page T181.

1. it
2. him
3. is
4. sip
5.
6.
7.
8.
9.
10.

TEACHER TIP

Guess the words! The Surprise Words are application words. Their purpose is to show whether children can apply the spelling principle, going beyond the memorization of specific words. After a while, kids will start trying to guess what the Surprise Words might be early in the week.

Cumulative Vocabulary

Review Vocabulary

LEARNING OBJECTIVES

- **Language** Explain and use academic vocabulary words.
- Use newly acquired vocabulary to identify real-life connections between word and their use.
- Identify the meaning of words with the affix *-ed*.

MATERIALS   Online

Vocabulary Cards *1.1–1.3, 1.10–1.15, 1.22–1.27, 1.36–1.40*

myBook *Book 1, pp. 10–11*

- Tell children you will review the Big Idea Words and Power Words from this module together.

- Display Vocabulary Cards 1.1–1.3, 1.10–1.15, 1.22–1.27, and 1.36–1.40 one at a time. If children would like you to refresh their memories about a word, they should raise their hand when you display that Vocabulary Card.

- Read aloud the student-friendly meaning on each Vocabulary Card, as needed. Encourage children who didn't raise their hands to explain the word's meaning and/ or use it in a sentence.

Vocabulary Cards

 ENGLISH LEARNER SUPPORT: Build Vocabulary

ALL LEVELS As the class works together to identify the Power Words they need help with, give English learners an opportunity to request assistance, not only by employing nonverbal cues, such as raising their hand, but also by verbalizing their request by using simple questions, such as these: *Can you say that word again? What does that word mean? Can you show me?*

 LEARNING MINDSET

Seeking Challenges

Normalize Remind children that it's normal to be challenged when they read words. Explain that they will learn new vocabulary throughout their lives. *Readers always see words that they don't know or understand. That is one of our challenges as readers. But it's fun to learn and use new words. We understand that new words help us understand the world around us.*

Teacher's Choice

Display the Vocabulary Cards, or write the Big Idea Words and Power Words from this module on the board so children can refer to them as they complete one or more of the following activities. Assign an activity from the following options to the whole class, or assign different activities based on children's needs.

VOCABULARY NETWORK

- Revisit the Vocabulary Network on *myBook* pages 10–11 that children started at the beginning of the module.

- Tell children that as they learned about the module topic through their reading, they may have learned other words or ideas that could be added to the network.

- Have children add more synonyms, antonyms, or details to their drawings to complete their Vocabulary Network.

- Ask partners to share and compare their completed networks.

WORD SORT

- Remind children that when they sort words, they group words together that are alike. Have small groups look at the Big Idea Words and the Power Words and discuss how to sort them.

- Children may choose to group the words by a topic, such as Feelings. The words *excited, enjoy,* and *nervous* could all be used to talk about how someone feels.

- Children may also choose to group the words by part of speech, such as past-tense verbs. The words *wished, paddled,* and *changed* are all past-tense verbs.

- Children may also choose to group the words by other categories that are meaningful to them.

- Have children write their completed word sort on a sheet of paper.

VOCABULARY IN WRITING

- Remind children that they can practice using new vocabulary they have learned in conversations and in their writing.

- Have children work independently, with a partner, or in a small group to compose a short piece of writing that uses as many of the vocabulary words as possible.

- Since this module's topic and literature are related to social studies concepts, children may gravitate towards a social studies-related topic. Don't discourage them from writing about those topics, but you may point out that these words can be used in many different contexts. For example, they may want to write a journal entry about how they have grown and *changed* since the summer, or a comic strip about a person who *paddled* down a river in *chilly* weather.

- Have children share their writing with a small group.

Professional Learning

RESEARCH FOUNDATIONS

"When teachers made children aware of the meaning of the words and then engaged them in using those words in a meaningful context, children achieved greater gains than from explicit instruction alone."
—Dr. Susan B. Neuman and Dr. Tanya S. Wright (2014)

See the **GPS guide** to learn more.

READING WORKSHOP

Wrap Up the Topic

Reflect on the Topic

- Project Display and Engage: <u>Knowledge Map 1.1</u> to reflect on the module topic, new friends, and experiences. As you point to various parts of the Knowledge Map, prompt children to recall texts about the topic and share what they learned. Alternatively, you may name texts from the module and have children point out parts of the map that relate.

- Encourage children to discuss similarities and differences between the texts and how they approach the same topic. *What is the same about* (Suki's Kimono) *and* (Big Dilly's Tale)? *What is different? What did you learn about making friends from each of these texts? What did you learn about new experiences from each of these texts?*

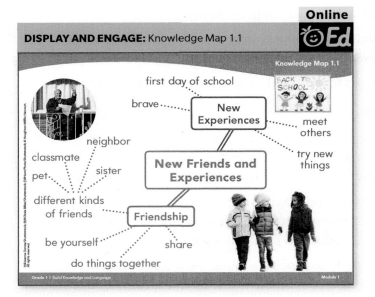

DISPLAY AND ENGAGE: Knowledge Map 1.1

Online

Knowledge Map 1.1

first day of school

brave

New Experiences

meet others

try new things

neighbor

classmate

pet   sister

New Friends and Experiences

different kinds of friends

Friendship

be yourself   share

do things together

Grade 1 · Build Knowledge and Language   Module 1

 LEARNING MINDSET

Seeking Challenges

Reflect Point out specific examples of how children have sought challenges and grown in Module 1. For example, say: *At first, it was hard to find text evidence, because that was new for many of you, but as you kept trying and practicing, you got better at it. You even found text evidence I didn't notice!*

 ENGLISH LEARNER SUPPORT: Facilitate Discussion

ALL LEVELS Use classroom objects to help children develop understanding of the words *same* and *different*. Hold up two similar objects and say: *These objects are the same.* Then hold up two different objects and say: *These objects are different.* Then have children choose objects, and tell whether they are the same or different.

Go to Your
Teaching Pal

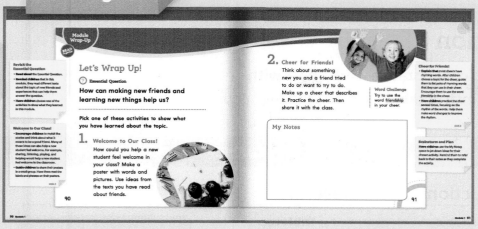

Synthesize Information

In your Teaching Pal, pages 90–91, use the prompts to have children revisit the Essential Question: *How can making new friends and learning new things help us?*

- Then have children choose one of the activities to demonstrate what they have learned about the topic from reading the texts in this module. Use the supports in your Teaching Pal to guide them.

- As children share their final work with a partner or with the class, remind them to follow these tips for presenting:
  - » speak clearly so people can understand you
  - » speak at an appropriate pace, not too fast or too slow
  - » work together or take turns if you are presenting with a partner

---

PERFORMANCE TASK OPTION

Instead of the wrap-up activities in the Teaching Pal, you may choose to have children complete a Performance Task. Remind children that they read many texts about making a new friend. Tell them they will tell how a character makes a friend by writing. Display the prompt:

Choose two characters from different texts. Write a paragraph to tell how they meet. Be sure to include the important events in order.

Guide children through the steps of the writing process: plan, draft, revise, and present. In each of the steps, remind children to continually refer back to the texts to support their ideas.

 LINK TO SMALL-GROUP INSTRUCTION

REINFORCE SYNTHESIZING Review or extend the skill as needed during small-group time to support children's need for differentiation. *See the lesson on p. T239.*

READING WORKSHOP

Options for Differentiation

As the class engages in independent and collaborative work, meet with Guided Reading Groups or differentiate instruction based on student need.

GUIDED READING GROUPS

Match Children to Books + Instruction

- Choose just-right books based on level, skill, topic, or genre.

C D E F G H I J K

Leveled Readers

- Deliver instruction with each book's Take and Teach Lesson, choosing appropriate sessions based on need.

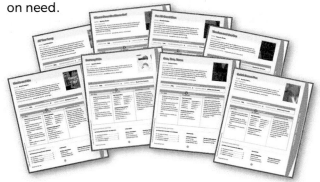

- Check comprehension, reinforce instruction, and extend learning with suggested supporting activities.

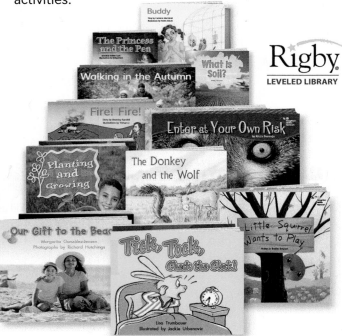

Rigby® LEVELED LIBRARY

EL ENGLISH LEARNER SUPPORT

Describe

- Use **Tabletop Minilessons: English Language Development 3.3 (Collaborative Problem Solving)** to reinforce and practice the language skill.

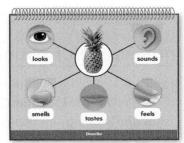

Tabletop Minilessons: English Language Development

- Then use the following prompts to guide application of the language skill. Begin with the prompt at the child's identified language proficiency level. As children are able, use lighter supports to encourage increased language proficiency.

SUBSTANTIAL
Remind children that readers can describe characters both on the "outside" and on the "inside." Ask: *What do you know about the characters?* Allow children to point to pictures and/or to use single words to respond.

MODERATE
Ask children how readers learn about characters in a story. Ask questions and supply frames: *What can we learn from the pictures? We can learn _____ from the pictures. What can we learn from the text? We can learn _____ from the text.*

LIGHT
Allow children to reference books from previous lessons. Ask: *How can we describe characters in a story? How can a character's actions tell us what he or she might be thinking or feeling?*

REINFORCE SYNTHESIZE

Demonstrate

- Use **Tabletop Minilessons: Reading 9** to remind children that readers can put together, or **synthesize**, information and ideas from different parts of the text and also from different texts that they read. Explain that bringing together different elements of a text lets readers see the author's ideas in new ways. Thinking about how all these different parts of a text fit together helps readers decide, "What does this text mean to me?"

- Model filling out Printable: **Reading Graphic Organizer 6** as you lead a discussion that requires children to synthesize information from one or more selections they have read.

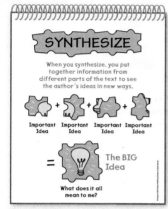

Tabletop Minilessons: Reading 9

Apply to Independent Reading

- Now have children synthesize information in an appropriate just-right book that they are reading independently. Customize these prompts to the books children choose.

  » *What idea in this book could you use in your own life?*

  » *What is the big idea in this book?*

  » *What does the text mean to you?*

- Have children complete Printable: **Reading Graphic Organizer 6** for their independent reading book.

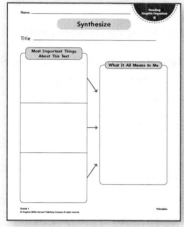

Printable:
Reading Graphic Organizer 6

SCAFFOLD AND EXTEND

ALMOST THERE

READY FOR MORE

- Lead children to put two ideas from their book together. Guide them to draw a conclusion.

- Have children use pictures and key words that repeat to identify important ideas, and draw a conclusion.

- Have partners compare information from two books on the same topic. Ask them to synthesize and state what they know about the topic.

EL ENGLISH LEARNER SUPPORT

SUBSTANTIAL
Prompt children to tell what they know about the topic based on the pictures in the story. They may point, gesture, or use single words to express their ideas.

MODERATE
Help children complete these frames about their book: *At the beginning, I thought _____. At the end I thought _____.*

LIGHT
Ask children to identify important ideas in the text. Ask: *Why does the author include them? What do they mean to the reader?*

READING WORKSHOP

Options for Differentiation

Start Right Reader, *Book 1*, pp. 68–99

REINFORCE FOUNDATIONAL SKILLS

Read Decodable Text

Review Remind children of the Start Right Reader stories they read this week about the characters Pam, Tim, and Fin.

- *Tim and Pam*
- *Dab, Dab, Dab!*
- *Tin Cans Tip!*
- *Fin*

Allow a few minutes for children to page through the stories to recall what they are about.

Make Text Connections Prompt children to explain how the four stories are connected.

- *Who are the main characters in these stories?* (Pam, Tim, and Fin)

- *What is the main thing that each story is about?* (Possible responses: In Tim and Pam, *Tim and Pam look for a bat; in* Dab, Dab, Dab!, *Tim and Pam paint a picture, but then rip it; in* Tin Cans Tip!, *Pam fixes the picture and then spills paint on the cat; in* Fin, *Tim and Pam clean the cat.*)

- *What problem in* Tin Cans Tip! *has a solution in* Fin? (The tin cans tip and spill paint on the table, floor, and Fin. Then Pam and Tim clean up the mess in the story Fin.)

- *Based on these stories, what can you tell about Pam and Tim?* (Possible response: They like to work together and help each other.)

- *What might happen to Pam, Tim, and Fin in a new story about them?* (Accept reasonable responses.)

Reread for Fluency Have children select one of the stories to reread. Use the **ECHO READING** routine and have children focus on reading with natural phrasing.

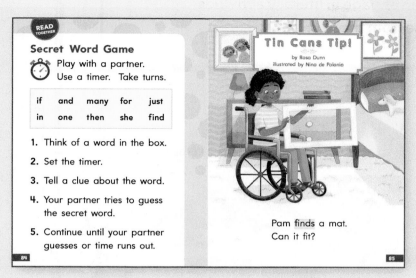

Secret Word Game

Play with a partner.
Use a timer. Take turns.

if	and	many	for	just
in	one	then	she	find

1. Think of a word in the box.
2. Set the timer.
3. Tell a clue about the word.
4. Your partner tries to guess the secret word.
5. Continue until your partner guesses or time runs out.

84

Tin Cans Tip!
by Rosa Dunn
illustrated by Nina de Polonia

Pam finds a mat.
Can it fit?

85

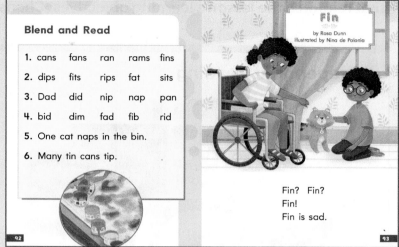

Blend and Read

1. cans   fans   ran   rams   fins
2. dips   fits   rips   fat   sits
3. Dad   did   nip   nap   pan
4. bid   dim   fad   fib   rid
5. One cat naps in the bin.
6. Many tin cans tip.

92

Fin
by Rosa Dunn
illustrated by Nina de Polonia

Fin? Fin?
Fin!
Fin is sad.

93

Make Minutes Count

As you meet with small groups to review the week's decodable stories, use one or both of these related activities, as needed, at the beginning or the end of the small-group session.

- **Connect to Phonics** Display these Picture Cards, picture side down: *can, cat, map, pin*. Write the words naming the Picture Cards on separate index cards, and place the index cards on top of the corresponding Picture Cards. Call on a child to read one of the words. Then have the child turn over the card and look at the picture to confirm that he or she correctly read the word. Continue until all of the cards are picture side up. Then have children choose a word card, add *-s* to the end of the word, read the new word, and explain how adding the *-s* changed the meaning of the original word.

- **Connect to Handwriting** Display the High-Frequency Word cards *like* and *this* from Printable: <u>Word List 3</u>. Have children write two sentences that begin *I like this*. As they write, reinforce proper pencil grip and paper position, correcting as needed. Then have partners switch papers. Partners should take turns providing feedback on proper letter formation, legibility, and spacing between letters and words.

LESSON 15

READING WORKSHOP

Options for Independent and Collaborative Work

While you meet with small groups, have other children engage in literacy activities that reinforce the lesson's learning objectives. Choose from these options.

Independent Reading

Student Choice Library

Rigby LEVELED LIBRARY

APPLY READING SKILL

Synthesize Children complete Printable: <u>Reading Graphic Organizer 6</u> for an independent reading book.

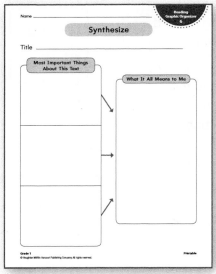

Printable: Reading Graphic Organizer 6

APPLY LANGUAGE SKILL

Describe Children complete Printable: <u>Language Graphic Organizer 6</u> for an independent reading book.

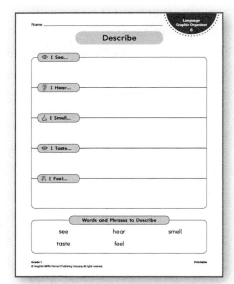

Printable: Language Graphic Organizer 6

Literacy Centers

See pp. T174–T175.

 WORD WORK

 CREATIVITY CORNER

 DIGITAL STATION

 READING CORNER

 TEAMWORK TIME

Start Right Reader

Tim and Pam
by Rosa Dunn
illustrated by Nina de Polonia

Pam sat. Tim ran in.
Tim is sad.
Did Pam see a bat for Tim?

69

Read Decodable Text Book 1:
pp. 68–99

Wrap-Up

Share Time

At the end of Reading Workshop, have children reflect on their learning by sharing how they applied **Synthesize** or another area of focus during independent work time. Choose from these options:

- **SHARE CHAIR** Select a reader each day to come to the front of the class and tell what he or she learned from the reading by using a skill or strategy.

- **THINK-PAIR-SHARE** Children share their thinking with a partner. Select a few children each day to share with the whole class.

- **RETURN TO ANCHOR CHART** Have children add sticky notes about their independent reading book to the Synthesize Anchor Chart. Call on a few children to explain what they added.

Online

ANCHOR CHART 9: Synthesize

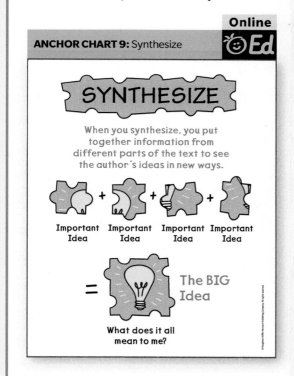

SYNTHESIZE

When you synthesize, you put together information from different parts of the text to see the author's ideas in new ways.

Important Idea + Important Idea + Important Idea + Important Idea

= The BIG Idea

What does it all mean to me?

Notes

My Family, My Community

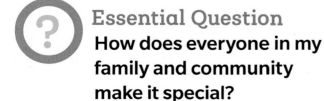

Essential Question
How does everyone in my family and community make it special?

SOCIAL STUDIES CONNECTION:
Communities

Young children seek to discover their place in the world. They begin their search by exploring how they fit within their family and their local community. It is important that they feel a sense of belonging to both.

This module describes communities as special places to live. It explains how the people who live there, including family members, work together to make it better for everyone.

Building Knowledge Networks

As children read, view, and interact with the texts and media in this module, they build deep topic knowledge about different kinds of communities and families and how everyone in a family and community make it special.

DISPLAY AND ENGAGE: Knowledge Map 2.1

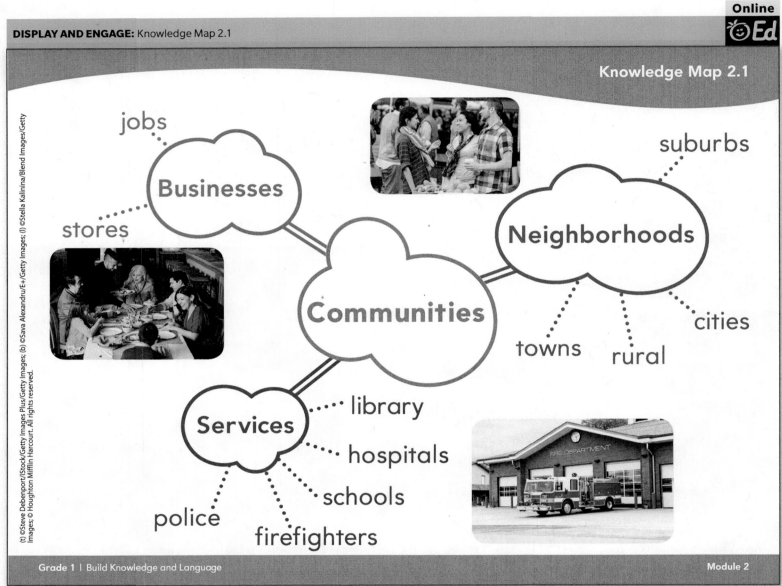

Knowledge Map 2.1

jobs

Businesses

stores

Communities

Neighborhoods

suburbs

cities

towns

rural

Services

library

hospitals

schools

police

firefighters

Grade 1 | Build Knowledge and Language

Module 2

Synthesizing Knowledge

1 At the beginning of the module, introduce the module topic. Use Display and Engage: **Knowledge Map 2.1** to preview what children can expect to learn about families and communities.

2 After reading each text, share the Knowledge Map again to help children visualize and discuss that everyone lives in a community and has a family and that there are many ways for people to make their communities and families special.

3 At the end of the module, have children synthesize what they have learned about the topic during **Let's Wrap Up!**

Fostering a Learning Mindset

Throughout this module, look for the Learning Mindset feature to introduce the Learning Mindset focus—**belonging**—and use the suggestions to weave it throughout children's literacy instruction as they encounter new texts and practice new skills.

Key Messages

- You are a valuable member of our class/learning community; you each have something important to offer.
- Just because we're different doesn't mean that we're not part of a community.
- Being different helps make my community great!
- Display **Anchor Chart 53: My Learning Mindset** throughout the year. Refer to it to introduce belonging and to reinforce the skills you introduced in previous modules.
- Recognize when children consistently exhibit a Learning Mindset focus, using Printable: **Learning Mindset Certificate**.

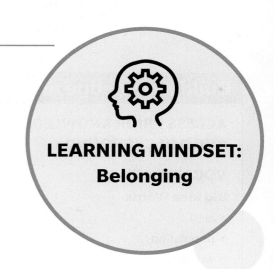

LEARNING MINDSET: Belonging

ANCHOR CHART 53: My Learning Mindset

Online Ed

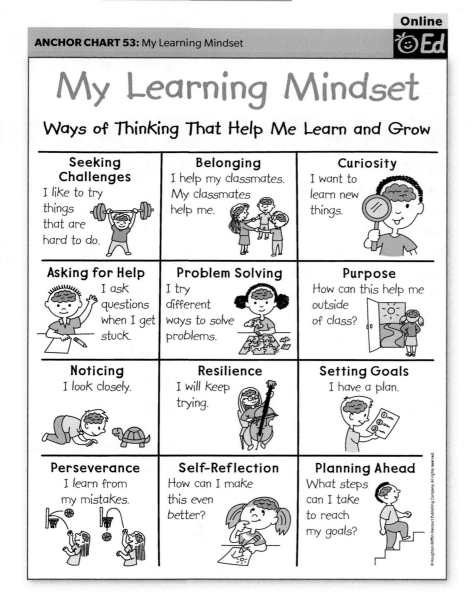

My Learning Mindset

Ways of Thinking That Help Me Learn and Grow

Seeking Challenges
I like to try things that are hard to do.

Belonging
I help my classmates. My classmates help me.

Curiosity
I want to learn new things.

Asking for Help
I ask questions when I get stuck.

Problem Solving
I try different ways to solve problems.

Purpose
How can this help me outside of class?

Noticing
I look closely.

Resilience
I will keep trying.

Setting Goals
I have a plan.

Perseverance
I learn from my mistakes.

Self-Reflection
How can I make this even better?

Planning Ahead
What steps can I take to reach my goals?

Developing Knowledge and Skills

Children build topic knowledge and develop foundational reading, writing, and oral language skills through daily whole- and small-group instruction.

? **Essential Question**
How does everyone in my family and community make it special?

LEARNING MINDSET:
Belonging

Build Knowledge and Language

ACCESS PRIOR KNOWLEDGE/ BUILD BACKGROUND

VOCABULARY

Big Idea Words

- area
- population
- working

MULTIMEDIA

Active Listening and Viewing

- Get Curious Video: *Come to the Fair!*

Online
Ed

GET CURIOUS VIDEO

Foundational Skills

PHONOLOGICAL AWARENESS

- Blend Onset and Rime
- Blend Phonemes
- Segment Onset and Rime
- Segment Phonemes
- Alliteration; Isolate Phonemes
- Isolate Phonemes
- Isolate, Segment Phonemes
- Isolate Phoneme: Identify Vowel

PHONICS

- Consonants *g, k*
- Review Short *a, i*
- Consonants *l, h*; Short *o*
- Review Short *a, i, o*
- Consonants *w, j, y, v*; Short *u*
- Review Short *i, o, u*

SPELLING

- Short *i*
- Short *o*
- Short *u*

HIGH-FREQUENCY WORDS

CONCEPTS OF PRINT

- Words in Sentences
- Commas
- Quotation Marks

FLUENCY

- Expression
- Intonation
- Accuracy and Self-Correction

Reading Workshop & Vocabulary

VOCABULARY

Power Words

Reader's Vocabulary

Generative Vocabulary

- Words About Places and Things
- Words About Actions and Directions

Vocabulary Strategy

- Antonyms

MULTIPLE GENRES

Discuss Genre Characteristics

- Opinion Writing
- Informational Text
- Realistic Fiction
- Fantasy
- Video

SPEAKING AND LISTENING

- Social Communication

COMPREHENSION

Use Metacognitive Skills

- Retell
- Summarize
- •Make Connections
- •Ask and Answer Questions

Literary Elements/Author's Purpose and Craft

- Ideas and Support
- Text Organization
- Setting
- Text Features
- Content-Area Words

RESPONSE TO TEXT

- Interact with Sources
- Written Response

FLUENCY

- Expression
- Intonation
- Accuracy and Self-Correction

Writing Workshop

WRITING FORM

- Descriptive Essay

FOCAL TEXT

- *Nana in the City* by Lauren Castillo

GRAMMAR MINILESSONS

- Adjectives: Size and Shape; Articles
- Adjectives: Color and Number
- Complete Sentences

Demonstrate Knowledge

INQUIRY & RESEARCH PROJECT

- Our Community News

ASSESS LEARNING

Formative Assessments

- Selection Quizzes
- Weekly Assessments

Performance-Based Assessments

- Informational Text
- Inquiry and Research Project

Summative Assessment

- Module Assessments
- Summative Assessments

Teaching with Text Sets

Carefully selected, content-rich text sets help children build topic knowledge and reading skills.

WEEK 1

Come to the Fair

Children view and respond to the video *Come to the Fair* to learn more about family and community cooperation.

Genre: Opinion Writing
Lexile Measure: 210L
Guided Reading Level: D

Genre: Informational Text
Lexile Measure: AD420L

Genre: Realistic Fiction
Lexile Measure: 250L
Guided Reading Level: E

WEEK 2

Genre: Realistic Fiction
Lexile Measure: AD580L

Genre: Informational Text
Lexile Measure: 240L
Guided Reading Level: C

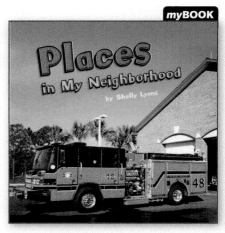

Genre: Informational Text
Lexile Measure: IG470L
Guided Reading Level: I

Essential Question

All texts in this set address the question:
How does everyone in my family and community make it special?

WEEK 3

READ ALOUD BOOK

Genre: Fantasy
Lexile Measure: 510L

*my*BOOK

Genre: Informational Text
Lexile Measure: 420L
Genre Reading Level: G

*my*BOOK

Online Ed

Genre: Video

WRITING FOCAL TEXT

Genre: Realistic Fiction
Lexile Measure: AD360L

Reading Workshop

During Reading Workshop, children will engage daily in a variety of whole-group, small-group, and independent literacy activities. Multiple options for differentiated instruction allow teachers to tailor instruction based on student need.

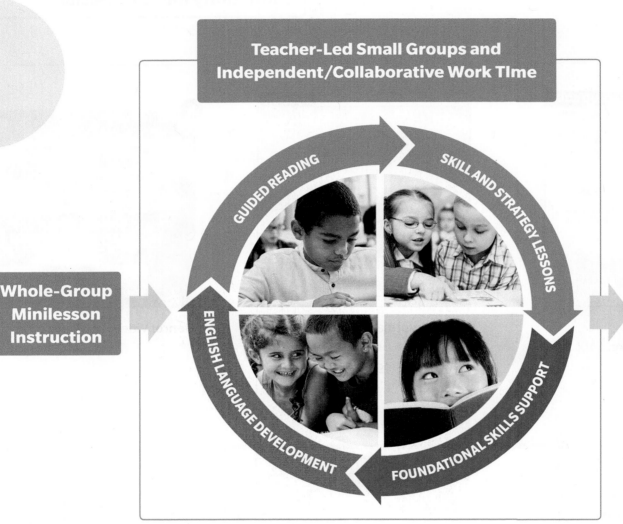

Whole-Group Minilesson Instruction

Teacher-Led Small Groups and Independent/Collaborative Work Time

GUIDED READING

SKILL AND STRATEGY LESSONS

ENGLISH LANGUAGE DEVELOPMENT

FOUNDATIONAL SKILLS SUPPORT

Wrap Up and Share

GUIDED READING

Teacher works with children at their instructional guided reading level.

Using the Rigby Leveled Library, pull just-right books to facilitate guided reading lessons.

SKILL AND STRATEGY LESSONS

Teacher works with small groups to reinforce reading skills and strategies.

Group children for targeted support. Lessons may be connected to the daily whole-group minilesson or based on student need.

FOUNDATIONAL SKILLS SUPPORT

Teacher works with needs-based groups.

Group children according to need to reinforce foundational skills through additional lessons and activities.

ENGLISH LANGUAGE DEVELOPMENT

Teacher works with small groups to support English language acquisition.

Lessons provide children with opportunities to engage in language skills across all the literacy domains in a safe small-group environment.

Forming Small Groups

Guided Reading Groups

- Assess children periodically, using running records or other diagnostic assessments to determine each child's guided reading level.
- Choose books from the Rigby Leveled Library based on reading level, or choose strategies that you plan to teach or practice with each group.
- Use assessment data and information from conferences to frequently regroup children based on reading level.
- Refer to Take & Teach lessons to guide reading instruction, check comprehension, and extend learning.
- Access online Printables, comprehension quizzes, and additional resources that promote revisiting the Leveled Readers for multiple purposes.

English Language Development

- Use Tabletop Minilessons: English Language Development to teach and practice language skills. Guide children to apply them to each lesson's text at their identified language proficiency level
- Access online Printables for children to apply the skill to an independent reading book.

Skill and Strategy Groups

- Observe children during whole-group minilessons to determine who may benefit from targeted support or extension of the day's reading skill. Use assessment data and information to pull groups according to need.
- Use Tabletop Minilessons: Reading to scaffold children's understanding of the skill through an Anchor Chart and supporting lesson.
- Access online Printables for children to apply their understanding of the skill to an independent reading book.

Foundational Skills Support

- Guide children to apply phonics and fluency skills in the Start Right Reader decodable texts and connect the related texts from across the week.
- Use the suggestions in Make Minutes Count to reinforce other foundational skills from the lesson, as needed.

SETTING READING GOALS AND CONFERRING

- Talk to children about their strengths and areas for growth during conferences.
- Work with children to set realistic reading goals that will support them with reaching the next guided reading level.
- Teach strategies that will help children achieve their goals, and remind them to use the strategies when they read. Review strategies frequently with different books.

Writing Workshop

Children will engage in the full writing process to produce a descriptive essay during this three-week module. The Writing Workshop Teacher's Guide provides explicit instruction and ample opportunity for children to write daily.

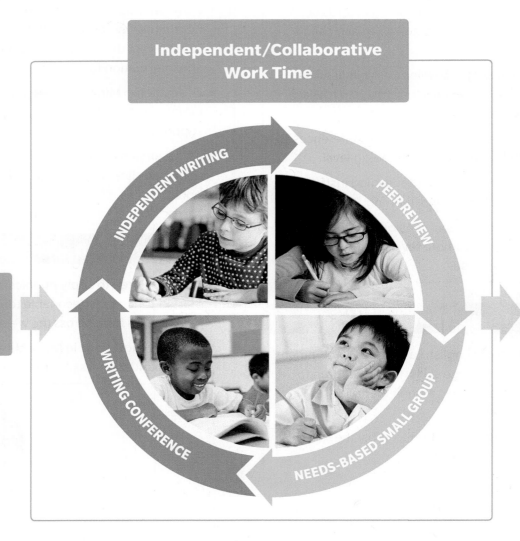

Independent/Collaborative Work Time

INDEPENDENT WRITING · PEER REVIEW · NEEDS-BASED SMALL GROUP · WRITING CONFERENCE

Launch Writing Workshop

Share

INDEPENDENT WRITING

Children work independently to:
- generate ideas/research
- prewrite
- draft
- write
- revise and edit
- publish

PEER REVIEW

Children work in small groups to peer edit.
Children engage in analytic talk and clocking activities to provide comments and suggestions that peers may consider incorporating into their writing.

NEEDS-BASED SMALL GROUP

Teacher works with small needs-based groups on grammar and writing skills.
Targeted minilessons support development of writing and grammar skills in areas of need.

WRITING CONFERENCE

One-on-One Conferring
Teachers meet with children one-on-one to set writing goals and to provide feedback throughout the writing process.

Descriptive Essay Writing Module Overview

Writing Workshop Teacher's Guide, pp. W17–W32

WEEK 1
- Introducing the Focal Text
- The Read
- Vocabulary
- Prewriting I: Finding a Topic
- Prewriting II: Planning a Descriptive Essay

WEEK 2
- Drafting I: Elements of a Descriptive Essay
- Drafting II: Using Sensory Words
- Drafting III: Adding Art
- Revising I: Grouping
- Revising II: Incorporating Feedback

WEEK 3
- Revising III: Capitalization
- Editing I: Reviewing for Grammar
- Editing II: Preparing to Publish
- Publishing
- Sharing

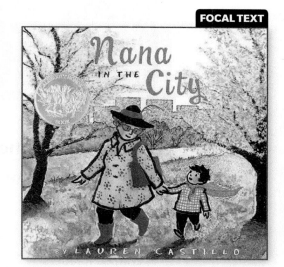

FOCAL TEXT

Nana in the City by Lauren Castillo

WRITING MODE Informational Text

WRITING FORM Descriptive Essay

FOCAL STATEMENT Our world is a special place.

Writing Prompt

- **WRITE** a short description of what makes your world wonderful.

Assessment and Progress Monitoring

Ongoing formative assessment guides daily instruction while performance-based assessments demonstrate student progress toward mastery of module skills and standards.

Selection Quizzes

Assess comprehension of the *my*Book text selections.

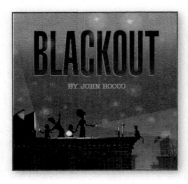

Weekly Assessments

Assess children's understanding of the key Reading, Writing, and Foundational Skills covered during each week of instruction.

Ongoing Formative Assessment Tools

- Leveled Readers
- Comprehension Quizzes
- Running Records
- 1:1 Observation Records
- Daily Lesson Checks and Correct & Redirect opportunities in the Teacher's Guide

Module Assessment

Measure children's proficiency in the critical skills covered in this module:

- Foundational Skills
- Generative Vocabulary
- Vocabulary Strategies
- Comprehension/Literary Analysis
- Grammar
- Writing

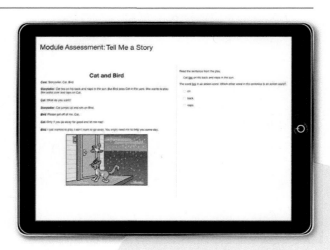

Performance-Based Assessments

Children synthesize what they have learned from the module's text set and demonstrate their topic knowledge by completing one of the module's culminating activities. An optional written Performance Task is also provided at the end of each module in the Teacher's Guide.

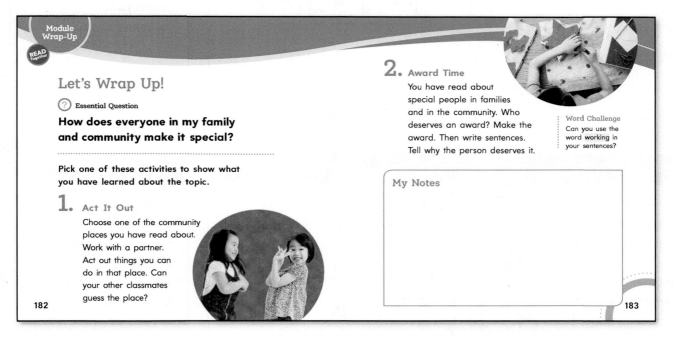

Writing Assessment

Throughout the course of the module, children work through the stages of the writing process in Writing Workshop. Children's writing can be evaluated according to the rubric provided for the module's writing form in the Teacher Resource Book.

Teaching with Instructional Routines

Use recursive, research-informed instructional routines to support lesson planning and maximize children's learning.

Active Viewing

Build and extend children's knowledge about the module topic by actively viewing and responding to the Get Curious Videos at the beginning of each module.

Blending: Sound-by-Sound

Lead children to decode unfamiliar one-syllable words, using consistent language.

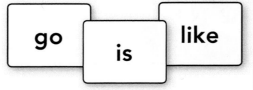

Blending: Continuous Blending

Provide this intermediate strategy as a transition between sound-by-sound blending and reading words with automaticity.

Blending: Vowel-First Blending

Provide additional support to children who have difficulty with the other types of blending and need to focus on vowel sounds.

High-Frequency Words

Teach children to read and spell common high-frequency words with automaticity.

FOCUS ROUTINE

Vocabulary

Explicitly teach the meaning of topic-related and academic vocabulary words from the texts, provide relevant examples, and practice using the words in familiar contexts.

Additional Routines

ENGAGEMENT ROUTINES
- Choral Reading
- Partner Reading
- Echo Reading
- Turn and Talk
- Write and Reveal
- Think-Pair-Share

CLASSROOM MANAGEMENT ROUTINES
- Quiet Cue
- Silent Signals
- Give Me Five!
- Ask Three, Then Me
- Partner Up

Refer to the **GPS guide** for support with using the **ENGAGEMENT** routines and **CLASSROOM MANAGEMENT** routines embedded throughout the lessons.

FOCUS ROUTINE

Vocabulary

Use the **VOCABULARY** routine to

- teach Big Idea Words at the beginning of each module and Power Words from the module's texts.

- provide explicit vocabulary instruction in the context of reading.

- give children the opportunity to acquire new words and explore their meanings through relevant, student-friendly examples.

- support children in building word knowledge and rich vocabularies that contribute to future reading success.

ROUTINE MATERIALS

Use the **Vocabulary Cards** when teaching Big Idea Words and Power Words.

- Display the front of the card so that it's visible to all children as you teach the word.

- Use the back of the card as a quick reference for the routine steps, child-friendly meaning, and examples.

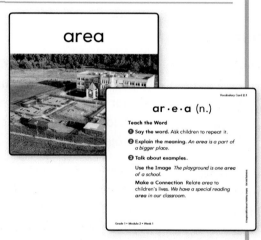

ROUTINE IN ACTION

ROUTINE STEP	MODEL LANGUAGE
1 **Say the word.** Ask children to repeat it.	*The first word we are going to learn today is area. Repeat after me: area.* *(area) Again. (area) Now let's say it in syllables. Repeat: ar-e-a. (ar-e-a) Area (area)*
2 **Explain the meaning.** Read aloud the child-friendly meaning.	*The word area is a noun—a word that names a person, place, or thing. An **area** is a part of a bigger place.*
3 **Talk about examples.** Use the image or a strategy to give examples of the word.	*Look at the picture on the Vocabulary Card. The playground is one **area** of a school.*

Professional Learning

RESEARCH FOUNDATIONS

"When teachers made children aware of the meaning of the words and then engaged them in using those words in a meaningful context, children achieved greater gains than from explicit instruction alone."

—Neuman & Wright (2014)

See the **GPS guide** to learn more.

IMPLEMENTATION SUPPORT

Consider these tips when you teach new words explicitly:

- Guide children to practice pronouncing the word a few times chorally so they become comfortable with saying the word aloud.

- Use the student-friendly meanings provided to avoid defining words on the spot or using complicated dictionary definitions.

- Reinforce grammar and word knowledge by telling children the part of speech for new words using a child-friendly meaning.

- Ensure that additional examples you provide are relevant to the children in your class and their experiences.

- Point out other common forms of the word when the class encounters them in different contexts (e.g., *success/successful; discover/discovery*).

Inquiry and Research Project

OUR COMMUNITY NEWS Over the next three weeks, children will collaborate to generate ideas, research, complete, and present an inquiry-based project.

WEEK 1 Launch the Project

LEARNING OBJECTIVES

- Participate in shared research projects.
- Generate questions for inquiry and develop a research plan.
- Gather information and evidence from sources.

MATERIALS

- Photographs of places in the local community
- Informational books
- Approved websites

WEEKLY FOCUS Set a Goal and Gather Information

Build Background Remind children that they will be learning about their community in this module.

- Help children recall that a community is made up of many different places, such as neighborhoods, fire stations, schools, parks, and libraries.

Clarify Project Goals Tell children that over the next few weeks, they will find out more about their community and make a video or presentation about how they add to community life.

Generate Research Questions Have children brainstorm places in their community and questions about each place that they hope their research will help answer. Make a note of children's questions to revisit after they have completed their projects.

Develop a Research Plan Guide children to come up with a research plan that will help them answer their research questions. Prompt children to look at informational books, magazines, newspapers, and approved websites for information about places in their community. If possible, bring in brochures or newsletters about your community and community places.

Create Curiosity Boards Have children start researching.

- Create a classroom Curiosity Board on which groups can post images, facts, or other ideas about places in their community. Discuss the display with children, and explain how you want them to use it.

- As children post to the board, have them think about why each place is important to the community.

EL ENGLISH LEARNER SUPPORT: Share Ideas

Show photographs of various places in a community. Have children name each place and discuss what they would do at that place. Provide sentences frames if necessary, such as *Firemen help _____. I can find _____ at the library.*

WEEK 2 Take Action

LEARNING OBJECTIVE

- Record information.
- Create a video.

MATERIALS

- Drawing paper
- Writing paper
- Video equipment

WEEKLY FOCUS Develop Ideas

Write About a Place in the Community Have children draw and write about a place in their community.

- With children, make a list of places in your community. Organize children into groups based on the place they choose.
- Have groups draw the place they chose and write a complete sentence to tell about the place.
- Then have each group discuss who they might find in the place and what he or she might be doing there. For example, at the library, you might find librarians or people from the community reading books. Have children write their ideas.

Create a "Spotlight" News Report Have groups work together to create a list of questions they can ask other groups about the places they chose and who might be there.

- Clarify for children that groups will film each other and ask questions about the community places. The on-camera group will answer these questions based on what they wrote.

 ENGLISH LEARNER SUPPORT: Generate Ideas

To help children decide what to write and draw about, display a graphic organizer with two columns labeled *Where I Go* and *What I Do There*. Provide one example and then ask children to provide additional examples.

 WEEK 3 Reflect and Celebrate

LEARNING OBJECTIVE

- Participate in a video or presentation.

MATERIALS

- List of research questions from Week 1
- Drawings and writings from Week 2

WEEKLY FOCUS Practice and Present

Practice Presenting Have children practice their presentations.

- Tell children in each group to take turns showing their drawings and reading their sentences about a place in the community. You may want to have group members ask each other questions to prepare for other groups' questions.

Present and Reflect Establish a time for children to present their news report to the whole class using the **SHARE CHAIR** routine.

- Tell presenters to speak loudly and clearly and to self-correct mistakes. The group filming should address the child they are questioning.
- Revisit the list of research questions children generated in Week 1 and discuss which ones they were able to answer.

✓ ASSESS LEARNING

See the **Inquiry and Research Project Rubric**.

ENGLISH LEARNER SUPPORT: Present Ideas

Have more proficient readers present first, and encourage other children to observe them carefully. Remind presenters that they should try to correct any mistakes that they make.

Introduce this module's Signposts, using these lessons. Revisit the Anchor Charts, as needed, as you encounter the Signposts during Shared Reading.

FICTION Aha Moment

INTRODUCE THE SIGNPOST

- Tell children that at a certain point in some stories, a character might suddenly understand something clearly, as if saying "Aha!" When this happens, it is important to pause because that understanding means something. It might tell something new about the character or change the events in the story.

- **Look for Clues!** Explain that there are usually clues in the story that help readers identify the Aha Moment Signpost. Phrases such as "All of a sudden, I knew" or "I finally understood" might mean that an Aha Moment is happening. Phrases that tell that something happened quickly or that something was just understood tell the reader to pause and think about what the character learned or how things might change.

NOTICE & NOTE IN ACTION!

- Tell children that you will pause as you read certain *my*Book stories in this module to prompt them to notice the Aha Moment Signpost and explain how they would apply it to that page or pages. You will also ask children to note in their books things in the text or pictures that will help them remember the Signpost and why it is important to the story.

ANCHOR QUESTION

- Display <u>Anchor Chart 55: Aha Moment</u>, and discuss the Anchor Question. Tell children that they will ask themselves this question after noticing the Aha Moment Signpost. Answering this question will help them think about how the story, events, character, or setting change.

ANCHOR CHART 55: Aha Moment

This module's Signposts are featured with the texts below, which contain strong examples of the Signposts as well as complementary comprehension skills. Encourage children to use their growing bank of known Signposts as they read different texts.

LESSON	TEXT	GENRE	COMPREHENSION SKILL	SIGNPOST
3	Dan Had a Plan	Realistic Fiction	Retell	Aha Moment
7	On the Map	Informational Text	Summarize	3 Big Questions
9	Places in My Neighborhood	Informational Text	Make Connections	3 Big Questions
12	Who Put the Cookies in the Cookie Jar?	Informational Text	Ask and Answer Questions	3 Big Questions

● *Professional Learning*

RESEARCH FOUNDATIONS

"Reading looks like a solitary act as you sit alone with a book, but you are surrounded by a community of characters, writers, and other readers, all of whom become a part of the reading experience."

—Beers & Probst (2017)

See the **GPS guide** to learn more.

NONFICTION 3 Big Questions

INTRODUCE

- Remind children that you already introduced them to the 3 Big Questions in the previous module. If children successfully applied the questions to that module's texts, focus on the Anchor Questions section.

- Review with children that when they read nonfiction texts, it is important to remember that the author is saying something about the world or a certain topic. Readers cannot assume that everything the author says is true or correct. Remind children that the author might include his or her opinions. Readers should question what the author says and how it relates to what they already know.

NOTICE & NOTE IN ACTION!

- Tell children that you will pause as you read certain *my*Book selections in this module to prompt them to ask themselves the 3 Big Questions about a page or pages. You will also ask children to note in their books things in the text or pictures that will help them remember the questions, help them answer the questions, or tell why the questions are important to the text.

ANCHOR QUESTIONS

- Display **Anchor Chart 65: 3 Big Questions**, and discuss the Anchor Questions. Share that children will ask themselves these questions when they see new, confusing, or challenging information in a nonfiction text.

ANCHOR CHART 65: 3 Big Questions

Online
Ed

Kicking Off the Module!

Get started with Module 2 by setting goals with children and connecting with families.

Set Goals with Children

Tell children that over the next few weeks they will build and strengthen their reading, writing, listening, and speaking skills as they explore family and community:

- Encourage children to reflect on their prior learning and set personal goals for the upcoming module.

- Share the sentence frames to the right to support children with setting goals. Model examples and record goals for each child.

- Revisit children's goals throughout the module to help them track progress and reflect on their learning.

> I want to read stories about _____.
>
> I want to learn about _____.
>
> I will _____ so I can _____.

Connect with Families

Share Printable: **Family Letter 2** to support children's learning at home:

- Offer support to help families discuss the module topic and the module's Big Idea Words.

- Encourage children to read at home with their families, and provide ideas for families to talk about books together.

- Suggest word play activities to support literacy development.

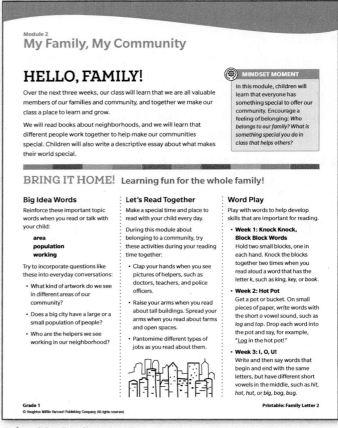

Printable: Family Letter 2

 SOCIAL STUDIES CONNECTION: Communities

My Family, My Community

(?) Essential Question How can making new friends and learning new things help us?

Essential Skills

FOUNDATIONAL SKILLS

- Phonics: Consonants *g*, *k*; Review Short *a*, *i*
- High-Frequency Words: *are, buy, little, said, too, up, will, you*
- Fluency: Expression
- Spelling: Short *i*

VOCABULARY

- Power Words: *belong, gifted, help, market, mess, neighbors, persists, sell, set, sketch, smeared, toiled*
- Generative Vocabulary: Words About Places and Things
- Vocabulary Strategy: Antonyms

READING WORKSHOP

- Ideas and Support
- Text Organization
- Retell
- Setting
- Speaking and Listening: Social Communication

WRITING WORKSHOP

- Writing Form: Descriptive Essay
- Grammar Minilessons: Adjectives: Size and Shape; Articles

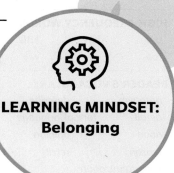

LEARNING MINDSET:
Belonging

THIS WEEK'S TEXTS

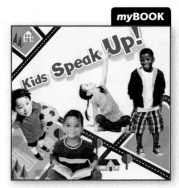

Kids Speak Up!

Whose Hands Are These?

Dan Had a Plan

Decodable Texts
Cab! Cab!
Go, Big Cab!
A Big Pit
Big Pat

Rigby®
LEVELED LIBRARY

⏱ Suggested Daily Times

- **BUILD KNOWLEDGE & LANGUAGE/ VOCABULARY**   10–15 minutes
- **FOUNDATIONAL SKILLS**   15–30 minutes
- **READING WORKSHOP**   60–75 minutes
- **WRITING WORKSHOP**   20–30 minutes

This Week's Words

BIG IDEA WORDS

area	population	working

POWER WORDS

belong	gifted	help
market	mess	neighbors
persists	sell	set
sketch	smeared	toiled

HIGH-FREQUENCY WORDS

are	buy	little	said
too	up	will	you

READER'S VOCABULARY

antonym	describe	description
detail	formal language	informal language
noun	opinion	persuade
reason	retell	setting
text organization		

Assessment Options

 **Online Ed**

- ✓ **Selection Quiz:** *Dan Had a Plan*
- ✓ **Weekly Assessment**
  - High-Frequency Words
  - Phonics: Consonants *g, k*; Short *a, i*
  - Comprehension: Ideas and Support; Setting
  - Generative Vocabulary: Words About Places and Things
  - Vocabulary Strategy: Antonyms
  - Grammar: Adjectives: Size and Shape; Articles

Intervention

For children needing strategic intervention, use *Tabletop Minilessons: Intervention.*

- Module 2, Week 1 Daily Lessons

LESSON 1

BUILD KNOWLEDGE & LANGUAGE

Module Launch, pp. T272–T273   *Teaching Pal*

- Introduce the Topic: Communities
- Big Idea Words: *area, population, working*

FOUNDATIONAL SKILLS

Word Work Warm-Up, pp. T274–T275

- High-Frequency Words: *are, buy, little, said, too, up, will, you*
- Phonological Awareness

Phonics, pp. T276–T277

- Consonants *g, k*

Spelling, pp. T278–T279

- Short *i*

READING WORKSHOP

Kids Speak Up!   *Teaching Pal*
GENRE Opinion Writing
Shared Reading: MINILESSON, pp. T280–T281

- Connect and Teach: Ideas and Support
- Apply to Text: *Kids Speak Up!*
- Engage and Respond: Speaking & Listening

SMALL-GROUP INSTRUCTION 👥

Options for Differentiation

- Guided Reading Groups, p. T282
- English Learner Support: Recount Information, p. T282
- Reinforce Ideas and Support, p. T283
- Reinforce Foundational Skills: Read *Cab! Cab!*, pp. T284–T285

Options for Independent and Collaborative Work, pp. T286–T287

WRITING WORKSHOP

Descriptive Essay, p. W18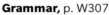

- Introducing the Focal Text

Grammar, p. W306

- Adjectives

LESSON 2

FOUNDATIONAL SKILLS

Word Work Warm-Up, pp. T288–T289

- High-Frequency Words: *go, is, like, see, the, this, to, we*
- Phonological Awareness

Phonics, pp. T290–T291

- Consonants *g, k*

VOCABULARY

Academic Vocabulary, pp. T292–T293

- Introduce Oral Language: *toiled, belong, gifted, persists, smeared, sketch*

READING WORKSHOP

Whose Hands Are These?   **Book Stix**
GENRE Informational Text
Shared Reading: MINILESSON, pp. T294–T295

- Connect and Teach: Text Organization
- Apply to Text: *Whose Hands Are These?*
- Engage and Respond: Writing

SMALL-GROUP INSTRUCTION 👥

Options for Differentiation

- Guided Reading Groups, p. T296
- English Learner Support: Recount Information, p. T296
- Reinforce Text Organization, p. T297
- Reinforce Foundational Skills: Read *Go, Big Cab!*, pp. T298–T299

Options for Independent and Collaborative Work, pp. T300–T301

WRITING WORKSHOP

Descriptive Essay, p. W19

- The Read

Grammar, p. W307

- Adjectives for Size and Shape

LESSON 3

FOUNDATIONAL SKILLS

Word Work Warm-Up, p. T302
- High-Frequency Words: *go, is, like, see, the, this, to, we*
- Phonological Awareness

Fluency, p. T303
- Reading Rate

Phonics, pp. T304–T305
- Review Short *a, i*

VOCABULARY

Academic Vocabulary, pp. T306–T307
- Introduce Power Words: *mess, market, sell, help, neighbors, set*

READING WORKSHOP

Dan Had a Plan
GENRE Realistic Fiction
Shared Reading: MINILESSON, pp. T308–T309
- Connect and Teach: Retell
- Apply to Text: *Dan Had a Plan*
- Engage and Respond: Speaking & Listening

SMALL-GROUP INSTRUCTION

Options for Differentiation
- Guided Reading Groups, p. T310
- English Learner Support: Recount Information, p. T310
- Reinforce Retell, p. T311
- Reinforce Foundational Skills: Read *A Big Pit,* pp. T312–T313

Options for Independent and Collaborative Work, pp. T314–T315

WRITING WORKSHOP

Descriptive Essay, p. W20
- Vocabulary

Grammar, p. W308
- Using Articles

LESSON 4

FOUNDATIONAL SKILLS

Word Work Warm-Up, p. T316
- High-Frequency Words: *go, is, like, see, the, this, to, we*
- Phonological Awareness

Phonics, p. T317
- Phonics Review

VOCABULARY

Academic Vocabulary, p. T318
- Review Power Words: *mess, market, sell, help, neighbors, set*

Generative Vocabulary, p. T319
- Words About Places and Things

READING WORKSHOP

Dan Had a Plan
GENRE Realistic Fiction
Shared Reading: MINILESSON, pp. T320–T321
- Connect and Teach: Setting
- Apply to Text: *Dan Had a Plan*
- Engage and Respond: Writing

SMALL-GROUP INSTRUCTION

Options for Differentiation
- Guided Reading Groups, p. T322
- English Learner Support: Recount Information, p. T322
- Reinforce Setting, p. T323
- Reinforce Foundational Skills: Read *Big Pat,* pp. T324–T325

Options for Independent and Collaborative Work, pp. T326–T327

WRITING WORKSHOP

Descriptive Essay, p. W21
- Prewriting I: Finding a Topic

Grammar, p. W289
- Spiral Review: Action Verbs

LESSON 5

FOUNDATIONAL SKILLS

Word Work Warm-Up, p. T328
- High-Frequency Words: *go, is, like, see, the, this, to, we*
- Phonological Awareness

Spelling, p. T329
- Spelling Assessment

VOCABULARY

Vocabulary Strategy, pp. T330–T331
- Antonyms

READING WORKSHOP

Speaking and Listening: MINILESSON, pp. T332–T333
- Connect and Teach: Social Communication
- Apply to Text
- Engage and Respond: Writing

SMALL-GROUP INSTRUCTION

Options for Differentiation
- Guided Reading Groups, p. T334
- English Learner Support: Recount Information, p. T334
- Reinforce Social Communication, p. T335
- Reinforce Foundational Skills: Make Text Connections, pp. T336–T337

Options for Independent and Collaborative Work, pp. T338–T339

WRITING WORKSHOP

Descriptive Essay, p. W22
- Prewriting II: Planning a Descriptive Essay

Grammar, p. W310
- Connect to Writing: Using Adjectives and Articles

Week at a Glance T267

Preview Lesson Texts

Build understanding of this week's texts so that you can best support children in making connections, understanding key ideas, and becoming lifelong readers.

Kids Speak Up!

GENRE Opinion Writing

WHY THIS TEXT?

In this text, first-graders share their thoughts about why their hometown is a great place to live. By reflecting on the opinions of these children, readers will be encouraged to recognize what is special about their own communities.

KEY LEARNING OBJECTIVES

- Identify characteristics of opinion writing.
- Identify an author's opinion and the reasons given to support it.

TEXT COMPLEXITY

LEXILE MEASURE 210L • **GUIDED READING LEVEL** D

OVERALL RATING Slightly Complex

The text is told from different points of view but in easy-to-understand language.

MAKE CONNECTIONS

🔗 **BUILD KNOWLEDGE AND LANGUAGE**

- **Social Studies Connection:** Communities

🔗 **VOCABULARY**

- **Words About Places and Things:** *ball, books, fires, lake, library, park, town*

🔗 **FOUNDATIONAL SKILLS**

- **High-Frequency Words:** *up, you*
- **Consonants *g, k*:** *big, books, get, go, great, kids, lake, like, make, park, speak, think, workers*
- **Review Short *a, i*:** *and, big, can, dad, fast, fishing, has, is, it, kids, live, think*

TEXT X-RAY

KEY IDEAS	🔵 LANGUAGE
Key Idea *p. 96* Different children explain what makes each of their hometowns special. One child likes a big park. Another likes the town's library.	**Phrasal Verb** ***speak up*** (p. 96): Explain that when people "speak up," they tell others their thoughts or opinions about something.
Key Idea *p. 97* Town workers, such as firefighters, help make the town great. A boy enjoys fishing at the lake in the town.	**Informal Language** ***tons of*** (p. 96): In this text, *tons of* is an informal way of saying "a lot of" or "a very large number/amount of."

Dan Had a Plan by Wong Herbert Yee

GENRE Realistic Fiction

WHY THIS TEXT?

Dan's older sister thinks he's too little to help with her fundraising project, but Dan has a plan! He helps sell all the bug and bat snacks his sister made to raise money for the library. Children will learn that no one is too young to be helpful.

KEY LEARNING OBJECTIVES

- Identify features of realistic fiction.
- Retell story events in sequence and in a way that shows understanding.
- Use details in the text and illustrations to identify and describe a story's setting.

TEXT COMPLEXITY

LEXILE MEASURE 250L • **GUIDED READING LEVEL** E

OVERALL RATING Slightly Complex

The story's chronological order helps communicate its somewhat subtle theme.

MAKE CONNECTIONS

🔗 BUILD KNOWLEDGE AND LANGUAGE

- **Social Studies Connection:** Communities

🔗 VOCABULARY

- **Words About Places and Things:** *bats, books, bugs, library, market, money, sign*

🔗 FOUNDATIONAL SKILLS

- **High-Frequency Words:** *are, buy, little, said, too, up, will, you*
- **Consonants g, k:** *asked, big, books, bugs, go, good, great, kids, Kim, like, market*
- **Review Short a, i:** *and, asked, at, bats, big, can, Dad, Dan, did, had, is, it, kids, Kim, last, little, Pam, plan, ran, sad, Sam, Tim, will*

📖 TEXT X-RAY

KEY IDEAS	🔵 LANGUAGE
Key Idea *pp. 100–103* Dan's sister, Kim, is making creative bug and bat snacks. She will sell them at an outdoor market to raise money for the library.	**Word Play** ***Fruit Flyers*** (p. 101): The author is making a little joke by saying that the snacks fly because they are in the shape of bugs and bats.
Key Idea *pp. 104–109* Dan has a plan to help. He and his friend, Sam, encourage people at the market to buy the bugs and bats.	**Phrasal Verb** ***set up*** (p. 103): Explain that when you set something up, you get it ready to work properly. Here, people set up by putting up tables and displaying items for sale.
Key Idea *pp. 110–112*	**CULTURAL REFERENCES**
The sale is a success! To thank Dan for all his help, Kim gives him the last bug snack. Dan and Sam are proud that they helped raise money to buy new books for the library.	***farmers' market*** (p. 101): Although farmers' markets are found around the world, they may differ from country to country. Explain how farmers' markets generally operate in the United States.

While you meet with small groups, have children work independently in Literacy Centers. At the beginning of the week, explain what is expected of children in each center. Post a daily rotation schedule.

WORD WORK

Word Search Puzzle

- Provide graph paper in the center. Display the Word Cards for this week's High-Frequency Words.

- Have children make a word search puzzle by writing each of the High-Frequency Words on graph paper and then filling in the empty squares with random letters.

- Have children exchange puzzles with a partner. Have children search for, circle, and write the hidden words.

- For an extra challenge, have children include previously learned High-Frequency Words in their puzzles.

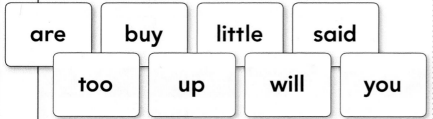

are	buy	little	said
too	up	will	you

Short *i*

- Display the week's Spelling Words and copies of Printable: **Spelling & Handwriting**. Have children choose one of the activities to practice writing this week's Spelling Words in their best handwriting.

- Have children complete the activity on a separate sheet of paper.

Printable:
Spelling & Handwriting

CREATIVITY CORNER

Readers' Theater

- Preview Printable: **Readers' Theater 2**, "Help Find Bud," and assign parts to mixed-ability groups of five children. The part of the Nurse is ideal for a struggling reader, while the part of Mom should be read by a proficient reader.

- Have groups write in the missing parts to make their script unique and then practice reading it aloud several times.

- Remind children to read their lines loudly and clearly.

Printable: Readers' Theater 2

Reading Remake

- Display in the center and have children complete the activity for *Dan Had a Plan* on Printable: **Write a News Story**.

- Tell partners to explain to one another how their news story shows their understanding of the selection.

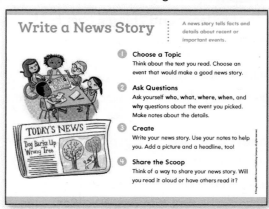

Printable: Write a News Story

DIGITAL STATION

Listener's Choice

- Have children listen to the Big Book *Whose Hands Are These?* or a Leveled Reader of their choice.
- Tell them to add the book to their Printable: **Listening Log**, as well as the active listening skills they used, a summary, and a question they have about the book.

Phonics Practice

- Have children continue their personalized, adaptive learning for foundational skills in *iRead*.

TEAMWORK TIME

Inquiry and Research Project: Our Community News

- Have groups work on the module project.
- Remind children that their focus this week is to think about and research places in their community. *See pp. T260–T261.*

READING CORNER

Independent Reading

- Have children self-select or continue reading an independent reading book.
- Remind children to set a purpose for reading and to record their progress on their Printable: **Reading Log**.
- You may want to choose from these additional options to have children interact with their books:

  » **Read for Fluency** Children use the **PARTNER READING** routine to practice the week's fluency skill, expression, or another area of need.

  » **Annotate the Text** Children practice a strategy and use sticky notes to record questions or what they are thinking as they read. Review the sticky notes while you confer with children.

  » **Response Journal** Children draw or write about what they read.

Student Choice Library

LEVELED LIBRARY

BUILD KNOWLEDGE AND LANGUAGE

 Introduce the Topic: Communities

Access Prior Knowledge

LEARNING OBJECTIVES

- **Language** Answer questions using multi-word responses.
- Share information and ideas about a topic under discussion.
- Identify real-life connections between words and their use.

MATERIALS   Online

Display and Engage *Knowledge Map 2.1*

Teaching Pal *Book 1, pp. 92–95*

myBook *Book 1, pp. 92–95*

Get Curious Video *Come to the Fair!*

Vocabulary Cards *2.1–2.3*

- Reveal the module topic by projecting Display and Engage: <u>Knowledge Map 2.1</u>. Point to the center of the Knowledge Map. Tell children that the texts they will read about all tell something about communities. Use the Knowledge Map to point out some things that children can expect to read about in this module.

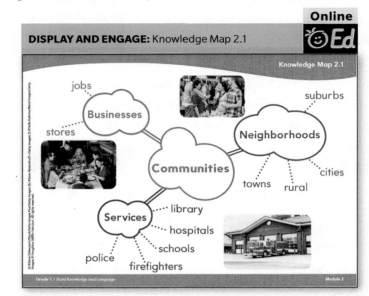

- Have children brainstorm word associations for *communities* and add them to a web.

 LEARNING MINDSET

Belonging

Introduce Tell children that every person in a classroom is a valuable, important member of the school community. Throughout the module, children will encounter examples of story characters who belong to a community. Children will also engage in their own school learning community.

Give feedback when you notice children participating. *Even if you feel you don't belong, you do! Everyone's ideas are helpful. Our community benefits when everyone joins in and shares ideas!*

● *Professional Learning*

TEACHING TERMS

Knowledge maps are powerful tools to visually represent what children will learn or have learned about a topic. Encourage children to discuss, reflect on, and add to the knowledge maps throughout the module.

See the **GPS guide** to learn more.

Teaching Pal, pp. 92–93

Build Background

In your Teaching Pal, pages 92–95, use the prompts to begin developing the module topic as children follow along in their *my*Book.

- **Discuss the Quotation** Lead a discussion about the Hispanic proverb *(p. 92).*

- **Essential Question** Introduce the Essential Question: *How does everyone in my family and community make it special?* Then use the **ACTIVE VIEWING** routine with the Get Curious Video: **Come to the Fair!** *(p. 93).*

- **Big Idea Words** Use the **VOCABULARY** routine and Vocabulary Cards 2.1–2.3 to introduce the Big Idea Words: *area, population, working.* Then have children begin the Vocabulary Network *(pp. 94–95).* Encourage them to add to it throughout the module.

Online
Ed
GET CURIOUS VIDEO

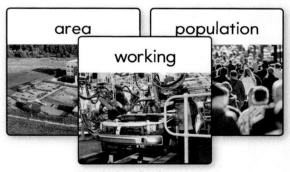

area population working

Vocabulary Cards

(EL) ENGLISH LEARNER SUPPORT:
Build Background

SUBSTANTIAL
To build background about families, ask children to name the people in their family: *Who is in your family? What are their names?*

MODERATE
Ask children to share the names of people in their family with a partner.

LIGHT
To build background about family and community, ask open-ended questions: *Why is your family special? Why is your community special?*

Professional Learning

RESEARCH FOUNDATIONS

"We must recognize that knowledge is not just accumulating facts; rather, children need to develop knowledge networks, comprised of clusters of concepts that are coherent, generative, and supportive of future learning in a domain."
—Dr. Susan B. Neuman, Dr. Tanya Kaefer, and Dr. Ashley Pinkham (2014)

See the **GPS guide** to learn more.

FOUNDATIONAL SKILLS

High-Frequency Words

Teach the Words

Use Word Cards *are, buy, little, said, too, up, will,* and *you* and the **HIGH-FREQUENCY WORDS** routine below to introduce the week's High-Frequency sight words.

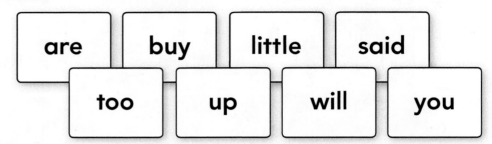

1. **See the word.** Display a Word Card. Say the word, and have children repeat it twice.

2. **Say the word.** Have children repeat it chorally. Use the word in a sentence or two. *This is my little finger. An ant is a little bug.* (Use gestures.)

3. **Spell the word.** Point to the letters, and have children spell the word aloud. Point out any familiar spelling patterns. Little *begins with l. Can you think of an animal name that begins with l?* (lion, lizard) *Do you know any other words that begin with l?*

4. **Write and check the word.** Hide the word, and have children use the **WRITE AND REVEAL** routine to write the word. Then have them check it against the Word Card.

Have children add this week's words to their individual Word Rings. Tell them to write a word on the front of each card and write a sentence or draw a picture about the word on the back. Alternatively, you may have children complete Know It, Show It page 33.

LEARNING OBJECTIVES

- Identify and read high-frequency words.
- **Language** Recognize, recite, and write basic sight vocabulary.
- Blend onsets and rimes to say one-syllable words.
- Blend phonemes to say one-syllable words.

MATERIALS   Online

Word Cards *are, buy, little, said, too, up, will, you*

Know It, Show It *p. 33*

Picture Cards *bell, boat, cup, gate, hay, pan, peas, pen, pin*

 ENGLISH LEARNER SUPPORT: Build Vocabulary

SUBSTANTIAL
Act out word meanings to reinforce understanding. For example, hold up a small bit of chalk and say, *The chalk is little.*

MODERATE
Reinforce the meaning of *buy.* Contrast it to *by,* and then have children complete the frame: *I will buy _____ at the store.*

LIGHT
Have children take turns using High-Frequency Words in sentences.

 CORRECT & REDIRECT

Guide children who have trouble identifying any of the words. Say the correct word, and have children repeat it. Example:

- Said. *What is the word?* (said)
- Have children spell the word. *(s-a-i-d) How do we say this word?* (said)
- Have children reread all the cards in random order.

Phonological Awareness

Blend Onset and Rime

- Remind children that listening for and working with the sounds in words they hear can help them when they read and write. Explain that blending word chunks can help them notice the sounds in words.

- Display Picture Cards *bell, boat, cup, gate, hay,* and *peas.*

- Tell children that you will say word chunks and that they will blend the chunks to say each word. Display Picture Card *bell* and model: *I will say a word in two chunks: the word's beginning and the rest of the word. You blend the beginning chunk and the rest of the word to say the word. I will do the first one and give you a hint by showing a picture for the word. Listen to the two chunks of the word: /b/ /ĕl/. I can blend the chunks to say the word: /b/ /ĕl/, /b-ĕl/,* bell. Point to Picture Card *bell. The word is* bell.

- *Now you try it. I will say one of these picture names in two chunks, the beginning and the rest of the word. You blend the word chunks and say the word. I will call on someone to bring me the matching Picture Card. Listen: /k/ /ŭp/. What is the word?* (cup) *Who can give me the matching card?*

- Continue having children blend onset and rime to say words. Have children give a "thumbs up" sign if there is a matching Picture Card, and ask a volunteer to bring you the card: /h/ /ā/ (hay), /p/ /ŏd/ (pod), /m/ /ăd/ (mad), /g/ /āt/ (gate), /b/ /ōt/ (boat), /r/ /ŭn/ (run), /p/ /ēz/ (peas).

Blend Phonemes

- Remind children that they know how to blend all the sounds in a word to say the word.

- Say: *I will say all the sounds in a word, and you will blend the sounds to say the word. I will do the first one. Listen, the sounds are: /r/ /ā/ /n/. When I blend /r/, /ā/, and /n/, I say the word* rain. /r/ /ā/ /n/, rain.

- Display Picture Cards *pan, pen,* and *pin.*

- *Are you ready to try? What's the word for these sounds? Listen: /p/ /ĭ/ /n/. Point to the Picture Card for the word you say when you blend /p/ /ĭ/ /n/.* (pin) *Now try: /p/ /ĕ/ /n/* (pen), /p/ /ă/ /n/ (pan).

- *Let's blend some more. Ready? /w/ /ē/* (we), /ă/ /d/ (add), /b/ /ŭ/ /d/ (bud), /p/ /ĭ/ /k/ (pick), /g/ /ō/ (go), /s/ /ĭ/ /p/ (sip)

 CORRECT & REDIRECT

For children who blend incorrectly, differentiate instruction by modeling. Enunciate the sounds separately, then say them more closely together before finally blending them. Example:

The sounds are /g/ and /ō/. The first sound is /g/. Listen: /g/. The next sound is /ō/. Listen: /ōōō/. Say each sound with me: /g/, /ō/. Now listen as I blend the two sounds together: /g/ /ō/, /g-ō/, go. *What is the word?* (go)

FOUNDATIONAL SKILLS

PHONICS

LEARNING OBJECTIVES

- Learn the sound-spellings for the consonants *g* (hard *g*), *k*.
- **Language** Recognize sound-letter relationships and use them to decode words.
- Blend letter sounds and decode regularly spelled one-syllable words with /g/, /k/.

MATERIALS Online

Sound/Spelling Cards *goat, kangaroo*
Letter Cards *a, b, d, g, i, k, s*
Articulation Videos /g/, /k/

 # Consonants *g, k*

Spotlight on Sounds

- Tell children that they will be reading words with the sounds for the consonants *g* and *k*. Explain that first they will practice identifying the beginning sounds in words you say. *I am going to say a word, and you say the beginning sound. I will do the first one. Listen: The word is gas. The beginning sound in gas is /g/. Listen again: gas, /g/. Now listen to each word and say the beginning sound:* kite *(/k/);* go *(/g/);* key *(/k/);* give *(/g/);* good *(/g/);* keep *(/k/).*

- Next, model how to identify the ending sound in *tag, /g/*. Have children continue with these words: *dog (/g/); back (/k/); big (/g/); rag (/g/); pick (/k/).*

- Conclude the activity by having children suggest words with final sounds. Say: *Now you think of more words that end with /g/. Repeat for final /k/.*

I Do It

Spotlight on Letters Display the Sound/Spelling Card for *g: goat*. Name the picture, say the hard /g/ sound, and give the spelling. *Goat begins with the /g/ sound. The letter* g *is a consonant. It can stand for the /g/ sound at the beginning or end of a word.*

Write *gap*. Say the letter sounds and blend the word. *The word* gap *begins with the letter* g *and the sound /g/.* Point out the vowel and the final consonant. *When there is only one vowel and it is followed by a consonant, what sound does the vowel usually stand for?* (the short vowel sound) *Blend the word with me: /g/ /ă/ /p/,* gap.

Repeat for *k*, using Sound/Spelling Card *kangaroo* and the word *kit*.

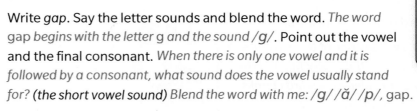

g
—gg

TEACHER TIP

Now decodable! After this lesson, children will be able to decode the High-Frequency Words *big, ran, sit, did,* and *its!* Children will practice these words along with the other High-Frequency Words for this week to build fluent word recognition.

 ENGLISH LEARNER SUPPORT: Facilitate Language Connections

ALL LEVELS Speakers of Hmong, Cantonese, Korean, and Khmer may have trouble hearing and producing /g/. Play the Articulation Video for /g/. Then have children practice the sound. Say words that begin with /g/ for children to repeat: *girl, goat, go, give.* Finally, say word pairs that begin with /g/ and /k/. Have children repeat the word with /g/: *cave/gave; get/cat; good/could.* If children need practice with /k/, play the Articulation Video for /k/.

Online
ARTICULATION VIDEO

We Do It

Write *gas* and use Letter Cards *g, a, s* with the **SOUND-BY-SOUND BLENDING** routine below to model blending the word.

1 **Display** cards as shown. Say the first letter and sound.

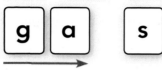

2 **Slide** the second letter over. Say its sound. Then blend the two sounds.

3 **Slide** the last letter over. Say its sound. Say the first two blended sounds, the last sound, and the blended word: /gă/ /s/, gas.

Sound-by-Sound Blending Repeat the **SOUND-BY-SOUND BLENDING** routine with cards for the words *kid* and *gab*, having children say the sounds and blend.

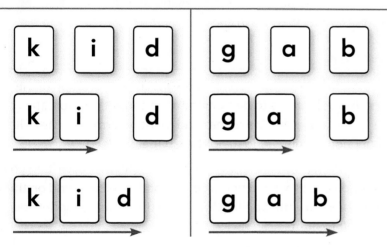

You Do It

INDEPENDENT PRACTICE

Blending Practice Write the words below. Then choose two volunteers to model the activity. The first child points to any word and says the letter sounds. The second child blends the sounds to read the word. Children then switch roles to choose and read another word. Continue until each child has had a turn and all words have been blended and read.

| bag | gag | kit | kin |
| gap | kid | pig | kim |

✓ CORRECT & REDIRECT

- If a child mispronounces a word during Blending Practice, make note of the error type and address it.
- If a child reads *bag* as *gab*, cover the word and blend it together as you uncover one letter at a time, left to right. Then have the child blend and read the word.
- If a child reads *pig* as *pick*, contrast the /g/ and /k/ sounds, using the Sound/Spelling Cards *goat* and *kangaroo*. Use sound-by-sound blending to read the word, having the child repeat the steps after you.

👥 LINK TO SMALL-GROUP INSTRUCTION

REINFORCE FOUNDATIONAL SKILLS Use *Cab! Cab!* during small-group time to review or reinforce blending and decoding words with consonants *g, k*. Meet with children to work through the story, or assign it as independent work. *See the lesson on p. T284.*

Short *i*

Administer the Pretest

- Read the first Spelling Word and the Dictation Sentence. Repeat the word as children write it.

- Write the Spelling Word, and have children correct their spelling if needed. Repeat for words 2–6 and for the Review Words.

- Assign the Basic and Review Spelling Words as needed for practice this week. If children do well on the pretest, assign the Challenge Words.

LEARNING OBJECTIVES

- Spell words with short *i* (closed syllables).
- **Language** Identify relationships between sounds and letters.
- Develop handwriting.

MATERIALS   Online

Sound/Spelling Card *igloo*
Printable *Word List 4*
Know It, Show It *p. 34*

DICTATION SENTENCES

BASIC

1. **in**   We go *in* that door.
2. **pig**   A *pig* is a farm animal.
3. **did**   What *did* you do yesterday?
4. **sit**   Please *sit* in the chair.
5. **dig**   Use a shovel to *dig* a hole.
6. **big**   An elephant is very *big*.

REVIEW

7. **pin**   She uses a *pin* to hold her hair.
8. **fit**   All my markers *fit* in the box.
9. **it**   Put *it* away.
10. **sip**   Take a *sip* of the drink.

CHALLENGE

11. **ship**   The *ship* crossed the ocean.
12. **fish**   Many *fish* swim in the lake.

Teach the Principle

- Remind children that they have learned to read and spell some words with short *i*. Write *pig* on the board, underlining *i*, and read it aloud. Remind children that the /ĭ/ sound can be spelled with the letter *i*.

- Tell children that this week all the Spelling Words have the short *i* sound, /ĭ/, spelled *i*. Explain that short *i* sound can be at the beginning or in the middle of a word.

- If children have difficulty, review Sound/Spelling Card *igloo*. Remind them that *i* is a vowel that can stand for many sounds and that one of those sounds is /ĭ/, as in *igloo*.

Model Handwriting

- Remind children that they have learned that as they write, the position of the paper is important. Ask volunteers to demonstrate the correct position: the paper should be slanted along the line of the child's writing arm, and the child should use his or her non-writing hand to hold the paper in place.

- Remind children that when they read, they read left to right. Model writing your name on the board. Point out that you begin writing on the left and end on the right. Then ask volunteers to write Spelling Words on the board to model how to write words from left to right.

- Ask children to demonstrate the correct paper position and left-to-right directionality as they write practice writing this week's Spelling Words.

ENGLISH LEARNER SUPPORT:
Build Vocabulary

ALL LEVELS Make sure children understand the meanings of the Spelling Words and Dictation Sentences. Have volunteers act out word meanings for others to guess.

Professional Learning

TEACHING TERMS

What is the difference between **decoding** and **encoding**? **Decoding** is the ability to apply knowledge of letter-sound relationships and word parts to recognize and read written words. **Encoding** is the ability to apply knowledge of letter-sound relationships and word parts to spell words.

See the **GPS guide** to learn more.

Word Sort

1 **Introduce** Display both the Basic and the Review Spelling Word cards from Printable: <u>Word List 4</u>, and read each one aloud.

2 **Columns 1–3** Display the Spelling Word cards *dig* and *sit* as headings for columns 1 and 2. Write *other* as a third column heading. Explain: *I will put* dig *and* sit *at the top of columns 1 and 2. I will put* other *at the top of column 3. I will read a word. You will tell me if the word has the same ending sounds as* dig *or* sit *or if it belongs in* other.

3 **Model** Display the Spelling Word card *pig* and read it aloud. Explain: *Pig. Pig ends with the letters* -ig *and the sounds* /ĭg/. *So I'll put* pig *under* dig. Repeat for *fit*, placing it under *sit*, and *did*, placing it under *other*.

4 **Continue** Sort the remaining words, including the Review Words.

5 **Discuss** Read each column together. Discuss what children notice about the words in each column. If no one mentions it, guide children to identify the words in column 1 as ending with *-ig* and rhyming with *dig* and the words in column 2 as ending with *-it* and rhyming with *sit*. Tell children they can think about these patterns when they spell words with short *i*.

6 **Repeat** Have children work together to repeat the sort, using the Spelling Word cards from Printable: <u>Word List 4</u>. Make additional copies of the page and the Spelling Word cards for use all week.

dig	sit	other	
pig	fit	did	in
big	it	pin	sip

INDEPENDENT PRACTICE

For additional practice, have children complete Know It, Show It page 34. Encourage them to use their best handwriting and pay particular attention to the position of their papers and writing from left to right.

ENGLISH LEARNER SUPPORT:
Facilitate Language Connections

ALL LEVELS Some English learners may need support pronouncing the vowel sound /ĭ/. Have children listen carefully to the following pairs of words: *in/an, pin/pan, big/bag, sit/sat, did/dad*. Then repeat each pair of words, and have children say them after you.

LEARNING MINDSET

Belonging

Model Encourage children to feel comfortable asking for help when they get stuck. Use the following example. *I'm having trouble learning how to sort words by their ending sounds, but I can ask a member of our community for help. To sort this week's Spelling Words, I can ask a partner to work with me. Then I can get the help I need, and the two of us can work together and have fun.*

READING WORKSHOP

 Ideas and Support

Step **1**   **Connect and Teach**

LEARNING OBJECTIVES

- Recognize characteristics of opinion writing.
- Identify an author's opinion and supporting reasons.
- **Language** Discuss the reasons an author gives for an opinion.
- Share ideas in cooperative learning interactions.

MATERIALS   Online

Anchor Chart 15
Ideas and Support

Printable
Anchor Chart 15: Ideas and Support

Teaching Pal *Book 1, pp. 96–97*

myBook *Kids Speak Up!, Book 1, pp. 96–97*

READER'S VOCABULARY

- **persuade** to try to convince someone of an idea or to try to get the person to do something
- **opinion** ideas or beliefs that cannot be proved
- **reason** a statement or fact that explains an idea

- Ask children to think of a time they wanted to **persuade** others to play with them. Explain that when you persuade someone to play, you try to get that person to agree to play with you or to play the game you want to play.

- Project or display <u>Anchor Chart 15: Ideas and Support</u>. Explain that when authors write to persuade, they try to get readers to agree with an idea or to do something.

- Point out that an author of **opinion** writing usually starts by telling his or her opinion, or what they think about something. Then the author gives **reasons** or facts that support the opinion.

ANCHOR CHART 15: Ideas and Support   **Online**

> ## IDEAS and SUPPORT
>
> When authors write to persuade, they want readers to do or believe something.
>
> **OPINION**
> What does the author think or feel?
>
> I think...
> I believe...
> I feel...
> _____ is the best _____.
>
> **REASONS**
> What reasons support the opinion? Look for facts, or things that can be proved.
>
> **EXAMPLES**
> What examples or details tell more about the reasons?

- Explain that when children read opinions, they should figure out what the author is trying to persuade them to think or do. They should also think about the reasons the author used to support the opinion and whether those reasons make sense.

- Tell children they will practice identifying an author's opinion and supporting reasons when they read an opinion writing selection called *Kids Speak Up!*

TEACHER TIP

Why, why, why? Tell children that asking "Why?" is a good way to figure out the reasons for an opinion. Model by making an opinion statement, such as "I think blue is the best color." Have two or three different children ask why, and give several reasons for your opinion.

ENGLISH LEARNER SUPPORT: Facilitate Language Connections

ALL LEVELS For Spanish-speaking children, point out that the English words *persuade, opinion, reason,* and *ideas* have Spanish cognates: *persuadir, opinión, razón,* and *ideas.* Also point out that the English word *support* has a false cognate, *soportar,* which most often means "to put up with."

**Go to Your
Teaching Pal**

 Online
Ed

ANNOTATE IT!

Children may use the annotation
tools in their eBook.

Step 2 Apply to Text

In your Teaching Pal, pages 96–97, use the blue **READ FOR
UNDERSTANDING** prompts to guide discussion of *Kids Speak
Up!* as children follow along in their *my*Book.

- **Genre Study** Remind children that opinion writing shows an
  author's thoughts, beliefs, or ideas. Ask them to preview the
  title, text features, and illustrations, and tell what opinion they
  think they will read about.

- **Set a Purpose** Prompt children to set their own purpose for
  reading, based on their preview. As needed, use this model:
  I will read to find out why these children think their town is great.

- **Read and Comprehend** Guide children to read the
  selection. Pause occasionally, using the prompts in your
  Teaching Pal to gauge children's understanding and to have
  them identify the children's opinions and the reasons for their
  opinions, and tell what the children want the readers to think.
  Refer back to the Anchor Chart to help children identify each
  opinion and reason in *Kids Speak Up!*

Step 3 Engage and Respond

INDEPENDENT PRACTICE: Speaking & Listening

- Remind children of the Essential Question: *How does everyone
  in my family and community make it special?* Then have children
  look at *Kids Speak Up!* again to see if they can find any
  information that will help them answer the question.

- Have partners use the **THINK-PAIR-SHARE** routine to discuss
  their ideas and then share with the group. Remind children to
  stay on topic and tell their ideas in full sentences.

- You may want to have children conduct their discussions
  during daily small-group time.

 *Getting Started*

ENGAGEMENT ROUTINE

Use the **THINK-PAIR-SHARE** routine when:

- greater participation in the lesson is desired.

- there is a question that requires higher order thinking to answer.

See the **GPS guide** to learn more.

 LINK TO SMALL-GROUP INSTRUCTION

REINFORCE IDEAS AND SUPPORT Review or extend the skill as
needed during small-group time to support children's need for
differentiation. *See the lesson on p. T283.*

Options for Differentiation

As the class engages in independent and collaborative work, meet with Guided Reading Groups or differentiate instruction based on student need.

GUIDED READING GROUPS

Match Children to Books + Instruction

- Choose just-right books based on level, skill, topic, or genre.

C D E F G H I J K

Leveled Readers

- Deliver instruction with each book's Take and Teach Lesson, choosing appropriate sessions based on need.

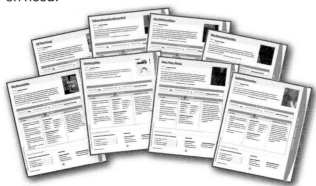

- Check comprehension, reinforce instruction, and extend learning with suggested supporting activities.

Rigby®
LEVELED LIBRARY

🗨 ENGLISH LEARNER SUPPORT

Recount Information

- Use **Tabletop Minilessons: English Language Development 4.1 (Listening)** to introduce and practice the language skill.

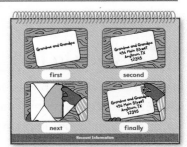

Tabletop Minilessons: English Language Development

- Then use the following text-based prompts with *Kids Speak Up!* to guide application of the language skill. Begin with the prompt at the child's identified language proficiency level. As children are able, use lighter supports to encourage increased language proficiency.

SUBSTANTIAL
Have children recount information from *Kids Speak Up!* by answering questions, using single words or short phrases, or by explaining in their home language. Ask questions such as: *Who likes to play ball? Where can you read books? Where can you go fishing?*

MODERATE
Ask children to recount the information from *Kids Speak Up!* Supply these frames: *You can go fishing at the _____. _____ put out fires. You can read books at the _____.*

LIGHT
Ask children to recount information from *Kids Speak Up!* Ask: *What is there to do in this town?*

REINFORCE IDEAS AND SUPPORT

Demonstrate

- Use **Tabletop Minilessons: Reading 15** to remind children that when authors write to **persuade,** they want readers to do or try something. To persuade readers, authors state an **opinion** about something, or say what they think or feel about it. They also give **reasons** to **support** their opinion, or tell why they think or feel the way they do. Readers of persuasive texts should determine what the author is trying to persuade them to think or do. Readers should also consider the reasons the author uses to support his or her opinion.

- Model filling out Printable: **Reading Graphic Organizer 16** to identify and explain the author's ideas and support in *Kids Speak Up!*

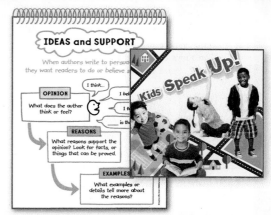

Tabletop Minilessons: Reading

Apply to Independent Reading

- Now have children identify an author's ideas and supporting reasons in an appropriate just-right book that they are reading independently. Before children read their books, guide them to set a purpose for reading. Remind them to pay attention to the author's opinion and supporting reasons. Customize these prompts to the books children choose.

  » *What does the author want to persuade you to think or do?*

  » *What reasons does the author give?*

  » *Do these reasons persuade you to agree with the author?*

- Have children complete Printable: **Reading Graphic Organizer 16** for their independent reading book.

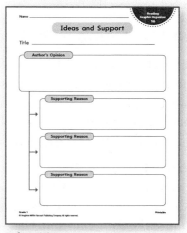

Printable:
Reading Graphic Organizer 16

ALMOST THERE

↓

READY FOR MORE

SCAFFOLD AND EXTEND

- Help children identify the opinions. Then work with children to ask *why* questions about those opinions to help them identify the reasons.

- Have children identify the opinions. Guide them to identify the reasons the author gives to support the opinions.

- Have children discuss whether the reasons the author gives for the opinions are strong or not and why they think so.

 ENGLISH LEARNER SUPPORT

SUBSTANTIAL
Read aloud opinion words, such as *think* or *feel*, for children and have them repeat. Ask children to point to the words as they say them again.

MODERATE
Focus children's attention on opinion words. Supply this frame: *I know this is an opinion because _____.*

LIGHT
Guide children to use opinion words, such as *think* or *feel*, in opinion sentences. Have them use *because* to give a reason.

Options for Differentiation

Cab! Cab!, *Start Right Reader, Book 1,* pp. 100–107

REINFORCE FOUNDATIONAL SKILLS

Read Decodable Text

Get Started Have children turn to Start Right Reader page 100. Explain that this week's stories are about the characters Kim, Nan, Sam, and Dan. Have children point to each character in the illustration. Then read page 100 together and discuss the questions.

Preview the Story Draw attention to page 101, the title page. Read aloud the title and have children look at the pictures on the first few pages. Have them predict where Kim will take Sam, Dan, and Nan.

Concepts of Print: Words in Sentences Use page 102 to model identifying words, sentences, and end punctuation. Review that sentences are made up of individual words. The first word in a sentence starts with a capital letter, and the sentence ends with a punctuation mark. As you read a new sentence, have children point to the first word and end punctuation.

Fluency Focus: Expression Read aloud page 103 as children follow along. Ask: *What emotion did I show when I read the words "Dan can fit!"? (excitement) What is the end punctuation in that sentence? (exclamation point)* Point out that end punctuation can guide your expression. Then lead children in reading the page chorally with appropriate expression.

Reflect on Reading Have children read to find out where Kim is taking Sam, Dan, and Nan. Have them read each page silently and then chorally. Pause for these prompts:

- **Pages 101–102:** *Where do Sam and Dan want to go? (to Big Pat) Look at the pictures. What are Sam and Dan holding? Why do you think they want to go to Big Pat? (Possible response: They are holding wrapped items that say "To Big Pat"; they want to give Big Pat the gifts.)*

- **Page 105:** *Who is in the cab now? (Sam, Dan, and Nan)*

- **Page 106:** *Can Kim fit in the cab? Why? (Yes; she is little.)*

What Is the Word? Read aloud the directions and clues on page 107. Have children find and read the matching words in the story. *(big; Kim)* Then have them page through the story for ideas for their own clue writing. Have partners find and read the words that match each other's clues.

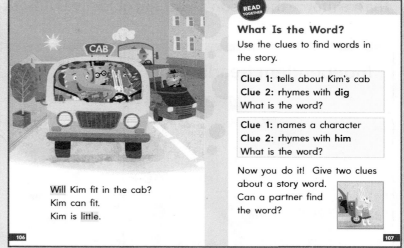

Nan ran.
Cab! Cab!
"Go to Big Pat," said Nan.

104

Can Nan fit?
"My cab is big," said Kim.
Nan can fit in it.

105

Will Kim fit in the cab?
Kim can fit.
Kim is little.

106

READ TOGETHER

What Is the Word?
Use the clues to find words in the story.

Clue 1: tells about Kim's cab
Clue 2: rhymes with **dig**
What is the word?

Clue 1: names a character
Clue 2: rhymes with **him**
What is the word?

Now you do it! Give two clues about a story word. Can a partner find the word?

107

Make Minutes Count

As you meet with small groups to read *Cab! Cab!*, use one or more of these related activities, as needed, at the beginning or the end of the small-group session.

- **Connect to Phonics** Model using Letter Cards to spell the word *big* sound by sound. Blend the sounds, and then read the word smoothly. Display these Letter Cards: *a, b, g, i, k, m, n, p, s, t.* Call on a child to use the cards to build a word, blend the sounds, and read the word aloud. Continue until all children have had a turn.

- **Connect to Spelling** Have children sort the Spelling Words from Printable: Word List 4 into two categories: words that rhyme with *wig* and words that do not. Have them explain how the words that rhyme with *wig* are the same. *(They all end with the letters -ig and the sounds /ig/.)*

- **Connect to Handwriting** Model writing the Spelling Words *did, pig,* and *sit.* Point out your paper position and review how your hand moves from left to right across the paper as you write. Have children write each word in the same order as your model, focusing on writing each letter from left to right.

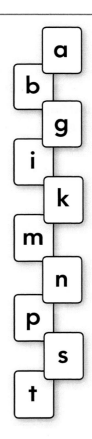

a
b
g
i
k
m
n
p
s
t

👥 **INDEPENDENT APPLICATION**

Options for Independent and Collaborative Work

While you meet with small groups, have other children engage in literacy activities that reinforce the lesson's learning objectives. Choose from these options.

Independent Reading

Student Choice Library

Rigby
LEVELED LIBRARY

APPLY READING SKILL

Ideas and Support Children complete Printable: **Reading Graphic Organizer 16** for an independent reading book.

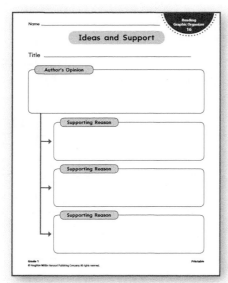

Printable: Reading Graphic Organizer 16

APPLY LANGUAGE SKILL

Recount Information Children complete Printable: **Language Graphic Organizer 11** for an independent reading book.

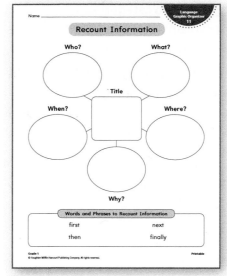

Printable: Language Graphic Organizer 11

Literacy Centers

See pp. T270–T271.

 WORD WORK

 CREATIVITY CORNER

 DIGITAL STATION

 READING CORNER

 TEAMWORK TIME

Start Right Reader

Cab! Cab!
by Jesse Cortez
illustrated by Brian Fitzgerald

Sam ran.
Dan ran.
Cab! Cab!

101

Read Decodable Text *Cab!*
Cab!, Book 1: pp. 100–107

Speaking & Listening

Partners use Think-Pair-Share to discuss the Essential Question.
See Engage & Respond, p. T281.

Additional Skills Practice

HIGH-FREQUENCY WORDS

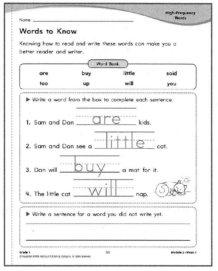

Know It, Show It, p. 33

SPELLING

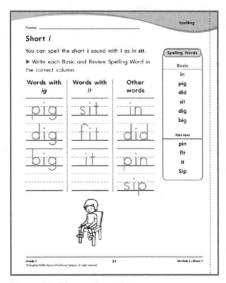

Know It, Show It, p. 34

Wrap-Up

Share Time

At the end of the Reading Workshop, have children reflect on their learning by sharing how they applied **Ideas and Support** or another area of focus during independent work time. Choose from these options:

- **SHARE CHAIR** Select a reader each day to come to the front of the class and tell what he or she learned from the reading by using a skill or strategy.

- **THINK-PAIR-SHARE** Children share their thinking with a partner. Select a few each day to share with the whole class.

- **RETURN TO ANCHOR CHART** Have children add sticky notes about their independent reading book to the Ideas and Support Anchor Chart. Call on a few children to explain what they added.

ANCHOR CHART 15: Ideas and Support

Online **Ed**

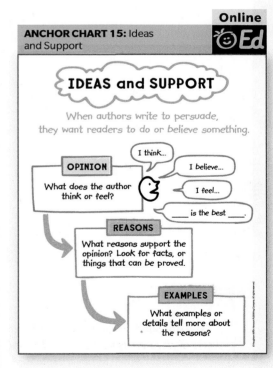

FOUNDATIONAL SKILLS

LEARNING OBJECTIVES

- Identify and read high-frequency words.
- **Language** Recognize and recite basic sight vocabulary.
- Blend onsets and rimes to say one-syllable words.
- Blend phonemes to say one-syllable words.

MATERIALS   Online

Word Cards *are, big, buy, did, its, little, ran, said, sit, too, up, will, you*

Printable *Word List 4*

Picture Cards *duck, keys, yak*

 # High-Frequency Words

Review the Words

Repeat the **HIGH-FREQUENCY WORDS** routine to review this week's High-Frequency Words: *are, buy, little, said, too, up, will,* and *you,* and the decodable High-Frequency Words *big, did, its, ran,* and *sit.*

Odd One Out

- Have children cut out the High-Frequency Word cards and decodable High-Frequency Word cards from Printable: **Word List 4**.

- Assign partners. Each pair of children will use two sets of cutout word cards.

- Tell partners to mix the two sets of cards and then remove a single card without looking at it. (This creates an odd number of cards.) All the remaining cards are dealt to the two players. Both players check for matching word cards. When a player has a match, the player reads aloud the High-Frequency Word for each match and places the matching cards on the table.

High-Frequency Words	Decodable High-Frequency Words	Spelling Words	
		Basic	Review
are	big	in	pin
buy	ran	pig	fit
little	sit	did	it
said	did	sit	sip
too	its	dig	
up		big	
will			
you			
			Challenge
			ship
			fish

Printable: Word List 4

- One child holds his or her cards without showing the words the partner. The other child takes one of the first child's cards. If the child who picked a card has a match, he or she reads the word aloud and places the matching pair of cards on the table.

- Players switch roles and continue the game. The first player with no cards left wins.

TEACHER TIP

Play on! Send children home with two sets of word cards so they can play Odd One Out with a family member.

Phonological Awareness

Blend Onset and Rime

- Remind children that they know how to blend word chunks to say words.

- Display Picture Cards *duck, keys,* and *yak.*

- Tell children they are going to help you say some words. Model: *I will say a word in two chunks: the beginning and the rest of the word. Blend the chunks to say the word. Then say whether there is a matching Picture Card for the word you say. Listen as I do the first one: I want to say the word for these chunks: /j/, /ŏg/. I can blend the chunks and say the word: /j/ /ŏg/, jog. The word is jog. Does jog have a Picture Card match? No. There is no Picture Card for jog.*

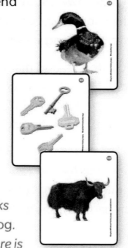

- *Now you try! Listen and blend the word chunks. Then tell whether there is a Picture Card match. Not all the words you say will have a Picture Card match. Here are the chunks: /d/ /ŭk/. What is the word?* (duck) *Great! Does* duck *have a picture match?* (yes)

- *Let's keep going. Point to the Picture Card when there is a picture match with a word you say: /k/ /ēz/* (keys), */r/ /ŏd/* (rod), */y/ /ăk/* (yak), */d/ /ĭg/* (dig), */l/ /āk/* (lake).

Blend Phonemes

- Remind children that they also know how to blend individual sounds to say words.

- Say: *I am going to say a sentence, and you will help me finish it. I will say the sounds in the last word, and you will blend the sounds to say the last word. Listen as I do the first one: The bus is /b/ /ĭ/ /g/. When I blend /b/, /ĭ/, and /g/, I say the word big. /b/ /ĭ/ /g/, big. The sentence is: The bus is big.*

- *Your turn! Listen: I lost my /h/ /ă/ /t/. What word do you say when you blend these sounds: /h/ /ă/ /t/?* (hat) *Good! When you blend the sounds /h/, /ă/, and /t/, you say hat. /h/ /ă/ /t/, hat. The sentence is: I lost my hat.*

- Have children practice blending phonemes to say the last word in each of the following sentences:

  » *Please come /ĭ/ /n/.* (in)

  » *The game is /f/ /ŭ/ /n/.* (fun)

  » *Joe rides in a /k/ /ă/ /b/.* (cab)

  » *Ann swims in the /s/ /ē/.* (sea)

  » *I will sleep on the /k/ /ŏ/ /t/.* (cot)

  » *Did you break a /b/ /ō/ /n/?* (bone)

 ENGLISH LEARNER SUPPORT: Build Vocabulary

SUBSTANTIAL
Ask children *yes/no* questions about the words. Examples: *Does a duck swim? Do you eat keys? Can you ride in a cab? Can you see your bones?*

MODERATE
Have children answer *either/or* questions about the words. Examples: *Is a duck a bird or a fish? Are keys big or little? What is bigger, a lake or a sea?*

LIGHT
Prompt children to create their own *yes/no* questions about Picture Cards *duck, keys,* and *yak* to ask their classmates.

 CORRECT & REDIRECT

To support children who blend phonemes incorrectly, model the task by saying the sounds more and more closely together, as in the example below.

- Say each sound in the word. */f/ /ŭ/ /n/* Have the child repeat. (*/f/ /ŭ/ /n/*)

- Repeat, each time blending the sounds a little more closely together, and then say the word. */f/, /ŭ/, /n/; /f/ /ŭ/ /n/; /f-ŭ-n/;* fun

- Ask the child to blend and say the word. (*/f/ /ŭ/ /n/,* fun)

- Continue, having children blend individual sounds to say other words.

FOUNDATIONAL SKILLS

LEARNING OBJECTIVES

- Blend letter sounds and decode and build regularly spelled one-syllable words with /g/ (hard g), /k/.
- **Language** Recognize sound-letter relationships and use them to decode words.

MATERIALS Online

Sound/Spelling Cards *goat, kangaroo*
Letter Cards *a, g, i, k, p, t*
Display and Engage *Blend and Read 2.2*
Start Right Reader *Book 1, p. 108*
Printable *Letter Cards*
Know It, Show It *p. 35*

Consonants *g, k*

Spotlight on Sounds

Remind children that vowels stand for many sounds, and that they have been learning about the short vowel sounds for *a*, /ă/ and *i*, /ĭ/. Explain that the vowels *a* and *i* can also stand for long vowel sounds that match the letter names, /ā/, /ī/.

Guide children to listen for and distinguish vowel sounds. *I will say a word, and you say the vowel sound. I will do the first one. Listen: The word is* kite. *The vowel sound in* kite *is /ī/. Say it with me:* kite, /ī/. *Now you try it. Tell me what vowel sound you hear:* back (/ă/); gave (/ā/); dig (/ĭ/); kick (/ĭ/); bike (/ī/); wag (/ă/).

Now I will say two words, and you say which word has a short vowel sound. Let's try it: bite/bit. *Which word has the short vowel?* (bit) *What is the short vowel sound?* (/ĭ/, short i) Continue: mate/mat (mat, /ă/, short a); fig/fine (fig, /ĭ/, short i); pan/pain (pan, /ă/, short a); kit/kite (kit, /ĭ/, short i).

I Do It

Spotlight on Letters Review Sound/Spelling Cards *goat, kangaroo*. Remind children that the letters *g* and *k* are consonants.

Write *kit* for children to see, and use the **SOUND-BY-SOUND BLENDING** routine below to model blending the word using Letter Cards *k, i, t*.

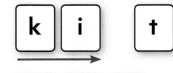

1. **Display** Letter Cards as shown. Say the first letter and sound.

2. **Slide** the second letter over. Say its sound. Then blend the two sounds.

3. **Slide** the last letter over. Say its sound. Say the first two blended sounds, the last sound, and the blended word: /kĭ//t/, kit.

Repeat the routine with the cards for *gap*.

TEACHER TIP

Blend and talk! All year, remember that the conversations *about* the words in Blend and Read are just as important as the decoding! Children discover valuable patterns by comparing words.

 ENGLISH LEARNER SUPPORT:
Facilitate Language Connections

SUBSTANTIAL
Isolate pairs of words in Blend and Read for comparison. For example, name the letters in *gas* and *sag*, and then have children compare the words.

MODERATE
Have children identify Blend and Read rhyming words (*sag/bag, gab/cab, big/fig/gig, kid/did*). Prompt discussion about word spellings and sounds.

LIGHT
Have children compare the words *gap, gaps,* and *gasp*. Discuss the meanings of the words and have children use them in oral sentences.

We Do It

Blend and Read

Project Display and Engage: **Blend and Read 2.2** or use Start Right Reader page 108.

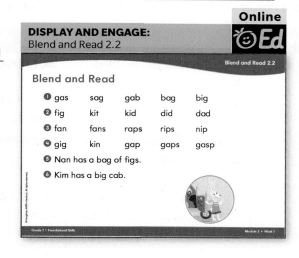

❶ **Line 1** Have children read the line. Then prompt a conversation about the words: *What do you notice about the words? Which words have the same letters? How are those words different?* If necessary, lead children to find similarities (same letters: *gas/sag, gag/bag*), and differences (letters in different order). Point to each word, and have children read the line chorally. Provide corrective feedback as needed.

❷ **Line 2** Continue with these words. Then call on volunteers to reread selected words until children can identify the words quickly.

❸ **Review** For Line 3, have children read the words chorally.

❹ **Challenge** Have children who are ready for a challenge read the less familiar words in Line 4. Have them demonstrate how they blended the words and share what they know about them. Discuss word meanings with the group.

❺ **Sentences** For Lines 5–6, call on children to blend selected decodable words. Then have the group read the sentences chorally.

You Do It

INDEPENDENT PRACTICE

- **Option 1** Model how to write and spell the word *gas* sound by sound. Then have children identify sounds and use Printable: **Letter Cards** to form these words: *sag, bag, big, kid*. Have a child spell each word aloud while others check their own work.

- **Option 2** Children complete Know It, Show It page 35.

 CORRECT & REDIRECT

- If a child mispronounces a word during Blend and Read, make note of the error type and address it.

- If a child misreads the final sounds in *gas, gab,* and *gap*, make sure the child is blending the whole word and not partially blending and then guessing. Model blending the first two sounds, and then the last. Have children repeat. Point to each word and say: /gă/ /s/; /gă/ /b/; /gă/ /p/. *How are the words alike?* (*same beginning sound and vowel sound*) *How are they different?* (*different ending sounds*)

LINK TO SMALL-GROUP INSTRUCTION

REINFORCE FOUNDATIONAL SKILLS Use *Go, Big Cab!* during small-group time to review or reinforce blending and decoding words with consonants *g, k*. Meet with children to work through the story, or assign it as independent work. *See the lesson on p. T298.*

Go, Big Cab!

Go, big cab!
The big cab sat.
Kim is sad.

LEARNING OBJECTIVES

• **Language** Answer questions and discuss meanings to develop vocabulary.

• Identify real-life connections between words and their use.

MATERIALS   Online

Vocabulary Cards *2.4-2.9*
Big Book *Whose Hands Are These?*
Classroom materials *scrap paper*

 ## Introduce Oral Language

Use the steps **I Do It, We Do It, You Do It** with the information in the chart below to teach the oral Power Words from the Big Book *Whose Hands Are These?*

❶ Power Word	❷ Meaning	❸ Example
toiled (v.) *(p. 4)*	If you **toiled**, you worked hard for a long time.	**ACT IT OUT** Act out cleaning the classroom. *I have* ***toiled*** *to clean the classroom.*
belong (v.) *(p. 5)*	When things **belong** to you, you own them or they are part of you.	**USE A PROP** Point to personal items you own. *These shoes* ***belong*** *to me.*
gifted (adj.) *(p. 7)*	If you are **gifted** at doing something, you are able to do it very well.	**MAKE A CONNECTION** Connect being very good at a skill to the concept of *gifted*. *A person who can sing very, very well is a* ***gifted*** *singer.*
persists (v.) *(p. 11)*	When someone **persists**, that person keeps doing something even if it's hard.	**USE A PROP** Toss crumpled balls of paper into a container, deliberately missing. *Someone who* ***persists*** *at doing something keeps trying over and over.*
smeared (v.) *(p. 17)*	If something is **smeared**, something dirty has been spread onto it.	**MAKE A CONNECTION** Connect mud to the concept of *smeared*. *If I put mud all over my hands, they are* ***smeared*** *with mud.*
sketch (v.) *(p. 19)*	When you **sketch** something, you draw a simple picture of it quickly.	**ACT IT OUT** Draw a simple sketch of an animal on the board or on paper. *I can* ***sketch*** *a picture of a dog.*

TEACHER TIP

Multiple meanings! Children will encounter two meanings of the word *belong* in this module. The meaning of the Power Word *belong* relates to ownership. In the Learning Mindset focus for this module, *belong* relates to being a member of a group. Have children explain how the two meanings for *belong* are different.

I Do It

Use the **VOCABULARY** routine and Vocabulary Cards 2.4–2.9 to introduce the oral Power Words from *Whose Hands Are These?* You may wish to display the corresponding Vocabulary Card for each word as you discuss it.

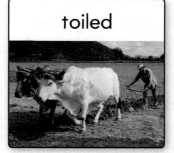

toiled

Vocabulary Cards

1. **Say the Power Word.** Ask children to repeat it.

2. **Explain the meaning.** Read aloud the student-friendly meaning.

3. **Talk about examples.** Use the image or a strategy to give examples of the word.

We Do It

Guide children to make connections between each word's meaning and how they can use it in their own lives. Use these prompts. Encourage children to explain or justify their answers.

- Would a **gifted** artist **sketch** a good picture or bad picture? Explain.

- Name some things that might **belong** to a teacher.

- When might a farmer's hands be **smeared** in dirt? Explain.

- If a kitten **persists** trying to catch a mouse, does the kitten give up if the mouse is hard to catch? Why or why not?

- If you **toiled** in a garden, what are some things you might have done?

You Do It

INDEPENDENT PRACTICE

Have partners work together to complete each of the activities below. Circulate and observe partners as they work, providing corrective feedback as necessary.

- **Draw** *Sketch two things that **belong** to you.*

- **Discuss** *Why might people watch a **gifted** soccer player? Would someone who **persists** to learn to play a sport give up easily if it was hard to do? Explain.*

- **Role-Play** *Demonstrate how you have **toiled** to clean your room. Show how you would pick up a piece of paper **smeared** with fingerpaint.*

EL **ENGLISH LEARNER SUPPORT:**
Elicit Participation

SUBSTANTIAL
Ask children to demonstrate the meanings of *belong, sketch, smeared,* and *toiled.* Have them repeat each word after you.

MODERATE
Supply frames such as these: *A **gifted** artist _____. I **toiled** _____. A farmer's hands may be **smeared** in dirt when _____.*

LIGHT
What does a teacher need to do his/her job? What are some things you do to take care of a garden?

READING WORKSHOP

 Text Organization

Step **1** Connect and Teach

LEARNING OBJECTIVES

- Recognize characteristics of informational text.
- Identify the text's organization as description.
- **Language** Describe how an author organizes a text.
- Respond to an informational text by drawing and writing.

MATERIALS Online

Anchor Chart 35
Text Organization
Printable
Anchor Chart 35:
Text Organization
Big Book *Whose Hands Are These?*
BookStix *2.1*

📖 READER'S VOCABULARY

- **text organization** the way a text is arranged to help readers understand the information
- **description** a way to organize a text that gives details about one topic or subtopic at a time
- **detail** small bit of information that supports a central idea or describes something in a text

- Explain that organizing classroom materials, such as paper and crayons, helps people find them. Point out that authors organize information so readers can find it, too!

- Project or display <u>Anchor Chart 35: Text Organization</u>.

- Tell children that **text organization** is the way an author arranges information in a text. Authors organize their text based on their purpose, or reason, for writing.

- Explain that one kind of text organization, or structure, is **description**. In this kind of organization, an author tells **details** about one thing after another. For example, an author writing about whales could tell about a humpback whale, then a fin whale, and then a blue whale.

- Explain that the details an author includes can tell what each thing looks, sounds, smells, feels, or acts like. The author can also give examples.

- Tell children that they will practice identifying and analyzing text organization as they listen to a Big Book called *Whose Hands Are These?*

ANCHOR CHART 35:
Text Organization

Online

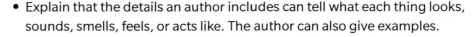

Text Organization
◁ **Description** ▷

Informational texts have a structure, or type of organization, that fits the topic and the author's purpose.

Description is one kind of structure or organization. Authors choose description to tell details about what something is like.

It smells like…
It looks like…
It sounds like…
It feels like…
It acts like…

Examples

● Professional Learning

RESEARCH FOUNDATIONS

"Increasing young children's contact with print during shared reading represents an empirically validated approach to fostering children's short-term gains in print knowledge."

–Dr. Shayne B. Piasta et al. (2012)

See the **GPS guide** to learn more.

🗨 **ENGLISH LEARNER SUPPORT:**
Facilitate Language Connections

ALL LEVELS For Spanish-speaking children, point out that the English words *text organization*, *detail*, and *description* have the following Spanish cognates: *organización del texto*, *detalle*, and *descripción*.

Go to
BookStix 2.1

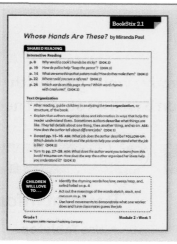

Step 2 Apply to Text

- **Genre Study** Read aloud the title *Whose Hands Are These?* and introduce the book. *Today we will read an informational text about what different workers do with their hands.* Have children examine the cover. Prompt them to think about what the book will be about. *What are the hands doing? Whose hands are they?*

- **Set a Purpose** Remind children that the purpose for reading informational text is to find out about a topic. *What do you think you will learn about in this text? Use your idea to set a purpose for reading.*

- **Model Fluency** Tell children that as you read, you are going to demonstrate how to read with expression, or varying your voice to show excitement, surprise, or other feelings, based on what the text says. Model reading a few different kinds of sentences with expression.

- **Concepts of Print** As you read, point to a sentence. Help children find the first word and the end punctuation. Have children find the beginning and end of a few more sentences.

- **Read and Comprehend** Do a shared reading of the Big Book, pausing occasionally to ask the questions on BookStix 2.1 and to help children recognize the descriptive text organization. As needed, refer back to the Anchor Chart to identify text organization in *Whose Hands Are These?*

Step 3 Engage and Respond

INDEPENDENT PRACTICE: Writing

- Remind children that in the Big Book *Whose Hands Are These?*, children learn about different jobs by learning what the hands of the workers do.

- Have children draw what one worker in the text does with his or her hands. Encourage them to include details from the book. Then have them write the name of worker at the bottom of the page and fold up a flap to hide the label.

- Ask partners to share their drawings and guess which worker's hands are shown. Have children compare drawings, discussing how the hands are the same or different.

- You may want to have children complete their writing during daily small-group time.

LEARNING MINDSET

Belonging

Apply Point out that all of the hands in *Whose Hands Are These?* do important tasks that help their community. Discuss how children can use *their* hands to help *their* communities. *What can you do with your hands to help in our classroom? What can you do to help at home? Where else can you use your hands to help?*

LINK TO SMALL-GROUP INSTRUCTION

REINFORCE TEXT ORGANIZATION Review or extend the skill as needed during small-group time to support children's need for differentiation. *See the lesson on p. T297.*

👥 **SMALL-GROUP INSTRUCTION**

Options for Differentiation

As the class engages in independent and collaborative work, meet with Guided Reading Groups or differentiate instruction based on student need.

GUIDED READING GROUPS

Match Children to Books + Instruction

- Choose just-right books based on level, skill, topic, or genre.

C D E F G H I J K ➡

Leveled Readers

- Deliver instruction with each book's Take and Teach Lesson, choosing appropriate sessions based on need.

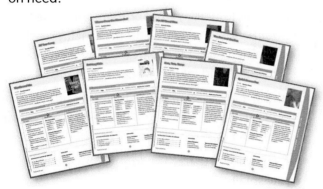

- Check comprehension, reinforce instruction, and extend learning with suggested supporting activities.

Rigby®
LEVELED LIBRARY

EL ENGLISH LEARNER SUPPORT

Recount Information

- Use **Tabletop Minilessons: English Language Development 4.1 (Speaking)** to reinforce and practice the language skill.

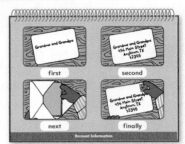

Tabletop Minilessons: English Language Development

- Then use the following text-based prompts with *Whose Hands Are These?* to guide application of the language skill. Begin with the prompt at the child's identified language proficiency level. As children are able, use lighter supports to encourage increased language proficiency.

SUBSTANTIAL
Have children recount what some of the hands do by completing this sentence frame: *These hands _____.* Allow children to point, respond in single words or short phrases, or explain in their home language.

MODERATE
Ask children to recount the information about what the different hands do by completing this frame: *The text says these hands _____.*

LIGHT
Ask children to recount information that describes the different helping hands in *Whose Hands Are These?* Ask: *What can these hands do?*

REINFORCE TEXT ORGANIZATION

Demonstrate

- Use **Tabletop Minilessons: Reading 35** to remind children that authors of informational texts organize their writing so that it fits the topic and their purpose for writing. A common type of **text organization**, or structure, is **description**. A text organized in this way gives **details** that describe each thing or idea, one by one.

- Model filling out Printable: <u>**Reading Graphic Organizer 22**</u> to identify and explain text organization in *Whose Hands Are These?*

Apply to Independent Reading

- Now have children identify text organization in an appropriate just-right book that they are reading independently. Customize these prompts to the books children choose.

  » *What is the author describing?*

  » *What details does the author include about each thing or idea?*

  » *Why do you think the author wrote this book?*

  » *How does the descriptive text organization help you understand the author's purpose for writing this book?*

- Have children complete Printable: <u>**Reading Graphic Organizer 22**</u> for their independent reading book.

Tabletop Minilessons: Reading

Printable:
Reading Graphic Organizer 22

SCAFFOLD AND EXTEND

ALMOST THERE

↓

READY FOR MORE

- Help children understand that each odd and even pair of pages belongs together and tells about one kind of worker.

- Help children identify descriptive words that help them identify the type of worker being described.

- Have children compose several sentences that describe the hands of a different type of worker. Challenge children to use rhyming words.

 ENGLISH LEARNER SUPPORT

SUBSTANTIAL

Read aloud descriptive words and phrases to children. Ask children to point to the words as they say them after you.

MODERATE

Ask questions to help children recognize description, such as: *What does the author tell about on this page? What does this item look like? What words tell you that?*

LIGHT

Have children restate a description from the book in their own words.

Options for Differentiation

Go, Big Cab!, *Start Right Reader, Book 1*, pp. 108–115

REINFORCE FOUNDATIONAL SKILLS

Read Decodable Text

Blend and Read Have children turn to Start Right Reader page 108. Use the **CHORAL READING** routine to read aloud the Blend and Read lines. Use challenge line 4 with children who are ready.

Preview the Story Read aloud the title on page 109. Have children look at the picture and identify the characters in the cab as Kim, Dan, Sam, and Nan from *Cab! Cab!* Then have children look at the first two pages and predict the problem in this story.

Fluency Focus: Expression Read aloud page 109 as children follow along. Point out that you read with expression—you used your voice to show the characters' emotions. For example, you read the sentence "Go, big cab!" with excitement. Then lead children in reading the page chorally. Remind them to read with expression to show the characters' actions and emotions.

Reflect on Reading Have children use a finger to track the words from left to right as they read each page silently. Then have them read the page chorally. Pause for these prompts:

- **Pages 109–110:** *What is the problem with the cab? (It will not go.) What do the characters think might be causing the problem? (There are too many animals in the cab.)*

- **Page 111:** *How does Sam, Nan, and Dan feel? (sad) How does Kim feel? (mad)*

- **Page 112:** *What does Nan think the cab might need? (gas)*

- **Page 114:** *Did the cab need gas? How do you know? (Yes; Kim added gas and then the cab could go.)*

Hunt for Words with g Read aloud the first numbered item on page 115. Have children list words from the story that start or end with *g*. Then read the second numbered item. Allow time for children to review their lists and circle words that begin with *g* and underline words that end with *g*.

Kim! Kim!
Is it gas?
Did you buy gas, Kim?

Sam sat.
Dan sat.
Nan sat.

112

113

Can the big cab go, Kim?
It can! It can!

114

READ TOGETHER

Hunt for Words with g

1. Look in the story for words with the letter **g**. Write each word you find.

2. Look at your list of **g** words. Circle each word that begins with **g**. Draw a line under each word that ends with **g**.

115

(?) Make Minutes Count

As you meet with small groups to read *Go, Big Cab!*, use one or more of these related activities, as needed, at the beginning or the end of the small-group session.

- **Connect to Phonics** Play Word Match. Use two sets of the Spelling Word cards from Printable: <u>Word List 4</u>. Shuffle the cards and place them face down in a grid on the tabletop. Children take turns selecting two cards, turning them over, and reading the words. If the words match, the child leaves the cards facing up. If the words do not match, the child turns the cards face down again and the next player takes a turn. Play continues until all of the words are matched.

- **Connect to Spelling** Play Eruption. Write the Spelling Words on the board or chart paper. Point to a word and have children spell it in a whisper. Then have children pretend they are a volcano erupting as they raise their arms and spell the word in a normal speaking voice. Continue with the remaining words.

- **Connect to Handwriting** Write this sentence on the board: *The big pig can dig*. Have children write the sentence two times, making sure to leaving appropriate space between letters and words. As they write, check that they are writing from left to right across their papers, and correct as needed. Then have children self-assess the legibility of their writing, putting a star next to the sentence that best matches the model.

Name _____

Word List 4

High-Frequency Words	Decodable High-Frequency Words	Spelling Words	
		Basic	Review
are	big	in	pin
buy	ran	pig	fit
little	sit	did	it
said	did	sit	sip
too	its	dig	
up		big	
will			
you			
			Challenge
			ship
			fish

Grade 1
© Houghton Mifflin Harcourt Publishing Company. All rights reserved.   Printable

Printable: Word List 4

Options for Independent and Collaborative Work

While you meet with small groups, have other children engage in literacy activities that reinforce the lesson's learning objectives. Choose from these options.

Independent Reading

Student Choice Library

LEVELED LIBRARY

APPLY READING SKILL

Text Organization Children complete Printable: <u>Reading Graphic Organizer 22</u> for an independent reading book.

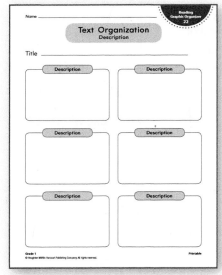

Printable: Reading Graphic Organizer 22

APPLY LANGUAGE SKILL

Recount Information Children complete Printable: <u>Language Graphic Organizer 11</u> for an independent reading book.

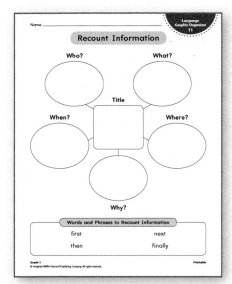

Printable: Language Graphic Organizer 11

Literacy Centers

See pp. T270–T271.

 WORD WORK

 CREATIVITY CORNER

 DIGITAL STATION

 READING CORNER

 TEAMWORK TIME

Start Right Reader

Go, big cab!
The big cab sat.
Kim is sad.

109

Read Decodable Text *Go, Big Cab!*, Book 1: pp. 108–115

Writing

Children use details from the Big Book to draw and label a picture that partners then share and compare. *See Engage & Respond, p. T295.*

Additional Skills Practice

PHONICS

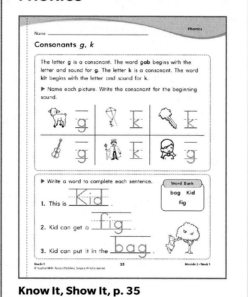

Know It, Show It, p. 35

Wrap-Up
Share Time

At the end of the Reading Workshop, have children reflect on their learning by sharing how they applied **Text Organization** or another area of focus during independent work time. Choose from these options:

- **SHARE CHAIR** Select a reader each day to come to the front of the class and tell what he or she learned from the reading by using a skill or strategy.

- **THINK-PAIR-SHARE** Children share their thinking with a partner. Select a few each day to share with the whole class.

- **RETURN TO ANCHOR CHART** Have children add sticky notes about their independent reading book to the Text Organization Anchor Chart. Call on a few children to explain what they added.

ANCHOR CHART 35: Text Organization **Online Ed**

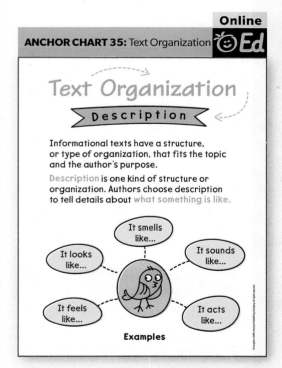

LESSON 3

FOUNDATIONAL SKILLS

LEARNING OBJECTIVES

- Identify and read high-frequency words.
- **Language** Recognize and recite basic sight vocabulary.
- Segment onsets and rimes in one-syllable words.
- Segment spoken one-syllable words into individual phonemes.

MATERIALS Online Ed

Word Cards *are, big, buy, did, its, little, ran, said, sit, too, up, will, you*
Printable *Word List 4*

 # High-Frequency Words

Review the Words

Repeat the **HIGH-FREQUENCY WORDS** routine to review this week's High-Frequency Words: *are, buy, little, said, too, up, will,* and *you,* and the decodable High-Frequency Words *big, did, its, ran,* and *sit.*

> you

Word Match

- Have children play the game with partners. Each pair will use two sets of cutout High-Frequency Word cards from Printable: **Word List 4**.

- Have players mix the cards and spread them out face down on a desk. Players take turns flipping over two cards and reading them aloud. If the words match, the player keeps the two cards. If the cards do not match, the player puts them face down again. Players take turns until all cards have been matched.

 # Phonological Awareness

Segment Onset and Rime

- Remind children that they know how to separate words into chunks. Say: *I will say a word, and you will say the word in two chunks: the beginning and the rest of the word. Listen:* men. *I hear /m/ at the beginning. The rest of the word is /ĕn/. Men, /m/ /ĕn/. Now you try:* code (/k/ /ōd/), neck (/n/ /ĕk/), tip (/t/ /ĭp/), game (/g/ /ām/), rug (/r/ /ŭg/), chest (/ch/ /ĕst/), phone (/f/ /ōn/).

- *Now I will say the first sound and you will say the rest of the word. Listen:* hope. *The first sound is /h/. What is the rest of the word?* (/ōp/) *Great! Let's do some more:* bin, /b/ (/ĭn/); sale, /s/ (/āl/); tent, /t/ (/ĕnt/); bug, /b/ (/ŭg/); peek, /p/ (/ēk/).

Segment Phonemes

- Remind children that they can break words into individual sounds. Say: *I will say a word, and you say the sounds in the word. Listen:* pie. *I hear /p/ at the beginning. After /p/, I hear /ī/. Pie, /p/ /ī/. The sounds in pie are /p/ and /ī/.*

- *Your turn!* at (/ă/ /t/), so (/s/ /ō/), me (/m/ /ē/), ten (/t/ /ĕ/ /n/), lip (/l/ /ĭ/ /p/), tack (/t/ /ă/ /k/), rich (/r/ /ĭ/ /ch/), leaf (/l/ /ē/ /f/)

● Professional Learning

RESEARCH FOUNDATIONS

"Children who have well-developed phonological awareness are much more likely to learn to read quickly and be readers over time".

    —Dr. Anne E. Cunningham and Dr. Jamie Zibulsky (2014)

See the **GPS guide** to learn more.

 CORRECT & REDIRECT

If children segment phonemes incorrectly, say the word repeatedly, emphasizing a phoneme each time. Example for *tack:*

- /tăk/: *The beginning sound is /t/.*
- /tăăăk/: *The middle sound is /ă/.*
- /tăk:/ *The last sound is /k/.*
- *The sounds in tack are /t/ /ă/ /k/.*

Expression

 I Do It

- Explain to children that good readers make their reading flow and sound like they do when are speaking to someone. Tell children that they can use their voices to show how characters feel at different points in a story. This is called reading with expression.

- Have children turn to page 109 of the Start Right Reader (*Go, Big Cab!*). Tell children to close their eyes and listen as you read the first sentence. Sound excited as you read it. Discuss with children how the speaker who says "Go, big cab!" is feeling and why they think so. Then ask whether they could hear excitement in your voice as you read. Point out that you used the exclamation point as a clue to how to read the line.

- Read the rest of the page, sounding sad and disappointed at the last sentence. Point out that the word *sad* in the sentence helped you know what feelings to express while reading.

We Do It

- Read aloud pages 110 and 111 using the proper expression. Use the **ECHO READING** routine to have children follow your model to reread the sentences.

- Guide children to point out clues in the punctuation or in the words that let them know how to express feelings with their voices.

You Do It

INDEPENDENT PRACTICE

- Have small groups use the **PARTNER READING** routine with one of the Start Right Reader stories about Kim and her cab or *Dan Had a Plan* from their *my*Book. Remind children to use clues in the words and punctuation to help them read with appropriate expression.

LEARNING OBJECTIVE

- Read aloud fluently and with appropriate expression (prosody).

MATERIALS   Online

Start Right Reader *Book 1, pp. 109–114*

 ENGLISH LEARNER SUPPORT:
Elicit Participation

ALL LEVELS English learners who need additional support reading expressively in English can benefit from reading aloud with more fluent partners. The more fluent reader can act as a coach for the less fluent, offering encouragement, help with difficult words, and feedback on expression.

Review Short *a, i*

Spotlight on Sounds

LEARNING OBJECTIVES

- Review the sound-spellings for short *a* and short *i*.
- **Language** Recognize sound-letter relationships and use them to decode words.
- Blend letter sounds and decode regularly spelled one-syllable words with short *a* and *i*.

MATERIALS   Online ⊙*Ed*

Sound/Spelling Cards *alligator, igloo*
Letter Cards *a, b, g, i, m, r*
Articulation Videos /ă/, /ĭ/

- Tell children that today they will be reading words with the short *a* and *i* sounds. Then have them practice identifying the middle sounds in words you say. *I am going to say a word, and you will repeat the word and say the middle sound.*

- *I will do the first one. Listen:* Kim. Repeat the word, emphasizing the middle sound. *The middle sound in Kim is /ĭ/, short i. Now you do it. Repeat the word I say, then say the middle sound:* gab (gab, /ă/, *short* a); kit (kit, /ĭ/, *short* i); tag (tag, /ă/, *short* a); pin (pin /ĭ/, *short* i).

- Then model how to distinguish the vowel sound in two words. *This time, I will say two words. You will tell me if the words have the same middle sound or different middle sounds. Listen:* pat/pit. *Is the vowel sound the same or different?* (different) *That's right! Let's try it with some more words:* pick/tip (same); Dan/Sam (same); fin/fan (different); kit/cat (different); bag/map (same); fin/fan (different).

▌I Do It

Spotlight on Letters Display the Sound/Spelling Card for /ă/ *alligator.* Name the picture, say the sound, and give the spelling. *The letter* a *is one of the vowel letters. Vowels stand for many sounds. One sound for* a *is the short* a *sound you hear at the beginning of* alligator: /ă/.

Write *an.* Say the letter sounds, and blend the word. *Remember, when there is only one vowel and it is followed by a consonant, the vowel usually stands for its short sound.* Repeat with the word *fan.*

Continue with /ĭ/, using Sound/Spelling Card *igloo* and the words *it* and *kit.*

●— *Professional Learning*

RESEARCH FOUNDATIONS

"Systematic and explicit phonics instruction significantly improves kindergarten and first grade children's word recognition and spelling"
—Dr. Bonnie B. Armbruster, Fran Lehr, & Jean Osborn (2001)

See the **GPS guide** to learn more.

EL **ENGLISH LEARNER SUPPORT: Facilitate Language Connections**

ALL LEVELS Spanish, Vietnamese, Hmong, Cantonese, Korean, and Haitian Creole speakers may need practice distinguishing between short *a* and *i.* Play the **Articulation Videos** for /ă/ and /ĭ/. Then have children distinguish the vowel sounds in these word pairs: *tin/tan, bat/bit, rig/rag, had/hid, has/his.*

▶ **ARTICULATION VIDEO**   **Online** ⊙*Ed*

We Do It

Write *ram* and use Letter Cards *r, a, m* with the SOUND-BY-SOUND BLENDING routine below to model blending the word.

1 **Display** the cards as shown. Say the first letter and sound.

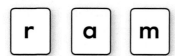

2 **Slide** the second letter over. Say its sound. Then blend the two sounds.

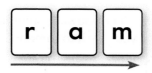

3 **Slide** the last letter over. Say its sound. Say the first two blended sounds, the last sound, and the blended word: /ră/ /m/, ram.

Sound-by-Sound Blending Repeat the SOUND-BY-SOUND BLENDING routine with cards for the words *rim* and *gab*, having children say the sounds and blend.

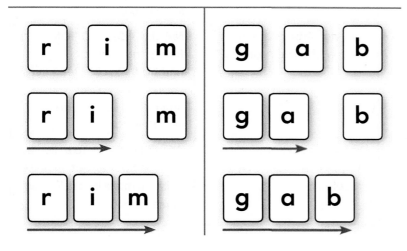

You Do It

INDEPENDENT PRACTICE

Blending Practice Write the words below. Then choose a volunteer to model the activity. Explain that you will point to two words in random order and the child will read them aloud. Repeat the blending routine as needed. Continue until each child has had a turn.

fin	can	dip	sat
sit	man	fig	kid
pin	kit	gas	bag

✓ CORRECT & REDIRECT

- If a child mispronounces a word during Blending Practice, make note of the error type and address it.
- If a child reads *fin* as *fan*, contrast the short *a* and short *i* vowel sounds and use Sound/Spelling Card *igloo* to reinforce short *i*, /ĭ/. Use sound-by-sound blending to read the word, and then have the child repeat the steps after you.
- If a child reads *nip* as *pin*, cover the word and blend it together as you uncover one letter at a time, left to right. Then have the child blend and read the word.

👥 LINK TO SMALL-GROUP INSTRUCTION

REINFORCE FOUNDATIONAL SKILLS Use *A Big Pit* during small-group time to review or reinforce blending and decoding words with consonants *g, k* and short vowels *a, i*. Meet with children to work through the story, or assign it as independent work. *See the lesson on p. T312.*

LEARNING OBJECTIVES

- **Language** Answer questions and discuss meanings to develop vocabulary.
- Identify real-life connections between words and their use.

MATERIALS   Online

Vocabulary Cards 2.10–2.15
Classroom materials *books, coin, paper, chair*

 ## Introduce Power Words

Use the steps **I Do It, We Do It, You Do It** with the information in the chart below to teach the Power Words from *Dan Had a Plan*.

❶ Power Word	❷ Meaning	❸ Example
mess (n.) *(p. 100)*	If something is a **mess**, it is not neat.	**ACT IT OUT** Make a mess with classroom objects, such as books. *This is a mess!*
market (n.) *(p. 101)*	A **market** is a place where people can buy things.	**MAKE A CONNECTION** Talk about things you buy at a market. *People can buy fruit, juice, and eggs at a market.*
sell (v.) *(p. 101)*	When you **sell** something, you give it to someone who gives you money for it.	**USE A PROP** Give a child a coin to exchange with you for a piece of paper. *If I sell this paper to you, you give me money and I give you the paper.*
help (v.) *(p. 102)*	When you **help**, you make it easier for someone to do something.	**ACT IT OUT** Try to lift a chair and then ask a volunteer to lift it with you. *I need help to lift this chair.*
neighbors (n.) *(p. 103)*	Your **neighbors** are the people who live near you.	**MAKE A CONNECTION** Relate the concept of neighbors to children's lives. *The people who live around you at home are your neighbors.*
set (v.) *(p. 103)*	When you **set** something up, you make it so that it is useful.	**ACT IT OUT** Set up a display of three books. *I set up these books to make it easy for you to see them.*

 LEARNING MINDSET

Belonging

Model Demonstrate using the words *help* and *neighbors* to discuss ways friends and neighbors can support each other. *An important part of belonging to a group is helping other people. If I see that my **neighbors** have a problem, I can ask if they need me to **help**. What could you do if a classmate needed **help**?*

I Do It

Use the **VOCABULARY** routine and Vocabulary Cards 2.10–2.15 to introduce the Power Words from *Dan Had a Plan*. You may wish to display the corresponding Vocabulary Card for each word as you discuss it.

mess

Vocabulary Cards

1. **Say the Power Word.** Ask children to repeat it.

2. **Explain the meaning.** Read aloud the student-friendly meaning.

3. **Talk about examples.** Use the image or a strategy to give examples of the word.

We Do It

Guide children to make connections between each word's meaning and how they can use it in their own lives. Use these prompts. Encourage children to explain or justify their answers.

- *Describe how the classroom would look if it were a **mess**.*
- *Would you go to a **market** to dance? Why or why not?*
- *What could you **sell** to make money?*
- *How do you **help** friends at school?*
- *Would you like friendly **neighbors** or grumpy **neighbors**? Why?*
- *How do you **set** up your desk to get ready for school?*

You Do It

INDEPENDENT PRACTICE

Have partners work together to complete each of the activities below. Circulate and observe partners as they work, providing corrective feedback as necessary.

- **Draw** *Draw a picture of things that people **sell** at a **market**.*
- **Discuss** *Talk about how **neighbors** can **help** clean up a **mess**.*
- **Role-Play** *Act out how you would **set** up art supplies to get ready to draw or paint.*

 ENGLISH LEARNER SUPPORT: Facilitate Discussion

SUBSTANTIAL
Point out examples in the classroom related to the Power Words, and ask *yes/no* questions: *Is this a **mess**? Did we **set** up the books?*

MODERATE
Supply frames such as these: *I go to a **market** to _____. I could **sell** _____. I **help** my friends _____.*

LIGHT
Have children work with a partner to take turns using each word in a simple sentence.

 **Retell**

Step 1 Connect and Teach

- Remind children that, in stories and in life, things usually happen in an order that makes sense.

- Project or display **Anchor Chart 5: Retell**.

- Tell children that one way to remember and understand a story is to **retell** it by telling the story using their own words. Telling the parts of the story in order will help the story make sense to others.

- Explain that children should use sequence words to tell the parts of a story in order. Tell them to use *first* to tell about events at the beginning, *next* and *then* to tell about events in the middle, and *last* to tell about events at the end.

ANCHOR CHART 5: Retell

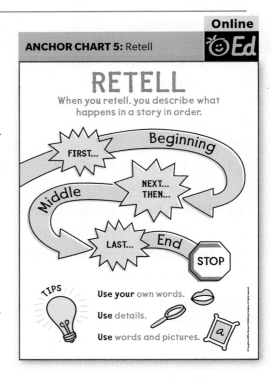

- Finally, point out that children can use details from the words and pictures to help them retell a story. Remind them to tell the story in their own words.

- Tell children they will practice retelling when they read the realistic fiction story called *Dan Had a Plan*.

LEARNING OBJECTIVES

- Identify the features of realistic fiction.
- Retell a story in sequential order, maintaining meaning.
- **Language** Narrate a story from beginning to end, using sequence words.
- Share and respond to story retellings.

MATERIALS Online

Anchor Chart 5 *Retell*
Printable *Anchor Chart 5: Retell*
Teaching Pal *Book 1, pp. 98–113*
myBook *Dan Had a Plan, Book 1, pp. 98–113*

 READER'S VOCABULARY

- **retell** to tell a story in your own words

Notice & Note

Aha Moment

- The Teaching Pal prompts in this lesson feature the **Notice & Note signpost: Aha Moment**.
- As needed, refer to p. T263 to review the signpost with children.

 ASSESSMENT OPTION

Assign the **Selection Quiz** to check comprehension of *Dan Had a Plan*.

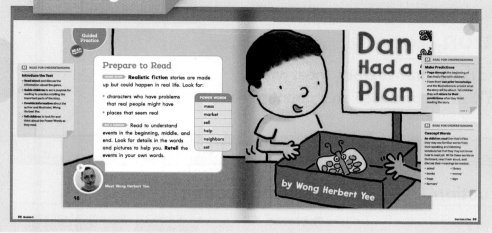

Step 2 Apply to Text

In your Teaching Pal, pages 98–113, use the blue **READ FOR UNDERSTANDING** prompts to read *Dan Had a Plan* with children as they follow along and annotate in their *my*Book.

- **Genre Study** Read the genre information on page 98. Discuss the kinds of things children would expect to find in a realistic fiction story and compare them to a fantasy story.

- **Set a Purpose** Read the Set a Purpose section on page 98. Prompt children to set their own purpose for reading *Dan Had a Plan*.

- **Meet the Author and Illustrator** Play the audio about Wong Herbert Yee. Help children make connections between the information about Wong Herbert Yee and the features of realistic fiction.

- **Read and Comprehend** Guide children to read the story all the way through. Pause occasionally, using the prompts in your Teaching Pal to gauge children's understanding and to have them retell parts of the story. As children retell, have them refer back to the Anchor Chart and use the sequence words and tips.

Step 3 Engage and Respond

INDEPENDENT PRACTICE: Speaking & Listening

- Use the **TURN AND TALK** routine with the questions on Teaching Pal and *my*Book page 113. Remind children to use text evidence and the words *first, next, then,* and *last* as they retell the story in their own words.

- Read the Listening Tip. Remind children to listen actively by looking at their partners and showing interest, and by asking questions when they don't understand something.

- You may want to have children conduct their discussions during daily small-group time.

ENGLISH LEARNER SUPPORT:
Build Background

ALL LEVELS Develop meaning for the term *farmers' market* using the illustration on page 103. If possible, show magazine pictures of a farmers' market to help children understand that it is a place where farmers and different merchants bring food and other goods to sell to people. Encourage children to tell about their own experiences at farmers' markets, if appropriate.

LINK TO SMALL-GROUP INSTRUCTION

REINFORCE RETELL Review or extend the skill as needed during small-group time to support children's need for differentiation. *See the lesson on p. T311.*

👥 SMALL-GROUP INSTRUCTION

Options for Differentiation

As the class engages in independent and collaborative work, meet with Guided Reading Groups or differentiate instruction based on student need.

GUIDED READING GROUPS

Match Children to Books + Instruction

- Choose just-right books based on level, skill, topic, or genre.

C D E F G H I J K ➡
Leveled Readers

- Deliver instruction with each book's Take and Teach Lesson, choosing appropriate sessions based on need.

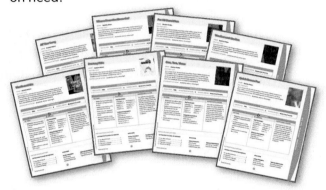

- Check comprehension, reinforce instruction, and extend learning with suggested supporting activities.

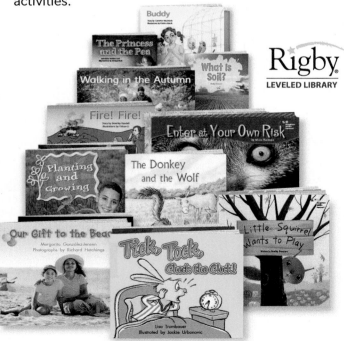

Rigby
LEVELED LIBRARY

🔵 ENGLISH LEARNER SUPPORT

Recount Information

- Use **Tabletop Minilessons: English Language Development 4.2 (Reading)** to reinforce and practice the language skill.

Tabletop Minilessons: English Language Development

- Then use the following text-based prompts with *Dan Had a Plan* to guide application of the language skill. Begin with the prompt at the child's identified language proficiency level. As children are able, use lighter supports to encourage increased language proficiency.

SUBSTANTIAL

Have children turn to page 100. Ask: *What is on the table?* Allow children to point, respond in single words or simple phrases, or explain in their home language.

MODERATE

Ask children to recount how Kim responds to Dan on page 102. Supply this frame: *Kim says Dan is _____.*

LIGHT

Ask children to recount what Dan's plan is. Ask: *What is Dan doing on page 106? Why is he doing this?*

REINFORCE RETELL

Demonstrate

- Use **Tabletop Minilessons: Reading 5** to remind children that retelling what you read is a good way to understand and remember a text. To **retell,** they should use their **own words** to say what happened in a story. They should also tell the events in order: explain the beginning, middle, and end. They should give enough information so that someone who has not read the story can understand it. They should also use information from the text and pictures to retell the story.

- Model filling out Printable: **Reading Graphic Organizer 4** to retell *Dan Had a Plan.*

Tabletop Minilessons: Reading

Apply to Independent Reading

- Now have children retell an appropriate just-right book that they are reading independently. Before children read their books, guide them to set a purpose for reading. Remind them to pay attention to the main events that happen in the story. Customize these prompts to the books children choose.

  » *Pause after you read the first part of the book. What has happened so far?*

  » *Pause after you read another section. What happened in this section?*

  » *When you get to the end, stop and think about it. What happens at the end?*

  » *How can you use your own words to retell the whole story in order?*

- Have children complete Printable: **Reading Graphic Organizer 4** for their independent reading book.

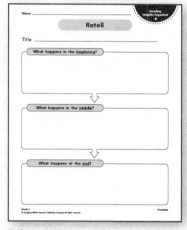

Printable:
Reading Graphic Organizer 4

ALMOST THERE

READY FOR MORE

SCAFFOLD AND EXTEND

- Help children use the pictures while they retell events in order.

- Prompt children to use the pictures and words in the text to retell what happens in the beginning, middle, and end of the book.

- Have children retell what happens in the beginning, middle, and end of the book, using their own words.

EL **ENGLISH LEARNER SUPPORT**

SUBSTANTIAL
Ask children what is happening at different points in the story. Allow them to answer using single words or short phrases.

MODERATE
Supply frames to help children retell: *In the beginning, _____. In the middle, _____. In the end, _____.*

LIGHT
Guide children to retell the story in their own words, using information from the text and pictures.

Options for Differentiation

A Big Pit, Start Right Reader, *Book 1*, pp. 116–123

REINFORCE FOUNDATIONAL SKILLS

Read Decodable Text

Story Break: High-Frequency Word Review Have children turn to Start Right Reader page 116. Have partners take turns reading the story. Then have them discuss what they think will happen next.

Preview the Story Call attention to page 117. Read aloud the title and have children look at the pictures on the first few pages. Have them use their preview to predict the problem in this story.

Concepts of Print: Words in Sentences Have children draw a finger under each sentence on page 120. Periodically prompt: *What is the first word in this sentence? What is the last word? What is the end punction? Point to the word _____.*

Fluency Focus: Expression Read aloud page 117 as children follow along. Remind them to use end punctuation, such as exclamation points, to guide their expression. Then lead children in reading the page chorally with appropriate expression.

Reflect on Reading Have children use a finger to track the words from left to right as they read each page silently. Then have them read the page chorally. Pause for these prompts:

- **Pages 117–118:** *Oh, no! Kim's cab has a problem. What do the words say the cab does? (It hits a pit. It dips.) What do the pictures show about the cab? (The cab is driving toward the pit. Then one of its back tires falls off.)*

- **Page 120:** *What is Kim looking for? (a kit) What do you think the kit is for? (fixing the tire that fell off)*

- **Page 121:** *What does Kim do with the kit? (She fixes the tire that fell off.)*

- **Page 122:** *Is the problem fixed? How do you know? (Yes; a character says the cab will go.)*

Personal Response Read aloud the directions and numbered items on page 123. Have children think about the questions and write their answers on a sheet of paper. Then have them share their responses with a partner or the group.

Big bins? Rags in bits?
Gas cans? Tin pans?
Kim finds the kit!

120

Kim taps it a little bit.
Tap! Tap! Tap!

121

Dan taps it, too. Big taps!
Tap! Tap! Tap!
The cab will go, Kim!

122

READ TOGETHER

Personal Response

Think about the stories. Then write to answer the questions.

1. Who is your favorite character? Why?

2. Which story do you like best? Draw and write about your favorite part.

Talk about the stories with a partner or a group.

123

⏱ Make Minutes Count

As you meet with small groups to read *A Big Pit*, use one or more of these related activities, as needed, at the beginning or the end of the small-group session.

- **Connect to Phonics** Display the Sound/Spelling Cards *alligator* and *igloo*. Then write these words on the board: *bad, big, car, Kim, kit, Nan, tan, tin*. Have each child read a word and point to the Sound/Spelling Card that names the vowel sound in the word.

- **Connect to Spelling** Play Tic-Tac-Toe. Have partners draw a three-by-three grid and assign who will be *X* and who will be *O*. One partner calls out a Spelling Word from Printable: <u>Word List 4</u> for the other partner to spell. If the other partner spells the word correctly, he or she writes his or her assigned letter anywhere on the grid. Play continues until one partner has three *X*s or *O*s in a row.

- **Connect to High-Frequency Words** Play Word Jar. Place the High-Frequency Word cards from Printable: <u>Word List 4</u> in a jar or box. Have children take turns choosing a word and reading it aloud. Continue until all the words have been selected.

a

Options for Independent and Collaborative Work

While you meet with small groups, have other children engage in literacy activities that reinforce the lesson's learning objectives. Choose from these options.

Independent Reading

Student Choice Library

Rigby®
LEVELED LIBRARY

APPLY READING SKILL

Retell Children complete Printable: **Reading Graphic Organizer 4** for an independent reading book.

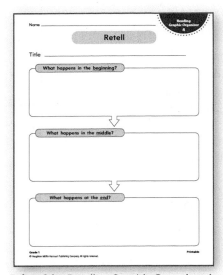

Printable: Reading Graphic Organizer 4

APPLY LANGUAGE SKILL

Recount Information Children complete Printable: **Language Graphic Organizer 11** for an independent reading book.

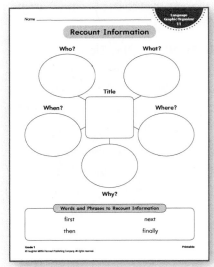

Printable: Language Graphic Organizer 11

Notice & Note

Aha Moment

When children encounter this signpost in their independent reading, encourage them to ask the Anchor Question: *How might this change things?*

Literacy Centers

See pp. T270–T271.

 WORD WORK

 CREATIVITY CORNER

 DIGITAL STATION

 READING CORNER

 TEAMWORK TIME

Start Right Reader

A Big Pit
by Jesse Cortez
illustrated by Brian Fitzgerald

Kim! Kim!
It is a big pit, Kim!

117

Read Decodable Text *A Big Pit,*
Book 1: pp. 116–123

Speaking & Listening

Partners discuss the Turn and Talk questions while using sequence words to retell the story. *See Engage & Respond, p. T309.*

Additional Skills Practice

SPELLING

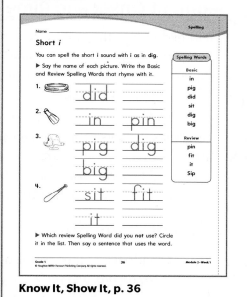

Know It, Show It, p. 36

Wrap-Up
Share Time

At the end of Reading Workshop, have children reflect on their learning by sharing how they applied **Retell** or another area of focus during independent work time. Choose from these options:

- **SHARE CHAIR** Select a reader each day to come to the front of the class and tell what he or she learned from the reading by using a skill or strategy.

- **THINK-PAIR-SHARE** Children share their thinking with a partner. Select a few each day to share with the whole class.

- **RETURN TO ANCHOR CHART** Have children add sticky notes about their independent reading book to the Retell Anchor Chart. Call on a few children to explain what they added.

ANCHOR CHART 5: Retell

Online Ed

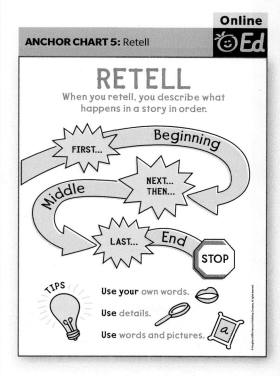

FOUNDATIONAL SKILLS

LEARNING OBJECTIVES

- Identify and read high-frequency words.
- **Language** Recognize and recite basic sight vocabulary.
- Segment onsets and rimes in one-syllable words.
- Segment spoken one-syllable words into individual phonemes.

MATERIALS   Online

Word Cards *are, big, buy, did, its, little, ran, said, sit, too, up, will, you*

 # High-Frequency Words

Review the Words

Repeat the **HIGH-FREQUENCY WORDS** routine to review this week's High-Frequency Words: *are, buy, little, said, too, up, will,* and *you,* and the decodable High-Frequency Words *big, did, its, ran,* and *sit.*

Eruption

- Write the High-Frequency Words and decodable High-Frequency Words on the board or display the Word Cards for the week's words.
- Point to a word, and have children whisper-read it. Then have them pretend to be an erupting volcano and read it loudly. Continue in a similar manner for the rest of the words.

 # Phonological Awareness

Segment Onset and Rime

- Tell children that they will be separating words into chunks. Say: *I will say a word, and you will say the word in two chunks: the beginning, and the rest of the word. Listen as I do one:* leap. *The beginning is /l/. The rest of the word is /ēp/.* Leap, */l/ /ēp/. Now, say these words in two chunks:* cold (*/k/ /ōld/*), gap (*/g/ /ăp/*), tin (*/t/ /ĭn/*), set (*/s/ /ĕt/*), ripe (*/r/ /īp/*).

- *Now I will say the word and the beginning, and you will say the rest of the word. Listen:* pick. *The first chunk is /p/. What is the rest of the word?* (*/ĭk/*) *Good! Let's do some more:* line, */l/ (/īn/);* rob, */r/ (/ŏb/);* make, */m/ (/āk/);* hen, */h/ (/ĕn/);* dug, */d/ (/ŭg/);* shut, */sh/ (/ŭt/);* rest, */r/ (/ĕst/);* pump, */p/ (/ŭmp/).*

Segment Phonemes

- Remind children that they can also separate words into their individual sounds. Say: *I will say a word, and you will say all the sounds in the word. Listen as I do one:* low. *I hear /l/ at the beginning and then /ō/. The sounds in low are /l/ and /ō/.*

- *It's your turn! Say all the sounds in these words:* high (*/h/ /ī/*), say (*/s/ /ā/*), toe (*/t/ /ō/*), cut (*/k/ /ŭ/ /t/*), rope (*/r/ /ō/ /p/*), head (*/h/ /ĕ/ /d/*), fill (*/f/ /ĭ/ /l/*).

TEACHER TIP

Add actions! Work with children to choose two actions to perform while segmenting onset and rime: one to do as they say the onset and one as they say the rime. Have children use these actions to remind them to say each chunk of the word.

✓ **CORRECT & REDIRECT**

If children have trouble segmenting onset and rime, guide them to first say the beginning sound and then say the rest of the word. Have children repeat after you. Example:

- Cold. *I hear /k/ at the beginning of cold. Say it with me:* cold, */k/.*
- Cold. */k/ and then the rest of the word: /ōld/. Say it with me:* /ōld/.
- Cold: *the beginning chunk is /k/, and the rest of the word is /ōld/. Say cold in two chunks.* (*/k/ /ōld/*)

Phonics Review

I Do It

Spotlight on Letters Use the **SOUND-BY-SOUND BLENDING** routine to review this week's phonic elements: short vowels *a, i* and consonants *g* /g/ (hard *g*), *k*. Model blending *bag* with Letter Cards (or display the written word). Say the first two sounds separately, then together; then say the last sound and add it to the blended sounds. Repeat for *Kim*.

LEARNING OBJECTIVE

• Blend, decode, and build regularly spelled one-syllable words with consonants *g* /g/ (hard *g*), *k*, and short vowels *a, i*.

MATERIALS   Online

Letter Cards *a, b, i, g, K, m*
Display and Engage *Blend and Read 2.3*
Start Right Reader Book 1, p. 124
Know It, Show It *p. 37*

We Do It

Blend and Read Project Display and Engage: **Blend and Read 2.3** or use Start Right Reader page 124.

DISPLAY AND ENGAGE:
Blend and Read 2.3

Online

Blend and Read 2.3

Blend and Read

❶ pig   rig   big   bag   rag
❷ kit   ram   rim   kid   rid
❸ bad   did   dig   big   gag
❹ rig   ring   kid   skid
❺ Kim hits a big pit.
❻ Kim digs in the cab.

Grade 1 | Foundational Skills   Module 2 • Week 1

① **Line 1** Have children read the line. Then prompt a conversation about the words. Ask: *How are all of the words alike? different? Do any of them rhyme?* Reread the line chorally.

② **Line 2** Continue. Then have volunteers reread selected words until they can identify them quickly.

③ **Review** Display Line 3, and have children read it chorally.

④ **Challenge** Children who are ready for a challenge can read Line 4, tell how the words in columns 2 and 4 differ from the words in columns 1 and 3, and demonstrate how they blended the words with four letters.

⑤ **Sentences** Display Lines 5–6. Call on children to blend selected words. Point to each word as children read the sentences chorally.

You Do It

INDEPENDENT PRACTICE

• **Option 1** Dictate these words for children to write: *bag, rag, pig, kid.* Have children work with partners to check their spelling against the Blend and Read lines. Then have children draw a picture for each word and share.

• **Option 2** Have children complete Know It, Show It page 37.

 ENGLISH LEARNER SUPPORT:
Build Vocabulary

ALL LEVELS Have children share what they know about each Blend and Read word. Confirm or clarify word meanings as needed. Provide oral clues, and have children find and read the word that matches the clue: *I can clean my desk with this. (rag) I can carry things in this. (bag) This word names a child or a baby goat. (kid)*

 **LINK TO SMALL-GROUP INSTRUCTION**

REINFORCE FOUNDATIONAL SKILLS Use *Big Pat* during small-group time to review or reinforce blending and decoding words with consonants *g, k* and short vowels *a, i*. Meet with children to work through the story, or assign it as independent work. *See the lesson on p. T324.*

Big Pat
by Jesse Cortez
illustrated by Brian Fitzgerald

Kim sees a tag for Big Pat.
Kim is sad.

VOCABULARY

LEARNING OBJECTIVES

- **Language** Respond using newly acquired vocabulary.
- Use newly acquired vocabulary to identify real-life connections between words and their use.
- Identify and use words that name places, things, and actions.

MATERIALS   Online

Vocabulary Cards *2.10–2.15*
Know It, Show It *p. 38*

 # Review Power Words

Revisit the Power Words

- Use Vocabulary Cards 2.10–2.15 to review the Power Words from *Dan Had a Plan.*
- Guide children to discuss how the image helps them understand each word's meaning.

Vocabulary Chat

- Display the Power Words. Have children break into small groups.
- One child in each group says clues about a Power Word without saying the word itself. Clues can be real-world examples, words with similar or opposite meanings, or descriptions of times the children may have used or might use the Power Word.
- For example, for the Power Words *mess* and *market*, children can say "Something your room would be if you never cleaned it" or "I can buy eggs here."
- The rest of the group guesses the word. If necessary, children may ask the speaker questions to get clarification about the word or what he/she is saying.
- Have children continue the activity until all the words have been guessed.
- **Get Up and Move!** *Think of times when people **help** each other with chores or work. Act out some examples.* Have small groups take turns demonstrating how they help doing things like cleaning up the classroom. Ask them to share times when they might do or see this.
- For additional practice with the Power Words from *Dan Had a Plan,* have children complete Know It, Show It page 38.

mess

Vocabulary Cards

(EL) ENGLISH LEARNER SUPPORT:
Facilitate Discussion

SUBSTANTIAL
Ask: *Would you buy food at a **market** or at a school? If something is a **mess**, is it clean or dirty?*

MODERATE
Simplify clues as needed. Prompt responses with questions: *Where do you go to shop? What does your room look like when it is not picked up?*

LIGHT
Ask: *Where do you see **neighbors**? How can a **mess** be a problem?*

Words About Places and Things

I Do It

- Project Display and Engage: **Generative Vocabulary 2.4**. Read aloud the introduction.

- Discuss the examples *market* and *apple*. Remind children that they read the word *market* in *Dan Had a Plan*.

- Model determining each type of **noun**. *Market is a noun that names a place. People go to a market to buy things, like an apple. Apple is a noun that names a thing.*

- Continue with Examples 1 and 2. Discuss how each word names a place or a thing. Tell children that if they do not know the meaning of one of these words, they can look it up in a dictionary. Model looking up one of the words.

DISPLAY AND ENGAGE:
Generative Vocabulary 2.4

Online

Generative Vocabulary 2.4

Words About Places and Things

Nouns are words that name a person, a place, or a thing.

- A noun that names a **place** tells **where** something is happening.
- A noun that names a **thing** tells **what** something is.

Examples
1 Places: house, mountain, beach, field
2 Things: ball, toy, pencil, flower

market   apple

Grade 1 | Vocabulary   Module 2 • Week 1

We Do It

- Lead children in a discussion about other nouns that name places and things. Prompt them with questions such as these: *Where are some places you might go to play? (playground, beach) What are some things you use to learn? (book, computer)*

- Ask volunteers to look up one of the nouns in a picture dictionary and explain its meaning.

You Do It

INDEPENDENT PRACTICE

- **Option 1** Have partners write lists. One partner identifies and writes a list of three things, and the other partner identifies and writes a list of three places. Have them exchange lists and draw a picture of the words on their partner's list to demonstrate meaning. Tell them to use a dictionary if they need help.

- **Option 2** Have children complete Know It, Show It page 39.

LEARNING OBJECTIVES

- Understand and use common nouns that name places and things.

- **Language** Identify words that name places and things.

- Use a dictionary to find the meaning of unknown words.

MATERIALS   Online Ed

Display and Engage *Generative Vocabulary 2.4*

Know It, Show It *p. 39*

READER'S VOCABULARY

- **noun** a word that names a person, place, or thing

 ENGLISH LEARNER SUPPORT:
Build Vocabulary

ALL LEVELS To support children's understanding of the noun categories, use realia/photographs. Guide children to sort the items in two columns or piles. Label them "Place" and "Thing." Ask: *Is this a place? Or is this a thing?* Prompt children to point to the correct column. After all have been sorted, hold up each visual and prompt children to repeat simple statements after you, such as these: *This is an apple. An apple is a thing.*

READING WORKSHOP

Setting

Step 1   **Connect and Teach**

LEARNING OBJECTIVES

- Identify and describe the setting of a story.
- **Language** Share information about the setting, using describing words.
- Write steps in order, using evidence to support ideas.

MATERIALS   Online

Anchor Chart 11 *Setting*

Printable *Anchor Chart 11: Setting*

Teaching Pal *Book 1, pp. 98–115*

myBook *Dan Had a Plan, Book 1, pp. 98–115*

Know It, Show It *p. 40*

READER'S VOCABULARY

- **setting** where and when a story takes place
- **describe** to tell what someone or something is like by giving details
- **detail** small bit of information that supports a central idea or describes something in a text

- Project or display <u>Anchor Chart 11: Setting</u>.

- Tell children that the **setting** of a story is where and when the story takes place. The setting can be the place, time of day, time of year, or season where the story takes place.

- Point out that sometimes a setting stays the same through a whole story. In other stories, the setting changes. For example, if the characters go to a different place, or if the season or time of day changes.

- Tell children that when they **describe** a setting, they tell what the setting is like. To know what the setting is like, they can look for small pieces of information, or **details**, in the text and the pictures.

- Finally, point out that children can also use the details to tell how the setting is important to the story.

- Tell children they will reread parts of *Dan Had a Plan* to practice identifying and describing the setting.

Online

ANCHOR CHART 11: Setting

Professional Learning

RESEARCH FOUNDATIONS

"Writing about reading had a positive impact on the comprehension of weaker readers and writers."

–Dr. Steve Graham and Dr. Michael Hebert (2011)

See the **GPS guide** to learn more.

 LEARNING MINDSET

Belonging

Reflect Explain that one way of belonging to a community is to help others. Tell children there are all kinds of ways to help your community. *In Dan Had a Plan, Dan's sister makes fruit snacks to raise money for the local library. Dan, his friend Sam, and other community members help too. How do you think what they are doing helps other people?*

ANNOTATE IT!

Online
Ed

Children may use the annotation tools in their eBook.

Step 2 Apply to Text

In your Teaching Pal, use the purple **TARGETED CLOSE READ** prompts to guide children to apply the describing setting skill to *Dan Had a Plan*. Children may refer to the questions on Know It, Show It page 40 as you discuss them.

- Read aloud the first question on Teaching Pal page 102 and have children look for details in the words and pictures to answer it. *(Their home and then the farmers' market.)*

- Then read the follow-up question. Tell children to describe the text evidence they used to answer the question. *(The pictures show them at those places.)*

- Read aloud the question on Teaching Pal page 110. Tell children to look back at the words and pictures to figure out how the setting has changed. *(The family is at their house and the farmers' market one day and at the library on a different day.)*

- Refer back to the Anchor Chart to support the discussion. Children may add sticky notes to the chart to tell where and when the parts of *Dan Had a Plan* take place, and to explain why the library setting is important to the story.

Step 3 Engage and Respond

INDEPENDENT PRACTICE: Writing

- Read aloud the prompt on Teaching Pal page 114. Have children use the planning space to draw or write about what Dan and Sam do first, next, and last to sell the fruit snacks.

- Then have children write their responses to the prompt. Remind children to refer back to *Dan Had a Plan* and use the words and pictures from the story for ideas. Remind them to use sequence words and begin each sentence with a capital letter and end it with a period.

- You may want to have children complete their writing during daily small-group time.

ENGLISH LEARNER SUPPORT:
Scaffold Writing

SUBSTANTIAL
Review the pictures in *Dan Had a Plan* with children. Use *first, next,* and *last* to describe what is happening. Have children repeat.

MODERATE
Provide sentence frames for children to complete: *First, Sam and Dan _____. Next, they _____. Last, they _____.*

LIGHT
Have partners describe events in the story before writing their answers.

LINK TO SMALL-GROUP INSTRUCTION

REINFORCE SETTING Review or extend the skill as needed during small-group time to support children's need for differentiation. *See the lesson on p. T323.*

Options for Differentiation

As the class engages in independent and collaborative work, meet with Guided Reading Groups or differentiate instruction based on student need.

GUIDED READING GROUPS

Match Children to Books + Instruction

- Choose just-right books based on level, skill, topic, or genre.

C D E F G H I J K
Leveled Readers

- Deliver instruction with each book's Take and Teach Lesson, choosing appropriate sessions based on need.

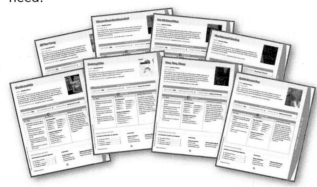

- Check comprehension, reinforce instruction, and extend learning with suggested supporting activities.

Rigby®
LEVELED LIBRARY

🔵EL ENGLISH LEARNER SUPPORT

Recount Information

- Use **Tabletop Minilessons: English Language Development 4.2 (Writing)** to introduce and practice the language skill.

Tabletop Minilessons: English Language Development

- Then use the following text-based prompts with *Dan Had a Plan* to guide application of the language skill. Begin with the prompt at the child's identified language proficiency level. As children are able, use lighter supports to encourage increased language proficiency.

SUBSTANTIAL
Turn to page 110. Ask children who got the last treat. Ask: *How does Dan feel?* Allow children to point, respond with single words, or use their home language to respond.

MODERATE
Have children use short phrases to complete these frames as they recount details from the story: *Kim makes _____. Dan and Sam help by _____.*

LIGHT
Ask children to recount what happens at the farmers' market. Ask: *Who sets up? What does the sign say? What do Dan and Sam do?*

REINFORCE SETTING

Demonstrate

- Use **Tabletop Minilessons: Reading 11** to remind children that the **setting** is where and when a story takes place. It can be the time of day or the time of year. The setting can be the same for a whole story, or it might change throughout a story. Authors might **describe** where the setting is as well as what it looks or sounds like. **Details** in the text and pictures help readers identify the setting and why it is important.

- Model filling out Printable: **Reading Graphic Organizer 18** to identify and describe the setting in *Dan Had a Plan*.

Apply to Independent Reading

- Now have children identify and describe the setting in an appropriate just-right book that they are reading independently. Customize these prompts to the books children choose.

  » *Where does the story take place? What words tell you what the place is like?*

  » *When does the story take place? What words tell you when the story happens?*

  » *What details describe the setting?*

- Have children complete Printable: **Reading Graphic Organizer 18** for their independent reading book.

Tabletop Minilessons: Reading

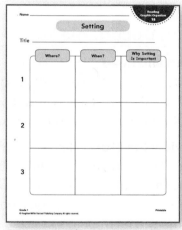

Printable:
Reading Graphic Organizer 18

ALMOST THERE

READY FOR MORE

SCAFFOLD AND EXTEND

- Guide children to locate details that tell *where* and *when* events happen.

- Prompt children to describe the setting using words from the text.

- Guide children to describe the different settings of the story in their own words.

ENGLISH LEARNER SUPPORT

SUBSTANTIAL
Read aloud or say words that describe the setting. Ask children to point to what you are describing in the pictures and to repeat the words after you.

MODERATE
Supply these frames to discuss the setting of different parts of the book: *The story takes place in _____. The story takes place at _____.*

LIGHT
As children answer prompts, encourage them to use their own words to describe in detail the setting of the story.

Options for Differentiation

Big Pat, *Start Right Reader, Book 1,* pp. 124–131

REINFORCE FOUNDATIONAL SKILLS

Read Decodable Text

Blend and Read Have children turn to Start Right Reader page 124. Use the **CHORAL READING** routine to read aloud the Blend and Read lines. Use challenge line 4 with children who are ready.

Preview the Story Help children recall that Kim is taking Nan, Dan, and Sam to see Big Pat. Then read aloud the title on page 125 and have children look at the pictures on the first few pages. Have them predict what will happen on the way to see Big Pat.

Fluency Focus: Expression Read aloud page 127 as children follow along. Point out how you used the end punctuation to guide your expression. Then have children read the selection, focusing on using appropriate expression.

Reflect on Reading Have children read to find out who Big Pat is. Have them read each page silently and then chorally. Pause for these prompts:

• **Page 125:** *What does Kim see? (a tag for Big Pat) Why do you think Kim is sad when she sees the tag? (She does not have a gift for Big Pat.)*

• **Pages 126–127:** *Where does Kim run to? (a store) What does she get? (a big fan to give Big Pat)*

• **Page 128:** *How does Kim fit the fan into the cab? (She ties it to the roof of the cab.)*

• **Page 129:** *Why do you think Nan, Sam, and Dan have come to see Big Pat? What details support your response? (Big Pat has a hurt arm; the picture shows a bandage around one of Big Pat's arms.*

• **Pages 125–130:** *Was your prediction correct? Explain. (Responses will vary.)*

Turn and Talk Allow time for children to reread the week's four Start Right Reader stories. Then use the **TURN AND TALK** routine to guide partners to discuss the questions on page 131.

Rip! Rip! Nan rips rags.
Kim rigs up the fan.
Kim did it! It can fit.

128

"Nan! Sam! Dan! Kim!"
Big Pat sees the tags.
"You are good!" he said.

129

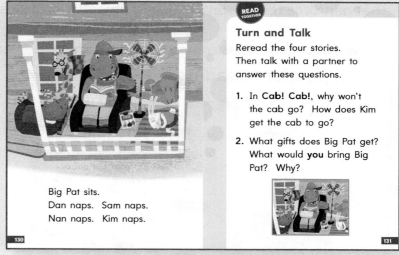

Big Pat sits.
Dan naps. Sam naps.
Nan naps. Kim naps.

130

READ TOGETHER

Turn and Talk

Reread the four stories. Then talk with a partner to answer these questions.

1. In **Cab! Cab!**, why won't the cab go? How does Kim get the cab to go?

2. What gifts does Big Pat get? What would **you** bring Big Pat? Why?

131

(?) Make Minutes Count

As you meet with small groups to read *Big Pat*, use one or more of these related activities, as needed, at the beginning or the end of the small-group session.

- **Connect to Phonics** Write these words on separate self-stick notes: *bag, bin, cab, fan, fig, kit, pan, sit, tag, tip*. Then draw a two-column chart on chart paper with the columns labeled *short* a and *short* i. Have children take turns selecting a note, reading the word, and sticking the note in the appropriate column.

- **Connect to Spelling** Play Hot Potato. Have children gather in a circle. Take a soft item, such as a beanbag, and hand it to a child. Have children pass the beanbag around the circle until you say, "Hot potato!" Then whoever has the beanbag must spell the Spelling Word that you say. Repeat until each child has had a turn.

- **Connect to High-Frequency Words** Play Ask and Answer. Place these High-Frequency Word cards from Printable: **Word List 4** face down in a pile: *buy, little, sit, up, will, you*. Call on a child to take the top card, read aloud the word, and ask the group a question that contains that word. Call on another child to answer the question using the same High-Frequency Word. Continue until each child has had a turn to ask and answer a question.

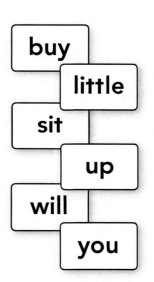

buy
little
sit
up
will
you

Options for Independent and Collaborative Work

While you meet with small groups, have other children engage in literacy activities that reinforce the lesson's learning objectives. Choose from these options.

Independent Reading

Student Choice Library

LEVELED LIBRARY

APPLY READING SKILL

Setting Children complete Printable: <u>Reading Graphic Organizer 18</u> for an independent reading book.

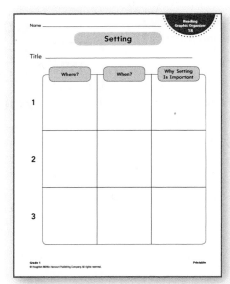

Printable: Reading Graphic Organizer 18

APPLY LANGUAGE SKILL

Recount Information Children complete Printable: <u>Language Graphic Organizer 11</u> for an independent reading book.

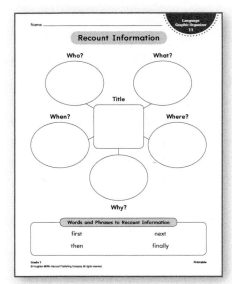

Printable: Language Graphic Organizer 11

Literacy Centers

See pp. T270–T271.

 WORD WORK

 CREATIVITY CORNER

 DIGITAL STATION

 READING CORNER

 TEAMWORK TIME

Start Right Reader

Big Pat
by Jesse Cortez
illustrated by Brian Fitzgerald

Kim sees a tag for Big Pat.
Kim is sad.

125

Read Decodable Text *Big Pat,*
Book 1: pp. 124–131

Writing

Children respond to the prompt referring to the story for ideas. *See Engage & Respond, p. T321.*

Close Reading

Together

READ How do the kids help? Underline words that tell.

Kim, Pam, and Sam are friends.
The kids like this neighborhood.
The kids like to help the neighbors.
A neighbor asked, "Can you help dig?"
"We will help you dig!"
Kim, Pam, and Sam did it together. ▶

Close Reading Tip
Number the main events in order.

CHECK MY UNDERSTANDING
Describe the setting of the story.

a neighborhood yard
on a fall day

117

***my*Book, Book 1, pp. 116–119**

Additional Skills Practice

PHONICS AND VOCABULARY

Know It, Show It, pp. 37, 38, 39

Wrap-Up
Share Time

At the end of Reading Workshop, have children reflect on their learning by sharing how they applied **Setting** or another area of focus during independent work time. Choose from these options:

- **SHARE CHAIR** Select a reader each day to come to the front of the class and tell what he or she learned from the reading by using a skill or strategy.

- **THINK-PAIR-SHARE** Children share their thinking with a partner. Select a few each day to share with the whole class.

- **RETURN TO ANCHOR CHART** Have children add sticky notes about their independent reading book to the Setting Anchor Chart. Call on a few children to explain what they added.

ANCHOR CHART 11: Setting

Online
Ed

LEARNING OBJECTIVES

- Identify and read high-frequency words.
- **Language** Recognize and recite basic sight vocabulary.
- Blend onsets and rimes or individual phonemes to say one-syllable words.
- Segment one-syllable words into onsets and rimes or into individual phonemes.

MATERIALS   Online

Word Cards *are, big, buy, did, its, little, ran, said, sit, too, up, will, you*

Printables *Phonological Awareness 4; Word List 4*

 # High-Frequency Words

Children's Choice

- Remind children of the High-Frequency Words they have been practicing this week: *are, buy, little, said, too, up, will,* and *you,* and the decodable High-Frequency Words: *big, did, its, ran,* and *sit.*

- Review any words that posed difficulty for children this week, using Word Cards and the **HIGH-FREQUENCY WORDS** routine.

- In Lessons 2–4, children used these practice activities: Odd One Out (p. T288), Word Match (p. T302), and Eruption (p. T316). Have children vote on their favorite, and use it to review the week's words for word recognition fluency.

> ## too

 # Phonological Awareness

Teacher's Choice

- In Lessons 1–4, children practiced blending onsets and rimes and blending phonemes (pp. T35, T51). They also practiced segmenting onsets and rimes and segmenting phonemes (pp. T64, T76).

- Use Printable: **Phonological Awareness 4** to gauge which blending or segmenting tasks need reinforcement.

  » **Blend Onset and Rime** Have children blend onset and rime to say these words: /r/ /āk/ (rake), /m/ /ŭg/ (mug).

  » **Blend Phonemes** Have children blend the sounds to say these words: /m/ /ă/ /n/ (man), /r/ /ŏ/ /k/ (rock).

  » **Segment Phonemes** Have children orally segment the following words into individual sounds and then count the sounds in each word: up (/ŭ/ /p/, 2); soak (/s/ /ō/ /k/, 3).

- To determine whether children need reinforcement for segmenting onsets and rimes, tell children to segment these words into chunks: tie (/t/ /ī/), mill (/m/ /ĭl/), hum (/h/ /ŭm/), dot (/d/ /ŏt/), bee (/b/ /ē/).

EL **ENGLISH LEARNER SUPPORT:**
Build Vocabulary

SUBSTANTIAL
Point out classroom objects that are different sizes. Have children describe different objects as *big* or *little.*

MODERATE
Have children use sentence frames to describe the objects' sizes. For example: *The chair is _____. (big) The pen is _____. (little)*

LIGHT
Ask children to share sentences that compare the sizes of objects. For example: *The globe is bigger than the paperclip.*

 CORRECT & REDIRECT

If children have difficulty, model the tasks by emphasizing the sounds. Examples:

- Model blending phonemes. Listen: /r/ /ŏ/ /k/, /r/-/ŏŏŏ/-/k/, rock. *The word is rock. Say the sounds with me: /r/ /ŏ/ /k/, /r-ŏŏŏ-k/, rock. What is the word for the sounds /r/, /ŏ/, and /k/? (rock)*

- Model segmenting phonemes. *We can segment, or break, words into their individual sounds. Listen as I segment the sounds in the word soak: /sss/-/ōōō/-/k/. I hear /s/ at the beginning, /ō/ in the middle, and /k/ at the end. What are the sounds in soak? (/s/ /ō/ /k/) How many sounds are in soak? (3)*

Short *i*

Spelling Assessment

1 Say each Spelling Word, and read the Dictation Sentence. Repeat the word and then have children write it. Remind them to use their best handwriting.

2 Add the Surprise Words *fin*, *bit*, and *rid*. If you prefer a shorter test, replace three of the Basic Words with the Surprise Words.

- **fin** The shark has a big *fin*.
- **bit** I *bit* into an apple.
- **rid** She got *rid* of the old toys.

3 Include the Challenge Words for children who practiced them this week.

4 Review any words that children misspell. If they miss two or more words, then revisit the Lesson 1 Word Sort activity on page T279.

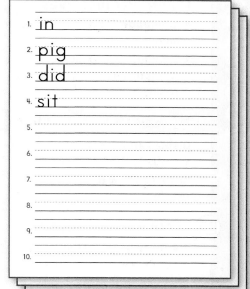

1. in
2. pig
3. did
4. sit
5.
6.
7.
8.
9.
10.

LEARNING OBJECTIVE

- Spell words with short *i* (closed syllables).

DICTATION SENTENCES

BASIC

1. **in** We go *in* that door.
2. **pig** A *pig* is a farm animal.
3. **did** What *did* you do yesterday?
4. **sit** Please *sit* in the chair.
5. **dig** Use a shovel to *dig* a hole.
6. **big** An elephant is very *big*.

REVIEW

7. **pin** She uses a *pin* to hold her hair.
8. **fit** All my markers *fit* in the box.
9. **it** Put *it* away.
10. **sip** Take a *sip* of the drink.

CHALLENGE

11. **ship** The *ship* crossed the ocean.
12. **fish** Many *fish* swim in the lake.

VOCABULARY

LEARNING OBJECTIVES

- **Language** Discuss and compare antonyms.
- Identify and use antonyms, including words that name actions and positions.

MATERIALS   Online

Display and Engage *Vocabulary Strategy 2.5*

Know It, Show It *p. 41*

READER'S VOCABULARY

- **antonym** a word that is opposite in meaning to another word

---

 # Antonyms

I Do It

- Project Display and Engage: <u>Vocabulary Strategy 2.5</u>. Read aloud the first section.

- Discuss the concept of opposite positions, using **antonyms** *open* and *closed*. *If a word is the opposite of another word, it has a completely different meaning. This door is open. The opposite of* open *is* closed. *This door is closed.* Closed *has a completely different meaning. It means "not open."*

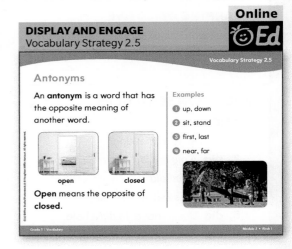

- Then read aloud the first word in Example 1. Model identifying the antonym for *up,* or a word that tells the opposite position. *This word is up. What is the opposite of up? I know that an opposite has a completely different meaning. So I have to think of a word that means "not up." A word that means "not up" is* down. *So* up *and* down *are antonyms.*

- Continue with the remaining examples in the same way. Tell children that learning antonyms for words they already know is a good way to help them remember the meaning of new words.

- Point out that they can think of an antonym for a word they see in their reading to help them make sure they understand the word's meaning. Write this sentence on the board: *I walk through the open door.* Model using the antonym of *open* to show understanding of its meaning. *I can change the word* open *to* closed *and see if the sentence still makes sense. It doesn't! I can't walk through a closed door.*

TEACHER TIP

Opposite theme day! Deepen children's understanding of opposites by celebrating an Opposite Theme Day. Brainstorm a set of rules for fun, safe ways to do the opposite of regular classroom routines, such as turning off the lights, staying inside for recess, or standing at their desks.

 ### LEARNING MINDSET

Belonging

Normalize Explain to children that it's normal to feel the opposite of belonging from time to time. *Everyone feels like they don't belong from time to time. It's okay to feel that way. The best way to get back that belonging feeling is to help a friend or schoolmate. Ask, "How can I help?" Pretty soon, you'll get that belonging feeling back! How might you help a friend who is struggling to understand words with opposite meanings?*

We Do It

- Write antonym pairs on separate slips of paper, one word on each slip, using pairs such as *front/back*, *run/walk*, *happy/ sad*, *cold/hot*, *old/new*, and *early/late*.

- Demonstrate finding an antonym partner by reading aloud a word, such as *new*, and asking "What is the opposite of *new*?" Ask different children if the word on their papers is the opposite of *new*. Stop when you find the child with the word *old*. Explain that you and the child are antonym partners. Then have children move around the room looking for their antonym partners.

- After all children have found their antonym partners, ask pairs to use the following sentence frame to share their antonyms: _____ *is the opposite of* _____.

- Have pairs act out the antonyms to demonstrate the opposite meanings.

You Do It

INDEPENDENT PRACTICE

- **Option 1** Have children practice thinking of an antonym for an action or position word in a book they are reading independently. Have them explain to a partner how replacing the word with its antonym in the original sentence helps them to understand the meaning of the word.

- **Option 2** Have children complete Know It, Show It page 41.

ENGLISH LEARNER SUPPORT:
Facilitate Language Connections

ALL LEVELS For Spanish-speaking children, point out that the word *opposite* has the cognate *opuesto*.

Professional Learning

BEST PRACTICES

Why teach **antonyms** before **synonyms**? Opposites are easier to learn than nuanced similarities in meaning, especially for younger children. In the early grades, attention to synonyms can begin after a few lessons on antonyms. For elementary students more broadly, it is helpful when children are stepping back and thinking more metacognitively about the categories of antonym and synonym to begin with antonyms because they are so straightforward.

See the **GPS guide** to learn more.

Social Communication

Step **1**   **Connect and Teach**

- Remind children that the children in the selection *Kids Speak Up!* tell their opinions and express their feelings about their town.

- Project or display **Anchor Chart 45: Social Communication**. Explain that it shows important listening and talking tips to follow while discussing ideas with other people.

- Discuss the rules on the Anchor Chart. Point out that when children first meet someone new or start a conversation, they should introduce themselves and others.

- Tell children that there are other rules for conversations that will make them communicate better: be polite and listen carefully, look at the speaker, use complete sentences, speak loudly and clearly, and (if you need to) draw a picture to help others understand your ideas.

- Point out that it is also important to decide what kind of language to use in different situations. Explain the difference between **formal language**, which is the language people use at school and with people they do not know well, and **informal language**, which is the language people use with family and friends.

- Tell children they will practice following these rules for social communication as they look back at the the selection *Kids Speak Up!*

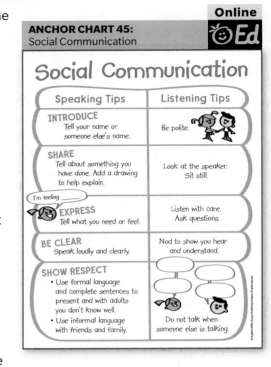

Online

ANCHOR CHART 45: Social Communication

LEARNING OBJECTIVES

- Understand rules of social communication.
- Discuss and follow agreed-upon rules for discussion.
- **Language** Write dialogue in cooperative learning interactions.

MATERIALS   Online

Anchor Chart 45 *Social Communication*

Printable *Anchor Chart 45: Social Communication*

myBook *Kids Speak Up!, Book 1, pp. 96-97*

Know It, Show It *pp. 42–43*

📖 READER'S VOCABULARY

- **formal language** a style for speaking or writing, following the rules of English
- **informal language** a style for speaking or writing that you use with people you know, like friends and family

---

  LEARNING MINDSET

Seeking Challenges

Review Tell children that the way we talk in school can be more formal than at home. Explain that it can take time to get used to the formal language of school, but it is a very good skill to have. *Don't worry if you don't learn all the rules of social communication at once. If you keep practicing, you will get better at it, and it will get easier.*

Step 2 Apply to Text

- Display *Kids Speak Up!* Remind children that the text tells about different things the children like in their community. Explain that when children talk to people in their own community, it is good for them to know how to follow the rules for social communication.

- Model conversations that might take place with people at the different places the children discuss in *Kids Speak Up!* For example, you might model what you might say if you were joining a baseball team at the park, asking a librarian for help finding a book, asking a firefighter about his or her job, or talking to a family member about fishing in a lake.

- Have children refer back to the Anchor Chart, and name the rules being followed in each conversation.

- Have partners use the **THINK-PAIR-SHARE** routine and act out one of the conversations on their own. Remind them to think about whether to use formal or informal language.

Step 3 Engage and Respond

INDEPENDENT PRACTICE: Writing

- **Option 1** Ask children to imagine that there is a new student in the class. Have partners role-play one of the following conversations with the new student: telling their names, telling how they feel about their school, or giving an opinion about the best lunch choice. Have children work together to write down their dialogue to share with others.

- **Option 2** Have children complete Know It, Show It pages 42–43.

EL ENGLISH LEARNER SUPPORT:
Facilitate Discussion

SUBSTANTIAL
Supply sentence frames such as these: *My name is _____. It's nice to meet you, _____.* Have children recite the dialogue.

MODERATE
Supply sentence frames such as these: *Hello, my name is _____. My friend's name is _____. It's nice to meet you, _____.*

LIGHT
Review formal language, such as *please, thank you,* and *excuse me.* Then have children use the phrases in sentences.

 LINK TO SMALL-GROUP INSTRUCTION

REINFORCE SOCIAL COMMUNICATION Review or extend the skill as needed during small-group time to support children's need for differentiation. *See the lesson on p. T335.*

Options for Differentiation

As the class engages in independent and collaborative work, meet with Guided Reading Groups or differentiate instruction based on student need.

GUIDED READING GROUPS

Match Children to Books + Instruction

- Choose just-right books based on level, skill, topic, or genre.

C D E F G H I J K →

Leveled Readers

- Deliver instruction with each book's Take and Teach Lesson, choosing appropriate sessions based on need.

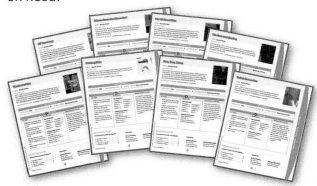

- Check comprehension, reinforce instruction, and extend learning with suggested supporting activities.

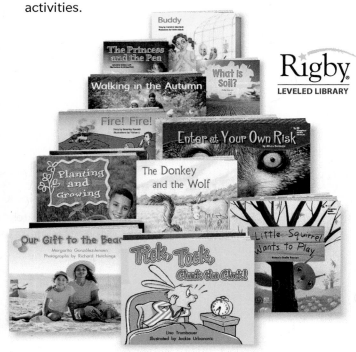

Rigby®
LEVELED LIBRARY

EL ENGLISH LEARNER SUPPORT

Recount Information

- Use **Tabletop Minilessons: English Language Development 4.3 (Collaborative Problem Solving)** to reinforce and practice the language skill.

Tabletop Minilessons: English Language Development

- Then use the following text-based prompts with the text *Kids Speak Up!* to guide application of the language skill. Begin with the prompt at the child's identified language proficiency level. As children are able, use lighter supports to encourage increased language proficiency.

SUBSTANTIAL

Point to each child in the text. Ask: *What does this child like about the town?* Allow children to respond using single words. Then model how to turn their responses into complete sentences and have children repeat them.

MODERATE

Have children work with a partner to recount what there is to do in the town. Supply these frames: *The text says _____. The pictures show _____.*

LIGHT

Have partners recount what there is to do in the town and why the kids think their town is great. Ask: *What activities can you do in this town? Why do the kids think their town is great?*

REINFORCE SOCIAL COMMUNICATION

Demonstrate

- Use **Tabletop Minilessons: Reading 45** to remind children that when they meet someone new or have conversations with classmates or teachers, they should think about how they **communicate.** We use **formal language** with people we do not know very well and **informal language** with people we do know well. It is important to be polite, to listen respectfully to others, to look at others as they speak, and to speak loudly and clearly enough to be understood. In classroom conversations, it is important to take turns so that everyone can **participate** in the conversation.

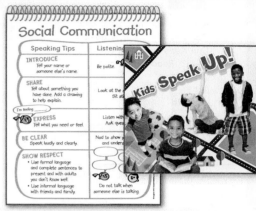

Tabletop Minilessons: Reading

Apply to Independent Reading

- Now have children practice effective social communication as they discuss an appropriate just-right book that they are reading independently. Customize these prompts.

  » *What is a good way to start the conversation?*

  » *What can you say to introduce two people who don't know each other?*

  » *What can you do or say if you want to share an idea or opinion?*

  » *How can you make sure others participate in the conversation?*

ALMOST THERE

READY FOR MORE

SCAFFOLD AND EXTEND

- Model speaking clearly and looking at others when speaking. Have children practice with a partner.

- Prompt children to share an idea from their reading and practice speaking clearly and looking at others when they speak.

- Have children share an idea from their reading and practice rules of social communication.

 ### ENGLISH LEARNER SUPPORT

SUBSTANTIAL

Model introducing yourself and starting a conversation using formal language. Then have partners do the same.

MODERATE

Model how to start a conversation and share an idea using formal language. Have children share an idea from the book they are reading by using the frame: *I think this book _____.*

LIGHT

Prompt children to share an idea from their book and to have a class conversation while following and discussing rules.

LESSON 5

READING WORKSHOP

Options for Differentiation

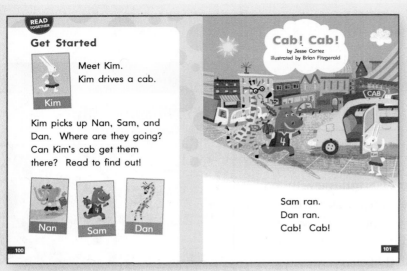

Start Right Reader, *Book 1*, pp. 100–131

REINFORCE FOUNDATIONAL SKILLS

Read Decodable Text

Review Remind children of the Start Right Reader stories they read this week about the characters Kim, Nan, Sam, Dan, and Big Pat.

- *Cab! Cab!*

- *Go, Big Cab!*

- *A Big Pit*

- *Big Pat*

Allow a few minutes for children to page through the stories to recall what they are about.

Make Text Connections Prompt children to explain how the four stories are connected.

- *Who are the main characters in these stories? (Kim, Sam, Dan, and Nan)*

- *What connects the four stories? (Kim is driving Sam, Dan, and Nan to Big Pat's home.)*

- *What are some problems the characters have with the cab? (Possible responses: It needs gas; it hits a big pit; it loses a tire; the characters cannot fit the big fan inside of it.)*

- *Why do Dan, Sam, and Nan get in the cab? (They want to go see Big Pat.) When does the cab get to Big Pat? (in the last story, Big Pat) What do the other characters give Big Pat? (gifts—a hat, a bat, figs, and a fan)*

- *What might happen to Kim, Dan, Sam, and Nan in a new story about them? (Accept reasonable responses.)*

Reread for Fluency Have children select one of the stories to reread. Use the **ECHO READING** routine and have children focus on reading with appropriate expression.

Story Break

Read this story with a friend.

1. "I am **little**," **said** Kim.

2. "Nan, **are you little, too?**"

3. "I am big!" **said** Nan.

4. "Can **you** see?"

What **will** happen next? Share ideas with your friend.

116

A Big Pit
by Jesse Cortez
illustrated by Brian Fitzgerald

Kim! Kim!
It is a big pit, Kim!

117

Blend and Read

1. pig   rig   big   bag   rag
2. kit   ram   rim   kid   rid
3. bad   did   dig   big   gag
4. rig   ring   kid   skid
5. Kim hits a big pit.
6. Kim digs in the cab.

124

Big Pat
by Jesse Cortez
illustrated by Brian Fitzgerald

Kim sees a tag for Big Pat.
Kim is sad.

125

Make Minutes Count

As you meet with small groups to review the week's decodable texts, use one or both of these related activities, as needed, at the beginning or the end of the small-group session.

- **Connect to Phonics** Play Word Path. Review any phonic elements that were problematic in this week's Start Right Reader stories. Then display Letter Cards *a, b, c, f, g, m, n, i, s, t.* Call on a child to use the Letter Cards to build a word with short *a* or *i*. Then call on another child to use one letter in the word to start a new word. For example, the first child might build *tag* and the next might use the *t* to start *tin*. After each child has had a turn, have the group read all the words chorally.

- **Connect to Handwriting** Have children write sentences that include the week's Spelling Words. Remind children to write from left to right. Check children's paper position and pencil grip and correct as needed.

INDEPENDENT APPLICATION

Options for Independent and Collaborative Work

While you meet with small groups, have other children engage in literacy activities that reinforce the lesson's learning objectives. Choose from these options.

Independent Reading

Student Choice Library

LEVELED LIBRARY

APPLY READING SKILL

Ask and Answer Questions Children complete Printable: <u>Reading Graphic Organizer 1</u> for an independent reading book.

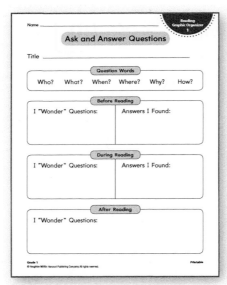

Printable: Reading Graphic Organizer 1

APPLY LANGUAGE SKILL

Recount Information Children complete Printable: <u>Language Graphic Organizer 11</u> for an independent reading book.

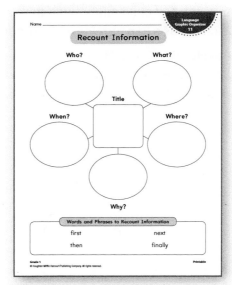

Printable: Language Graphic Organizer 11

Literacy Centers

See pp. T270–T271.

 WORD WORK

 CREATIVITY CORNER

 DIGITAL STATION

 READING CORNER

 TEAMWORK TIME

Start Right Reader

Read Decodable Text Book 1: pp. 100–131

Writing

Children act out or complete the Know It, Show It pages. *See Engage & Respond, p. T333.*

Additional Skills Practice

VOCABULARY STRATEGY

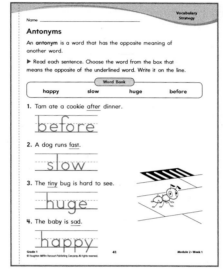

Know It, Show It, p. 41

SPEAKING & LISTENING

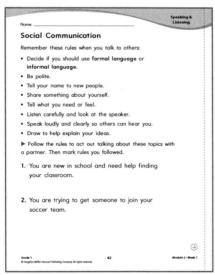

Know It, Show It, pp. 42–43

Wrap-Up
Share Time

At the end of Reading Workshop, have children reflect on their learning by sharing how they applied **Social Communication** or another area of focus during independent work time. Choose from these options:

- **SHARE CHAIR** Select a reader each day to come to the front of the class and tell what he or she learned about the skill.

- **THINK-PAIR-SHARE** Children share their thinking with a partner. Select a few each day to share with the whole class.

- **RETURN TO ANCHOR CHART** Revisit the Social Communication Anchor Chart. Call on a few children to explain what they learned.

ANCHOR CHART 45: Social Communicaion

Notes

 SOCIAL STUDIES CONNECTION: Communities

My Family, My Community

(?) **Essential Question** How can making new friends and learning new things help us?

Essential Skills

FOUNDATIONAL SKILLS

- Phonics: Consonants *l, h*; Short *o*; Review Short *a, i, o*
- High-Frequency Words: *do, live, of, our, wants, what, with, your*
- Fluency: Intonation
- Spelling: Short *o*

VOCABULARY

- Power Words: *canvas, clinic, community, decorated, dipped, gazed, gloom, heart, map, places, purpose, town*
- Generative Vocabulary: Words About Places and Things

READING WORKSHOP

- Setting
- Summarize
- Text Features
- Make Connections
- Content-Area Words

WRITING WORKSHOP

- Writing Form: Descriptive Essay
- Grammar Minilessons: Adjectives: Color and Number

LEARNING MINDSET:
Belonging

THIS WEEK'S TEXTS

READ ALOUD BOOK

Maybe Something
BEAUTIFUL
HOW ART TRANSFORMED A NEIGHBORHOOD

Maybe Something Beautiful

*my*BOOK

On the Map!

by Lisa Fleming

On the Map!

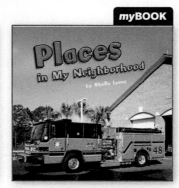

*my*BOOK

Places
in My Neighborhood
by Shelly Lyons

Places in My Neighborhood

START RIGHT READER

Tap, Bam! Rip! Bam!
by Jordan Moore
illustrated by Teresa Martinez

Bob sits with Sal.
Bob and Sal live with Dad.
Pop lives with Dad, too.

Decodable Texts
Tap, Bam! Rip! Bam!
A Map
Dot Is on It!
Hop on It, Dot!

Rigby®
LEVELED LIBRARY

Week at a Glance

Suggested Daily Times

- **VOCABULARY** — 10–15 minutes
- **FOUNDATIONAL SKILLS** — 15–30 minutes
- **READING WORKSHOP** — 60–75 minutes
- **WRITING WORKSHOP** — 20–30 minutes

This Week's Words

BIG IDEA WORDS

area	population	working

POWER WORDS

canvas	clinic	community
decorated	dipped	gazed
gloom	heart	map
places	purpose	town

HIGH-FREQUENCY WORDS

do	live	of	our
wants	what	with	your

READER'S VOCABULARY

bold text	connection	context clue
describe	detail	experience
label	map	noun
setting	summarize	symbol

Assessment Options

Online  **Ed**

- ✓ **Selection Quizzes:** *On the Map!*; *Places in My Neighborhood*
- ✓ **Weekly Assessment**
  - High-Frequency Words
  - Phonics: Consonants *l, h*; Short *o*; Review Short *a, i, o*
  - Comprehension: Text Features; Content-Area Words
  - Generative Vocabulary: Words About Places and Things
  - Grammar: Adjectives: Color and Number

Intervention

For children needing strategic intervention, use *Tabletop Minilessons: Intervention*.

- Module 2, Week 2 Daily Lessons

LESSON 6

FOUNDATIONAL SKILLS

Word Work Warm-Up, pp. T348–T349
- High-Frequency Words: *do, live, of, our, wants, what, with, your*
- Phonological Awareness

Phonics, pp. T350–T351
- Consonants *l, h*; Short *o*

Spelling, pp. T352–T353
- Short *o*

VOCABULARY

Academic Vocabulary, pp. T354–T355
- Introduce Oral Language: *heart, gazed, dipped, gloom, decorated, canvas*

READING WORKSHOP

Maybe Something Beautiful **Book Stix**
GENRE Realistic Fiction
Read Aloud: MINILESSON, pp. T356–T357
- Connect and Teach: Setting
- Apply to Text: *Maybe Something Beautiful*
- Engage and Respond: Writing

SMALL-GROUP INSTRUCTION 👥

Options for Differentiation
- Guided Reading Groups, p. T358
- English Learner Support: Compare and Contrast, p. T358
- Reinforce Setting, p. T359
- Reinforce Foundational Skills: Read *Tap, Bam! Rip! Bam!*, pp. T360–T361

Options for Independent and Collaborative Work, pp. T362–T363

WRITING WORKSHOP

Descriptive Essay, p. W23
- Drafting I: Elements of a Descriptive Essay

Grammar, p. W311
- Adjectives

LESSON 7

FOUNDATIONAL SKILLS

Word Work Warm-Up, pp. T364–T365
- High-Frequency Words: *do, live, of, our, wants, what, with, your*
- Phonological Awareness

Phonics, pp. T366–T367
- Consonants *l, h*; Short *o*

VOCABULARY

Academic Vocabulary, pp. T368–T369
- Introduce Power Words: *heart, gazed, dipped, gloom, decorated, canvas, town, map, community, places, purpose, clinic*

READING WORKSHOP

On the Map! **Teaching Pal**
GENRE Informational Text
Shared Reading: MINILESSON, pp. T370–T371
- Connect and Teach: Summarize
- Apply to Text: *On the Map!*
- Engage and Respond: Speaking & Listening

SMALL-GROUP INSTRUCTION 👥

Options for Differentiation
- Guided Reading Groups, p. T372
- English Learner Support: Compare and Contrast, p. T372
- Reinforce Summarize, p. T373
- Reinforce Foundational Skills: Read *A Map*, pp. T374–T375

Options for Independent and Collaborative Work, pp. T376–T377

WRITING WORKSHOP

Descriptive Essay, p. W24
- Drafting II: Using Sensory Words

Grammar, p. W312
- Adjectives for Color

LESSON 8

FOUNDATIONAL SKILLS

Word Work Warm-Up, p. T378
- High-Frequency Words: *do, live, of, our, wants, what, with, your*
- Phonological Awareness

Fluency, p. T379
- Intonation

Phonics, pp. T380–T381
- Review Short *a, i, o*

VOCABULARY

Academic Vocabulary, pp. T382–T383
- Review Power Words: *heart, gazed, dipped, gloom, decorated, canvas*

READING WORKSHOP

On the Map!
GENRE Informational Text
Shared Reading: MINILESSON, pp. T384–T385
- Connect and Teach: Text Features
- Apply to Text: *On the Map!*
- Engage and Respond: Writing

SMALL-GROUP INSTRUCTION

Options for Differentiation
- Guided Reading Groups, p. T386
- English Learner Support: Compare and Contrast, p. T386
- Reinforce Text Features, p. T387
- Reinforce Foundational Skills: Read *Dot Is on It!*, pp. T388–T389

Options for Independent and Collaborative Work, pp. T390–T391

WRITING WORKSHOP

Descriptive Essay, p. W25
- Drafting II: Adding Art

Grammar, p. W313
- Adjectives for Number

LESSON 9

FOUNDATIONAL SKILLS

Word Work Warm-Up, p. T392
- High-Frequency Words: *do, live, of, our, wants, what, with, your*
- Phonological Awareness

Phonics, p. T393
- Phonics Review

VOCABULARY

Generative Vocabulary, pp. T394–T395
- Words About Places and Things

READING WORKSHOP

Places in My Neighborhood
GENRE Informational Text
Shared Reading: MINILESSON, pp. T396–T397
- Connect and Teach: Make Connections
- Apply to Text: *Places in My Neighborhood*
- Engage and Respond: Speaking & Listening

SMALL-GROUP INSTRUCTION

Options for Differentiation
- Guided Reading Groups, p. T398
- English Learner Support: Compare and Contrast, p. T398
- Reinforce Make Connections, p. T399
- Reinforce Foundational Skills: Read *Hop on It, Dot!*, pp. T400–T401

Options for Independent and Collaborative Work, pp. T402–T403

WRITING WORKSHOP

Descriptive Essay, p. W26
- Revising I: Grouping

Grammar, p. W269
- Spiral Review: Subject Pronouns

LESSON 10

FOUNDATIONAL SKILLS

Word Work Warm-Up, p. T404
- High-Frequency Words: *do, live, of, our, wants, what, with, your*
- Phonological Awareness

Spelling, p. T405
- Spelling Assessment

VOCABULARY

Academic Vocabulary, pp. T406–T407
- Review Power Words: *community, places, purpose, clinic*

READING WORKSHOP

Places in My Neighborhood
GENRE Informational Text
Shared Reading: MINILESSON, pp. T408–T409
- Connect and Teach: Content-Area Words
- Apply to Text: *Places in My Neighborhood*
- Engage and Respond: Writing

SMALL-GROUP INSTRUCTION

Options for Differentiation
- Guided Reading Groups, p. T410
- English Learner Support: Compare and Contrast, p. T410
- Reinforce Content-Area Words, p. T411
- Reinforce Foundational Skills: Make Text Connections, pp. T412–T413

Options for Independent and Collaborative Work, pp. T414–T415

WRITING WORKSHOP

Descriptive Essay, p. W27
- Revising II: Incorporating Feedback

Grammar, p. W315
- Connect to Writing: Using Adjectives for Color and Number

Build understanding of this week's texts so that you can best support children in making connections, understanding key ideas, and becoming lifelong readers.

On the Map! by Lisa Fleming

myBOOK

GENRE Informational Text

WHY THIS TEXT?

In this informational text, children compare photographs of a town and a city with maps of the same places. They see the relationship between the two kinds of graphics and learn the important life skill of using a key to read a map.

KEY LEARNING OBJECTIVES

- Identify characteristics of informational texts.

- Summarize a text by telling the main idea and the most important details.

- Use print and graphic features to locate and understand information.

TEXT COMPLEXITY

LEXILE MEASURE 240L • **GUIDED READING LEVEL** C

OVERALL RATING Simple

The graphics are integral to understanding the text, which consists of simple, repetitive sentences.

MAKE CONNECTIONS

🔗 BUILD KNOWLEDGE AND LANGUAGE

- **Social Studies Connection:** Communities

🔗 VOCABULARY

- **Words About Places and Things:** *bank, bridge, city, farm, hospital, house, library, map, neighborhood, office, park, restaurant, river, school, store, street, suburb, town*

🔗 FOUNDATIONAL SKILLS

- **High-Frequency Words:** *do, live, of, what, your*

- **Consonants *l, h*; Short *o*:** *hospital, house, library, like, live, on, school*

- **Review Short *a, i, o*:** *bank, big, bridge, city, hospital, in, is, live, map, office, on, river, this*

📖 TEXT X-RAY

KEY IDEAS	🔵 LANGUAGE
Key Idea *pp. 122–123* A photograph of a town and a map of the same town are alike in some ways and different in others. **Key Idea** *pp. 124–125* A photograph of a big city and a map of the same big city are alike in some ways and different in others. **Key Idea** *p. 126* There are many kinds of neighborhoods. The map of each neighborhood looks different.	**Multiple Meanings** ***key*** (p. 123): English learners may know that a key is something used to unlock a door. Explain that another kind of key is a list of symbols used on a map. This kind of key unlocks the meaning of the map!

Places in My Neighborhood by Shelly Lyons

GENRE Informational Text

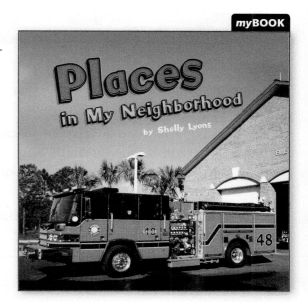

WHY THIS TEXT?

Neighborhoods are diverse places that meet people's needs in different ways. Children will read about places to live, places that help keep them safe, and places to get things. They will think about the special places in their own neighborhoods.

KEY LEARNING OBJECTIVES

- Identify characteristics of informational texts.

- Connect a text with personal experiences, society, and ideas in other texts.

- Use clues in the text and pictures to determine the meanings of unknown content-area words.

TEXT COMPLEXITY

LEXILE MEASURE IG470L • **GUIDED READING LEVEL** I

OVERALL RATING Moderately Complex

The text uses subject-specific vocabulary, but the connections between ideas are clear.

MAKE CONNECTIONS

🔗 **BUILD KNOWLEDGE AND LANGUAGE**

- **Social Studies Connection:** Communities

🔗 **VOCABULARY**

- **Words About Places and Things:** *apartment, bandage, books, building, city, clinic, fire, fire station, fruit, grocery store, home, house, library, milk, neighborhood, police station, street, town*

🔗 **FOUNDATIONAL SKILLS**

- **High-Frequency Words:** *do, live, our, wants, what, with, your*

- **Consonants *l, h*; Short *o*:** *building, clinic, feels, filled, her, him, his, home, house, library, Lila, lined, live, places, police, not, shot, small, special*

- **Review Short *a, i, o*:** *and, at, big, can, city, dad, filled, gives, has, him, his, in, is, Jack, live, milk, shot, that, visits*

TEXT X-RAY

KEY IDEAS	🟢 LANGUAGE
Key Idea *pp. 136–138* Neighborhoods have different places in them, each place having its own purpose. There are places for people to live.	**Common Expression** *lined with [homes]* (p. 138): If you say that a street or other place is "lined with" something, such as homes, you mean that those things form a line along the sides or edges.
Key Idea *pp. 139–141* There are places that help with safety, such as the fire station, police station, and health clinic.	**Phrasal Verb** *put out* (p. 139): Explain that when firefighters "put out" a fire, they make it stop burning.
Key Idea *pp. 142–144* There are places such as the library and the grocery store where people get things they need.	**Multiple Meanings** *bikes* (p. 142): English learners may know what a bike is and may have ridden one. Point out that here, *bikes* is an action word that means "to ride a bike."

Literacy Centers

While you meet with small groups, have children work independently in Literacy Centers. At the beginning of the week, explain what is expected of children in each center. Post a daily rotation schedule.

WORD WORK

Word Pictures

- Provide magazines in the center. Display the Word Cards for this week's High-Frequency Words.

- Have children find or draw a picture that reminds them of one of the High-Frequency Words. Have them write a caption or label containing the High-Frequency Word to go with their picture.

- For an extra challenge, have children include two High-Frequency Words in their captions.

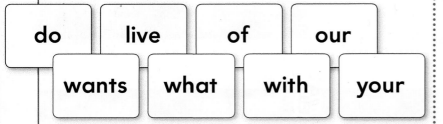

do	live	of	our
wants	what	with	your

Short o

- Display the week's Spelling Words and copies of Printable: **Spelling & Handwriting**. Have children choose one of the activities to practice writing this week's Spelling Words in their best handwriting.

- Have children complete the activity on a separate sheet of paper.

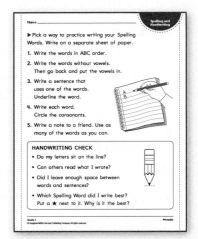

Printable:
Spelling & Handwriting

CREATIVITY CORNER

Readers' Theater

- Have children read Printable: **Readers' Theater 2**, "Help Find Bud," and ask them to think of suitable props to use in the production. For example, children might suggest a firefighter's helmet, a police badge, and a nurse's thermometer.

- Point out the importance of using expression when speaking. Then read aloud the Performance Tip and the Read with Fluency tip and have groups rehearse.

- Encourage children to identify unfamiliar words in the script and look them up in a dictionary.

Printable: Readers' Theater 2

Reading Remake

- Display in the center and have children complete the activity for *On the Map!* on Printable: **Make a Postcard**.

- Tell partners to explain to one another how their postcard shows their understanding of the selection.

Printable: Make a Postcard

DIGITAL STATION

Listener's Choice

- Have children listen to the Read Aloud Book *Maybe Something Beautiful* or a Leveled Reader of their choice.

- Tell them to add the book to their Printable: **Listening Log**, as well as the active listening skills they used, a summary, and a question they have about the book.

Phonics Practice

- Have children continue their personalized, adaptive learning for foundational skills in *iRead*.

TEAMWORK TIME

Inquiry and Research Project:
Our Community News

- Have groups continue work on the module project.

- Remind children that their focus this week is to write or draw about places in their community and to create a news report. *See pp. T260–T261.*

READING CORNER

Independent Reading

- Have children self-select or continue reading an independent reading book.

- Remind children to set a purpose for reading and to record their progress on their Printable: **Reading Log**.

- You may want to choose from these additional options to have children interact with their books:

  » **Read for Fluency** Children use the **PARTNER READING** routine to practice the week's fluency skill, intonation, or another area of need.

  » **Annotate the Text** Children practice a strategy and use sticky notes to record questions or what they are thinking as they read. Review the sticky notes while you confer with children.

  » **Response Journal** Children draw or write about what they read.

Student Choice Library

LEVELED LIBRARY

FOUNDATIONAL SKILLS

Teach the Words

Use Word Cards *do, live, of, our, wants, what, with,* and *your* and the **HIGH-FREQUENCY WORDS** routine below to introduce the week's High-Frequency sight words.

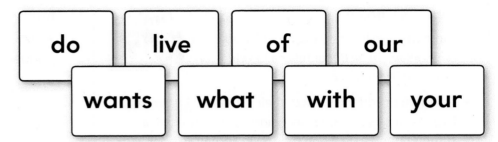

1 **See the word.** Display a Word Card. Say the word, and have children repeat it twice.

2 **Say the word.** Have children repeat it chorally. Use the word in a sentence or two. Point to a child and say: *Your name is [child's name]. Show me your pencil.* (Use gestures.)

3 **Spell the word.** Point to the letters, and have children spell the word aloud. Point out any familiar spelling patterns. *Your begins with y. Can you think of a color word that begins with y?* (*yellow*) *Do you know any other words that begin with y?*

4 **Write and check the word.** Hide the word, and have children use the **WRITE AND REVEAL** routine to write the word. Then have them check it against the Word Card.

Have children add this week's words to their individual Word Rings. Tell them to write a word on the front of each card and write a sentence or draw a picture about the word on the back. Alternatively, you may have children complete Know It, Show It page 44.

LEARNING OBJECTIVES

- Identify and read high-frequency words.
- **Language** Recognize, recite, and write basic sight vocabulary.
- Blend phonemes to say one-syllable words.

MATERIALS Online

Word Cards *do, live, of, our, wants, what, with, your*

Know It, Show It *p. 44*

Picture Cards *bed, bee, cube, duck, gate, hoe, kite, mitt, web, yak*

 ENGLISH LEARNER SUPPORT: Build Vocabulary

ALL LEVELS Use objects and gestures to help reinforce word meanings. For example, point to the clock as you say: *Our classroom has a clock.* Then have children point to and name something else in the classroom as they complete the sentence frame: *Our classroom has a _____.*

 CORRECT & REDIRECT

Guide children who have trouble identifying any of the words. Say the correct word, and have children repeat it. Example:

- With. *What is the word?* (**with**)
- Have children spell the word. (**w-i-t-h**) *How do we say this word?* (**with**)
- Have children reread all the cards in random order.

Phonological Awareness

Blend Phonemes

- Tell children that today they will be blending sounds to say words. Remind them that they know how to blend sounds, or phonemes. Model the task: *I will say all the sounds in a word, and you blend the sounds to say the word. Listen as I do the first one: /n/ /ā/ /m/. When I blend /n/, /ā/, and /m/, I say the word name. Are you ready to try? Listen: /m/ /ō/. What's the word?* (mow) *Very good!*

- Have children practice blending phonemes to say words. Say: *Let's see if you can blend the sounds to say these words: /l/ /ĭ/ /p/* (lip); */ă/ /d/* (add); */d/ /ĕ/ /n/* (den); */h/ /ō/ /l/* (hole); */f/ /ŭ/ /n/* (fun).

- Then display Picture Cards *bed, bee, cube, duck, gate, hoe, kite, mitt, web,* and *yak* in different spots around the classroom where children can see them. Tell children they will be playing "I Spy."

- *Now let's play "I Spy." I will say the sounds in a word. You will blend the sounds to say the word and then find the matching Picture Card. Ready? I spy with my little eye a /k/ /ī/ /t/. What do I spy?* (kite) *Yes! You blended /k/, /ī/, and /t/ to say kite. /k/ /ī/ /t/,* kite. Ask a child to point to Picture Card *kite.*

- *Let's keep playing: /h/ /ō/* (hoe); */d/ /ŭ/ /k/* (duck); */w/ /ĕ/ b/* (web); */y/ /ă/ /k/* (yak); */b/ /ē/* (bee); */m/ /ĭ/ /t/* (mitt); */k/ /yōō/ /b/* (cube); */b/ /ĕ/ /d/* (bed); */g/ /ā/ /t/* (gate).

- Tell children that they will keep playing but now you will say the sounds of words that name classroom objects.

- Say: *Now I am going to "spy" things in our classroom. I will say the sounds in the name of something in our classroom, and you will blend the sounds to say the word. Then you will find the object and the person I call on points to it. Listen: I spy with my little eye a /p/ /ĕ/ /n/. What do I spy?* (pen) *That's right!* Invite a child to find a pen and point to it or hold it up for the class to see.

- Continue having children blend phonemes to say these words (or similar words for objects in your classroom): */k/ /ŭ/ /p/* (cup), */k/ /ē/* (key), */t/ /ā/ /p/* (tape), */p/ /ĭ/ /n/* (pin), */m/ /ă/ /p/* (map), */b/ /ă/ /g/* (bag), */k/ /ā/ /s/* (case), */p/ /ĕ/ /t/* (pet).

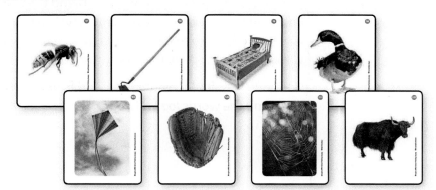

 Professional Learning

TEACHING TERMS

What is **phonological awareness?** Phonological awareness is the ability to identify and manipulate words, syllables, and sounds in oral language.

See the **GPS guide** to learn more.

 CORRECT & REDIRECT

To support children who blend incorrectly, model the task by saying the sounds more and more closely together, as in the example below.

- Say each sound in the word and have the child repeat. */d/ /ŭ/ /k/*

- Repeat, each time blending the sounds a little more closely together, and then say the word. */d/ /ŭ/ /k/, /d-ŭ-k/,* duck

- Ask the child to blend and say the word.

Consonants *l*, *h*; Short *o*

Spotlight on Sounds

- Tell children that today they will be reading words with a new vowel, short *o*, and the consonants *l* and *h*. Explain that first they will practice identifying the sounds in words. *I am going to say a word, and you say the beginning sound. I will do the first one. Listen: The word is* lock. *The beginning sound in* lock *is* /l/. *Listen again, and repeat after me:* lock, /l/. *Now tell me the beginning sound in these words:* hop (/h/); happy (/h/); laugh (/l/); look (/l/); hot (/h/); like (/l/).

- Then model how to identify the ending sound in *pal*, (/l/). Have children listen for the ending sounds in these words: *ball* (/l/); *log* (/g/); *doll* (/l/); *lock* (/k/); *pull* (/l/); *had* (/d/); *hill* (/l/).

- Conclude the activity by having children suggest words that end with the /l/ sound. Say: *Think of words you know that end with* /l/.

 I Do It

Spotlight on Letters Display the Sound/Spelling Card for short *o*: *octopus*. *Remember, the vowels are a, e, i, o, u, and each one stands for many sounds.* Name the card's picture, say the sound, and give the spelling. *Octopus begins with the short o sound,* /ŏ/. *The letter o can stand for the sound* /ŏ/ *at the beginning or middle of a word.*

Write *on*. Say the letter sounds, and blend the word: /ŏ/ /n/, on. Point out the vowel and consonant. Say: *You have learned that when there is only one vowel and it is followed by a consonant, the vowel usually stands for the short vowel sound.*

Continue in a similar manner for *l* and *h*, using Sound/Spelling Cards *lion* and *horse* and the words *log* and *hog*.

TEACHER TIP

Role play! Call on volunteers to play "teacher" and model the blending routine for the class. Make sure that all children who wish to model the routine have an opportunity to do so.

EL **ENGLISH LEARNER SUPPORT:**
Facilitate Language Connections

ALL LEVELS Children whose first language is Spanish, Tagalog, or Korean may have trouble pronouncing the short *o* sound. Play the **Articulation Video** for /ŏ/. Then have children listen as you pronounce words with the /ŏ/ sound: *clock, pot, mop, hot, lock, hop*. Have children repeat each word, say the middle sound, and then say the word again.

If children need practice with the consonant sounds, use the **Articulation Videos** in the Materials list.

Online
ARTICULATION VIDEO

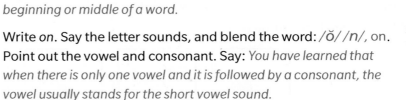

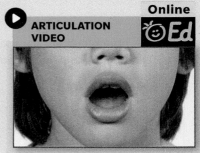

We Do It

Write *hot* and use Letter Cards *h, o, t* with the **SOUND-BY-SOUND BLENDING** routine below to model blending the word.

1 **Display** cards as shown. Say the first letter and sound.

2 **Slide** the second letter over. Say its sound. Then blend the two sounds.

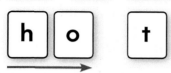

3 **Slide** the last letter over. Say its sound. Say the first two blended sounds, the last sound, and the blended word: /hŏ//t/, hot.

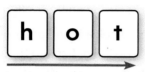

Sound-by-Sound Blending Repeat the **SOUND-BY-SOUND BLENDING** routine with cards for the words *lot* and *hop,* having children say the sounds and blend.

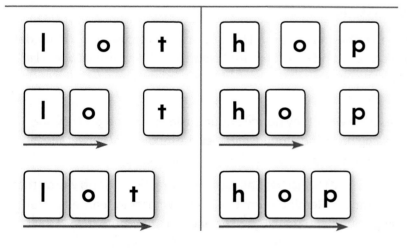

You Do It

INDEPENDENT PRACTICE

Blending Practice Write the words below. Then choose a volunteer to model the activity. Explain that you will point to two words in random order and the child will read them aloud. Repeat the blending routine as needed. Continue until each child has had a turn.

mop	log	lap	hip
pot	Hal	lot	hat

✓ CORRECT & REDIRECT

- If a child mispronounces a word during Blending Practice, make note of the error type and address it.
- If a child reads *mop* as *map*, frame the vowel and use Sound/Spelling Card *octopus* to reinforce short *o*, /ŏ/. Then use sound-by-sound blending to read the word, and have the child repeat the steps after you.
- If a child reads *lap* as *pal*, cover the word and blend it together as you uncover one letter at a time, left to right. Then have the child blend and read the word.

👥 LINK TO SMALL-GROUP INSTRUCTION

REINFORCE FOUNDATIONAL SKILLS Use *Tap, Bam! Rip! Bam!* during small-group time to review or reinforce blending and decoding words with the short *o* vowel and consonants *l, h.* Meet with children to work through the story, or assign it as independent work. *See the lesson on p. T360.*

Short o

Administer the Pretest

- Read the first Spelling Word and the Dictation Sentence. Repeat the word as children write it.

- Write the word, and have children correct their spelling if needed. Repeat for words 2–6 and for the Review Words.

- Assign the Basic and Review Words as needed for practice this week. If children do well on the pretest, assign the Challenge Words.

Teach the Principle

- Write *not* on the board, underlining *o*, and read it aloud. Explain that the /ŏ/ sound can be spelled with the letter *o*.

- Tell children that this week all the Spelling Words have the short *o* sound, /ŏ/, spelled *o*. Explain that short *o* sound can be at the beginning or in the middle of a word.

- If children have difficulty, review Sound/Spelling Card *octopus*. Remind them that *o* is a vowel that can stand for many sounds and that one of those sounds is /ŏ/, as in *octopus*.

Model Handwriting

- Remind children that they have learned how to write lowercase *a* and *d*. Model how to write lowercase *o* and *g*. *o: Start just below the middle line. Pull back and around. g: Start just below the middle line. Pull back, around, down past the bottom line, and curve around.*

- Have children describe what they notice about the letters *o* and *g*. (*They are both formed by pulling back and around, and they are made up of curved lines.*) Model writing one or more of the Spelling Words that include *o* or *g*.

- Have children use the **WRITE AND REVEAL** routine to practice writing words that include lowercase *o* and *g*. Remind them to also use what they learned about the correct paper position and pencil grip. As needed, distribute the handwriting models on Printable: Manuscript Gg, Oo. Printables for Continuous Stroke letter forms are also available online.

LEARNING OBJECTIVES

- Spell words with short *o* (closed syllables).
- **Language** Identify relationships between sounds and letters.
- Develop handwriting.

MATERIALS   Online Ed

Sound/Spelling Card *octopus*
Printables *Manuscript Gg, Oo; Word List 5*
Know It, Show It p. 45

DICTATION SENTENCES

BASIC

1. **log**   Mom put a *log* on the fire.
2. **not**   Stop at the sign, and do *not* go.
3. **top**   Put a cherry on *top* of the cake.
4. **hot**   The stove is *hot*.
5. **hop**   A rabbit can *hop* away.
6. **on**   I stood *on* a ladder.

REVIEW

7. **big**   An elephant is very *big*.
8. **sit**   Please *sit* in the chair.
9. **pig**   A *pig* is a farm animal.
10. **dig**   Use a shovel to *dig* a hole.

CHALLENGE

11. **shop**   We bought milk in the *shop*.
12. **block**   He built a *block* tower.

TEACHER TIP

Hanging down! Point out to children that some letters have descenders, which are parts of the letter that extend below the bottom line. When they write a letter with a descender, such as *g*, it should touch the middle line and the bottom line and then extend below the bottom line. A lowercase letter without a descender, such as *o*, should touch the middle line and the bottom line.

 ENGLISH LEARNER SUPPORT: Build Vocabulary

ALL LEVELS Make sure children understand the meanings of the Spelling Words and Dictation Sentences. Work with children to ask and answer questions, such as the following. For each *no* answer, encourage them to add explanations, as they are able.

- Is a *log* made out of wood?
- Which is usually *hot*, cocoa or lemonade?
- Which is the opposite of *on*, up or off?

Word Sort

1 **Introduce** Display both the Basic and Review Spelling Word cards from Printable: **Word List 5**, and read each one aloud.

2 **Columns 1 and 2** Display the word cards *log* and *big* as column headings. Explain: *I will put* log *at the top of one column and* big *at the top of another. I will read a word, and you will tell me if the vowel sound is the same as in* log *or as in* big. *I'll sort the first word to show you.*

3 **Model** Display the word card *not* and read it aloud. Explain: Not. *Listen for the vowel sound. Nooooot. That sounds the same as the vowel sound in* log, *looooog, so I'll put* not *under* log. Repeat for *pig*, placing it under *big*.

4 **Continue** Sort the other words. Model if necessary.

5 **Discuss** Read each column together. Discuss what children notice about the words in each column. If no one mentions it, guide children to identify the words in column 1 as having the short *o* sound and the words in column 2 as having the short *i* sound. Tell children they can think about this pattern when they spell words with short *o* and short *i*.

6 **Repeat** Have children work together to repeat the sort, using the Spelling Word cards from Printable: **Word List 5**. Remind children to save the rest of the page and the Spelling Word cards for use all week.

log		big
not	top	pig
hot	hop	sit
on		dig

INDEPENDENT PRACTICE

For additional practice, have children complete Know It, Show It page 45. Encourage them to use their best handwriting and pay particular attention to writing the letters *o* and *g* correctly.

TEACHER TIP

What's the pattern? Help children identify the spelling patterns. Explain that if they know how to spell *not*, they can also spell *cot, dot, got, hot, jot, lot, pot, rot,* and *tot*. Repeat for the following sets of words:

- **log:** *bog, cog, dog, fog, hog, jog*
- **top:** *bop, cop, hop, mop, top*
- **on:** *Don, Lon, Ron*

Point out that it doesn't always help to think of rhymes, but it may be a helpful clue.

(EL) **ENGLISH LEARNER SUPPORT:**
Facilitate Language Connections

ALL LEVELS Some Spanish speakers may pronounce the short vowel sound /ŏ/ as /ō/. Read the list of spelling words, elongating the short o sound in each word. Then read the words normally. Have children repeat the words after you.

LEARNING OBJECTIVES

- **Language** Answer questions and discuss meanings to develop vocabulary.
- Identify real-life connections between words and their use.

MATERIALS   Online

Vocabulary Cards *2.16–2.21*

Read Aloud Book *Maybe Something Beautiful*

Classroom materials *cup of water, spoon, piece of drawing paper*

 # Introduce Oral Language

Use the steps **I Do It, We Do It, You Do It** with the information in the chart below to teach the oral Power Words from the Read Aloud Book *Maybe Something Beautiful*.

① Power Word	② Meaning	③ Example
heart (n.) (*p. 3*)	If you are in the **heart** of a place, you are in its most important part.	**MAKE A CONNECTION** Make a connection to the importance of the heart in the body. *The heart in your body is like the* **heart** *of a place. It is in the center and very important.*
gazed (v.) (*p. 8*)	If you **gazed** at something, you looked at it for a long time.	**ACT IT OUT** Gaze at the clock or flag for a minute. *I just* **gazed** *at the clock.*
dipped (v.) (*p. 11*)	If you **dipped** something, you put it in another thing and took it out quickly.	**USE A PROP** Dip a spoon in a cup of water. *I just* **dipped** *the spoon in the water.*
gloom (n.) (*p. 11*)	A place filled with **gloom** is dark and makes you feel sad.	**MAKE A CONNECTION** Talk about places that could be filled with gloom. *A foggy night can give you a feeling of* **gloom***.*
decorated (v.) (*p. 24*)	If you **decorated** something, you added to it to make it look nicer.	**USE A PROP** Point to a bulletin board or other decorated space in the classroom. *We* **decorated** *our wall to make it look nice.*
canvas (n.) (*p. 26*)	A **canvas** is a kind of cloth that people paint a picture on.	**USE A PROP** Hold up a piece of drawing paper. *A* **canvas** *is a similar to drawing paper, but it is made of cloth.*

● Professional Learning

TEACHING TERMS

Why does mindset matter? Children with a **learning mindset** are curious, challenge-seeking students who recognize that taking on challenges and learning from mistakes creates opportunities to develop their intelligence, practice skills, and increase their potential to be successful.

See the **GPS guide** to learn more.

 LEARNING MINDSET

Seeking Challenges

Review Remind children that seeking challenges and trying new things can make them smarter. *Remember that trying new things makes your brain grow. This even happens when you learn new words. Challenge yourself to learn new words every day. It's as if your brain grows with every new word you learn! With a partner, you can challenge each other to use each oral Power Word in a sentence.*

I Do It

Use the **VOCABULARY** routine and Vocabulary Cards 2.16–2.21 to introduce the oral Power Words from *Maybe Something Beautiful*. You may wish to display the corresponding Vocabulary Card for each word as you discuss it.

Vocabulary Cards

1. **Say the Power Word.** Ask children to repeat it.

2. **Explain the meaning.** Read aloud the student-friendly meaning.

3. **Talk about examples.** Use the image or a strategy to give examples of the word.

We Do It

Guide children to make connections between each word's meaning and how they can use it in their own lives. Use these prompts. Encourage children to explain or justify their answers.

- How would it look if you **dipped** a spoon into soup?
- Tell what you would do with a **canvas**.
- Which might be filled with **gloom**, a forest or a flower garden? Explain.
- Name some things you have **decorated**.
- Which area is the **heart** of our classroom? Why do you think that?
- When have you **gazed** at something?

You Do It

INDEPENDENT PRACTICE

Have partners work together to complete each of the activities below. Circulate and observe partners as they work, providing corrective feedback as necessary.

- **Draw** *Draw pictures to show what people look like in a room full of **gloom**. Then draw what they look like after they have **decorated** the room with colorful balloons.*

- **Discuss** *Which do you think is the **heart** of a home—the kitchen or a closet? Tell why.*

- **Role-Play** *Demonstrate how you have **gazed** at a beautiful painting. Then show how the painter **dipped** a brush into paint and used a **canvas** to make the painting.*

EL ENGLISH LEARNER SUPPORT:
Build Vocabulary

SUBSTANTIAL
Act out the words *decorated*, *gazed*, and *dipped*. Have children repeat the actions as they say each word.

MODERATE
Supply frames such as these: *I **gazed** at a beautiful* _____ .
*I **dipped*** _____ .

LIGHT
Ask children to explain the meanings of the words before answering the questions in the We Do It activity.

TEACHER TIP

Put tired words to bed! Tell children that sometimes we use certain words so much that they become worn out and tired. Luckily, there is often a more interesting word that can be used in place of a tired word. Encourage children to replace *looked* in their speaking and writing with the synonym *gazed*.

READING WORKSHOP

Setting

Step 1 **Connect and Teach**

LEARNING OBJECTIVES

- Recognize characteristics of realistic fiction.
- Describe the setting of a story.
- **Language** Explain how the setting of a story changes over time.
- Write sentences to describe a story's setting.

MATERIALS Online

Anchor Chart 11
Setting

Printable *Anchor Chart 11: Setting*

Read Aloud Book
Maybe Something Beautiful

BookStix *2.2*

READER'S VOCABULARY

- **setting** where and when a story takes place
- **describe** to tell what someone or something is like by giving details
- **detail** small bit of information that supports a central idea or describes something in a text

- Project or display <u>Anchor Chart 11: Setting</u>.

- Remind children that the **setting** of a story is where and when the story takes place.

- Point out that sometimes a setting can change in a story. For example, the characters in a story might go to a different place, or the season might change.

- Tell children that when they **describe** a setting, they tell what the setting is like. To know what the setting is like, they should look for small pieces of information, or **details**, in the text and the pictures.

- Finally, explain that knowing why a setting is important will help them understand the story better.

- Tell children they will practice describing the setting when they listen to a Read Aloud Book called *Maybe Something Beautiful*.

Online
ANCHOR CHART 11: Setting

 Professional Learning

RESEARCH FOUNDATIONS

"Interactive read alouds are important learning opportunities for emergent readers because teachers and peers can actively model and scaffold comprehension strategies, engage readers, and cultivate a community of learners."

–Dr. Angela Wiseman (2011)

See the **GPS guide** to learn more.

LEARNING MINDSET

Belonging

Reflect *In Maybe Something Beautiful, two artists share their passion for making art with a whole community. Everyone takes part and they make big changes in their neighborhood.* Ask children to find text and picture details that show who in the community helped, and how they changed their neighborhood by working together.

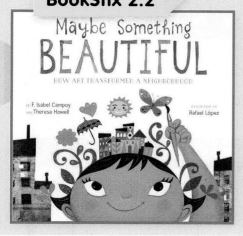
Go to
BookStix 2.2

Step 2 Apply to Text

- **Genre Study** Read aloud the title *Maybe Something Beautiful* and introduce the book. *Today we will read a realistic fiction story about a girl and the neighborhood where she lives.* Read the subtitle aloud. Then discuss with children how they think art could transform a real neighborhood.

- **Set a Purpose** Discuss the illustration on the cover. *What do you think the girl will do with the paintbrush? Use your idea to set a purpose for reading.*

- **Model Fluency** Tell children that you are going to demonstrate how to read with intonation, by changing the sound, or pitch, of your voice to reflect end marks in the text. As you read, demonstrate how to read a few sentences and questions with and without the correct intonation.

- **Read and Comprehend** Read aloud the book *Maybe Something Beautiful*, pausing occasionally to ask the questions on BookStix 2.2 and to have children describe the book's setting and how it changes over time. Refer back to the Anchor Chart to discuss questions children can ask about the setting in *Maybe Something Beautiful,* as needed.

Step 3 Engage and Respond

INDEPENDENT PRACTICE: Writing

- Remind children that in the Read Aloud Book *Maybe Something Beautiful,* Mina and others work together to change the way their neighborhood looks.

- Have children draw a picture and write a sentence that shows what the girl's neighborhood looks like at the beginning and at the end of the story. Encourage them to recall details from the book to support their responses.

- Ask partners to share and compare their pictures and sentences. Encourage them to recognize how they are similar or different.

- You may want to have children complete their writing during daily small-group time.

ENGLISH LEARNER SUPPORT:
Build Background

SUBSTANTIAL
Take a picture walk through the book and help children name details. Ask questions such as: *Who is the girl? Can you point to something that is (grey)? Where is the apple? Who is painting?*

MODERATE
Help children tell about the pictures with sentences frame such as: *The city is _____. _____ is painting.*

LIGHT
Ask children to name things and describe details in the illustrations.

LINK TO SMALL-GROUP INSTRUCTION

REINFORCE SETTING Review or extend the skill as needed during small-group time to support children's need for differentiation. *See the lesson on p. T359.*

LESSON 6

READING WORKSHOP

Options for Differentiation

As the class engages in independent and collaborative work, meet with Guided Reading Groups or differentiate instruction based on student need.

GUIDED READING GROUPS

Match Children to Books + Instruction

- Choose just-right books based on level, skill, topic, or genre.

C D E F G H I J K →

Leveled Readers

- Deliver instruction with each book's Take and Teach Lesson, choosing appropriate sessions based on need.

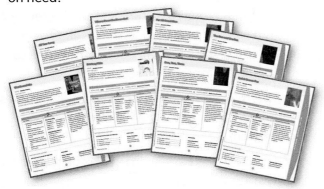

- Check comprehension, reinforce instruction, and extend learning with suggested supporting activities.

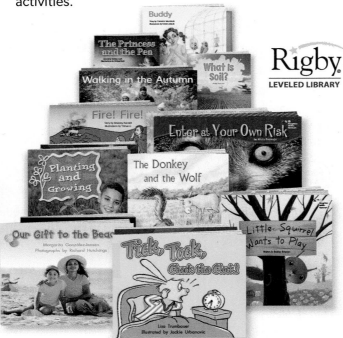

Rigby® LEVELED LIBRARY

EL ENGLISH LEARNER SUPPORT

Compare and Contrast

- Use **Tabletop Minilessons: English Language Development 5.1 (Listening)** to introduce and practice the language skill.

Tabletop Minilessons: English Language Development

- Then use the following text-based prompts with *Maybe Something Beautiful* to guide application of the language skill. Begin with the prompt at the child's identified language proficiency level. As children are able, use lighter supports to encourage increased language proficiency.

SUBSTANTIAL

Read aloud page 3. Ask: *What color is the city in the beginning?* Then ask children to name the colors of the city on pages 22–23. Allow children to point to the pictures and use single words to respond.

MODERATE

Have children describe the city in the beginning of the story and contrast it with the city's appearance at the end of the story. Supply these frames: *In the beginning, the city _____. At the end, the city _____.*

LIGHT

Read aloud page 3. Ask children to describe the similarities and differences in the setting from the beginning to the end of the story. Supply this frame: *At the beginning, the city ____. At the end, the city ____. At the beginning and at the end, the city ____.*

REINFORCE SETTING

Demonstrate

- Use **Tabletop Minilessons: Reading 11** to remind children that the setting is where and when the story happens. Readers can look for **details** in the text and illustrations to identify and **describe** the place or places, time of day, and time of year where the story takes place. These details help us understand how the setting is important to the story. In some texts, there is just one setting; in others, the setting changes throughout the text.

- Model filling out Printable: **Reading Graphic Organizer 18** to identify and describe the setting in *Maybe Something Beautiful*.

Apply to Independent Reading

- Now have children identify and describe the setting in an appropriate just-right book that they are reading independently. Customize these prompts to the books children choose.

  » *What words tell where and when the story takes place?*

  » *What pictures show when and where the story takes place?*

  » *What details help you understand how the setting is important to the story?*

- Have children complete Printable: **Reading Graphic Organizer 18** for their independent reading book.

Tabletop Minilessons: Reading

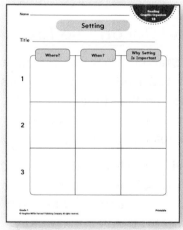

Printable:
Reading Graphic Organizer 18

ALMOST THERE

READY FOR MORE

SCAFFOLD AND EXTEND

- Help children identify words that tell where and when the story takes place.

- Prompt children to use pictures and describing words in the text to help identify and describe the setting.

- Have children discuss details of the setting that change from the beginning to the end of the story.

 ENGLISH LEARNER SUPPORT

SUBSTANTIAL

Read aloud words from the text that describe the setting. Have children repeat them after you and identify pictures that relate to the descriptive words.

MODERATE

Provide these frames so that children can tell about the setting of their book: *The words _____ tell where the story takes place. The words _____ tell when the story takes place.*

LIGHT

As children answer the prompts, encourage them to share the details in the text and pictures that helped them respond.

LESSON 6

READING WORKSHOP

Options for Differentiation

Tap, Bam! Rip! Bam!, Start Right Reader, *Book 1,* pp. 132–139

REINFORCE FOUNDATIONAL SKILLS

Read Decodable Text

Get Started Have children turn to Start Right Reader page 132. Explain that this week's stories are about the characters Bob, his family, and his friends. Have children point to and name the characters pictured on page 132. Then read the page together.

Preview the Story Read aloud the title on page 133 and discuss the sound words in the title. Then have children look at the pictures on the first few pages and predict the problem in the story.

Concepts of Print: Commas Use page 133 to model identifying a comma. Explain that a comma is often used before the word *too.* Then have children turn to page 134 and point to the comma. Explain that a comma is also often used before a person's name. Remind children that commas can show readers where to pause when reading aloud. Read aloud the sentence to model.

Fluency Focus: Intonation Read aloud page 134 as children follow along. Remind them that reading with intonation means changing the pitch of your voice to reflect the end punctuation in the text. For example, when you read the exclamatory sentences, you gradually

went from a higher pitch down. When you read the question, you raised your pitch at the end of the sentence. Then lead children in reading page 134 chorally, using appropriate intonation.

Reflect on Reading Have children read to find out why the story title has sound words in it. Have them read each page silently and then chorally. Pause for these prompts:

- **Page 133:** *Who does Bob live with? (Sal, Dad, Pop)*

- **Page 135:** *What problem does Bob have? (He cannot see what is happening behind the wall.) How will Bob solve his problem? (He will hop on Dad.)*

- **Page 137:** *What is making the noise? (a big rig)*

- **Page 138:** *What do you think* din *means? What details in the text give you clues to the meaning of* din? *(Possible response:* Din *means "noise"; The text says "Rip! Bam!" right before saying "What a big din!")*

Story Word Clues Read aloud the directions on page 139. Then have children read the clues and find the word in the story that fits each clue. *(Bob; Pop; rod)*

Bob did it!
Bob sat on top of Dad.
Bob can see!

136

It is a big rig!
Its big rod taps as it hits.
Tap! Bam! Tap! Bam!

137

This rig can dig pits. Rip!
Tip it in, big rig. Bam!
Rip! Bam! What a big din!

138

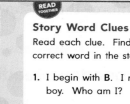

READ TOGETHER

Story Word Clues

Read each clue. Find the correct word in the story.

1. I begin with **B**. I name a boy. Who am I?

2. I begin with **P**. I live with Dad. Who am I?

3. I am part of a rig. I can tap. What am I?

139

(?) Make Minutes Count

As you meet with small groups to read *Tap, Bam! Rip! Bam!,* use one or more of these related activities, as needed, at the beginning or the end of the small-group session.

h l o p t

- **Connect to Phonics** Play Letter Swap. Gather multiple Letter Cards for *h, l, o, p, t*. Build the word *lot* and have children blend and read the word. Ask what letter must be swapped in order to change *lot* to *hot*. Make the change, and have children blend and read *hot*. Repeat the process to change *hot* to *hop*. Guide children in using the Letter Cards to make new words, changing only one consonant at a time.

- **Connect to Spelling** Play Tap and Clap. Display the basic and review Spelling Words from Printable: <u>Word List 5</u>. Point to each word and have children spell the word chorally with you, tapping the table for each consonant and softly clapping for each vowel.

- **Connect to Handwriting** Have children "air write" the letter *o*. Then model writing the letter *o*. As you model, point out that *o* is a backward circle letter—your hand starts at the top and then moves backward and down, or counterclockwise, to form the letter. Then write the Spelling Words *hot* and *top* on the board. Have children write each word three times, putting a star next to the word in each set that best matches the model. As children write, check their paper position and pencil grip and correct as needed.

👥 INDEPENDENT APPLICATION

Options for Independent and Collaborative Work

While you meet with small groups, have other children engage in literacy activities that reinforce the lesson's learning objectives. Choose from these options.

Independent Reading

Student Choice Library

Rigby
LEVELED LIBRARY

APPLY READING SKILL

Setting Children complete Printable: **Reading Graphic Organizer 18** for an independent reading book.

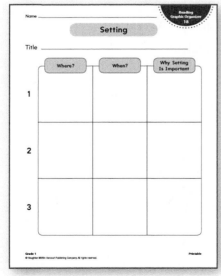

Printable: Reading Graphic Organizer 18

APPLY LANGUAGE SKILL

Compare and Contrast Children complete Printable: **Language Graphic Organizer 5** for an independent reading book.

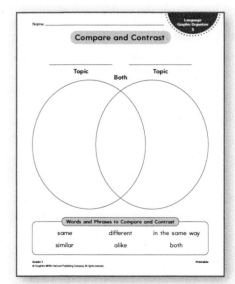

Printable: Language Graphic Organizer 5

Literacy Centers

See pp. T346–T347.

 WORD WORK

 CREATIVITY CORNER

 DIGITAL STATION

 READING CORNER

 TEAMWORK TIME

Start Right Reader

Read Decodable Text *Tap, Bam! Rip! Bam!*, Book 1: pp. 132–139

Writing

Partners write and draw about a neighborhood. *See Engage & Respond, p. T357.*

Additional Skills Practice

HIGH-FREQUENCY WORDS

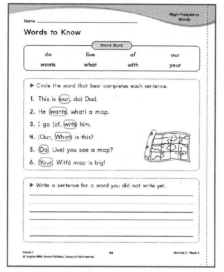

Know It, Show It, p. 44

SPELLING

Know It, Show It, p. 45

Wrap-Up
Share Time

At the end of Reading Workshop, have children reflect on their learning by sharing how they applied **Setting** or another area of focus during independent work time. Choose from these options:

- **SHARE CHAIR** Select a reader each day to come to the front of the class and tell what he or she learned from the reading by using a skill or strategy.

- **THINK-PAIR-SHARE** Children share their thinking with a partner. Select a few each day to share with the whole class.

- **RETURN TO ANCHOR CHART** Have children add sticky notes about their independent reading book to the Setting Anchor Chart. Call on a few children to explain what they added.

ANCHOR CHART 11: Setting **Online** 🌞**Ed**

FOUNDATIONAL SKILLS

LEARNING OBJECTIVES

- Identify and read high-frequency words.
- **Language** Recognize and recite basic sight vocabulary.
- Blend phonemes to say one-syllable words.

MATERIALS Online

Word Cards *do, got, had, has, him, his, live, not, of, our, wants, what, with, your*

Printable *Word List 5*

Picture Cards *bee, boat, cat, eel, fox, goat, hat, ox*

High-Frequency Words

Review the Words

Repeat the **HIGH-FREQUENCY WORDS** routine to review this week's High-Frequency Words: *do, live, of, our, wants, what, with,* and *your,* and the decodable High-Frequency Words *got, had, has, him, his,* and *not.*

Around the World

- Have children cut out word cards for the week's High-Frequency Words and decodable High-Frequency Words from Printable: <u>Word List 5</u> and sit in a circle.

- Each child selects a word card from his or her pile. (Make sure that all High-Frequency Words and decodable High-Frequency Words are represented in the cards children select.)

- Call on one child to stand inside the circle in front of one of the seated children.

- All the seated children hold up their word cards for the child in the middle to see.

High-Frequency Words	Decodable High-Frequency Words	Spelling Words	
		Basic	Review
do	got	log	big
live	had	not	sit
of	has	top	pig
our	him	hot	dig
wants	his	hop	
what	not	on	
with			
your			
			Challenge
			shop
			block

Printable: Word List 5

- The standing child reads the word in front of him or her and then moves to the next seated child to read the next word. The object is to read all the words quickly and to read the words all the way around the circle.

- Continue until all children have had a turn and can read the words fluently.

TEACHER TIP

Watch out for tricky letters!
Explain that many High-Frequency Words, such as *got* and *has,* have regular spellings. Others, however, may have some letter-sounds that children know, such as *wh* and *t* in *what,* but other letters that don't follow phonics rules. Children can use what they know about phonics to learn to read and spell the words, but remind them to look out for the tricky letters!

LEARNING MINDSET

Belonging

Apply Point out to children that playing games and learning together is one way to come together as a community of learners. Say: *We're a community of learners! When we work together, we can help each other practice and learn. We can make learning fun for our class!* Talk with children about how holding up the words in Around the World helps their classmates become better readers.

Phonological Awareness

Blend Phonemes

- Tell children that they will blend more sounds to say words.

- Model: *Let's practice blending sounds to say words. Listen as I do the first one. These are the sounds: /s/ /ā/ /f/. When I blend /s/, /ā/, and /f/, I say the word safe. /s/ /ā/ /f/, safe.*

- *Now it's your turn. Listen to the sounds. Then blend the sounds and say the word: /h/ /ī/. What's the word?* (hi) *Yes, when you blend /h/ and /ī/, you say hi.*

- *Let's do some more. Blend the sounds and say the words: /m/ /ē/ (me), /h/ /ŏ/ /p/ (hop), /d/ /o͞o/ (do), /b/ /ī/ /t/ (bite), /w/ /ī/ /z/ (wise), /j/ /ŭ/ /g/ (jug).*

- Display Picture Cards *bee, boat, cat, eel, fox, goat, hat,* and *ox* in random order along the chalkboard ledge.

- Tell children that now they will practice blending as you sing the song "Down by the Bay."

- Sing the song as usual until you reach the line: "Did you ever see a . . . ?": *Down by the bay, / Where the watermelons grow, / Back to my home / I dare not go. / For if I do, / My mother will say, / Did you ever see a _____ _____ing a _____ / Down by the bay?*

- Pause before each rhyming word and provide the phonemes for children to blend to complete the lyric. For example:

  » *Did you ever see a /k/ /ă/ /t/ (cat) wearing a /h/ /ă/ /t/ (hat)?*

  » *Did you ever see a /g/ /ō/ /t/ (goat) rowing a /b/ /ō/ /t/ (boat)?*

  » *Did you ever see a /b/ /ē/ (bee) flying out to /s/ /ē/ (sea)?*

  » *Did you ever see an /ē/ /l/ (eel) talking to a /s/ /ē/ /l/ (seal)?*

  » *Did you ever see a /f/ /ŏ/ /ks/ (fox) sitting on an /ŏ/ /ks/ (ox)?*

- Ask children to point to Picture Card matches for any of the words they blended to sing.

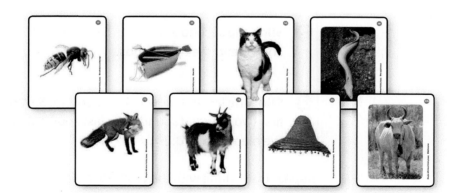

 CORRECT & REDIRECT

For children who blend incorrectly, differentiate instruction by modeling. Enunciate the sounds separately, then say them more closely together, and finally blend them. Example:

The sounds are /m/ and /ē/. The first sound is /m/. Listen: /mmm/. The next sound is /ē/. Listen: /ēēē/. Say each sound with me: /mmm/ /ēēē/. Now listen as I blend the two sounds together: /m/ /ē/, /m-ē/, me. What word do you say when you blend /m/ and /ē/? (me)

 ENGLISH LEARNER SUPPORT:
Build Vocabulary

SUBSTANTIAL
Tell children to point to Picture Cards as you say the picture names: *bee, boat, cat, eel, fox, goat, hat, ox.* Have children repeat each word.

MODERATE
Prompt children to sort the Picture Cards into categories: living things and objects. Have them share their sort with the class.

LIGHT
Have children tell a fact about each Picture Card image. For example: *A goat is a farm animal.*

Consonants *l*, *h*; Short *o*

Spotlight on Sounds

- Remind children that they have been reading words with short vowel sounds. Guide them to listen for and distinguish vowel sounds in words. *I will say a word, and you will listen for and say the middle sound and its name.*

- *I will do the first one. Listen: The word is* pot. Repeat, emphasizing the vowel sound. *The middle sound in* pot *is /ŏ/, short o. Listen again, and repeat after me:* pot, /ŏ/, short o.

- *Now it's your turn. Repeat each word I say and tell me the middle sound:* tip (tip, /ĭ/, short i); lap (lap, /ă/, short a); hog (hog, /ŏ/, short o); lip (lip, /ĭ/, short i); hat (hat, /ă/, short a); hot (hot, /ŏ/, short o).

I Do It

Spotlight on Letters　Review Sound/Spelling Cards *octopus, horse, lion*.

Write *hop* for children to see, and use the **SOUND-BY-SOUND BLENDING** routine below to model blending the word using Letter Cards *h, o, p*.

1 **Display** Letter Cards as shown. Say the first letter and sound.

2 **Slide** the second letter over. Say its sound. Then blend the two sounds.

3 **Slide** the last letter over. Say its sound. Say the first two blended sounds, the last sound, and the blended word: /hŏ//p/, hop.

Repeat the routine with the cards for *lot*.

EL **ENGLISH LEARNER SUPPORT:**
Build Vocabulary

SUBSTANTIAL
Use gestures to show the meaning of the Blend and Read words *hot, hid, fan, top,* and *stop*. Point to show the meanings of *lap, lip, hat,* and *lid*.

MODERATE
Discuss the multiple meanings of Blend and Read words, such as *lot, rig, fan,* and *top*. Have children use the words in oral sentences.

LIGHT
Have children tell what they know about the Blend and Read words. Use context sentences to help them determine the meaning of unknown words.

We Do It

Blend and Read

Project Display and Engage: **Blend and Read 2.6** or use Start Right Reader page 140.

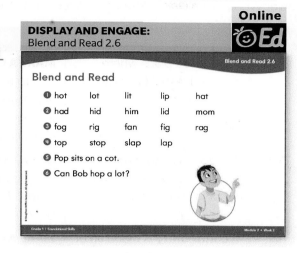

1 **Line 1** Have children read the line. Then prompt a conversation about the words: *How are the first two words the same? How are they different?* If necessary, lead children to compare the words. (same: *rhyming; middle and end sounds;* different: *beginning consonants*) Point to each word, and have children read the line chorally. Provide corrective feedback as needed.

2 **Line 2** Continue with these words. Then call on volunteers to reread selected words until children can identify the words quickly.

3 **Review** For Line 3, have children read the words chorally.

4 **Challenge** Have children who are ready for a challenge read Line 4. Ask them to compare any two words that differ by one letter, and to demonstrate how they read the words with consonant blends. Discuss word meanings with the group.

5 **Sentences** For Lines 5–6, call on children to blend selected decodable words. Then have the group read the sentences chorally.

You Do It

INDEPENDENT PRACTICE

- **Option 1** Write the following Blend and Read words: *hot, lid, top.* Have children read the words and write them. Then ask children to find and write a rhyming word for each one from the Blend and Read lines 1-4. Have a child read his or her rhyming words while others check their own work.

- **Option 2** Children complete Know It, Show It page 46.

✓ **CORRECT & REDIRECT**

- If a child mispronounces a word during Blend and Read, make note of the error type and address it.
- If a child reads *hot* as *hat*, point to the word and read it, emphasizing the short *o* sound. Name the letters, and say the sounds. Then have the child blend with you to read the word: /h/ /ŏ/ /t/, hot.

👥 **LINK TO SMALL-GROUP INSTRUCTION**

REINFORCE FOUNDATIONAL SKILLS Use *A Map* during small-group time to review or reinforce blending and decoding words with the vowel short *o* and consonants *l, h.* Meet with children to work through the story, or assign it as independent work. *See the lesson on p. T374.*

A Map
by Jordan Munro
Illustrated by Teresa Martinez

Dad has a big map.
Find the X, Bob!
Find it, Dom!

VOCABULARY

LEARNING OBJECTIVES

- **Language** Answer questions and discuss meanings to develop vocabulary.
- Identify real-life connections between words and their use.

MATERIALS   Online

Vocabulary Cards 2.22–2.27
Classroom materials *map*

 # Introduce Power Words

Use the steps **I Do It, We Do It, You Do It** with the information in the chart below to teach the Power Words from *On the Map!* and *Places in My Neighborhood.*

❶ Power Word	❷ Meaning	❸ Example
town (n.) *(p. 122)*	A **town** is a place where people live that is smaller than a city.	**MAKE A CONNECTION** Talk about the town or city where your school is located. *Our school (is/is not) in a* **town**.
map (n.) *(p. 123)*	A **map** is a picture that shows streets, rivers, and other parts of a place.	**USE A PROP** Point to a map in the classroom. *I can use a* **map** *to find where our state is.*
community (n.) *(p. 136)*	A **community** is made up of people who live near each other and the places around them.	**MAKE A CONNECTION** Talk about the people and places in your community. *Your home, your neighbors, and our school are in one* **community**.
places (n.) *(p. 136)*	**Places** are certain parts of a city or town.	**MAKE A CONNECTION** Give examples of places in your community. *The library, firehouse, and park are all* **places** *in our (city/town).*
purpose (n.) *(p. 136)*	A **purpose** is a reason for doing or having something.	**MAKE A CONNECTION** Relate the meaning of *purpose* to children's lives. *The* **purpose** *of this lesson is to learn new words!*
clinic (n.) *(p. 141)*	A **clinic** is a place where people go to see a doctor or nurse.	**ACT IT OUT** Place your hand on your forehead as if you are sick. *When I feel sick, I might go to a* **clinic** *to see the doctor.*

 ENGLISH LEARNER SUPPORT:
Facilitate Language Connections

ALL LEVELS For Spanish-speaking students, point out that the English words *community, map, purpose,* and *clinic* have the following cognates: *comunidad, mapa, propósito, clínica.*

• *Professional Learning*

RESEARCH FOUNDATIONS

"Direct instruction of vocabulary relevant to a given text leads to better reading comprehension."
—Dr. Bonnie B. Armbruster, Fran Lehr, and Jean Osborn (2001)

See the **GPS guide** to learn more.

I Do It

Use the **VOCABULARY** routine and Vocabulary Cards 2.22–2.27 to introduce the Power Words from *On the Map!* and *Places in My Neighborhood.* You may wish to display the corresponding Vocabulary Card for each word as you discuss it.

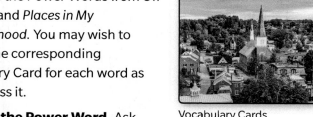

Vocabulary Cards

1. **Say the Power Word.** Ask children to repeat it.

2. **Explain the meaning.** Read aloud the student-friendly meaning.

3. **Talk about examples.** Use the image or a strategy to give examples of the word.

We Do It

Guide children to make connections between each word's meaning and how they can use it in their own lives. Use these prompts. Encourage children to explain or justify their answers.

- *What is one **purpose** for going to a store?*
- *What **places** might you find on a **map** of a **town**?*
- *How is your family a part of your **community**?*
- *When would you go to a **clinic**?*

You Do It

INDEPENDENT PRACTICE

Have partners work together to complete each of the activities below. Circulate and observe partners as they work, providing corrective feedback as necessary.

- **Draw** *Draw a **map** of your **community**. Include our school and your home.*
- **Write** *Write a list of **places** that you go to in a **town**.*
- **Compare** *Talk about a **purpose** for going on a trip. Then talk about a purpose for going to a **clinic**.*

 ENGLISH LEARNER SUPPORT: Build Vocabulary

SUBSTANTIAL
Use a map to talk about your community, incorporating the words *map, places, town,* and *community.* Have children repeat each word after you.

MODERATE
Supply frames such as these: *A **map** helps me to _____.*
*A **town** is _____ . Two **places** in my **community** are _____.*

LIGHT
If children respond with a phrase or short sentence, encourage them to elaborate. Use questions as prompts.

Summarize

LEARNING OBJECTIVES

- Identify the features of informational text.
- Summarize a text by telling its important ideas and details.
- **Language** Share important ideas and details about a text.
- Ask questions to clarify ideas or information.

MATERIALS   Online

Anchor Chart 4
Summarize

Printable *Anchor Chart 4: Summarize*

Teaching Pal *Book 1, pp. 120–127*

myBook *On the Map!, Book 1, pp. 120–127*

READER'S VOCABULARY

- **summarize** to tell the most important ideas of a text in your own words
- **detail** small bit of information that supports a central idea or describes something in a text

- Point out to children that when they share an experience with a friend, they tell the most important parts they remember about it. Tell children you can do that with books, too!

- Project or display the <u>Anchor Chart 4: Summarize</u>.

- Tell children that they can **summarize** a text to better understand and remember it.

- Explain to children that when you summarize, you tell the most important ideas in your own words. Walk through Steps 1–3 on the Anchor Chart, and point out that summarizing *as* you read helps you think about the information in the text so you can understand it better.

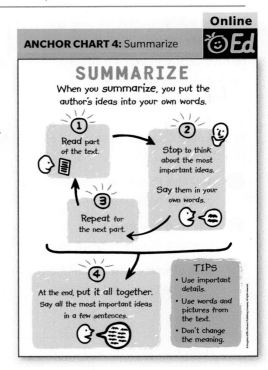

ANCHOR CHART 4: Summarize

Online

- Read aloud Step 4. Point out that to summarize *after* you read, you put the information from Steps 1–3 in order. Explain that you don't change the meaning of the text, you just tell the most important ideas in an order that makes sense.

- Read aloud the Tips. Tell children that a summary does not include every **detail**, or piece of information, from a text. It includes only the most important details from the words and pictures.

- Tell children they will practice summarizing when they read the informational text called *On the Map!*

Notice & Note

Big Questions

- The Teaching Pal prompts in this lesson feature the **Notice & Note Big Questions** for nonfiction.
- As needed, refer to p. T263 to review the Big Questions with children.

 ## ASSESSMENT OPTION

Assign the <u>Selection Quiz</u> to check comprehension of *On the Map!*

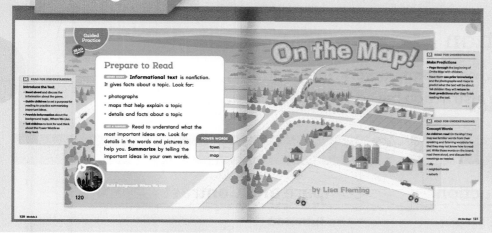

ANNOTATE IT!

Children may use the annotation tools in their eBook.

Step 2 — Apply to Text

 In your Teaching Pal, pages 120–127, use the blue **READ FOR UNDERSTANDING** prompts to read *On the Map!* with children as they follow along and annotate in their *my*Book.

- **Genre Study** Read the genre information on page 120. Discuss the kinds of things children would expect to find in an informational text and compare them with what they might find in a story.

- **Set a Purpose** Read the Set a Purpose section on page 120. Prompt children to set their own purpose for reading *On the Map!*

- **Build Background** Play the audio about **Where We Live**. Discuss with children the connection between the topic and the features of informational texts.

- **Read and Comprehend** Guide children to read the selection all the way through. Pause occasionally, using the prompts in your Teaching Pal to gauge children's understanding and to have them summarize the text in their own words. Have children refer back to the Anchor Chart to help them decide which details from the words and pictures are most important to include in their summaries.

Step 3 — Engage and Respond

INDEPENDENT PRACTICE: Speaking & Listening

- Use the **TURN AND TALK** routine with the questions on Teaching Pal and *my*Book page 127. Remind children to include only the most important ideas in their summaries of *On the Map!*

- Read the Talking Tip. Remind children that active listeners "stay awake" and ask questions when they do not understand something.

- You may want to have children conduct their discussions during daily small-group time.

 ENGLISH LEARNER SUPPORT: Support Comprehension

SUBSTANTIAL
Help children point to each feature in the photos and name them.

MODERATE
Help children match features in the photos to the maps: *Where is the (bridge/river/school) in the photo? Where is the (bridge/river/school) on the map?* Have children point to each feature and name it.

LIGHT
Have partners name and compare the features in the photo to the features in the map.

LINK TO SMALL-GROUP INSTRUCTION

REINFORCE SUMMARIZE Review or extend the skill as needed during small-group time to support children's need for differentiation. *See the lesson on p. 373.*

Options for Differentiation

As the class engages in independent and collaborative work, meet with Guided Reading Groups or differentiate instruction based on student need.

GUIDED READING GROUPS

Match Children to Books + Instruction

- Choose just-right books based on level, skill, topic, or genre.

C D E F G H I J K
Leveled Readers

- Deliver instruction with each book's Take and Teach Lesson, choosing appropriate sessions based on need.

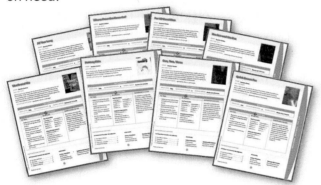

- Check comprehension, reinforce instruction, and extend learning with suggested supporting activities.

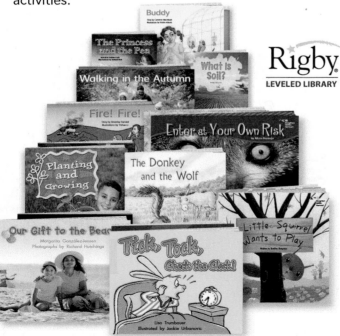

Rigby®
LEVELED LIBRARY

🔵 ENGLISH LEARNER SUPPORT

Compare and Contrast

- Use **Tabletop Minilessons: English Language Development 5.1 (Speaking)** to reinforce and practice the language skill.

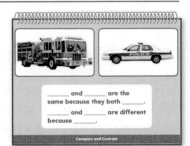

Tabletop Minilessons: English Language Development

- Then use the following text-based prompts with *On the Map!* to guide application of the language skill. Begin with the prompt at the child's identified language proficiency level. As children are able, use lighter supports to encourage increased language proficiency.

SUBSTANTIAL

Guide children to tell what is the same and different about the photo and the map of the town on pages 122–123. Ask: *What is the same? What is different?* Allow children to respond in single words, in short phrases, or in their home language.

MODERATE

Have children identify what is the same and different about the photo and the map of the town on pages 122–123. Supply these frames: *The photo and the map are (different/the same) because* _____.

LIGHT

Ask children to identify what is the same and different about the photo and the map of the town on pages 122–123. Ask: *What is the same about the photo and the map? What is different?*

REINFORCE SUMMARIZE

Demonstrate

- Use **Tabletop Minilessons: Reading 4** to remind children that when readers **summarize** a text, they use their own words to tell the most important ideas. Thinking about how to tell the important ideas in the text using their own words can help readers understand the text better. A **summary** includes the most important **details** from the words and visuals in a text, and it does not change the meaning of the text.

- Model filling out Printable: **Reading Graphic Organizer 5** to summarize *On the Map!*

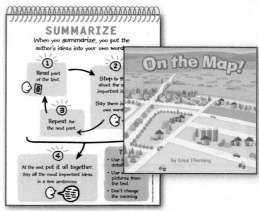

Tabletop Minilessons: Reading

Apply to Independent Reading

- Now have children summarize the information in an appropriate just-right book that they are reading independently. Before children read their books, guide them to set a purpose for reading. Remind them to pay attention to the most important ideas in the text. Customize these prompts to the books children choose.

  » *In your own words, what is the text about?*

  » *What are the most important details?*

  » *How can you tell about this (idea/event/character) in your own words?*

- Have children complete Printable: **Reading Graphic Organizer 5** for their independent reading book.

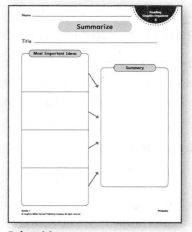

Printable:
Reading Graphic Organizer 5

SCAFFOLD AND EXTEND

ALMOST THERE

READY FOR MORE

- Help children identify the most important idea on each page or pages as a first step toward summarizing.

- Ask children to tell what each page or group of pages is about. Then guide them to use those statements to construct a summary.

- Have children summarize the book by referencing the text and pictures.

ⓔⓛ ENGLISH LEARNER SUPPORT

SUBSTANTIAL

For each page, ask: *What is this page about?* Allow children to give one- or two-word responses. Model using their responses in complete sentences.

MODERATE

Guide children to tell what each page is about. Provide this frame: *This page is about _____.*

LIGHT

As children answer the prompts, encourage them to use their own words to respond.

SMALL-GROUP INSTRUCTION

Options for Differentiation

A Map, Start Right Reader, *Book 1*, pp. 140–147

REINFORCE FOUNDATIONAL SKILLS

Read Decodable Text

Blend and Read Have children turn to Start Right Reader page 140. Use the **CHORAL READING** routine to read aloud the Blend and Read lines. Use challenge line 4 with children who are ready.

Preview the Story Call attention to page 141. Have children read the title and look at the picture and identify the characters Bob and Dad from *Tap, Bam! Rip! Bam!* Ask children who they think the new character is. Then have them look at the pictures on the first few pages and predict Bob's problem.

Fluency Focus: Intonation Read aloud page 142 as children follow along. Ask: *How could you tell when I read a question? (I saw the question mark at the end of the sentence; you raised your pitch at the end of the sentence.)* Then lead children in reading the page chorally, using appropriate intonation to reflect the end punctuation.

Reflect on Reading Have children use a finger to track the words from left to right as they read each page silently. Then have them read the page chorally. Pause for these prompts:

• **Page 141:** *What do Bob and Dom need to find? (the X)*

• **Pages 142–143:** *In what places do Bob and Dom look for the X? (the bin, the log)*

• **Page 144:** *Why are Bob and Dom sad? (They cannot find the X.)*

• **Page 146:** *Think about the prediction you made about the problem in the story. Was your prediction correct? Explain. (Responses will vary.)*

Rhyming Word Hunt Read aloud the directions on page 147. Have children read the clues, look through the story for the answers, and write the answers on a sheet of paper. *(Bob; log; pops)*

Bob is sad.
Dom is sad.
Dad, what is it?

144

It is hot.
Bob sits on the log.
Dom sits. Dom fits on it.

145

146

"It is your Pop!" said Dom.
"Pop has an **X**!" said Bob.
"Pop has pops!"

READ TOGETHER

Rhyming Word Hunt
Read each clue to a word in the story. Write each word.

1. This word rhymes with **sob**. It names a boy.

2. This word rhymes with **dog**. Bob sits on one.

3. This word rhymes with **mops**. It is what Pop has.

147

Make Minutes Count

As you meet with small groups to read *A Map*, use one or more of these related activities, as needed, at the beginning or the end of the small-group session.

- **Connect to Phonics** Display these Picture Cards, picture side down: *hat, log, map, pot*. Write the words naming the Picture Cards on separate index cards, and place the index cards on top of the corresponding Picture Cards. Call on a child to read one of the words. Then have the child turn over the card and look at the picture to confirm that he or she correctly read the word. Continue until all of the cards are picture side up. Then have children read the words chorally.

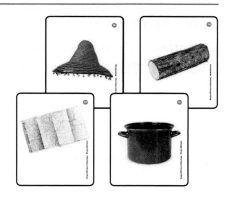

- **Connect to Spelling** Play Tic-Tac-Toe. Have partners draw a three-by-three grid and assign who will be *X* and who will be *O*. One partner calls out a Spelling Word from Printable: <u>Word List 5</u> for the other partner to spell. If the other partner spells the word correctly, he or she writes his or her assigned letter anywhere on the grid. Play continues until one partner has three *X*s or *O*s in a row.

- **Connect to Handwriting** Draw a triple-track line on the board, and write the letter *g* on the track. As you model, point out that you form the letter by moving in a backward circle direction, and then pulling down past the bottom line almost as far as the distance between the middle and bottom lines. Then write this sentence on the track: *Hop on the big log, Bob.* Have children write the sentence, focusing on correctly forming the letters *o* and *g*. Have children circle the word in their sentence that best matches the model.

👥 INDEPENDENT APPLICATION

Options for Independent and Collaborative Work

While you meet with small groups, have other children engage in literacy activities that reinforce the lesson's learning objectives. Choose from these options.

Independent Reading

Student Choice Library

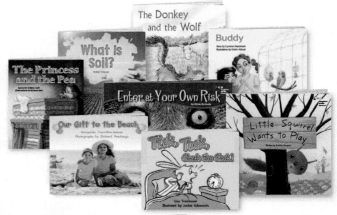

Rigby®
LEVELED LIBRARY

APPLY READING SKILL

Summarize Children complete Printable: <u>Reading Graphic Organizer 5</u> for an independent reading book.

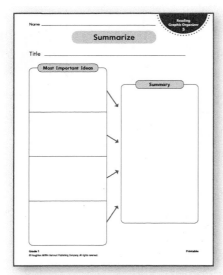

Printable: Reading Graphic Organizer 5

APPLY LANGUAGE SKILL

Compare and Contrast Children complete Printable: <u>Language Graphic Organizer 5</u> for an independent reading book.

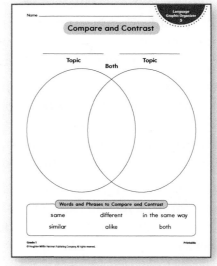

Printable: Language Graphic Organizer 5

Notice & Note
Big Questions

Encourage them to ask the Big Questions for nonfiction: *What surprised me? What did the author think I already knew? What challenged, changed, or confirmed what I already knew?*

Literacy Centers

See pp. T346–T347.

 WORD WORK

 CREATIVITY CORNER

 DIGITAL STATION

 READING CORNER

 TEAMWORK TIME

Start Right Reader

Read Decodable Text *A Map,* Book 1: pp. 140–147

Speaking & Listening

Children discuss the Turn and Talk questions using only the most important ideas in their summaries. *See Engage & Respond, p. T371.*

Additional Skills Practice

PHONICS

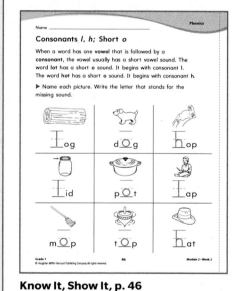

Know It, Show It, p. 46

Wrap-Up

Share Time

At the end of Reading Workshop, have children reflect on their learning by sharing how they applied **Summarize** or another area of focus during independent work time. Choose from these options:

- **SHARE CHAIR** Select a reader each day to come to the front of the class and tell what he or she learned from the reading by using a skill or strategy.

- **THINK-PAIR-SHARE** Children share their thinking with a partner. Select a few each day to share with the whole class.

- **RETURN TO ANCHOR CHART** Have children add sticky notes about their independent reading book to the Summarize Anchor Chart. Call on a few children to explain what they added.

Online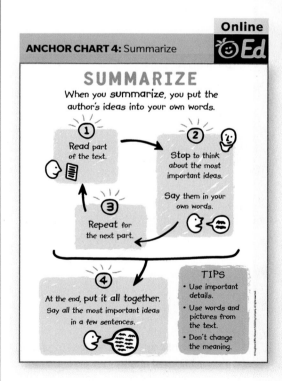

ANCHOR CHART 4: Summarize

FOUNDATIONAL SKILLS

LEARNING OBJECTIVES

- Identify and read high-frequency words.
- **Language** Recognize basic sight vocabulary.
- **Language** Compose oral sentences using basic sight vocabulary.
- Recognize spoken alliteration.
- Isolate initial and final phonemes in spoken one-syllable words.
- Segment spoken one-syllable words into individual phonemes.

MATERIALS   Online

Word Cards *do, got, had, has, him, his, live, not, of, our, wants, what, with, your*

Picture Cards *bridge, cherries, flowers, giraffe, horse, milk, phone, pillow*

 # High-Frequency Words

Review the Words

Repeat the **HIGH-FREQUENCY WORDS** routine to review this week's High-Frequency Words: *do, live, of, our, wants, what, with,* and *your,* and the decodable High-Frequency Words *got, had, has, him, his,* and *not.*

> him

Picture Card Challenge

- Display this week's High-Frequency Word Cards and an assortment of Picture Cards, such as *bridge, cherries, flowers, giraffe, horse, milk, phone,* and *pillow.*

- Have each child choose a Picture Card, such as *milk,* and suggest a sentence about it that includes a High-Frequency Word. For example: *Do you have milk?*

- Have others identify the High-Frequency Word or words in each sentence.

 # Phonological Awareness

Alliteration; Isolate Phonemes

- Tell children to listen and raise their hands if the all words you say begin with the same sound. Model: *The words are:* bike, bath, books. *Hands up! I hear* /b/ *at the beginning of* bike, bath, *and* books. **Continue:** cabin, code, kit *(up)*; heat, hide, wide *(down)*; gap, cave, game *(down)*; mind, moon, mail *(up)*.

- Have children isolate initial sounds. Model: feet. *What is the sound at the beginning of* feet? Feet, /f/. **Continue:** top (/t/), neck (/n/), soak (/s/), give (/g/).

- Ask children to isolate final sounds in these words: pod (/d/); mess (/s/); luck (/k/); tide (/d/); real (/l/).

Segment Phonemes

- Have children say every sound in a word. Model: head. *The sounds in* head *are* /h/, /ĕ/, *and* /d/. Head, /h/ /ĕ/ /d/.

- *It's your turn! Say each sound you hear:* ill (/ĭ/ /l/), no (/n/ /ō/), tea (/t/ /ē/), wait (/w/ /ā/ /t/), five (/f/ /ī/ /v/), pole (/p/ /ō/ /l/), hop (/h/ /ŏ/ /p/).

TEACHER TIP

Double up! Children looking for an additional challenge can choose two Picture Cards or High-Frequency Words to work into their sentences.

✓ CORRECT & REDIRECT

If children segment incorrectly, say the word repeatedly, emphasizing one phoneme at a time. Example for *five:*

- *What are the sounds in* five?
- /fīv/: *The beginning sound is* /f/.
- /fīīīv/: *The middle sound is* /ī/.
- /fīv/: *The last sound is* /v/.
- *The sounds in* five *are* /f/, /ī/, *and* /v/.

Intonation

I Do It

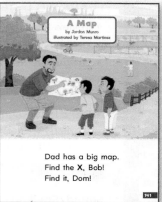

- Explain to children that good readers can make the words they read sound like they do in conversation. Point out that in conversation our voices go up and down to express meaning and give emphasis to what we're saying.

- Tell children that when they read, they can use the punctuation marks as clues to how certain phrases and sentences should sound. They can help with intonation, or making our reading sound like conversation.

- Have children look at the text on page 141 of the Start Right Reader (*A Map*). Model changing pitch to read the first sentence as a statement, an exclamation, and a question. Ask children how your voice changed. Guide them to see that the changes in intonation changed the meaning of the sentence.

We Do It

- Point to the end punctuation in sentences on pages 141 and 142. Then read the pages, using proper intonation for each sentence. Use the **ECHO READING** routine to have children follow your model.

- Use the **CHORAL READING** routine to have children reread pages 141–142 sentence by sentence, paying attention to the type of sentence they are reading so they know how to read it. Coach them as needed to read accurately and with appropriate intonation, rate, and expression.

You Do It

INDEPENDENT PRACTICE

- Have children use the **PARTNER READING** routine with one of the Start Right Reader stories about Bob and his family or *On the Map!* from their *my*Book. Coach children to change their intonation to match the kind of sentence they are reading. Ask volunteers to read one or two pages aloud.

LEARNING OBJECTIVE

- Read aloud fluently and with appropriate intonation (prosody).

MATERIALS   Online

Start Right Reader *Book 1, pp. 141–146*

 ENGLISH LEARNER SUPPORT:
Facilitate Language Connections

ALL LEVELS Speakers of Cantonese, Mandarin, and Vietnamese may need extensive modeling and practice to adjust to the patterns of stress and intonation of English. These Asian languages are "tonal" languages and use tonal variation for each individual syllable as part of expressing its meaning. In English, syllables within a word and words within a sentence get different amounts of stress. In addition to explicitly teaching and modeling patterns of oral language in English, you may wish to engage children in frequent choral readings, repeated readings, and partner reading of varied texts.

Professional Learning

RESEARCH FOUNDATIONS

"Students who read and reread passages orally as they receive guidance and/or feedback become better readers. Repeated oral reading substantially improves word recognition, speed, and accuracy as well as fluency."
    —Dr. Bonnie B. Armbruster, Fran Lehr, and Jean Osborn (2001)

See the **GPS guide** to learn more.

PHONICS

 # Review Short *a, i, o*

Spotlight on Sounds

- Tell children that they will be reading more words with short vowel sounds. Explain that first, they will practice identifying the middle sounds in words you say. *I am going to say words, and you repeat the word, say the middle sound, and name it.*

- *I will do the first one. Listen: The word is* hot. Repeat the word, emphasizing the middle sound. *The middle sound in hot is /ŏ/, short o. Repeat after me:* hot, /ŏ/, *short o. Great! Now you do it. Repeat the word I say, and then say the middle sound and its name:* lock *(lock, /ŏ/, short o);* had *(had, /ă/, short a);* lid *(lid, /ĭ/, short i);* lap *(lap, /ă/, short a);* his *(his, /ĭ/, short i);* hog *(hog, /ŏ/, short o).*

- Next, have children listen for the middle sounds in word pairs. *Now I will say two words. If the words are the same, say "same" and name the vowel. If the words are different, say "different" and tell what is different. Listen:* hot/hat. *Are* hot *and* hat *the same or different? (different) What is different? (short o, short a) Very good. Let's continue:* tap/tip *(different; short a, short i);* lock/lock *(same, short o);* him/him *(same; short i);* pin/pan *(different; short i, short a).*

▌I Do It

Spotlight on Letters Have children name the vowels with you and tell what is special about them. (a, e, i, o, u; *each stands for many sounds*)

Display the Sound/Spelling Card for /ă/, *alligator.* Name the picture, say the sound, and give the spelling. *Alligator begins with the short a vowel sound, /ă/. The letter a can stand for the sound /ă/ at the beginning or middle of a word.*

Write *pal.* Say the letter sounds, and blend the word. *What sound do you hear in the middle of* pal? *(/ă/) What letter stands for that sound? (a)*

Repeat for /ĭ/ and /ŏ/, using Sound/Spelling Cards *igloo* and *octopus* and the words *his* and *log.*

LEARNING OBJECTIVES

- Review the sound-spellings for short vowels *a, i,* and *o.*
- **Language** Recognize sound-letter relationships and use them to decode words.
- Blend letter sounds and decode regularly spelled one-syllable words with short *a, i,* and *o.*

MATERIALS   Online

Sound/Spelling Cards *alligator, igloo, octopus*

Letter Cards *a, d, h, i, k, l, o, t*

Articulation Videos /ă/, /ĭ/, /ŏ/

TEACHER TIP

Round robin! Have children sit in a circle and take turns saying words with short *a.* See how far around the circle children can go. Then repeat for words with short *i* and short *o.* See which vowel sound gets the most words!

🔘 ENGLISH LEARNER SUPPORT: Facilitate Language Connections

ALL LEVELS Continue to monitor speakers of Spanish, Vietnamese, Hmong, Cantonese, Haitian Creole, and Korean for any difficulty pronouncing or distinguishing short vowel sounds. Replay the **Articulation Video** for /ă/, /ĭ/, or /ŏ/ as needed. Have children practice saying the sounds as they look in a mirror to see how their mouth forms each sound.

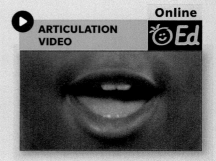

▶ **ARTICULATION VIDEO**   Online 🍊 *Ed*

We Do It

Write *lot* and use Letter Cards *l, o, t* with the **SOUND-BY-SOUND BLENDING** routine below to model blending the word.

1 **Display** cards as shown. Say the first letter and sound.

2 **Slide** the second letter over. Say its sound. Then blend the two sounds.

3 **Slide** the last letter over. Say its sound. Say the first two blended sounds, the last sound, and the blended word: /lŏ/ /t/, lot.

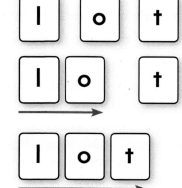

Sound-by-Sound Blending Repeat the **SOUND-BY-SOUND BLENDING** routine with cards for the words *hat* and *kid*, having children say the sounds and blend.

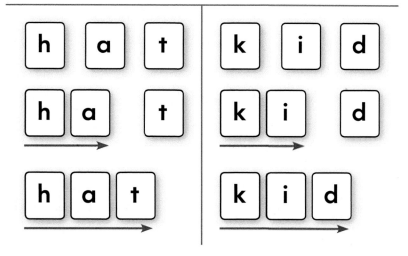

You Do It

INDEPENDENT PRACTICE

Blending Practice Write the words below. Then choose a volunteer to model the activity. Point to any word. Have the volunteer spell the word, blend the sounds, and read the word. Repeat the blending routine as needed. Continue until each child has had a turn.

him	gas	lit	pop
lap	hip	had	hid
pan	pin	cot	cat

✓ CORRECT & REDIRECT

- If a child mispronounces a word during Blending Practice, make note of the error type and address it.
- If a child reads *him* as *ham*, read the correct word. Then point to each letter and say its sound. As needed, use the Sound/Spelling Cards *igloo* and *alligator* to contrast the vowel sounds. Have the child repeat the short *i* sound several times. Then guide the child to use the sound-by-sound blending routine to blend the word.

👥 LINK TO SMALL-GROUP INSTRUCTION

REINFORCE FOUNDATIONAL SKILLS Use *Dot Is on It!* during small-group time to review or reinforce blending and decoding words with short vowels *a, i, o*. Meet with children to work through the story, or assign it as independent work. *See the lesson on p. T388.*

Review Power Words

Revisit the Power Words

LEARNING OBJECTIVES

- **Language** Respond to questions using multi-word responses.
- Use newly acquired vocabulary to identify real-life connections between words and their use.
- Identify and use words that name locations.

MATERIALS   Online

Know It, Show It *p. 48*

- Revisit the Power Words from *On the Map!* Display the questions and sentence frames below word by word.

- Model the task for the first word, using a child as your partner. Read aloud the question, and have the child repeat it. Respond using the sentence frame.

- Have partners use the **TURN AND TALK** routine to respond to each question using the sentence frame.

- For each word, ask one or two children to share their responses with the class. Then have them discuss the next question.

Power Word	Question	Sentence Frame
town	Is a **town** bigger or smaller than a city?	A **town** is _____.
map	What can a **map** help you to do?	A **map** can help me _____.

TEACHER TIP

Talk about towns! Locate and display a map of your school's town or a map of a nearby town. Guide children to find different locations on the map, such as schools, police stations, hospitals, and libraries. Compare the map of this town to a map of a city!

Getting Started

ENGAGEMENT ROUTINE

Model and practice engagement routines until they are automatic. For example, role-play **TURN AND TALK** in front of the class and show examples (and non-examples) of how to be a good partner.

See the **GPS guide** to learn more.

Vocabulary Chat

- Read aloud the following questions:

  1 *What are some places you would not find in a* **town**?

  2 *When would you need to use a* **map**?

- After you read aloud each question, have children use the **THINK-PAIR-SHARE** routine to discuss. Call on pairs to share their answers. Use positive feedback to reinforce correct usages of words.

- For additional practice with the Power Words from *On the Map!*, have children complete Know It, Show It page 48.

ENGLISH LEARNER SUPPORT:
Facilitate Discussion

SUBSTANTIAL
Ask: *Would you find an airplane in a* **town**? *Would you use a* **map** *if you knew where you were going or if you did not know where you were going?*

MODERATE
Repeat questions as needed. Prompt responses with sentence stems. *In a* **town**, *I would not see _____. I can use a* **map** *to _____.*

LIGHT
Ask: *What are some places you would not find in a* **town**? *What would you use a* **map** *to do?*

READING WORKSHOP

Text Features

Step 1 Connect and Teach

LEARNING OBJECTIVES

- Use text and graphic features to locate information.
- **Language** Explain why an author uses certain text features.
- Write directions, using sequence and location words.

MATERIALS Online *Ed*

Anchor Chart 22 *Text Features*

Printable *Anchor Chart 22: Text Features*

Teaching Pal *Book 1, pp. 120–129*

myBook *On the Map!, Book 1, pp. 120–129*

Know It, Show It *p. 49*

READER'S VOCABULARY

- **bold text** text that is dark to make it stand out as important
- **label** words on a diagram that name the parts of a picture
- **map** a graphic picture of an area that shows places such as towns, roads, and bodies of water to help you get somewhere
- **symbol** small pictures that stand for something else

- Project or display <u>Anchor Chart 22: Text Features</u>.

- Tell children that authors of informational texts often use different kinds of text features to help explain an idea or to help readers locate information. Authors choose the features that will best help readers understand the information.

- As you point to the corresponding parts of the Anchor Chart, explain each text feature. Point out that special text like **bold text** makes readers pay special attention to that part of the text.

- Explain that a **label** tells what a picture or part of a picture is.

- Tell children that a **map** is a small picture of a big place that shows where everything is.

- Finally, explain that a **symbol** is a small picture that stands for something else.

- Tell children they will reread parts of *On the Map!* to practice using text features to get information.

Online

ANCHOR CHART 22: Text Features *Ed*

Words in **bold text** are **darker** than other words. It means they are `important!`

Labels name parts of a picture.

window | door
house

Text Features

Authors choose text and graphic features to help explain ideas or to help readers locate information.

Maps are small pictures of **big** places.

Symbols are pictures that stand for something else.

TEACHER TIP

I spy a text feature! Help children connect text features to things they see in the classroom. Have children look at the classroom walls and displays to find examples of each feature: bold text or other special text, labels, symbols, and maps.

Professional Learning

RESEARCH FOUNDATIONS

"Reading aloud to children or shared book reading has been closely linked to children's reading achievement, emergent literacy ability, and language development."

–Dr. Justina Ong (2014)

See the **GPS guide** to learn more.

Go to Your
Teaching Pal

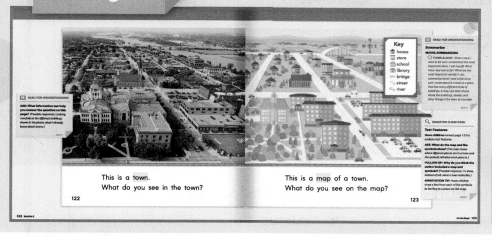

This is a town.
What do you see in the town?

122

This is a map of a town.
What do you see on the map?

123

ANNOTATE IT!

Online
Ed

Children may use the annotation tools in their eBook.

Step 2 Apply to Text

 In your Teaching Pal, use the purple **TARGETED CLOSE READ** prompts to guide children to apply the text features skill to *On the Map!* Children may refer to the questions on Know It, Show It page 49 as you discuss them.

- Read aloud the first question on Teaching Pal page 123. Tell children to look at details in the graphic features to answer it. *(The map shows where different places are in a town and the symbols tell what each place is.)*

- Then read aloud the follow-up question. Have children use evidence from the selection to make an inference about the author's purpose for including the graphic features. *(Sample response: To show, instead of tell, what a town looks like.)*

- Read aloud the questions on Teaching Pal page 126. Tell children to pay attention to the details in the text and graphic features to answer the questions. *(to show places where people live; The labels name the places in the photos.)*

- Refer back to the Anchor Chart to support the discussion. Children may add sticky notes to the chart to tell what information they learned from each of the text features in *On the Map!*

Step 3 Engage and Respond

INDEPENDENT PRACTICE: Writing

- Read aloud the prompt on Teaching Pal page 128. Have children use the planning space to put the steps of the directions in order.

- Then have children write their responses to the prompt. Remind children to refer back to *On the Map!* to make sure their directions match the map they chose. Also remind them to tell the steps in order and use sequence words.

- You may want to have children complete their writing during daily small-group time.

 ENGLISH LEARNER SUPPORT:
Scaffold Writing

SUBSTANTIAL
Provide direction lines on index cards and act them out with children: *Turn left. Turn right. Pass the _____. Go straight to the _____.* Help children put the cards together to create their map directions.

MODERATE
Supply sentence frames for children to use: *Start at the _____. Turn (right/left). Go straight to the _____. Pass the _____.*

LIGHT
Have partners trace each other's directions and then write them out.

LINK TO SMALL-GROUP INSTRUCTION

REINFORCE TEXT FEATURES Review or extend the skill as needed during small-group time to support children's need for differentiation. *See the lesson on p. T387.*

LESSON 8

READING WORKSHOP

Options for Differentiation

As the class engages in independent and collaborative work, meet with Guided Reading Groups or differentiate instruction based on student need.

GUIDED READING GROUPS

Match Children to Books + Instruction

- Choose just-right books based on level, skill, topic, or genre.

C D E F G H I J K

Leveled Readers

- Deliver instruction with each book's Take and Teach Lesson, choosing appropriate sessions based on need.

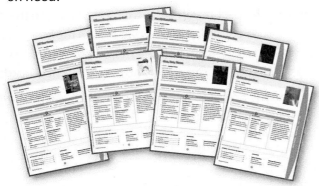

- Check comprehension, reinforce instruction, and extend learning with suggested supporting activities.

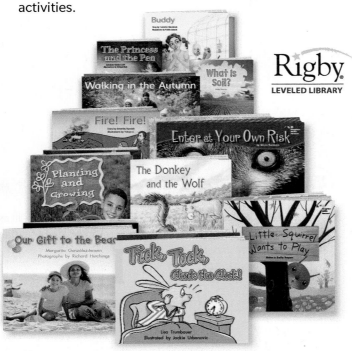

Rigby®
LEVELED LIBRARY

(EL) ENGLISH LEARNER SUPPORT

Compare and Contrast

- Use **Tabletop Minilessons: English Language Development 5.2 (Reading)** to reinforce and practice the language skill.

Both of these people are workers, but they do different jobs. One fixes cars, and the other builds houses. They are similar because they both wear uniforms.

Compare and Contrast

Tabletop Minilessons: English Language Development

- Then use the following text-based prompts with *On the Map!* to guide application of the language skill. Begin with the prompt at the child's identified language proficiency level. As children are able, use lighter supports to encourage increased language proficiency.

SUBSTANTIAL

Point to the photos of the suburb and the farm on page 126. Ask: *Which has more trees, the suburb or the farm? Which has more houses, the suburb or the farm?* Allow children to respond by pointing to the photos and text or by using single words.

MODERATE

Ask children to compare and contrast the photos of the suburb and the farm on page 126. Supply these frames: *The suburb and the farm are alike because they both_____. They are different because _____.*

LIGHT

Ask children to reread page 126 and compare and contrast the suburb and the farm. Ask: *What does the suburb have that the farm does not? What does the farm have that the suburb does not?*

REINFORCE TEXT FEATURES

Demonstrate

- Use **Tabletop Minilessons: Reading 22** to remind children that authors of **informational texts** often include different kinds of text and graphic features to explain an idea. These features can also help readers locate information. Some texts use **symbols**, or pictures that stand for something. **Maps** are small pictures of a large place that show where things are located. Maps often have a **key** that explains what each symbol means. A **diagram** is a picture with **labels** that tell what each part is. Special text, such as **bold text** or different colors, can call readers' attention to a certain part of the text.

- Model filling out Printable: <u>**Reading Graphic Organizer 19**</u> to identify and explain the text features in *On the Map!*

Tabletop Minilessons: Reading

Apply to Independent Reading

- Now have children identify text features and the information they give in an appropriate just-right book that they are reading independently. Customize these prompts to the books children choose.

  » *What text features does your book have?*

  » *How does this feature help you understand the text?*

  » *Why do you think the author included this text feature?*

- Have children complete Printable: <u>**Reading Graphic Organizer 19**</u> for their independent reading book.

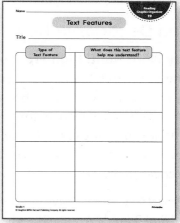

Printable:
Reading Graphic Organizer 19

ALMOST THERE

READY FOR MORE

SCAFFOLD AND EXTEND

- Help children match the text and pictures in their books with the relevant text features.

- Prompt children to use a text feature to explain a concept in the book.

- Have children create a text feature they could add to their books.

ENGLISH LEARNER SUPPORT

SUBSTANTIAL
Read aloud labels on diagrams for children and have them repeat. Ask children to point to the labels as they say the words again.

MODERATE
Supply this frame: *This text feature helps me because* _____.

LIGHT
As children answer prompts, encourage them to explain where they found details in the text or text features.

READING WORKSHOP

Options for Differentiation

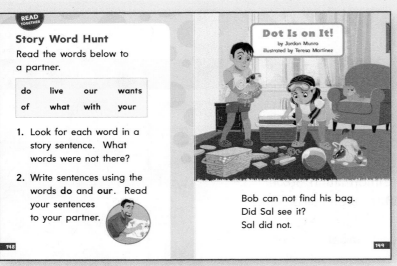

Dot Is on It!, Start Right Reader, *Book 1*, pp. 148–155

REINFORCE FOUNDATIONAL SKILLS

Read Decodable Text

Story Word Hunt: High-Frequency Word Review Have children turn to Start Right Reader page 148. Have partners read the boxed words. Then have them look for each word in the text and identify which words are not in the text. *(do, live, our, with)* Have children write sentences for the words *do* and *our* and read their sentences to their partners.

Preview the Story Have children briefly retell *Tap, Bam! Rip! Bam!* or *A Map.* Then have them turn to page 149. Read aloud the title and discuss the pictures on the first few pages. Have children use their preview to predict the problem in the story.

Concepts of Print: Commas Have children use a finger to point to commas as they read. Periodically prompt: *What word comes after this comma? What should you do when you are reading and you see a comma?*

Fluency Focus: Intonation Read aloud page 149 as children follow along. Remind them that good readers use end punctuation, such as question marks, to guide their intonation. Help children read the page chorally with appropriate intonation.

Reflect on Reading Have children use a finger to track the words from left to right as they read each page silently. Then have them read the page chorally. Pause for these prompts:

- **Page 150:** *Where is Bob's bag? (under Dot)*
- **Page 152:** *Who or what is on top of Sal's fin? (Dot)*
- **Page 153:** *Where do you think Bob, Sal, and Dad are going? (Possible responses: fishing; swimming) What details in the pictures and words make you think this? (Possible response: Dad is holding fishing poles and tackle boxes; Sal is looking for her fins and she is wearing goggles and a life jacket.)*
- **Pages 154:** *What is Pop looking for? Where does he find it? (his hat; under Dot)*

Characters Read aloud the directions on page 155. Have children choose a character and tell a partner three things they know about that character.

Sal! I see your fin.
Dot is on top of it!
Nab it, Sal.

152

Dad has big tan mats.
Dad has rods and maps.
Dad has kits, too.

153

Pop wants his big tan hat.
Did Dot see it?
Dot is on it!

154

READ TOGETHER

Characters

Look at the pictures.
Choose a character.

Bob   Dad   Dot

Sal   Pop

Tell a partner three things you
learned about the character
from the stories.

155

Make Minutes Count

As you meet with small groups to read *Dot Is on It!*, use one or more of these related
activities, as needed, at the beginning or the end of the small-group session.

- **Connect to Phonics** Play Letter Swap. Gather multiple Letter Cards for *a, e, g, h, i,
  l, o,* and *s.* Have children take turns using the Letter Cards to build words with the
  short *a, i,* or *o* vowel sounds. One child puts down 2–3 cards to build a word. The
  next child blends and reads the word, then swaps the vowel to make a new word
  for the next child to blend and read. When all vowels are used or no new word may
  be formed with a different vowel, the next child makes a new word and restarts the
  process.

- **Connect to Spelling** Write these words on the board: *an, at, bat, can, cap, pan.*
  Have children copy the words onto the blank cards on Printable: Word List 5. Then
  have children sort those words, as well as the basic and review Spelling Words, by
  vowel sounds. Have them write their sorts. If time permits, have children sort the
  cards again, this time by final consonant sounds.

- **Connect to High-Frequency Words** Play Card Flip. Spread out the
  High-Frequency Word cards from Printable:
  Word List 5 face up on the tabletop. Say a sentence that contains one of the
  High-Frequency Words. Call on a child to find the correct High-Frequency Word
  and flip over the card. Continue until all the cards are flipped over.

High-Frequency Words	Decodable High-Frequency Words	Spelling Words	
		Basic	Review
do	got	log	big
live	had	not	sit
of	has	top	pig
our	him	hot	dig
wants	his	hop	
what	not	on	
with			
your			
			Challenge
			shop
			block

Printable: Word List 5

Options for Independent and Collaborative Work

While you meet with small groups, have other children engage in literacy activities that reinforce the lesson's learning objectives. Choose from these options.

Independent Reading

Student Choice Library

Rigby
LEVELED LIBRARY

APPLY READING SKILL

Text Features Children complete Printable: **Reading Graphic Organizer 19** for an independent reading book.

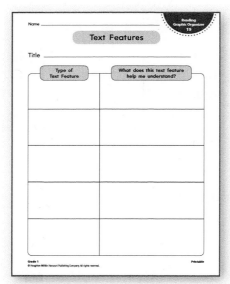

Printable: Reading Graphic Organizer 19

APPLY LANGUAGE SKILL

Compare and Contrast Children complete Printable: **Language Graphic Organizer 5** for an independent reading book.

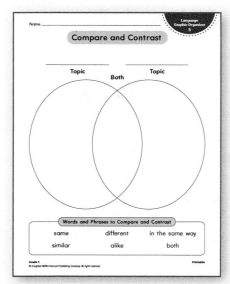

Printable: Language Graphic Organizer 5

Literacy Centers

See pp. T346–T347.

 WORD WORK

 CREATIVITY CORNER

 DIGITAL STATION

 READING CORNER

 TEAMWORK TIME

Start Right Reader

Bob can not find his bag.
Did Sal see it?
Sal did not.

Read Decodable Text *Dot Is on It!*, Book 1: pp. 148–155

Writing

Children respond to the prompt by writing the steps in order. *See Engage & Respond, p. T385.*

Close Reading

myBook, Book 1, pp. 130–133

Additional Skills Practice

SPELLING AND VOCABULARY

Know It, Show It, p. 47

Know It, Show It, p. 48

Wrap-Up
Share Time

At the end of Reading Workshop, have children reflect on their learning by sharing how they applied **Text Features** or another area of focus during independent work time. Choose from these options:

- **SHARE CHAIR** Select a reader each day to come to the front of the class and tell what he or she learned from the reading by using a skill or strategy.

- **THINK-PAIR-SHARE** Children share their thinking with a partner. Select a few each day to share with the whole class.

- **RETURN TO ANCHOR CHART** Have children add sticky notes about their independent reading book to the Text Features Anchor Chart. Call on a few children to explain what they added.

Online

ANCHOR CHART 22: Text Features

LESSON 9

FOUNDATIONAL SKILLS

LEARNING OBJECTIVES

- Identify and read high-frequency words.
- **Language** Recognize, recite, and spell basic sight vocabulary.
- Recognize spoken alliteration.
- Isolate initial and final phonemes in spoken one-syllable words.
- Segment spoken one-syllable words into individual phonemes.

MATERIALS   Online

Word Cards *do, got, had, has, him, his, live, not, of, our, wants, what, with, your*

Picture Cards *bag, bat, boat, book, gate, goat, hat, hook, lock, log*

Printable *Letter Cards*

 # High-Frequency Words

Review the Words

Repeat the **HIGH-FREQUENCY WORDS** routine to review this week's High-Frequency Words: *do, live, of, our, wants, what, with,* and *your,* and the decodable High-Frequency Words *got, had, has, him, his,* and *not.*

Letter Buddies

- Organize children into small groups. Give each group letter cards from Printable: <u>Letter Cards</u> for one of the week's words, one letter card per child.
- Each child takes one letter card from the group set. Children then look for their "letter buddies," group members with letters that will help them spell one of the words. Guide children as needed.
- When all children have found their letter buddies, ask them to stand with their group and display their letters in order. Have the class spell and say each word.

 # Phonological Awareness

Alliteration; Isolate Phonemes

- Tell children you will say sets of words. They should give a "thumbs up" if the first sound in all the words is the same. Model: *Listen:* two tiny toads. *Thumbs up! I hear /t/ at the beginning of all three words.* Continue with these: red rooster, yellow lemon, large round rock, busy bike builder, seven super suns.
- Have children sort the Picture Cards by beginning sound. Say: *The first card is* book. *What is the beginning sound? (/b/)* Call on children to choose a card, say the beginning sound, and tell whether or not the card goes with *book.* When the sort is complete, have the class say all the picture names that begin with the same sound and say the sound. Repeat the activity for final sounds.

Segment Phonemes

- Tell children that they will break words into individual sounds. Model: *Listen:* up. *I hear /ŭ/ at the beginning of up.* Up. /ŭ/ /p/. *The sounds in up are /ŭ/ and /p/.*
- *Now you try it! Listen and say each sound:* go (/g/ /ō/), hay (/h/ /ā/), us (/ŭ/ /s/), kick (/k/ /ĭ/ /k/), hide (/h/ /ī/ /d/), team (/t/ /ē/ /m/), sock (/s/ /ŏ/ /k/).

TEACHER TIP

Model it! Before beginning the Letter Buddies activity, invite one group to come to the front of the room. Guide them through a sample round of the game so the rest of the class can see how it is played.

 ### CORRECT & REDIRECT

If children have difficulty identifying alliteration, walk them through the process and provide additional supports. Example:

- *These are the words:* red rooster. *Let's say each word and then say the beginning sound in each word.* Red, /r/; rooster, /r/.
- *Are the beginning sounds the same or different? (**the same**)*
- *Let's try another set:* yellow lemon. *Repeat after me:* yellow lemon. *What sound do you hear at the beginning of yellow? (/y/)* Lemon? (/l/)
- *Are the beginning sounds the same or different? (**different**)*

Phonics Review

I Do It

Spotlight on Letters Use the **SOUND-BY-SOUND BLENDING** routine to review this week's phonic elements: short vowels *a, i, o,* and consonants *l, h.* Model blending *hop* with Letter Cards (or display the written word). Say the first two sounds separately, then together; then say the last sound and add it to the blended sounds. Repeat for *lid, had.*

We Do It

Blend and Read Project Display and Engage: **Blend and Read 2.7** or use Start Right Reader page 156.

DISPLAY AND ENGAGE:
Blend and Read 2.7

Online Ed

Blend and Read 2.7

Blend and Read

❶	hit	lot	lit	got	pot
❷	hot	hat	lap	not	hop
❸	bat	big	sit	bag	kit
❹	fog	frog	hop	shop	

❺ Bob, is the pot hot?
❻ Dot naps on the hat.

Grade 1 | Foundational Skills   Module 2 • Week 2

1. **Line 1** Have children read the line. Then prompt a conversation about the words. Ask: *Which words have the same vowel sounds? How are those words different?* Reread the line chorally.

2. **Line 2** Continue. Then have volunteers reread selected words until they can identify them quickly.

3. **Review** Display Line 3, and have children read it chorally.

4. **Challenge** Children who are ready for a challenge can read Line 4, tell how the words in columns 2 and 4 differ from the words in columns 1 and 3, and demonstrate how they blended the words with four letters.

5. **Sentences** Display Lines 5–6. Call on children to blend selected decodable words. Point to each word as children read the sentences chorally.

You Do It

INDEPENDENT PRACTICE

- **Option 1** Dictate sentences for children to write: *The big hat is on Bob. Dot is not hot.* Have them check their spelling using the Blend and Read lines.

- **Option 2** Have children complete Know It, Show It page 50.

LEARNING OBJECTIVES

- Blend, decode, and build regularly spelled one-syllable words with short vowels *a, i, o* and consonants *l, h.*

MATERIALS Online Ed

Letter Cards *a, d, h, i, l, o, p,*
Display and Engage *Blend and Read 2.7*
Start Right Reader Book 1, p. 156
Know It, Show It p. 50

 ENGLISH LEARNER SUPPORT:
Build Vocabulary

ALL LEVELS Ensure that children know the meanings of the Blend and Read words. Then pair beginning English learners with more proficient speaking partners. Have partners work together to illustrate several words, label the drawings, and then use the words in oral sentences.

LINK TO SMALL-GROUP INSTRUCTION

REINFORCE FOUNDATIONAL SKILLS Use *Hop on It, Dot!* during small-group time to review or reinforce blending and decoding words with short vowels *a, i, o* and consonants *l, h.* Meet with children to work through the story, or assign it as independent work. *See the lesson on p. T400.*

Hop on It, Dot!
by Jordan Moore

Sal has a big pot.
Sal wants Dot to hop on it.
"Hop, Dot! Hop!" said Sal.

Words About Places and Things

 I Do It

- Project Display and Engage: **Generative Vocabulary 2.8**. Read aloud the first section to discuss the two categories of **nouns**: words that name places and words that name things.

- Discuss the familiar nouns from *On the Map!*, *town* and *map*, using the images as support.

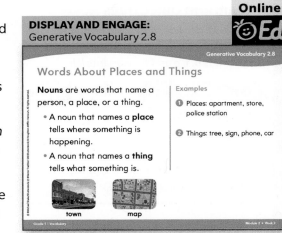

DISPLAY AND ENGAGE:
Generative Vocabulary 2.8

Online

Generative Vocabulary 2.8

Words About Places and Things

Nouns are words that name a person, a place, or a thing.

- A noun that names a **place** tells where something is happening.
- A noun that names a **thing** tells what something is.

Examples

1. Places: apartment, store, police station
2. Things: tree, sign, phone, car

town   map

- Then model determining each type of noun. *Town is a noun that names a place. Many people live in a town. Map is a noun that names a thing. A map shows you the different places and streets in a town.*

- Continue in the same way with Examples 1 and 2. Discuss how each word names a place or a thing. Tell children that if they do not know the meaning of one of these words, they can look it up in a dictionary. Model using a dictionary to find the meaning of an unfamiliar word.

LEARNING OBJECTIVES

- Understand and use common nouns that name places and things.
- **Language** Identify words that name places and things.
- Use a dictionary to find the meaning of unknown words.

MATERIALS   Online 📙 *Ed*

Display and Engage *Generative Vocabulary 2.8*

Know It, Show It *p. 51*

 READER'S VOCABULARY

- **noun** a word that names a person, place, or thing

 LEARNING MINDSET

Belonging

Apply Remind children that helping people in a community can make them feel like they belong. Explain that everyone needs some help at different times. *A school is a community where you can always ask for help. For example, when you are reading, if you come to a word that you don't know, ask someone in your school community—one of your classmates or a teacher. They will be happy that you asked for their help. That is one of the things that make a community special—helping each other.*

We Do It

Lead children to generate lists of other nouns that name places and things. Prompt them with questions such as these: *Where are some places you might go to learn? (school, library) What are some things you use to play? (bat, kite)*

- Remind children that if they do not know the meaning of one of these words, they can look up the word in a dictionary. Ask a volunteer to demonstrate how to look up a word in a picture dictionary.

- Then do the reverse. Name common places and things, and prompt children to name whether the noun is a place or a thing.

You Do It

INDEPENDENT PRACTICE

- **Option 1** Have children draw a picture to show the meaning of a word that names a place or a word that names a thing. Have partners exchange pictures and guess which kind of noun the pictures show. Then have children label their picture with the noun. Have children use a dictionary for support, as needed.

- **Option 2** Have children complete Know It, Show It page 51.

 ENGLISH LEARNER SUPPORT:
Elicit Participation

SUBSTANTIAL
For each noun, ask *yes/no* questions such as: *Can you go to a bat? Can you go to a school?*

MODERATE
Supply these frames: *What happens at a school? What do you do with a bat?*

LIGHT
Ask children to use nouns about places or things to describe experiences they have had, for example: *I went to school. I read a book there.*

READING WORKSHOP

 Make Connections

Step 1 Connect and Teach

LEARNING OBJECTIVES

- Identify the features of informational text.
- Make connections to personal experiences, other texts, and society.
- **Language** Compare information in two texts.
- State ideas clearly and loudly enough for others to hear.

MATERIALS   Online

Anchor Chart 7
Make Connections

Printable *Anchor Chart 7: Make Connections*

Teaching Pal *Book 1, pp. 134–145*

myBook *Places in My Neighborhood, Book 1, pp. 134–145*

READER'S VOCABULARY

- **connection** how things are linked or related in a way to help you remember them
- **experience** something that has happened to you

- Remind children that when they read, they should "stay awake" and think about what they are reading. One way to think about reading is to make **connections**.

- Project or display <u>Anchor Chart 7: Make Connections</u>. Explain to children that when you make connections, you find ways that a text is like and unlike things in your life. Point out that looking for things you can connect with in a text makes the reading more meaningful and memorable, and helps you learn more about the topic.

ANCHOR CHART 7:
Make Connections

Online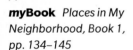

> **Make Connections**
>
> When you read, find ways that the text is like things in your own life and other texts you have read.
>
> **It all starts here!**
>
> **Text to Self**
> This reminds me of when I...
>
> **Text to Text**
> This is like another book I read...
>
> **Text to World**
> This is like something that happened in my community...

- Review the three types of connections on the Anchor Chart. Explain that in text-to-self connections, readers decide how a text is like or unlike their own life **experiences**.

- Explain that in text-to-text connections, readers decide how a text is like or unlike another text they have read.

- Finally, explain that in text-to-world connections, readers decide how a text is like or unlike something happening in their community.

- Tell children they will practice making connections when they read the informational text called *Places in My Neighborhood*.

Notice & Note

Big Questions

- The Teaching Pal prompts in this lesson feature the **Notice & Note Big Questions** for nonfiction.

- As needed, refer to p. T263 to review the Big Questions with children.

✓ ASSESSMENT OPTION

Assign the <u>Selection Quiz</u> to check comprehension of *Places in My Neighborhood*.

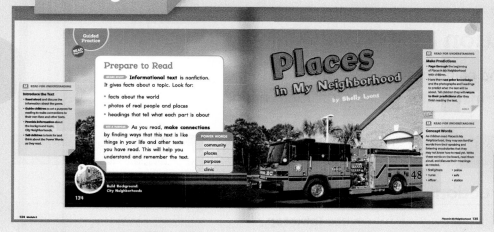

ANNOTATE IT!

Online
Ed

Children may use the annotation tools in their eBook.

Step 2 Apply to Text

In your Teaching Pal, pages 134–145, use the blue **READ FOR UNDERSTANDING** prompts to read *Places in My Neighborhood* with children as they follow along and annotate in their *my*Book.

- **Genre Study** Read the genre information on page 134. Discuss the kinds of things children would expect to find in an informational text and compare them with what they might find in a realistic fiction story.

- **Set a Purpose** Read the Set a Purpose section on page 134. Prompt children to set their own purpose for reading *Places in My Neighborhood*.

- **Build Background** Play the audio for **City Neighborhoods**. Guide children to connect informational text features to the information about city neighborhoods.

- **Read and Comprehend** Guide children to read the story all the way through. Pause occasionally, using the prompts in your Teaching Pal to gauge children's understanding and to have them make their own connections. As you discuss each connection, have children refer back to the Anchor Chart and tell what kind of connection it is.

Step 3 Engage and Respond

INDEPENDENT PRACTICE: Speaking & Listening

- Use the **TURN AND TALK** routine with the questions on Teaching Pal and *my*Book page 145. Remind children to look back at the words and pictures in both selections to make connections and find evidence.

- Read the Talking Tip. Tell children to use the sentence frame to tell their ideas. Remind them to speak clearly and loudly enough for others to hear them as they share their ideas.

- You may want to have children conduct their discussions during daily small-group time.

ENGLISH LEARNER SUPPORT:
Facilitate Discussion

Use the following supports for the Turn and Talk questions:

SUBSTANTIAL
Point to the photos and ask questions such as: *This neighborhood has (buildings). Do the photos in* On the Map! *have (buildings)?*

MODERATE
Supply frames such as these: *These neighborhoods are alike because _____. Both neighborhoods have _____.*

LIGHT
Have partners tell how neighborhoods are alike *and* different.

LINK TO SMALL-GROUP INSTRUCTION

REINFORCE MAKE CONNECTIONS Review or extend the skill as needed during small-group time to support children's need for differentiation. *See the lesson on p. T399.*

READING WORKSHOP

Options for Differentiation

As the class engages in independent and collaborative work, meet with Guided Reading Groups or differentiate instruction based on student need.

GUIDED READING GROUPS

Match Children to Books + Instruction

- Choose just-right books based on level, skill, topic, or genre.

C D E F G H I J K

Leveled Readers

- Deliver instruction with each book's Take and Teach Lesson, choosing appropriate sessions based on need.

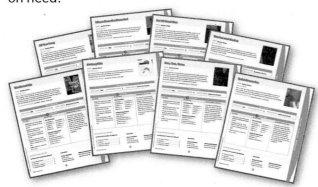

- Check comprehension, reinforce instruction, and extend learning with suggested supporting activities.

Rigby®
LEVELED LIBRARY

ENGLISH LEARNER SUPPORT

Compare and Contrast

- Use **Tabletop Minilessons: English Language Development 5.2 (Writing)** to reinforce and practice the language skill.

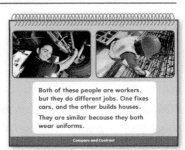

Both of these people are workers, but they do different jobs. One fixes cars, and the other builds houses. They are similar because they both wear uniforms.

Compare and Contrast

Tabletop Minilessons: English Language Development

- Then use the following text-based prompts with *Places in My Neighborhood* to guide application of the language skill. Begin with the prompt at the child's identified language proficiency level. As children are able, use lighter supports to encourage increased language proficiency.

SUBSTANTIAL
Focus on pages 142–143. Ask: *What do people get at the library? What do people get at a grocery store?* Allow children to respond using single words or short phrases.

MODERATE
Focus on pages 142–143. Have children compare and contrast the library and grocery store. Supply these frames: *At the library and at the grocery store, people _____. People get _____ at the library, but _____ at the grocery store.*

LIGHT
Ask children to compare and contrast the library and the grocery store. Ask: *How are these two places the same? How are they different?*

REINFORCE MAKE CONNECTIONS

Demonstrate

- Use **Tabletop Minilessons: Reading 7** to remind children that good readers make **connections** between a text and their own lives. This means that they find ways that the text is similar to or different from their own **experiences** and society. Good readers also make connections between the text they are reading and other texts they have read. Making connections helps readers understand and remember the text and makes reading it more meaningful.

- Model filling out Printable: **Reading Graphic Organizer 8** to help children make connections with *Places in My Neighborhood*.

Tabletop Minilessons: Reading

Apply to Independent Reading

- Now have children make connections between an appropriate just-right book that they are reading independently and their own lives, society, and other texts. Customize these prompts to the books children choose.

  » *Does something in this book remind you about a time when you _____? Tell how.*

  » *Is something in this book like something in your community? What?*

  » *How is this book similar to or different from another book you have read?*

- Have children complete Printable: **Reading Graphic Organizer 8** for their independent reading book.

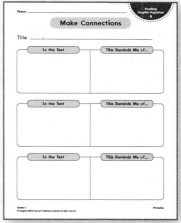

Printable:
Reading Graphic Organizer 8

ALMOST THERE

↓

READY FOR MORE

SCAFFOLD AND EXTEND

- Have children only make connections between things in the pictures and society, their own lives, and other books they have read.

- Have children focus their attention on making one type of connection before moving on to the others.

- Have children tell how the connections they made helped them understand the ideas in the text better.

(EL) ENGLISH LEARNER SUPPORT

SUBSTANTIAL
Model making a connection using this frame: *This reminds me of _____.*

MODERATE
Encourage children to make connections using this frame:
This reminds me of _____ because _____.

LIGHT
As children make connections, encourage them to use words such as *connection, same, similar, different, compare, contrast,* and *but.*

Options for Differentiation

Hop on It, Dot!, Start Right Reader, *Book 1,* pp. 156–163

REINFORCE FOUNDATIONAL SKILLS

Read Decodable Text

Blend and Read Have children turn to Start Right Reader page 156. Use the **CHORAL READING** routine to read aloud the Blend and Read lines. Use challenge line 4 with children who are ready.

Preview the Story Read aloud the title on page 157. Ask: *Who is Dot? (Bob and Sal's cat)* Then have children look at the pictures on the first few pages and predict what will happen in this story.

Fluency Focus: Intonation Read aloud page 157 as children follow along. Point out how you changed the pitch of your voice to reflect the end punctuation. Then have children read the selection, focusing on using appropriate intonation.

Reflect on Reading Have children read to find out what will happen between Dot, Bob, and Sal. Have them read each page silently and then chorally. Pause for these prompts:

- **Pages 157–158:** *What is Sal's problem? (Sal wants Dot to hop on the pot, but Sal will not.) According to Bob, how is Dot different than a dog? (Dogs can hop, but Dot cannot hop.)*

- **Page 160:** *According to Sal, how is Dot like a dog? (Dogs can sit, and so can Dot.)*

- **Pages 161–162:** *Does Dot hop where Sal wants her to hop? (no) Where does Dot hop? (onto Sal's lap)*

Think-Draw-Pair-Share Allow time for children to reread the week's four Start Right Reader stories. Then use the **THINK-DRAW-PAIR-SHARE** routine to guide children in drawing the answers to the questions on page 163. Have them share their work with a partner and then with the group.

Dot sat.
"Dot can sit!" said Sal.
"Our cat is like a dog!"

160

"Hop on it, Dot," said Sal.
"Dot can do it, Bob!"
Dot did not hop. Dot sat.

161

Sal is sad.
Dot hops up.
Dot can hop in a lap!

162

READ TOGETHER

Think-Draw-Pair-Share
Reread and think about the stories. Then draw to answer these questions.

1. What is one thing Bob does that is fun?

2. What would **you** like to do with Bob? Why?

Share your work with a partner and then with a group.

163

Make Minutes Count

As you meet with small groups to read *Hop on It, Dot!*, use one or more of these related activities, as needed, at the beginning or the end of the small-group session.

- **Connect to Phonics Play** Have children go on a word hunt in *Hop on It, Dot!* Choose a few pages for them to reread. Have them hunt for words with the short *a*, *i*, and *o* vowel sounds and write the words they find.

- **Connect to Spelling** Say a Spelling Word to a child. If the child correctly spells the word, he or she scores one point. Repeat with a different Spelling Word and child and continue until every word has been correctly spelled.

- **Connect to High-Frequency Words** Play Ask and Answer. Place the High-Frequency Word cards from Printable: **Word List 5** face down in a pile. Call on a child to take the top card and read aloud the word, without showing group members the card. Then have that child ask the group a question that contains that word. Call on another child to answer the question using the same High-Frequency Word and then spelling the word. Continue until each child has had a turn to ask and answer a question.

Name _____

Word List 5

High-Frequency Words	Decodable High-Frequency Words	Spelling Words	
		Basic	Review
do	got	log	big
live	had	not	sit
of	has	top	pig
our	him	hot	dig
wants	his	hop	
what	not	on	
with			
your			
			Challenge
			shop
			block

Grade 1
© Houghton Mifflin Harcourt Publishing Company. All rights reserved.
Printable

Printable: Word List 5

Options for Independent and Collaborative Work

While you meet with small groups, have other children engage in literacy activities that reinforce the lesson's learning objectives. Choose from these options.

Independent Reading

Student Choice Library

Rigby LEVELED LIBRARY

APPLY READING SKILL

Make Connections Children complete Printable: **Reading Graphic Organizer 8** for an independent reading book.

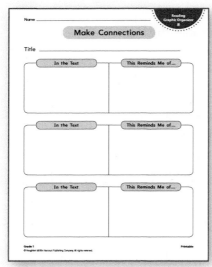

Printable: Reading Graphic Organizer 8

APPLY LANGUAGE SKILL

Compare and Contrast Children complete Printable: **Language Graphic Organizer 5** for an independent reading book.

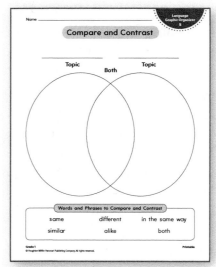

Printable: Language Graphic Organizer 5

Notice & Note

Big Questions

Encourage children to ask the Big Questions for nonfiction: *What surprised me? What did the author think I already knew? What challenged, changed, or confirmed what I already knew?*

Literacy Centers

See pp. T346–T347.

 WORD WORK

 CREATIVITY CORNER

 DIGITAL STATION

 READING CORNER

 TEAMWORK TIME

Start Right Reader

Read Decodable Text *Hop on It, Dot!,* Book 1: pp. 156–163

Speaking & Listening

Partners discuss the Turn and Talk questions to make connections.
See Engage & Respond, p. T397.

Additional Skills Practice

PHONICS

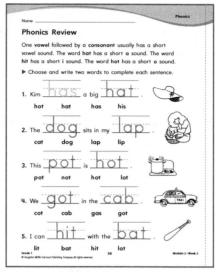

Know It, Show It, p. 50

GENERATIVE VOCABULARY

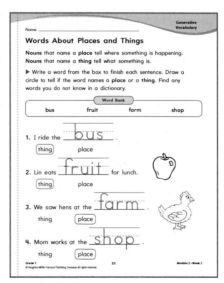

Know It, Show It, p. 51

Wrap-Up

Share Time

At the end of Reading Workshop, have children reflect on their learning by sharing how they applied **Make Connections** or another area of focus during independent work time. Choose from these options:

- **SHARE CHAIR** Select a reader each day to come to the front of the class and tell what he or she learned from the reading by using a skill or strategy.

- **THINK-PAIR-SHARE** Children share their thinking with a partner. Select a few each day to share with the whole class.

- **RETURN TO ANCHOR CHART** Have children add sticky notes about their independent reading book to the Make Connections Anchor Chart. Call on a few children to explain what they added.

ANCHOR CHART 7: Make Connections — Online **Ed**

High-Frequency Words

Children's Choice

- Remind children of the High-Frequency Words they have been practicing this week: *do, live, of, our, wants, what, with,* and *your,* and the decodable High-Frequency Words *got, had, has, him, his,* and *not.*

- Review any words that posed difficulty for children, using Word Cards and the **HIGH-FREQUENCY WORDS** routine.

- In Lessons 7–9, children used these practice activities: Around the World (p. T364), Picture Card Challenge (p. T378), and Letter Buddies (p. T392). Have children vote on their favorite, and use it to review the week's words for word recognition fluency.

> [!NOTE]
> not

Phonological Awareness

Teacher's Choice

- In Lessons 6–9, children practiced blending phonemes (pp. T349, T365). They also practiced identifying alliteration, isolating phonemes, and segmenting phonemes (pp. T378, T392).

- Use the following to gauge the need for phoneme isolation reinforcement.

  » **Isolate Phonemes** Ask children to identify the beginning sound in these words: keep (/k/), line (/l/). Then ask them to identify the ending sound in these words: made (/d/), hop (/p/).

- Use Printable: **Phonological Awareness 5** to gauge which other tasks need reinforcement.

  » **Blend Phonemes** Have children blend the sounds to say each word: /w/ /ĕ/ /b/ (web), /h/ /ă/ /t/ (hat).

  » **Alliteration** Use these word sets to check children's ability to recognize alliteration: bell, bed, boat; kite, gate, key. Ask whether any words in the second set begin with the same sound. *(kite, key)*

  » **Segment Phonemes** Have children segment these words into phonemes and say how many sounds are in each word. sale (/s/ /ā/ /l/, 3); pie (/p/ /ī/, 2)

LEARNING OBJECTIVES

- Identify and read high-frequency words.
- **Language** Recognize, recite, and spell basic sight vocabulary.
- **Language** Compose oral sentences using basic sight vocabulary.
- Blend phonemes to say one-syllable words.
- Recognize spoken alliteration.
- Isolate initial and final phonemes in spoken one-syllable words.
- Segment spoken one-syllable words into individual phonemes.

MATERIALS   Online 🍎Ed

Word Cards *do, got, had, has, him, his, live, not, of, our, wants, what, with, your*
Printables *Letter Cards; Phonological Awareness 5; Word List 5*

EL ENGLISH LEARNER SUPPORT: Build Vocabulary

SUBSTANTIAL
Help children use *him* and *his* correctly. Pass a book to a boy and say, *I give the book to him.* Point to the book. *The book is his.* Have children repeat and practice with other sentences.

MODERATE
Have children complete sentence frames using *him* or *his.*
Example: _____ *hair is brown. (His)* Give the ball to _____. *(him)*

LIGHT
Ask children to share complete sentences using *him* and *his.*

✓ CORRECT & REDIRECT

If children have difficulty distinguishing between High-Frequency Words that begin with the same letter, explain how to look for spelling differences in the words. Use Word Cards for *had* and *has.*

- Say: *Both words begin with* h-a, *but the last letters are different.*
- *Let's read* had. *Read it after me:* had. *How do we spell* had? *(h-a-d)* Had *begins with* h-a *and ends with* d.
- *Let's read* has. *How do we spell* has? *(h-a-s)* Has *ends with* s.
- *Let's read and spell both words once more.* Had, h-a-d. Has, h-a-s Discuss when to use *has* and *had* in speaking and writing.

Short o

Spelling Assessment

LEARNING OBJECTIVE

• Spell words with short *o* (closed syllables).

DICTATION SENTENCES

BASIC

1. **log** Mom put a *log* on the fire.
2. **not** Stop at the sign, and do *not* go.
3. **top** Put a cherry on *top* of the cake.
4. **hot** The stove is *hot*.
5. **hop** A rabbit can *hop* away.
6. **on** I stood *on* a ladder.

REVIEW

7. **big** An elephant is very *big*.
8. **sit** Please *sit* in the chair.
9. **pig** A *pig* is a farm animal.
10. **dig** Use a shovel to *dig* a hole.

CHALLENGE

11. **shop** We bought milk in the *shop*.
12. **block** He built a *block* tower.

1. Say each Spelling Word, and read the Dictation Sentence. Repeat the word and then have children write it. Remind them to use their best handwriting.

2. Add the Surprise Words *dog*, *lot*, and *mop*. If you prefer a shorter test, replace three of the Basic Words with the Surprise Words.

   • **dog** My *dog* barks often.

   • **lot** We read a *lot* of books.

   • **mop** He will *mop* the floor.

3. Include the Challenge Words for children who practiced them this week.

4. Review any words that children misspell. If they miss two or more words, then revisit the Lesson 6 Word Sort activity on page T353.

1. log
2. not
3. top
4. hot
5.
6.
7.
8.
9.
10.

VOCABULARY

LEARNING OBJECTIVES

- **Language** Respond to questions using multi-word responses.
- Use newly acquired vocabulary to identify real-life connections between words and their use.
- Identify and use words that name locations.

MATERIALS   Online

Know It, Show It *p. 52*

 # Review Power Words

Revisit the Power Words

- Revisit the Power Words from *Places in My Neighborhood*. Display the questions and sentence frames below word by word.
- Model the task for the first word, using a child as your partner. Read aloud the question, and have the child repeat it. Respond using the sentence frame.
- Have partners use the **TURN AND TALK** routine to respond to each question using the sentence frame.
- For each word, ask one or two children to share their responses with the class. Then have them discuss the next question.

Power Word	Question	Sentence Frame
community	Who are some of the people in a **community**?	*The people in a **community** are _____.*
places	What are some **places** you like to visit?	*Some **places** I like to visit are _____.*
purpose	What is the **purpose** of learning new words?	*The **purpose** of learning new words is _____.*
clinic	Why do people go to a **clinic**?	*People go to a **clinic** because _____.*

TEACHER TIP

People in places! Children might associate certain people with certain places. For instance, schools have teachers and students, while clinics have doctors and patients. Play a game where one child names a place in the community and the rest of the class names the people you might find there.

● *Getting Started*

ENGAGEMENT ROUTINE

Use **TURN AND TALK** routine when

- the topic is of high interest.
- there are quick and easy answers.
- you want a quick practice of a skill.

See the **GPS guide** to learn more.

Vocabulary Sentences

- Read aloud the following sentence frames:

  1 *People in our* **community** *help each other by _____.*

  2 *My favorite* **places** *to visit are _____.*

  3 *The* **purpose** *of having a phone is _____.*

  4 *You should go to a* **clinic** *if _____.*

- After you read aloud each sentence, have children use the **THINK-PAIR-SHARE** routine to discuss. Call on pairs to share their answers. Use positive feedback to reinforce correct usages of words.

- For additional practice with the Power Words from *Places in My Neighborhood,* have children complete Know It, Show It page 52.

ENGLISH LEARNER SUPPORT:
Facilitate Discussion

SUBSTANTIAL
Ask *yes/no* questions: *Are there teachers in a* **community**? *Is a* **clinic** *for sick people?*

MODERATE
Repeat sentence frames as needed. Prompt responses with questions. *What do people do in a* **community**? *What do people do at a* **clinic**?

LIGHT
Ask: *Who are the people in our* **community**? *What places can you visit? Who works at a* **clinic**?

READING WORKSHOP

⏱ Content-Area Words

Step **1** Connect and Teach

LEARNING OBJECTIVES

• Use context clues to clarify word meanings.

• **Language** Ask and answer questions about unknown words, using context clues.

• Write a description, using sensory details and evidence from the text.

MATERIALS   Online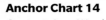

Anchor Chart 14
Content-Area Words

Printable *Anchor Chart 14: Content-Area Words*

Teaching Pal *Book 1, pp. 134–147*

myBook *Places in My Neighborhood, Book 1, pp. 134–147*

Know It, Show It *p. 53*

📖 READER'S VOCABULARY

• **context clue** the words and sentences around an unknown word that can be clues to its meaning

• Project or display the **Anchor Chart 14: Content-Area Words**.

• Remind children that they have read and listened to informational texts that tell about science or social studies topics.

• Explain that these kinds of informational texts have special vocabulary about science or social studies topics. Tell children that they can use **context clues** to figure out the meaning of these words.

• Read and explain each type of context clue on the Anchor Chart. Words and sentences around the unknown word can be clues to their meaning. Point out that text features such as titles, headings, pictures, or photographs can also be clues to a word's meaning.

• Explain that when children come to a word they don't know, they should ask themselves questions about the word, and look for context clues that can help them answer those questions and figure out the word's meaning.

• Tell children they will reread parts of *Places in My Neighborhood* to practice figuring out the meaning of unknown content-area words.

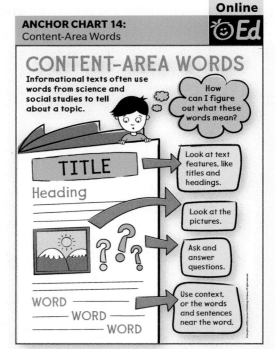

ANCHOR CHART 14:
Content-Area Words   Online

CONTENT-AREA WORDS
Informational texts often use words from science and social studies to tell about a topic.

How can I figure out what these words mean?

TITLE
Heading

WORD
— WORD —
WORD

Look at text features, like titles and headings.

Look at the pictures.

Ask and answer questions.

Use context, or the words and sentences near the word.

⚙ LEARNING MINDSET

Belonging

Apply *When people belong to a community, they go to places to do things like get food, get help staying healthy, or get information. Where do children go to get help, food, or information in* Places in My Neighborhood? *Have children look for examples, such as the doctor's office, the fire station, the police station, or the library. Then have children name places in their own community where they go for help, information, food, or to stay healthy.*

● *Professional Learning*

RESEARCH FOUNDATIONS

"Writing about material read enhances comprehension."

–Dr. Steve Graham and Dr. Michael Hebert (2011)

See the **GPS guide** to learn more.

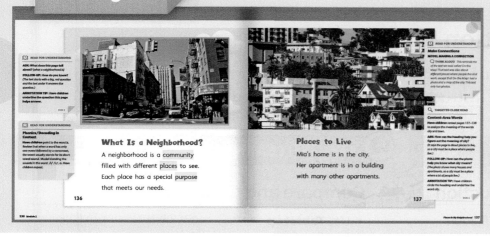

ANNOTATE IT!

Online
Ed

Children may use the annotation tools in their eBook.

Step 2 — Apply to Text

 In your Teaching Pal, use the purple **TARGETED CLOSE READ** prompts to guide children to apply the content-area words skill to *Places in My Neighborhood*. Children may refer to the questions on Know It, Show It page 53 as you discuss them.

- Read aloud the questions on Teaching Pal page 137 and have children answer them, using evidence from the text and pictures. *(Both tell about places to live.)*

- Read aloud the first question on Teaching Pal page 140. Have children generate questions that can help them figure out the meaning of *officer*. *(Sample response: What clues can I use to help me?)*

- Then read aloud the follow-up question. Prompt children to use details from the text and photos to answer their questions about unknown content-area words. *(Sample response: The text says that Devon is at the police station; the photo shows him with a policewoman.)*

- Refer back to the Anchor Chart to support the discussion. Children may add sticky notes to the chart to show which kinds of clues they used while reading *Places in My Neighborhood*.

Step 3 — Engage and Respond

INDEPENDENT PRACTICE: Writing

- Read aloud the prompt on Teaching Pal page 146. Have children use the planning space to write describing words that tell what the place looks, sounds, smells, or feels like.

- Then have children write their responses to the prompt. Remind children to refer back to *Places in My Neighborhood* and use the words and photos from the selection for ideas.

- You may want to have children complete their writing during daily small-group time.

 ENGLISH LEARNER SUPPORT: Scaffold Writing

SUBSTANTIAL
Ask questions such as: *Does the city look crowded or empty? Does it sound quiet or loud? Would it smell like flowers, food, or cars?* Record answers for children to refer to as they write.

MODERATE
Supply frames: *The city looks _____. It sounds _____. It smells _____.*

LIGHT
Have partners imagine they are in the city in the photos. Ask them to talk about what they would notice with their senses.

LINK TO SMALL-GROUP INSTRUCTION

REINFORCE CONTENT-AREA WORDS Review or extend the skill as needed during small-group time to support children's need for differentiation. *See the lesson on p. T411.*

Options for Differentiation

As the class engages in independent and collaborative work, meet with Guided Reading Groups or differentiate instruction based on student need.

GUIDED READING GROUPS

Match Children to Books + Instruction

- Choose just-right books based on level, skill, topic, or genre.

C D E F G H I J K →

Leveled Readers

- Deliver instruction with each book's Take and Teach Lesson, choosing appropriate sessions based on need.

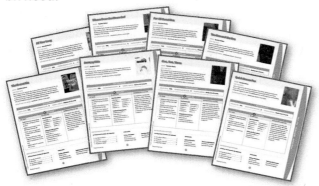

- Check comprehension, reinforce instruction, and extend learning with suggested supporting activities.

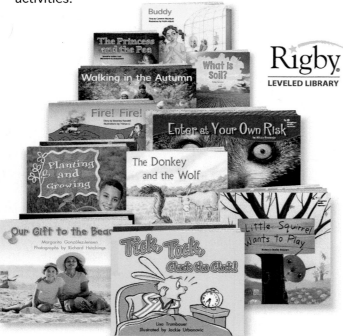

Rigby®
LEVELED LIBRARY

EL ENGLISH LEARNER SUPPORT

Compare and Contrast

- Use **Tabletop Minilessons: English Language Development 5.3 (Collaborative Problem Solving)** to reinforce and practice the language skill.

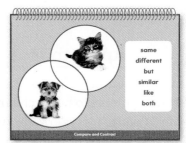

Tabletop Minilessons: English Language Development

- Then use the following text-based prompts with *Places in My Neighborhood* to guide application of the language skill. Begin with the prompt at the child's identified language proficiency level. As children are able, use lighter supports to encourage increased language proficiency.

SUBSTANTIAL

Focus children's attention on pages 137–138. Ask: *Where are different places you can live in a neighborhood?* Allow children to gesture to homes in the photographs or use single words to respond.

MODERATE

Focus children's attention on pages 137–138. Have children compare and contrast different places where people can live in a neighborhood. Supply these frames: *Mia lives in a(n) _____. Jack lives in a(n) _____. They are the same because _____. They are different because _____.*

LIGHT

Focus children's attention on pages 137–138. Ask: *What is different about where Mia and Jack live? What is the same about where they live?*

REINFORCE CONTENT-AREA WORDS

Demonstrate

- Use **Tabletop Minilessons: Reading 14** to remind children that some informational texts about science or social studies **topics** have special words about that topic they might not know. Readers can use different kinds of **context clues** to figure out what these words mean. Clues might be in the same sentence, in a different sentence, in pictures, or in other text features. Readers can ask themselves questions about the **vocabulary** and use the context from words and pictures to answer these questions and figure out the words' meanings.

- Model filling out Printable: **Reading Graphic Organizer 13** to identify and determine the meaning of content-area words in *Places in My Neighborhood*.

Apply to Independent Reading

- Now have children identify and discuss content-area words in an appropriate just-right book that they are reading independently. Customize these prompts to the books children choose.

  » *Is this text about science, social studies, math, or another content area?*

  » *What special words about the topic are in the text?*

  » *What clues in the text, text features, or pictures help you understand these words?*

- Have children complete Printable: **Reading Graphic Organizer 13** for their independent reading book.

Tabletop Minilessons: Reading

Printable:
Reading Graphic Organizer 13

ALMOST THERE

READY FOR MORE

SCAFFOLD AND EXTEND

- Choose content-area words, and help children ask questions about them. Guide them to identify context clues to answer the questions.

- Prompt children to use a content-area word in a question and answer it using context clues.

- Have children use a content-area word in a question. Provide a context clue so other children can answer.

ENGLISH LEARNER SUPPORT

SUBSTANTIAL

Read aloud content-area words in the text. Have children repeat the words and point to them as they say them.

MODERATE

Model finding clues that help children determine the meaning of important content-area words. Supply this frame: *I know what _____ means because _____.*

LIGHT

As children answer the prompts, have them cite specific words, text features, or pictures that support their thoughts.

Options for Differentiation

Start Right Reader, *Book 1*, pp. 132–163

REINFORCE FOUNDATIONAL SKILLS

Read Decodable Text

Review Remind children of the Start Right Reader stories they read this week about the characters Bob, Sal, Dad, Pop, Dom, and Dot.

• *Tap, Bam! Rip! Bam!*

• *A Map*

• *Dot Is on It!*

• *Hop on It, Dot!*

Allow a few minutes for children to page through the stories to recall what they are about.

Make Text Connections Prompt children to explain how the four stories are connected.

• *Which characters appear in all four stories? (Bob and Sal)*

• *What kind of person is Dad? Why do you think so? (Possible response: Dad is a fun and good father; he takes Bob to see the rig, does a map hunt with him, and takes him fishing.)*

• *What might happen to Bob and Sal in a new story about them? (Accept reasonable responses.)*

• *Which story would you recommend to a friend? Why? (Responses will vary.)*

Reread for Fluency Have partners select one of the stories to reread. Have them use the **PARTNER READING** routine and focus on reading with appropriate intonation.

Make Minutes Count

As you meet with small groups to review the week's decodable stories, use one or both of these related activities, as needed, at the beginning or the end of the small-group session.

- **Connect to Phonics** Play Cut and Connect. Assign each child a word with the short *a*, *i*, or *o* vowel sound. Have each child write his or her word onto a strip of construction paper. Then have children cut the strips to segment the words into sounds. Have partners swap their cut-up words. Partners must reconstruct the words and blend and read them aloud.

- **Connect to Handwriting** Have children write two sentences that each contain at least two High-Frequency or Spelling Words that have the letters *o* or *g*. Check children's paper position and pencil grip as they write and correct as needed.

👥 INDEPENDENT APPLICATION

Options for Independent and Collaborative Work

While you meet with small groups, have other children engage in literacy activities that reinforce the lesson's learning objectives. Choose from these options.

Independent Reading

Student Choice Library

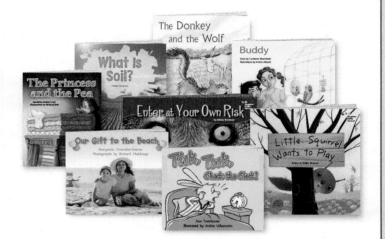

Rigby®
LEVELED LIBRARY

APPLY READING SKILL

Content-Area Words Children complete Printable: **Reading Graphic Organizer 13** for an independent reading book.

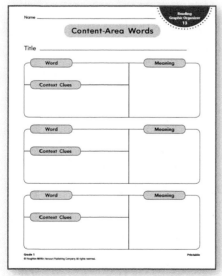

Printable: Reading Graphic Organizer 13

APPLY LANGUAGE SKILL

Compare and Contrast Children complete Printable: **Language Graphic Organizer 5** for an independent reading book.

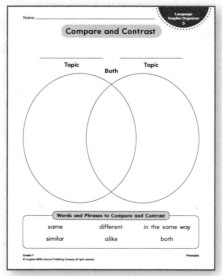

Printable: Language Graphic Organizer 5

Literacy Centers

See pp. T346–T347.

 WORD WORK

 CREATIVITY CORNER

 DIGITAL STATION

 READING CORNER

 TEAMWORK TIME

Start Right Reader

Read Decodable Text
Book 1: pp. 132–163

Writing

Children write describing words about a place from the text. *See Engage & Respond, p. T409.*

Close Reading

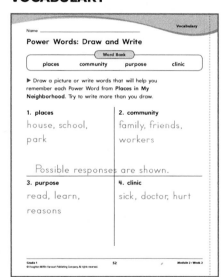

myBook, Book 1, pp. 148–151

Additional Skills Practice

VOCABULARY

Know It, Show It, p. 52

Wrap-Up
Share Time

At the end of the Reading Workshop, have children reflect on their learning by sharing how they applied **Content-Area Words** or another area of focus during independent work time. Choose from these options:

- **SHARE CHAIR** Select a reader each day to come to the front of the class and tell what he or she learned from the reading by using a skill or strategy.

- **THINK-PAIR-SHARE** Children share their thinking with a partner. Select a few each day to share with the whole class.

- **RETURN TO ANCHOR CHART** Have children add sticky notes about their independent reading book to the Content-Area Words Anchor Chart. Call on a few children to explain what they added.

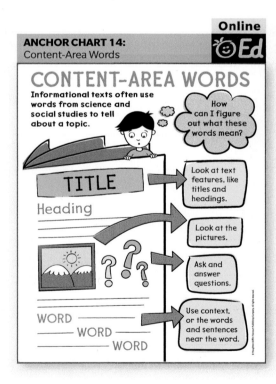

ANCHOR CHART 14:
Content-Area Words

Online

Notes

 SOCIAL STUDIES CONNECTION: Communities

My Family, My Community

 Essential Question How can making new friends and learning new things help us?

Essential Skills

FOUNDATIONAL SKILLS

- Phonics: Consonants *w, j, y, v*; Short *u*; Review Short *i, o, u*
- High-Frequency Words: *about, eat, how, make, out, put, takes, who*
- Fluency: Accuracy and Self-Correction
- Spelling: Short *u*

VOCABULARY

- Power Words: *against, churn, close, docked, drive, harbor, heal, pointing, spoon, stock, unload*
- Generative Vocabulary: Words About Actions and Directions

READING WORKSHOP

- Setting
- Ask and Answer Questions
- Text Organization
- Content-Area Words

WRITING WORKSHOP

- Writing Form: Descriptive Essay
- Grammar Minilessons: Complete Sentences

LEARNING MINDSET: Belonging

THIS WEEK'S TEXTS

Abuela

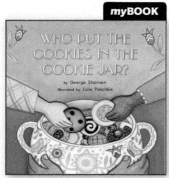

Who Put the Cookies in the Cookie Jar?

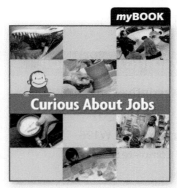

Curious About Jobs

Decodable Texts
Wags, Wags, Wags!
Yip! Yap!
Mud Pup
Bad Pup, Wags!

Rigby
LEVELED LIBRARY

T417

Suggested Daily Times

- VOCABULARY — 10–15 minutes
- FOUNDATIONAL SKILLS — 15–30 minutes
- READING WORKSHOP — 60–75 minutes
- WRITING WORKSHOP — 20–30 minutes

This Week's Words

BIG IDEA WORDS

area	population	working

POWER WORDS

against	chum	close
docked	drive	harbor
heal	pointing	spoon
stock	unload	

HIGH-FREQUENCY WORDS

about	eat	how	make
out	put	takes	who

READER'S VOCABULARY

action	context clue	describe
description	detail	evidence
setting	test organization	verb

Assessment Options

Online **Ed**

- ✓ **Selection Quiz:** *Who Put the Cookies in the Cookie Jar?*
- ✓ **Weekly Assessment**
  - High-Frequency Words
  - Phonics: Consonants *w, j, y, v;* Short *u;* Review Short *i, o, u*
  - Comprehension: Text Organization
  - Generative Vocabulary: Words About Actions and Directions
  - Grammar: Complete Sentences

Intervention

For children needing strategic intervention, use *Tabletop Minilessons: Intervention.*

- Module 2, Week 3 Daily Lessons

LESSON 11

FOUNDATIONAL SKILLS

Word Work Warm-Up, pp. T424–T425
- High-Frequency Words: *about, eat, how, make, out, put, takes, who*
- Phonological Awareness

Phonics, pp. T426–T427
- Consonants *w, j, y, v;* Short *u*

Spelling, pp. T428–T429
- Short *u*

VOCABULARY

Academic Vocabulary, pp. T430–T431
- Introduce Oral Language: *pointing, close, docked, unload, harbor*

READING WORKSHOP

Abuela
GENRE Fantasy
Read Aloud: MINILESSON,
pp. T432–T433

Book Stix

- Connect and Teach: Setting
- Apply to Text: *Abuela*
- Engage and Respond: Writing

SMALL-GROUP INSTRUCTION

Options for Differentiation
- Guided Reading Groups, p. T434
- English Learner Support: Classify, p. T434
- Reinforce Setting, p. T435
- Reinforce Foundational Skills: Read *Wags, Wags, Wags!,* pp. T436–T437

Options for Independent and Collaborative Work, pp. T438–T439

WRITING WORKSHOP

Descriptive Essay, p. W28
- Revising III: Capitalization

Grammar, p. W196
- Complete Sentences

LESSON 12

FOUNDATIONAL SKILLS

Word Work Warm-Up, pp. T4440–T441
- High-Frequency Words: *about, eat, how, make, out, put, takes, who*
- Phonological Awareness

Phonics, pp. T442–T443
- Consonants *w, j, y, v;* Short *u*

VOCABULARY

Academic Vocabulary, pp. T444–T445
- Introduce Power Words: *spoon, against, churn, stock, heal, drive*

READING WORKSHOP

Who Put the Cookies in the Cookie Jar?
GENRE Informational Text
Shared Reading: MINILESSON,
pp. T446–T447

Teaching Pal

- Connect and Teach: Ask and Answer Questions
- Apply to Text: *Who Put the Cookies in the Cookie Jar?*
- Engage and Respond: Speaking & Listening

SMALL-GROUP INSTRUCTION

Options for Differentiation
- Guided Reading Groups, p. T448
- English Learner Support: Classify, p. T448
- Reinforce Ask and Answer Questions, p. T449
- Reinforce Foundational Skills: Read *Yip! Yap!,* pp. T450–T451

Options for Independent and Collaborative Work, pp. T452–T453

WRITING WORKSHOP

Descriptive Essay, p. W29
- Editing I: Reviewing for Grammar

Grammar, p. W197
- Forming Complete Sentences

LESSON 13

FOUNDATIONAL SKILLS

Word Work Warm-Up, p. T454
- High-Frequency Words: *about, eat, how, make, out, put, takes, who*
- Phonological Awareness

Fluency, p. T455
- Accuracy and Self-Correct

Phonics, pp. T456–T457
- Review Short *i, o, u*

VOCABULARY

Academic Vocabulary, pp. T458–T459
- Review Power Words: *spoon, against, churn, stock, heal, drive*

READING WORKSHOP

Who Put the Cookies in the Cookie Jar?
GENRE Informational Text
Shared Reading: MINILESSON, pp. T460–T461
- Connect and Teach: Text Organization
- Apply to Text: *Who Put the Cookies in the Cookie Jar?*
- Engage and Respond: Writing

SMALL-GROUP INSTRUCTION

Options for Differentiation
- Guided Reading Groups, p. T462
- English Learner Support: Classify, p. T462
- Reinforce Text Organization, p. T463
- Reinforce Foundational Skills: Read *Mud Pup,* pp. T464–T465

Options for Independent and Collaborative Work, pp. T466–T467

WRITING WORKSHOP

Descriptive Essay, p. W30
- Editing II: Preparing to Publish

Grammar, p. W198
- Complete and Incomplete Sentences

LESSON 14

FOUNDATIONAL SKILLS

Word Work Warm-Up, p. T468
- High-Frequency Words: *about, eat, how, make, out, put, takes, who*
- Phonological Awareness

Phonics, p. T469
- Phonics Review

VOCABULARY

Generative Vocabulary, pp. T470–T471
- Words About Actions and Directions

READING WORKSHOP

Curious About Jobs
GENRE Video
Media Literacy: MINILESSON, pp. T472–T473
- Connect and Teach: Content-Area Words
- Apply to Media: *Curious About Jobs*
- Engage and Respond: Speaking & Listening

SMALL-GROUP INSTRUCTION

Options for Differentiation
- Guided Reading Groups, p. T474
- English Learner Support: Classify, p. T474
- Reinforce Content-Area Words, p. T475
- Reinforce Foundational Skills: Read *Bad Pub, Wags!,* pp. T476–T477

Options for Independent and Collaborative Work, pp. T478–T479

WRITING WORKSHOP

Descriptive Essay, p. W31
- Publishing

Grammar, p. W309
- Spiral Review: Adjectives and Articles

LESSON 15

FOUNDATIONAL SKILLS

Word Work Warm-Up, p. T480
- High-Frequency Words: *about, eat, how, make, out, put, takes, who*
- Phonological Awareness

Spelling, p. T481
- Spelling Assessment

VOCABULARY

Academic Vocabulary, pp. T482–T483
- Cumulative Vocabulary Review

READING WORKSHOP

Module Wrap-Up
pp. T484–T485
- Wrap Up the Topic
- Synthesize

SMALL-GROUP INSTRUCTION

Options for Differentiation
- Guided Reading Groups, p. T486
- English Learner Support: Recount Information, p. T486
- Reinforce Synthesize, p. T487
- Reinforce Foundational Skills: Make Text Connections, pp. T488–T489

Options for Independent and Collaborative Work, pp. T490–T491

WRITING WORKSHOP

Descriptive Essay, p. W32
- Sharing

Grammar, p. W200
- Connect to Writing: Using Complete Sentences

Preview Lesson Texts

Build understanding of this week's texts so that you can best support children in making connections, understanding key ideas, and becoming lifelong readers.

Who Put the Cookies in the Cookie Jar?
by George Shannon

GENRE Informational Text

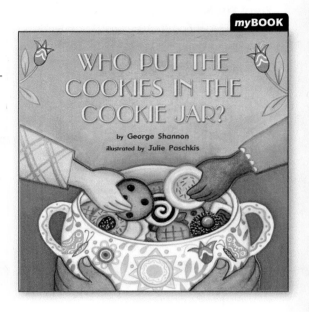
myBOOK

WHO PUT THE COOKIES IN THE COOKIE JAR?
by George Shannon
illustrated by Julie Paschkis

WHY THIS TEXT?

It takes just one hand to take a cookie from the cookie jar, but it takes many hands to put them there! In this informational text written as a poem, children will learn the many different jobs people do to make cookies appear in their homes.

KEY LEARNING OBJECTIVES

- Identify characteristics of informational texts.
- Ask and answer questions about a text before, during, and after reading, using text evidence to support responses.
- Identify a text's organization and how it supports the author's purpose.

TEXT COMPLEXITY

LEXILE MEASURE 420L • **GUIDED READING LEVEL** G

OVERALL RATING Moderately Complex

The illustrations are integral to understanding the text's implied purpose.

MAKE CONNECTIONS

 **BUILD KNOWLEDGE AND LANGUAGE**

- **Social Studies Connection:** Communities

🔗 **VOCABULARY**

- **Words About Actions and Directions:** *build, churn, cut, drive, eat, feed, gather, grind, guide, harvest, help, in, into, load, make, milk, mix, out, put, sow, takes, teach*

🔗 **FOUNDATIONAL SKILLS**

- **High-Frequency Words:** *about, eat, how, make, out, put, takes, who*
- **Consonants *w, j, y, v*; Short *u*:** *arrive, butter, clumps, cup, cut, drive, harvest, jar, shelves, trucks, until, us, vanilla, what, wheat, when, world's*
- **Review Short *i, o, u*:** *butter, clumps, cup, cut, drop, in, into, is, it, milk, mitts, mix, mixture, stock, things, trucks, until, us*

TEXT X-RAY

KEY IDEAS	LANGUAGE
Key Idea *pp. 154–157* Hands around the world help put cookies in the cookie jar. Some hands make the dough. Others make the cookie sheets and oven mitts.	**Multiple Meanings** ***spoon*** (p. 156); ***milk*** (p. 158): Children who are learning English may be familiar with the nouns *spoon* and *milk*. Here, these words name actions. Use illustrations in the text along with gestures to explain the meaning of each verb.
Key Idea *pp. 158–163* Workers on many farms produce the ingredients for cookies: milk, butter, flour, eggs, and sugar.	
Key Idea *pp. 164–169* Some hands help get the cookies to customers. There are many helping hands all around the world!	
Key Idea *p. 170* This recipe tells how to make sugar cookies.	

Curious About Jobs

GENRE Video

WHY THIS TEXT?

In this informational video, children are introduced to the work that airplane mechanics, potters, and museum educators do. Children see and hear details about what makes these jobs interesting and how these workers contribute to the community.

KEY LEARNING OBJECTIVES

- Identify features of videos.
- Use clues in the audio and visuals to determine the meanings of content-area words.

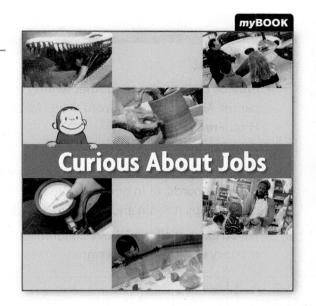

*my*BOOK

Curious About Jobs

TEXT COMPLEXITY

LEXILE MEASURE N/A • **GUIDED READING LEVEL** N/A

OVERALL RATING Slightly Complex

The video has a strong descriptive organization and straightforward language, but requires some discipline knowledge.

MAKE CONNECTIONS

🔗 **BUILD KNOWLEDGE AND LANGUAGE**

- **Social Studies Connection:** Communities

🔗 **VOCABULARY**

- **Words About Actions and Directions:** *are, be, come, doing, done, flies, gets, give, inside, is, knows, looks, makes, out, poke, rise, see, shapes, spins, tells, up, visit*

🔗 **FOUNDATIONAL SKILLS**

- **High-Frequency Words:** *about, how, make, out, who*
- **Consonants *w, j, y, v;* Short *u:*** *but, cups, fun, jobs, just, loves, up, us, we, wings, wires, works, wow, you*
- **Review Short *i, o, u:*** *but, cups, did, fun, give, is, it, job, just, lot, lump, not, on, rocks, spins, stuff, up, us, wings*

TEXT X-RAY

KEY IDEAS	🔵 **LANGUAGE**
Key Idea Some people work as airplane mechanics. A mechanic checks a plane's wires, screws, and other parts to make sure the plane is safe to fly.	**Informal Language** ***cool:*** Tell English learners that in this video, *cool* isn't describing the temperature. It's an informal way of saying that something is very good, or excellent.
Key Idea A potter makes things from clay. As a lump of clay spins around on a wheel, the potter shapes it into something beautiful.	***stuff:*** Here, *stuff means* "things." ***sweet:*** Explain that *sweet* isn't used here to describe something that tastes like sugar. It's an informal way to say "very good" or "great."
Key Idea Some people work in museums. A museum educator's job is to teach people about the great things they're seeing in the exhibits.	

Literacy Centers

While you meet with small groups, have children work independently in Literacy Centers. At the beginning of the week, explain what is expected of children in each center. Post a daily rotation schedule.

WORD WORK

Word Hunt

- Provide clipboards (or another writing surface) in the center. Also display the Word Cards for this week's High-Frequency Words.

- Have children copy two words and then try to find them in another place in the room, either on a word wall, on bulletin boards, or in books. When they find a word, they should copy it again and tell where they found it.

- For an extra challenge, have children find another mystery word that you designate in the classroom.

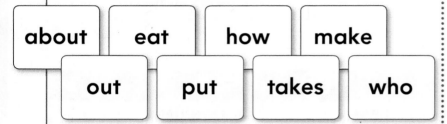

| about | eat | how | make |

| out | put | takes | who |

Short *u*

- Display the week's Spelling Words and copies of Printable: **Spelling & Handwriting**. Have children choose one of the activities to practice writing this week's Spelling Words in their best handwriting.

- Have children complete the activity on a separate sheet of paper.

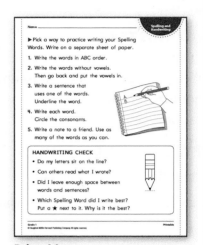

Printable:
Spelling & Handwriting

CREATIVITY CORNER

Readers' Theater

- Have children read Printable: **Readers' Theater 2**, "Help Find Bud," and ask them to pay attention to reading the script with accuracy. Encourage children to self-correct any errors they make while reading.

- Have groups of children perform the script. Then ask them to answer the questions on the last page of the script to assess their performance.

- Encourage group members to share what they liked best about the story.

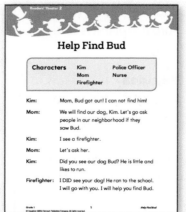

Printable: Readers' Theater 2

Reading Remake

- Display in the center and have children complete the activity for *Who Put the Cookies in the Cookie Jar?* on Printable: **Write a Poem**.

- Tell partners to explain to one another how their poem shows their understanding of the selection.

Printable: Write a Poem

DIGITAL STATION

Listener's Choice

Online Ed

- Have children listen to the Read Aloud Book *Abuela* or a Leveled Reader of their choice.
- Tell them to add the book to their Printable: Listening Log, as well as the active listening skills they used, a summary, and a question they have about the book.

Phonics Practice

- Have children continue their personalized, adaptive learning for foundational skills in *iRead*.

TEAMWORK TIME

Inquiry and Research Project: Our Community News

- Have groups continue work on the module project.
- Remind children that their focus this week is on presenting the news reports about people and places in the community. *See pp. T260–T261.*

READING CORNER

Independent Reading

- Have children self-select or continue reading an independent reading book.
- Remind children to set a purpose for reading and to record their progress on their Printable: Reading Log.
- You may want to choose from these additional options to have children interact with their books:

  » **Read for Fluency** Children use the **PARTNER READING** routine to practice the week's fluency skill, accuracy and self-correction, or another area of need.

  » **Annotate the Text** Children practice a strategy and use sticky notes to record questions or what they are thinking as they read. Review the sticky notes while you confer with children.

  » **Response Journal** Children draw or write about what they read.

Student Choice Library

Rigby
LEVELED LIBRARY

High-Frequency Words

Teach the Words

Use Word Cards *about, eat, how, make, out, put, takes,* and *who* and the **HIGH-FREQUENCY WORDS** routine below to introduce the week's High-Frequency sight words.

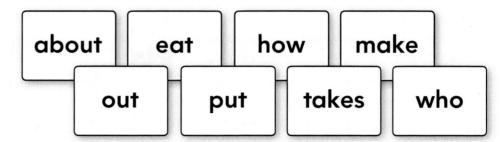

1 **See the word.** Display a Word Card. Say the word, and have children repeat it twice.

2 **Say the word.** Have children repeat it chorally. Use the word in a sentence or two. *I eat lunch at school. I can eat an apple.* (Use pantomime.)

3 **Spell the word.** Point to the letters, and have children spell the word aloud. Point out any familiar spelling patterns. *Eat begins with e. Does anyone in this class have a name that begins with E? Do you know any other words that begin with e?*

4 **Write and check the word.** Hide the word, and have children use the **WRITE AND REVEAL** routine to write the word. Then have them check it against the Word Card.

Have children add this week's words to their individual Word Rings. Tell them to write a word on the front of each card and write a sentence or draw a picture about the word on the back. Alternatively, you may have children complete Know It, Show It page 54.

LEARNING OBJECTIVES

- Identify and read high-frequency words.
- **Language** Recognize, recite, and write basic sight vocabulary.
- Blend phonemes to say one-syllable words.
- Isolate initial and final phonemes in spoken one-syllable words.

MATERIALS   Online

Word Cards *about, eat, how, make, out, put, takes, who*

Know It, Show It *p. 54*

Picture Cards *ax, bed, can, cow, sun, tie, tub*

 ENGLISH LEARNER SUPPORT:
Build Vocabulary

ALL LEVELS Explain to children that the word *about* has more than one meaning. Share the following sentences and discuss the meaning of *about* in each:

- I played soccer for *about* two hours.
- What is the movie *about*?

Provide additional opportunities for children to practice using *about* in sentences for both meanings of the word.

 CORRECT & REDIRECT

Guide children who have trouble identifying any of the words. Say the correct word, and have children repeat it. Example:

- Make. *What is the word? (make)*
- Have children spell the word. *(m-a-k-e) How do we say this word? (make)*
- Have children reread all the cards in random order.

Phonological Awareness

Blend Phonemes

- Remind children that they know how to blend sounds to say words. Say: *I will say all the sounds in a word, and you blend the sounds to say the word. Listen as I do the first one:* /l/ /ō/. *The word is* low.

- *Are you ready to try? Listen:* /n/ /ē/. *What's the word?* (knee)

- *Let's keep going:* /ŭ/ /p/ (up), /f/ /ŏ/ /g/ (fog), /r/ /ā/ /l/ (rail), /s/ /ă/ /g/ (sag), /z/ /ĭ/ /p/ (zip).

- Display Picture Cards *ax, bed, can, cow, sun, tie,* and *tub* in random order on the chalk ledge.

- Say: *Now we're going to try something different. I will say a sentence, but I won't say the last word. I will only say the sounds in the word. You will blend the sounds to say the last word in the sentence. I will do the first one. The sentence is: It is time to go to* /b/ /ĕ/ /d/. *When I blend* /b/, /ĕ/, *and* /d/, *I say the word* bed. /b/ /ĕ/ /d/, bed. Ask a volunteer to remove Picture Card *bed* from the chalk ledge.

- Continue with the following sentences. Have children remove each Picture Card after blending to say the picture name.

  » *Add some water to the* /t/ /ŭ/ /b/. (tub)

  » *Move away from the* /k/ /ou/! (cow)

  » *The cloud covers the* /s/ /ŭ/ /n/. (sun)

  » *Dan cut the tree with the* /ă/ /ks/. (ax)

  » *The soup is in a* /k/ /ă/ /n/. (can)

  » *Did you see Dad's* /t/ /ī/? (tie)

Isolate Phonemes

- Tell children that they will now listen for the sounds in different parts of the words you will say.

- Model finding the beginning sound with the word *red:* red. *The first sound in red is* /r/.

- *Now we will do one together: nut. What is the beginning sound in the word nut?* (/n/)

- *Let's keep going: jet* (/j/), *give* (/g/), *tell* (/t/), *vat* (/v/), *heat* (/h/), *mop* (/m/).

- Say: *Now you will listen for the sounds at the ends of words. Listen as I do one: cut. I hear* /t/ *at the end of* cut. Cut, /t/.

- *Your turn! What sound do you hear at the end of* leg? (/g/) *That's right. The last sound in* leg *is* /g/. Have children identify the final sound in these words: hum (/m/), soon (/n/), top (/p/), fall (/l/), mad (/d/), five (/v/).

- Then display Picture Cards *bed, can, sun,* and *tub,* one at a time. As you hold up each card, have children say the word and identify the beginning sound. (bed, /b/; can, /k/; sun, /s/; tub, /t/)

- Repeat, this time having children identify ending sounds in the same picture names. (bed, /d/; can, /n/; sun, /n/; tub, /b/)

✓ CORRECT & REDIRECT

For children who blend incorrectly, differentiate instruction by modeling. Enunciate the sounds, elongating the continuant sounds, then say them more closely together, and finally blend to say the word. Example:

Here are the sounds: /f/ /ŏ/ /g/. *The first sound is* /f/. *Listen:* /fff/. *The next sound is* /ŏ/, /ŏŏŏ/. *The last sound is* /g/. *Listen:* /g/. *Say each sound with me:* /fff/ /ŏŏŏ/ /g/. *Now listen as I blend the sounds:* /f/ /ŏ/ /g/, /f-ŏ-g/, fog. *What is the word?* (fog)

EL ENGLISH LEARNER SUPPORT:
Build Vocabulary

SUBSTANTIAL
Ask children *yes/no* questions about the Picture Card picture names. For example: *Do you see the sun at night? Can you wear a tie?*

MODERATE
Have children answer *either/or* questions about the words. *Is the sun in the sky or on the ground? Is a tie a person or a thing?*

LIGHT
Supply children with sentence frames for them to complete to tell about a Picture Card. *A _____ is _____. A _____ helps with _____.*

PHONICS

LESSON
11

FOUNDATIONAL SKILLS

LEARNING OBJECTIVES
- Learn the sound-spellings for short *u* and the consonants *w, j, y, v*.
- **Language** Recognize sound-letter relationships and use them to decode words.
- Blend letter sounds and decode regularly spelled one-syllable words with /ŭ/ and /w/, /j/, /y/, /v/.

MATERIALS Online 🍎Ed

Sound/Spelling Cards *jellyfish, umbrella, volcano, walrus, yak*
Letter Cards *a, g, j, m, n, t, u, v, w, y,*
Articulation Videos /j/,/ŭ/,/v/,/w/,/y/

 # Consonants *w, j, y, v*; Short *u*

Spotlight on Sounds

- Tell children that they will be reading words with a new vowel, short *u*, and the consonants *w, j, y, v*. Then have them practice identifying the beginning consonant sounds in words you say. *I am going to say a word, and you say the beginning sound. I will do the first one. Listen:* jump. *The beginning sound is /j/. Repeat after me:* jump, /j/. *Now listen for the beginning sound in these words:* win (/w/); vase (/v/); was (/w/); just (/j/); vacuum (/v/) yellow (/y/); yes (/y/).

- Then model how to identify the ending sound in *give, /v/.* Have children listen for the ending sound in these words: *cave (/v/); page (/j/); hive (/v/); huge (/j/).*

- Conclude the activity by having children think of more words that end with the /v/ sound.

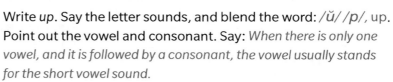 **I Do It**

Spotlight on Letters Display the Sound/Spelling Card for short *u, umbrella. Remember, the vowels are* a, e, i, o, u, *and each one stands for many sounds.* Name the card's picture, say the sound, and give the spelling. Umbrella *begins with the short* u *sound, /ŭ/. The letter* u *can stand for the /ŭ/ sound at the beginning or middle of a word.*

Write *up*. Say the letter sounds, and blend the word: /ŭ/ /p/, up. Point out the vowel and consonant. Say: *When there is only one vowel, and it is followed by a consonant, the vowel usually stands for the short vowel sound.*

Repeat for *w, j, y,* and *v,* using Sound/Spelling Cards *walrus, jellyfish, yak,* and *volcano* and the words *web, jug, yak,* and *vat.*

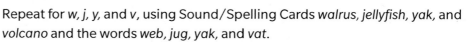

TEACHER TIP

Follow the leader! Have children use Printable: **Letter Cards** and duplicate your actions to the use **SOUND-BY-SOUND BLENDING** routine to blend and read *yum, jut, van,* and *wag.*

EL ENGLISH LEARNER SUPPORT: Facilitate Language Connections

ALL LEVELS Spanish and Korean speakers may have trouble distinguishing /v/ from /b/. Play the **Articulation Video** for /v/. Have children practice the sound. Then say word pairs, and have children say the word that begins with /v/: van/ban, bet/vet, bat/vat, vest/best. Speakers of Spanish, Cantonese, Tagalog, and Korean may pronounce /ŭ/ as /ŏ/. Use the **Articulation Video** for /ŭ/ to reinforce the sound. Use the other videos in the Materials list as needed.

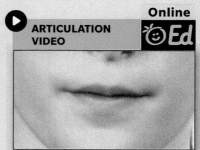
ARTICULATION VIDEO Online 🍎Ed

We Do It

Write *yum* and use Letter Cards *y, u, m* with the **SOUND-BY-SOUND BLENDING** routine below to model blending the word.

1. **Display** cards as shown. Say the first letter and sound.

2. **Slide** the second letter over. Say its sound. Then blend the two sounds.

3. **Slide** the last letter over. Say its sound. Say the first two blended sounds, the last sound, and the blended word: /yŭ/ /m/, yum.

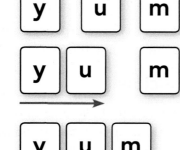

Sound-by-Sound Blending Repeat the **SOUND-BY-SOUND BLENDING** routine with cards for the words *jut, van,* and *wag,* having children say the sounds and blend.

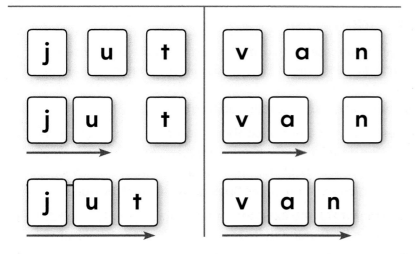

You Do It

INDEPENDENT PRACTICE

Blending Practice Display the words below. Then choose a volunteer to model the activity. Explain that you will point to two words in random order and the child will read them aloud. Repeat the blending routine as needed. Continue until each child has had a turn.

jug	wig	yam	van
tub	yip	vat	hut

✓ CORRECT & REDIRECT

- If a child mispronounces a word during Blending Practice, make note of the error type and address it.
- If a child reads *jug* as *jog*, read the word, emphasizing the vowel sound. Then have the child blend and read the word with you.
- Provide extra practice with the consonant sounds and the /ŭ/ sound for children who need it.

👥 LINK TO SMALL-GROUP INSTRUCTION

REINFORCE FOUNDATIONAL SKILLS Use *Wags, Wags, Wags!* during small-group time to review or reinforce blending and decoding words with the vowel short *u* and the consonants *w, j, y,* and *v.* Meet with children to work through the story, or assign it as independent work. *See the lesson on p. T436.*

FOUNDATIONAL SKILLS

 Short u

Administer the Pretest

- Read the first Spelling Word and the Dictation Sentence. Repeat the word as children write it.

- Write the word, and have children correct their spelling if needed. Repeat for words 2–6 and for the Review Words.

- Assign the Basic and Review Words as needed for practice this week. If children do well on the pretest, assign the Challenge Words.

Teach the Principle

- Write *not* on the board, underlining *u*, and read it aloud. Explain that the /ŭ/ sound can be spelled with the letter *u*.

- Tell children that this week the Spelling Words have the short *u* sound, /ŭ/, spelled *u*. Explain that short *u* sound can be at the beginning or in the middle of a word.

- If children have difficulty, review Sound/Spelling Card *umbrella*. Remind them that *u* is a vowel that can stand for many sounds and that one of those sounds is /ŭ/, as in *umbrella*.

Model Handwriting

- Model how to write lowercase *q* and *u*. *q: Start just below the middle line. Pull back, around and up to the middle line. Pull down past the bottom line, and curve up to the right. u: Start at the middle line. Pull down, around, up to the middle line, and down.* Point out that *q* is usually followed by *u* in words.

- Have children describe what they notice about the letters *q* and *u*. *(They are both formed by pulling down, around, up, and then down. Both are made up of straight and curved lines.)* Also help children note the differences between *q* and *g*. Then model writing one or more of the Spelling Words that include *u*.

- Have children use the **WRITE AND REVEAL** routine to practice writing words that include lowercase *q* and *u*. Remind them to also use what they have learned about the correct pencil grip. As needed, distribute the handwriting models on Printable: **Manuscript Qq, Uu**. Printables for Continuous Stroke letter forms are also available online.

 ENGLISH LEARNER SUPPORT: Build Vocabulary

AALL LEVELS Make sure children understand the meanings of the Spelling Words and Dictation Sentences. Use Picture Cards *ant* (for *bug*), *nuts*, and *tub* to show word meanings. Pantomime *up* and *hug*, as necessary.

LEARNING OBJECTIVES

- Spell words with short *u* (closed syllables).
- **Language** Identify relationships between sounds and letters.
- Develop handwriting.

MATERIALS Online

Sound/Spelling Card *umbrella*
Printables *Manuscript Qq, Uu; Word List 6*
Know It, Show It *p. 55*

DICTATION SENTENCES

BASIC

1. **up** The bird flew *up* in the sky.
2. **bug** An ant is a *bug*.
3. **mud** Rain may turn dirt to *mud*.
4. **nut** Almonds are a kind of *nut*.
5. **hug** My dad likes to *hug* me.
6. **tub** She washed the dog in a *tub*.

REVIEW

7. **log** Mom put a *log* on the fire.
8. **hop** A rabbit can *hop* away.
9. **hot** Be careful! The stove is *hot*.
10. **not** Stop at the sign, and do *not* go.

CHALLENGE

11. **puppy** We named our *puppy* Spot.
12. **bathtub** Water is in the *bathtub*.

TEACHER TIP

On the other hand!
Remind children that as they write, the position of the paper is important. The paper should be slanted along the line of the child's writing arm, and the child should use his or her non-writing hand to hold the paper in place. Right-handed writers should have the paper tilted slightly to the left. Left-handed writers should have the paper tilted slightly to the right.

Word Sort

1 Introduce Display both the Basic and the Review Spelling Word cards from Printable: **Word List 6**, and read each one aloud.

2 Columns 1 and 2 Display the word cards *nut* and *not* as column headings. Explain: *I will put* nut *at the top of one column and* not *at the top of another. I will read a word, and you will tell me if the vowel sound is the same as in* nut *or as in* not. *I'll sort the first word to show you.*

3 Model Display the word card *bug* and read it aloud. Explain: Bug. *Listen for the vowel sound.* Buuuuug. *Now I will compare the words.* Bug, not. Bug, nut. *The vowel sound in* bug *sounds the same as the vowel sound in* nut, *the short* u *sound, /ŭ/, so I'll put* bug *under* nut. *Repeat for* hot, *placing it under* not.

4 Continue Sort the other words. Model if necessary.

5 Discuss Read each column together. Discuss what children notice about the words in each column. If no one mentions it, guide children to identify the words in column 1 as having the short *u* sound and the words in column 2 as having the short *o* sound. Tell children they can think about this pattern when they spell words with short *u* and short *o*.

6 Repeat Have children work together to repeat the sort, using the Spelling Word cards from Printable: **Word List 6**. Remind children to save the rest of the page and the Spelling Word cards for use all week. Encourage them to make extra sets as necessary.

nut		not
bug	up	hot
mud	hug	log
tub		hop

INDEPENDENT PRACTICE

For additional practice, have children complete Know It, Show It page 55. Encourage them to use their best handwriting and pay particular attention to writing the letter *u* correctly.

(EL) ENGLISH LEARNER SUPPORT: Facilitate Language Connections

ALL LEVELS Speakers of Spanish, Cantonese, Tagalog, and Korean may pronounce the short vowel sound /ŭ/ as /ŏ/. Say the spelling word *up* several times, elongating the short *u* sound: uuuup. Then say the word normally, and have children repeat after you. Continue with other Spelling Words.

Professional Learning

TEACHING TERMS

There are two primary types of **word sorts**: open and closed. In **closed sorts,** the teacher provides the categories into which children will sort the words. After sorting, children discuss what spelling features they think distinguish the words in one category from the words in the other. In **open sorts,** children sort the words provided any way they wish—all options are open. They may sort by spelling features they notice or by meaning.

See the **GPS guide** to learn more.

Introduce Oral Language

Use the steps **I Do It, We Do It, You Do It** with the information in the chart below to teach the oral Power Words from the Read Aloud Book *Abuela*.

LEARNING OBJECTIVES

- **Language** Answer questions and discuss meanings to develop vocabulary.
- Identify real-life connections between words and their use.

MATERIALS   Online

Vocabulary Cards *2.28–2.32*

Read Aloud Book *Abuela*

Classroom materials *magazine or Internet photos of a docked ship and ships in a harbor*

❶ Power Word	❷ Meaning	❸ Example
pointing (v.) *(p. 14)*	If you are **pointing,** you are using a finger to show someone where to look.	**ACT IT OUT** Point at objects in the classroom. *I am pointing at the (clock).*
close (adv.) *(p. 18)*	If you are **close** to something, you are near it.	**ACT IT OUT** Stand next to your desk. *I am standing close to this desk.*
docked (v.) *(p. 20)*	If a ship is **docked,** it has stopped next to a place where people get on and off it.	**USE A PROP** Display a photo of a docked passenger ship. *When a ship is docked, it is not moving.*
unload (v.) *(p. 20)*	When you **unload** things, you take them off a ship, truck, or other thing that has carried them.	**ACT IT OUT** Unload books from a backpack. *I unload these books.*
harbor (n.) *(p. 22)*	A **harbor** is a place along the seacoast where boats go out or come in and can stay safely.	**USE A PROP** Display a photo of a harbor. *The water in a harbor is calm and unmoving.*

TEACHER TIP

New meaning! Children are probably familiar with the meaning and pronunciation of *close* for shutting a door or window. Eliminate confusion by explaining that some words can have the same spelling but different pronunciations and meanings. Have children use each meaning of *close* in a sentence.

⊸ *Professional Learning*

BEST PRACTICES

Children learn more when they are directly involved and clearly understand their own goals and objectives. Consider displaying and discussing the Learning Objectives at the beginning of the lesson and revisiting them at the end. These discussions can also serve as informal assessment so you can know what worked, what children learned, and what you can improve on.

See the **GPS guide** to learn more.

I Do It

Use the **VOCABULARY** routine and Vocabulary Cards 2.28–2.32 to introduce the oral Power Words from *Abuela*. You may wish to display the corresponding Vocabulary Card for each word as you discuss it.

pointing

Vocabulary Cards

1 **Say the Power Word.** Ask children to repeat it.

2 **Explain the meaning.** Read aloud the student-friendly meaning.

3 **Talk about examples.** Use the image or a strategy to give examples of the word.

We Do It

Guide children to make connections between each word's meaning and how they can use it in their own lives. Use these prompts. Encourage children to explain or justify their answers.

- *If a boat is **docked**, is it **close** to land? Explain.*

- *What might you see if you watched people **unload** items off a ship in a **harbor**?*

- *Why might you be **pointing** at a type of food in a market?*

You Do It

INDEPENDENT PRACTICE

Have partners work together to complete each of the activities below. Circulate and observe partners as they work, providing corrective feedback as necessary.

- **Draw** *Draw a picture of a boat that is **docked** in a **harbor**.*

- **Discuss** *Would you like to live **close** to your best friend? Why or why not?*

- **Role-Play** *Demonstrate **pointing** to a box. Then pantomime how you would **unload** it.*

 ENGLISH LEARNER SUPPORT:
Build Vocabulary

SUBSTANTIAL
Guide children to sketch and label a picture for each word. Refer to the Vocabulary Cards and other visuals as needed.

MODERATE
Supply these frames: *A boat that is **docked** is _____. I am **pointing** at _____. In a **harbor**, you can see _____.*

LIGHT
Ask: *What part of your body do you use when you are **pointing**? Explain what happens when a boat is **docked**.*

⏱ Setting

Step 1 Connect and Teach

ANCHOR CHART 11: Setting

LEARNING OBJECTIVES

- Recognize characteristics of fantasy.
- Describe the setting of a story.
- **Language** Describe differences between settings.
- Respond to a story by drawing and writing about one of its settings.

MATERIALS   Online ⊙ Ed

Anchor Chart 11 *Setting*

Printable *Anchor Chart 11: Setting*

Read Aloud Book *Abuela*

BookStix *2.3*

📖 READER'S VOCABULARY

- **setting** where and when a story takes place
- **describe** to tell what someone or something is like by giving details
- **detail** small bit of information that supports a central idea or describes something in a text

- Project or display <u>Anchor Chart 11: Setting</u>.

- Remind children that the **setting** of a story is where and when the story takes place.

- Point out that sometimes a story's setting can change in a story. For example, the characters in a story might go to a different place, or the time of day or season might change.

- Tell children that when they **describe** a setting, they tell what the setting is like. To know what the setting is like, they can look for small pieces of information, or **details**, in the text and the pictures.

- Explain that keeping in mind a story's setting is important will help children understand the story better.

- Tell children they will practice describing the setting when they listen to a Read Aloud Book called *Abuela*.

—● *Professional Learning*

TEACHING TERMS

Interactive read-alouds give children access to rich texts that they cannot read independently and opportunities to listen to models of fluent reading. Through purposeful prompts, teachers encourage children to actively engage with the text and participate in text-based collaborative conversations.

See the **GPS guide** to learn more.

LEARNING MINDSET

Belonging

Reflect Explain that when you belong to a community, you care for others and they care for you. Then discuss how Rosalba and Abuela show that they care about the community they live in. *What places do Rosalba and Abuela visit? Who do they see there? Why is each place important?* Help children understand that the places are important because they are part of the lives of people in their family.

Go to
BookStix 2.3

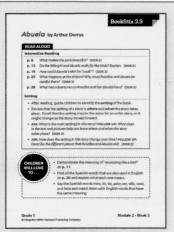

Step 2 Apply to Text

- **Genre Study** Read aloud the title *Abuela* and introduce the book. *Today we will read a fantasy. It tells about an adventure a girl has with Abuela, her grandmother.* Have children examine the cover. Prompt them to think about what makes this book a fantasy. *What looks make-believe? What do you think the girl and her Abuela do?*

- **Set a Purpose** Display the first few pages of the book. *What do you think might keep a reader interested in this story? Use your idea to set a purpose for reading.*

- **Model Fluency** Tell children that as you read, you are going to demonstrate how to use context to self-correct word recognition when a word doesn't sound right. As you read, mispronounce a few words and show how to use letter sounds and context to correct yourself.

- **Read and Comprehend** Read aloud *Abuela* to children, pausing occasionally to ask the questions on BookStix 2.3 and to have them identify and describe the setting and how it changes. Refer back to the Anchor Chart to discuss why the setting in *Abuela* is important.

Step 3 Engage and Respond

INDEPENDENT PRACTICE: Writing

- Remind children that in the Read Aloud Book *Abuela,* a girl and her grandmother fly to different places in their city.

- Have children draw a picture that shows the place in the city they think is the most interesting. Ask them to write what Rosalba and her Abuela did in that place. Encourage children to recall details from the book to support their responses.

- Ask partners to share and compare their responses. Encourage them to discuss how their writing is similar or different.

- You may want to have children complete their writing during daily small-group time.

 ENGLISH LEARNER SUPPORT:
Build Background

ALL LEVELS Children might not be familiar with New York City and its landmarks. They might benefit from seeing photographs of the places mentioned in the story. Point out that New York City is not one homogenous place but is made up of many different, diverse neighborhoods and communities.

 LINK TO SMALL-GROUP INSTRUCTION

REINFORCE SETTING Review or extend the skill as needed during small-group time to support children's need for differentiation. *See the lesson on p. T435.*

LESSON 11

READING WORKSHOP

Options for Differentiation

As the class engages in independent and collaborative work, meet with Guided Reading Groups or differentiate instruction based on student need.

GUIDED READING GROUPS

Match Children to Books + Instruction

- Choose just-right books based on level, skill, topic, or genre.

C — D — E — F — G — H — I — J — K →
Leveled Readers

- Deliver instruction with each book's Take and Teach Lesson, choosing appropriate sessions based on need.

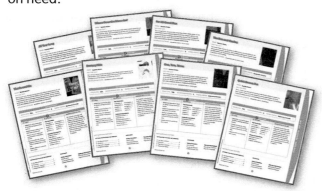

- Check comprehension, reinforce instruction, and extend learning with suggested supporting activities.

Rigby®
LEVELED LIBRARY

EL ENGLISH LEARNER SUPPORT

Classify

- Use **Tabletop Minilessons: English Language Development 6.1 (Listening)** to introduce and practice the language skill.

Tabletop Minilessons: English Language Development

- Then use the following text-based prompts with *Abuela* to guide application of the language skill. Begin with the prompt at the child's identified language proficiency level. As children are able, use lighter supports to encourage increased language proficiency.

SUBSTANTIAL
Have children focus on the kinds of transportation in the book. Ask: *What kinds of transportation are there in the city? In the ocean? In the sea?* Allow children to respond using single words or short phrases.

MODERATE
Ask children to focus on the kinds of transportation in the different areas. Supply this frame: *An example of transportation in the (city/sea/ocean) is _____.*

LIGHT
Ask children to classify the types of transportation Abuela and her granddaughter fly over. Ask: *What kinds of transportation are there in the (city)?*

REINFORCE SETTING

Demonstrate

- Use **Tabletop Minilessons: Reading 11** to remind children that the **setting** is where and when a story takes place. The setting can be the same for a whole story, or it can change throughout the story. **Details** in the text and illustrations help readers identify and describe the setting. Remind children to look for details that **describe** where characters are, the time of day, the season, or other information that helps identify where and when the story happens.

- Model filling out Printable: **Reading Graphic Organizer 18** to identify and describe the setting in *Abuela*.

Tabletop Minilessons: Reading

Apply to Independent Reading

- Now have children identify and describe the setting in an appropriate just-right book that they are reading independently. Before children read their books, guide them to set a purpose for reading. Remind them to think about where and when the story takes place. Customize these prompts to the books children choose.

  » *What details help you identify where the characters are?*

  » *What details help you identify when the action takes place?*

  » *How is the setting important to the story?*

- Have children complete Printable: **Reading Graphic Organizer 18** for their independent reading book.

Printable:
Reading Graphic Organizer 18

SCAFFOLD AND EXTEND

ALMOST THERE

READY FOR MORE

- Help children identify both pictures and text that tell about the setting of the story.

- Prompt children to identify words in the text that identify where and when the story takes place.

- Have children describe the setting, using their own words, and discuss why it is important to the story.

ENGLISH LEARNER SUPPORT

SUBSTANTIAL

Read aloud words that describe where characters are, the time of day, and/or the season. Have children repeat after you and point to the words when they say them.

MODERATE

Provide children with the following prompt to help their recognition of the setting: *The word _____ tells (where/when).*

LIGHT

As children answer the prompts, encourage them to use describing words from the text in complete sentences.

Options for Differentiation

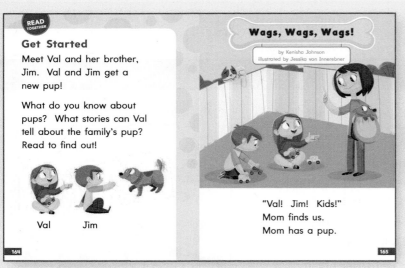

Wags, Wags, Wags!, Start Right Reader, *Book 1*, pp. 164–171

REINFORCE FOUNDATIONAL SKILLS

Read Decodable Text

Get Started Have children turn to Start Right Reader page 164. Explain that this week's stories are about Val and Jim and their new pup. Have children point to and read the names of the characters on page 164. Then read the page together and discuss the questions.

Preview the Story Draw attention to page 165, the title page. Discuss the title and the pictures on the first few pages. Have children predict what the pup will do.

Concepts of Print: Quotation Marks Use page 165 to model identifying quotation marks. Explain that quotation marks are used to show a character's dialogue, or the words he or she says out loud. Ask: *Who is speaking here? (Mom)* Then have children put a finger on the end quotation mark. Explain that the end quotation mark goes at the end of the character's dialogue, after the end punctuation. As you read, have children point to quotation marks and tell which character is speaking.

Fluency Focus: Accuracy and Self-Correction
Read aloud page 166 as children follow along. Omit *pats* and then model self-correcting. Ask children what they noticed about your reading. *(You corrected yourself.)* Remind children that it is important to read each word

accurately, or correctly, so the text makes sense. Then lead children in reading page 166 with accuracy.

Reflect on Reading Have children read each page silently and then chorally. Pause for these prompts:

Page 165: *What does Mom have? (a pup)*

Page 166: *Why do Jim and Val name the pup Wags? (because it wags a lot)*

Page 167: *Think about the prediction you made about the pup. Do you want to correct your prediction? Why? (Responses will vary.)*

Page 168: *What does Wags yap at? (a big bug)*

Page 170: *What happens to Wags? (Wags gets out of the yard.)*

Short *u* Picture Hunt Read aloud the directions and boxed words on page 171. Explain that not all of the words name things shown in the pictures. On a sheet of paper, have children write the words they find pictured in the story. *(rug, jug, pup, cup, bug)* Then have partners compare lists.

Yip! Yap! Yip! Yap!
Wags yaps at a big bug.
Can Wags eat it?

168

Jim takes the big bug.
I put it in a cup.
Jim gabs about Wags.

169

170

Wags? Wags? Wags!
Wags is not on the rug!
Wags got out!

READ TOGETHER

Short <u>u</u> Picture Hunt

Which words name pictures in the story?

rug	sun	jug
nut	pup	mud
cup	hug	bug

1. Make a list of pictures you find. Can you find 5 things?

2. Compare lists with a partner. Did you find the same things?

171

Make Minutes Count

As you meet with small groups to read *Wags, Wags, Wags!*, use one or more of these related activities, as needed, at the beginning or the end of the small-group session.

- **Connect to Phonics** Use Letter Cards *j, u, v, w,* and *y* to review the week's phonics skills. Then use additional Letter Cards to build words for children to blend and read, for example: *jot, run, Val, wig, yes.*

- **Connect to Spelling** Have children sort the basic and review Spelling Word cards from Printable: **Word List 6** by vowel sounds. Then have them draw a two-column chart on a sheet of paper, label one column *o* and the other *u,* and write the words in the appropriate columns.

- **Connect to Handwriting** Draw a triple-track line on the board, and write the letter *q* on the track. As you model, point out that you form the letter by moving in a backward circle direction, pulling down past the bottom line, and ending in a "hook." Then write the letter *u* on the track. Point out that in words with *q, q* is often followed by *u.* Then write the words *quit* and *quill* on the track and read them aloud. Have children repeat the words. Then have children write each word three times, putting a star next to the word in each set that most closely matches the model.

Name _____

Word List 6

High-Frequency Words	Decodable High-Frequency Words	Spelling Words	
		Basic	Review
about	but	up	log
eat	cut	bug	hop
how	run	mud	hot
make	up	nut	not
out	us	hug	
put	on	tub	
takes			
who			
			Challenge
			puppy
			bathtub

Grade 1
© Houghton Mifflin Harcourt Publishing Company. All rights reserved.
Printable

Printable: Word List 6

INDEPENDENT APPLICATION

Options for Independent and Collaborative Work

While you meet with small groups, have other children engage in literacy activities that reinforce the lesson's learning objectives. Choose from these options.

Independent Reading

Student Choice Library

Rigby
LEVELED LIBRARY

APPLY READING SKILL

Setting Children complete Printable: Reading Graphic Organizer 18 for an independent reading book.

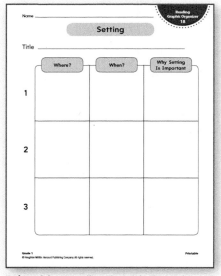

Printable: Reading Graphic Organizer 18

APPLY LANGUAGE SKILL

Classify Children complete Printable: Language Graphic Organizer 4 for an independent reading book.

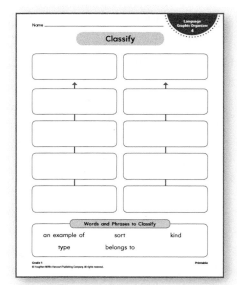

Printable: Language Graphic Organizer 4

Literacy Centers

See pp. T422–T423.

 WORD WORK

 CREATIVITY CORNER

 DIGITAL STATION

 READING CORNER

 TEAMWORK TIME

Start Right Reader

Read Decodable Text *Wags, Wags, Wags!*, Book 1: pp. 164–171

Writing

Children draw and write about an interesting place from the book.
See Engage & Respond, p. T433.

Additional Skills Practice

HIGH-FREQUENCY WORDS

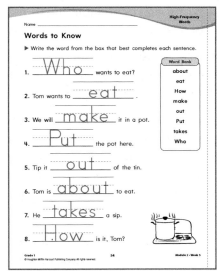

Know It, Show It, p. 54

SPELLING

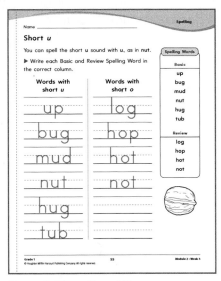

Know It, Show It, p. 55

Wrap-Up
Share Time

At the end of Reading Workshop, have children reflect on their learning by sharing how they applied **Setting** or another area of focus during independent work time. Choose from these options:

- **SHARE CHAIR** Select a reader each day to come to the front of the class and tell what he or she learned from the reading by using a skill or strategy.

- **THINK-PAIR-SHARE** Children share their thinking with a partner. Select a few each day to share with the whole class.

- **RETURN TO ANCHOR CHART** Have children add sticky notes about their independent reading book to the Setting Anchor Chart. Call on a few children to explain what they added.

ANCHOR CHART 11: Setting **Online** Ed

FOUNDATIONAL SKILLS

LEARNING OBJECTIVES

- Identify and read high-frequency words.
- **Language** Recognize and recite basic sight vocabulary.
- Blend phonemes to say one-syllable words.
- Isolate initial and final phonemes in spoken one-syllable words.

MATERIALS   Online

Word Cards *about, but, cut, eat, how, make, on, out, put, run, takes, up, us, who*

Printable *Word List 6*

Picture Cards *comb, keys, moon, pen, web*

Classroom materials *paper, markers or crayons*

 # High-Frequency Words

Review the Words

Repeat the **HIGH-FREQUENCY WORDS** routine to review this week's High-Frequency Words: *about, eat, how, make, out, put, takes,* and *who,* and the decodable High-Frequency Words *but, cut, on, run, up,* and *us.*

What Am I Thinking?

- Have children cut out the High-Frequency Words and decodable High-Frequency Words from Printable: **Word List 6.**

- Tell children to number a sheet of paper from 1 to 7, leaving a large space between numbers.

- Select a one of the week's words. Give three clues to help children guess which word you have in mind. For example: *This word has three letters. One of the letters is* t. *This word rhymes with* shout. *What word am I thinking of?* (out)

- Children place the corresponding word card next to the number 1 on their papers.

- Repeat for numbers 2 through 7. At the end of the game, have children read the list of words chorally.

- As time permits, play the game again with the remaining High-Frequency and decodable High-Frequency Words.

High-Frequency Words	Decodable High-Frequency Words	Spelling Words	
		Basic	Review
about	but	up	log
eat	cut	bug	hop
how	run	mud	hot
make	up	nut	not
out	us	hug	
put	on	tub	
takes			
who			
			Challenge
			puppy
			bathtub

Printable: Word List 6

TEACHER TIP

Write it out! After the game ends, tell children to write each word on their papers as they remove the word cards for use later in the week. Have them refer to the word card to make sure they have spelled each word correctly.

Phonological Awareness

Blend Phonemes

- Remind children that they can blend sounds to say words. Tell children they will listen to the sounds you say and blend the sounds to say words.

- Model the activity. Say: *I will say all the sounds in a word, and you will blend the sounds to say the word. Listen as I do the first one: /m/ /ī/. When I blend /m/ and /ī/, I say my. Are you ready to try? Listen. The sounds are: /p/ /ĕ/ /g/. Blend with me: /p-ĕ-g/. What's the word?* (peg)

- *Let's keep going. Blend these sounds to say words:* /h/ /ŏ/ /t/ (hot), /p/ /ă/ /k/ (pack), /ă/ /d/ (add), /s/ /ĭ/ /ks/ (six), /b/ /ŭ/ /g/ (bug), /h/ /ē/ /l/ (heel), /ă/ /m/ (am), /d/ /ĕ/ /n/ (den), /j/ /ŏ/ /b/ (job).

- Gather Picture Cards *comb, keys, moon, pen,* and *web,* and provide children with drawing supplies and paper. *Now we will practice blending sounds to say more words. I will say the sounds in a word. You blend the sounds and draw a picture of each word you say. Listen:* /w/ /ĕ/ /b/ (web), /k/ /ē/ /z/ (keys), /m/ /o͞o/ /n/ (moon), /k/ /ō/ /m/ (comb), /p/ /ĕ/ /n/ (pen).

- When children are finished drawing, check their work together. *Let's see if your pictures match! What did you draw for the sounds:* /w/ /ĕ/ /b/? Hold up Picture Card *web. Did you draw a web? Good!* Repeat for *keys, moon, comb,* and *pen.*

Isolate Phonemes

- Remind children that they can listen for sounds in different parts of words. Tell them they will be listening for beginning sounds in words you say.

- Model the task for the word *time.* Say: time. *The first sound I hear in* time *is* /t/. *The beginning sound in* time *is* /t/.

- *Now we will do one together. Listen:* cut. *What beginning sound do you hear in* cut? (/k/)

- *Let's keep going:* sack (/s/), deep (/d/), pit (/p/), will (/w/), fade (/f/), lid (/l/).

- Say: *Now listen for the ending sounds in words. Listen as I do one:* cone. *The last sound I hear in* cone *is* /n/.

- *Are you ready to try? What sound do you hear at the end of* name? (/m/) *Yes! The ending sound in* name *is* /m/. *Have children continue with the words:* hit (/t/), seal (/l/), hop (/p/), ride (/d/), back (/k/), lace (/s/).

- Display Picture Cards *comb, keys, moon, pen,* and *web* in random order. Ask children which two words have the same beginning sound. (*comb, keys;* /k/) Have children then tell which picture names end with the same sound. (*moon, pen;* /n/) Ask children to name other words that begin and end with those sounds.

✓ CORRECT & REDIRECT

To support children who blend incorrectly, model the task by saying the sounds more and more closely together, as in the example below.

- Repeat the sounds, each time saying the sounds a little more closely together. Then say the word. /h/, /ŏ/, /t/; /h/ /ŏ/ /t/; /h-ŏ-t/; hot

- Ask the child to blend the sounds to say the word.

- Continue, having children blend sounds to say other words.

● Professional Learning

TEACHING TERMS

Phonological awareness is the ability to identify and manipulate words, syllables, and sounds in oral language. **Phonemic awareness** refers specifically to this ability with phonemes, or individual speech sounds such as /b/ or /ă/.

See the **GPS guide** to learn more.

PHONICS

 Consonants *w, j, y v;* **Short u**

Spotlight on Sounds

Guide children to listen for and distinguish vowel sounds in words. *Today I will say a word, and you will repeat the word, say the middle sound, and name the vowel. I will do the first one. Listen: The word is* jug. Repeat, emphasizing the vowel sound. *The middle sound in* jug *is /ŭ/, short u. Listen again:* jug, /ŭ/, short u.

Now it's your turn. Repeat each word, say the middle sound, and name the vowel: with (with, /ĭ/ short i); van (van, /ă/ short a); jog (jog, /ŏ/ short o); cup (cup, /ŭ/ short u); wag (wag, /ă/ short a); jot (jot, /ŏ/ short o); yam (yam, /ă/ short a).

LEARNING OBJECTIVES

- Blend, decode, and build regularly spelled one-syllable words with the vowel short o and consonants *w, j, y, v.*
- **Language** Recognize sound-letter relationships and use them to decode words.

MATERIALS   Online

Sound/Spelling Cards *jellyfish, umbrella, volcano, walrus, yak*

Letter Cards *a, g, i, j, k, n, u, v, w, y*

Display and Engage *Blend and Read 2.9*

Start Right Reader *Book 1, p. 172*

Printable *Letter Cards*

Know It, Show It *p. 56*

I Do It

Spotlight on Letters Review Sound/Spelling Cards *umbrella, walrus, jellyfish, yak, volcano.*

Write *yak* for children to see, and use the **SOUND-BY-SOUND BLENDING** routine below to model blending the word using Letter Cards *y, a, k.*

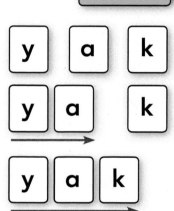

1. **Display** Letter Cards as shown. Say the first letter and sound.

2. **Slide** the second letter over. Say its sound. Then blend the two sounds.

3. **Slide** the last letter over. Say its sound. Say the first two blended sounds, the last sound, and the blended word: */yă//k/,* yak.

Repeat the routine with the letter cards for *wig, jug,* and *van.*

TEACHER TIP

Now decodable! Children can now decode the High-Frequency Words *but, cut, run, up,* and *us!* Children will practice these words along with the other High-Frequency Words for this week to build fluent word recognition.

 ENGLISH LEARNER SUPPORT:
Build Vocabulary

SUBSTANTIAL
Have children use gestures and pantomime to demonstrate their knowledge of the Blend and Read words. Share the meanings of any unknown words.

MODERATE
Ask questions about Blend and Read words to ensure understanding. *What does a dog's tail do? (wag) Where can you take a bath? (tub)*

LIGHT
Challenge children to use the words from Blend and Read in oral sentences to demonstrate meaning.

We Do It

Blend and Read

Project Display and Engage: **Blend and Read 2.9** or use Start Right Reader page 172.

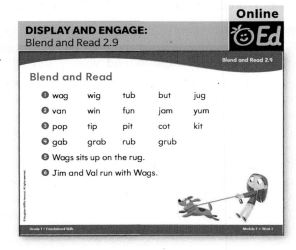

❶ **Line 1** Have children read the line. Then prompt a conversation: *What do you notice about the words? How can you compare the words?* If necessary, lead children to compare the words (same: *vowel sound in* tub, but, jug; *beginning sound in* wag, wig; different: *vowels in* wag, wig). Point to each word, and have children read the line chorally. Provide corrective feedback as needed.

❷ **Line 2** Continue with these words. Then call on volunteers to reread selected words until children can identify the words quickly.

❸ **Review** For Line 3, have children read the words chorally.

❹ **Challenge** If children are ready for a challenge, have them read the words with consonant blends in Line 4, share how they figured them out, and tell how each one differs from the word before it. Discuss word meanings with the group.

❺ **Sentences** For Lines 5–6, call on children to blend selected decodable words. Then have the group read the sentences chorally.

You Do It

INDEPENDENT PRACTICE

• **Option 1** Model how to write and spell the word *fun* sound by sound. Then have children identify sounds and use Printable: **Letter Cards** to form these words: *tub, van, jam, yum, wag.* Have a child spell each word aloud while others check their own work.

• **Option 2** Children complete Know It, Show It page 56.

✓ CORRECT & REDIRECT

• If a child mispronounces a word during Blend and Read, make note of the error type and address it.

• If a child reads *wag* as *wig*, read the word and point to the vowel: *The vowel sound is /ă/. Say each sound with me: /w/ /ă/ /g/. What is the word?* (wag)

• If a child reads *van* as *ban* or *jam* as *yam*, remember that many English learners have difficulty transferring these sounds. Reinforce the consonant sounds with the appropriate Sound/Spelling Cards (*volcano, jellyfish*). Then have the child blend the word with you.

👥 LINK TO SMALL-GROUP INSTRUCTION

REINFORCE FOUNDATIONAL SKILLS Use *Yip! Yap!* during small-group time to review or reinforce blending and decoding words with the vowel short *u* and the consonants *j, v, w, y.* Meet with children to work through the story, or assign it as independent work. *See the lesson on p. T450.*

Introduce Power Words

Use the steps **I Do It, We Do It, You Do It** with the information in the chart below to teach the Power Words from *Who Put the Cookies in the Cookie Jar?*

LEARNING OBJECTIVES

- **Language** Answer questions and discuss meanings to develop vocabulary.
- Identify real-life connections between words and their use.

MATERIALS   Online

Vocabulary Cards *2.33–2.38*
Classroom materials *spoon, two cups, water, books*

❶ Power Word	❷ Meaning	❸ Example
spoon (v.) (*p. 156*)	When you **spoon** food, you pick it up with a spoon.	**USE A PROP** Use a spoon and two cups (one empty, one with water). *I **spoon** the water from one cup to another.*
against (prep.) (*p. 157*)	If one thing is used **against** another, it keeps something from being harmed.	**MAKE A CONNECTION** Relate the concept of "protecting against" to children's lives. *We wear helmets when we bicycle to protect **against** injuries.*
churn (v.) (*p. 159*)	When you **churn** something, you stir it quickly for a long time.	**ACT IT OUT** Move a spoon inside a container in a churning motion. *This is how I would **churn** cream to make butter.*
stock (v.) (*p. 165*)	When you **stock** something, you fill it up with things.	**ACT IT OUT** Fill a shelf with books. *I **stock** this shelf with books.*
heal (v.) (*p. 166*)	When doctors **heal** sick or hurt people, they help them get well.	**MAKE A CONNECTION** Connect to children's experiences. *We can use a special cream and bandages to **heal** a scraped knee.*
drive (v.) (*p.164*)	When you **drive** something, you make it go where you want it to go.	**MAKE A CONNECTION** Talk about examples of driving. *I **drive** a car to work. The bus driver will **drive** the bus to school.*

TEACHER TIP

Fun with words! Children may be more familiar with the noun form of *spoon*. Point out that the two forms of *spoon* are often used together, such as *I **spoon** soup with a spoon.* Have children create similar sentences using both forms of the word *spoon*.

I Do It

Use the **VOCABULARY** routine and Vocabulary Cards 2.33–2.38 to introduce the Power Words from *Who Put the Cookies in the Cookie Jar?* You may wish to display the corresponding Vocabulary Card for each word as you discuss it.

spoon

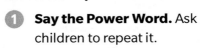
Vocabulary Cards

1. **Say the Power Word.** Ask children to repeat it.

2. **Explain the meaning.** Read aloud the student-friendly meaning.

3. **Talk about examples.** Use the image or a strategy to give examples of the word.

We Do It

Guide children to make connections between each word's meaning and how they can use it in their own lives. Use these prompts. Encourage children to explain or justify their answers.

- *What kinds of food can you **spoon**? What kinds of foods can you **churn**?*

- *When adults **drive** a car, what do seatbelts help protect **against**? Explain.*

- *What can you **stock** in your kitchen? Where would you put these things?*

- *What can you do to **heal** someone?*

You Do It

INDEPENDENT PRACTICE

Have partners work together to complete each of the activities below. Circulate and observe partners as they work, providing corrective feedback as necessary.

- **Role-Play** *Act out how you would **churn** a baby's food and then **spoon** it into a baby's mouth.*

- **Discuss** *Name some things you might **stock** in a closet to help you **heal** when you are hurt or sick. Then discuss some ways that you can protect yourself **against** getting hurt or sick.*

- **Write** *Make a list of things that people can **drive**.*

 ENGLISH LEARNER SUPPORT:
Build Vocabulary

SUBSTANTIAL
Act out the words *spoon, churn, stock,* and *drive.* Have children mimic your actions as they say each word.

MODERATE
Supply frames such as these: *I can **spoon** _____. I can **churn** _____. Adults might **drive** to _____. You might **stock** _____.*

LIGHT
Recast children's responses in complete sentences. Have them repeat the sentences after you.

Ask and Answer Questions

Step 1 Connect and Teach

LEARNING OBJECTIVES

- Identify the features of informational text.
- Generate questions about a text before, during, and after reading and answer them using text evidence.
- **Language** Ask and answer questions about key ideas in a text.
- Listen carefully and respond to others' ideas.

MATERIALS   Online

Anchor Chart 1 *Ask and Answer Questions*
Printable
Anchor Chart 1: Ask and Answer Questions
Teaching Pal *Book 1, pp. 152–171*
*my***Book** *Who Put the Cookies in the Cookie Jar?, Book 1, pp. 152–171*

📖 **READER'S VOCABULARY**

- **evidence** clues or details in the text that support an answer or idea
- **detail** small bit of information that supports a central idea or describes something in a text

- Remind children that good readers "stay awake," think, and ask questions about what they are reading.

- Project or display <u>Anchor Chart 1: Ask and Answer Questions</u>.

- Read the *when* and *why* parts of the Anchor Chart, explaining that readers ask questions before, during, and after reading to get information and to help them understand the text. They ask questions by putting into words the things they wonder about.

- Point to the *how* part of the chart and explain that starting questions with one of the words *who, what, where, why, when,* or *how* can help readers ask different kinds of questions and get different kinds of information.

- Tell children that **evidence** is information or clues in the text, and a **detail** is a small bit of information. Explain that to answer their questions, they should look for evidence and details in the text.

- Tell children they will practice asking and answering questions when they read the informational text called *Who Put the Cookies in the Cookie Jar?*

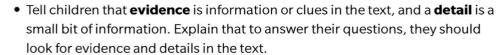

ANCHOR CHART 1: Ask and Answer Questions   Online 🍊*Ed*

Ask and Answer Questions

When?
- Before reading
- During reading
- After reading

Why?
- To get information
- To help you understand the text
- To practice being "awake" and thinking while reading
- To be curious and wonder as you read

How?
Use question words to **ASK**:
who   what   where
why   when   how

Look around in the text and pictures for evidence, or details, to help you **ANSWER.**

Notice **Note**

Big Questions

- The Teaching Pal prompts in this lesson feature the **Notice & Note Big Questions** for nonfiction.
- As needed, refer to p. T263 to review the Big Questions with children.

✓ **ASSESSMENT OPTION**

Assign the <u>Selection Quiz</u> to check comprehension of *Who Put the Cookies in the Cookie Jar?*

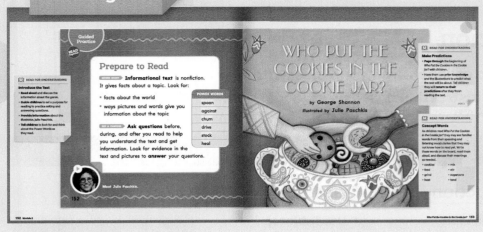

Step 2 Apply to Text

 In your Teaching Pal, pages 152–171, use the blue **READ
FOR UNDERSTANDING** prompts to read *Who Put the Cookies
in the Cookie Jar?* with children as they follow along and
annotate in their *my*Book.

- **Genre Study** Read the genre information on page 152.
Discuss what children would expect to find in an informational
text and compare that with what they might find in a fantasy.

- **Set a Purpose** Read the Set a Purpose section on page 152.
Prompt children to set their own purpose for reading *Who Put
the Cookies in the Cookie Jar?*

- **Meet the Illustrator** Play the audio about Julie Paschkis.
Help children make connections between the information
about Julie Paschkis and the features of informational text.

- **Read and Comprehend** Guide children to read the text all
the way through. Pause occasionally, using the prompts in
your Teaching Pal to gauge children's understanding and to
have them ask and answer questions. Have children refer back
to the Anchor Chart to note when, why, and how to ask and
answer questions.

Step 3 Engage and Respond

INDEPENDENT PRACTICE: Speaking & Listening

- Use the **TURN AND TALK** routine with the questions on
Teaching Pal and *my*Book page 171. Prompt children to
discuss how asking and answering questions before, during,
and after reading helped them understand the text.

- Read the Talking Tip. Remind children to follow agreed-
upon rules for discussion, such as listening carefully and
then adding to their partners' ideas. Tell children to use
the sentence frame to help them say more about their
partners' ideas.

- You may want to have children conduct their discussions
during daily small-group time.

 ENGLISH LEARNER SUPPORT:
Facilitate Discussion

Use the following supports for the Turn and Talk questions:

SUBSTANTIAL
Have children point to and act out jobs that help make cookies. Name
each job and have children repeat the word.

MODERATE
Use this sentence frame: *A _____ helps make cookies by _____.*
Encourage partners to name all the jobs from the book.

LIGHT
Have children use words with *-ing* to list jobs from the book.

LINK TO SMALL-GROUP INSTRUCTION

REINFORCE ASK AND ANSWER QUESTIONS Review or extend the
skill as needed during small-group time to support children's need for
differentiation. *See the lesson on p. T449.*

LESSON 12

READING WORKSHOP

Options for Differentiation

As the class engages in independent and collaborative work, meet with Guided Reading Groups or differentiate instruction based on student need.

GUIDED READING GROUPS

Match Children to Books + Instruction

- Choose just-right books based on level, skill, topic, or genre.

C — D — E — F — G — H — I — J — K

Leveled Readers

- Deliver instruction with each book's Take and Teach Lesson, choosing appropriate sessions based on need.

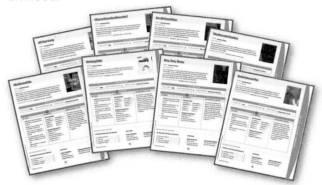

- Check comprehension, reinforce instruction, and extend learning with suggested supporting activities.

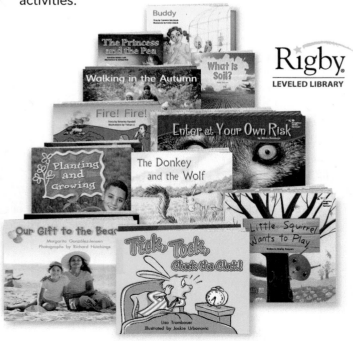

Rigby® LEVELED LIBRARY

EL ENGLISH LEARNER SUPPORT

Classify

- Use **Tabletop Minilessons: English Language Development 6.1 (Speaking)** to reinforce and practice the language skill.

Tabletop Minilessons: English Language Development

- Then use the following text-based prompts with *Who Put the Cookies in the Cookie Jar?* to guide application of the language skill. Begin with the prompt at the child's identified language proficiency level. As children are able, use lighter supports to encourage increased language proficiency.

SUBSTANTIAL

Have children describe the types of hands in the book, as well as how these hands help. Ask: *What do these hands do?* Allow children to use simple language to respond.

MODERATE

Ask children to describe the different types of hands that put the cookies in the cookie jar. Supply this frame: *These hands _____.*

LIGHT

Ask children to describe the different types of jobs that people do to put cookies in the cookie jar. Ask: *What kinds of jobs are described? What does that person do to help get the cookies in the cookie jar?*

REINFORCE ASK AND ANSWER QUESTIONS

Demonstrate

- Use **Tabletop Minilessons: Reading 1** to remind children that good readers ask questions before, during, and after reading in order to understand a text. Asking "I wonder . . ." questions helps readers think while reading the text. Remind children that questions can ask *who, what, where, when, why* or *how*. Then, readers look for **evidence**, or **details** in the text, to answer their questions.

- Model filling out Printable: **Reading Graphic Organizer 1** to ask and answer questions about *Who Put the Cookies in the Cookie Jar?*

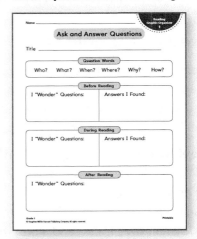

Tabletop Minilessons: Reading

Apply to Independent Reading

- Now have children ask and answer questions before, during, and after reading an appropriate just-right book that they are reading independently. Customize these prompts to the books children choose.

  » *Before you start reading, what are some questions you can ask about this text?*

  » *Now that you have read part of the text, what questions do you have?*

  » *Now that you are finished reading, what other questions can you ask?*

  » *What answers did you find to your questions?*

- Have children complete Printable: **Reading Graphic Organizer 1** for their independent reading book.

Printable:
Reading Graphic Organizer 1

ALMOST THERE

↓

READY FOR MORE

SCAFFOLD AND EXTEND

- Help children pause after every few pages to ask and answer this question: *What just happened?*

- Prompt children to ask questions before, during, and after reading by stopping and providing them with cues for asking questions.

- Have children ask questions throughout the process of reading and search for answers to their questions in the text.

🗨 ENGLISH LEARNER SUPPORT

SUBSTANTIAL

Model asking and answering a question before children begin reading. Have children repeat. Continue modeling asking and answering questions and encourage children to repeat them after you.

MODERATE

Review question words with children and prompt them to use the words when asking questions. Model as necessary.

LIGHT

As children answer the prompts, encourage them to include information from the questions in their answers.

Options for Differentiation

Yip! Yap!, Start Right Reader, *Book 1*, pp. 172–179

REINFORCE FOUNDATIONAL SKILLS

Read Decodable Text

Blend and Read Have children turn to Start Right Reader page 172. Use the **CHORAL READING** routine to read aloud the Blend and Read lines. Use challenge line 4 with children who are ready.

Preview the Story Help children recall what happens in *Wags, Wags, Wags!* and how the story ends. *(Val and Jim get a new pup that wags a lot so they name him Wags; Wags gets out of the yard.)* Then have children turn to page 173. Have them read aloud the title, look at the pictures on the first few pages, and predict whether Val, Jim, and Mom will find Wags.

Fluency Focus: Accuracy and Self-Correction Read aloud page 173 as children follow along. Misread *who* as *how* and discuss what you should do to self-correct. Ask: *Did I read this word correctly? (no) The word is who, but I said how. What should I do? (reread to say the correct word)* Then lead children in reading the page chorally, with accuracy.

Reflect on Reading Have children use a finger to track the words from left to right as they read each page silently. Then have them read the page chorally. Pause for these prompts:

- **Page 173:** *How does Jim feel about Wags getting out? (sad) What details in the picture support your answer? (He is crying.) What details in the words support your answer? ("Wags got out!" Jim sobs.)*

- **Page 174:** *How did Wags get out? (Wags dug a hole under the fence and ran.)*

- **Page 177:** *How does the family find Wags? (They hear Wags yipping and yapping.)*

- **Page 178:** *What is Wags doing? (Wags is in the mud playing with a bug.)*

Read It, Change It Read aloud the directions on page 179. Have children write their answers on a sheet of paper. *(jug; yap; run; win)* Then have them write a sentence for each new word and share their sentences with a partner.

Wags? Wags?
Is Wags in the log?
She is not in the log.

176

Yip! Yap! Yip! Yap!
Is it Wags?
Wags yaps at bugs.

177

It is Wags!
Wags has a big bug.
Wags is in mud!

178

Read It, Change It

Read each word, and follow the directions to write a new word. Read each new word.

1. bug   Change **b** to **j**.
2. yip   Change **i** to **a**.
3. ran   Change **a** to **u**.
4. in   Add **w** before **i**.

Check your work. Write a sentence for each new word. Share your work with a friend.

179

Make Minutes Count

As you meet with small groups to read *Yip! Yap!*, use one or more of these related activities, as needed, at the beginning or the end of the small-group session.

- **Connect to Phonics** Play Letter Swap. Gather multiples of Letter Cards *c, g, h, m, n, t,* and *u*. Build the word *mug* and have children blend and read the word. Ask what consonant must be swapped in order to change *mug* to *hug*. Make the change, and have children blend and read *hug*. Repeat the process for changing *hug* to *hut*. Guide children in using the letters to make new words, changing only one consonant at a time.

- **Connect to Spelling** Model segmenting sounds in the word *bug*. Have children repeat the sounds. Remind them that saying all the sounds in a word can help them spell the word. Then have children segment and write the remaining Spelling Words.

- **Connect to Handwriting** Model and explain how right-handed writers hold their papers tilted slightly to the left. Then model and explain how left-handed writers hold their papers tilted slightly to the right. Then write this sentence on the board: *The quick pup runs in the mud.* Have children write the sentence. Have them compare their sentence to the model and self-assess the legibility of their writing.

m	u	g

h	u	g

READING WORKSHOP

Options for Independent and Collaborative Work

While you meet with small groups, have other children engage in literacy activities that reinforce the lesson's learning objectives. Choose from these options.

Independent Reading

Student Choice Library

Rigby LEVELED LIBRARY

APPLY READING SKILL

Ask and Answer Questions Children complete Printable: <u>Reading Graphic Organizer 1</u> for an independent reading book.

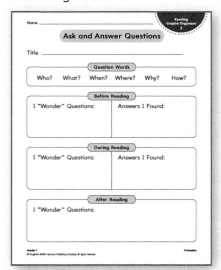

Printable: Reading Graphic Organizer 1

APPLY LANGUAGE SKILL

Classify Children complete Printable: <u>Language Graphic Organizer 4</u> for an independent reading book.

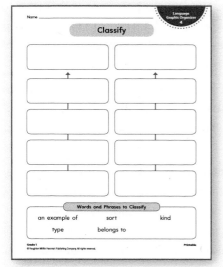

Printable: Language Graphic Organizer 4

Notice & Note

Big Questions

Encourage children to ask the Big Questions for nonfiction: *What surprised me? What did the author think I already knew? What challenged, changed, or confirmed what I already knew?*

Literacy Centers

See pp. T422–T423.

 WORD WORK

 CREATIVITY CORNER

 DIGITAL STATION

 READING CORNER

 TEAMWORK TIME

Start Right Reader

Yip! Yap!

by Kenisha Johnson
illustrated by Jessika von Innerebner

"Wags got out!" Jim sobs.
Who can find Wags?
Mom can!

173

Read Decodable Text *Yip! Yap!,*
Book 1: pp. 172–179

Speaking & Listening

Partners discuss the Turn and Talk questions using details from the text to help answer the questions. *See Engage & Respond, p. T447.*

Additional Skills Practice

PHONICS

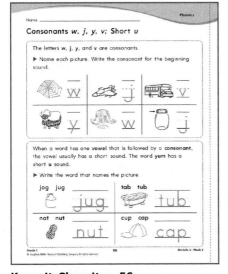

Name _____ Phonics

Consonants w, j, y, v; Short u

The letters w, j, y, and v are consonants.

▶ Name each picture. Write the consonant for the beginning sound.

w	j	v
y	u	j

When a word has one vowel that is followed by a consonant, the vowel usually has a short sound. The word **yum** has a short **u** sound.

▶ Write the word that names the picture.

jog jug	tab tub
jug	tub
not nut	cup cap
nut	cap

Know It, Show It, p. 56

Wrap-Up
Share Time

At the end of Reading Workshop, have children reflect on their learning by sharing how they applied **Ask and Answer Questions** or another area of focus during independent work time. Choose from these options:

- **SHARE CHAIR** Select a reader each day to come to the front of the class and tell what he or she learned from the reading by using a skill or strategy.

- **THINK-PAIR-SHARE** Children share their thinking with a partner. Select a few each day to share with the whole class.

- **RETURN TO ANCHOR CHART** Have children add sticky notes about their independent reading book to the Ask and Answer Questions Anchor Chart. Call on a few children to explain what they added.

ANCHOR CHART 1: Ask and Answer Questions

Online Ed

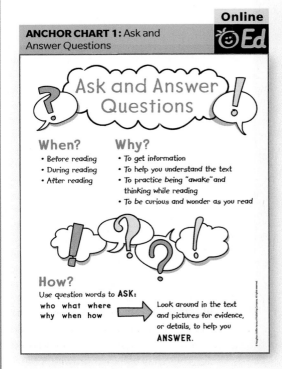

Ask and Answer Questions

When?
• Before reading
• During reading
• After reading

Why?
• To get information
• To help you understand the text
• To practice being "awake" and thinking while reading
• To be curious and wonder as you read

How?
Use question words to **ASK:**
who   what   where
why   when   how

→ Look around in the text and pictures for evidence, or details, to help you **ANSWER.**

LEARNING OBJECTIVES

- Identify and read high-frequency words.
- **Language** Recognize basic sight vocabulary.
- **Language** Ask and answer questions using basic sight vocabulary.
- Isolate initial, medial vowel, and final phonemes in spoken one-syllable words.
- Segment spoken one-syllable words into individual phonemes.
- Distinguish long from short vowel sounds in spoken one-syllable words.

MATERIALS Online

Word Cards *about, but, cut, eat, how, make, on, out, put, run, takes, up, us, who*

Printable *Word List 6*

Picture Cards *can, cape, cat, cup, pan, pot*

High-Frequency Words

Review the Words

Repeat the **HIGH-FREQUENCY WORDS** routine to review this week's High-Frequency Words: *about, eat, how, make, out, put, takes,* and *who,* and the decodable High-Frequency Words *but, cut, on, run, up,* and *us.*

> who

Questions and Answers

- Have partners use a a set of this week's High-Frequency Word cards from Printable: **Word List 6**. They place the cards facedown in a pile.
- The first player chooses a card and asks a question that uses the word on the card. The other player answers the question in a complete sentence that uses the same word. Partners swap roles and play until they have used all words.

Phonological Awareness

Isolate, Segment Phonemes

- Display Picture Cards *can, cape, cat, cup, pan,* and *pot.* Guide children to sort them by beginning sound. Point to *cat* and model: *The picture name is* cat. *What is the sound at the beginning of* cat? *(/k/)* Have children follow your model to sort the remaining cards. Repeat the activity for final sounds.
- Tell children they will now segment the picture names into their sounds. Point to *cape* and model: *The sounds in* cape *are /k/ /ā/ /p/.* Continue: pan (/p/ /ă/ /n/), can (/k/ /ă/ /n/), cat (/k/ /ă/ /t/), cup (/k/ /ŭ/ /p/), pot (/p/ /ŏ/ /t/).

Isolate Phonemes: Identify Vowel

- Have children compare two spoken words and tell whether the middle vowel sounds are the same or different. Model: *The two words are* pit, pat. Pit *and* pat *have different vowel sounds: /ĭ/, /ă/.*
- *Ready?* pan, pan (*same: /ă/*); bed, bead (*different: /ĕ/, /ē/*); hop, hop (*same: /ŏ/*); big, bag (*different: /ĭ/, /ă/*); hope, hop (*different: /ō/, /ŏ/*); sip, sip (*same: /ĭ/*)

TEACHER TIP

Illustrate it! Have children each draw a picture to illustrate one of their oral sentences from Questions and Answers. They may use their drawings as inspiration to write a short story!

 CORRECT & REDIRECT

Guide children who isolate a different phoneme by repeating the question with emphasis the target position.

- Tell children to listen carefully to the question as you repeat it: *What is the BEGINNING, or FIRST, sound in* cup?
- Ask: *What are you listening for?* (*the beginning sound*)
- Isolate the sounds in the word, emphasizing the beginning sound, and have children repeat: cup, /k/ /ŭ/ /p/.
- Ask: *What is the BEGINNING sound in* cup? (*/k/*)

Accuracy and Self-Correction

I Do It

"Wags got out!" Jim sobs.
Who can find Wags?
Mom can!

- Remind children that good readers think about what they are reading and whether the words make sense. They ask themselves questions, such as these: *What would make sense here? Does that sound right?*

- Ask children to follow along and to pay attention to whether the words make sense as you reread Start Right Reader page 173 (*Yip! Yap!*). Model misreading the first sentence, pointing to each word. "Wags goat out!" Jim sobs. *Does that sound right? No, the word* goat *doesn't make sense. I'll try again.* Reread the sentence and self-correct. Wags got out! *The word is* got, *not* goat.

We Do It

- Have children return to Start Right Reader page 173 (*Yip! Yap!*). Model misreading *find* in the second line as *fin* and then self-correcting. Who can fin Wags? Fin *doesn't make sense. I'll take another look. Oh, the word is* find. Who can find Wags? *makes sense.* Ask a volunteer to restate the process you used when you read a word that did not make sense.

- Have children use the **PARTNER READING** routine to read pages 174 and 175 to each other. As you circulate and listen, coach children to use context to confirm or self-correct word recognition. Encourage partners to help each other go back to find the words that caused difficulty and reread them correctly.

You Do It

INDEPENDENT PRACTICE

- Have children use the **PARTNER READING** routine to reread one of the Start Right Reader stories about Wags or *Who Put the Cookies in the Cookie Jar?* from their *my*Book. Remind them that rereading and self-correcting when things do not make sense will help them understand what they are reading and help them become better readers.

 LEARNING MINDSET

Belonging

Reflect Encourage children to reflect on how they support each other as learners when they use the **PARTNER READING** routine to practice fluency. *Think about how you and your partner have helped each other read better. You each have something important to offer to our classroom community. Also remember that when you get stuck, your partner or someone else in our class may be able to help you.*

 ENGLISH LEARNER SUPPORT:
Elicit Participation

ALL LEVELS It is important to note that English learners can demonstrate fluency while still struggling with English pronunciation. Rather than interrupting English learners' fluency practice to focus on pronunciation, ask children to focus on one sound that they would like to practice pronouncing as they record themselves reading. This way, children are not overwhelmed. Have them record, listen, and then rerecord to demonstrate improvement in pronouncing the sound they chose to practice.

LEARNING OBJECTIVES

- Read on-level text accurately.
- Use context to self-correct while reading on-level text.

MATERIALS   Online

Start Right Reader *Book 1, pp. 173–178*

Review Short *i, o, u*

Spotlight on Sounds

LEARNING OBJECTIVES

- Review the sound-spellings for short vowels *i, o,* and *u*.
- **Language** Recognize sound-letter relationships and use them to decode words.
- Blend letter sounds and decode regularly spelled one-syllable words with short *i, o,* and *u*.

MATERIALS   Online ⊙Ed

Sound/Spelling Cards *igloo, octopus, umbrella*

Letter Cards *b, g, i, j, m, o, u, w, y*

Articulation Video */ŭ/*

- Tell children that today they will be reading more words with the short vowel sounds. First, they will practice listening and telling how words are alike or different. *I will say two words. If the words are the same, say "same" and name the vowel. If the words are different, say "different" and tell what is different.*

- *Let's do the first one together. Listen:* hot/hat. *Are* hot *and* hat *the same or different? (different) What is different? (short o, short a) Very good. Let's continue:* pit/pot *(different, short i, short o);* jet/jet *(same, short e);* wag/wig *(different, short a, short i);* not/nut *(different, short o, short u);* hut/hot *(different, short u, short o);* tin/tin *(same, short i).*

▌Do It

Spotlight on Letters Have children name the vowels with you and tell what is special about them. *(a, e, i, o, u; each stands for many sounds)*

Display the Sound/Spelling Card for /ĭ/, *igloo*. Name the picture, say the sound, and give the spelling. *Igloo begins with the short i sound, /ĭ/. The letter i can stand for the sound /ĭ/ at the beginning or middle of a word.*

Write *win*. Say the letter sounds, and blend the word. *What sound do you hear in the middle of* win? *(/ĭ/) What letter stands for that sound?* (i)

Repeat for /ŏ/ and /ŭ/, using Sound/Spelling Cards *octopus* and *umbrella* and the words *jot* and *cup*.

● *Professional Learning*

TEACHING TERMS

What is the difference between phonemic awareness and phonics? **Phonemic awareness** deals only with sounds—not the letters that spell or represent those sounds—and so the activities are oral. **Phonics**, on the other hand, is the set of skills that deals with how letters represent those sounds. In other words, phonics is phonemic awareness written down!

See the **GPS guide** to learn more.

 ENGLISH LEARNER SUPPORT: Facilitate Language Connections

ALL LEVELS Speakers of Spanish, Chinese, Tagalog, or Korean may pronounce the sound /ŭ/ as /ŏ/. Play the **Articulation Video** for /ŭ/. Model the sound as children focus on your mouth. Then have children repeat each of these words and say the vowel sound: *cup, tub, but, gum, pup.*

ARTICULATION VIDEO   **Online** ⊙Ed

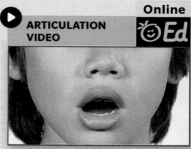

We Do It

Write *yum* and use Letter Cards *y, u, m* with the SOUND-BY-SOUND BLENDING routine below to model blending the word.

1. **Display** cards as shown. Say the first letter and sound.

2. **Slide** the second letter over. Say its sound. Then blend the two sounds.

3. **Slide** the last letter over. Say its sound. Say the first two blended sounds, the last sound, and the blended word: /yŭ/ /m/, yum.

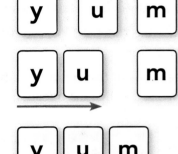

Sound-by-Sound Blending Repeat the SOUND-BY-SOUND BLENDING routine with cards for the words *job* and *wig*, having children say the sounds and blend.

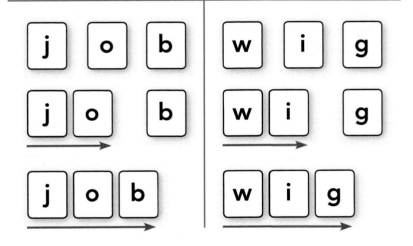

You Do It

INDEPENDENT PRACTICE

Blending Practice Write the words below. Then choose a volunteer to model the activity. Explain that you will point to a word and the child will blend and read the word. Then that child points to another word and calls on another child to blend and read it. Repeat the blending routine as needed. Continue until each child has had a turn.

win	jog	yum	Vin
cut	pot	his	rub

✓ CORRECT & REDIRECT

- If a child mispronounces a word during Blending Practice, make note of the error type and address it.
- If a child reads *cut* as *cot*, say the word and the vowel sound: *The word is cut, /ŭ/.* Point to the letters as you blend: /c/ /ŭ/ /t/, cut. Ask the child what the word is, and then have the child reread the line.
- If a child reads *pot* as *top*, cover the word and blend it together as you uncover one letter at a time, left to right. Then have the child blend and read the word.

👥 LINK TO SMALL-GROUP INSTRUCTION

REINFORCE FOUNDATIONAL SKILLS Use *Mud Pup* during small-group time to review or reinforce blending and decoding words with short vowels *i, o, u* and consonants *w, j, y, v.* Meet with children to work through the story, or assign it as independent work. *See the lesson on p. T464.*

LEARNING OBJECTIVES

- **Language** Respond to questions using multi-word responses.
- Use newly acquired vocabulary to identify real-life connections between words and their use.
- Identify and use words that name actions.

MATERIALS   Online

Know It, Show It   p. 58

Review Power Words

Revisit the Power Words

- Revisit the Power Words from *Who Put the Cookies in the Cookie Jar?* Display the questions and sentence frames below word by word.
- Model the task for the first word, using a child as your partner. Read aloud the question, and have the child repeat it. Respond using the sentence frame.
- Have partners use the **TURN AND TALK** routine to respond to each question using the sentence frame.
- For each word, ask one or two children to share their responses with the class. Then have them discuss the next question.

❶ Power Word	❷ Question	❸ Sentence Frame
spoon	Would it be easier to **spoon** cereal or an apple? Explain.	*It would be easier to* **spoon** *_____ because _____.*
against	What do gym mats protect us **against**?	*Gym mats protect us* **against** *_____.*
churn	Why would you **churn** food?	*I would* **churn** *food to _____.*
stock	What could a shop owner **stock** the shelves with in a grocery store?	*A shop owner could* **stock** *the shelves with _____.*
heal	How could a nurse **heal** a scraped knee?	*A nurse could* **heal** *a scraped knee with _____.*
drive	Where can people **drive** cars?	*People can* **drive** *cars _____.*

 ENGLISH LEARNER SUPPORT:
Facilitate Language Connections

ALL LEVELS Children whose first language is Cantonese, Hmong, Korean, or Vietnamese may have difficulty pronouncing or perceiving words that begin with the digraph *ch* or consonant blends. These sounds may not exist in their primary language, may be pronounced differently, or may be easily confused with another sound. Have children practice saying the sounds *ch*, *sp*, and *st*. Then have them practice saying words that begin with *ch*, *sp*, and *st*, including the Power Words *churn*, *spoon*, and *stock*.

Vocabulary Guess

- Display the Power Words. Have children break into small groups.

- One child in each group says clues about a Power Word without saying the word itself. Clues can be real-world examples, words with similar or opposite meanings, or descriptions of times the children may have used or might use the Power Word.

- For example, for the Power Word *spoon,* children might say "I do this when I eat soup" or "I would use this word to talk about eating."

- The rest of the group guesses the word. If necessary, children may ask the speaker questions to get clarification about the word or what he/she is saying.

- Have children continue the activity until all the words have been guessed.

- **Get Up and Move!** *Think of what someone does to* **drive** *a bus or a truck. Act out what that person does.* Have small groups take turns demonstrating how an adult would drive a bus or a truck. Ask them to share times when they might see someone do this.

- For additional practice with the Power Words from *Who Put the Cookies in the Cookie Jar?* Have children complete Know It, Show It page 58.

LEARNING MINDSET

Belonging

Normalize Explain to children that when we work in groups or with partners, everyone can add something useful to a discussion. *Everyone belongs in a group. We work in groups or with partners so that we can help and support each other. This is how we learn from each other, too!*

Getting Started

CLASSROOM MANAGEMENT

During lessons that are time- or thought-intensive, allow children to have breaks for movement at reasonable stopping points. Use movement to reinforce learning, as in the Get Up and Move! example on this page, or simply have children stretch to recharge and refocus.

See the **GPS guide** to learn more.

Text Organization

Step **1** Connect and Teach

LEARNING OBJECTIVES

- Recognize how an informational text is organized.
- Analyze description as a type of text organization.
- **Language** Describe how an author organizes a text.
- Write a thank-you note based on text evidence.

MATERIALS Online

Anchor Chart 35
Text Organization

Printable
*Anchor Chart 35:
Text Organization*

Teaching Pal *Book 1,
pp. 152–173*

myBook *Who Put the
Cookies in the Cookie Jar?,
Book 1, pp. 152–173*

Know It, Show It *p. 59*

📖 **READER'S VOCABULARY**

- **text organization** the way a text is arranged to help readers understand the information
- **description** a way to organize a text that gives details about one topic or subtopic at a time
- **detail** small bit of information that supports a central idea or describes something in a text

- Remind children that **text organization** is the way an author arranges information in a text. Authors organize informational texts to go with their purpose, or reason, for writing.

- Project or display **Anchor Chart 35: Text Organization**.

- Explain that one kind of text organization, or structure, is **description**.

- In this kind of organization, an author tells **details** about one thing after another. For example, an author writing about toys with wheels could tell about roller skates, then scooters, then skateboards, and then bicycles.

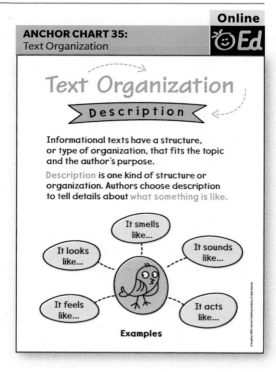

ANCHOR CHART 35:
Text Organization

Online

Text Organization
> Description <

Informational texts have a structure, or type of organization, that fits the topic and the author's purpose.

Description is one kind of structure or organization. Authors choose description to tell details about what something is like.

It smells like...
It looks like...
It sounds like...
It feels like...
It acts like...

Examples

- Point out that sometimes an author includes sensory details about what each thing looks, sounds, smells, feels, and acts like. Other times the author gives examples, one after the other.

- Tell children they will reread parts of *Who Put the Cookies in the Cookie Jar?* to practice recognizing text organization.

TEACHER TIP

Join in! Point out that *Who Put the Cookies in the Cookie Jar?* is an informational text that is also a poem. Read the poem aloud, having children clap to keep the rhythm of the text. Then invite them to chime in on rhyming words.

● *Professional Learning*

RESEARCH FOUNDATIONS

"One of the scaffolds that teachers identified as part of close reading instruction lies at the heart of this instructional approach: rereading the text. There is evidence that suggests that repeated reading of the same text is effective."

–Dr. Douglas Fisher and Dr. Nancy Frey (2014)

See the **GPS guide** to learn more.

Go to Your
Teaching Pal

ANNOTATE IT!

Online
Ed

Children may use the annotation tools in their eBook.

Step 2 Apply to Text

In your **Teaching Pal**, use the purple **TARGETED CLOSE READ** prompts to guide children to analyze the text organization in *Who Put the Cookies in the Cookie Jar?* Children may refer to the questions on Know It, Show It page 59 as you discuss them.

- Read aloud the first question on Teaching Pal page 158 and have children use information fro the text to answer it. *(The jobs people do to get ingredients.)*

- Then read the follow-up question. Tell children to think about how the author organized the information to answer it. *(He tells about each job and ingredient, one after the other.)*

- Read aloud the first question on Teaching Pal page 166. Have children use text evidence to infer the author's purpose for writing. *(to tell how each person's job helps everyone else)*

- Then read the follow-up question. Have children think about the text organization and how it contributes to the author's purpose for writing the text to answer it. *(The author describes each job, one after the other.)*

- Refer back to the Anchor Chart to support the discussion. As children name jobs in *Who Put the Cookies in the Cookie Jar?*, have them tell what examples and details the author used to describe each job.

Step 3 Engage and Respond

INDEPENDENT PRACTICE: Writing

- Read aloud the prompt on Teaching Pal page 172. Have children use the planning space to draw a worker from *Who Put the Cookies in the Cookie Jar?* that they think was helpful.

- Then have children write their responses to the prompt. Remind children to refer back to *Who Put the Cookies in the Cookie Jar?* and use the words and pictures to help them include specific details in their thank-you notes. Prompt children to write the word *I* and their names with a capital letter.

- You may want to have children complete their writing during daily small-group time.

ENGLISH LEARNER SUPPORT:
Scaffold Writing

SUBSTANTIAL
Have children complete this sentence frame with the name of the worker they chose: *Thank you, _____.*

MODERATE
Supply a thank-you note frame for children to use: *Dear_____, Thank you for _____. You help make cookies by _____.*

LIGHT
Model writing a thank-you note. Include variations in greetings and closings for children to choose from.

LINK TO SMALL-GROUP INSTRUCTION

REINFORCE TEXT ORGANIZATION Review or extend the skill as needed during small-group time to support children's need for differentiation. *See the lesson on p. T463.*

👥 SMALL-GROUP INSTRUCTION

Options for Differentiation

As the class engages in independent and collaborative work, meet with Guided Reading Groups or differentiate instruction based on student need.

GUIDED READING GROUPS

Match Children to Books + Instruction

- Choose just-right books based on level, skill, topic, or genre.

C D E F G H I J K

Leveled Readers

- Deliver instruction with each book's Take and Teach Lesson, choosing appropriate sessions based on need.

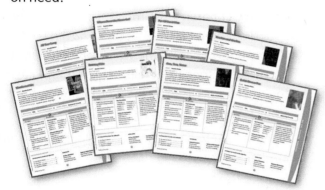

- Check comprehension, reinforce instruction, and extend learning with suggested supporting activities.

Rigby®
LEVELED LIBRARY

EL ENGLISH LEARNER SUPPORT

Classify

- Use **Tabletop Minilessons: English Language Development 6.2 (Reading)** to reinforce and practice the language skill.

Look at the different types of baked goods. Muffins are for breakfast. Cake is for dessert. What other foods do you see?

Classify

Tabletop Minilessons: English Language Development

- Then use the following text-based prompts with *Who Put the Cookies in the Cookie Jar?* to guide application of the language skill. Begin with the prompt at the child's identified language proficiency level. As children are able, use lighter supports to encourage increased language proficiency.

SUBSTANTIAL
Have children identify the items needed to bake cookies for the cookie jar. Ask: *What do you need to bake cookies?* Allow children to point to pictures or use single words or short phrases to respond.

MODERATE
Ask children to identify the items needed to bake cookies for the cookie jar. Supply this frame: _____ and _____ *are examples of items needed to bake cookies.*

LIGHT
Ask children to identify the types of items needed to bake cookies for the cookie jar. Ask: *What ingredients are needed to bake cookies for the cookie jar?*

REINFORCE TEXT ORGANIZATION

Demonstrate

- Use **Tabletop Minilessons: Reading 35** to remind children that authors organize informational texts to fit the topic and purpose for writing. **Text organization**, or structure, means how a text is set up. For example, a text might be a set of **descriptions**: first the text describes one thing, then it describes another thing, and so on. The author uses **details** in each description. Using this method of text organization allows an author to describe things or ideas one at a time.

- Model filling out Printable: **Reading Graphic Organizer 22** to identify and discuss text organization in *Who Put the Cookies in the Cookie Jar?*

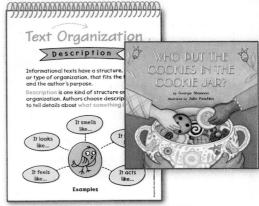

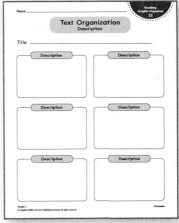

Tabletop Minilessons: Reading

Apply to Independent Reading

- Now have children identify and discuss text organization in an appropriate just-right book that they are reading independently. Customize these prompts to the books children choose.

  » *What is the topic of your text?*

  » *How does the text give information about the topic?*

  » *How does the organization help you understand the text?*

  » *Why do you think the author organized the information this way?*

- Have children complete Printable: **Reading Graphic Organizer 22** for their independent reading book.

Printable:
Reading Graphic Organizer 22

SCAFFOLD AND EXTEND

ALMOST THERE

READY FOR MORE

- Focus on two pages and help children understand that the text on each page describes one thing or idea, for the most part.

- Prompt children to identify details in the words and pictures that help them understand what is being described.

- Have children explain in their own words how information is organized by providing examples to explain their thinking.

 ENGLISH LEARNER SUPPORT

SUBSTANTIAL

Read aloud descriptive words on a page of the book. Have children repeat after you and point to the words as they say them. Help children connect the words to pictures.

MODERATE

Encourage children to identify words that describe what the hands on each page do: *The hands on this page _____.*

LIGHT

As children answer the prompts, have them explain their thinking by citing details or descriptive words that support their ideas.

READING WORKSHOP

Options for Differentiation

Mud Pup, *Start Right Reader, Book 1*, pp. 180–187

REINFORCE FOUNDATIONAL SKILLS

Read Decodable Text

Sentence Starters: High-Frequency Word Review Have partners read the boxed words on page 180. Then have them use words from the box and the sentence starters to talk about *Wags, Wags, Wags!* and *Yip! Yap!*

Preview the Story Have children recall where Val, Jim, and Mom found Wags in *Yip! Yap!* (the mud) Then have children turn to page 181. Read aloud the title and have children look at the pictures on the first few pages. Have them predict what will happen in this story.

Concepts of Print: Quotation Marks Remind children that quotation marks go before and after a character's dialogue, or a character's words. Have children use a finger to point to quotation marks as they read. Periodically prompt: *What is the dialogue? Which character said this dialogue?*

Fluency Focus: Accuracy and Self-Correction Read aloud page 182 as children follow along. Remind them that reading with accuracy means reading every word correctly and not skipping any words. When good readers read something that does not sound right, they

self-correct. Then help children read the page chorally with accuracy.

Reflect on Reading Have children read each page silently and then chorally. Pause for these prompts:

- **Page 181:** *What are Val, Jim, and Mom doing? Why? (They are giving Wags a bath; Wags got muddy at the end of* Yip! Yap!*)*

- **Page 183:** *How does the family feel? (mad) What details in the picture support your answer? (They are frowning; Val has her arms crossed.) What details in the words support your answer? ("Mom is mad at Wags.")*

- **Page 185:** *What is Mom doing? Why? (Mom is mopping up the mud; Wags splashed mud on everything when he wagged.)*

- **Page 186:** *Why does Mom put a log over the gap? (so Wags cannot get out again)*

Story Clues Have children read the clue on page 187 and answer it. *(bugs)* Then have them page through the week's Start Right Reader stories for ideas for their clue writing. Have partners listen to and answer each other's clues.

Jim got Wags in the tub.
"Sit, Wags! Sit!"
I rub Wags.

184

Mom mops up the mud.
Mom has a big job.
But Wags is not a mud pup!

185

186

Mom got a big log.
Mom fit it in the gap.
Wags can not go out.

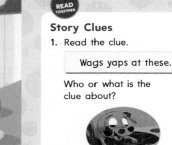

READ TOGETHER

Story Clues

1. Read the clue.

   Wags yaps at these.

   Who or what is the clue about?

2. Pick something in a story. Write a clue and read it to a friend. Can your friend find the answer?

187

Make Minutes Count

As you meet with small groups to read *Mud Pup,* use one or more of these related activities, as needed, at the beginning or the end of the small-group session.

- **Connect to Phonics** Play Letter Swap. Gather multiples of Letter Cards *b, d, i, m, n, o, p, s, t,* and *u.* Have children take turns using the cards to build words with the short *i, o,* or *u* vowel sound. One child puts down three cards to build a word. The next child blends and reads the word, then swaps the vowel to make a new word for the next child to blend and read. When all vowels are used or no new word may be formed with a different vowel, the next child makes a new word and restarts the process.

- **Connect to Spelling** Play Robot. Write the Spelling Words on the board or on chart paper. Then call on volunteers to demonstrate a "robot" voice and body movements. Point to a Spelling Word and have children quietly spell the word with you, chanting each letter in a robotic voice and moving like a robot. Repeat for all of the week's words.

- **Connect to High-Frequency Words** Give each child two High-Frequency Word cards from Printable: <u>Word List 6</u>. On a sheet of drawing paper, have them write a sentence that contains both words. On the other side of the paper, have them draw a picture that illustrates the sentence. Then have children trade pictures with a partner. The partners should take turns saying a sentence using two High-Frequency Words. Then partners discuss whether the two sentences about the pictures are similar and identify which High-Frequency Words they used in their sentences.

t	i	p
t	o	p

👥 **INDEPENDENT APPLICATION**

Options for Independent and Collaborative Work

While you meet with small groups, have other children engage in literacy activities that reinforce the lesson's learning objectives. Choose from these options.

Independent Reading

Student Choice Library

LEVELED LIBRARY

APPLY READING SKILL

Text Organization Children complete Printable: **Reading Graphic Organizer 22** for an independent reading book.

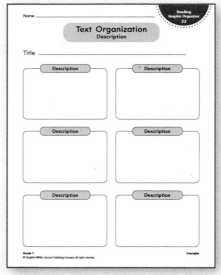

Printable: Reading Graphic Organizer 22

APPLY LANGUAGE SKILL

Classify Children complete Printable: **Language Graphic Organizer 4** for an independent reading book.

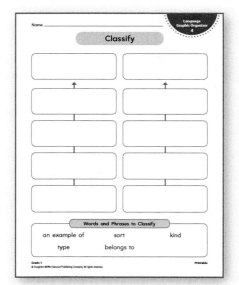

Printable: Language Graphic Organizer 4

Literacy Centers

See pp. T422–T423.

 WORD WORK

 CREATIVITY CORNER

 DIGITAL STATION

 READING CORNER

 TEAMWORK TIME

Start Right Reader

Wags is a mud pup!
Mom takes out a big tub.
Jim puts Wags in it.

Read Decodable Text *Mud Pup,*
Book 1: pp. 180–187

Writing

Children use specific details from the story to write thank-you notes.
See Engage & Respond, p. T461.

Close Reading

myBook, Book 1, pp. 174–177

Additional Skills Practice

SPELLING AND VOCABULARY

Know It, Show It, p. 57

Know It, Show It, p. 58

Wrap-Up
Share Time

At the end of Reading Workshop, have children reflect on their learning by sharing how they applied **Text Organization** or another area of focus during independent work time. Choose from these options:

- **SHARE CHAIR** Select a reader each day to come to the front of the class and tell what he or she learned from the reading by using a skill or strategy.

- **THINK-PAIR-SHARE** Children share their thinking with a partner. Select a few each day to share with the whole class.

- **RETURN TO ANCHOR CHART** Have children add sticky notes about their independent reading book to the Text Organization Anchor Chart. Call on a few children to explain what they added.

ANCHOR CHART 38:
Text Organization

Online
Ed

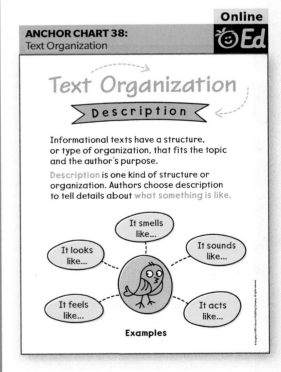

FOUNDATIONAL SKILLS

LEARNING OBJECTIVES

- Identify and read high-frequency words.
- **Language** Recognize, recite, and spell basic sight vocabulary.
- Isolate initial, medial vowel, and final phonemes in spoken one-syllable words.
- Segment spoken one-syllable words into individual phonemes.
- Distinguish long from short vowel sounds in spoken one-syllable words.

MATERIALS   Online

Word Cards *about, but, cut, eat, how, make, on, out, put, run, takes, up, us, who*
Picture Cards *cap, kite, map, mitt, mule, pool*

High-Frequency Words

Review the Words

Repeat the **HIGH-FREQUENCY WORDS** routine to review this week's High-Frequency Words: *about, eat, how, make, out, put, takes,* and *who,* and the decodable High-Frequency Words *but, cut, on, run, up,* and *us.*

Robot Game

- Display the Word Cards for the week's High-Frequency Words and decodable High-Frequency Words along the chalk ledge.
- Tell children that they will pretend to be robots for this activity. Ask for volunteers to demonstrate how a robot talks and moves. Then point to a Word Card and have children read it aloud. Have them spell the word in a robotic voice with accompanying robot motions. Repeat for the remaining words.

Phonological Awareness

Isolate, Segment Phonemes

- Display the Picture Cards. Tell children they will sort the cards by beginning sound. Say: *Listen for the beginning sound:* mule. *What is the beginning sound in* mule? (/m/) Call on children to say a picture name and initial sound, and group it with *mule* or begin a new pile. Repeat the activity for final sounds.

- Have children segment the picture names into phonemes. Hold up a Picture Card. Model with Picture Card *cap: The sounds in* cap *are* /k/, /ă/, *and* /p/. Have children segment the remaining picture names: mitt (/m/ /ĭ/ /t/), pool (/p/ /o͞o/ /l/), kite (/k/ /ī/ /t/), mule (/m/ /yo͞o/ /l/), map (/m/ /ă/ /p/).

Isolate Phonemes: Identify Vowel

- Tell children that you will say a pair of words, and they will tell whether the words are the same or different and how they differ. Model: *Listen:* rug, rag. *The words are different. The vowel sounds are different. Rug,* /ŭ/; *rag,* /ă/.

- *Now you try it! Are the words the same or different? If they are different, explain how. Listen:* fin, fine *(different vowel sound,* /ĭ/, /ī/*);* sun, sun *(same);* make, make *(same);* rack, rake *(different vowel sound,* /ă/, /ā/*);* main, man *(different vowel sound,* /ā/, /ă/*);* jet, jet *(same).*

TEACHER TIP

Choose the word! Once you have played a few rounds of the Robot Game, have children take turns choosing the High-Frequency Word or decodable High-Frequency Word for the class to spell.

✓ CORRECT & REDIRECT

If children segment incorrectly, say the word repeatedly, emphasizing a different phoneme each time. Example for *mitt:*

- */mmmĭt/: The beginning sound is* /m/.
- */mĭĭĭt/: The middle sound is* /ĭ/.
- */mĭt/: The last sound is* /t/.
- *The sounds in* mitt *are* /m/ /ĭ/ /t/.

Phonics Review

I Do It

Spotlight on Letters   Use the **SOUND-BY-SOUND BLENDING** routine to review this week's phonic elements: short vowels *i, o, u,* and consonants *w, j, y, v.* Model blending *jug* with Letter Cards (or display the written word). Say the first two sounds separately, then together; then say the last sound and add it to the blended sounds. Repeat for *win, van, jog, yum.*

LEARNING OBJECTIVE

• Blend, decode, and build regularly spelled one-syllable words with consonants *w, j, y, v,* and short vowels *i, o, u.*

MATERIALS   Online

Letter Cards *a, g, i, j, m, n, o, u, v, w, y*
Display and Engage *Blend and Read 2.10*
Start Right Reader *Book 1, p. 188*
Know It, Show It *p. 60*

We Do It

Blend and Read   Project Display and Engage: **Blend and Read 2.10** or use Start Right Reader page 188.

DISPLAY AND ENGAGE:
Blend and Read 2.10

Online **Ed**

Blend and Read 2.10

Blend and Read

❶ yam	cut	job	hum	mud
❷ us	fin	on	run	bus
❸ lip	hip	hot	has	got
❹ rub	scrub	hut	hunt	hint

❺ Jim puts Wags in the van.
❻ Val rubs Wags with rags.

Grade 1 / Foundational Skills   Module 2 • Week 3

❶ **Line 1**   Have children read the line. Then prompt a conversation about the words. Ask: *What do you notice about the words? How are any of them alike or different?* Reread the line chorally.

❷ **Line 2**   Continue. Then have volunteers reread selected words until they can identify them quickly.

❸ **Review**   Display Line 3, and have children read it chorally.

❹ **Challenge**   Children who are ready for a challenge can read Line 4, tell how they figured out the words, and compare *rub/scrub* and *hut/hunt.*

❺ **Sentences**   Display Lines 5–6. Call on children to blend selected decodable words. Point to each word as children read the sentences chorally.

You Do It

INDEPENDENT PRACTICE

• **Option 1**   Dictate sentences for children to write: *Jim has a cut lip. Val hums in the van.* Have them check their spelling using the Blend and Read lines.

• **Option 2**   Have children complete Know It, Show It page 60.

 ENGLISH LEARNER SUPPORT:
Build Vocabulary

ALL LEVELS Assign sets of partners different Blend and Read words. Have partners work together to decide how to present their words for the group to guess. Partners can use gestures, pantomime, or drawings to convey the meaning of each word.

 LINK TO SMALL-GROUP INSTRUCTION

REINFORCE FOUNDATIONAL SKILLS Use *Bad Pup, Wags!* during small-group time to review or reinforce blending and decoding words with short vowels *i, o, u,* and consonants *w, j, y, v.* Meet with children to work through the story, or assign it as independent work. *See the lesson on p. T476.*

Bad Pup, Wags!

Yip! Yip! Yip!
Who is it, Wags?
It is Nan!

LEARNING OBJECTIVES

- **Language** Identify words that name actions and directions.
- Understand and use words about actions and directions.
- Use a dictionary to find the meaning of unknown words.

MATERIALS   Online ⊙Ed

Display and Engage *Generative Vocabulary 2.11*

Know It, Show It *p. 61*

 READER'S VOCABULARY

- **action** what someone or something does
- **verb** an action word

 # Words About Actions and Directions

I Do It

- Project Display and Engage: <u>Generative Vocabulary 2.11</u>. Read aloud the introduction on the left side, explaining the difference between **action** words, or **verbs**, and direction words.

- Then discuss the phrase *drive straight*. Point out that the word *drive* is a verb, or an action word. It tells what the person is doing. The word *straight* is a direction word. It tells where the person is driving.

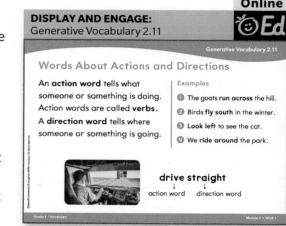

DISPLAY AND ENGAGE: Online ⊙Ed
Generative Vocabulary 2.11

Generative Vocabulary 2.11

Words About Actions and Directions

An **action word** tells what someone or something is doing. Action words are called **verbs**. A **direction word** tells where someone or something is going.

Examples
1. The goats **run across** the hill.
2. Birds **fly south** in the winter.
3. **Look left** to see the cat.
4. We ride **around** the park.

drive straight
↓   ↓
action word   direction word

Grade 1 | Vocabulary   Module 2 • Week 3

- Model determining the meaning of the phrase. *I know that* drive *means "to make something go where you want it to."* Straight *means "in a forward direction without turning." That means that* drive straight *means "to make something go forward without turning."*

- Continue by reading the example sentences, identifying each action and direction word and discussing the meanings of the phrases.

- Tell children that if they don't know the meaning of an action or direction word, they can look it up in a dictionary. Model looking up one of the words.

● *Professional Learning*

RESEARCH FOUNDATIONS

"Word reading ability may depend not only on basic reading skills but also on oral language skills such as vocabulary. As the ultimate goal of reading is reading for understanding, across developmental reading proficiency is less determined by technical reading skills and is more dependent on sophisticated vocabulary, background knowledge, and intelligence."

—Dr. Suzanne E. Mol (2011)

See the **GPS guide** to learn more.

 LEARNING MINDSET

Seeking Challenges

Review Remind children that having a learning mindset means trying new things and not being afraid to fail. *Sometimes in my reading, I come across words that I don't know. But I don't just give up and not learn the word's meaning. Instead, I think of it as a challenge! I know learning the word will help me to get smarter and build a bigger vocabulary. I try to learn as many words as I can!*

We Do It

- Write the following phrases on the board or chart paper:

  swim through

  go right

  march away

- Read each phrase aloud. Then point to each word. Have children tell whether the word is an action or direction word.

- Discuss the meaning of each phrase. If necessary, guide children to look up unknown words in the dictionary. Then have volunteers demonstrate the meaning of each phrase and use it in a sentence.

You Do It

INDEPENDENT PRACTICE

- **Option 1** Ask pairs to brainstorm lists of additional action and direction words. Prompt them with questions, such as these: *What are some other action words that tell how a person moves? What are some other direction words that explain where someone is going?* Have partners share their word lists and explain the meanings of the words they wrote. Have them look up unknown words in a dictionary.

- **Option 2** Have children complete Know It, Show It page 61.

ENGLISH LEARNER SUPPORT:
Build Vocabulary

SUBSTANTIAL
Say each phrase as you demonstrate its meaning. Have children repeat the actions and phrase after you.

MODERATE
Use these frames: *I swim through _____. I go right _____. I march away _____.*

LIGHT
Ask: *What do you swim through? When would you go right? When would you march away from something?*

TEACHER TIP

Use new words! Explain direction words like *east* and *west*, and have children point in the appropriate direction. Using their hands to indicate direction will help children to remember new words.

Content-Area Words

LEARNING OBJECTIVES

- Identify the features of videos.
- Use media and media features to clarify word meanings.
- **Language** Identify context clues that clarify word meaning.
- Speak clearly and at an appropriate rate.

MATERIALS   Online

Anchor Chart 14
Content-Area Words

Printable
Anchor Chart 14: Content-Area Words

Teaching Pal Book 1, pp. 178–181

*my*Book *Curious About Jobs,* Book 1, pp. 178–181

READER'S VOCABULARY

- **context clue** the words and sentences around an unknown word that can be clues to its meaning

- Remind children that people get information from videos as well as from books. Point out that videos can sometimes be about science or social studies topics.

- Project or display the **Anchor Chart 14: Content-Area Words**.

- Explain that some informational videos have special science or social studies vocabulary. Tell children that they can use **context clues** to figure out the meaning of these words.

- Read and explain each type of context clue on the Anchor Chart. Point out that some videos have titles or headings that appear on the screen. All videos have pictures that can be clues to a word's meaning. The spoken words or sounds around a word can also be clues.

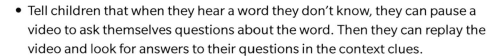

ANCHOR CHART 14:
Content-Area Words

Online

CONTENT-AREA WORDS

Informational texts often use words from science and social studies to tell about a topic.

How can I figure out what these words mean?

TITLE

Heading

WORD
WORD
WORD

Look at text features, like titles and headings.

Look at the pictures.

Ask and answer questions.

Use context, or the words and sentences near the word.

- Tell children that when they hear a word they don't know, they can pause a video to ask themselves questions about the word. Then they can replay the video and look for answers to their questions in the context clues.

- Tell children they will practice using media features to figure out the meaning of content-area words when they view *Curious About Jobs.*

LEARNING MINDSET

Seeking Challenges

Review Remind children that seeking challenges and learning new things helps our brains grow and learn. Point out that learning new words can also be a challenge: *If you come to a word you don't know, that is a challenge. Stopping to ask questions to figure out the word's meaning is a way to meet that challenge. Even if you don't understand the word the very first time you see it, you will know more about it the next time.*

● Getting Started

ENGAGEMENT ROUTINE

Use strategies that engage all children in listening and responding. For example, instead of calling on one child to answer a question, use the TURN AND TALK routine to have all children discuss ideas with a partner. Then select pairs to share with the whole class, allowing children to learn from the variety of responses.

See the **GPS guide** to learn more.

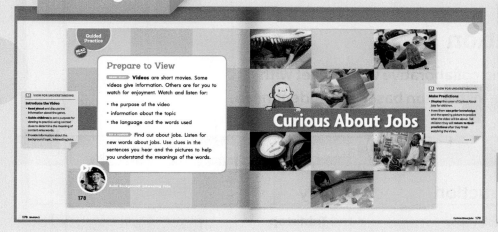

Step 2 Apply to Media

 In your Teaching Pal, pages 178–180, use the blue **VIEW FOR UNDERSTANDING** prompts to introduce and project *Curious About Jobs* as children follow along in their *my*Book.

- **Genre Study** Read the genre information on page 178. Discuss the kinds of things children would expect to find in an informational video. Remind children that the pictures, words, and sounds in a video all work together to give information.

- **Set a Purpose** Read the Set a Purpose section on page 178. Prompt children to set their own purpose for viewing *Curious About Jobs*.

- **Build Background** Play the audio for **Interesting Jobs** to set up the topic for the video.

- **As You View** Read page 180. Guide children to watch the video all the way through. Replay and have children raise their hands when they hear an unknown word. Pause the video and have them ask questions about the word and look for context clues to its meaning. Refer back to the Anchor Chart as necessary.

Step 3 Engage and Respond

INDEPENDENT PRACTICE: Speaking & Listening

- Use the **TURN AND TALK** routine with the questions on Teaching Pal and *my*Book page 181. Remind children to use new words they have learned in their responses.

- Read the Talking Tip. Discuss with children why it's important to speak clearly and not too fast or slow. Then have them use the sentence frame to tell their ideas.

- You may want to have children conduct their discussions during daily small-group time.

 ENGLISH LEARNER SUPPORT:
Support Comprehension

ALL LEVELS Pre-teach important terms before children view the video. Before viewing, write and read aloud the terms *airplane mechanic*, *potter*, and *museum educator*. Give simple definitions, and have children repeat the words with you. Ask them to listen for these words as they view the video.

LINK TO SMALL-GROUP INSTRUCTION

REINFORCE CONTENT-AREA WORDS Review or extend the skill as needed during small-group time to support children's need for differentiation. *See the lesson on p. T475.*

Options for Differentiation

As the class engages in independent and collaborative work, meet with Guided Reading Groups or differentiate instruction based on student need.

GUIDED READING GROUPS

Match Children to Books + Instruction

- Choose just-right books based on level, skill, topic, or genre.

C D E F G H I J K
Leveled Readers

- Deliver instruction with each book's Take and Teach Lesson, choosing appropriate sessions based on need.

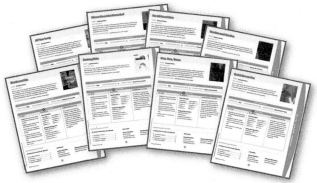

- Check comprehension, reinforce instruction, and extend learning with suggested supporting activities.

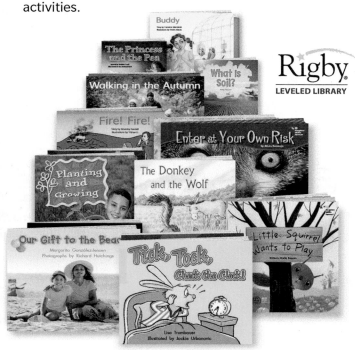

Rigby®
LEVELED LIBRARY

EL ENGLISH LEARNER SUPPORT

Classify

- Use **Tabletop Minilessons: English Language Development 6.2 (Writing)** to reinforce and practice the language skill.

Look at the different types of baked goods. Muffins are for breakfast. Cake is for dessert. What other foods do you see?

Classify

Tabletop Minilessons: English Language Development

- Then use the following text-based prompts with *Curious About Jobs* to guide application of the language skill. Begin with the prompt at the child's identified language proficiency level. As children are able, use lighter supports to encourage increased language proficiency.

SUBSTANTIAL
Encourage children to identify adjectives presented to describe each job. Ask: *What is the person doing to the plane? With the pottery? At the museum?* Allow children to respond using single words or short phrases.

MODERATE
Have children relate the kinds of tasks each type of job involves. Supply these frames: *When you fix a plane, you _____. When you make pottery, you _____. When you work at a museum, you _____.*

LIGHT
Ask children to describe each job. Ask: *What is part of the job of fixing planes? of making pottery? of working at a museum?*

REINFORCE CONTENT-AREA WORDS

Demonstrate

- Use **Tabletop Minilessons: Reading 14** to remind children that special vocabulary about a science or social studies topic is called **content-area vocabulary.** Readers can use **context clues** to understand the meanings of these words. These clues might be in the same sentence, in surrounding sentences, or in the visuals.

- Model filling out Printable: **Reading Graphic Organizer 13** to use context clues to determine the meaning of content-area words in *Curious About Jobs*.

Apply to Independent Reading

- Now have children use context clues to determine the meaning of content-area words in an appropriate just-right book that they are reading independently. Customize these prompts to the books children choose.

  » *What is the topic?*

  » *What are some words related to the topic?*

  » *What context clues help you understand these words?*

- Have children complete Printable: **Reading Graphic Organizer 13** for their independent reading book.

Tabletop Minilessons: Reading

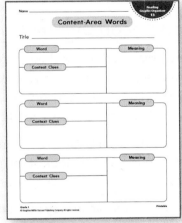

Printable:
Reading Graphic Organizer 13

| ALMOST THERE | | READY FOR MORE |

SCAFFOLD AND EXTEND

- Help children identify important content-area words and identify applicable context clues.

- Prompt children to say a content-area word from their text and to explain what it means, using context clues from the text.

- Have children identify content-area words and encourage them to explain their meaning, citing context clues to support their ideas.

🔵EL ENGLISH LEARNER SUPPORT

SUBSTANTIAL

Read aloud content-area words in the text. Have children point to the words and repeat them after you.

MODERATE

Have children identify important content-area words. Model finding clues that can help them determine their meaning. Supply this frame: *I know what _____ means because_____.*

LIGHT

Encourage children to cite specific words, text features, or pictures that support their thoughts about the meanings of content-area words.

Options for Differentiation

Bad Pup, Wags!, Start Right Reader, *Book 1*, pp. 188–195

REINFORCE FOUNDATIONAL SKILLS

Read Decodable Text

Blend and Read Have children turn to Start Right Reader page 188. Use the **CHORAL READING** routine to read aloud the Blend and Read lines. Use challenge line 4 with children who are ready.

Preview the Story Call attention to page 189. Have children read the title, look at the pictures on the first few pages, and predict what Wags does that is bad.

Fluency Focus: Accuracy and Self-Correction
Read aloud page 189 as children follow along. Misread *It is Nan!* as *Is it Nan?* and then model self-correcting. Point out that you self-corrected so the story made sense. Then have children read the story, paying attention to accuracy and self-correcting as needed.

Reflect on Reading Have children read to find out why Wags is a bad pup. Have them read each page silently and then chorally. Pause for these prompts:

- **Page 190:** *What does Wags do that is bad? (hops up on Nan)*

- **Pages 191–192:** *What other bad things does Wags do? (digs in pots, nips at Bud Cat, eats jam, almost tips the jugs) What do Val and Jim want Wags to do? (sit)*

- **Page 193:** *How does Nan help Wags sit? (She makes rag tugs.)*

- **Page 194:** *Why does Val say that Wags is a good pup? (because Wags sits on the rug)*

Show What You Know Allow time for children to reread the week's four Start Right Reader stories. Then have them answer the questions on page 195. Have partners discuss the stories.

Wags eats jam.
She is about to tip jugs.
"Bad pup, Wags! Sit!"

192

How can we make Wags sit?
Nan makes rag tugs.
Jim and I tug. Wags tugs.

193

Wags sits on the rug.
Jim and I hug Wags.
Wags is our good pup.

194

READ TOGETHER

Show What You Know
Reread the four stories to answer these questions.

1. How do Val and Jim feel about Wags? How can you tell?

2. What do Val and Jim learn about having a pup? Use details from the stories in your answer.

Talk about the stories with a partner.

195

⏱ Make Minutes Count

As you meet with small groups to read *Bad Pup, Wags!*, use one or more of these related activities, as needed, at the beginning or the end of the small-group session.

- **Connect to Phonics** Have children go on a word hunt in *Bad Pup, Wags!* Choose a few pages for them to reread. Have them hunt for words with short *i*, *o*, and *u* vowel sounds and write the words they find.

- **Connect to Spelling** On the board, write these words: *did, dig, fit, pig, sip, sit*. Have children copy those words onto the blank cards on Printable: <u>Word List 6</u>. Then have them sort those words, as well as the basic and review Spelling Words, by vowel sounds. After sorting, have them draw a three-column chart on a sheet of paper and label the columns *i*, *o*, and *u*. Have them write the words in the appropriate columns. If time permits, have children sort the cards again, this time by final consonant sounds.

- **Connect to High-Frequency Words** Play Word Match. Use two sets of High-Frequency Word cards from Printable: <u>Word List 6</u>. Shuffle the cards and place them face down in a grid on the tabletop. Children take turns selecting two cards, turning them over, and reading the words. If the words match, the child leaves the cards facing up. If the words do not match, the child turns the cards face down again and the next player takes a turn. Play continues until all of the words are matched.

Name _____   Word List 6

High-Frequency Words	Decodable High-Frequency Words	Spelling Words	
		Basic	Review
about	but	up	log
eat	cut	bug	hop
how	run	mud	hot
make	up	nut	not
out	us	hug	
put	on	tub	
takes			
who			
			Challenge
			puppy
			bathtub

Grade 1
© Houghton Mifflin Harcourt Publishing Company. All rights reserved.   Printable

Printable: Word List 6

READING WORKSHOP

Options for Independent and Collaborative Work

While you meet with small groups, have other children engage in literacy activities that reinforce the lesson's learning objectives. Choose from these options.

Independent Reading

Student Choice Library

Rigby
LEVELED LIBRARY

APPLY READING SKILL

Content-Area Words Children complete Printable: **Reading Graphic Organizer 13** for an independent reading book.

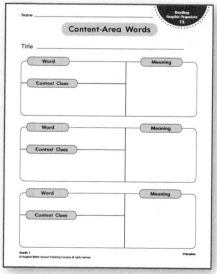

Printable: Reading Graphic Organizer 13

APPLY LANGUAGE SKILL

Classify Children complete Printable: **Language Graphic Organizer 4** for an independent reading book.

Printable: Language Graphic Organizer 4

Literacy Centers

See pp. T422–T423.

 WORD WORK

 CREATIVITY CORNER

 DIGITAL STATION

 READING CORNER

 TEAMWORK TIME

Start Right Reader

Read Decodable Text *Bad Pup, Wags!*, Book 1: pp. 188–195

Speaking & Listening

Partners discuss the Turn and Talk questions using new words. *See Engage & Respond, p. T473.*

Additional Skills Practice

PHONICS

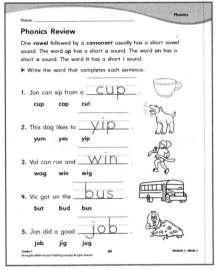

Know It, Show It, p. 60

GENERATIVE VOCABULARY

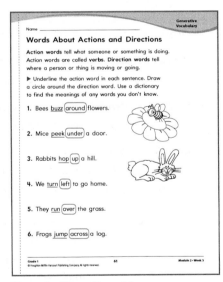

Know It, Show It, p. 61

Wrap-Up
Share Time

At the end of Reading Workshop, have children reflect on their learning by sharing how they applied **Content-Area Words** or another area of focus during independent work time. Choose from these options:

- **SHARE CHAIR** Select a reader each day to come to the front of the class and tell what he or she learned from the reading by using a skill or strategy.

- **THINK-PAIR-SHARE** Children share their thinking with a partner. Select a few each day to share with the whole class.

- **RETURN TO ANCHOR CHART** Have children add sticky notes about their independent reading book to the Content-Area Words Anchor Chart. Call on a few children to explain what they added.

ANCHOR CHART 14:
Content-Area Words

Online

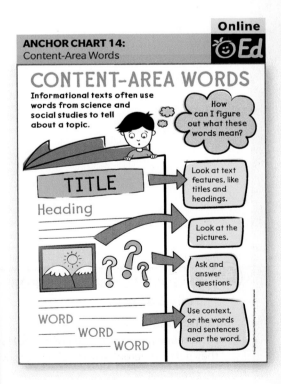

High-Frequency Words

Children's Choice

- Remind children of the High-Frequency Words they have been practicing this week: *about, eat, how, make, out, put, takes,* and *who,* and the decodable High-Frequency Words *but, cut, on, run, up,* and *us.*

- Review any words that posed difficulty for children this week, using Word Cards and the **HIGH-FREQUENCY WORDS** routine.

- In Lessons 12–14, children used these practice activities: What Am I Thinking? (p. T440), Questions and Answers (p. T454), and Robot Game (p. T468). Have children vote on their favorite, and use it to review the week's words for word recognition fluency.

LEARNING OBJECTIVES

- Identify and read high-frequency words.
- **Language** Recognize, recite, and spell basic sight vocabulary.
- **Language** Ask and answer questions using basic sight vocabulary.
- Blend phonemes to say one-syllable words.
- Isolate initial, medial vowel, and final phonemes in spoken one-syllable words.
- Segment spoken one-syllable words into individual phonemes.
- Distinguish long from short vowel sounds in spoken one-syllable words.

MATERIALS   Online

Word Cards *about, but, cut, eat, how, make, on, out, put, run, takes, up, us, who*

Printable *Phonological Awareness 6; Word List 6*

Phonological Awareness

Teacher's Choice

- In Lessons 11–14, children practiced blending and isolating phonemes (pp. T425, T441, T454, T468). They also practiced segmenting phonemes and identifying vowel sounds (pp. T454, T468).

- Use the following to gauge children's facility isolating initial and final phonemes.

  » **Isolate Phonemes** Ask children to identify the beginning sound: bug (/b/), side (/s/). Ask children to identify the ending sounds: note (/t/), bill (/l/).

- Use Printable: **Phonological Awareness 6** to gauge which other phonological awareness tasks need reinforcement.

  » **Blend Phonemes** Have children blend the sounds to say each word: /r/ /ŭ/ /g/ (rug), /h/ /ĕ/ /n/ (hen).

  » **Segment Phonemes** Have children segment the following words and write a tally mark for each phoneme: fox (/f/ /ŏ/ /ks/, 3); tag (/t/ /ă/ /g/, 3).

  » **Isolate Phoneme: Identify Vowel** Have children identify the medial vowel sound in each word and say whether the words are the same: neat, net (/ē/, /ĕ/, no); top, top (/ŏ/, / ŏ/, yes).

 ENGLISH LEARNER SUPPORT: Build Vocabulary

SUBSTANTIAL
Pantomime putting on a pair of pants. Have children act out how they *put on* different articles of clothing while they say *put on.*

MODERATE
Have children use sentence frames with *put* and *on.*
When it is cold, I put on _____. When it is hot, I put on _____.

LIGHT
Ask children to share oral sentences about things they *put on* in different weather and tell why.

 CORRECT & REDIRECT

To support children who struggle to distinguish vowel sounds in similar words, elongate the vowel sounds as you say the words. Example:

- *Listen for the vowel sound in the middle of this word:* neat. *Listen as I say it again:* /n-ēēē-t/. Have children repeat. *Now let's say just the vowel sound:* /ē/.

- *Now let's do the same for* net: /n-ĕĕĕ-t/. Have children repeat. *Say the vowel sound with me:* /ĕ/.

- *Listen:* Neat, /ē/. Net, /ĕ/. *Are the vowel sounds the same or different?* (different)

Short u

Spelling Assessment

LEARNING OBJECTIVE
- Spell words with short *u* (closed syllables).

DICTATION SENTENCES

BASIC

1. **up** The bird flew *up* in the sky.
2. **bug** An ant is a *bug*.
3. **mud** Rain may turn dirt to *mud*.
4. **nut** Almonds are a kind of *nut*.
5. **hug** My dad likes to *hug* me.
6. **tub** She washed the dog in a *tub*.

REVIEW

7. **log** Mom put a *log* on the fire.
8. **hop** A rabbit can *hop* away.
9. **hot** Be careful! The stove is *hot*.
10. **not** Stop at the sign, and do *not* go.

CHALLENGE

11. **puppy** We named our *puppy* Spot.
12. **bathtub** Water is in the *bathtub*.

1. Say each Spelling Word, and read the Dictation Sentence. Repeat the word, and then have children write it. Remind them to use their best handwriting.

2. Add the Surprise Words *jug, rub,* and *pup*. If you prefer a shorter test, replace three of the Basic Words with the Surprise Words.

   - **jug** The milk *jug* was in the fridge.
   - **rub** I *rub* my arm where it hurts.
   - **pup** The mother dog licked her *pup*.

3. Include the Challenge Words for children who practiced them this week.

4. Review any words that children misspell. If they miss two or more words, then revisit the Lesson 11 Word Sort activity on page T429.

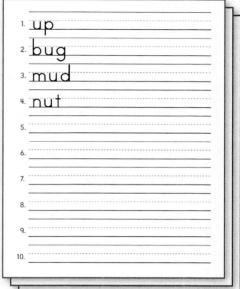

⏱ Cumulative Vocabulary

Review Vocabulary

LEARNING OBJECTIVES

- **Language** Explain and use academic vocabulary words.

- Use newly acquired vocabulary to identify real-life connections between words and their use.

- Identify and use words that name locations.

MATERIALS   Online ⓔ**Ed**

Vocabulary Cards 2.1–2.3, 2.10–2.15, 2.22–2.27, 2.33–2.38

myBook Book 1, pp. 94–95

- Tell children you will review the Big Idea Words and Power Words from this module together.

- Display Vocabulary Cards 2.1–2.3, 2.10–2.15, 2.22–2.27, 2.33–2.38 one at a time. If children would like you to refresh their memories about a word, they should raise their hand when you display that Vocabulary Card.

- Read aloud the student-friendly meaning on each Vocabulary Card, as needed. Encourage children who didn't raise their hands to explain the word's meaning and/or use it in a sentence.

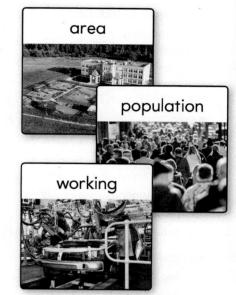

Vocabulary Cards

LEARNING MINDSET

Belonging

Apply Point out that helping each other is an important part of being in a learning community. *Don't be shy to ask for help learning a new word. When someone helps you, he or she gets extra practice using that word. So when we ask for help, we are actually helping the person who helps us!*

Teacher's Choice

Display the Vocabulary Cards, or write the Big Idea Words and Power Words from this module on the board so children can refer to them as they complete one or more of the following activities. Assign an activity from the following options to the whole class, or assign different activities based on children's needs.

VOCABULARY NETWORK

- Revisit the Vocabulary Network on *my*Book pages 94–95 that children started at the beginning of the module.

- Tell children that as they learned about the module topic through their reading, they may have learned other words or ideas that could be added to the network.

- Have children add more synonyms, antonyms, or details to their drawings to complete their Vocabulary Network.

- Ask partners to share and compare their completed networks.

WORD SORT

- Remind children that when they sort words, they group words together that are alike. Have small groups look at the Big Idea Words and the Power Words and discuss how to sort them.

- Children may choose to group the words by a topic, such as Community. The words *market, neighbors, help, town, community,* and *places* could all be used to talk about the community.

- Children may also choose to group the words by part of speech, such as Nouns. The words *market, clinic, community, town, map, places,* and *neighbors* are all nouns. Some of them will be easily identified as nouns that name places or nouns that name things. Encourage children to group the words into those noun categories. Children might need some guidance with the categories.

- Children may also choose to group the words by other categories that are meaningful to them.

- Have children write their completed word sort on a sheet of paper.

VOCABULARY IN WRITING

- Remind children that they can practice using new vocabulary they have learned in conversations and in their writing.

- Have children work independently, with a partner, or in a small group to compose a short piece of writing that uses as many of the vocabulary words as possible.

- Since this module's topic and literature are related to social studies concepts, children may gravitate towards a social studies-related topic. Don't discourage them from writing about those topics, but you may point out that these words can be used in many different contexts. For example, they may want to write a personal narrative about what it means to live in a *community* or an essay about why it important for *neighbors* to *help* each other.

- Have children share their writing with a small group.

ENGLISH LEARNER SUPPORT:
Scaffold Writing

SUBSTANTIAL
Encourage children to use their first languages to start their writing.

MODERATE
Provide model sentences such as this: *My neighbors help us wash our car. My neighbors help us go to school.*

LIGHT
Prompt children with questions, such as these: *Who lives in your community? How do neighbors help each other?*

Professional Learning

BEST PRACTICES

Frequent exposure to words in a variety of contexts builds and strengthens word knowledge. By revisiting vocabulary throughout the week, children can practice using the words in different contexts and across content areas.

See the **GPS guide** to learn more.

READING WORKSHOP

LEARNING OBJECTIVES

- **Language** Discuss and compare texts.
- Synthesize information from multiple texts about the same topic.
- Compare and contrast texts on the same topic.
- Write about communities.
- Speak clearly at an appropriate pace and using the conventions of language.

MATERIALS   Online

Display and Engage *Knowledge Map 2.1*
Teaching Pal *Book 1, pp. 182–183*
myBook *Book 1, pp. 182–183*

 Wrap Up the Topic

Reflect on the Topic

- Project Display and Engage: <u>**Knowledge Map 2.1**</u> to reflect on the module topic, communities. As you point to various parts of the Knowledge Map, prompt children to recall texts about the topic and share what they learned. Alternatively, you may name texts from the module and have children point out parts of the map that relate to them.

- Encourage children to discuss similarities and differences between the texts and how they approach the same topic. *What did you learn about communities from these texts? What is the same about* Places in My Neighborhood *and* Who Put the Cookies in the Cookie Jar? *What is different about them?*

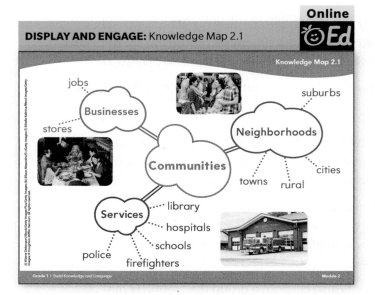

 LEARNING MINDSET

Belonging

Reflect Point out specific examples of how children contributed to their classroom or school community or made others feel like they belonged during Module 2. For example, *I noticed that you helped _____,* or *I noticed that you were kind and caring when you _____.*

 ENGLISH LEARNER SUPPORT:
Scaffold Writing

Use these supports with the Award Time activity.

SUBSTANTIAL
Have children draw why the winner deserves the award. Help them write captions: _____ *wins the award for best _____.*

MODERATE
Supply this frame: _____ *wins the _____ award because _____.*

LIGHT
Have children give at least two reasons in their response. Encourage them to use the word *because* in their responses.

Go to Your
Teaching Pal

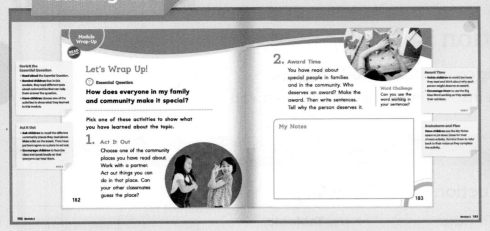

Synthesize Information

In your **Teaching Pal**, pages 182–183, use the prompts to have children revisit the Essential Question: *How does everyone in my family and community make it special?*

- Have children choose one of the activities to demonstrate what they have learned about the topic from reading the texts in this module. Use the supports in your Teaching Pal to guide them.

- As children share their final work with a partner or with the class, remind them to follow these tips for presenting:

  » speak clearly

  » speak at an appropriate pace, not too fast or too slow

  » speak in complete sentences to express a complete thought

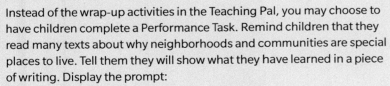

PERFORMANCE TASK OPTION

Instead of the wrap-up activities in the Teaching Pal, you may choose to have children complete a Performance Task. Remind children that they read many texts about why neighborhoods and communities are special places to live. Tell them they will show what they have learned in a piece of writing. Display the prompt:

> *Think about the texts you read. What makes each community special? Write to tell what special things all communities have.*

Guide children through the steps of the writing process: plan, draft, revise, and present. In each of the steps, remind children to continually refer back to the texts to support their ideas.

 ### LINK TO SMALL-GROUP INSTRUCTION

REINFORCE SYNTHESIZING Review or extend the skill as needed during small-group time to support children's need for differentiation. *See the lesson on p. T487.*

LESSON 15

READING WORKSHOP

👥 **SMALL-GROUP INSTRUCTION**

Options for Differentiation

As the class engages in independent and collaborative work, meet with Guided Reading Groups or differentiate instruction based on student need.

GUIDED READING GROUPS

Match Children to Books + Instruction

- Choose just-right books based on level, skill, topic, or genre.

C D E F G H I J K →
Leveled Readers

- Deliver instruction with each book's Take and Teach Lesson, choosing appropriate sessions based on need.

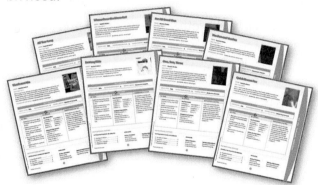

- Check comprehension, reinforce instruction, and extend learning with suggested supporting activities.

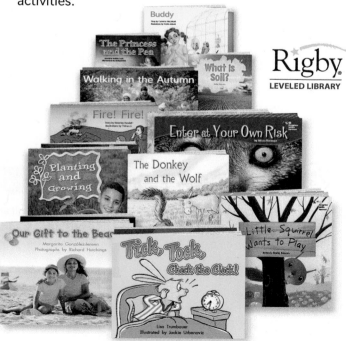

Rigby
LEVELED LIBRARY

🗨 ENGLISH LEARNER SUPPORT

Classify

- Use **Tabletop Minilessons: English Language Development 6.3 (Collaborative Problem Solving)** to reinforce and practice the language skill.

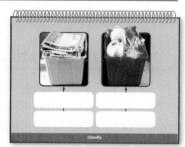

Tabletop Minilessons: English Language Development

- Then use the following prompts to guide application of the language skill. Begin with the prompt at the child's identified language proficiency level. As children are able, use lighter supports to encourage increased language proficiency.

SUBSTANTIAL
Have children recall how to classify ideas. Ask: *How have we grouped ideas?* Allow children to reference or point to a text as they respond.

MODERATE
Ask children to recount how to classify ideas or objects. Supply these frames: *We can group ideas by _____. We can group objects by _____.*

LIGHT
Ask children to summarize the different ways that ideas or objects can be grouped or classified. Ask: *What are ways to group ideas or objects that are described in a text?*

REINFORCE SYNTHESIZE

Demonstrate

- Use **Tabletop Minilessons: Reading 9** to remind children that to better understand a text, readers can synthesize, or put together, information that they learn from different parts of a text or from several texts. To synthesize, readers identify the most important parts of the text. They also bring in their own **perspective**—their own ideas and way of seeing things. Then, they figure out what each text means to them.

- Model filling out Printable: <u>Reading Graphic Organizer 6</u> as you lead a discussion that requires children to synthesize information from one of more of the selections they have read.

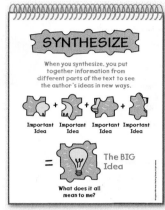

Tabletop Minilessons: Reading

Apply to Independent Reading

- Now have children synthesize information in an appropriate just-right book that they are reading independently. Customize these prompts to the books children choose.

  » *What are the most important ideas in this book?*

  » *What do you think or feel about the ideas in this book?*

  » *What do the ideas in this text mean to you?*

- Have children complete Printable: <u>Reading Graphic Organizer 6</u> for their independent reading book.

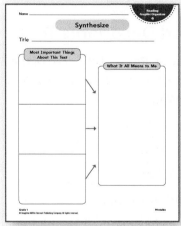

Printable: Reading Graphic Organizer 6

ALMOST THERE

READY FOR MORE

SCAFFOLD AND EXTEND

- Lead children to put two ideas from their book together and to draw a conclusion about them.

- Prompt children to use pictures and key words in the book to identify important ideas. Guide children to draw a conclusion from those ideas.

- Have partners compare information from two different books on the same topic. Ask them to synthesize and state what they know about the topic.

 ENGLISH LEARNER SUPPORT

SUBSTANTIAL

Ask children to tell everything they know about the topic, based on the pictures. They may point or use single words.

MODERATE

Encourage children to identify important ideas in the text and state what the idea means to them. Supply this frame: *This idea is important and means _____ because _____.*

LIGHT

Have children identify important ideas in the text. Ask: *Why does the author include these ideas? What meaning do they have for you?*

READING WORKSHOP

Options for Differentiation

Start Right Reader, *Book 1*, pp. 164–195

REINFORCE FOUNDATIONAL SKILLS

Read Decodable Text

Review Remind children of the Start Right Reader stories they read this week about the characters Val, Jim, and Wags.

- *Wags, Wags, Wags!*

- *Yip! Yap!*

- *Mud Pup*

- *Bad Pup, Wags!*

Allow a few minutes for children to page through the stories to recall what they are about.

Make Text Connections Prompt children to explain how the four stories are connected.

- *Who are the main characters in these stories?* (Val, Jim, and Wags)

- *What is the main thing that each story is about? (Possible response: Val and Jim's new pup, Wags, and the trouble Wags gets into.)*

- *What problem in* Wags, Wags, Wags! *has a solution in* Yip! Yap! *and* Mud Pup? *What is the solution? (Wags gets out of the yard; in* Yip! Yap!*, Mom finds Wags, and in* Mud Pup*, Mom puts a log in the gap under the fence so Wags cannot get out again.)*

- *What might Wags do in a new story about him? (Accept reasonable responses.)*

Reread for Fluency Select one of the stories to reread. Use the **CHORAL READING** routine and have children focus on reading with accuracy, self-correcting as needed.

Make Minutes Count

As you meet with small groups to review the week's decodable stories, use one or both of these related activities, as needed, at the beginning or the end of the small-group session.

- **Connect to Phonics** Play Pair Up! Gather the Spelling and High-Frequency Words from Printable: **Word List 6** from all children in the group. Shuffle and deal all of the cards. Children take turns sorting through their cards, making as many pairs as possible, placing the pairs face up on the tabletop, and reading the words. Then, the first child fans out his or her remaining cards face down and the child on the left takes a card. If that card makes a pair for the second child, he or she places the pair face up on the table and reads the word. Play continues until one child gets rid of all of his or her cards.

- **Connect to Handwriting** Dictate previously taught letters, as well as this week's focus letters *q* and *u*. Have children write each letter from memory. Then have them self-assess their letter formation and put a star next to letters they formed correctly.

Options for Independent and Collaborative Work

While you meet with small groups, have other children engage in literacy activities that reinforce the lesson's learning objectives. Choose from these options.

Independent Reading

Student Choice Library

Rigby®
LEVELED LIBRARY

APPLY READING SKILL

Synthesize Children complete Printable: <u>Reading Graphic Organizer 6</u> for an independent reading book.

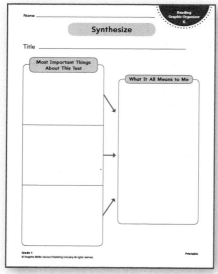

Printable: Reading Graphic Organizer 6

APPLY LANGUAGE SKILL

Classify Children complete Printable: <u>Language Graphic Organizer 4</u> for an independent reading book.

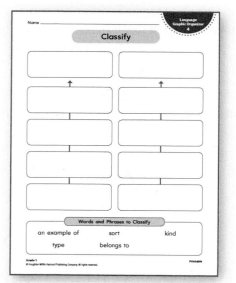

Printable: Language Graphic Organizer 4

Literacy Centers

See pp. T422–T423.

 WORD WORK

 CREATIVITY CORNER

 DIGITAL STATION

 READING CORNER

 TEAMWORK TIME

Start Right Reader

Wags, Wags, Wags!

by Kenisha Johnson
illustrated by Jessika von Innerebner

"Val! Jim! Kids!"
Mom finds us.
Mom has a pup.

165

Read Decodable Text Book 1:
pp. 164–195

Wrap-Up
Share Time

At the end of the Reading Workshop, have children reflect on their learning by sharing how they applied **Synthesize** or another area of focus during independent work time. Choose from these options:

- **SHARE CHAIR** Select a reader each day to come to the front of the class and tell what he or she learned from the reading by using a skill or strategy.

- **THINK-PAIR-SHARE** Children share their thinking with a partner. Select a few each day to share with the whole class.

- **RETURN TO ANCHOR CHART** Have children add sticky notes about their independent reading book to the Synthesize Anchor Chart. Call on a few children to explain what they added.

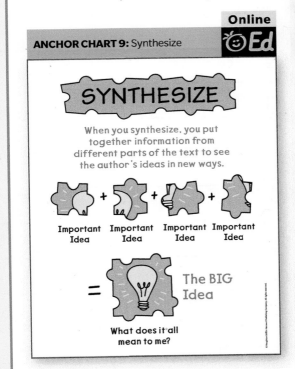

ANCHOR CHART 9: Synthesize

Online **Ed**

SYNTHESIZE

When you synthesize, you put together information from different parts of the text to see the author's ideas in new ways.

Important Idea + Important Idea + Important Idea + Important Idea

= The BIG Idea

What does it all mean to me?

Notes

Resources

Professional Learning R2

Credits R3

Online
Ed

FIND MORE ONLINE!

Into Reading Scope and Sequence

Rubrics

Index

Standards Correlations

Word Lists
- Start Right Readers (Decodable Texts)
- Academic Vocabulary: Big Idea Words and Power Words

Glossary of Professional Terms

Handwriting Models

Articulation
- Consonant Sounds
- Vowel Sounds

Phoneme-Grapheme Correspondences

Language Differences
- Alphabet
- Sound-Spellings
- Word Parts

Professional Learning

Access these professional resources to learn more about the research foundations for *Into Reading*.

Armbruster, Bonnie B., Fran Lehr, and Jean Osborn. *Put Reading First: The Research Building Blocks for Teaching Children to Read: Kindergarten Through Grade 3*. Edited by C. Ralph Adler. Jessup, Maryland: National Institute for Literacy at ED Pubs, 2001.

Barber, Angela. "Multilinguistic Components of Spelling: An Overview." *Perspectives on Language Learning and Education* 20, no. 4 (2013): 124–128.

Blachowicz, Camille L. Z., and Peter Fisher. "Vocabulary Lessons." *Educational Leadership* 61, no. 6 (2004): 66–69.

Cunningham, Anne E., and Jamie Zibulsky. *Book Smart: How to Develop and Support Successful, Motivated Readers*. New York: Oxford University Press, 2014.

Dean, Heather. "Creating Critical Readers: Connecting Close Reading and Technology." *California Reader* 50, no. 4 (2017): 8–11.

Dougherty Stahl, K. A. "Complex Text or Frustration-Level Text: Using Shared Reading to Bridge the Difference." *The Reading Teacher* 66, no. 1 (2012): 47–51.

Ehri, Linnea C. "Learning to Read Words: Theory, Findings, and Issues." *Scientific Studies of Reading* 9, no. 2 (2005): 167–188.

Ehri, Linnea C., and Julie Rosenthal. "The Spellings of Words: A Neglected Facilitator of Vocabulary Learning." *Journal of Literacy Research* 39, no. 4 (2007): 389–409.

Fisher, Douglas, and Nancy Frey. *Better Learning Through Structured Teaching: A Framework for the Gradual Release of Responsibility*. 2nd ed. Alexandria, Virginia: ASCD, 2014.

Fisher, Douglas, and Nancy Frey. "Contingency Teaching During Close Reading." *Reading Teacher* 68, no. 4 (2014): 277–286.

Graham, Steve, and Michael Hebert. "Writing to Read: A Meta-Analysis of the Impact of Writing and Writing Instruction on Reading." *Harvard Educational Review* 81, no. 4 (2011): 710–744.

Hirsch, E. D., Jr. "Reading Comprehension Requires Knowledge — of Words and the World: Scientific Insights into the Fourth-Grade Slump and Stagnant Reading Comprehension." *American Educator* 27, no. 1 (2003): 10–22, 28–29, 48.

"Learning Mindsets." *Mindset Scholars* Network. Last modified 2015. http://mindsetscholarsnetwork.org/learning-mindsets/.

Lyster, Roy, Kazuya Saito, and Masatoshi Sato. "Oral Corrective Feedback in Second Language Classrooms." *Language Teaching* 46, no. 1 (2013): 1–40.

Mol, Suzanne E. "To Read or Not to Read: A Meta-Analysis of Print Exposure from Infancy to Early Adulthood." *Psychological Bulletin* 137, no. 2 (2013): 267–296.

Neuman, Susan B., Tanya Kaefer, and Ashley Pinkham. "Building Background Knowledge." *The Reading Teacher* 68, no. 2 (2014): 145–148.

Neuman, Susan B., and Tanya S. Wright. "The Magic of Words: Teaching Vocabulary in the Early Childhood Classroom." *American Educator*, Summer 2014: 4–13.

Ong, Justina. "A Tension Between Theory and Practice: Shared Reading Program." *Reading Matrix: An International Online Journal* 14, no. 2 (September 2014): 20–33.

Piasta, Shayne B., Laura M. Justice, Anita S. McGinty, and Joan N. Kaderavek. "Increasing Young Children's Contact with Print During Shared Reading: Longitudinal Effects on Literacy Achievement." *Child Development* 83, no. 3 (2012): 810–820.

Puranik, Cynthia S., and Stephanie Al Otaiba. "Examining the Contribution of Handwriting and Spelling to Written Expression in Kindergarten Children." *Reading and Writing* 25, no. 7 (2012), 1523–1546.

Richards, Todd L., Virginia W. Berninger, Pat Stock, Leah Altemeier, Pamala Trivedi, and Kenneth R. Maravilla. "Differences Between Good and Poor Child Writers on fMRI Contrasts for Writing Newly Taught and Highly Practiced Letter Forms." *Reading and Writing* 24, no. 5 (2011): 493–516.

U.S. Public Health Service. *Report of the Surgeon General's Conference on Children's Mental Health: A National Action Agenda*. Washington, DC: Department of Health and Human Services, 2000.

Wiseman, Angela. "Interactive Read Alouds: Teachers and Students Constructing Knowledge and Literacy Together." *Early Childhood Education Journal* 38, no. 6 (2011): 431–438.

Credits

T8 TL ©Monkey Business images/Shutterstock, **TR** ©Tania Kolinko/Shutterstock, **BL** ©FatCamera/E+/Getty Images, **BR** ©paulaphoto/Shutterstock; **T9** ©Monkey Business/Fotolia; **T10 TL** ©Romrodphoto/Shutterstock, **TR** ©Jonathan Cohen/iStock/Getty Images, **BL** ©Getty Images, **BR** ©Monkey Business Images/Shutterstock; **T11** ©Getty Images; **T16** ©Houghton Mifflin Harcourt; **T252 TL** ©Monkey Business images/Shutterstock, **TR** ©Tania Kolinko/Shutterstock, **BL** ©FatCamera/E+/Getty Images, **BR** ©paulaphoto/Shutterstock; **T253** ©Monkey Business/Fotolia; **T254 TL** ©Romrodphoto/Shutterstock, **TR** ©Jonathan Cohen/iStock/Getty Images, **BL** ©Getty Images, **BR** ©Monkey Business Images/Shutterstock; **T255** ©Getty Images; **T260** ©Houghton Mifflin Harcourt